GIN INSIDE

Eine inspirierende Reise
mit Rezepten, Tipps & Trends

IMPRESSUM

CALLWEY 1884

© 2022 Callwey GmbH
Klenzestraße 36
80469 München
buch@callwey.de
Tel.: +49 89 8905080-0
www.callwey.de

Wir sehen uns auf Instagram:
www.instagram.com/callwey

ISBN 978-3-7667-2603-2
1. Auflage 2022

Originalausgabe: © 2022 by VT-Verlag
VT-Verlags GmbH
Victor Hochheiden, Tom Channir
Lise-Meitner-Straße 39/41
D-10589 Berlin

Bei Fragen und Anregungen:
info@vt-verlag.de

Bibliografische Information der Deutschen Nationalbibliothek
Die Deutsche Nationalbibliothek verzeichnet diese Publikation in der Deutschen Nationalbibliografie; detaillierte bibliografische Daten sind im Internet über <http://dnb.d-nb.de> abrufbar.

Das Werk einschließlich aller seiner Teile ist urheberrechtlich geschützt. Jede Verwertung außerhalb der engen Grenzen des Urheberrechtsgesetzes ist ohne Zustimmung des Verlages unzulässig und strafbar. Das gilt insbesondere für Vervielfältigungen, Übersetzungen, Mikroverfilmungen und die Einspeicherung und Verarbeitung in elektronischen Systemen.

Dieses Buch wurde in CALLWEY-QUALITÄT für Sie hergestellt:
Beim Inhaltspapier haben wir uns für ein MagnoMatt in 150 g/m² entschieden – ein matt gestrichenes Bilderdruckpapier. Diese gestrichene, matte Oberfläche gibt dem Inhalt einen edlen und hochwertigen
Charakter. Die Hardcover-Gestaltung besteht aus bedrucktem Surbalin-Papier und wurde mit Heißfolienprägung veredelt. Dieses Buch wurde in Europa gedruckt und gebunden bei Graspo CZ.

Viel Freude mit diesem Buch wünschen Ihnen:
Cover, Satz & Layout: Julia Jung
Texte: Leonore Piper, Josephine Rosse, Robert Rau & Tara Gottmann
Expertenbeiträge: Lu Geipel, Magnus Tobler, Martin Thibault, Frank Thelen, Steffen Zimmermann & Kristof Mulack
Lektorat: Frank Elminowski,
Anne Fries Lektorat
Übersetzung: Peter Cox

Bildnachweis:
Fotografie: Julia Jung
© Adobe Stock: S.14 / © iStockphoto:
S. 454, S. 474, S. 512, S. 520, S. 523, S. 524
Darüber hinaus wurden uns Fotos von Gin-Herstellern zur Verfügung gestellt. Hierfür möchten wir uns ganz herzlich bedanken!

Druck und Bindung: Graspo CZ, a.s., Zlín,
Gedruckt in der Tschechischen Republik

Hinweis: Uns ist es ein Anliegen, dass sich alle Geschlechter wahrgenommen und wertgeschätzt fühlen. Im Sinne einer besseren Lesbarkeit der Texte verzichten wir jedoch auf die gleichzeitige Verwendung der Sprachformen männlich, weiblich und divers (m/w/d). Wo dies möglich ist, bemühen wir uns darum alle Formen miteinzubeziehen oder um neutrale Formulierungen. Sämtliche Personenbezeichnungen gelten gleichermaßen für alle Geschlechter.

G:INHALT

PREFACE 12

WTF... is Gin?

HOW TO MAKE A GREAT GIN OR HOW IS GIN MADE? 17

A JOURNEY AROUND THE WORLD OF GINS OF 7 TYPES 22

HOW TO MAKE A GIN 28

Stories

THE GIN-STORY 36

THE TONIC-STORY 42

Journey

GERMANY

The Northman Gin 52	Calluna Lüneburger Heide Gin 76
GIN-HUDE 54	Flow Gin 78
WATER Nörder Dry Gin 56	Schwarzer Walfisch Gin 80
Raven Hills Gin 58	AAGIN 82
SILKGIN Brombyrina 60	BER Dry Gin 86
Gin Sul 62	Mampe Gin 89
Hamburg-Zanzibar Tumeric No. 1 Gin 64	Mariposa Gin 90
LUV & LEE Hanseatic Dry Gin 68	Sundown Gin 92
Skywater Gin 70	The Earl of Gin 94
Elephant London Dry Gin 72	UNKNOWN Lands | GIN 99
Müritz Gin 74	Wild Child Gin 100

vaGINa – the Hibiscus Gin	103	Murre Gin	152
GIN	104	Little Darling Gin	154
Moritzburger Gin	106	Inkognito Gin	157
Friedrichs Dry Gin	109	Gießen Dry Gin	158
Jos. Garden Gin	110	Koka Destillat	161
UrGin	112	LA SU Gin	162
Alpako Gin	114	Mandarina Dry Gin	164
Renton-Gin	118	Amato Mediterranean Dry Gin	166
Rinocero Gin	120	Schloss Gin	168
Yoshi Nama – Little Tokyo Dry Gin	124	Pure Gin	170
AMETHYST London Dry Gin	126	Aquamarin Gin	174
Proud, Strong & Noble Gin	129	Little Big Hill	176
moersGIN	130	Natural Dry Gin	180
HerGINg	132	Momotarō Gin	182
Keller's Gin	134	Gin dry – Pfälzer Edelgin	186
Woodland Sauerland Dry Gin	138	GIN 24/7 – Stübinger's DRY Gin	188
Naturbummler Gin	140	Ferdinand's Gin	190
GINSAN!TY White Truffle Premium Dry Gin	142	Hoos London Gin	192
MATS Dry Gin	144	Böser Kater Two Faced Gin	194
Raspmary Gin	146	Satoshi Gin	197
Big Moose Gin	148	Erich Schwäbischer Dry Gin	198

Gin under Construction	200	Bernstein Brothers Prohibited Dry Gin	228
Mädchen & Jungs gin	202	KULTUR.GUT London Dry Gin	230
Monkey 47 Schwarzwald Dry Gin	204	Illegal Gin Outlaw	232
Crypto-Gin	209	Kaiser Hill 16	234
Delicium Gin	210	SHADOWS Franconian Dry Gin classic	236
Needle Blackforest Masterpiece	212	Eisvôgel Gin	239
WEISSBART Gin	215	HUMULUS Dry Gin	240
Liquid Emotions & Leviathan Gin	216	KONKANI Goa Inspired Gin	244
GIN FICHTE	ZITRONE	218	Lindwurm Gin – Sommer Edition	248
MUNDART – KAISERSTUHL DRY GIN	220	MUNiG – Munich Premium Gin	252
GINklin	222	ORO IBIZA GIN	254
Longitude London Dry Gin	224	Lorbär Gin	256
Red Beard Gin	226	JOSEF Bavarian Gin	258

AUSTRIA

Löwen Green Gin	262	GIN.milla Magic Distilled Gin	274
Elfer-Gin	266	The Good Gin	276
ZIRBIN Dry Gin	268	Skoff oriGINal	279
5020 London Dry Gin	270	STIN Classic Proof	281
Gin FIOR	272	GIN_Uh!	282

SWITZERLAND

Chameleon Gin	286	Sir Dry Gin	298
Edelwhite Gin	290	Porto Sofie Dry Gin	300
Deux Frères Gin	292	GIN 27	302
Dr. Becker's Gin	296		

GREAT BRITAIN

Tanqueray	306	Beefeater Dry Gin	321
Tanqueray London Dry Gin	308	BROCKMANS Gin	322
Tanqueray Flor de Sevilla Distilled Gin	310	Hayman's Old Tom Gin	324
Tanqueray Blackcurrant Royale Distilled Gin	313	Oxley Gin	326
Lind & Lime Gin	314	Sipsmith London Dry Gin	328
Bombay Sapphire Premier Cru	316	Tarquin's Cornish Dry Gin	330

FROM AROUND THE GLOBE

Death's Door Gin	334	Z44 Distilled Dry Gin	360
Brooklyn Gin	336	Sabatini London Dry Gin	362
Canaïma	338	The Artisan Gin	364
Bobby's Schiedam Dry Gin	340	Hernö Dry Gin	367
Sir Edmond Gin	342	Kyrö Gin	368
Hanami Dry Gin	344	Junimperium Blended Dry Gin	370
Solar Gin	346	Benguela Diamonds Gin	374
Citadelle Gin Original	348	KAIZA 5 Gin	377
Citadelle Gin Jardin d'Été	350	Unit 43 Original	378
MistralGin	352	399 on Albert – Original Gin Woodstock Gin	380
Le Tribute Gin	354	Etsu Handcrafted Japanese Gin	382
La Valdôtaine Acqueverdi Gin delle Alpi	356	KI NO TEA Kyoto Dry Gin	384
Malfy Gin Rosa	359	Roku Gin	386

Filler

Rosebottel Tonic Essences	392
ÖselBirch Mixers	394
Le Tribute Tonic Water & Lemonade	396
Schreieck Indian Tonic	398
Ginger & Fred Syrups	401
HITCHCOCK Juice Collection	402
Aqua Monaco Tonics	405
Fitch & Leedes – Premium Mixers	406
Barker & Quin Tonic Waters	409
Doctor Polidori Fine Tonic Waters	410
Erich Bee Tonic Water	412
Fever-Tree Tonic Waters	414
Schweppes Tonic Waters	416

Bars

Bellboy Berlin	422
Bellucci Bar	424
House of Gin	426
Stue Bar	429

Gin Insider

MARTIN THIBAULT: WITH SMALL AND BIG IDEAS, MAKING THE WORLD A LITTLE BIT BETTER 435

FRANK THELEN: BLOODY MARY FOR BREAKFAST? NOT QUITE! 446

MAGNUS TOBLER: TALKING FAIRY DUST & GLITTER CONFETTI: 457

LU GEIPEL: LU ALONE IN THE BAR 466

STEFFEN ZIMMERMANN: PRETTY MUCH BEST FRIENDS 475

Cocktails & Their Creators

Kate	487
Hottie	488
Devil's Tears	491
Yuzu Blizzard	492
Ballroom Beauty	495
Rosehip Renaissance	496
The Milky Way	499
Berlin Breakfast Club	500
The Fragrance	503
Faye's Valentine	504
Royal Fashion	507
Touch of Winter	508

Gin & Food

KRISTOF MULACK: FROM INSURANCE SALESMAN TO CATERING HERO 512

Salmon with gin-schwips on cucumber-apple salad	522
Cold vegan basil & coconut soup with gin and caramelized walnut crunch ᵛ	525
Spaghetti with gin & tomato sauce and meatballs	526
Gin-chicken with sage risotto with leeks and peas	529
Tipsy pralines in chocolate coating	530
Gin & Tonic cake with lemon cream	532

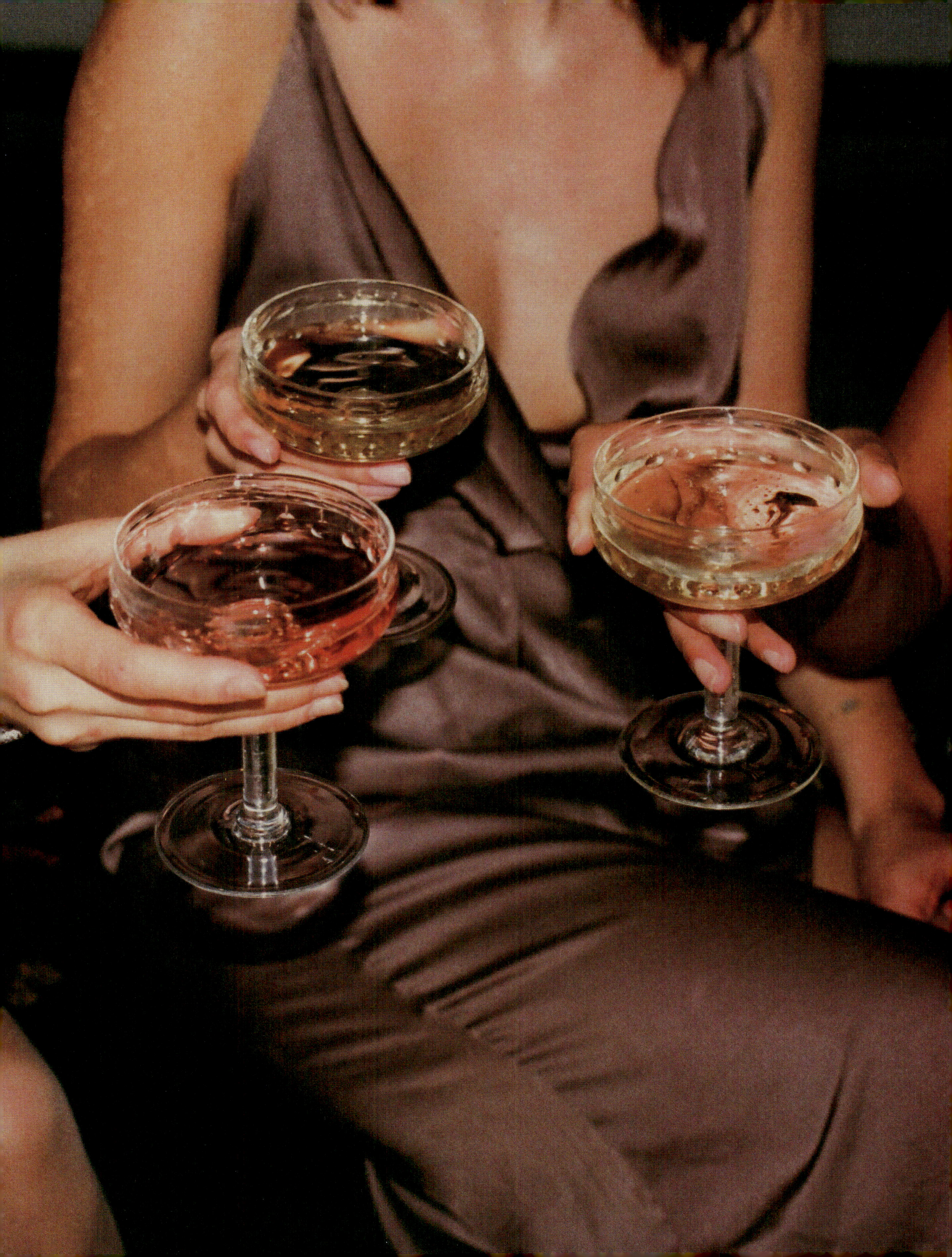

LOVE IS LIKE A BOTTLE OF GIN

But A Bottle Of Gin Is Not Like Love

PREFACE

to all gin connoisseurs and those who want to be...

Ein Blick, ein kurzes Augenzwinkern, gefolgt von einem zaghaften „Ist der Platz neben dir noch frei?". Wir trafen uns in der Uni, an Tag eins unseres Studiums. Wir, das sind Victor und Tom aus Berlin. Wir mochten uns, hatten dieselben Interessen – unter anderem auch kurzweilige Partynächte. Wir tranken Gin Tonics, bis der Himmel seinen schwarzen Umhang gegen Morgenröte eintauschte. Auch mehr als fünf Jahre nach unserem ersten Treffen zwischen den Sitzreihen des Seminarraums hat sich an der Sympathie füreinander und unseren Interessen wenig geändert. Wir sind weniger grün hinter den Ohren – oh ja! Aber wir trinken immer noch gern Gin. Seit es auf einer der unzähligen Studentenpartys klick in unseren Köpfen machte, dass es mehr geben muss als die üblichen Verdächtigen, sind wir auf einer Mission: Wir trinken uns durch die schier unendliche Welt des Gins und schreiben auf, was wir dabei lernen, entdecken und erleben. Unsere Superkräfte: herausragender Geschmack, ein tadellos funktionierender Geruchssinn, Fachwissen und ein munter wachsendes Netzwerk ausgezeichneter Spirituosenexperten und -hersteller.

Aus einer anfänglichen Backpack-Tour durch exotische Gefilde wurde eine abenteuerliche Wacholder-Reise rund um die Welt. Wir besuchten Destillerien, ausgezeichnete Bars, unterhielten uns mit erstklassigen Bartendern – unser Kompass leitete uns direkt in die Häfen der regionalen und internationalen Gin-Renaissance. Inzwischen haben wir mehr als 2.500 Sorten dieses wunderbar abwechslungsreichen Drinks verkostet – natürlich stets im Auftrag des guten Geschmacks. Nicht alle konnten unsere Gaumen erobern. Diejenigen, die es im Sturm geschafft haben, nehmen Platz auf der Tribüne unseres Herzensprojektes „Gin Inside II". Greift zu diesem Buch, wenn ihr Lust auf spannende Storys und Insights habt, wenn ihr die passenden Rezepte für eure Date Night sucht oder wenn ihr einen Berater am Gin-Regal braucht. Nehmt Freunde, Familie und Bekannte mit auf diese abwechslungsreiche Expedition durch das Gin-Universum. Wir weisen euch den Weg – ihr werdet staunen!

Als wir 2018 mit unserem neu gegründeten VT-Verlag an den Start gingen, wollten wir als Genussbotschafter die Spirituosen-Szene

A glance, a quick wink, followed by a tentative "Is the seat next to you still free?". We met at university, on day one of our studies. We, that's Victor and Tom from Berlin. We liked each other, had the same interests – including entertaining party nights. We drank gin tonic till the sky drifted from the darkness of juniper to the glow of oranges. Even now, more than five years on from our first meeting between the rows of seats in the seminar room, little has changed in our liking for each other or our interests. We're less wet behind the ears – oh yes! But we still like to drink gin. Ever since it clicked in our heads, at one of countless student parties, that there must be more to gin than the usual suspects, we've been on a mission; drinking our way through the seemingly endless world of gin and writing down what we learn, discover and experience along the way. Our superpowers: outstanding taste, an impeccably functioning sense of smell, expertise, and a lively and growing network of excellent spirits experts and producers.

An initial backpack tour through exotic climes turned into an adventurous juniper journey around the world. We visited distilleries, excellent bars, talked to first-class bartenders – our compass guided us directly to the ports of the regional and international gin renaissance. To date we've tasted more than 2,500 varieties of this wonderfully varied drink – always on a mission seeking good taste, of course. Not all of them were able to conquer our palates. Those that stormed through gained a seat on the grandstand of our heartfelt project, "Gin Inside II". Pick up this book if you're in the mood for exciting stories and insights, if you're looking for the right recipes for your date night, or if you need an adviser by the gin shelf. Take friends, family and acquaintances with you on this wide-ranging expedition through the gin universe. We'll show you the way – you'll be amazed!

When we launched our newly founded VT publishing house in 2018, we wanted to shake up the spirits scene as ambassadors of delight. We launched "Gin Inside" and hit the bull's eye. That gin euphoria has remained unbroken ever since. Forecasts show that the market for this trendy drink will continue to grow strongly

aufmischen. Wir brachten „Gin Inside" heraus und trafen mitten ins Schwarze. Die Gin-Euphorie ist seitdem ungebrochen. Prognosen zeigen: Der Markt rund um das Trendgetränk wird auch in den kommenden Jahren weiter stark wachsen. Diese Dynamik treibt uns an, sie reißt uns mit. Wir wollen weiter neue Gipfel erklimmen und ferne Gestade erobern – mit und für euch. Deshalb haben wir in diesem Jahr www.sipsta.de gelauncht, eine unabhängige Genuss-Boutique, auf der ihr eine Auswahl unserer persönlichen Lieblingsspirituosen findet. www.sipsta.de ist damit die ideale Ergänzung zu unseren Büchern.

Wenn uns heute jemand fragt, welchen Gin wir am liebsten trinken, lautet unsere Antwort: „Es kommt darauf an". Die Antwort zeigt, wie wunderbar vielfältig Gin sein kann. In jeder Situation, passend zu jeder Stimmung, zu jedem Wetter, zu jeder Begleitung: Es gibt den passenden Gin. Vielleicht finden wir irgendwann eine eindeutige Antwort. Doch vorher bestreiten wir die nächste Etappe unserer Juniper-Journey.

in the coming years. We are driven by this dynamism, and we are carried along by it. We want to keep climbing new peaks and diving uncharted depths – with and for you. That's why we launched www.sipsta.de this year, an independent boutique of delights where you can find a selection of our personal favorite spirits. www.sipsta.de is thus the ideal complement to our books.

Today, when someone asks us which gin we like best, our answer is "it depends". The answer shows how wonderfully diverse gin can be. In every situation, suitable for every mood, regardless of the weather, whatever the company; there is a suitable gin. Perhaps we'll find an unambiguous answer at some point. But, ahead of that, we'll press on with the next stage of our juniper journey.

In that spirit, cheers!

Victor & Tom

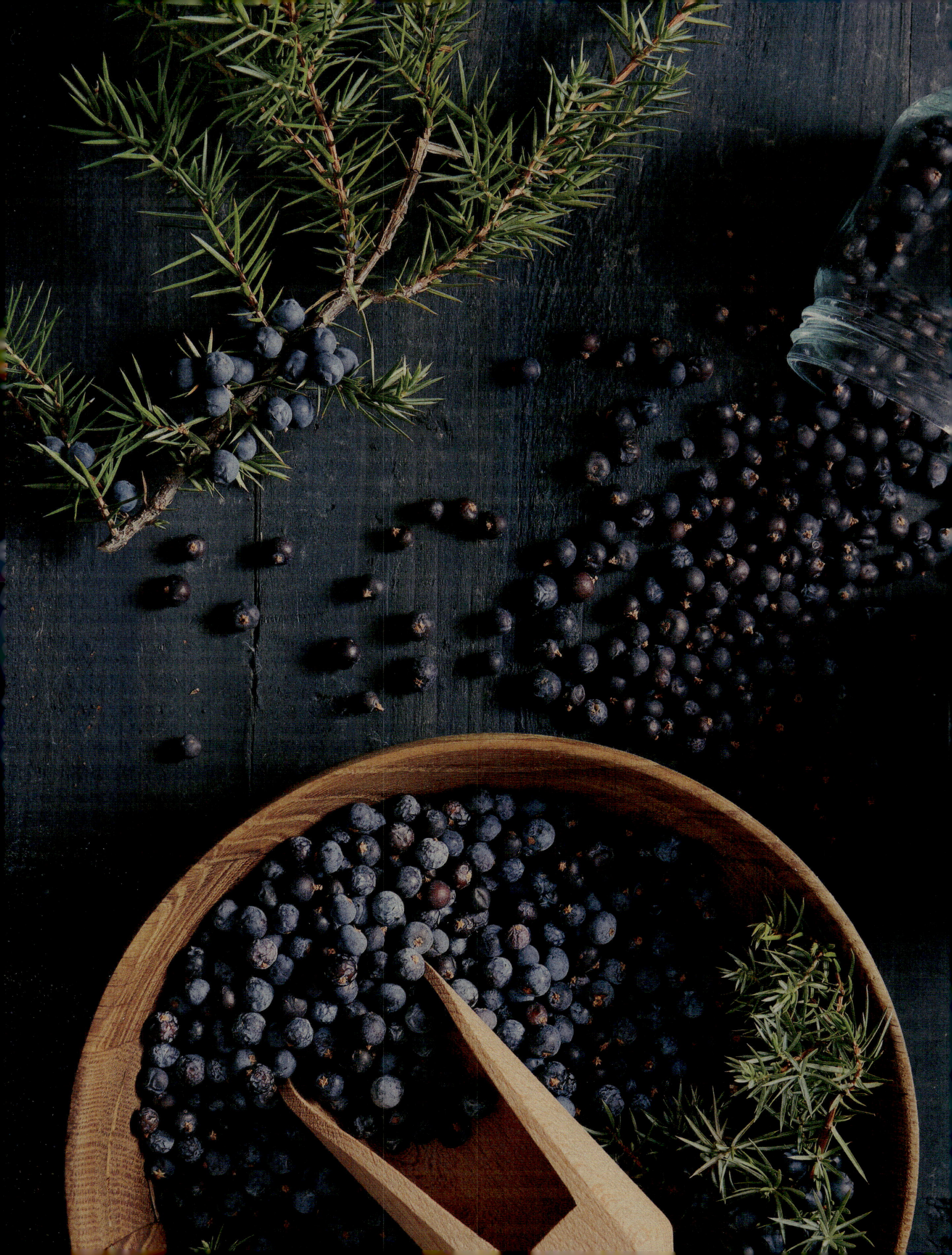

1

WTF...
IS GIN?

Mit Fotos aus der Berlin Distillery

HOW TO MAKE A GREAT GIN OR HOW IS GIN MADE?

Every smooth gin has a tough past

Die Zutaten

BeGINnen wir am Anfang (und wir haben uns geschworen, auf diese albernen und schon total durchgekaute Gin-Wortspiele zu verzichten!), und zwar mit den Basiszutaten, die man benötigt, um einen Gin herzustellen.

Das wäre hochprozentiger, fast reiner Alkohol. Vater Alkohol hat ein sehr strenges Händchen in der Herstellung, mit einem Aggressionsgehalt von harten 96 % – also don't drink and try before it's Dry. Der Alkohol wird in der Regel aus Getreiden wie Gerste, Roggen, Mais oder Weizen gewonnen – manchmal auch aus Zuckerrüben, Melasse und Kartoffeln. Nichts geht ohne Wacholder: Juniperus (Latein) ist eine festgelegte Zutat für einen Gin. Ohne Wacholder ist es kein Gin. Ein Gin muss einen Alkoholgehalt von mindestens 37,5 % haben.

Wie aber bekommt der Gin seinen charakteristischen Geschmack? Was macht Gin nicht einfach zu einem Schnaps wie Wodka und Co? Seine Botanicals. Die hauchen ihm erst die komplexen Noten ein und machen ihn zu einem Geschmackserlebnis, das man genießen kann und nicht runterstürzen muss. Ein Botanical, das in keinem Gin fehlen darf, ist der Wacholder. Oft kommen dann auch noch Orangen, Limetten- und/oder Zitronenschalen mit rein. Aber auch Gewürze, Pflanzen, Kräuter, Blüten, Schalen und Beeren – whatever. Hier sind der Kreativität keine Grenzen gesetzt. Das ist gut, um immer wieder etwas geschmacklich Neues zu entdecken, aber so mancher Hersteller schießt ab und an mit seinem „außergewöhnlichen" Gin über das Ziel hinaus. Nicht Wasser oder Alkohol sind für einen guten Gin verantwortlich, erst die Botanicals machen aus einem Destillat einen großartigen Gin. Mit den Botanicals wird jeder Gin geschmacklich orchestriert, bis er die gewünschte leichte, hohe, tiefe, erdige, fruchtige oder trockene Note bekommt.

Die Mischung

Hier macht nicht der Ton die Musik, hier machen die Botanicals den Geschmack: Je nachdem, wie die Mischung der Botanicals ausfällt und komponiert wird, entscheidet sich das finale Aroma, die geschmackliche Komplexität und die Textur des Gins. Einige Destillateure schwören in der Herstellung auf Minimalismus und zaubern mit 5–10 Botanicals

The ingredients:

Let's start at the beGINning (and we've sworn to desist from those silly, well-worn gin puns) with the basic ingredients needed to make a gin.

First, high-proof, almost pure alcohol. Alcohol Sen. has a very strict role in production, with an alcohol aggression level of a tough old 96 % ABV – so don't drink and try before it's dry. The alcohol is usually made from grains like barley, rye, corn or wheat – sometimes sugar beet, molasses or potatoes.

But how does gin get its characteristic flavor? What makes gin not simply a liquor like vodka &Co.? Its botanicals. They're what breathe the complex notes into it in the first place and make it a taste experience that can be enjoyed and doesn't have to be downed. A botanical that cannot be absent from any gin is juniper. Often then oranges, lime and/or lemon peel come in with it. But also spices, plants, herbs, flowers, peels and berries – whatever. There are no limits to creativity here. All very laudable, discovering something new in terms of taste, but some producers overshoot the mark with their "extraordinary" gins. It's not water or alcohol that makes a good gin, it's the botanicals that turn a distillate into a great gin. What were Bruce Lee's smart words back then? "Be water my friend." Today, he might say, "BeGIN my friend."

The mix

It's not the sound that makes the music here, it's the botanicals that make the taste. Depending on how the blend of botanicals turns out and is composed is what decides the final aroma, flavor complexity and texture of the gin. Some distillers swear by minimalism in the production and conjure up a first-class gin with 5-10 botanicals, others create more in the belief that "more is more" and pimp their gin with 30 to 50 or more botanicals. Every year, heck, every month, new "extraordinary" botanicals are "discovered" to set a particular gin apart from all the others. To date, it is said that probably around 120 different botanicals have been used in gin production – common and well-known

einen erstklassigen Gin, andere kreieren eher nach dem Motto „mehr ist mehr" und pimpen ihren Gin mit 30 bis 50 oder mehr Botanicals. Jedes Jahr, ach was, jeden Monat werden neue „außergewöhnliche" Botanicals „entdeckt", um den eigenen Gin von allen anderen abzusetzen. Heute, sagt man, werden wohl über 100 verschiedene Botanicals für die Gin-Herstellung verwendet – gewöhnliche und bekannte Zutaten und ungewöhnliche und völlig unbekannte Botanicals. Die Frage ist: Wo wird das noch hinführen? In ein Gin-Zeitalter, in dem wir voller Begeisterung ständig Neues entdecken, oder in dem wir uns gelangweilt von der gigantischen Flut an neuen Gins abwenden und nach einem neuen Lieblingsgetränk suchen? We will see.

Aber wie genau kommt der Geschmack der Botanicals in den Gin? Dafür hat man verschiedene Methoden erfunden, geprüft und für erfolgreich befunden. Diese wären:

1. Mazeration
2. Digestion
3. Perkolation

Äh – wie bitte? Genau, darum klären wir mal ganz kurz auf:

Aller guten Dinge sind drei bei der Gin-Herstellung
Die Mazeration

Die Mazeration oder das Mazerieren klingt wie malträtieren und tatsächlich ist es nicht weit davon entfernt. Es ist lateinisch und bedeutet: mürbe machen oder auch quälen. Bei der Gin-Herstellung aber passiert den Botanicals das Beste, was ihnen vielleicht passieren kann: Sie

ingredients and unusual and completely unknown botanicals. The question is, where will this lead? To a gin age in which we enthusiastically discover new things all the time, or in which we turn away bored by the giant flood of new gins and search for a new favorite drink? We shall see.

But how exactly does the flavor of the botanicals get into the gin? For this, various methods have been invented, tested and found to be successful, namely:

1. *Maceration*
2. *Digestion*
3. *Percolation*

Uh – what? Exactly, that's why we'll briefly explain:

All good things come in threes in gin production
Maceration

Maceration sounds like maltreatment and, in fact, that's not far from the truth. It's from the Latin and means to soften or also to torture. But in gin production, the botanicals experience perhaps the best thing that could happen to them. They're chopped up or pressed and put into a large vat to be steeped in alcohol for several days or weeks. So no hint of torture. Softening? Maybe a little. But, in return, the botanicals have a great, glorious future and end up in a pretty bottle as a coveted treat for gin lovers. Through maceration, the botanicals release their flavors to the alcohol. The distillate is then filtered, diluted and bottled directly.

> ## Mixing is possible.

werden meistens zerkleinert oder gepresst in einen großen Bottich gegeben und so für mehrere Tage oder Wochen in Alkohol gelagert. Von Quälen also keine Spur. Mürbe machen? Vielleicht ein bisschen. Aber dafür haben die Botanicals eine große, ruhmvolle Zukunft und landen als begehrtes Genussmittel für Gin-Liebhaber in einer hübschen Flasche. Durch die Mazeration geben die Botanicals ihr Aroma an den Alkohol ab. Danach wird das Destillat gefiltert, verdünnt und direkt abgefüllt.

Die Digestion

Bei der Digestion, der bekanntesten Methode, geht es im Gegensatz zur Mazeration etwas heißer zu: Wie bei der Mazeration kommen die Botanicals zusammen mit dem Alkohol in einen Bottich. Dann wird ihnen ordentlich eingeheizt – auf ca. 70 Grad. So werden ätherische Öle und Aromen aus den Botanicals gelöst.

Die Perkolation

Die Methode ist weniger verbreitet. Die Perkolation wird auch als Dampfextraktion bezeichnet. Weil die Botanicals in einen sogenannten Geistkorb (Botanical-Tray) mit Siebeinsatz gefüllt werden, der über der Brennblase in den Geisthelm eingehängt wird. Das Besondere dabei: Diese Botanicals kommen nicht mit dem flüssigen Alkohol in Berührung, nur mit den Alkoholdämpfen, und werden so aromatisiert. Eine Art Sanftgaren. Dadurch ergeben sich besonders feine Noten. Manche Gin-Hersteller kombinieren auch gern die Mazeration und die Perkolation-Methode miteinander.

Digestion, Mazeration, Libération… Perkolation!

Die einen Gin-Macher schwören auf die Perkolation, die anderen auf die Digestion und wieder andere stellen verschiedene Gin-Varianten her, wofür sie die Mazeration und die Perkolation kombinieren oder die Digestion. Wie auch immer, wichtig bei jeder Methode ist, so perfekt wie möglich die Aromen der Botanicals in den Gin zu übertragen. Das ist echtes Handwerk und echte Kunst. Dann gibt es noch das gewisse Extra, das sich einige Gin-Macher nicht nehmen lassen: Sie aromatisieren im Nachgang den Gin mit ausgewählten Essenzen. Dafür kommen natürliche Botanicals erst nach der Destillation dazu. Beim Hendrick's Gin sind das zum Beispiel Rosen- und Gurkenessenzen. Ja, die besten Gin-Macher machen es sich schwer, damit wir es leichter haben, unseren Lieblings-Gin zu finden. Oder wird es dadurch nicht noch schwerer, weil es immer mehr und mehr großartige Gins gibt …? Auf jeden Fall verneigen wir uns vor der Kunst, einen großartigen, wohl orchestrierten Gin herzustellen – wir heben unser Glas auf die Digestion, Mazeration, Libération… äh… Perkolation!

Digestion

In contrast to maceration, digestion is a hotter process. As in maceration, the botanicals are placed in a vat with the alcohol. Then they are heated up to about 70 degrees. This dissolves essential oils and flavors from the botanicals.

Percolation

This method is less common. Percolation is also known as vapor extraction. Because the botanicals are placed in a so-called gin basket (botanical tray) with a sieve insert, which is suspended above the still in the head. What's special here is that the botanicals don't come into contact with the liquid alcohol, only with the alcohol vapors, yielding their aroma. A kind of gentle cooking. This results in particularly fine notes. Some gin producers also like to combine the maceration and percolation methods.

Digestion, maceration, libération …er….percolation!

Some gin makers swear by percolation, others by digestion and still others make different gin variants, for which they combine maceration and percolation or digestion. Whatever the case, the important thing in any method is to transfer as perfectly as possible the flavors of the botanicals into the gin. This is true craft and truly an art. Yes, the best gin makers make it hard for themselves so that we can have it easier and enjoy our favorite gin. We bow in appreciation and raise our glasses to digestion, maceration, libération …er….percolation!

"
Gin & Tonic – Two friends helping to make family gatherings ginuinely bearable.

21

A JOURNEY AROUND THE WORLD OF GINS OF 7 TYPES

Gin ist nicht gleich Gin. Obwohl die Geschichte des Gins relativ weit zurück reicht, gab es früher nicht annähernd die vielfältige Auswahl an Gins, die wir heute genießen dürfen. Die Geschichte geht sogar bis zu einer Zeit, da gab es nur eine Sorte: Genever – der Urvater des Gins. Aber heute ist der Gin so vielfältig wie seine Genießer. Und zum Glück gibt es für jeden noch so anspruchsvollen Gin-Gaumen den passenden Gin. Wer sich mit Gin und seinen Sorten noch nicht so gut auskennt, bekommt hier einen Fahrplan für seine Gin-Geschmacksreise. Am besten ist, nicht auf das zu hören, was andere sagen, sondern immer auszuprobieren. Das macht nicht nur Spaß, es ist auch interessant, sich mit den verschiedenen Gin-Sorten zu befassen. So könnt ihr herausfinden, welcher Gin-Typ ihr seid.

London Dry Gin

Bezeichnet die klassische Herstellungsmethode des Gins. Damit hat alles angefangen – in England. Bei der London Dry Gin-Variante dominiert die Wacholdernote und es ist die reinste Variante des Gins. Ein Gin, der nach der London-Dry-Gin-Methode hergestellt wird, kann von überall herkommen: aus Deutschland, der Schweiz, Spanien, Italien, Amerika – woher auch immer. Aber was der Gin erfüllen muss, um als London Dry Gin durchzugehen, ist Folgendes: Der Gin muss destilliert werden. Zugabe von Farbstoffen, künstlichen Aromen oder Zucker ist verboten. Die Botanicals für den Gin müssen während der Destillation zugegeben werden. Für manche Hersteller ein enges Korsett, um der eigenen Kreativität freien Lauf zu lassen, aber auch ein guter Rahmen, um mit Handwerk, Kreativität und minimalistischen Mitteln ganz Großes zu kreieren.

Dry Gin

Bezeichnet ebenfalls die Herstellungsmethode des Gins und auch bei dieser Variante wird der Gin mit seinen Botanicals destilliert. Der Unterschied zur London Dry Gin-Variante: Beim Dry Gin dürfen nachträglich naturidentische Aromen und Farbstoffe und Zucker zugesetzt werden. Auch verschiedene Brände dürfen vermischt werden. Im Gegensatz zum London Dry Gin haben hier andere

Not all gins are created equal. Although the history of gin goes back relatively far, in the past there was nowhere near the diverse selection of gins we enjoy today. In fact, the story goes back to a time when there was only one variety: genever – the forefather of gin. But today, gin is as diverse as its connoisseurs. Fortunately, there is a gin to suit every gin palate, no matter how discerning. For those not yet familiar with gin and its varieties, here's a roadmap for your gin flavor journey. The best thing to do is not to listen to what others say, but always to try it out. Not only is it fun, it's also interesting to look at the different types of gin. That way you can find out what gin-type you are.

London Dry Gin

Refers to the classic method of production of gin. It all started with this – in England. In the London Dry Gin variant, the juniper note dominates and it's the purest type of gin. A gin made by the London Dry Gin method can come from anywhere: Germany, Switzerland, Spain, Italy, America – wherever. But what the gin must fulfill to pass as a London Dry Gin is this: it must be distilled. Addition of colorants, artificial flavors or sugar is prohibited. Botanicals for the gin must be added during distillation. For some producers, it's a tight corset in which to give free rein to their own creativity, but also a good framework to create great things with craft, creativity and minimalist means.

Dry Gin

Also refers to the production method of the gin and, in this variant too, the gin is distilled with its botanicals. The difference from the London Dry Gin type is that, in Dry Gin, nature-identical flavors, colorants and sugar may be added subsequently. Different spirits may also be blended. In contrast with London Dry Gin, other botanicals have the opportunity here to push the traditional juniper somewhat into the background. For gin connoisseurs who want to take their palate down a complex path every now and then, this is a very good way to discover new nuances. So let's try a Dry Gin.

New Western Dry Gin

The New Western Dry Gin variant does not designate the production method, but a taste category. Here, the juniper note does not necessarily play the main role. In New Western Dry Gin, botanicals such as citrus, herbs or spices also have the opportunity to stand out and give the gin its dominant note. Good for gin connoisseurs who are not quite so inclined to juniper. Or for those who simply don't always want to drink the same gin. Good to know: New Western Dry Gin is made just like a Dry Gin.

Sloe Gin

One immediately thinks of slow gin, i. e. carefully produced gin. But it isn't. Sloe is also known as blackthorn. This gin still gets time: for sloe gin, red sloe berries are soaked in gin for days or weeks. So here it isn't distilled, but steeped. If we were being petty (which we are not), we would say that Sloe Gin is not a gin at all, but a gin-

> "I drank so much gin last night I've woken up with a London Dry accent.

Sloe Gin

Man denkt sofort an Slow Gin, also behutsam hergestellter Gin. Ist es aber nicht. Sloe bedeutet übersetzt Schlehen-Gin. Aber Zeit bekommt er trotzdem: Für den Sloe Gin werden rote Schlehenbeeren tage- oder wochenlang in Gin eingelegt. Hier wird also nicht destilliert, sondern angesetzt. Wenn wir kleinlich wären (was wir aber nicht sind), würden wir sagen, der Sloe Gin ist gar kein Gin, sondern ein Likör auf Gin-Basis, weil der Alkoholgehalt unter 37,5 % liegt und Zucker hinzugefügt wird. Aber zum Glück sind wir nicht kleinlich, sondern Freunde des guten Geschmacks und ein guter Sloe Gin ist ein guter Sloe Gin ist ein guter Sloe Gin. Meistens sehr fruchtig, komplex, mit einem angenehm langen Abgang.

Plymouth Gin

Eine Herkunftsbezeichnung, die früher einmal geschützt war. Für den Plymouth Gin werden intensive Botanicals und weniger Wacholder verwendet. Darum schmeckt er meistens eher mild, erdig, süßlich-fruchtig und hat oft einen langen, angenehmen Abgang. Wie es der Name schon sagt, ist die Herstellung geknüpft an ihren Standort. Nur ein Gin, der innerhalb der Stadtgrenzen von Plymouth destilliert wurde, darf sich auch so nennen. Heute gibt es nur noch eine Destillerie, die den Plymouth Gin nach dem ursprünglichen Rezept herstellt: die Black Friars Distillery in Plymouth – England – und das bereits seit 1793.

Old Tom Gin

Dieser Variante wird etwas Zucker hinzugefügt. Das Ergebnis ist eine spezielle Gin-Variante mit einem süßlichen Geschmack und einer oft wunderschön gelb-goldenen Farbe. Könnte auch Whisky sein, ist aber Gin, ein Gin für Genießer, die gerne ausprobieren und mischen. Denn die Old Tom Gin-Variante ist ideal für Cocktails, aber weniger geeignet als ein Dry Gin für den perfekten Gin Tonic. Einmal im Leben eines Gin-Genießers sollte man einen guten Old Tom Gin probieren – und wer weiß, sich dabei vielleicht sogar verlieben, wie es gerade die New Yorker und Londoner tun? Dort ist der gute alte Old Tom Gin in der Bar-Szene gerade wieder voll am Kommen und genießt bereits große Beliebtheit. Old Tom Gin, wann hältst du endlich Einzug in Berlin?

based liqueur, because the alcohol content is less than 37.5 % and sugar is added. But fortunately, rather than petty, we're friends of good taste and a good sloe gin is a good sloe gin is a good sloe gin. Usually very fruity, complex, with a pleasant long finish.

Plymouth Gin

A designation of origin that was once protected. Plymouth Gin uses intense botanicals and less juniper. That's why it usually tastes rather mild, earthy, sweet-fruity and often has a long, pleasant finish. As the name suggests, its production is tied to its location. Only a gin distilled within the city limits of Plymouth can call itself so. Today, there is only one distillery that still produces Plymouth Gin according to the original recipe: the Black Friars Distillery in Plymouth – England – and has been doing so since 1793..

Old Tom Gin

This variant receives a little sugar. The result is a special gin type with a sweet taste and often a beautiful yellow-gold color. Could also be whiskey, but is actually gin, one for connoisseurs who like to try and mix. Because the Old Tom gin type is ideal for cocktails, but less suitable than a Dry Gin for the perfect gin tonic. Every gin connoisseur should try a good Old Tom Gin at least once in their lifetime – and who knows, maybe even fall in love with it, as New Yorkers and Londoners are doing right now. There, good Old Tom Gin is on the rise again in the bar scene and already enjoys great popularity. Old Tom Gin, when will you finally come to Berlin?

Bathtub Gin

The name says it all: this gin variant used to be made in secret in people's own bathtubs. It was so quick and easy that the gin supply ran smoothly. It didn't take much – just a little experimentation and a bathtub. In terms of taste, of course, it is far removed from today's gin varieties and they don't use a bathtub in production. But, to this day, the technique of cold maceration is still used. For this – just as in the past – herbs and plants are cut into small pieces, chopped or pressed and placed in alcohol. The aromas of the botanicals dissolve and combine with the clear spirit. After a

Bathtub Gin

Der Name sagt es schon: Diese Gin-Variante wurde früher schwarz und heimlich in der eigenen Badewanne hergestellt. Das ging so einfach und schnell, dass der Gin-Nachschub reibungslos verlief. Dafür brauchte es nicht viel – nur ein wenig Experimentierfreude und eben eine Badewanne. Geschmacklich ist er natürlich von den heutigen Gin-Sorten weit entfernt und man verzichtet bei der Herstellung auf eine Badewanne. Aber auch derzeitig wird die Technik der kalten Mazeration angewendet. Dafür werden – genau wie früher – Kräuter und Pflanzen klein geschnitten, gehackt oder gepresst und in Alkohol eingelegt. Die Aromen der Botanicals lösen sich und verbinden sich mit der klaren Spirituose. Nach ein paar Tagen oder Wochen, je nachdem, welchen Anspruch man an das Destillat hat, ist der Gin fertig. That's it.

Einfach, einfallsreich und früher sehr erfolgreich. Heute eher unpopulär bei den Genießern, aber bei den Machern, die ihren ersten eigenen Gin herstellen wollen, ein Hit. Weil – das liegt auf der Hand – es einfach ist und eine Badewanne hat auch fast jeder zu Hause. Die Frage ist nur: Wer will den Gin danach auch trinken? Gut, dass es auch experimentierfreudige Gin-Anfänger gibt, die nicht nur genießen, sondern auch kreieren wollen. Good luck in the bathtub!

Die Suche nach dem besten Gin der Welt

Und dann gibt es noch etwas ganz Besonderes... wer dem Whisky nicht abgeneigt ist, der wird Gefallen finden an einem großartigen Barrel Aged Gin. Diese Sorte Gin verlangt viel Ruhe und Zeit und bekommt sie auch. Lange bis sehr lange darf das Destillat in Holz-Fässern reifen, wo der Gin und seine Botanicals sich so richtig schön entfalten können. Das Ergebnis: Ein charaktervoller Gin, in den sich auch Whisky-Liebhaber verlieben...

Wie auch immer, es gibt viele Sorten und noch mehr Gins. Welche darf es für den Gaumen sein? Stopp – bevor ihr die Frage für euch beantwortet – ihr müsst euch gar nicht auf eine einzige Sorte festlegen. Wir schauen auf Netflix ja auch nicht immer nur eine Serie an. Es gibt unsere Lieblingsserien und andere Serien, die vielleicht speziell sind, aber auch ihren Reiz haben. Manchmal entscheidet die Stimmung, die Jahreszeit, der Gaumen oder der Bartender eures Vertrauens. Oder wie es der große, leider schon verstorbene Anthony Bourdain gesagt hat: Der beste Wein ist der, der dir schmeckt. Das gilt nicht nur für Wein, das gilt... für alles, auch für den Gin.

Also: Der beste Gin der Welt ist immer der, der euch am besten schmeckt. Punkt. Und wie findet ihr diesen Gin? Ausprobieren, experimentieren, testen, vergleichen. Lasst euch führen, hört auf euren Gaumen und auf eure Zunge: Eure Geschmacksknospen werden euch leiten.

In diesem Sinne: Viel Freude und Genuss beim Entdecken!

> **Drink responsibly – Don't spill any.**

few days or weeks, depending on the expectations of the distillate, the gin is ready. That's it.

Simple, inventive and once very successful. Today tending to be unpopular with connoisseurs, but a hit with crafters who want to make their own first gin. Because – it's obvious – it's easy, and almost everyone has a bathtub at home, too. The only question is, who wants to drink the gin afterwards? It's a good thing that there are also gin beginners who are eager to experiment, who not only want to enjoy, but also create. Good luck in the bathtub!

The search for the best gin in the world

And then there is something very special... anyone who is not averse to whiskey will find pleasure in a great Barrel Aged Gin. This type of gin requires a lot of rest and time, and it gets it. The distillate is allowed to mature in wooden barrels for a long to very long time, where the gin and its botanicals can really develop. The result, a gin full of character, with which even whiskey lovers fall in love...

Anyway, there are many types and even more gins. Which one would you like for your palate? Stop – before you answer that question for yourself – you don't have to commit to just one type. We don't always watch just one series on Netflix. There are our favorite series and other series that may be different, but also have their own appeal. Sometimes it's the mood, the season, the palate or the bartender you trust that decides. Or as the great, sadly departed Anthony Bourdain said: The best wine is the one that tastes the best to you. That's not just true for wine, it's true... for everything, including gin.

So, the best gin in the world is always the one that tastes best to you, period. How to track this gin down? Try, experiment, test, compare. Let yourself be guided, listen to your palate and your tongue – your taste buds will guide you.

In that spirit: Have fun and enjoy discovering!

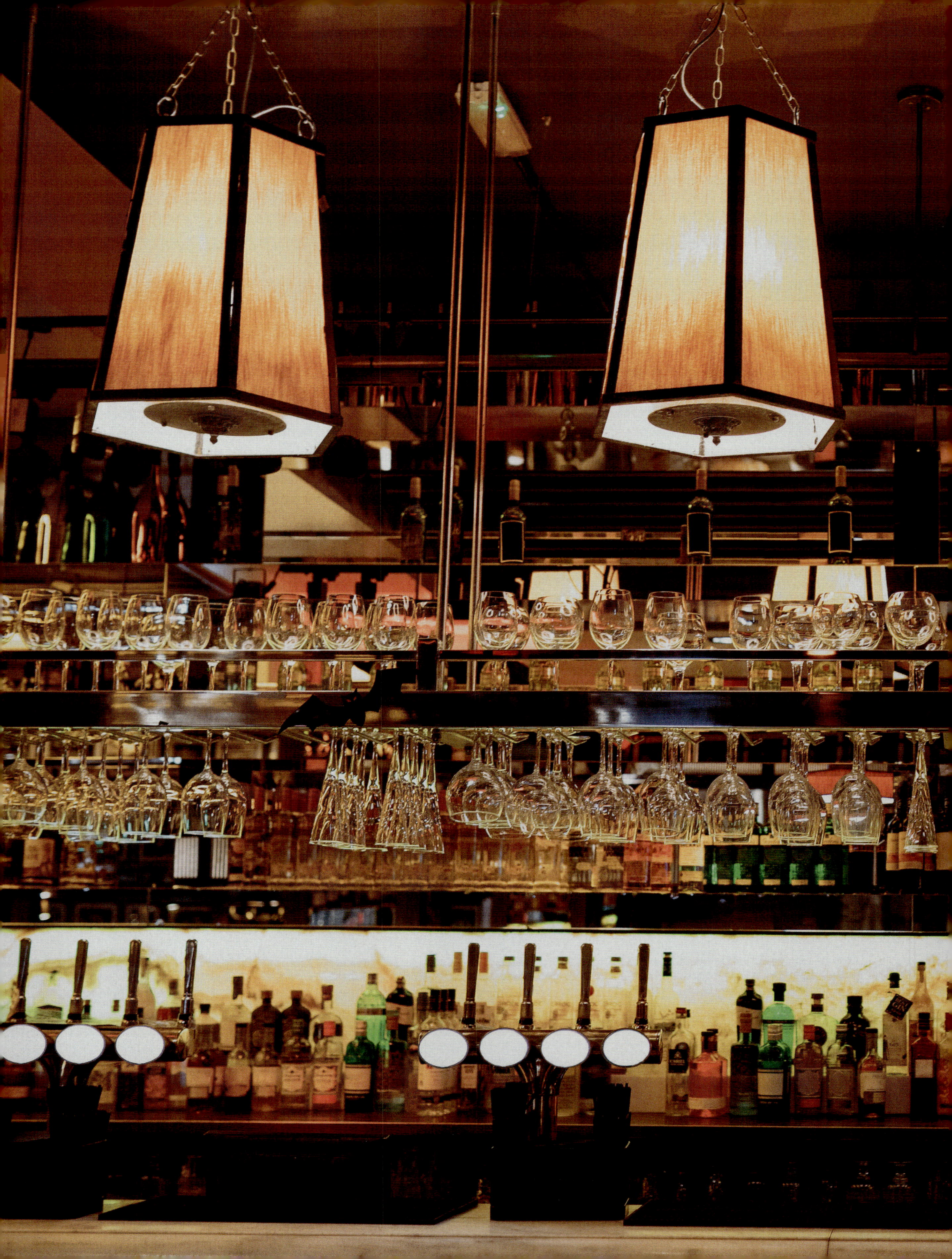

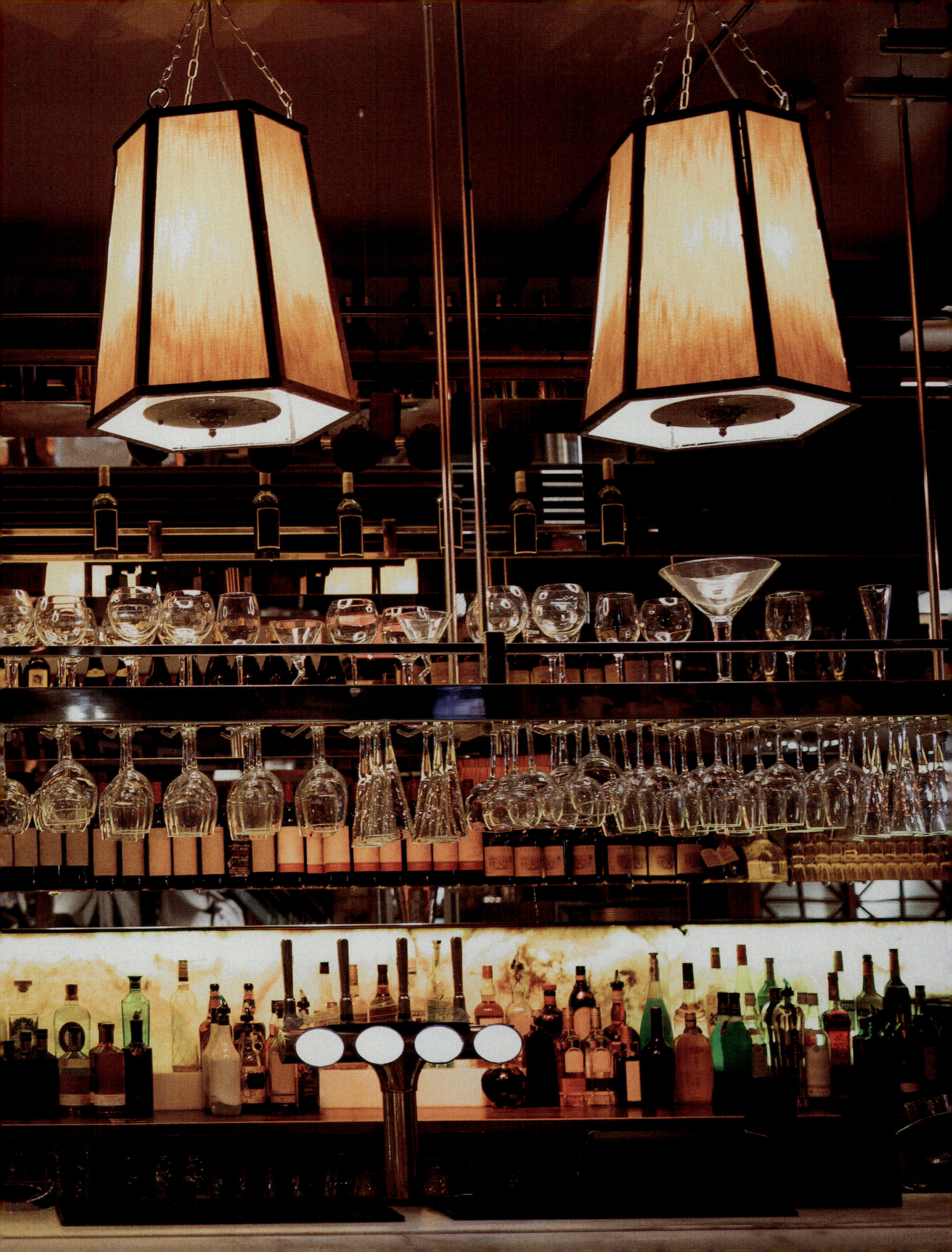

HOW TO MAKE A GIN

The ultimate guide to your homemade gin

Ihr wolltet schon immer mal euren eigenen Homemade-Gin machen? Ihr habt eine Badewanne? Scherz, ihr braucht keine Badewanne, trotzdem ist es super einfach, seinen eigenen Gin zu Hause herzustellen. Das Ergebnis ist vielleicht kein Spitzen-Premium-Gin, der mit den ganz großen Gins mithalten kann, aber er ist genießbar und es macht Spaß. Am besten geht ihr das Homemade-Gin-Projekt mit zwei, drei Freunden zusammen an. Übrigens ist der selbstgemachte Gin mit einem liebevoll gestalteten Etikett auch ein geniales Geburtstagsgeschenk – wer kann so ein Geschenk schon toppen? Wer weiß, vielleicht ist das ja auch der Start einer großen Gin-Macher-Karriere. Dann habt ihr schon mal eine gute Story, die bei euch zu Hause in eurer Küche ihren Anfang genommen hat..

Always wanted to make your own homemade gin? You have a bathtub? Jus kidding, you don't need a bathtub, yet it's super easy to make your own gin at home. The result may not be a top-of-the-line premium gin that can compete with the really big gins, but it's enjoyable and it's fun. It's best to tackle the homemade gin project with two or three friends. By the way, homemade gin with a lovingly designed label is also a brilliant birthday gift – who can top a gift like that? Who knows, maybe this is the start of a great gin-making career. Then you'll already have a good story that starts in your kitchen at home....

Zutaten für eine Flasche Gin (750 ml)

- 2 EL getrocknete Wacholderbeeren
- 1 EL schwarze Pfefferkörner
- 1 EL Koriandersamen
- 6 Kardamomkapseln
- 2 Zimtstangen
- 1 Bio-Zitrone
- 1 Bio-Orange
- 2 Zweige Rosmarin
- 3 kleine Lorbeerblätter
- 30 g Ingwerknolle
- 750 ml Korn oder Wodka
- 1 großes Schraubglas mit einem Fassungsvermögen von 1-1,5 Liter

Ingredients for a bottle of gin (750 ml)

- *2 tbsp dried juniper berries*
- *1 tbsp black peppercorns*
- *1 tbsp coriander seeds*
- *6 cardamom pods*
- *2 cinnamon sticks*
- *1 organic lemon*
- *1 organic orange*
- *2 sprigs rosemary*
- *3 small bay leaves*
- *30 g ginger bulb*
- *750 ml grain spirit or vodka*
- *1 large screw-top jar with a capacity of 1-1.5 liters*

Homemade-Gin Step #1: Aller Anfang ist leicht – super leicht

Die Wacholderbeeren in einem Mörser zerstoßen. Ab in die Pfanne damit und zusammen mit Pfefferkörnern, Koriandersamen, Kardamom und Zimtstangen ohne Fett kurz anrösten. Auf einen kalten Teller schütten und abkühlen lassen.

Homemade gin step #1: getting going is easy – super easy.

Crush the juniper berries in a mortar. Put them in the pan with the juniper berries and, together with peppercorns, coriander seeds, cardamom and cinnamon sticks, roast briefly without oil. Tip onto a cold plate and let cool.

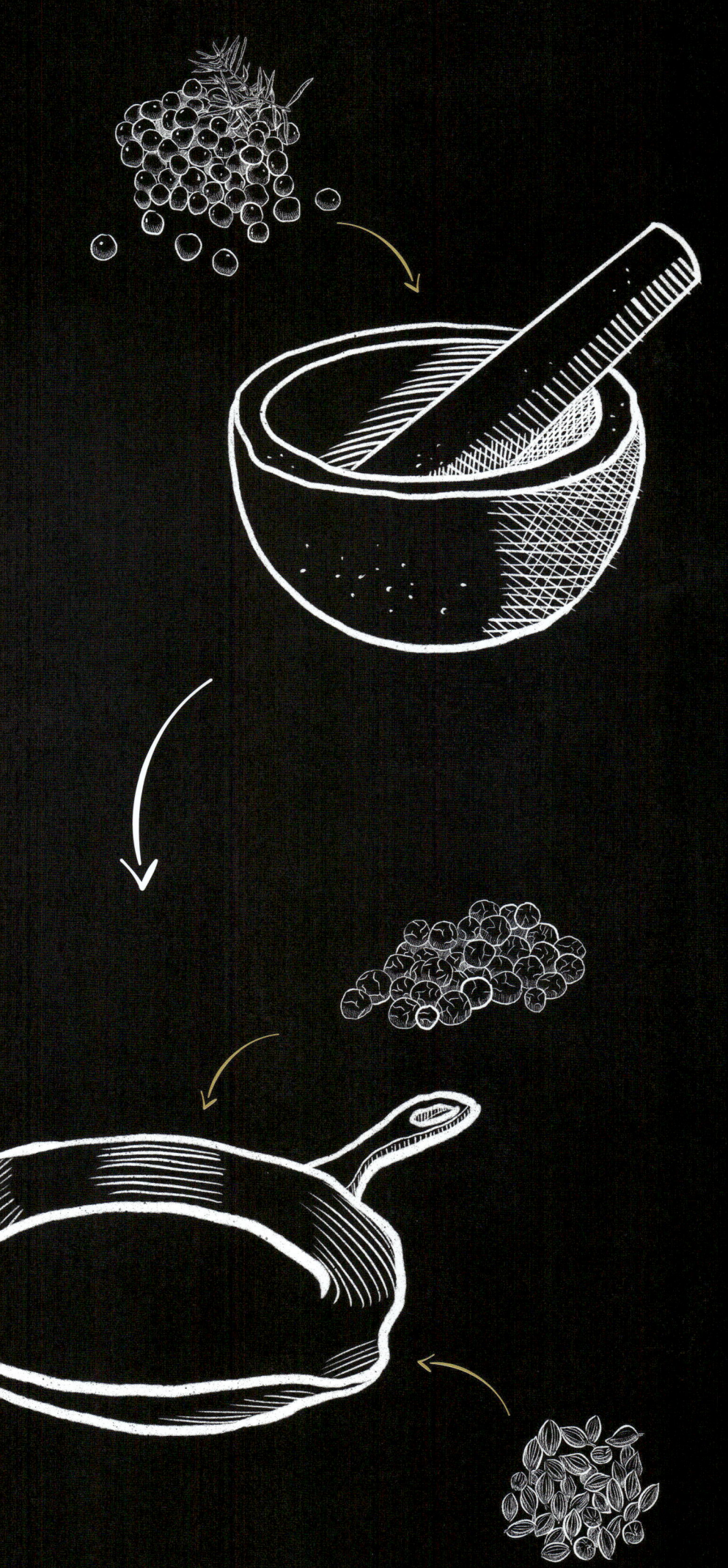

2

Homemade-Gin Step #2: Halbzeit – Gin o' clock

Zitrone und Orange heiß waschen und abtrocknen. Die Hälfte der Schale von Zitrone und Orange als dünne Streifen (Zesten) abschneiden. Lorbeer, Ingwer und Rosmarin waschen und mit einem Küchentuch trocken tupfen. Ingwer ungeschält in feine Scheiben schneiden.

Homemade gin step #2: half-time – gin o'clock

Wash lemon and orange hot and dry. Cut off half of the peel from the lemon and orange as thin strips (zests). Wash bay leaf, ginger and rosemary and pat dry with kitchen towel. Cut unpeeled ginger into thin slices.

Mit Händchen und Näschen für Botanicals zum World Gin Award

Fertig? That's it. So einfach ist es, einen Homemade-Gin zu produzieren. Das ist das Gin-Grundrezept. Und das ist nur der Anfang. Fügt ganz nach Belieben eure Traum-Botanicals hinzu: Minze, Beeren, Blüten, Basilikum, Fenchel, Pflanzen, Wurzeln, Grüner Tee – was auch immer. Lasst euch dafür am besten von den Brand Portraits hier im Buch inspirieren. Testet, probiert, experimentiert – genau so haben viele große und geniale Gin-Macher angefangen. Wenn ihr ein Händchen und ein Näschen für Botanicals habt, sehen wir uns vielleicht schon bald bei den World Gin Awards.

With a knack and a nose for botanicals, off to the World Gin Awards

Ready? Done – that's it. It's that easy to produce a homemade gin. That's the basic gin recipe. But that's just the beginning. You can add your dream botanicals however you like: mint, berries, flowers, basil, fennel, plants, roots, green tea – whatever. Let yourself be inspired by the Brand Portraits here in the book. Test, try, experiment – that's exactly how many great and brilliant gin makers started. If you have a knack and a nose for botanicals, maybe we'll see you soon at the World Gin Awards.

3

**Homemade-Gin Step #3:
Das große Finale**

Geröstete Gewürze, Zitronen- und Orangenschale, Rosmarin, Lorbeer und Ingwer zusammen mit dem Korn oder Wodka in das große Schraubglas geben. Deckel drauf und fest verschließen. Jetzt braucht ihr etwas Geduld, aber ihr müsst nicht davorsitzen und warten, bis das Ganze drei Tage durchgezogen ist. Macht, was immer ihr so macht: Trinkt Gin, geht zur Arbeit, in die Bar, schaut Netflix und dann, endlich nach drei Tagen...

... dürft ihr euer Destillat durch ein feines Sieb filtern, kurz stehenlassen, damit die feinsten Wacholderbeerteilchen sich am Boden absetzen, und dann vorsichtig (ohne Bodensatz) zurück in das (sauber ausgewaschene und getrocknete) Schraubglas gießen.

*Homemade gin step #3:
The grand finale.*

Add roasted spices, lemon and orange zest, rosemary, bay leaf and ginger to the large screw-top jar along with the grain spirit or vodka. Put the lid on and close tightly. Now you need some patience, but you don't have to sit in front of it and wait for it to infuse for all three days. Do whatever you do: drink gin, go to work, go to the bar, watch Netflix and then, finally, after three days....

... you can filter your distillate through a fine sieve, let it stand for a short time, so that the finest juniper berry particles settle at the bottom, and then carefully (without sediment) back into the (cleanly washed and dried) screw-top jar.

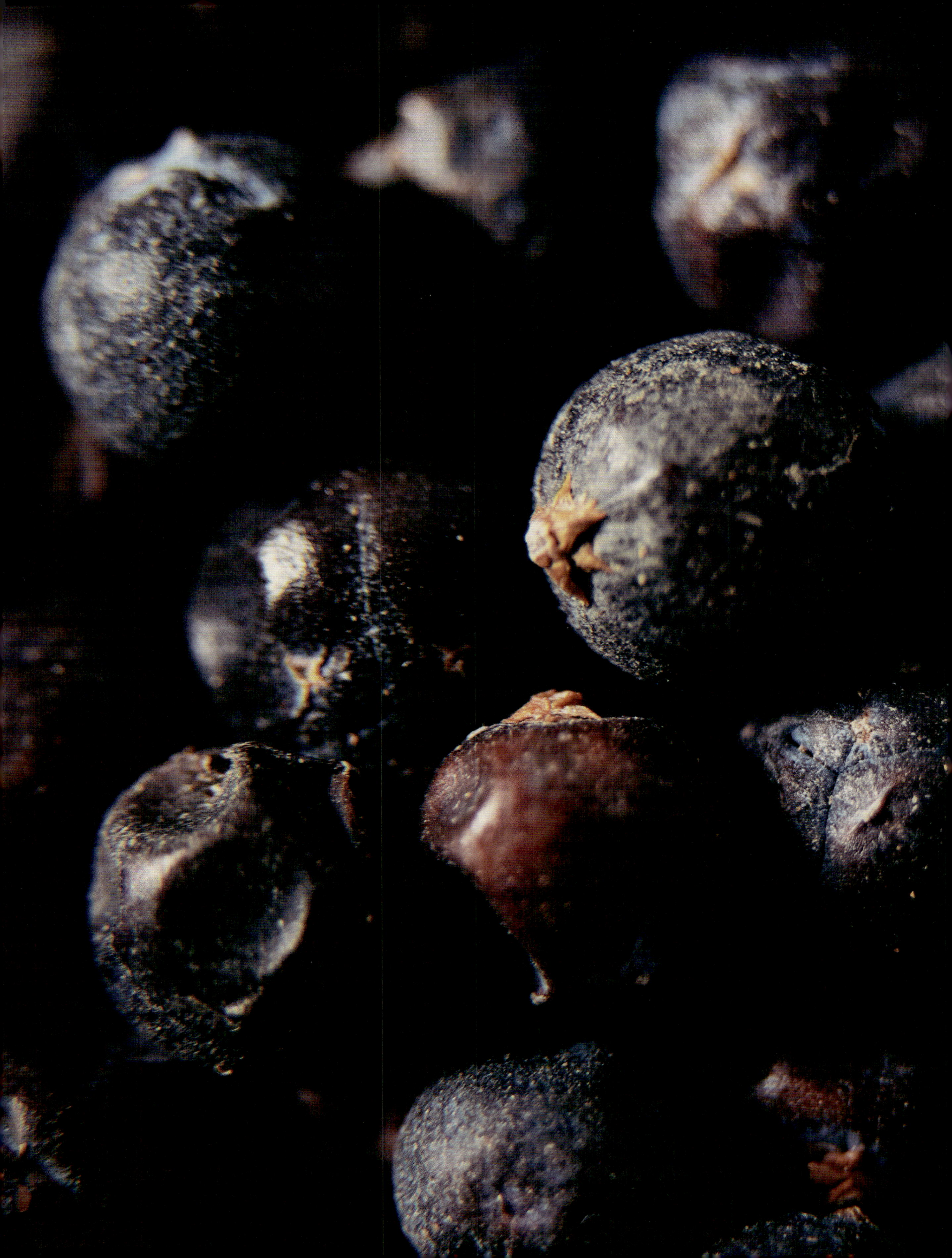

> "Once upon a time there was juniper. And it became gin.

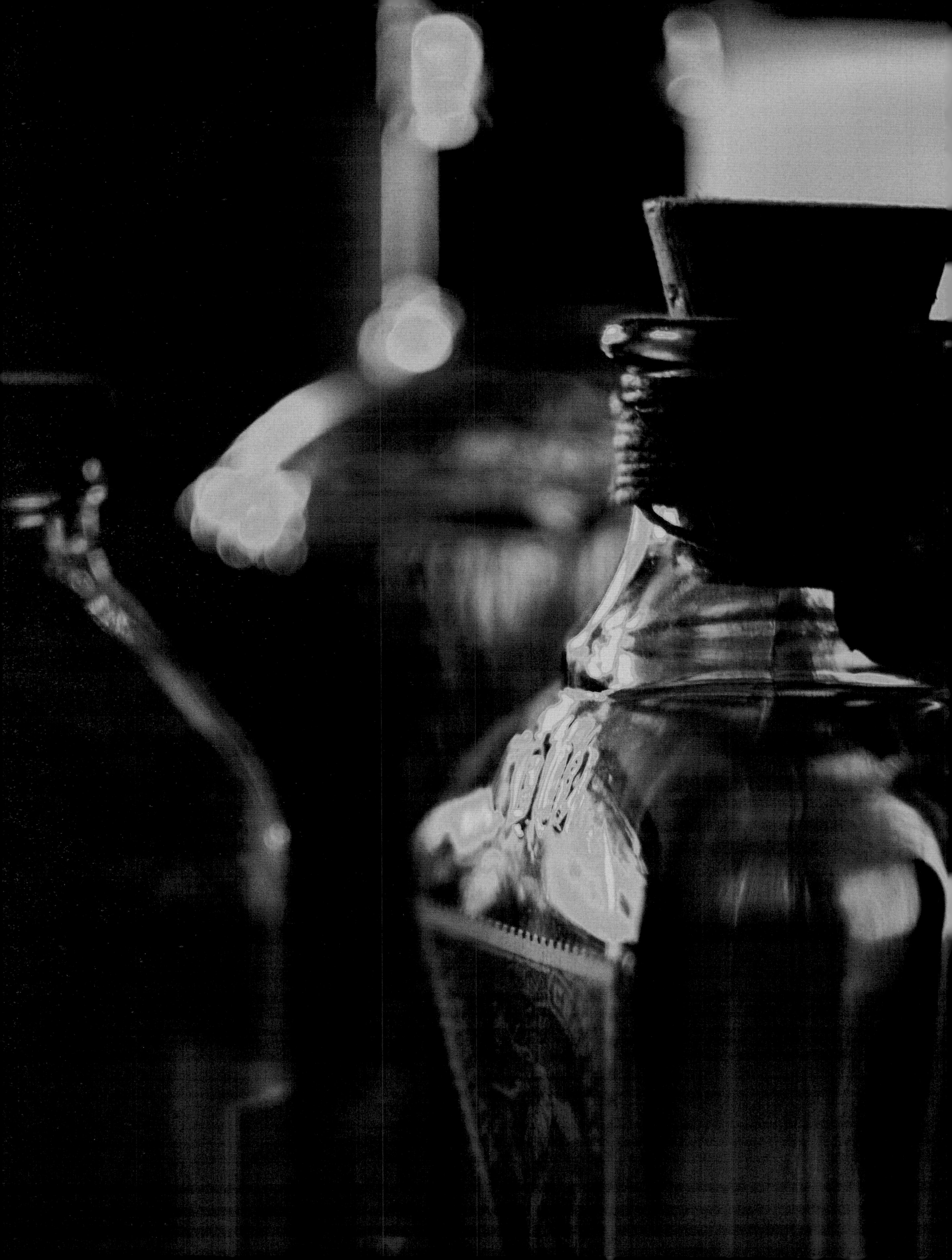

2
STORIES

THE GIN-STORY

Die Suche nach dem Wunderheilmittel

Es ist das frühe 17. Jahrhundert. Der in Hanau geborene Francois de la Boë studiert in der kleinen Stadt Leiden in der niederländischen Provinz Südhollands. Dort widmet sich der angehende junge Mediziner seinen Studien. Voller Forscherdrang und Experimentierfreude stürzt er sich in die Suche nach einer neuartigen Medizin und mischt Wacholder mit Alkohol. Das ist nicht ganz neu. Ganz und gar nicht. Ähnliche Experimente wurden schon 1.000 Jahre nach Christi Geburt an der medizinischen Lehr- und Forschungsanstalt in Salerno durchgeführt, eine der ältesten Universitäten Europas.

Schon damals war der Wacholder für seine positive und heilende Wirkung bekannt. Wenn Wacholder in der Lage ist, Sodbrennen, Verdauungsstörungen und Harnprobleme zu lindern, dann ist die Wunderpflanze vermutlich noch zu viel Größerem fähig, denkt de la Boë. Dem jungen Studenten erscheint es nur logisch und sehr vielversprechend, diesen Weg weiter zu verfolgen. Intensiver und genauer als seine Vorgänger. Ja, er würde nicht eher aufgeben, bevor er mit seinem Experiment erfolgreich wäre. De la Boë entwickelt die Wacholder-Alkohol-Mischung und gibt weitere Pflanzen hinzu.

Von der Manie zum Meilenstein in der modernen Medizin

De la Boë ist fasziniert von seinem Experiment und arbeitet wie besessen weiter, oft bis zum frühen Morgen. Dann wandelt er völlig übermüdet, aber zuversichtlich durch die Innenstadt von Leiden, vorbei an den Grachten und den Kanälen, in denen das dunkle Wasser gegen die Stadtmauern schwappt. Mit dem Kopf voller Gedanken an sein Experiment lässt er sich ziellos durch die Gassen treiben. Bemerkt kaum die ersten Passanten, die an ihm vorbeieilen, auf ihrem Weg zur Arbeit oder zum Markt. Die Absätze seiner einzigen Schuhe klappern rhythmisch zu den Gedankenblitzen in seinem Kopf. Eine Symphonie, die das Flackern seines Schattens an den Häuserfassaden begleitet. Bis die lauten Glocken des Kirch-

The search for the miracle cure

It is the early 17th century. Born in Hanau, Francois de la Boë is studying in the small town of Leiden in the Netherlands province of South Holland. There, the budding young physician devotes himself to his studies. Full of the urge to explore and experiment, he plunges into the search for a new kind of medicine and mixes juniper with alcohol. This is not entirely new. Not at all. Similar experiments were conducted as early as 1,000 years after the birth of Christ at the medical teaching and research institute in Salerno, one of the oldest universities in Europe.

Even then, juniper was known for its positive and healing effects. If juniper is able to relieve heartburn, indigestion and urinary problems, then the miracle plant is probably capable of much greater things, reasons De la Boë. To this young student, it seems only logical and very promising to pursue this path further.

„ Even children love Genever

turms ihn aus seiner Gedankenwelt herausreißen und er sich auf den Weg macht zurück zur Universität.

Zuversichtlich feilt er die nächsten Wochen an seiner Wacholder-Kreation und tauft sie eines Nachts auf den Namen Genever – abgeleitet von dem lateinischen Namen des Wacholders: Juniperus. Nach seinem erfolgreichen Abschluss an der Universität macht er sich als Mediziner selbständig und verabreicht seinen ersten Patienten seinen Genever, um deren Magenbeschwerden und Nierenerkrankungen zu bekämpfen. Mit seinen Ergebnissen und Erkenntnissen aus den Experimenten und deren positiven Auswirkungen auf die moderne Medizin begründet de la Boë die naturwissenschaftliche Medizin und die klinische Chemie. Seine Aufzeichnungen und Ergebnisse sind ein Meilenstein in der modernen Medizin.

Sogar Kinder lieben den Genever

Unterdessen schlägt seine Medizin bei den Patienten an – vor allem geschmacklich. Kaum eine andere Medizin wird von ihnen

More intensively and more precisely than his predecessors. Indeed, he has no intention of giving up before achieving success with his experiments. De la Boë develops the juniper-alcohol mixture and adds other plants.

From mania to a milestone in modern medicine

De la Boë is fascinated by his experiment and continues to work obsessively, often till the early hours. Then, completely overtired but confident, he wanders through downtown Leiden, past the canals and sewers where the dark water laps against the city walls. With his head full of thoughts about his experiment, he drifts aimlessly through the alleys. Barely noticing the first passersby, who hurry past him on their way to work or to the market. The heels of his only shoes clack rhythmically alongside the flashes of thought in his head. A symphony that accompanies the flickering of his shadow on the facades of the houses. Until the loud bells of the church tower pull him out of his world of thoughts and he sets off back to the university.

Confidently, he spends the next few weeks fine-tuning his juniper creation and, one night, christens it Genever – derived from the Latin name of the juniper: Juniperus. Following his successful graduation from the university, he becomes a self-employed physician and administers his Genever to his first patients to combat their stomach complaints and kidney diseases. With his results and findings from the experiments and their positive impact on modern medicine, De la Boë founded scientific medicine and clinical chemistry. His records and results are a milestone in modern medicine.

so begrüßt, denn die meisten anderen Tinkturen und Aufgüsse schmecken grässlich. Aber dieses Heilmittel, das dieser junge Arzt hier entwickelt hat, wird wegen seines hervorragenden Geschmacks und, ja, auch wegen seiner heilenden Wirkung sehr geschätzt. Seine Patienten sind – ohne es zu wissen – Gin-Fans der ersten Stunde und ebnen dem Gin seinen Siegeszug. Die Medizin erobert die Stadt wie im Sturm – ach was, wie ein Tornado fegt sie über Leiden hinweg. Jeder schluckt schon binnen Kurzem die Medizin – den wohltuenden Genever aus Leiden. Bald darauf eilt sein guter und heilender Ruf über die Stadtgrenzen hinaus und erobert die Niederlande. Der Bedarf nach de la Boës Wunderheilmittel steigt so rasant an, dass Apotheken die Nachfrage kaum mehr abdecken können. De la Boë grübelt, wandelt durch Leiden, vorbei an den Grachten und den Kanälen, lauscht dem dunklen Wasser und dann hat er die Idee, wie er seine Patienten mit dem dringend benötigten Genever versorgen kann.

De la Boë besucht umliegende Brennereien und stellt ihnen erfolgreich seine Idee vor. Man beginnt mit der Herstellung und damit ist die industrielle Produktion des Genevers geboren. Aber noch eine andere Tatsache spielt de la Boë bei der Verbreitung seiner „Medizin" in die Hände und in die Gaumen der Patienten (Gin-Genießer): Der Handel nimmt zeitgleich rasant zu. Es werden immer mehr Boote gezimmert, man baut die Handelstätigkeit zu anderen Ländern aus und den Rest tut der Niederländisch-Spanische Krieg: Durch die bereitwillige Unterstützung englischer Soldaten – die von dieser „Medizin" ebenfalls sehr angetan sind – gelangt der Genever in Kürze und in rauen Mengen auf die britischen Inseln, wo er bald darauf liebevoll auf den Namen „Gin" getauft wird.

Von hier aus erobert die „Medizin" ganz England – aber fortan an als das, was die Medizin in Wahrheit auch ist: eine wunderbar köstliche Spirituose, die vielleicht keine Wunderheilung vollbringen kann, dafür aber herrlich trunken und glückselig macht. 1740 trinkt jeder Engländer – Kinder eingeschlossen – durchschnittlich einen halben Liter Gin am Tag.

Die Eroberung der Welt

Aus den Patienten – männlich oder weiblich, ganz egal – werden leidenschaftliche Trunkenbolde. In kürzester Zeit verfällt das finstere England dem Dauersuff. Kaum ein Engländer hat noch irgendwelche Krankheitssymptome, dafür sind so gut wie alle Bürger durchgehend besoffen. Das geht nun doch zu weit. Man versucht, die Gin-Herstellung zu regulieren. Das Gesetz erfreut Schwarzbrenner, in ihrem Hobby und ihrer Leidenschaft ihre Berufung zu finden. 1743 verschärft man die Vorschriften weiter. Ohne Erfolg. Es wird immer mehr Gin ohne Lizenz gebrannt.

Bevor der Gin sich später zu einem qualitativ hochwertigen Produkt und zu einer der beliebtesten Spirituosen weltweit entwickelt, sollte noch einige Zeit vergehen, in der weitere Verbote und Reglementierungen verhängt werden. Aber das ist eine andere Geschichte, von der ihr Auslöser und der Erfinder des „Gins" de la Boë nichts mehr mitbekommen wird.

Even children love Genever

Time passes and his medicine is striking a chord with patients – especially in terms of taste. Few other medicines are so welcomed by their patients, because most other tinctures and infusions taste dreadful. But this remedy, developed by our young doctor, is highly appreciated for its excellent taste and yes, also for its healing properties. His patients are – without knowing it – early-adopting gin fans and pave the way for gin's triumphal procession. The medicine takes the city by storm; for goodness' sake, like a tornado it sweeps over ailments. Soon enough, everyone is swallowing the medicine – the soothing Genever from Leiden. Soon after, its good and healing reputation breaches the city limits and conquers the Netherlands. The demand for De la Boë's miracle remedy increases so rapidly that pharmacies can hardly keep up with the demand. De la Boë ponders, wanders through Leiden, past the canals and sewers, listening to the dark water, and then he has an idea of how to supply his patients with that urgently-needed Genever.

De la Boë visits surrounding distilleries and successfully presents his idea to them. Production begins, and the industrial production of Genever is born. But, in the distribution of his "medicine", another factor plays into De la Boë's hands as well as the palates of those patients (gin fans): trade increases rapidly at the same time. More and more boats are built, trade with other countries is expanded, and the Dutch-Spanish War does the rest. Thanks to the willing support of English soldiers, who are also very fond of this "medicine", Genever soon reaches the British Isles in great quantities, where, shortly afterwards, it is affectionately christened "gin". From here, the "medicine" conquers the whole of England , albeit henceforth as what the medicine is in truth, a wonderfully delicious spirit that may not be able to perform a miracle cure, but renders the "patient" agreeably drunk and blissful. In 1740, every Englishman, children included, drank an average of half a liter of gin a day.

The conquest of the world

The "patients" – male or female, it doesn't matter – become passionate drunkards. In no time at all, gloomy England falls into a permanent drunken stupor. Scarcely any of the English have any symptoms of illness any more, given almost all citizens are permanently drunk. This has gone too far. Attempts are made to regulate gin production. The law prompts moonshiners to escalate their hobby and passion to a vocation. In 1743, the regulations are further tightened. Without success. Ever more gin is distilled without a license.

Before gin ultimately developed into a high-quality product, and one of the most popular spirits in the world, some time was to pass during which further prohibitions and regulations were imposed. But that's another story, which its initiator and the inventor of "gin", De la Boë, will never hear.

"
Gin there,
done that.

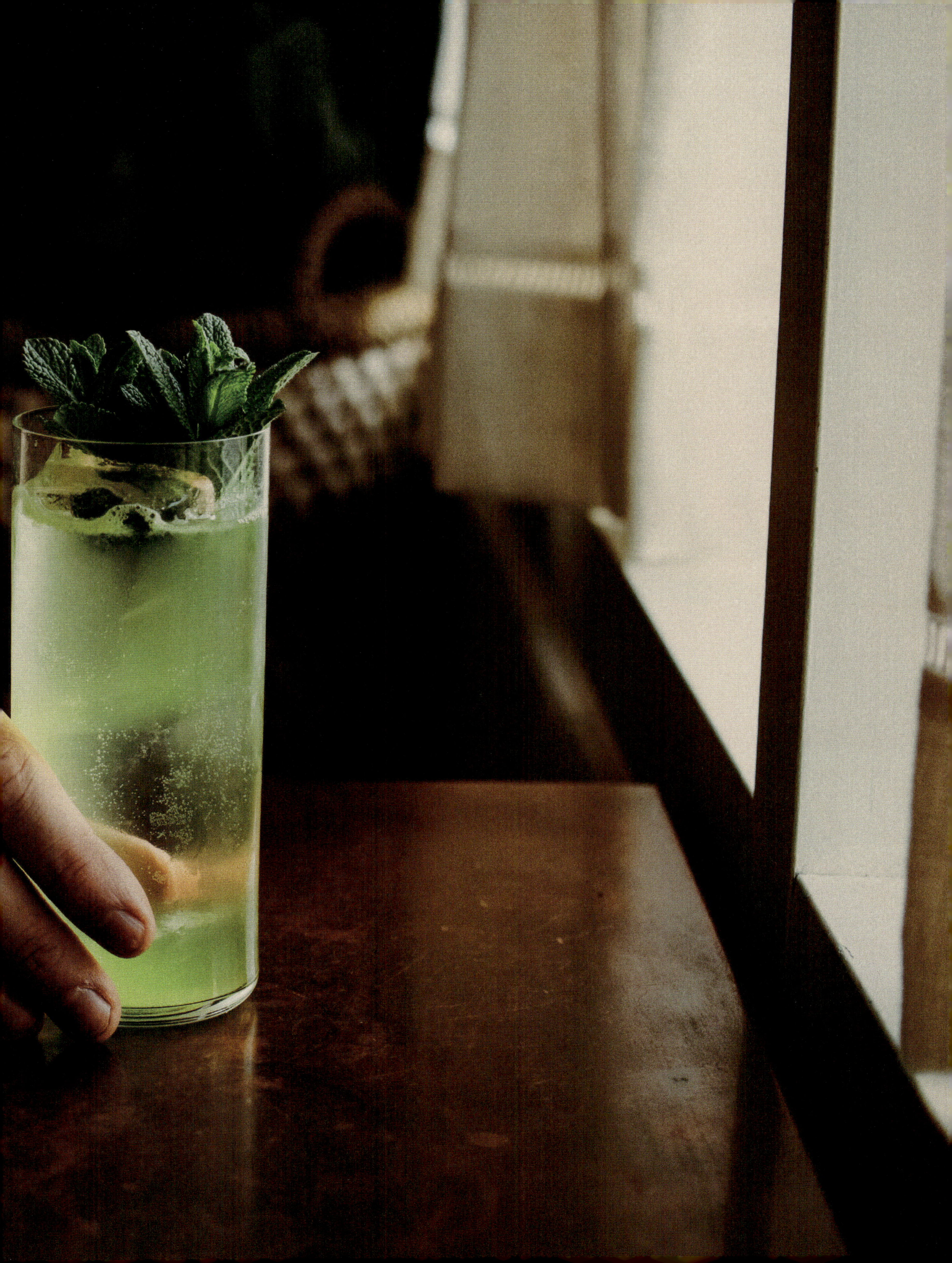

Die peruanischen Inkas bieten ihren Gästen kleine Schätze und Kostbarkeiten an. Darunter auch die Rinde des sogenannten Chinarinden-Baumes.

THE TONIC-STORY

Das un:bekannte Jahr der großen Entdeckung

... ist nicht mehr genau zuzuordnen. Es muss wohl zwischen 1620 und 1630 gewesen sein. Aber was machen schon zehn Jahre aus in einer Zeit, die fast 400 Jahre zurück liegt?

Im 17. Jahrhundert also werden spanische Jesuiten „im Auftrag Gottes" zur Eroberung Südamerikas ausgesandt, wo sie der indigenen Bevölkerung zu ihrem Glück verhelfen und sie missionieren sollen. Noch angetan vom Besuch der Spanier bieten die peruanischen Inkas ihren Gästen kleine Schätze und Kostbarkeiten an. Darunter

The year of the great discovery

... can no longer be precisely identified. It must have been between 1620 and 1630. But what difference does ten years make in a time that goes back almost 400 years?

So, in the 17th century, Spanish Jesuits are sent out "on a mission from God" to the ongoing conquest of South America, where they are to help the indigenous population find contentment and to missionize them. Still somewhat taken by the Spaniards' visit, the Peruvian Incas offer their guests small treasures and precious

auch die Rinde des sogenannten Chinarinden-Baumes (Cinchona pubescens). Die Spanier fragen sich zuerst, was es mit dieser seltsamen Rinde auf sich hat und was sie damit anfangen sollen. Stolz machen die Inkas sie auf die heilsame Wirkung der Rinde aufmerksam. Erst skeptisch, werden die von Gott ausgesandten Spanier jedoch schon bald von der heilenden Wirkung dieser Rinde überzeugt.

Wettlauf mit der Zeit und hoffen auf ein Wunder

1638 erkrankt die Countess of Chinchon, Ehefrau des nun amtierenden Vizekönigs von Peru, an Malaria. Man verabreicht ihr Tinkturen und Pulver. Keine Medizin hilft. Die Zeit wird knapp. Wenn man nichts findet, was der Frau hilft, wird sie in wenigen Tagen tot sein. Fast schon vergessen, kramt man die Rinde hervor. „Was ist das?", fragt der Vizekönig. Die Rinde des Chinarinden-Baumes, antwortet man ihm. Er hat... er soll eine heilende Wirkung haben. Der Vizekönig zögert, blickt auf seine sterbende Frau. Er nickt, macht eine kaum merkliche Geste mit dem Zeigefinger.

Man verabreicht der Countess of Chinchon das geriebene Pulver der Rinde. Die Wunder-Medizin schlägt an und die Vizekönigsgattin erholt sich schon bald vollständig von der Malaria. Das ist er Beweis für die heilsame Wirkung dieser Wunderrinde. Schon bald setzt man das aus der Rinde gewonnene Pulver erfolgreich zur Bekämpfung von Malaria und zur Fiebersenkung ein. Der Chinarinden-Baum wird zu Ehren der Countess of Chinchon umbenannt zu „Chinchona-Baum".

Eine schmackhafte Lösung für ein ungenießbares Problem

Das Timing könnte nicht besser sein für eine Medizin, die bei der Bekämpfung von Malaria hilft: Die Britische Ostindien-Gesellschaft benötigte große Mengen Chinin, um die britischen Soldaten vor den grassierenden Symptomen der Malaria zu schützen. Man schluckt die „bittere Pille" – das bittere Chinin-Pulver aufgelöst in Wasser – täglich als Prophylaxe. Bis ein vergesslicher, aber findiger Offizier auf die Idee kommt, wie man das bittere Pulver auch schmackhafter einnehmen kann.

Der Auslöser ist Vergesslichkeit. Während Offiziere und Soldaten bei ihrem abendlichen Gin zusammensitzen, fällt besagtem Offizier ein, dass er am Morgen vergessen hatte, das Chinin-Pulver zu schlucken. Dieser Geistesblitz ist der Aus-löser: Er gibt das Pulver in seinen Gin, den er mit Sodawasser aufgefüllt hat, und trinkt das Glas in einem Zug leer. Man ist begeistert von diesem wahrlich grandiosen Geistesblitz und gibt von nun an das Chinin-Pulver in den allabendlichen Gin. Eine kreative und schmackhafte Lösung für ein ungenießbares Problem.

Eine kleine Idee erobert als Gin & Tonic die ganze Welt

Auch wenn zu diesem Zeitpunkt noch keiner wissen kann, was es mit dieser kleinen großen Idee auf sich hat – es ist die Geburtsstunde des original Gin & Tonic, der schon bald die Welt erobern sollte.

> ## About a healing miracle bark.

objects. Among them is the bark of the so-called cinchona tree (Cinchona pubescens). The Spaniards initially wonder what the significance of this strange bark might be and what they should do with it. The Incas proudly point out the healing properties of the bark. Skeptical at first, the Spaniards sent by God are soon convinced of the healing properties of this bark.

Race against time and hope for a miracle

In 1638, the Countess of Chinchon, wife of the incumbent Viceroy of Peru, falls ill with malaria. She is given tinctures and powders. No medicine helps. Time is running out. If nothing is found to help the woman, she will be dead in a few days. Almost forgotten, they dig out the bark. What is it, asks the viceroy. The bark of the cinchona tree, he is told. It has... is said to have a healing effect. The viceroy hesitates, looks at his dying wife. He nods, makes a barely perceptible gesture with his index finger.

The grated powder of the bark is administered to the Countess of Chinchon. The miracle medicine takes effect and the Countess of Chinchon soon recovers completely from malaria. Now there is proof of the healing effect of this miracle bark. Soon, powder extracted from the bark is successfully used to fight malaria and reduce fever. The tree that yields the bark is renamed in honor of the Countess of Chinchon to "Chinchona tree".

A tasty solution to an inedible problem

The timing couldn't have been better for a medicine that helps fight malaria. The British East India Company needed large amounts of quinine to protect British soldiers from the raging symptoms of malaria. People swallowed the "bitter pill" – bitter quinine powder dissolved in water – daily as a prophylactic. Until, that is, a forgetful but resourceful officer came up with an idea for taking the bitter powder in a more palatable way.

The trigger was forgetfulness. As the officers and soldiers were sitting together over their evening gin, the officer remembered that he had forgotten to take his quinine powder in the morning. This flash of recollection was the trigger; he added the powder to his gin, which he filled up with soda water, and downed the glass in one. Delighted with this truly great flash of inspiration, from this moment on he added the quinine powder to the gin he drank every evening. A creative and tasty solution to an unpalatable problem.

A small idea conquers the whole world as Gin & Tonic

Even if, at this point, no one could know what the consequence of this little big idea might be – it heralded the birth of the original Gin & Tonic, which was soon to conquer the world.

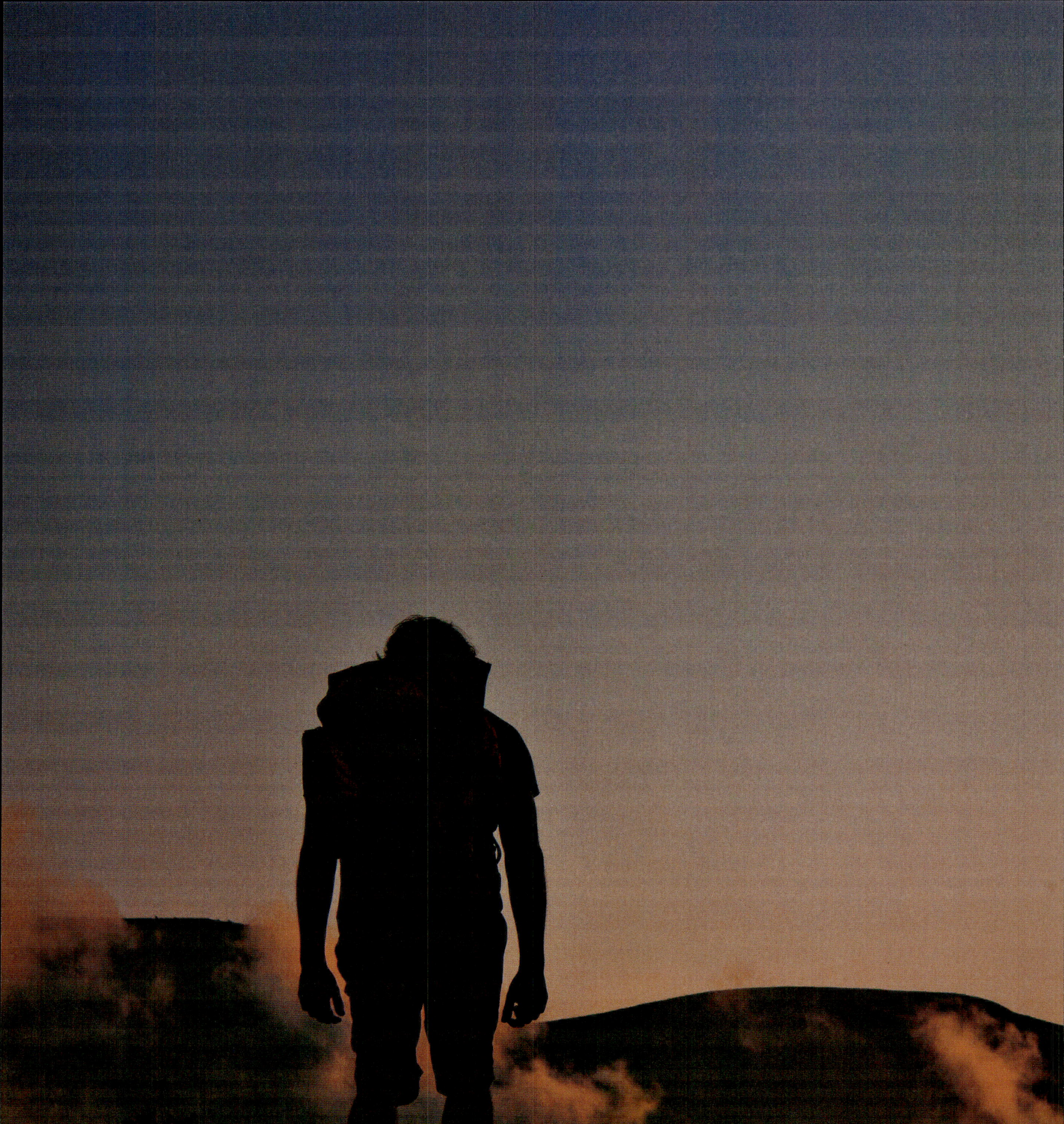

3

JOURNEY

GERMAN GIN DISTILLERIES

Schleswig-Holstein

Luschendorf
1. *The Northman Gin*

Kayhude
2. *GIN-HUDE*

Norden
3. *Water Nörder Dry Gin*

Bremerhaven
4. *Raven Hills Gin*

Hamburg

5. *Brombyrina SILKGIN*
6. *Gin Sul*
7. *Hamburg-Zanzibar Tumeric No. 1 Gin*
8. *LUV & LEE Hanseatic Dry Gin*

Mecklenburg-Western Pomerania

Schwerin
9. *Skywater Gin*

Wittenburg
10. *Elephant London Dry Gin*

Waren (Müritz)
11. *Müritz Gin*

Lower Saxony

Rotenburg (Wümme)
12. *Flow Gin*

Bad Bevensen
13. *Calluna Gin*

Brandenburg

Bergfelde
14. *Schwarzer Walfisch Gin*

Berlin

15. *AAGIN Berlin*
16. *BER Dry Gin*
17. *Mampe Gin*
18. *Mariposa Gin*
19. *Sundown Gin*
20. *The Earl of Gin*
21. *UNKNOWN Lands Gin*
22. *Wild Child Gin*

Saxony-Anhalt

Wernigerode
23. *vaGINa – the Hibiscus Gin*

Schloss Neuenburg (Freyburg)
24. *Gin*

Saxony

Moritzburg
25. *Moritzburger Gin*

North Rhine-Westphalia

Oelde
26. *Friedrichs Dry Gin*

Werne
27. *Jos. Garden Gin*

Recklinghausen
28. *UrGin*

Herne
29. *Alpako Gin*
30. *Renton Gin*

GERMAN GIN DISTILLERIES

Düsseldorf

31 *Rinocero Gin*
32 *Yoshi Nama – Little Tokyo Dry Gin*

Gelsenkirchen

33 *AMETHYST London Dry Gin*

Wesel

34 *Proud, Strong & Noble Gin*

Moers

35 *moersGIN*

Rüthen

36 *HerGing*

Eslohe

37 *Keller's Gin*

Lüdenscheid

38 *Woodland Gin*

Neuss

39 *Naturbummler Gin*

Cologne

40 *GINSAN!TY White Truffle Premium Dry Gin*
41 *MATS Dry Gin*
42 *Raspmary Gin*

Much

43 *Big Moose Gin*

St. Augustin

44 *Murre Gin*

Bonn

45 *Little Darling Gin*
46 *Inkognito Gin*

Hesse

Gießen

47 *Gießen Dry Gin*
48 *Koka Macerat*

Altenstadt

49 *LA SU Gin*

Kriftel

50 *Mandarina Dry Gin*

Wiesbaden

51 *Amato Mediterranean Dry Gin*

Geisenheim

52 *Schloss Gin*

Rhineland-Palatinate

Kail

53 *Vallendar Pure Gin*

Kirschweiler

54 *Aquamarin Gin*

Gau-Odernheim

55 *Little Big Hill*

Mettenheim

56 *Natural Dry Gin*

Westhofen

57 *Momotarō Gin*

St. Martin

58 *Gin dry – Pfälzer Edelgin*

Leinsweiler

59 *GIN 247 – Stübinger's DRY Gin*

Wincheringen

60 *Ferdinand's*

Baden-Wuerttemberg

Karlsruhe

61 *HOOS LONDON GIN*

Eppingen

62 *Böser Kater Two Faced Gin*

Ludwigsburg

63 *Satoshi Gin*

Berglen

64 *Erich Schwäbischer Dry Gin*

Esslingen am Neckar

65 *Gin under Construction*

Filderstadt

66 *Mädchen & Jungs Gin*

Loßburg

67 *Monkey 47 Schwarzwald Dry Gin*

Bühl

68 *Crypto Gin*

Achern

69 *Delicium Gin*
70 *Needle Blackforest Masterpiece*

Offenburg

71 *Weissbart Gin*

Neuried

72 *Liquid Emotions & Leviathan Gin*

GERMAN GIN DISTILLERIES

Mühlenbach

73 *Buchholzenhof Gin*

Vogtsburg im Kaiserstuhl

74 *Mundart Gin*

Eichstetten am Kaiserstuhl

75 *GINklin*

Weil am Rhein

76 *Longitude Gin*

Leutkirch im Allgäu

77 *Red Beard Gin*

Munich

85 *KONKANI Goa Inspired Gin*
86 *Lindwurm Gin – Sommer Edition*
87 *MUNiG – Munich Premium Gin*

Eggenfelden

88 *ORO IBIZA GIN*

Tattenhausen

89 *Lorbär Gin*

Hausham

90 *Josef Bavarian Gin*

GIN

GERMAN GIN DISTILLERIES

51

12 BEAUFORT UG

THE NORTHMAN GIN

CATEGORY
Dry Gin

ORIGIN
Germany

ESTABLISHED
2019

SIZE
● ○ ○ ○

TASTING NOTES
Beim The Northman Gin treffen elegant inszenierter Rosmarin und frische Zitrusnoten auf den kernigen Wacholder. Seine wirklich interessanten Nuancen erhält der Gin aber vom Kombu Royal, dem regional in Schleswig-Holstein gezüchteten Zuckertang. Dieser verleiht dem Gin die salzige Note und versetzt euch augenblicklich an die Küsten des Nordens. Ein klassischer Dry mit dem gewissen nördlichen Etwas.

In The Northman Gin, elegantly staged rosemary and fresh citrus notes meet the robust juniper. Yet the gin gets its really interesting nuances from Kombu Royal, the sugar kelp cultivated regionally in Schleswig-Holstein. This gives the gin its salty note and transports you instantly to the coasts of the north. A classic Dry Gin with that certain northern something.

Alles begann mit einer Idee

Sagen wir es mal so: Einige Ideen müssen erst verworfen werden, bis man zur richtigen kommt. So erging es auch Lars und Claas, die ausgiebig überlegten, warum sie Geld für einen Gin-Workshop raushauen sollten, statt sich selbst etwas Gutes zu gönnen. Alle Wege führen zum Gin, sagt man. Das Gute kam in Form einer Tischdestille. Nach einigem Probieren begannen schon die ersten Proben auf magische Weise zu überzeugen. Man arbeitete mit einzelnen und gemischten Aromen und kam schnell auf einige Kombinationen, welche die Jungs und später auch Familie, Freunde und Kollegen überzeugten. Man war bereit! Bereit, aus einer Idee „Meer" werden zu lassen als nur eine Windböe am Strand. Bereit, die Segel zu hissen.

Aus Meer wird mehr

Lars und Claas sind zwei waschechte Nordlichter und schon lange gute Freunde. An der Ostsee, in der schönen Lübecker Bucht in Schleswig-Holstein gelegen, produzieren die Jungs heute alles im Small-Batch-Verfahren. Gerade mal 220 Flaschen werden pro Brennvorgang produziert, von Hand abgefüllt, etikettiert und signiert. Die Nähe zur See brachte die Jungs darauf, die verschiedenen lebhaften und bekannten Eindrücke, die jeder von uns kennt, in einer Flasche zu verkorken. Es entstand der The Northman Calm Sea Gin, der die salzig schmeckende Seeluft, den Strandspaziergang entlang der windgepeitschten See oder die sonnenverwöhnten Sommer wiedergibt. Gegensätzlich und doch harmonisch, mild und ebenso kraftvoll verbindet dieser Dry Gin viele Elemente mit seiner ganz besonderen Eigenart. Es war den norddeutschen Jungs wichtig, das einzufangen, womit sie groß geworden sind. Das wiederzugeben, was in ihren Adern pulsiert: der Geschmack und das Lebensgefühl der Küste.

> Experience the North.

It all started with an idea

Let's put it this way: you have to discard some ideas first to get to the right one. That's what happened to Lars and Claas, who thought long and hard about why they should shell out money for a gin workshop instead of treating themselves to something good. All roads lead to gin, they say. Resolution came in the form of a table still. After some tasting, the first samples were already somehow magically convincing. They worked with single and mixed flavors and quickly came up with some combinations that convinced the guys themselves, followed by family, friends and colleagues. They were ready! Ready to turn an idea into "sea", rather than just a gust of wind on the beach. Ready to hoist the sails.

Sea the way forward

Lars and Claas are two true northerners and have been good friends for a long time. Located on the Baltic Sea in beautiful Lübeck Bay in Schleswig-Holstein, the guys produce everything today in a small-batch process. Just 220 bottles are produced per distillation, bottled by hand, labeled and signed. Proximity to the sea made the guys think of corking the various vivid and familiar impressions that each of us knows in a bottle. Thus the exemplary Northman Calm Sea Gin was born, reflecting that salty-tasting sea air, a beach walk along the windswept sea or sun-drenched summers. Contrasting yet harmonious, mild and equally powerful, this Dry Gin combines many elements with its very special character. It was important to these young north Germans to capture what they grew up with. To reflect what pulsates in their veins: the taste and the attitude to life of the coast.

Luschendorf, Germany

JÖRG HILDEBRAND

GIN-HUDE

" A gin whose soul tastes soft, mild and round.

Von innerer Unruhe getrieben

Das kann ich auch, vielleicht kann ich das sogar besser, dachte sich Jörg Hildebrand als er 2017 auf seine Gin-Sammlung starrte. Vorausgegangen waren nächtelange Recherchen über Gin aus aller Welt, über Brennverfahren und Botanicals. Er blickte auf seine Hausbar, die inzwischen besser ausgestattet war als die meisten Cocktailbars. Gemeinsam mit seiner Frau Karina zog er um die Häuser, probierte Gin-Empfehlungen und besuchte Brenn-Seminare, angetrieben von dem inneren Reiz den ultimativen Gin zu finden. Oder ihn sogar selbst zu entwickeln? Drei Jahre später hielt das Paar seine erste Flasche in der Hand. Eine von insgesamt 799 aus ihrer ersten Charge.

Eine spannende Affäre

Diese eigene von Jörg Hildebrand ausschließlich mit bio-zertifizierten Zutaten entwickelte GIN-HUDE Rezeptur ist die perfekte Mixtur und ein absolutes Markenzeichen. Herausstechend: Der Wacholder wird zart geküsst von der Minze und umgarnt von der Kokosnuss. Eine spannende Affäre, die nur als Dreierbeziehung funktioniert. Eine eigene Destillerie haben Jörg und Karina Hildebrand nicht, der Gin wird auf Gut Basthorst in der Feingeisterei von Fabian Rohrwasser produziert. Der Bezug zum beschaulichen schleswig-holsteinischen Kayhude sticht beim GIN-HUDE aufgrund seiner Namensgebung jedoch deutlich heraus. Und Karina und Jörg Hildebrand? Die haben inzwischen einen RESERVE London Dry Gin in Fassstärke mit einem 58 %-igen Alkoholgehalt aus einem Triple Sec Fass mit warmen floralen Orangennoten abgefüllt.

CATEGORY
London Dry Gin

ORIGIN
Germany

ESTABLISHED
2019

SIZE
● ○ ○ ○

TASTING NOTES
Vollmundig, rund, mild und weich, Wacholder umgarnt von Minze und Kokos, im Abgang mit leichten Minznoten.

Full-bodied, round, mild and soft, juniper entwined with mint and coconut, with light mint notes in the finish.

Kayhude, Germany

Driven by inner restlessness

I can do that too, maybe I can even do it better, Jörg Hildebrand thought to himself as he stared at his gin collection in 2017. This had been preceded by many nights of research into gins from all over the world, distilling processes and botanicals. He looked at his home bar, which was now better equipped than most cocktail bars. Together with his wife Karina, he traveled around, tasting gin recommendations and attending distilling seminars, driven by the inner thrill of finding the ultimate gin. Or even to develop it himself? Three years later, the couple held their first bottle in their hands. One of a total of 799 from their first batch.

An exciting affair

This proprietary GIN-HUDE recipe, developed by Jörg Hildebrand exclusively with certified organic ingredients, is the perfect mixture and an absolute trademark. What stands out is juniper delicately kissed by mint and ensnared by coconut. An exciting affair that only works as a three-way relationship. Jörg and Karina Hildebrand do not have their own distillery; the gin is produced at Gut Basthorst in Fabian Rohrwasser's Feingeisterei. However, the reference to the tranquil Schleswig-Holstein Kayhude stands out clearly in GIN-HUDE due to its name. And Karina and Jörg Hildebrand? They have since bottled a RESERVE London Dry Gin at cask strength with 58 % alcohol content and with warm floral orange notes from a Triple Sec cask.

ROMANTIK HOTEL REICHSHOF

WATER NÖRDER DRY GIN

CATEGORY
Dry Gin

ORIGIN
Germany

ESTABLISHED
2019

SIZE
● ● ● ●

TASTING NOTES
Mild und ausgewogen, frisch-fruchtig mit würzigen Nuancen, dominierende Zitrusfruchtaromen, leicht kräuterig, zurückhaltender Wacholder, Tonkabohnen und Vanille erzeugen eine zarte Süße.

Mild and balanced, fresh-fruity with spicy nuances, dominant citrus aromas, slightly herbal, restrained juniper, tonka beans and vanilla create a delicate sweetness.

> If your glass is low, 'WATER Nörder Dry Gin' tide helps.

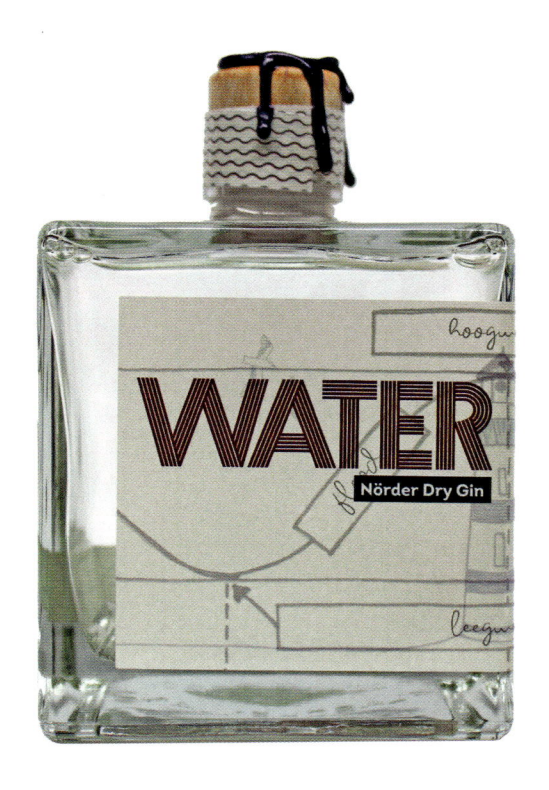

In Norden spricht man Platt

Das Leben an der Nordseeküste ist geprägt von den Gezeiten. Das Wasser geht, das Wasser kommt, Ebbe und Flut oder besser: Ebb un Flood. Denn im Norden spricht man Platt und im ostfriesischen Städtchen Norden sowieso. Dort, wo die Menschen Nörder genannt werden, hat das Wasser eine wichtige Bedeutung, und das nicht nur weil es dem Ort das Siegel „Nordseeheilbad" beschert und dem Tourismus Aufwind gibt, sondern auch weil seine vitalisierenden Eigenschaften so besonders sind, dass ihm direkt ein Gin gewidmet wurde. Der WATER Nörder Dry Gin wurde 2019 zum Leben erweckt. Sein Markenzeichen: Er ist so frisch wie die Nordsee und kombiniert würzige Kräuternoten mit fruchtigen Aromen.

Der Spargel des Meeres

Queller, der Spargel des Meeres, hat einen Stammplatz in der Rezeptur. Das Gewächs, das im Watt beheimatet ist, bringt einen kräftigen und leicht salzigen Eigengeschmack mit. Dazu gesellen sich 15 weitere Botanicals. Für den fruchtigen Teil sorgen Birne, Grapefruit und Zitrone. Das süßsaure Erlebnis wird durch Kaffirblätter und Zitronenthymian untermalt. Die würzigen Aromen werden durch Schokopfeffer, Tonkabohne, Vanille, Kardamom und Koriander erzeugt. Der Gin-Ansatz wird in der Bar-Lounge Wolbergs in Norden komplett in Eigenregie hergestellt. Dabei werden sämtliche Botanicals per Hand vorbereitet, portioniert und abgewogen. Das Destillieren übernimmt dann aber Wein Wolff in Leer.

In Norden they speak Platt

Life on the North Sea coast is guided by the tides. The water goes, the water comes, ebb and flow, or better: "Ebb un Flood". Because in the North they speak Low Saxon "Platt", and specifically in the East Frisian town of Norden. There, where the people are called Nörder, the water has an important meaning, and not only because it has conferred the title "North Sea spa" and gives tourism a boost, but also because its vitalizing properties are so special that a gin was dedicated to it directly. WATER Nörder Dry Gin was born in 2019. Its hallmark: It's as fresh as the North Sea and combines spicy herbal notes with fruity aromas.

The asparagus of the sea

Salicornia, the asparagus of the sea, has place of honor in the recipe. The plant, which is native to the mudflats, brings a strong and slightly salty flavor of its own. It is joined by 15 other botanicals. Pear, grapefruit and lemon provide the fruity part. The sweet and sour experience is underlined by kaffir leaves and lemon thyme. The spicy flavors are created by chocolate pepper, tonka bean, vanilla, cardamom and coriander. This gin concept is produced completely in-house at the Bar-Lounge Wolbergs in Norden. All botanicals are prepared, portioned and weighed by hand, while distillation is then handled by Wein Wolff in Leer.

Norden, Germany

COPPER & BRAVE

RAVEN HILLS GIN

Bremerhaven, Germany

CATEGORY
New Western Dry Gin

ORIGIN
Germany

ESTABLISHED
2019

SIZE
● ● ○ ○

TASTING NOTES
Aufregend edel und elegant, vordergründig angenehmes Wacholderaroma, begleitet von Orangen- und Zitrusnoten sowie Nuancen von frischen Kräutern aus dem englischen Garten; der Nachklang überzeugt mit einer subtilen und angenehmen Süße und einer dezenten Minzexplosion.

Excitingly noble and elegant, pleasant juniper aroma in the foreground, accompanied by orange and citrus notes and nuances of fresh herbs from an English garden; compelling finish with subtle and pleasant sweetness and subtle mint explosion.

Nichts für schwache Nerven

Westengland, 1892: Der junge, ambitionierte Apotheker Charles Layton wird in die abgelegene Anstalt für kriminelle Geistesgestörte „Raven Hills" beordert, um mit seinem neu entwickelten Alcoholicum-Elixir die Insassen zu heilen. Die vermeintliche Anstaltsleiterin Dr. Hermine Schlegel stellt ihm alle Insassen vor; nur Patientin Nr. 23 fehlt, ihr Gefahrenpotenzial ist zu hoch. Von Neugierde und Selbstbewusstsein angetrieben, sucht Layton die Patientin auf und die hat eine schauderliche Bitte: „Helfen Sie mir! Ich bin Dr. Hermine Schlegel!" Die Geschichte rund um den Raven Hills Gin liest sich wie eine Horrorstory mit offenem Ende, mit Raum für eine Fortsetzung. Wer wissen will, ob der erste und einzige Asylum Gin der Welt wirklich heilende Kräfte hat, muss einen Schluck kosten. Doch wer ist mutig genug?

Zeit für ein Wundermittel

Es ist das ätherische Zusammenspiel von reinstem, klar destilliertem Getreide, erfrischenden Minzblatt-Essenzen, Wacholder, Zitrusfrüchten und Heilkräutern, die diesen New Western Dry Gin zu einem Sinne schärfenden Wundermittel gedeihen lassen. Untermauert wird die Geschichte rund um den Raven Hills Gin durch die edle, braune, handgefertigte Apotheker-Flasche mit aufwendig gestaltetem Etikett, das die handschriftlichen Notizen von Charles Layton abbildet. „Raven Hills" stammt aus der Ideenschmiede von Copper & Brave aus Bremerhaven, die rund um ihre Spirituosen Zeitreise-Geschichten platzieren. Die Zeitreisenden sind dabei die Wissenschaftler Gabriel Copper und Tyler Brave, die im 19. Jahrhundert waghalsige Expeditionen auf sich nahmen, um einzigartige Destillate aufzuspüren.

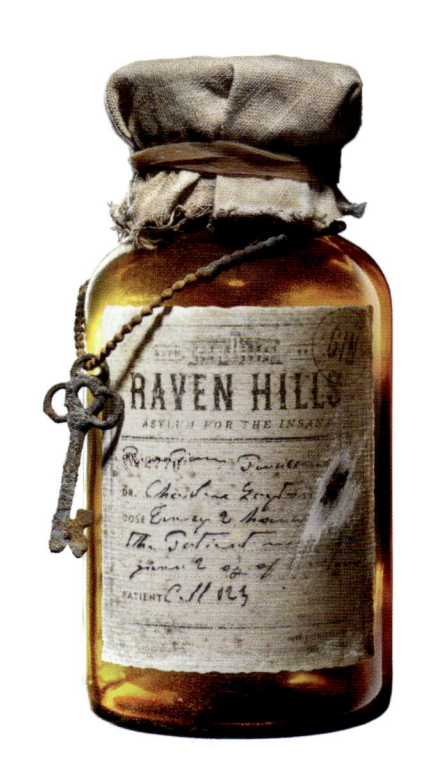

Not for the faint of heart

Western England, 1892: The young, ambitious pharmacist Charles Layton is ordered to "Raven Hills", a remote asylum for the criminally insane, to cure the inmates with his newly developed "Alcoholicum Elixir". Dr. Hermine Schlegel, presumably head of the asylum, introduces him to all the inmates, albeit patient No. 23 is missing, her potential danger being too high. Driven by curiosity and self-confidence, Layton seeks out the patient and she has a gruesome request: "Help me! I'm Dr. Hermione Schlegel!" The story surrounding Raven Hills Gin reads like an open-ended horror story, with room for a sequel. Anyone who wants to know if the world's first and only Asylum Gin really has healing powers needs to taste a sip. But who is brave enough?

Time for a miracle cure

It is the ethereal interplay of the purest, clear-distilled grain, refreshing mint leaf essences, juniper, citrus and medicinal herbs that allow this New Western Dry Gin to flourish into a miracle cure to sharpen the senses. Underpinning the story surrounding Raven Hills Gin is the classy, brown, handcrafted apothecary bottle with intricately designed label depicting Charles Layton's handwritten notes. "Raven Hills" comes from the think tank of Copper & Brave in Bremerhaven, Germany, which places time travel stories around its spirits. The time travelers are the scientists Gabriel Copper and Tyler Brave, who undertook daring expeditions in the 19th century to track down unique distillates.

> ❞
> Horror, but not in taste.
> A gin like Netflix in a
> glass – spoilers allowed.

PORT OF SILK OSTASIATISCHER SEIDENIMPORT

SILKGIN BROMBYRINA

CATEGORY
Dry Gin

ORIGIN
Germany

ESTABLISHED
2018

SIZE
● ○ ○ ○

TASTING NOTES
Der SILKGIN Brombyrina überrascht mit einer kräftigen Note der Maulbeeren. Im Hintergrund vernehmen wir eine würzige Note des Wacholders und eine leichte Frische von Zitrus, die allgegenwärtig den beerigen Hauptcharakter begleitet. Der perfekte Gegenpart wird zum Ende von einer dezenten Schärfe gespielt, die an Pfeffer und Ingwer denken lässt.

SILKGIN Brombyrina surprises with a strong note of mulberries. In the background we discern a spicy note of juniper and a slight freshness of citrus that constantly accompanies the main berry character. The perfect counterpart is played at the end by a subtle spiciness, reminiscent of pepper and ginger.

Hamburg, Germany

Der Weg der Seide

Hinter „Port of Silk" steht ein Traditionsunternehmen aus Hamburg, das seit seiner Gründung im Jahr 1959 hochwertige Seide in Indien produzieren und von dort importieren lässt. Als das Team von Port of Silk eines Tages das Reisetagebuch der mittlerweile verstorbenen Gründerin Lieselotte Roloff im Keller der Firma fand, entdeckten sie die Welt der Seide aus einer neuen Perspektive. Auf Liselottes Reisen entlang der exotischen „Seidenstraße" schwärmte sie auf mitreißende Art über die unterschiedlichsten Stoffe und Farben. Sie sprach jedoch ebenso fasziniert von den Düften, der Farbenwelt von Pflanzen und Gebäuden sowie den überwältigenden Geschmäckern der Gerichte. Eine packende Faszination, die das Team auf eine besondere Idee brachte: diese Zutaten der Seidenstraße im SILKGIN Brombyrina zu vereinen.

Ein seidiges Kleid für den Geschmack

Nicht nur Seide ist ein hochwertiges Produkt, auch Lebensmittelzutaten aus asiatischen Ländern können sich mit stolzen Preisen schmücken. Das macht den SILKGIN Brombyrina ebenso besonders wie seine Herstellung. Um diese kümmert sich kein Geringerer als Hubertus Vallendar, mehrfach mit Gold ausgezeichneter Destillateur. In seiner Brennerei sorgt er für die Umsetzung des exotischen Gins. Klassische Mazeration, anschließendes Destillieren und das Herabsetzen des Gins mit durch Seide gefiltertem Wasser geben dem Gin seinen unvergleichlichen Charakter. Während mit Wacholder, Orangen, Zitronen und Ceylon klassische Zutaten Verwendung finden, sind Safran, Maulbeeren und vietnamesischer Pfeffer schon etwas Besonderes. Ebenfalls wurde das ursprüngliche Business nie vergessen und geschickt in das Vorhaben „eingewebt". So ziert jede Flasche ein individuell gefertigtes Seidenkleid.

> "Taste the botanicals of the Silk Road."

In the way of silk

Behind "Port of Silk" is a traditional company from Hamburg, which has been producing high-quality silk in India and importing it from there since its foundation in 1959. When, one day, the Port of Silk team found the travel diary of the now deceased founder, Lieselotte Roloff, in the company's basement, they came to see the world of silk from a new perspective. During Liselotte's travels along the exotic "Silk Road", she raved in a captivating way about the most diverse fabrics and colors. However, she wrote with equal fascination about the scents, the colors of plants and buildings, and the overwhelming flavors of the dishes. A gripping fascination that gave the team a special idea: to combine these ingredients of the Silk Road in SILKGIN Brombyrina.

A silken dress for the taste

It isn't just silk that's a high-quality product; food ingredients from Asian countries can also command impressive prices. This makes SILKGIN Brombyrina just as special as its production. No less a person than Hubertus Vallendar, a distiller who has won several gold awards, is responsible for its production. In his distillery, he takes care of the implementation of this exotic gin. Classic maceration, subsequent distillation and the dilution of the distillate with water filtered through silk give this gin its incomparable character. While with juniper, oranges, lemons and Ceylon-cinnamon, classic ingredients are used, saffron, mulberries and Vietnamese pepper are altogether something special. Likewise, the original business was never forgotten and cleverly "woven" into the project. Thus, each bottle is adorned with an individually manufactured silk dress.

ALTONAER SPIRITUOSEN MANUFAKTUR

GIN SUL

Hamburgs portugiesische Ader

In Hamburg sagt man „Moin", in Portugal „Olá" und in der Altonaer Spirituosen Manufaktur „Gin Sul". Aber hallo! Der beliebte Weltenbummler aus Norddeutschland zeigt nicht nur Londoner Klasse, sondern auch seine mediterranen Wurzeln. Immerhin werden die 14 Botanicals hauptsächlich von der Costa Vincentina im Südwesten Portugals importiert, zum Beispiel Koriander, Rosmarin, Piment, Lavendel, Zimt und frische Zitronen. Diese werden mazeriert und in einer Kupferbrennblase von Arnold Holstein mit einem Fassungsvermögen von rund 100 Litern destilliert. Bei diesem Vorgang müssen alle Alkoholdämpfe durch einen metallenen Geistkorb hindurch, der unter anderem frische Zitronenschalen, Rosmarin und Rosenblüten enthält. Dadurch nimmt der flüssige Alkohol ganz behutsam die wichtigen Aromen auf, bevor er wieder abkühlt. Dazu gesellt sich das klare, weiche Wasser aus der Lüneburger Heide.

Konservierte Saudade

Die Altonaer Spirituosen Manufaktur wurde 2013 von Stephan Garbe gegründet. Dieser verliebte sich bereits vor vielen Jahren in Portugal und dessen Menschen, sodass er eines Tages zwischen seiner Heimat und der rauen Atlantikküste hin- und herpendelte. Am Strand von Odeceixe entstand die Idee zu einem portugiesisch inspirierten Gin, der die Düfte, Geschmäcke und die „Saudade" des Südens einfängt. „Saudade" findet keine Übersetzung – ein Wort von den Portugiesen für die Portugiesen. Es beschreibt Sehnsucht, Wehmut, Weltschmerz, schön und traurig zugleich, unvergleichbar, unvergesslich – so wie der Sonnenuntergang am Atlantik oder ein Glas Gin Sul aus der typisch weißen Tonflasche.

Hamburg, Germany

Hamburg's Portuguese streak

In Hamburg they say "Moin", in Portugal "Olá" and, in the Altona spirits operation, "Gin Sul". But hello... the popular globetrotter from northern Germany shows not only London class, but also its Mediterranean roots. After all, the 14 botanicals are imported mainly from the Costa Vincentina in southwestern Portugal, for example, coriander, rosemary, allspice, lavender, cinnamon and fresh lemons. These are macerated and distilled in an Arnold Holstein copper still with a capacity of around 100 liters. During this process, all alcohol vapors must pass through a metal botanical basket containing, among other things, fresh lemon peel, rosemary and rose petals. As a result, the alcohol vapor very gently absorbs the important aromas before cooling down again. This is joined by clear, soft water from the Lüneburg heathlands.

Preserved saudade

Altonaer Spirituosen Manufaktur was founded in 2013 by Stephan Garbe. He fell in love with Portugal and its people many years ago, with the result that at one time he commuted back and forth between his home country and the rugged Atlantic coast. It was on the beach at Odeceixe that the idea for a Portuguese-inspired gin was born, capturing the scents, flavors and "saudade" of the south. "Saudade" has no direct translation – a word from the Portuguese for the Portuguese. It describes longing, melancholy, world-weariness, beautiful and sad at the same time, incomparable, unforgettable – just like the sunset on the Atlantic Ocean or a glass of Gin Sul from that typical white clay bottle.

> The scent of the south. Distilled in the North.

CATEGORY
Dry Gin

ORIGIN
Germany

ESTABLISHED
2013

SIZE

TASTING NOTES
Weich und ausgeglichen, klassisch, sommerlich-mediterran, fruchtig-würzig, frisch, zart-süß, holzige Noten treffen auf die Würze des Wacholders und die herbalen Nuancen des Rosmarins, dazu gesellen sich das fruchtige Aroma der Zitronen sowie die würzigen Nuancen von Koriander, Piment und Zimt.

Soft and balanced, classic, evocative of a Mediterranean summer, fruity-spicy, fresh, delicately sweet, woody notes meet the spiciness of juniper and the tart nuances of rosemary, joined by the fruity aroma of lemons and the spicy nuances of coriander, allspice and cinnamon.

ALTONAER SPIRITUOSEN MANUFAKTUR // GIN SUL

GIN

0,5 L // 43,0 %

STADTRAND & CO.

HAMBURG-ZANZIBAR TUMERIC NO. 1 GIN

Hamburg, Germany

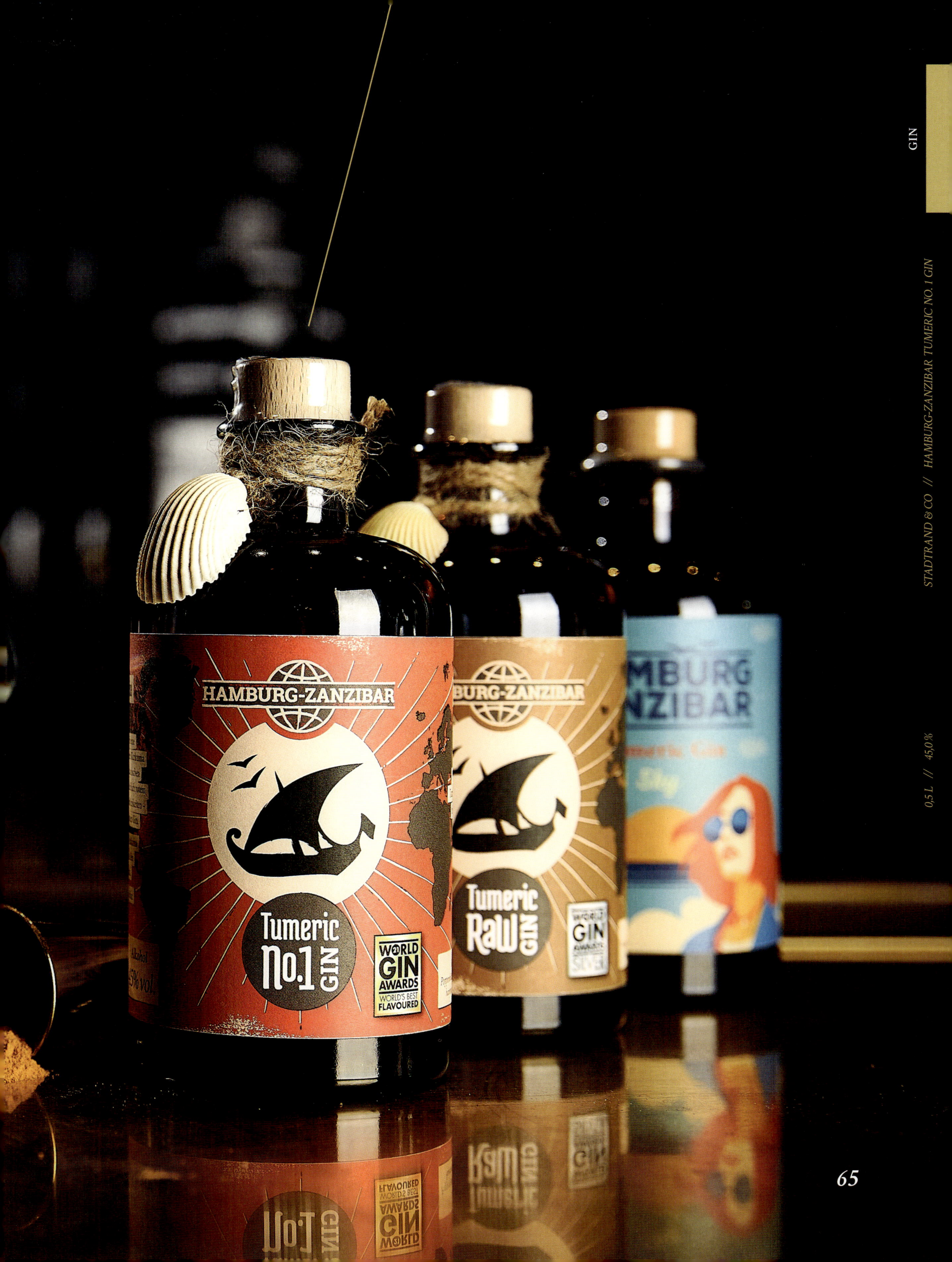

STADTRAND & CO // HAMBURG-ZANZIBAR TUMERIC NO. 1 GIN

0,5 L // 45,0 %

Ein bisschen Sansibar aus Hamburg

Der weiße Sand so fein wie Puderzucker, der azurblaue Indische Ozean angenehm warm, mit Kokosnüssen bestückte Palmen, die im Wind sanft hin- und hertanzen: Sansibar präsentiert sich märchenhaft. Doch die Insel kann mehr als Sonne und Meer. Sansibar duftet. Nach Blumen und Gewürzen. Neben Pfeffer gedeihen hier Nelken, Kardamom, Ingwer, Zimt, Vanille und Muskatnuss. Genau hier, inmitten dieses Paradieses, beginnt die Geschichte des Tumeric No. 1 Gin. Im Sommer 2017 experimentierten Yuka Suzuki und ihr Mann Hauke Günther in der eigenen Küche mit den letzten Resten Kurkuma (engl. „tu(r)meric") ihrer vergangenen Sansibar-Reise. Das Ergebnis war ihr erster selbstgebrannter Gin, außergewöhnlich im Geschmack und golden in der Farbe.

Kurkuma gibt den Ton an

Anfang 2020 bezogen die Spirituosen-Quereinsteiger am Stadtrand von Hamburg ihre eigene Destille, die kleinste der Stadt. Neben Kurkuma gehören Mandeln, Rosmarin, roter Pfeffer, Zimtblüten, aber auch Nadelhölzer sowie Klassiker wie Piment, Koriander, Kardamom und natürlich Wacholder in den Tumeric No. 1. Die Botanicals werden in einer genau abgestimmten Choreografie aus Mazeration und Destillation zu einem klaren Destillat gebrannt. Abschließend erfolgt eine zweite Mazeration mit Kurkuma. Auf diese Weise bekommt der Gin seine goldgelbe Farbe. Die Spirituose reift anschließend noch einige Wochen, wird abgefüllt und per Hand auf ihre nächste Reise vorbereitet. Pro Batch brennt das Paar zwischen 250 und 350 Flaschen – klein, aber fein, so wie Sansibar.

> "A gin like an adventurous journey to the 'island of spices'.

CATEGORY
New Western Dry Gin

ORIGIN
Germany

ESTABLISHED
2017

SIZE
● ○ ○ ○

TASTING NOTES
Ausgewogen und weich, würzig und facettenreich, frisch und wuchtig, herb und intensiv, Kurkuma im Vordergrund, im Wechselspiel mit Wacholder und rotem Pfeffer.

Balanced and soft, spicy and multifaceted, fresh and powerful, tart and intense, turmeric in the foreground, playing back and forth with juniper and red pepper.

A pinch of Zanzibar from Hamburg

The white sand as fine as powdered sugar, the azure Indian Ocean pleasantly warm, palm trees studded with coconuts that gently swing to and fro in the wind; the fairytale image of Zanzibar. But the island can offer more than sun and sea. Zanzibar has a fragrance. Of flowers and spices. Not only pepper but also cloves, cardamom, ginger, cinnamon, vanilla and nutmeg thrive here. Right here, in the middle of this paradise, the story of Tumeric No. 1 Gin begins. In the summer of 2017, Yuka Suzuki and her husband Hauke Günther experimented in their own kitchen with the last remnants of tu(r)meric from their past trip to Zanzibar. The result was their first self-distilled gin, extraordinary in taste and golden in color.

Turmeric sets the tone

At the beginning of 2020, the spirits quartet moved into their own distillery on the outskirts of Hamburg, the smallest in the city. In addition to turmeric, almonds, rosemary, red pepper, cinnamon blossoms, and conifers as well as classics such as allspice, coriander, cardamom and, of course, juniper, all are included in Tumeric No. 1. The botanicals are distilled in a precisely coordinated choreography of maceration and distillation to a clear distillate. Finally, a second maceration with turmeric takes place. This gives the gin its golden yellow color. The spirit then matures for a few more weeks, is bottled and prepared by hand for its next journey. The pair distills between 250 and 350 bottles per batch – small but superb, just like Zanzibar.

HEINRICH VON HAVE SPIRITUOSEN

LUV & LEE HANSEATIC DRY GIN

Hamburg, Germany

Seediensttauglichkeit bestanden

„Vor Gericht und auf der See sind wir in Gottes Hand", sagten schon die alten Seefahrer und meinten damit ihre lebensbedrohliche Abhängigkeit vom Wetter. Eine zentrale Bedeutung wird dabei dem Wind zugesprochen. Wer an der Küste zu Hause ist, wo die Auswirkungen einer steifen Brise nicht nur beim Haarstyling deutlich werden, sondern wo die See- und Schifffahrt Geschichte und Traditionen geprägt hat, der weiß um die Kraft der Luftbewegungen. Klar, dass der waschechte Hanse-Gin LUV & LEE entsprechend seediensttauglich daherkommt. Dabei ist Luv die dem Wind zugewandte und Lee die vom Wind abgewandte Seite – oder damit sich Nicht-Seefahrer das besser merken können: „Luv ist da, wo die ‚Luvt' herkommt."

Darfs ein bisschen Meer sein?

Der Hamburger Jung gibt sich betont nordisch-hanseatisch. Neben den klassischen Gin-Botanicals wie Wacholder und Koriander bedient sich LUV & LEE des Aquavits, dessen typische Sternanis- und Kümmelnoten gekonnt hervorgekitzelt werden. Ergänzt wird das Gefühl, an der Waterkant zu stehen und sich den salzigen Wind der See um die Nase wehen zu lassen, durch eine Prise Sylter Meersalzkristalle. Destilliert wird der edle Tropfen in Hamburgs ältester Spirituosen-Manufaktur Heinrich von Have. So weit, so gut. Fast. Denn Gutes tun bedeutet für den LUV & LEE Schöpfer Christian Heck, sich mithilfe seines Produktes gesellschaftlich zu engagieren. Als geborener Fischkopp arbeitet er mit der Deutschen Seemannsmission Hamburg-Altona zusammen, um das Leben der Seeleute zu erleichtern.

Sea worthiness confirmed

"In court and at sea, we are in God's hands," said the ancient seafarers, referring to their life-threatening dependence on the weather. Here, the wind is assigned central significance. Anyone who's at home on the coast, where the effects of a stiff breeze are evident not only in hairstyling and where seafaring and shipping have indeed shaped history and traditions, knows about the power of air movements. It goes without saying that LUV & LEE genuine Hanseatic gin is sea worthy. Here, "Luv" is the windward side and "Lee" the leeward, or, to make it easier for non-seafarers around here to remember: "Luv" sounds like "Luft", the German for air.

A drop more sea, perhaps?

This Hamburg youth is emphatically Nordic-Hanseatic. In addition to the classic gin botanicals such as juniper and coriander, LUV & LEE makes use of aquavit, whose typical star aniseed and caraway notes are skillfully tickled out. The feeling of standing on the water's edge and letting the salty wind of the sea blow around your nose is complemented by a pinch of Sylt sea salt crystals. This fine spirit is distilled in Hamburg's oldest distilling operation, Heinrich von Have. So far, so good. Almost. Because for LUV & LEE creator Christian Heck, doing good means social engagement with the help of his product. As a born fisherman, he works with the Hamburg-Altona German seamen's Mission to make life easier for seafarers.

" **Fresh wind in the glass.**

CATEGORY
Dry Gin

ORIGIN
Germany

ESTABLISHED
1868

SIZE
● ○ ○ ○

TASTING NOTES
Komplex, mild und fruchtig-würzig, norddeutsch-frisch; Fenchel, Kümmel und Anis übernehmen im Zusammenspiel mit den Zitrusnoten die Hauptrolle, der Wacholder sticht hervor, im Abgang leicht scharf.

Complex, mild and fruity-spicy, with north-German freshness; fennel, caraway and aniseed take on the main role, interplaying with the citrus notes; the juniper stands out, slightly spicy in the finish.

MAENNERHOBBY DESTILLERIE

SKYWATER GIN

*Schwerin
Germany*

Wenn der Himmel aufbricht

Eigentlich liegt die Expertise der Schweriner Firma GreenLife im dezentralen Wassermanagement und im Verkauf von Zisternen. Dass in ihrer Produktpalette neben Pumpen und Tanks nun auch ein Gin zu finden ist, ist einer verrückten Idee zu verdanken. 2019 erhielt GreenLife auf einer Festveranstaltung für Immobilienfirmen in Warschau einen Nachhaltigkeitspreis und wollte wichtigen Geschäftspartnern ein nettes Gimmick überreichen. Auf den klassischen Kalender wollte das Unternehmen dabei verzichten. Wie wäre es also mit einem Wacholderschnaps? Der Skywater Gin erlebte seine Geburtsstunde. Für die Produktion des Gins wird ausschließlich aufbereitetes Regenwasser verwendet, das in Schwerin in riesigen unterirdischen Tanks aufgefangen und vor Ort gefiltert wird.

Tropfen perlen von Tannennadeln

Regenwasser ist die Quelle allen Lebens für Tiere und Pflanzen, Ursprung menschlichen Trinkwassers und natürlicher Luftfilter. Neben Wacholder, Zitrone und heimischem Sanddorn findet sich das Aroma der Küstentanne im Skywater wieder. Ergänzt werden diese Ingredienzien um fünf weitere geheim gehaltene Botanicals. Zu haben ist der Gin in erster Linie in lokalen Verkaufsräumen – ganz bewusst verzichten die Macher auf Supermärkte oder große Handelsplattformen im Internet. Sie wollen keine Massenproduktion und sehen sich in regionalen Feinkostgeschäften genau richtig platziert, in ausgewählten Hof- und Unverpacktläden, in kleinen Bars oder Cafés und in ihrem eigenen Online-Shop.

CATEGORY
Dry Gin

ORIGIN
Germany

ESTABLISHED
2020

SIZE
● ○ ○ ○

TASTING NOTES
Fruchtig, zitronig, herb, natürlich, rein, mit Nadeln der Küstentanne, Zitrusschalen, Sanddorn vom Darß und belebender Grapefruit.

Fruity, lemony, tart, natural, pure, with needles of the coastal fir, citrus zest, sea buckthorn from the Darss and invigorating grapefruit.

When the heavens open

Actually, the expertise of the Schwerin-based company GreenLife lies in decentralized water management and the sale of cisterns. The fact that their product range now includes a gin in addition to pumps and tanks is thanks to a crazy idea. In 2019, GreenLife received a sustainability award at a formal event for real estate companies in Warsaw and wanted to present a nice gimmick to important business partners. The company wanted to skip the classic calendar. So how about a juniper spirit? Skywater Gin was born. For the production of the gin, only treated rainwater is used, which is collected in huge underground tanks in Schwerin and filtered on site.

Drops bead on pine needles

Rainwater is the source of all life for animals and plants, the origin of human drinking water and a natural air filter. In addition to juniper, lemon and native sea buckthorn, the aroma of coastal fir is found in Skywater. These ingredients are supplemented by five other secret botanicals. The gin is available primarily in local outlets – the makers deliberately avoid supermarkets or large trading platforms on the Internet. They don't want mass production and see themselves as being just rightly placed in regional delicatessens, in selected farm and unpackaged stores, in small bars or cafés, and in their own online store.

> Clear and fresh – like a walk through the forest after a strong shower.

ELEPHANT GIN LTD.

ELEPHANT LONDON DRY GIN

Wittenburg, Germany

Von Afrika inspiriert, in Deutschland von Hand gefertigt

Tessa und Robin Gerlach reisen nach Afrika und entwickeln eine unbändige Leidenschaft für den afrikanischen Kontinent, seine Kultur, die beeindruckende Landschaft – und für Gin. Nach ihren abenteuerlichen Tagen in der Wildnis genießen sie abends als Sundowner einen Gin Tonic, während die afrikanische Sonne wie ein leuchtend roter Ball am Horizont untergeht. Inspiriert von der Natur Afrikas und ihren Erlebnissen kreieren die beiden einen Gin, in dem sie den „African Spirit" einfangen wollen. Daher verwenden sie für ihr Destillat seltene afrikanische Kräuter und Früchte wie Buchu, Baobab, afrikanischen Wermut und Teufelskralle. Diese mischen sie mit klassischen Gin-Zutaten wie Wacholder, Orangen und frischen Äpfeln. Die verschiedenen Aromen verbinden sich zu einer einzigartigen Geschmackskomposition: dem Elephant London Dry Gin.

Hommage an den Afrikanischen Elefanten

Der Elephant Gin wird handwerklich hergestellt und entspricht höchsten Qualitätsanforderungen. Die handverlesenen Botanicals werden in einer traditionellen Kupferbrennblase in kleinen Chargen destilliert und in einzigartige Flaschen abgefüllt. Das Etikett ziert eine alte illustrierte Karte Südafrikas und wird von einer Kalligrafin jeweils mit dem Namen eines Elefanten handbeschriftet. Auf ihren Reisen konnten Tessa und Robin den Afrikanischen Elefanten in freier Wildbahn sehen – ein Tier, das die beiden zutiefst beeindruckt hat. Der Elephant Gin ist eine Hommage an diese majestätische Kreatur. Um das Überleben dieser Dickhäuter für zukünftige Generationen zu sichern, spendet das Unternehmen 15 Prozent des Erlöses jeder verkauften Flasche Gin an afrikanische Stiftungen, die sich für den Schutz des vom Aussterben bedrohten Afrikanischen Elefanten und dessen Lebensraums einsetzen. Elephant Gin: „Gutes trinken. Gutes tun." Darauf sollten wir alle das Glas erheben!

CATEGORY
London Dry Gin

ORIGIN
Germany

ESTABLISHED
2013

SIZE
● ● ● ○

TASTING NOTES
In der Nase ist ein intensives Wacholderaroma präsent, das sich mit leichten Anklängen von Latschenkiefer mischt. Der Geschmack ist ausgeglichen und zart, florale, fruchtige und pikante Noten vereinen sich zu einem harmonischen Ganzen.

An intense juniper aroma is present on the nose, blended with light hints of Mountain pine. The taste is balanced and delicate, while floral, fruity and spicy notes combine to form a harmonious whole.

Inspired by Africa, handmade in Germany

Tessa and Robin Gerlach traveled to Africa and developed an irrepressible passion for the African continent, its culture, the impressive landscape - and for gin. After their adventurous days in the wilderness, they enjoyed a gin and tonic as a sundowner in the evening, while the African sun set on the horizon like a glowing red ball. Inspired by the nature of Africa and their experiences, the two created a gin in which they sought to capture the "African Spirit". So they use rare African herbs and fruits such as buchu, baobab, African wormwood and devil's claw for their distillate. They mix these with classic gin ingredients including juniper, oranges and fresh apples. The different flavors combine to create a unique taste composition: Elephant London Dry Gin.

Homage to the African Elephant

Elephant London Dry Gin is handcrafted and meets the highest quality standards. The hand-picked botanicals are distilled in small batches in a traditional copper still and bottled in unique bottles. The label is adorned with an old illustrated map of South Africa and each is hand-lettered with the name of an elephant by a calligrapher. During their travels, Tessa and Robin were able to see the African Elephant in the wild - an animal that impressed them both deeply. Elephant London Dry Gin is a tribute to this majestic creature. To ensure the survival of these pachyderms for future generations, the company donates 15 percent of the proceeds from each bottle of gin sold to African foundations working to protect the endangered African elephant and its habitat. Elephant London Dry Gin: "A good drink that does good." We should all raise a glass to that!

> A gin that tastes like an adventure.

GENUSSWUNDER GBR

MÜRITZ GIN

CATEGORY
Dry Gin

ORIGIN
Germany

ESTABLISHED
2016

SIZE
● ● ● ●

TASTING NOTES
Ein ausgeprägter und kräftiger Wacholdergeschmack, der von zarter Blumigkeit über Zitrusfrische mit weichen Sanddorn-Noten begleitet wird. Eine leichte angenehme Schärfe zeichnet sich auf dem Weg zum Abgang ab und lässt den Gin warm nach hinten gleiten.

A pronounced and strong juniper flavor, which is accompanied by delicate florality over citrus freshness with soft sea buckthorn notes. A light pleasant spiciness stands out on the way to the finish and lets the gin glide warmly to the backand cinnamon, slightly spicy-peppery tone, floral nuances.

Geschenke der Natur genießen.

Wer die Mecklenburgische Seenlandschaft rund um die Müritz kennt, weiß diese teils unberührte Naturlandschaft mit satten Wäldern und Wiesen zu schätzen. Hier, mitten in der Natur, leben Thomas Engels und Jens-Peter Schaffran einen kleinen Traum. Was sie hier machen? Sie sind auf jeden Fall nicht allein. In der geschützten Natur des Müritz-Nationalparks, direkt vor der Haustür, liegt eine 300 Hektar große Wacholderheide. Einmal jährlich, im Februar/März, wird diese unter der Leitung des Nationalparkamtes Müritz von einigen freiwilligen Naturschützern kontrolliert zurückgeschnitten, damit die dort wachsenden, äußerst seltenen Orchideenarten nicht verdrängt werden. Der Schutz der Kulturlandschaft ermöglicht eine limitierte Ernte der grünen und blauen Früchte. Der so gewonnene Wacholder ist in seiner Größe und Beschaffenheit anders als am Markt erhältliche Beeren und bildet die Basis des Müritz Gin. Die Liebe zur Natur, zu ihrer Region und zu klaren Spirituosen brachte sie zu dieser einzigartigen Idee. Eine Liebe, die es wert ist, im Geschmack gezeigt zu werden.

Mehr als nur Wacholder

Neben dem einzigartigen Wacholder spielt auch der Sanddorn eine wichtige Rolle. Er verleiht zusätzlich einen weichen Charakter und harmoniert auf sanfte Weise mit dem Wacholder. In einer weiteren spannenden Kreation – dem Hanse Gin – kommt zusätzlich Manufaktursalz aus der Nord- und Ostsee zum Einsatz, das dem Gin eine elegante Meeresbrise verleiht und zusammen mit dem Wacholder eine schöne Liaison eingeht. Das Meersalz ist für seine besondere Milde bekannt, stammt aus kleinen Manufakturen entlang ehemaliger Handelswege und rundet den Hanse Gin ab. Mit beiden Gins erlebt ihr die Müritzregion und die norddeutschen Küsten so, wie sie Thomas und Jens-Peter für sich jeden Tag erleben.

> **Two wonders of delight bring the region to life in terms of taste.**

Enjoy gifts of nature

Anyone who knows the Mecklenburg lake district around the Müritz can appreciate this partly untouched natural landscape with lush forests and meadows. Here, in the middle of nature, Thomas Engels and Jens-Peter Schaffran are living a little dream. What are they doing here? Well, they're definitely not alone. In the protected natural environment of the Müritz National Park, right on their doorstep, lies a 300-hectare juniper heath. Once a year, in February/March, this is cut back in a controlled manner by a few volunteer conservationists under the direction of the Müritz National Park Authority, so that the extremely rare orchid species growing there don't get displaced. The protection of the cultivated landscape allows a limited harvest of the green and blue fruits. The juniper obtained in this way is different in size and texture from berries available on the market and forms the basis of Müritz Gin. The love for nature, for their region and for clear spirits brought them to this unique idea. A love worth expressing in the taste.

More than just juniper

Alongside that unique juniper, sea buckthorn also plays an important role. It adds a soft character and harmonizes gently with the juniper. In another fascinating creation named Hanse Gin, the distillery also uses natural salt from the North and Baltic Seas, giving this gin an elegant sea breeze and forming a beautiful liaison with the juniper. The sea salt is known for its special mildness, and comes from small businesses along former trade routes, rounding off Hanse Gin. With both gins, you will experience the Müritz region and the North German coasts; just as Thomas and Jens-Peter experience them for themselves every day.

Waren (Müritz), Germany

HEINZ EGGERT GMBH

CALLUNA LÜNEBURGER HEIDE GIN

Von Dichtern, der Liebe und dem Schnaps

"Das wichtigste Stück des Reisegepäcks ist und bleibt das fröhliche Herz" – dem Heimatschriftsteller Hermann Löns wird nachgesagt, kein Kostverächter gewesen zu sein, zumindest was Frauen und den Alkohol betrifft. Ihm wird auch nachgesagt, dass er eine dritte Liebe pflegte, und die fand er in der Natur- und Pflanzenwelt der Lüneburger Heide. Diese Liebe packte er in stimmungsvolle Gedichte. Eine Hommage an die Heidschnucken, Heideköniginnen, Heideböcke, Honigfeste, Wölfe und echte Heidjer kann aber auch ganz anders aussehen: hochprozentig, in einer weißen Flasche mit pinkem Etikett. Vom Rande der Lüneburger Heide kommt der Calluna Gin – aus einer Gegend zwischen Fischbek und Celle, die geprägt ist durch weitläufige, mit Heidekraut (Calluna vulgaris) bewachsene Torfmoore.

Flüssiges Glück der Heidjer

Das Landschaftsbild der Heide bestimmt das Geschmacksprofil des Calluna Gins. Heimischer Wacholder und Heidekraut harmonieren mit destillierten Lavendel- und Holunderblüten. Ein feiner Hauch von kostbarem Rosendestillat vollendet den besonderen Geschmack. Hergestellt wird der Gin in der Spirituosenmanufaktur Heinz Eggert in Bad Bevensen. In dem familiengeführten Unternehmen, das für den Import von Wein und Spirituosen aus Übersee und Europa bekannt ist, werden bereits seit 1948 vor allem traditionelle Heide-Spezialitäten produziert. Dieser regionale Bezug, der auch im Calluna Gin steckt, ist das, was die Manufaktur bei ihren Eigenmarken auszeichnet: Lokalpatriotismus – und zwar so, wie ihn schon Hermann Löns beschrieb.

> A rendezvous with Lüneburg Heath.

Lüneburger Heide, Germany

Of poets, love and schnapps

"The most important piece of luggage is and remains a cheerful heart" – the local writer Hermann Löns is said to have been no taster, at least when it came to women and alcohol. He is also said to have cultivated a third love, which he found in the natural environment and flora of Lüneburg Heath. He put this love into atmospheric poems. But a homage to the special characters of that setting can also look quite different: high-proof, in a white bottle with a pink label. Calluna Gin comes from the outskirts of Lüneburg Heath – from an area between Fischbek and Celle that is characterized by extensive peat bogs overgrown with heather (Calluna vulgaris).

Liquid happiness of the Heidjer

The landscape of the heath determines the flavor profile of Calluna Gin. Native juniper and heather harmonize with distilled lavender and elderflower. A fine touch of precious rose distillate completes the special taste. The gin is produced at the Heinz Eggert spirits factory in Bad Bevensen. At this family-run company, which is known for importing wine and spirits from overseas and Europe, mainly traditional Heide specialties have been produced since 1948. This regional reference, also present in Calluna Gin, is what distinguishes the operation's own brands; local patriotism – indeed as Hermann Löns already described it.

CATEGORY
Dry Gin

ORIGIN
Germany

ESTABLISHED
1948

SIZE
● ○ ○ ○

TASTING NOTES
Würzig und frisch, leicht scharf, hervorstechende Heidekräuter, fein-florale Süße der Rose, nachträglich begleitet von kräftigem Wacholder und einem dezenten Zitronengeschmack.

Tangy, bold and elegant, fresh fruit aromas of grapefruit, with subtly sweet influences of rosehip, classic juniper notes subtly round out the profile.

HEINRICH BRUNS
SPIRITUOSENFABRIK

FLOW GIN

Rotenburg (Wümme), Germany

Hoher Anspruch an die Qualität

Viel kleiner als die meisten anderen Hersteller und selten im Lebensmitteleinzelhandel zu finden sind die Produkte der Heinrich Bruns Spirituosenfabrik. Als inhabergeführtes Unternehmen produziert die Bruns-Spirituosenfabrik in Rotenburg (Wümme) seit 1906 geistige Getränke von erlesenem Geschmack. Schon dem Firmengründer Ludwig Bruns kam nur das Beste in die Flasche, produziert wird seitdem mit handwerklichem Können, langjähriger Erfahrung und hohem Anspruch an die Qualität der eigenen Arbeit. Die Tradition des Hauses wird inzwischen in vierter Generation fortgeführt. Eins der durchweg gehobenen Qualitätsprodukte aus dem Hause Bruns ist der Flow Gin. Ein Dry Gin mit Aromen von Wildrosen, Zitrus und Wacholder.

Goldene Farbe von Wildrosen

Der Flow Gin wird nach einem besonderen und geheim gehaltenen Verfahren in der historischen Schnapsfabrik unter Verwendung von Getreide-Destillat und anderen Destillaten hergestellt. Nach der Mazeration in 30-Liter-Badges wird er in historischen Steingut-Fässern gelagert. Mit selbst erzeugtem Solarstrom werden maximal 300 Flaschen am Tag hergestellt. Der handwerkliche Anteil ist ungefähr zehnmal so hoch wie in der Massenherstellung großer und größter Hersteller, worauf die Unternehmer sehr stolz sind. Das für den Gin verwendete Wasser kommt aus einem Tiefbrunnen des Rotenburger Wasserschutzgebietes. Die verwendeten Wild-

CATEGORY
Dry Gin

ORIGIN
Germany

ESTABLISHED
1906

SIZE
● ● ○ ○

TASTING NOTES

Wildrosen bestimmen den dominierenden floralen Geschmack – mit dem Wacholder entsteht ein runder, lang anhaltender Geschmack. Abgerundet mit Hopfen- und Lavendelblüten, Kardamom und Zitronenschale.

Wild roses are the dominant aspect in this floral tasting gin – in combination with juniper it creates a long lasting taste. Rounded off with hop and lavender blossoms, cardamom and citrus peel.

0,5 L // 40,0 %

> Wild roses, craftsmanship and many years of experience – true guarantees of success!

Top quality aspiration

Much smaller than most other manufacturers and rarely found in grocery stores are the products of Heinrich Bruns Spirituosenfabrik. As an owner-managed company, the Bruns Spirituosenfabrik distillery in Rotenburg (Wümme) has been producing "spiritual" beverages of exquisite taste since 1906. The company's founder, Ludwig Bruns, only put the best in the bottle. Since then, production has been carried out with craftsmanship, many years of experience and an aspiration for top quality in the work carried out. The firm's family tradition now continues into the fourth generation. One of the consistently elevated quality products from the house of Bruns is Flow Gin, a dry gin with aromas of wild roses, citrus and juniper.

Golden color of wild roses

Flow Gin is produced according to a special and secret process in the historic distillery using distillates of grain and other sources. After maceration in 30-liter tanks, it is stored in historic earthenware barrels. A maximum of 300 bottles a day are produced using solar power generated in-house. The manual effort is about ten times higher than in the mass production of large and the largest manufacturers, a source of pride for the entrepreneurs. The water used for the gin comes from a deep well in the Rotenburg water conservation area. The wild roses used originate in Iran and Morocco. Rather than being bred and planted there, they're picked wild in the countryside locally and then air-dried. They give Flow Gin its golden color.

HUTMACHERS MARITIME SPIRITUOSEN

SCHWARZER WALFISCH GIN

> "A light salty breeze wafts into the palate

Zuckertang trifft Sanddorn

"Im schwarzen Walfisch zu Askalon" ist ein Spottlied von Joseph Victor von Scheffel aus dem Jahr 1854, das die Trinkkultur der Studenten aufs Korn nimmt und eine Melodie von 1783 aufgreift. Es geht um einen Kneipengast, der sich unrühmlich betrinkt. In jeder Strophe wird er auf eine andere Weise aus der Bar geworfen. Wie passend, dass es sich beim "Schwarzen Walfisch" aus dem Jahr 2018 um Gin handelt – und zwar um einen, der auf vielfältige Weise mit dem Meer verbunden ist, zum Beispiel hinsichtlich der verwendeten Botanicals. In der Spirituose stecken nämlich nicht nur Wacholder und Zitrusfrüchte, sondern auch Zuckertang aus Schleswig-Holstein und Sanddorn aus dem malerischen Mecklenburg-Vorpommern. Beide Komponenten verleihen dem Gin seinen fruchtig-frischen maritimen Charakter.

Zum Schutz der Meere

Von seinem Vater, einem Diplombraumeister, bekam der Kopf hinter dem Schwarzen Walfisch, Bjarne Hutmacher, die Wertschätzung für die Getränkekultur in die Wiege gelegt. Ihn überzeugte allerdings nicht der väterliche Whisky, sondern der trendbewusste Gin. Hinzu kommt, dass der Gründer ein begeisterter Ruderer und Segler ist. Auf hoher See hörte er das Lied, das namensgebend für seinen Schnaps sein sollte, zum ersten Mal. Der Wal ist dabei zugleich Sinnbild für die Schutzbedürftigkeit der Meeresbewohner. Diese Anspielung ist nicht zufällig gewählt: Der Wahlberliner unterstützt mit jeder verkauften Flasche Organisationen, die sich für den Schutz und den Erhalt der Meere und seiner Bewohner einsetzen.

Sugar kelp meets sea buckthorn

"Im schwarzen Walfisch zu Askalon" [In Ashkelon's Black Whale] is a mocking song by Joseph Victor von Scheffel from 1854 that takes aim at the drinking culture of students and picks up a melody from 1783. It is about a tavern guest who gets ingloriously drunk. In each verse he is thrown out of the bar in a different way. How fitting that the "Black Whale" of 2018 is a gin – and one that's connected to the sea in many ways, for example in terms of the botanicals used. The spirit contains not only juniper and citrus fruits, but also sugar kelp from Schleswig-Holstein and sea buckthorn from Mecklenburg-Western Pomerania. Both components give the gin its fruity-fresh maritime character.

To protect the seas

Bjarne Hutmacher, the mastermind behind Schwarzer Walfisch, inherited his appreciation for the culture of beverages from his father, a graduate brew master. However, it was not his father's whiskey that convinced him, but trendsetting gin. Moreover, the founder is an avid rower and sailor. It was on the high seas that he first heard the song that was to give his schnapps its name. The whale is also a symbol of the need for protection of sea creatures. This allusion was not chosen by chance. Whilst now happily resident in Berlin, with every bottle sold he supports organizations that work to protect and preserve the oceans and their inhabitants.

Bergfelde, Germany

CATEGORY
London Dry Gin

ORIGIN
Germany

ESTABLISHED
2018

SIZE
● ● ● ○   0,5 L // 45,0 %

TASTING NOTES
Vielfältig, kräftig und intensiv, mit einem komplexen Zusammenspiel aus Wacholder- und Zitrusnoten, umrahmt von dem sanften und fruchtigen Charakter der Beeren, leichte Kräuternoten und florale Akzente komplettieren den Geschmack, der durch die süß-salzige Note des Zuckertangs abgerundet wird.

Multifaceted, powerful and intense, with a complex interplay of juniper and citrus notes, framed by the gentle and fruity character of berries; light herbal notes and floral accents complete the taste, which is rounded off by the sweet-salty note of sugar kelp.

WEINDIMENSIONAL GMBH

AAGIN

*Berlin,
Germany*

WEINDIMENSIONAL GMBH // AAGIN

GIN

0,5 L // 43,0 %

83

"
The spirit of Berlin.

CATEGORY
Dry Gin

ORIGIN
Germany

ESTABLISHED
2019

SIZE
● ● ○ ○

TASTING NOTES
Samtig-weiches Aroma. Wacholderbetont. Ingwer und Kardamom verleihen ihm Würze und Schwarze Johannisbeere und Grapefruit sorgen für den fruchtig-komplexen Geschmack mit feinen Zitrusnuancen.

Velvety smooth aroma. Juniper accented. Ginger and cardamom add spice and blackcurrant and grapefruit provide the fruity complex flavor with subtle citrus nuances.

Ein Gin mit Geschichte

Einen hochwertigen Gin zu produzieren, der pur getrunken werden sollte und mit Soda gemischt auch Menüs begleiten kann: Das war die Vision von AAGIN-Gründer und Winemaker Markus Haas, als er 2017 das 1908 errichtete Kesselhaus der ehemaligen Berliner Luxuspapierfabrik Albert und Meister an der Aroser Allee/Holländerstraße fand. Zusammen mit dem Gin-Experten und Meister-Destillateur Dr. Klaus Hagmann wurde an diesem historischen Ort nach einer alten Rezeptur eine hochwertige Gin-Komposition entwickelt: AAGIN. – Please call me [eɪdʒɪn]. Durch den Gründungsort, seine Geschichte und den mit ihm verbundenen Assoziationen soll er eine Hommage an die prachtvolle Berliner Belle Époque in seiner inneren und äußeren Ästhetik widerspiegeln. In der JVA Kapfenburg in Baden-Württemberg fanden Markus und Klaus eine von Hand gehämmerte, 150 Liter fassende Kupferbrennblase und ließen diese liebevoll aufarbeiten und modernisieren.

Botanicals werden pur und schonend destilliert

In dieser wird heute langsam und schonend destilliert. Durch die Bauart erfolgt eine intensive Durchmischung bei der Geistherstellung. Dabei werden die Aromen durch die von Hand gehämmerte Oberfläche der Brennblase auf besondere Weise intensiv verwirbelt und erlauben die Freisetzung selbst feinster Aromen. In kleinen Chargen werden elf sorgfältig erlesene Botanicals, pur und ohne Mazeration, mit hochwertigem Wittenberger Weizenfeindestillat verarbeitet. Die schonende Destillation verleiht dem AAGIN sein samtiges Aroma. Durch die Zugabe einer extra großen Portion an reinen Wacholderbeeren schmeckt er wacholderbetont. Ingwer und Kardamom verleihen ihm Würze und Schwarze Johannisbeere und Grapefruit sorgen für den fruchtig-komplexen Geschmack mit feinen Zitrusnuancen.

A gin with history

To produce a high-quality gin intended to be drunk neat whilst also suited to accompanying menus when mixed with soda; that was the vision of AAGIN founder and winemaker Markus Haas when he came upon the 1908 boiler house of the former Berlin luxury paper factory Albert und Meister on Aroser Allee/Holländerstraße in 2017. Together with gin expert and master distiller Dr. Klaus Hagmann, a high-quality gin composition was developed at this historic location, based on an old recipe: AAGIN. – please call me [eɪdʒɪn]. Through the founding location, its history and the associations linked to it, it's intended to reflect a tribute to the magnificent Berlin Belle Époque in its internal and external aesthetics. In the Kapfenburg correctional facility in Baden-Württemberg, Markus and Klaus found a hand-hammered, 150-liter copper still and had it lovingly refurbished and modernized.

Botanicals distilled purely and gently

In this still now, distillation runs slowly and gently. Due to the design, intensive mixing takes place during spirit production. In the process, the aromas are thoroughly swirled in a special way by the hand-hammered surface of the still and allow the release of even the finest aromas. Eleven carefully selected botanicals are processed in small batches, pure and without maceration, with high-quality Wittenberg wheat fine spirit. This gentle distillation gives AAGIN its velvety smooth aroma. The addition of an extra large portion of pure juniper berries gives it a juniper-accented taste. Ginger and cardamom give it spice and blackcurrant and grapefruit provide the fruity-complex taste with subtle citrus nuances.

BER BERLINER GIN MANUFAKTUR

BER DRY GIN

CATEGORY
Dry Gin

ORIGIN
Germany

ESTABLISHED
2019

SIZE
● ○ ○ ○

TASTING NOTES
Spritzig, frech und elegant, frische Fruchtaromen der Pampelmuse, mit dezent süßen Einflüssen der Hagebutte, klassische Wacholdernoten runden zurückhaltend das Profil ab.

Tangy, bold and elegant, fresh fruit aromas of grapefruit, with subtly sweet influences of rosehip, classic juniper notes subtly round out the profile.

Das dicke B

„Du kannst so hässlich sein, so schön schrecklich sein", sang der deutsche Hip-Hop-Musiker und Ur-Berliner Peter Fox im Jahr 2008 in seinem Song „Schwarz zu blau" über die deutsche Hauptstadt und betonte im gleichen Atemzug: „Ich weiß, ob ich will oder nicht, dass ich dich zum Atmen brauch." Berlin ist die Stadt der Gegensätze. Die freche Schnauze mischt sich in die schönste Literatur, die dreckigsten Sneaker werden zu den teuersten Kleidern getragen. Berlin ist laut, Berlin ist dreckig, und dazwischen stecken all die Schönheiten der Stadt. Berlin ist frech, wild, wunderbar und niemals langweilig – und der BER Dry Gin aus der BER Berliner Gin Manufaktur eine Hommage an die „Muddastadt".

Das rosa Glücksbärchen

Die Intention dahinter: den Lifestyle Berlins mit seinen ständig wechselnden Trends in einem Getränk verewigen, das so beliebt ist wie die Stadt selbst. Ein echter Berliner trägt den Bären auf dem Bauch. Das Wappentier der Stadt ziert den BER Dry Gin in fulminanter Größe. Doch was steckt in dem Tierchen? Ganz viel Rosa! Die Farbgebung ist das Resultat zweier Botanicals: Hagebutte und Pampelmuse. Den Wacholder gibt es einfach dazu – herb, bitter, krautig und frisch. Die Namenswahl BER erinnert an den gleichnamigen Flughafen, das Tor zu Welt einerseits, das Tor nach Berlin andererseits. Das Einfache, Gewohnte wird ergänzt durch Einflüsse aus aller Welt. Zusammen ergeben sie die Essenz von Berlin.

> „
> A gin that gives the feeling of a city where everything is possible.

The big B

[You can be so ugly, be so wonderfully terrible], translated lyrics by Peter Fox, the German hip-hop musician and native of Berlin, describing the German capital in his 2008 song "Schwarz zu blau," emphasizing in the same breath, [I know, whether I want to or not, that to breathe, I need you]. Berlin is the city of contrasts. Cheeky townsfolk dig into the most beautiful literature, the dirtiest sneakers complement the most expensive clothes. Berlin is loud, Berlin is dirty, and in between are all the beauties of the city. Berlin is bold, wild, wonderful and never boring – and the BER Dry Gin from the BER Berliner Gin Manufaktur is a tribute to the "mom-city".

The pink lucky bear

The intention behind it is to immortalize Berlin's lifestyle with its constantly changing trends in a drink that is as popular as the city itself. As a real Berliner, it wears the bear on his belly. The city's heraldic animal adorns the BER Dry Gin in rampant style. But what's inside this little creature? A whole lot of pink! The coloring is the result of two botanicals: rosehip and grapefruit. Juniper is simply added – tart, bitter, herbaceous and fresh. The choice of name BER is reminiscent of the airport with that code, gateway to the world on the one hand, gateway to Berlin on the other. What is simple and familiar is complemented by influences from all over the world. Together they result in the essence of Berlin.

Berlin, Germany

CATEGORY
Dry Gin

ORIGIN
Germany

ESTABLISHED
1920

SIZE
● ● ● ○

TASTING NOTES
Los geht's mit einer angenehmen, aber nicht zu dominanten Wacholdernote. Es folgt eine sehr ausgeglichene Würze mit smarter Zitrusnote. Frisch und leicht, liegt der Gin zart im Mundraum und der Abgang ist kurz und schnell. Im G&T beweist der Gin ebenfalls seine Stärke und die Simplizität überzeugt durch seine ehrliche Kraft.

Mampe Dry Gin starts with a pleasant though not too dominant juniper note. There follows a very balanced spiciness with smart citrus note. Fresh and light, the gin settles delicately in the mouth and the finish is short and quick. In G&T, the gin also proves its strength and the simplicity convinces with its honest power.

MAMPE SPIRITUOSEN

MAMPE GIN

Berliner Geschichte

In einer 150 Jahre ehemaligen alten Weißbierbrauerei mit riesigen Fenster, Backsteinmauern und hohen Decken geht die 1831 gegründete Berliner Marke Mampe ihrem Tagewerk nach. In dieser historischen Atmosphäre wird allerdings mehr als nur gebrannt. Die Berliner Ur-Marke steht wofür Berlin bekannt ist: Offenheit, Ehrlichkeit und ein bisschen Verrücktheit. So finden hier Dreharbeiten, Brennkurse, Seminare und außergewöhnliche Events statt. Man nutzt alte Rezepte aus über 190 Jahren Erfahrung und Brennkunst. In den 1920er Jahren wurde sich in einem "Tier-Casting" für den weißen Elefanten als starkes Wappentier für den Gin entschieden. Daraufhin bekam der kleine Zwergelefant im Berliner Zoo seinen Namen "Mampe" und steht für eine lange Partnerschaft zwischen dem Berliner Zoo und der Marke Mampe.

Ein echter Berliner

Der Mampe Gin basiert auf einem Rezept aus den 1910er Jahren, welches bis heute Bestand hat. Hier treffen spannende Zutaten auf altes handwerkliches Geschick. Manufakturleiter Danny Krüger geht hier seinem Handwerk nach und schaut mit seinem strengem Auge über jeden Herstellungsschritt. Heute blickt Mampe auf ein großes Portfolio verschiedener Spirituosen und hat auch den wohl ältesten alkoholfreien Gin der Welt im Angebot. Einst entwickelt, um der eingeführten amerikanischen Prohibition zu entgehen. Der Mampe Dry Gin mag ein Berliner sein, ehrlich, direkt und etwas laut aber in Wirklichkeit ist er ein klassischer Gin mit ehrlichen und soliden Gin-Noten, der hervorragend zu einem Dry Tonic passt. Übrigens wird der weiße Elefant mit der Kordel in den Berliner Gefängnissen an Elefanten geknotet.

Story of Berlin

In a 150-year-old former wheat-beer brewery with huge windows, brick walls and high ceilings, the Berlin brand Mampe, founded in 1831, goes about its day-to-day work. But, in this historic atmosphere, it's more than just brewing that takes place. The original Berlin brand stands for what Berlin is known for: openness, honesty and a bit of craziness. Film shoots, distilling courses, seminars and unusual events take place here. Old recipes from over 190 years of experience and distilling art are used here. In the 1920s, an "animal casting" decided on the white elephant as a strong emblematic animal for the gin. As a result, the small dwarf elephant in the Berlin Zoo got its name "Mampe" and stands for a long partnership between Berlin Zoo and the Mampe brand.

A true Berliner

Mampe Gin is based on a recipe from the 1910s, still holding its own to this day. Here, exciting ingredients meet old craftsmanship. Head of manufacture Danny Krüger oversees every step of the production process with his strict eye. Today, Mampe can boast a large portfolio of different spirits and has probably the oldest non-alcoholic gin in the world on offer, MAMPE NULL NULL - developed to circumvent the introduction of American Prohibition. Mampe Dry Gin may be a Berliner, honest, direct and a bit loud but in reality it is a classic gin with honest and solid gin notes that goes great with a dry tonic. By the way, the white elephant with its cord is tied in quite locally in Berlin prisons - a Berlin original through and through.

Berlin, Germany

0,7 L // 40,0%

" Classic, honest and straightforward.

MONOPOL SPIRITUOSEN

MARIPOSA GIN

Florale Leichtigkeit aus dem Weserbergland

Im Sommer 2018 entspannt Fabian Simon auf seiner Sonnenliege, mit einem kühlen Gin Tonic in der Hand. Garniert mit Himbeeren, fruchtig und herb zugleich – das perfekte Sommergetränk. Er nimmt einen Schluck und plötzlich ist da dieser Gedanke: Wieso hat seine Heimatstadt Hameln eigentlich keinen eigenen Gin? Der Unternehmer findet: So eine Idee darf nicht ungenutzt bleiben! Doch wie sollte ein Gin aus Hameln aussehen? Inspiration findet er am Ufer der Weser. Die Rattenfängerstadt ist nicht nur für ihre Geschichte berühmt, sondern auch eingebettet ins wunderschöne Weserbergland, umringt von Bergen, Flüssen und Blumenwiesen. Was wäre da passender als ein floraler Gin mit natürlichen Botanicals, wild gewachsen und handverlesen? Süß und fruchtig soll er sein. Und so mild, dass er eine Alternative zum klassischen London Dry Gin bietet. Fabian Simon wendet sich an eine lokale Brennerei. Nach unzähligen Proben und Verkostungen entsteht schließlich Mariposa Gin: der erste Gin aus Hameln.

Süßes Aroma mit leichter Schärfe

Der Mariposa Gin wird im Einmalbrennverfahren gebrannt und über drei weitere Destillationsböden verfeinert. Die Botanicals werden vor der Destillation hinzugegeben. Natürliches Quellwasser bringt den Gin auf Trinkstärke. Das Zusammenspiel von Erdbeeren, Himbeeren, Orangen und Limetten, kombiniert mit Lavendelblüten, verleiht dem Mariposa Gin ein süßlich-unbeschwertes Aroma. Koriandersamen, Zimtrinde und Ingwer entfesseln eine leichte Schärfe auf der Zunge. Da der Gin nur wenig Wacholder enthält, ist er besonders mild.

> *A getaway onto the butterfly meadow.*

Floral lightness from the Weser Uplands

In summer 2018, Fabian Simon was relaxing on his sun lounger with a cool gin and tonic in his hand. Garnished with raspberries, fruity and tart at the same time – the perfect summer drink. He took a sip and suddenly came this thought: Why does his hometown of Hamelin not actually have its own gin? The entrepreneur thought an idea like that shouldn't go to waste. But what should a gin from Hamelin look like? He found inspiration on the banks of the Weser. This town of the Pied Piper is not only distinguished by its history, but also by its setting, nestling in the beautiful Weser Uplands, surrounded by mountains, rivers and flower meadows. What could be more fitting than a floral gin with natural botanicals, grown wild and handpicked? It should be sweet and fruity. And so mild that it offers an alternative to the classic London Dry Gin. Fabian Simon approached a local distillery. After countless samples and tastings, Mariposa Gin was finally created: the first gin from Hamelin.

Sweet aroma with slight spiciness

Mariposa Gin is distilled in a single distillation process and refined over three additional distillation trays. The botanicals are added before distillation. Natural spring water brings the gin to drinking strength. The interplay of strawberries, raspberries, oranges and limes, combined with lavender flowers, gives Mariposa Gin a sweet, light-hearted aroma. Coriander seeds, cinnamon bark and ginger unleash a slight spiciness on the tongue. Since the gin contains only a little juniper, it is particularly mild.

CATEGORY
Dry Gin

ORIGIN
Germany

ESTABLISHED
2018

SIZE
● ○ ○ ○

TASTING NOTES
Ein fruchtiges Zusammenspiel verschiedener Beeren mit eher dezentem Wacholder – leicht scharf im Abgang.

A fruity composition of different berries and rather subtle juniper with a spicy finish.

BERLIN DISTILLERY KREUTZ

SUNDOWN GIN

CATEGORY
Dry Gin

ORIGIN
Germany

ESTABLISHED
2019

SIZE
● ● ○ ○

TASTING NOTES
Kräftige Sanddorn- und Orangennote, dadurch ein fruchtiges und frisches Aroma, feine Würze durch Wacholder und Kardamom.

Strong sea buckthorn and orange notes, resulting in a fruity and fresh aroma, subtle spice from juniper and cardamom.

The Spirit of Berlin

Die reifen Sanddornbeeren leuchten orange wie der perfekte Sonnenuntergang. Und es kommt noch besser: Mit dem Sundown Gin aus Berlin bereiten sie einen fruchtig-entspannten Gin-Moment! Erfrischend leicht ist diese Rezeptur aus elf harmonisch abgestimmten Botanicals aus nachhaltigem Anbau. Sanddornbeeren, Wacholderbeeren, Orangenzesten, Zitronenmelisse, Kardamom und Grapefruitzesten sorgen für ein besonderes Aroma.

Klimaneutral und mit frischen Zutaten

Die Berliner Gin-Manufaktur arbeitet klimaneutral. Verwendet werden nur frische, nachhaltige, biozertifizierte und überwiegend regionale Zutaten. Neben den Botanicals kommt nur selbst gebranntes Destillat und Wasser in den Gin. Es werden keine getrockneten Früchte verwendet, sondern frische, deren Zesten direkt vor dem Brennvorgang abgeschnitten werden. Das Ergebnis ist eine kräftige Sanddorn- und Orangennote im Gin. Gebrannt wird alles per Hand in einer sehr kleinen, 40 Liter fassenden Brennblase in der Destillerie in Berlin-Zehlendorf. Dadurch ist die Kupferoberfläche größer und die Destillationszeiten sind kürzer. Das macht den Sundown Gin besonders aromatisch, rund, weich und frei von Bitterstoffen. Wer neben Sanddorn mehr Abwechslung haben möchte: Von der Berlin Distillery Kreutz gibt es nicht nur den Sundown Gin. Außerdem werden Berliner Nacht Gin, Urban Garden Gin, BBQ Dry Gin, Bratapfel Gin, Reserve Gin aus dem Sherry-Fass und ein Spargel Gin produziert. Da ist für jeden etwas dabei! Das Ziel der Produzenten: Besondere Genussmomente in die Flasche bringen – inspiriert von Berlin und ebenso vielfältig.

> *Homemade Berlin Gin – With botanicals that grow on the roof, which go directly into the kettle.*

Berlin, Germany

The Spirit of Berlin

The ripe sea buckthorn berries glow orange like the perfect sunset, and it gets even better. In Sundown Gin from Berlin they prepare a fruity and relaxed gin moment. Refreshingly light is this recipe of eleven harmoniously matched botanicals from sustainable cultivation. Sea buckthorn berries, juniper berries, orange zest, lemon balm, cardamom and grapefruit zest provide a special flavor.

Climate-neutral and with fresh ingredients

This Berlin gin operation works on a climate-neutral basis. Only fresh, sustainable, certified organic and predominantly regional ingredients are used. In addition to the botanicals, only home-produced distillate and water are used in the gin. No dried fruits are used, only fresh ones, their zests peeled off directly before the distilling process. The result is a strong sea buckthorn and orange note in the gin. Everything is distilled by hand in a very small 40-liter still at the distillery in Berlin-Zehlendorf. This means that the copper surface is larger and the distillation times shorter. This makes Sundown Gin particularly aromatic, round, soft and free of bitterness. If you want more variety besides sea buckthorn, Berlin Distillery Kreutz doesn't offer just Sundown Gin. They also produce Berliner Nacht Gin, Urban Garden Gin, BBQ Dry Gin, Bratapfel Gin, Reserve Gin from the sherry cask and an asparagus gin. There's something for everyone. The goal of the producers is to bring special moments of pleasure into the bottle – inspired by Berlin and just as diverse.

EARL SPIRITS

THE EARL OF GIN

Berlin,
Germany

EARL SPIRITS // THE EARL OF GIN

0,5 L // 45,0 %

GIN

95

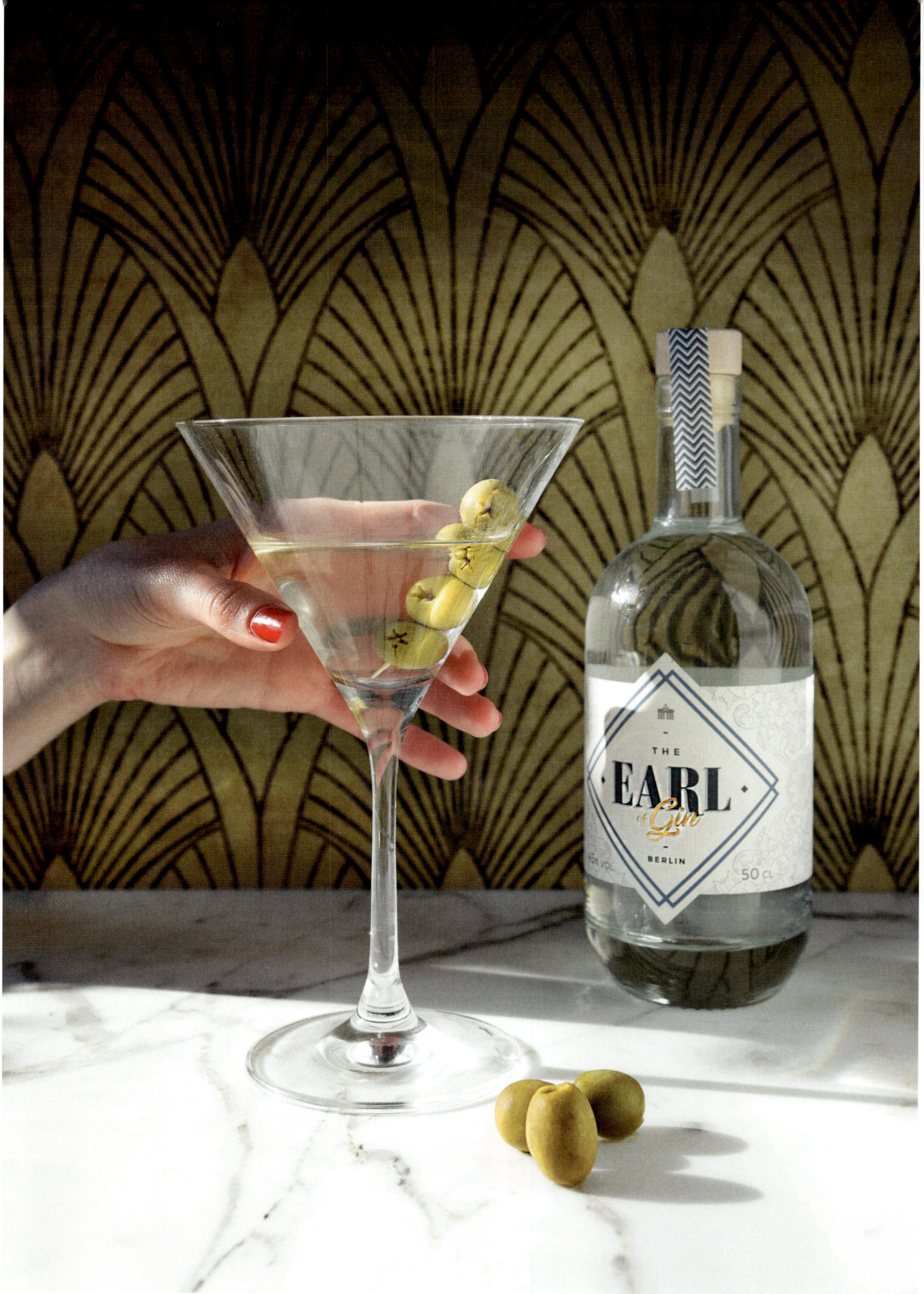
THE
EARL
of Gin
BERLIN
50 CL

CATEGORY
Dry Gin

ORIGIN
Germany

ESTABLISHED
2015

SIZE
● ● ○ ○

TASTING NOTES
Raffiniert, fruchtig-herb, komplex, mit präsenten Schwarztee-Aromen, markanten Zitrusnoten und einer leichten Ingwer-Schärfe sowie einem kräftigen Wacholder-Nachhall.

Refined, fruity-tart, complex, with black tea aromas present, distinctive citrus notes and a slight ginger spiciness, as well as a strong juniper aftertaste.

Ein Gin für die Queen?

Die einen lieben ihn pur, die anderen mit Milch, Honig oder einem Hauch Zucker: Earl Grey. Der geadelte Tee gehört im britischen Königshaus zum Pflichtgetränk. Es ranken sich zahlreiche Geschichten um seine Entstehung, am wahrscheinlichsten ist jedoch folgende: In seiner Zeit als Premierminister hob Charles Grey das Preismonopol der East India Tea Company auf. Der mit Bergamotteöl beträufelte chinesische Schwarztee wurde zum Dank nach dem Earl benannt. Beträufelt wurde er, um ihn auf der monatelangen Schiffsreise nach Europa vor Gerüchen zu schützen. Noch heute verleiht das fruchtige Öl dem Earl Grey sein mediterranes Zitronen-Aroma und dem The Earl of Gin aus dem Hause Earl Spirits seinen dominanten Geschmack.

Gepflegt einen im Tee haben

Die Seele des Earl of Gin ist ein kräftiger, intensiv duftender Earl Grey-Tee aus China, der mit frischem Zitronengras und Ingwer angereichert wird. Die Basis bildet ein fünffach destillierter Weizenbrand. Die Köpfe hinter Earl Spirits wollen einzigartige Tee-Spirituosen in die Welt bringen. Dabei suchen sie nach neuen Wegen, mit Tee auf das Leben anzustoßen – und zwar nicht nachmittags um drei an der Kaffeetafel, sondern nachts um eins in der Cocktailbar. Für die Gründer aus Berlin hat die Aromenvielfalt von Tee großes Potenzial. Die besten Bars der Welt hantieren mit eigenen Teeextrakten. Mit The Earl of Gin können nun auch Gin-Liebhaber gepflegt einen im Tee haben.

A gin for the Queen?

Some love it neat, others with milk, honey or a little sugar: Earl Grey. The ennobled tea is a compulsory drink among British royalty. There are numerous stories about its origins, but the most likely is the following. During his time as prime minister, Charles Grey lifted the East India Tea Company's price monopoly. Chinese black tea sprinkled with bergamot oil was named after the Earl in gratitude. It was sprinkled to protect it from odors during the month-long sea voyage to Europe. Even today, the fruity oil gives Earl Grey its Mediterranean lemon aroma and, to The Earl of Gin from Earl Spirits, its dominant flavor.

Distinguished tea guest

The core of Earl of Gin is a strong, intensely fragrant Earl Grey tea from China, enriched with fresh lemongrass and ginger. The base is a fivefold distilled wheat spirit. The minds behind Earl Spirits want to bring unique tea spirits to the world. They are looking for new ways to toast life with tea – not at the coffee table at three in the afternoon, but at the cocktail bar at one in the morning. For the founders from Berlin, the diversity of tea aromas has great potential. The best bars in the world work their own tea extracts. With Earl of Gin, gin lovers can now also have a distinguished tea guest.

> **When tea drinkers become gin lovers and gin lovers become tea drinkers.**

CATEGORY
New Western Dry Gin

ORIGIN
Germany

ESTABLISHED
2019

SIZE
● ○ ○ ○

TASTING NOTES
Rund und ausbalanciert, floral-blumig, mit einem ausgeprägten Geschmack von süßen Himbeeren und Lavendel, ergänzt durch die herbe Note der Cranberrys und des Rosa Pfeffers, ein Hauch von Wacholder, im Abgang frisch durch die Kaffirlimettenblätter.

Round and balanced, floral-blossomy, with a pronounced taste of sweet raspberries and lavender, complemented by the tart notes of cranberries and pink pepper, a touch of juniper, fresh on the finish with the addition of kaffir lime leaves.

❞
The Spirit of Adventure.

UNKNOWN LANDS | SPIRITS

UNKNOWN LANDS | GIN

Aufbruch ins Unbekannte

Die Sehnsucht nach Freiheit und Abenteuer, abseits von bekannten Pfaden zu wandeln, das Vertraute hinter sich zu lassen und sich ins Unbekannte zu stürzen – der UNKNOWN Lands | GIN ließe sich bestens in einem Glas mit der Aufschrift "Fernweh" servieren. Darunter die Definition: "der starke Wunsch zu reisen und die Welt zu entdecken". Inspiriert vom Freigeist Peter Pans, dorthin zu gehen, wo Träume geboren werden, überlegten sich Maxim Matthew und Sebastian Panneck die Rezeptur für ihren Gin. Die Botanicals und ihre aromatischen Eigenschaften schaffen es, Sehnsüchte zu wecken, Erinnerungen aufzurufen oder sogar ein Abenteuer in den "Unknown Lands" zu erleben.

Viele Wege führen zum Gin

Dabei wollten die Gründer, zwei ehemalige Filmemacher, ursprünglich mit einem Fashion-Label für Lifestyle & Accessoires auf neuen Wegen wandeln. Sie wollten einen Look für Abenteurer kreieren. Eine Wasserflasche mit Ledereinband braucht jedoch ein Getränk, das am Ende eines langen Tages mit Freunden am Lagerfeuer geteilt werden kann. In Zusammenarbeit mit dem Master Distiller Thomas Häberer brachten sie den UNKNOWN Lands | GIN auf den Markt, der mit Wacholder, Sternmoos, wilden Himbeeren, Cranberrys, Lavendel, Hibiskus, Rosenknopsen, Kaffirlimettenblättern, Koriander, Basilikum, Zimt, Angelikawurzel und Rosa Pfeffer auftrumpft. Je nach Temperatur und Füllstand der Flasche entwickeln die Botanicals ein unterschiedliches Profil. Wer den Gin genießt, betritt immer wieder geschmackliches Neuland. Auch das Flaschendesign greift das Reiselust-Konzept auf. Das Etikett, auf dem das Höhenprofil einer unbekannten Landschaft dargestellt ist, umrundet die Glasflasche.

Berlin, Germany

Setting off into the unknown

The longing for freedom and adventure, to wander off the beaten track, to leave the familiar behind and plunge into the unknown – the UNKNOWN Lands | GIN would be best served in a glass with the inscription "wanderlust". Then below that, the definition: "the strong desire to travel and discover the world". Inspired by Peter Pan's free spirit of going where dreams are born, Maxim Matthew and Sebastian Panneck mulled over the recipe for their gin. The botanicals and their aromatic properties manage to awaken longings, evoke memories and even the experience of adventuring in "Unknown Lands".

Many roads lead to gin

The founders, two former filmmakers, originally wanted to tread new paths with a fashion label for lifestyle & accessories. They wanted to create a look for adventurers. But a leather-bound water bottle needs a drink that can be shared with friends around the campfire at the end of a long day. Working with Master Distiller Thomas Häberer, they launched UNKNOWN Lands | GIN, which boasts juniper, star moss, wild raspberries, cranberries, lavender, hibiscus, rosebuds, kaffir lime leaves, coriander, basil, cinnamon, angelica root and pink pepper. Depending on the temperature and fill level of the bottle, the botanicals develop a different profile. Anyone who enjoys gin always enters new taste territory. The bottle design also picks up on that adventurous concept. The label, which depicts the altitude profile of an unknown landscape, encircles the glass bottle.

SASH & FRITZ GMBH

WILD CHILD GIN

> " A gin that embodies the spirit of the capital – born to be wild!

Born to be... Berlin Dry Gin

Der Wild Child Gin ist eine Hommage an Berlin und die Freiheit des Geistes – hochprozentig regional! Verwendet werden wilde, von Hand gelesene Wacholderbeeren, Gin-Botanicals wie Rosmarin und Koriander sowie Zitronatzitronen und Bergamotte aus Kalabrien. Pur verkostet eröffnet dieser Dry Gin ein intensives und sehr komplexes Universum verschiedenster floraler, herbaler und fruchtiger Noten. In Cocktails und Gin Tonics entwickeln sich die Kopfnoten zu den Trägern des Aromenspektrums und treten sehr klar hervor. Die behutsame traditionelle Gin-Destillation sowie das weiche Wasser aus den Ausläufern des Erzgebirges geben diesem „wilden Brand" einen weichen Kern.

Eine Hommage an die Freiheit des Geistes

Als Grundlage dient das Basisdestillat des Sash & Fritz-Wodkas. Hier wird unter Verwendung von klassischen und einigen besonderen, aus der Weinherstellung bekannten Arbeitsschritten ein besonders feiner, weicher und cremiger Brand aus deutschem Weizen destilliert. Darin werden die verschiedenen Gin-Botanicals bei unterschiedlichen Temperaturen nacheinander mazeriert. Die auf komplexe Basis- und Herznoten gesetzten Kopfnoten sind Earl-Grey-Tee, Rosmarin und Bergamotte. Zusammen mit der balancierten Wacholderwürze und dem Konzert aller anderen Zutaten erzeugen sie einen spannenden und frisch-herben, irgendwie wilden Kontrast. Dieser Gin aus Berlin steht für das Lebensgefühl der Hauptstadt. Er feiert das Leben und lässt sich in keine Schublade stecken. Freier Geist aus einer freien Stadt! Wild Child Gin... Born to be wild!

CATEGORY
Dry Gin

ORIGIN
Germany

ESTABLISHED
2015

SIZE

TASTING NOTES
Der Wacholder ist präsent, deutlich frisches Aroma von Zitrone, markante und ausgeprägte Würze mit Koriander, Ingwer, Kardamom, Rosmarin und Pfeffer, florale Note mit einem Hauch von Süße, dezente Note von Kräutern und eine angenehm scharfe Note.

The juniper is present, distinct fresh aroma of lemon, prominent and pronounced spice with coriander, ginger, cardamom, rosemary and pepper, floral note with a touch of sweetness, subtle note of herbs and a pleasant spicy note.

Berlin, Germany

Born to be... Berlin Dry Gin

Wild Child Gin is a tribute to Berlin and the freedom of the spirit – spiritedly regional! Ingredients are wild, hand-picked juniper berries, gin botanicals such as rosemary and coriander, as well as citron lemons and bergamot from Calabria. Tasted neat, this dry gin opens an intense and very complex universe of diverse floral, herbal and fruity notes. In cocktails and gin and tonics, the top notes become the carriers of the aromatic spectrum and emerge very clearly. The careful traditional distillation of gin and the soft water from the foothills of the Ore Mountains give a soft core to this "wild spirit".

A tribute to the freedom of the spirit

The base distillate of Sash & Fritz vodka serves as the foundation. Here, using classical and some special working steps known from wine production, a particularly fine, soft and creamy spirit is distilled from German wheat. In it, the various gin botanicals are successively macerated at different temperatures. The top notes, founded on complex base and heart notes, are Earl Grey tea, rosemary and bergamot. Together with the balanced juniper flavor and the concert of all other ingredients, they create an exciting and freshly-tart, somehow wild contrast. This gin from Berlin stands for the attitude to life of the capital city. It celebrates life and can not be pigeonholed. Free spirit from a free city! Wild Child Gin ... born to be wild!

CATEGORY
Infused Gin

ORIGIN
Germany

ESTABLISHED
2020

SIZE
● ● ●

TASTING NOTES
Weich, orientalisch und leicht herb sowie zuckersüß am Gaumen, milde mediterrane Wacholderaromen in Kombination mit einer spritzigen Zitrus- und einer herzhaften Angelikawurzel-Note, im Nachhall leicht pfeffrig.

Soft, oriental and slightly tart as well as sugary sweet on the palate, mild Mediterranean juniper aromas combined with a tangy citrus and a lusty angelica note, slightly peppery in the aftertastetaste being rounded off by berries and nuances of pepper.

GINZEIT GMBH

VAGINA – THE HIBISCUS GIN

Verlangen nach einem Hibis-Kuss

Es scheint, als würde die junge Dame, die sich lasziv aus einer Blume räkelt, nonchalant „I want you naked" flüstern. Ihr wallendes Haar fällt ihr locker ins Gesicht, ihr Blick ist ein wenig schüchtern, der Mund leicht geöffnet. Auf ihrem tattooverzierten Arm leuchtet rot eben jene Blüte, der eine aphrodisierende Wirkung nachgesagt wird: der Hibiskus. Vagina heißt die Lady, die freudige Erwartungen auslöst. Sie ist die Göttin des Gins und Namensgeberin des gleichnamigen Destillats aus der GinZeit-Schmiede. Der vaGINa-Gin ist in vielerlei Hinsicht ein Hingucker – und das nicht nur wegen des provokanten Namens und des Frauendesigns auf dem Etikett. Es ist vor allem die leuchtend rote Farbe, die Lust auf mehr macht.

Konventionslos, aber traditionsbewusst

In der Basis entspricht der vaGINa-Gin der Herstellung eines London Dry Gin. Der süßlich-herbe Gin wird dreifach in einer Kupferbrennblase im Small-Batch-Verfahren destilliert und anschließend per Hand abgefüllt. Neben Wacholder bilden hierbei klassische Botanicals wie Angelikawurzel, Koriandersamen, Zitrus sowie Kubebenpfeffer als Exot die Eckpfeiler. Verfeinert wird das Destillat mit echten getrockneten Hibiskusblüten. Auf diese Weise erhält die Göttin ihre charakteristisch natürliche Rotfärbung. vaGINa ist die Nummer eins einer gottesgleichen Gin-Familie. Ihre schüchterne und weniger offensive Schwester Virgina als alkoholfreie Variante hat sich bereits zu ihr gesellt.

Wernigerode, Germany

Yearning for a hibis kiss

It seems as if the young lady, lolling lasciviously from a flower, might be nonchalantly whispering "I want you naked". Her flowing hair falls loosely into her face, her gaze a little shy, her mouth slightly open. On her tattooed arm glows red the very flower that is said to have an aphrodisiac effect: the hibiscus. Vagina is the name of the lady who excites joyful expectations. She is the goddess of gin and namesake of the eponymous distillate from the GinZeit operation; vaGINa gin is an eye-catcher in many respects – and not just because of the provocative name and female design on the label. It is above all the bright red color that makes you want more.

Unconventional, but conscious of tradition

Essentially vaGINa gin corresponds with the production of a London Dry Gin. This sweet-tart gin is distilled three times in a copper still using the small-batch method and then bottled by hand. In addition to juniper, classic botanicals such as angelica root, coriander seeds, citrus and cubeb pepper as an exotic together form the cornerstones. The distillate is refined with real dried hibiscus flowers. This gives the goddess her characteristic natural red color. vaGINa is the number one of a goddess-like gin family. Her shy and less offensive sister Virgina as an alcohol-free variant has already joined her.

0,7 L // 45,0 %

> **This gin is certainly unique – but no angel!**

EDELBRENNEREI
SCHLOSS NEUENBURG

GIN

CATEGORY
Dry Gin

ORIGIN
Germany

ESTABLISHED
2011

SIZE

TASTING NOTES
Mild und ausgewogen, leicht herb, sehr blumig, ein Hauch von Zitrus, kräftiger Gintyp mit viel Volumen am Gaumen durch asiatische Gewürze.

Mild and balanced, slightly tart, very floral, a hint of citrus, strong gin type with lots of volume on the palate due to Asian spices.

Ohne viel Chichi

Einfach nur GIN. Drei Buchstaben. Mehr Trara braucht die Spirituose aus der Edelbrennerei Schloss Neuenburg nicht in ihrem Namen, um für das zu stehen, was in der schlichten, glasklaren Hülle, geschmückt mit einer goldenen stilisierten Lilie auf dem Etikett, steckt: einfach GIN. Trocken und wacholderbetont. Die Lilie als Symbol der Reinheit verkörpert die Lebensphilosophie von Matthias Hempel, dem Inhaber der Brennerei. Er war es, der im Alter von 25 Jahren einen Weinberg kaufte und der sich seit der Finanzkrise 2008 der Pflege und dem Erhalt alter Obstsorten widmet. Das Einfangen und Konservieren von natürlichen Aromen sowie die Veredelung von Rohstoffen gipfeln in Weinen, Whiskys und Edelbränden.

Elf kräuterige Freunde

Der GIN ist aus einer Auftragsarbeit heraus entstanden und gehört inzwischen zur festen Größe in der Produktpalette der Edelbrennerei. Das Besondere: Der Wacholder wird getrennt von den anderen Botanicals gebrannt. Um einen betont milden, aromatischen Geschmack zu erzielen, wird das Wacholderdestillat ganz eng geschnitten. Die genaue Botanical-Liste bleibt unter Verschluss. Nur so viel: Die dominierende Holunderblüte verleiht dem GIN zusätzlich eine feine Floralität. Bei der Komposition wurde Wert darauf gelegt, dass sich keines der elf verwendeten Kräuter geschmacklich in den Vordergrund drängt. Sie alle dienen dem Gesamtgeschmacksbild. Auf das Anreichern der Destillate mit Zucker verzichtet Matthias Hempel vollständig, alles bleibt naturbelassen. Die Lizenz zum Destillieren hat er seit 2013. Allen seinen Bränden wird mindestens ein Jahr oder länger Zeit zur Reifung im Gewölbekeller gegeben.

> ## No dime-a-dozen spirit with a one-dimensional citrus flavor.

Without much fuss

Simply GIN. Three letters. That's all the fanfare this spirit from the Schloss Neuenburg distillery needs in its name to stand for what's inside its simple, crystal-clear container, adorned with a golden stylized lily on the label: simply GIN. Dry and juniper accented. The lily, as a symbol of purity, embodies the philosophy of life of Matthias Hempel, the owner of the distillery. It was he who bought a vineyard at the age of 25 and who, ever since the financial crisis of 2008, has devoted himself to the care and preservation of old fruit varieties. Capturing and preserving natural flavors, as well as refining raw materials, culminates in wines, whiskies and fine spirits.

Eleven herbal friends

GIN arose from a commissioned work and is now a permanent fixture in the product range of this distillery of fine spirits. The special feature is that the juniper is distilled separately from the other botanicals. In order to achieve an emphatically mild, aromatic taste, the juniper distillate is cut very closely. The exact botanical list remains under lock and key. What can be revealed: the dominant elderflower gives the GIN an additional fine florality. In the composition, emphasis was placed on ensuring that none of the eleven herbs used pushes itself to the fore in terms of taste. They all serve the overall flavor picture. Matthias Hempel does not add sugar to the distillates at all; everything remains natural. He has been licensed to distill since 2013, and all his spirits are given at least a year or more to mature in the vaulted cellar.

Schloss Neuenburg (Freyburg), Germany

DESTILLATE PRINZ VON SACHSEN

MORITZBURGER GIN

" Only the best for the prince.

Ein Prinz aus Sachsen

Das Besondere am Moritzburger Gin ist nicht nur seine Herkunft. Mitten in Moritzburg, der Jagdresidenz des Kurfürsten von Sachsen, befindet sich die Brennerei „Prinz von Sachsen", die von Prinz Nils von Sachsen gekauft und von Brennmeister Michael Gerlach betrieben wird. Hier weht noch Geschichte durch die Luft, die von vergangenen Fürsten und ihre berauschenden Festen berichtet. Von dieser geschichtsträchtigen Luft beflügelt, können wir von einer „Genussgeneration" sprechen, die Michael zu nichts Geringerem treibt, als das Beste in der Brennerei zusammen zu bringen. Tradition verpflichtet und so nimmt Michael nicht nur die Herstellung sehr ernst, sondern auch die Herkunft seiner Zutaten.

Pure Reinheit

Denn für den Moritzburger Gin wird der Moritzburger Wodka verwendet. Ein aus biozertifiziertem Kartoffelalkohol gewonnener Brand, der aus regionalen Biokartoffeln hergestellt wird. Sage und schreibe 51 mal wird der Wodka destilliert, um zu seiner absoluten Reinheit zu kommen. Eine Reinheit, die sich im Charakter des Moritzburger Gins auf sanfte Art und Weise widerspiegelt. Verschiedene Brennanlagen und Filtertechniken machen es möglich einen reinen Wodka zu schaffen, den der Fürst mit Sicherheit nicht mehr so schnell aus der Hand gelegt hätte. Dieser hochwertige Kartoffel-Spirit dient als Ausgangsbasis für den Moritzburger Gin. Lediglich vier Zutaten kommen in dem Gin zum Zuge. Alle werden einzeln destilliert und anschließend in einer geheimen Komposition mit dem Kartoffel-Wodka vermählt.

CATEGORY
Distilled Gin

ORIGIN
Germany

ESTABLISHED
2009

SIZE
● ○ ○ ○

TASTING NOTES
Der Gin beginnt mit einem sanften Charakter, der an leicht erdig-nussige Noten erinnert, schnell gefolgt von einer gut abgestimmten Wacholdernote. Fruchtige Aromen wie Blutorange und der Schärfe von Ingwer lassen sich ebenfalls herausschmecken.

The gin starts with a smooth character reminiscent of slightly earthy and nutty notes, quickly followed by a well-balanced juniper note. Fruity aromas such as blood orange and the spiciness of ginger can also be tasted.

Moritzburger, Germany

A prince from Saxony

The special thing about Moritzburger Gin is not just its origin. In the middle of Moritzburg, the hunting residence of the Prince Elector of Saxony, is the distillery "Prince of Saxony", bought by Prince Nils of Saxony and run by master distiller Michael Gerlach. History still wafts through the air here, telling of past princes and their intoxicating feasts. Fueled by this history breeze, we can speak of a "generation of delectation" that drives Michael to do nothing less than bring the best together in the distillery. Tradition is an obligation and so Michael takes very seriously not just production, but also the origin of ingredients.

Sheer purity

Because Moritzburger Gin is based on Moritzburger Vodka. A spirit obtained from certified organic potato alcohol, which is made from regional organic potatoes. The vodka is distilled no fewer than 51 times to reach its absolute purity. A purity that is gently reflected in the character of Moritzburger Gin. A selection of distillation equipment and filtering techniques makes it possible to create a pure vodka that the prince would certainly not have put back down that quickly. This high-quality potato spirit serves as the starting point for Moritzburger Gin. Only four ingredients are used in the gin. All are distilled individually and then combined in a secret composition with the potato vodka.

> With a lot of love down to the smallest detail, a true masterpiece is created here.

CATEGORY
Dry Gin

ORIGIN
Germany

ESTABLISHED
1766

SIZE
● ● ○ ○

TASTING NOTES
Trocken, aromatisch, blumig. Ausgeprägte Wacholdernote, dazu intensive Aromen von Orangenblüten, Koriander und Rosmarin.

Dry, aromatic, floral. Pronounced juniper note, plus intense aromas of orange blossom, coriander and rosemary.

SCHWARZE UND SCHLICHTE GMBH & CO. KG

FRIEDRICHS DRY GIN

Der Tradition treu bleiben

Tradition seit 1766: Die Steinhagen Brennerei hat eine längere Erfahrung in der Wacholderbrennerei als jeder andere Betrieb in Deutschland. Der Friedrichs Dry Gin basiert auf dieser jahrhundertelangen Brenntradition und der damit verbundenen Expertise. Seit jeher brennt man hier mit einer handgefertigten kupfernen Brennblase, auf der der Friedrichs Dry Gin dreifach destilliert wird. Die besonders sorgfältige, mehrfache Destillation sorgt dafür, dass ein Gin mit besonders mildem Geschmack entsteht. Die traditionelle Steinhäger Brennmethode hat sich über die Jahrhunderte nicht verändert. Denn Brennmeister Nollmann weiß: Sie macht den Unterschied, den man beim Friedrichs Dry Gin schmecken kann.

Eine meisterhafte Komposition

Tradition, echtes Handwerk und viel Liebe zum Detail – so entsteht ein wahres Meisterstück. Durch die sorgfältig verlesenen Wacholderbeeren erhält der Friedrichs Dry Gin eine ausgeprägte Wacholdernote. Diese wird um zwölf, mit besonderer Sorgfalt ausgewählte Botanicals ergänzt. Zutaten wie Koriander, Curaçaoschale, Süßholzwurzel, Rosmarin, Sternanis, Jasmin- und Lavendelblüten lassen diesen aromatisch-blumigen Gin zu einem einzigartigen Geschmackserlebnis werden. Unsere Empfehlung: den Friedrichs Dry Gin als Apple Tonic genießen. Dafür mischt man 6 cl Friedrichs Dry Gin mit 4 cl Apfelsaft und füllt das Ganze mit Tonic Water auf. Zum Schluss gibt man einen Schuss Zitronensaft hinzu und garniert den Drink mit einer dünnen Apfelscheibe und einem Stängel Rosmarin. Et voilà.

Oelde, Germany

Staying true to tradition

Tradition since 1766: Steinhagen Distillery has gained experience of distilling juniper over a period longer than that of any other company in Germany. Friedrichs Dry Gin is based on this centuries-long distilling tradition and the expertise associated with it. Since time immemorial, the distillery has used a handmade copper still on which Friedrichs Dry Gin is triple distilled. The particularly careful, multiple distillation ensures that a gin with a particularly mild taste is created. The traditional Steinhäger distilling method has not changed over the centuries. Because, as master distiller Nollmann knows, it makes the difference that you can taste in Friedrichs Dry Gin.

A masterful composition

Tradition, genuine craftsmanship and great attention to detail – this is how a true masterpiece is created. The carefully selected juniper berries give Friedrichs Dry Gin a distinctive juniper note. This is complemented by twelve botanicals selected with special care. Ingredients such as coriander, curaçao peel, licorice root, rosemary, star anise, jasmine and lavender flowers make this aromatic-floral gin a unique taste experience. Our recommendation: enjoy Friedrichs Dry Gin in an Apple Tonic. Mix 6 cl Friedrichs Dry Gin with 4 cl apple juice and fill up with tonic water. Finally, add a dash of lemon juice and garnish the drink with a thin slice of apple and a sprig of rosemary. Et voilà.

BRENNEREI EHRINGHAUSEN

JOS. GARDEN GIN

CATEGORY
New Western Dry Gin

ORIGIN
Germany

ESTABLISHED
2014

SIZE

TASTING NOTES
Im Geschmack reichen sich im ersten Eindruck herber Wacholder und frische Zitrusnoten die Hände, die allerdings schnell umgarnt werden von der süßen Frucht der Himbeere. Im Anschluss baut sich eine leichte und willkommene Schärfe auf, die an würzigen Koriander und Pfeffer erinnert. Im Ganzen ist der Jos. Garden milder als erwartet und gibt einen tollen Gin zum puren Genuss und im Gin Tonic.

In the taste, tart juniper and fresh citrus notes join hands in the first impression, then to be quickly ensnared by the sweet fruit of raspberry. Subsequently, a slight and welcome spiciness builds up, reminiscent of spicy coriander and pepper. Overall, Jos. Garden Gin is milder than expected, offering a great gin for pure enjoyment and in gin tonic.

Ein Geschenk aus der Vergangenheit

Wie oft stöberte jeder von uns einmal im Keller der Eltern, dem Dachboden der Großeltern oder kroch durch staubbedeckte Ecken. Die Nase kitzelt, die gedämpfte Atmosphäre lockt, der Geruch des Geheimnisvollen liegt in der Luft und hinter jeder Truhe und in jedem Regal könnte er liegen: der unbekannte Schatz. Vollkommen egal, welcher. Man weiß es, wenn man ihn sieht. Ob sich die Geschwister Theres und Georg so fühlten, als sie den Dachboden des alten Speichers aufräumten, wissen wir nicht, aber der Schatz, den sie entdeckten, sollte vieles verändern. Denn sie fanden eine unglaublich große und detailliert dokumentierte Sammlung konservierter Pflanzen. Dieses Herbarium stammt von ihrem Urgroßonkel Josef Ehringhausen, damals Apotheker und wie viele seines Schlags zu dieser Zeit: ein Kräuterkundler und Wissenschaftler mit Büchlein in der Hand. Ein Geschenk aus einer längst vergangenen Zeit, die zu einem weiteren „brennenden" Abenteuer am Kessel führte.

Sammelsurium der Sinne

Mit dieser einzigartigen Sammlung verschiedenster Pflanzen begannen die beiden zu experimentieren. Sie brannten einzelne und kombinierten Aromen und der Jos. Garden Gin nahm 2014 seine finale Form an. Benannt nach Urgroßvater Josef, werden auch die Jos. Garden Gins nachhaltig, CO2-neutral und mit Zutaten ausschließlich aus anerkannt ökologischem Anbau produziert. Die Brennerei zeichnete schon immer aus, dass man mit sehr viel Leidenschaft und Liebe an die Ideen und Produkte geht. Diese Liebe ist nicht nur im Jos. Garden Gin und dem Barrel Aged Gin wiederzufinden, sondern in jedem Produkt der Familienbrennerei.

Werne, Germany

A present from the past

How often has each of us rummaged in the parents' basement, the grandparents' attic or crawled through dust-covered corners. The nose tickles, the muffled atmosphere entices, the smell of mystery is in the air, and behind every chest or on every shelf it might lie: unknown treasure. It doesn't matter which. You know it when you see it. We don't know if that's how siblings Theres and Georg felt when they were cleaning out the attic of the old storehouse, but the treasure they discovered was to change a great deal. For they found an incredibly large and detailed documented collection of preserved plants. This herbarium came from their great-granduncle Josef Ehringhausen, back then a pharmacist and, like many of his ilk at the time, a herbalist and scientist with notebook to hand. A present from a bygone era that led to another "burning" adventure at the still.

Compendium of the senses

With this unique collection of diverse plants, the two began to experiment. They distilled individual and combined flavors and Jos. Garden Gin took its final form in 2014. Named after great-grandfather Josef, the Jos. Garden Gins are also produced sustainably, CO_2-neutral and with ingredients exclusively from recognized organic cultivation. The distillery has always been characterized by the fact that one approaches the ideas and products with a great deal of passion and love. This love is not only found in Jos. Garden Gin and the barrel-aged gin, but in every product of the family distillery.

0,5 L // 44,0 %

„
The globetrotter and his garden.

PRIVATBRENNEREI BOENTE

URGIN

Das Original – mehr Tradition geht nicht

Es ist bekannt: Um das Jahr 1600 herum erzeugte der aus Hanau stammende und im niederländischen Leiden praktizierende Arzt Franz de le Boë (1614–1672) mit wenigen Zutaten ein Destillat aus Wacholderbeeren, Koriander und Alkohol: Genever, das holländische Wort für Wacholder und wurde damit zum Vater des Gins. Nun hat die Privatbrennerei Boente aus Recklinghausen mit dem UrGin einen Gin herausgebracht, der dem Originalrezept aus dem 17. Jahrhundert wie kaum ein anderer nachempfunden ist.

Aus Medizin wurde Genuss

Das Destillat von de la Boë war ursprünglich Medizin und sollte Magenleiden und Sodbrennen seiner Patienten lindern. Man wusste um die positive Wirkung des Wacholders bei diesen Beschwerden. Zu dieser Zeit wütete auch der Niederländisch-Spanische Krieg. In diesem kamen die Briten den Holländern zu Hilfe. Hier lernten sie Genever kennen. Wegen des guten Geschmacks nahmen sie ihn mit in die Heimat auf die Insel. Dort wurde er nicht mehr bloß zu medizinischen Zwecken getrunken. Der Einfachheit halber kürzten sie den Namen ab und nannten das Destillat schlicht und ergreifend Gin. Seitdem entstand eine Vielzahl verschiedener Gins unterschiedlicher Kategorien. Doch dem Original kommt wohl kaum einer so nahe wie der UrGin.

Recklinghausen, Germany

The original – can't have more tradition

It is known: around the year 1600, Franz de le Boë (1614-1672), a physician from Hanau who practiced in Leiden, the Netherlands, produced a distillate from juniper berries, coriander and alcohol with just a few ingredients: Genever, the Dutch word for juniper. Thus he became the father of gin. Now, the Boente private distillery from Recklinghausen has brought out a gin that is like hardly any other based on the original recipe from the 17th century.

Medicine became pleasure

The distillate from de la Boë was originally a medicine intended to relieve his patients' stomach ailments and heartburn. People knew about the positive effect of juniper on these ailments. At that time, the Dutch-Spanish War was raging. In this war the British came to the aid of the Dutch. Here they got to know Genever. Because of its good taste, they took it back to their island home. There it was drunk not simply for medicinal purposes. For the sake of simplicity, they shortened the name and simply called the distillate gin. Since then, a variety of different gins of different categories has emerged. But few are this close to the original as the UrGin.

CATEGORY
Dry Gin

ORIGIN
Germany

ESTABLISHED
2020

SIZE

TASTING NOTES
Ein ehrlicher Gin mit dominantem Wacholder und intensivem Koriander.

An honest gin with dominant juniper and intense cilantro.

"A gin in the spirit of Franz de la Boë.

ALPAKO GMBH

ALPAKO GIN

*Herne,
Germany*

ALPAKO GMBH // ALPAKO GIN – "THE MODERN TASTE OF DRY GIN". 0,5 L // 43,0 %

GIN

115

CATEGORY
Distilled Dry Gin

ORIGIN
Germany

ESTABLISHED
2019

SIZE
● ● ○ ○

TASTING NOTES
Die Wacholdernote wird dezent zurückgestellt, dominierend sind die 25 sorgsam ausgewählten Botanicals. Beim Aroma sind vor allem Mango und Drachenfrucht vorherrschend, der Geschmack wird hauptsächlich von Açaí-Beere und Mango getragen.

The juniper note is discreetly restrained, the 25 carefully selected botanicals are dominant. The aroma is dominated by mango and dragon fruit, the taste is mainly conveyed by açaí berry and mango.

> „A modern gin with an unprecedented flavor."

Herne, Germany

Von der Schnapsidee zur Geschäftsidee

Die drei Gin-Liebhaber Patrick Hanel, Marcel Werth und Marcel Hupe probieren sich durch die Gin-Welt, um den perfekten Gin zu finden. Jedoch müssen sie feststellen, dass dieser nicht zu existieren scheint. Dem wollen sie kurzerhand ein Ende setzen. Und wie? Ganz einfach – indem sie ihren eigenen perfekten Gin kreieren. So wird eine Schnapsidee zur Geschäftsidee. Doch was macht den perfekten Gin aus? Die drei Herren sind sich einig: Sie wollen Gin modern interpretieren und eine komplett neue, nie da gewesene Geschmackskomposition kreieren. Durch eine Kombination von 25 erlesenen Botanicals ist dies gelungen. Ein Großteil der Botanicals stammt aus Peru – aus dem Land, in dem das Alpaka sein Zuhause hat. So gibt das Alpaka dem Alpako Gin seinen Namen und schmückt jede einzelne Flasche.

Der Gin für abenteuerlustige Genießer

Der Alpako ist ein Gin für echte Abenteurer. Er kombiniert außergewöhnliche und exotische Botanicals wie Mango und Açaí-Beere mit Drachen- und Sternfrucht – und wird so zu einem einmaligen und unvergesslichen Geschmackserlebnis. Durch diese harmonische Symbiose verschiedenster komplexer Aromen entsteht ein komplett neuartiger Gin: So wird der Alpako Gin zum „Modern Taste of Dry Gin". Doch nicht nur die erlesenen Botanicals sind für den Geschmack entscheidend, sondern auch die Liebe und Sorgfalt, mit der dieser Gin hergestellt wird. Übrigens wird seit Kurzem unter Verwendung von Handwerkskunst aus dem Jahre 1878 auch der Gin in der Rosé-Variante produziert – ebenfalls ein einmaliges Geschmackserlebnis. Also: Genießt ein Glas Alpako Gin und überzeugt euch selbst.

From spirited inspiration to business idea

The three gin lovers Patrick Hanel, Marcel Werth and Marcel Hupe feel their way through the world of gin to find that perfect gin. But what they discover is it doesn't seem to exist. Without further ado, they want to bring this to an end. How? Quite simply – by creating their own perfect gin. This is how spirited inspiration becomes a business idea. But what makes the perfect gin? The three gentlemen agree: they want to interpret gin in a modern way and create a completely new, unprecedented flavor composition. Through a combination of 25 exquisite botanicals, they have succeeded in doing so. A large part of the botanicals comes from Peru – home of the alpaca. Thus, the alpaca gives Alpako Gin its name and decorates each bottle.

The gin for adventurous connoisseurs

Alpako is a gin for real adventurers. It combines unusual and exotic botanicals such as mango and açaí berry with dragon and star fruit – and thus becomes a unique and unforgettable taste experience. This harmonious symbiosis of a wide variety of complex flavors creates a completely new kind of gin: making Alpako Gin the "Modern Taste of Dry Gin". However, it isn't just the exquisite botanicals that decide the taste, but also the love and care with which this gin is produced. Incidentally, using craftsmanship dating back to 1878, the gin has also recently been produced in a rosé variant – also a unique taste experience. So, enjoy a glass of Alpako Gin and convince yourself.

DESTILLERIE EICKER & CALLEN PETER MEINKEN

RENTON-GIN

CATEGORY
Dry Gin

ORIGIN
Germany

ESTABLISHED
–

SIZE
● ○ ○ ○

TASTING NOTES
Der Renton-Gin beginnt mit frischen Zitrusnoten und einem sehr floralen Part sehr blumig. Während sich zum Finale Orangennoten und ein leichter Hauch von Rosen versammeln, baut sich im Hintergrund schon eine elegant erdige Note auf, die von Angelikawurzel und anderen Kräutern stammt. Der Abgang wird von einer würzigen Schärfe abgerundet, die an Pfeffer erinnert. Ein sehr harmonisches Aufeinanderfolgen der verschiedenen Zutaten.

Renton-Gin gives an initial impression of blossom with fresh citrus notes and a very floral part. While orange notes and a slight hint of roses gather for the finale, an elegant earthy note is already building up in the background, which comes from angelica root and other herbs. The finish is rounded off by a spicy pungency reminiscent of pepper. A very harmonious succession of the various ingredients.

Ein Offizier und GINtleman

Offizier Jim Renton blickt auf die zerstörten Gebäude des Ruhrgebietes. Ruinen, graue Landschaften und aufsteigender Rauch sind im Blickfeld des erfahrenen Soldaten. Es ist 1945 und die Region war aufgrund seiner wichtigen Infrastruktur ein priorisiertes Angriffsziel der alliierten Luftstreitkräfte. Jim Renton, ehemaliger Bergbauspezialist, blieb nach dem Krieg, um der zerstörten Gegend wieder Leben einzuhauchen. Eine Geschichte, die England und das Ruhrgebiet verbindet wie nur wenige. Bryn Jones, Gründer des Importunternehmens „House of Ruhr", ist langjähriger Freund von Peter Meinken, Besitzer der Destillerie Eicker und Callen. Die Brennerei schaut heute auf eine ebenso lange Geschichte zurück, aber auch auf eine lange Freundschaft mit einer starken Verbindung. Zusammen wollten die beiden Freunde nicht nur uralte Rezepte aus der Brennerei wieder zum Leben erwecken, sondern sie auch in die Bars und Geschäfte bringen. Die Gemeinsamkeit?

Enge Verbindungen

Jim Renton war Bryns Urgroßvater, der beim Wiederaufbau im Ruhrgebiet großen Anteil hatte. Zu Ehren des Mannes bekam der Gin seinen Namen und gehört zu einem Gin-Trio, das die Geschichte der Bergbauregion widerspiegeln sollte, aber ebenso die Herkunft des britischen Soldaten. Ein Grund, warum der Gin vornehmlich auf dem britischen Markt erhältlich ist. Der Renton-Gin schmückt sich mit insgesamt zwölf Botanicals wie Wacholder, Orangenschalen, verschiedenen Zitrusnoten, Lavendel, Rosenwasser und spannenden Gewürzen. Mit über 130 Jahren Brennerfahrung hat die Destillerie Eicker und Callen nicht nur das Wissen zu bieten, sondern auch das nötige Feingefühl, um durch ihre Produkte eine lebendige Geschichte erzählen zu lassen. Der Renton-Gin mit seiner pikanten Note und dem scharf-würzigen Charakter hätte Jim Renton sicher gefallen.

> *A gin that connects England and the Ruhr like no other.*

An officer and a GINtleman

Officer Jim Renton looked out over the ruined buildings of the Ruhr. Ruins, gray landscapes and rising smoke were in the experienced soldier's field of vision. It was 1945 and the region was a prioritized target for Allied air forces because of its vital infrastructure. Jim Renton, former mining specialist, stayed after the war to breathe life back into the devastated area. It's a story that connects England and the Ruhr like few others. Bryn Jones, founder of the import company "House of Ruhr", is a longtime friend of Peter Meinken, owner of the Eicker and Callen distillery. Today, the distillery looks back on an equally long history, but also on a long friendship with a strong connection. Together, the two friends wanted not only to bring age-old recipes from the distillery back to life, but also to bring them to bars and stores. The common ground?

Close connections

Jim Renton was Bryn's great-grandfather, who played a major role in the reconstruction of the Ruhr. In honor of the man, the gin received his name, and belongs to a trio of gins that should reflect the history of the mining region, but equally the origin of the British soldier. One reason why the gin is mainly available on the British market. Renton-Gin adorns itself with a total of twelve botanicals such as juniper, orange zest, various citrus notes, lavender, rose water and exciting spices. With over 130 years of distilling experience, the Eicker and Callen distillery not only has the knowledge to offer, but also the sensibilities to let their products tell a vivid story. Renton-Gin, with its spicy note and hot and spicy character, would certainly have pleased Jim Renton.

Herne, Germany

DESTILLERIE EICKER UND CALLEN PETER MEINKEN

RINOCERO GIN

Düsseldorf, Germany

GIN

DESTILLERIE ECKER UND CALLEN PETER MEINKEN // RINK BRAND

0,5 L // 41,0%

121

Brennfreude

Wenn Freunde für etwas brennen und daraus eine Unternehmung entsteht, kann man sich auch durchaus „Brennfreunde" nennen. Genau hinter diesem Namen stecken drei Jungs, die einer gemeinsamen Leidenschaft nachjagen. Zusammen mit der alten Familienbrennerei Destillerie Eicker und Callen in Herne, die in 4. Generation auf eine über 130 Jahre alte Geschichte zurückblicken kann, entwickeln und produzieren sie einzigartige und charakterstarke Spirits. Wenn dann noch jeder Schritt handgemacht ist, entwickelt man eine persönliche Bindung zu seinen Produkten und kreiert in kleinen Chargen besondere Unikate. Die Brennerei ist bekannt für ihre aufwendige Handarbeit und das nahmen sich die Jungs zu Herzen. So wird jedes Etikett liebevoll designt und von einem lokalen Unternehmen im Letterpressverfahren hergestellt, vom Brennmeister unterschrieben und nummeriert.

Fruchtige Außergewöhnlichkeit

Der Rinocero Gin ist einer dieser Dry Gins, die geschmacklich schon im extravaganten Bereich ein Tänzchen aufführen. Denn die beiden Hauptzutaten sind hier Physalis und Gojibeere. Diese werden in einer zarten, aber abgestimmten Harmonie zum Wacholder, Yerba Mate, Zitronenmelisse, zarten Rosenblüten und weiteren geheimen Zutaten gebracht – eine Herausforderung für den Destilliermeister bei solch einzigartigen und ausgeprägten Geschmacksaromen. Dennoch wird eine Brücke zwischen den so unterschiedlichen Aromen gebaut, was beweist, was Geduld und Erfahrung alles bewirken können. Das Rhinozeros steht sinnbildlich für die Stärke und Einzigartigkeit der Zutaten, die uns auf eine Reise über verschiedene Kontinente mitnehmen.

> From Flingern. For Flingern. For everyone.

Still friends

When friends are inflamed with enthusiasm for something and an enterprise is born out of it, the German name "Brennfreunde" [burning/distilling friends] hits the spot. Behind this very name are three guys chasing a common passion. Together with the Eicker and Callen family distillery in Herne, which can look back on a history of over 130 years, now into the 4th generation,

CATEGORY
London Dry Gin

ORIGIN
Germany

ESTABLISHED
—

SIZE
● ○ ○ ○

TASTING NOTES
Ein harmonisches Zusammenspiel von aufeinander abgestimmter Physalis und Gojibeere, die zusammen mit Wacholder ihre Aufwartung machen. Im Hintergrund zarte Zitrusnoten, die eine solide Grundlage bilden und im Einklang mit den Hauptzutaten stehen.

A harmonious interplay of well-matched physalis and goji berry, which together with juniper pay their respects. In the background, delicate citrus notes that form a solid foundation and are in harmony with the main botanicals.

Fruity exceptionality

Rinocero Gin is one of those dry gins that put on a show in the more extravagant sector in terms of taste. Because the two main ingredients here are physalis and goji berry. These are brought in a delicate but coordinated harmony with the juniper, yerba mate, lemon balm, delicate rose petals and other secret ingredients – a challenge for the master distiller with such

they develop and produce unique spirits with a strong character. If every step involves handcraft, you develop a personal connection to your products and create something unique in small batches. The distillery is known for its intricate handwork, and the guys took that to heart. So each label is intricately designed and letterpressed by a local company, signed and numbered by the master distiller.

unique and distinct flavors. Nevertheless, a bridge is built between such diverse flavors, proving what patience and experience can accomplish. The rhinoceros is emblematic of the strength and uniqueness of the ingredients, which take us on a journey across different continents.

FAUDE FEINE BRÄNDE

YOSHI NAMA – LITTLE TOKYO DRY GIN

CATEGORY
London Dry Gin

ORIGIN
Germany

ESTABLISHED
2020

SIZE
● ○ ○ ○

TASTING NOTES
Komplex, erfrischendes Aroma von Grapefruit und Zitronenschalen, angenehme Würze der Wacholderbeere, unterstrichen von einer subtilen spritzigen Fruchtnote durch Preiselbeere und Schlehe, langanhaltender Nachgang mit Kubebenpfeffer, Enzian und Safran.

Complex, refreshing aroma of grapefruit and lemon zest, pleasant spiciness of juniper berry, underlined by a subtly tangy fruit note from cranberry and sloe, long-lasting finish with cubeb pepper, gentian and saffron.

Japanische Philosophie trifft deutsches Handwerk

In Düsseldorf ist die größte japanische Community Deutschlands zuhause – und mittendrin Maximilian Bergfried, der happy ist, mit einem Schritt vor die Haustür in die Welt von Little Tokyo einzutauchen. Dort, in den japanischen Restaurants und Supermärkten, lernte er erstmals die fernöstliche Aromenwelt kennen. Seine Neugierde war geweckt. Je intensiver er in die japanische Kultur eintauchte, desto mehr inspirierte ihn die Philosophie von Kaiseki, Zen und Co. Denn hier dient die Natur als Vorbild, getreu dem Motto: „Was zusammen wächst, gehört zusammen." Und so bilden die vier natürlichen Nachbarn Wacholder, Schlehe, Preiselbeere und Enzian das Grundgerüst seines Yoshi Nama Gin.

Mit Yoshi um die Häuser ziehen

Der Yoshi Nama Gin ist der Inbegriff deutsch-japanischer Freundschaft. Destilliert wird das in Flaschen abgefüllte Little Tokyo von Florian Faude, dem Gründer von Faude feine Brände. Das Ergebnis ist ein erfrischender, intensiver deutscher Gin, der ein Stück Japan in sich trägt. Letzteres verkörpert auch das Flaschendesign, für das alte, japanische Streichholzschachteln als Vorbild dienten. Yoshi, das Männchen in der Mitte, stellt ein Fabelwesen dar. Er zieht gerne von Bar zu Bar, immer auf der Suche nach neuen Bekanntschaften – also ein sehr geselliger Zeitgenosse.

> **Cheers and kanpai! An aromatic declaration of love for Germany's Little Tokyo.**

Japanese philosophy meets German craftsmanship

Dusseldorf is home to Germany's largest Japanese community – and right in the middle of it is Maximilian Bergfried, who's happy

to dive into the world of Little Tokyo with just one step outside his front door. It was there, in the Japanese restaurants and supermarkets, that he first got to know the Far Eastern world of aromas. His curiosity was awoken. The more intensively he immersed himself in Japanese culture, the more he was inspired by the philosophy of Kaiseki, Zen and the like. For here, nature serves as a guiding principle, true to the motto "What grows together, belongs together." So it is that the four natural neighbors, juniper, sloe, cranberry and gentian, form the basic structure of his Yoshi Nama Gin.

Get around with Yoshi

Yoshi Nama Gin is the epitome of German-Japanese friendship. Bottled Little Tokyo is distilled by Florian Faude, founder of Faude fine brandies. The result is a refreshing, intense German gin that has a piece of Japan in it. The latter is also embodied in the bottle design, for which old Japanese matchboxes served as a model. Yoshi, the little man in the middle, represents a mythical creature. He likes to move from bar to bar, always looking for new acquaintances – quite a sociable contemporary.

Düsseldorf, Germany

OLEJNIK & STEFANSKI GBR

AMETHYST LONDON DRY GIN

Gelsenkirchen, Germany

Vermächtnis eines Sommerabends

Sie harmonieren wie Gin und Tonic: Dennis und Manuel, zwei Kumpel aus dem Ruhrgebiet, schrieben 2018 ihr eigenes Theaterstück. Eine Geschichte, geprägt von Höhen und Tiefen, vom Lernen und Reifen, von Spannungen und Gespanntsein. Eine Komödie? Nein! Eine Tragödie? Keinesfalls! Vielmehr eine Geschichte über Mut und Wagnis. Was an einem lauschigen Sommerabend mit kühlen Getränken und philosophischen Ergüssen begann, trägt heute den Namen AMETHYST Gin. Ihre eigene Spirituose wollten die beiden kreieren, einen wandlungsfähigen Gin, der pur, mit Tonic oder im Cocktail immer wieder neu und immer wieder ein bisschen nach Sommer schmeckt.

Der Stein des Ruhr-Gins

Dem Amethysten werden besondere Fähigkeiten zugesprochen. Soll er doch beruhigend und reinigend auf die Nerven und das Herz wirken. Ein Edelstein, der die Konzentrationsfähigkeit erhöht und unter das Kopfkissen gepackt vor Albträumen schützt. Ähnlich wie der Lavendel, der in diesem London Dry Gin steckt und dessen lila Farbe so ausgezeichnet zum Amethysten passt. Er ist eines von insgesamt acht verwendeten Botanicals, die größtenteils auch im heimischen Ruhrgebiet-Garten von Dennis und Manuel zu finden sind. Die Heimatverbundenheit ist den Freunden wichtig – wurde hier doch die Idee für ihren Gin geboren.

CATEGORY
London Dry Gin

ORIGIN
Germany

ESTABLISHED
2020

SIZE
● ○ ○ ○

TASTING NOTES
Blumiger, leicht herb-bitterer, außergewöhnlicher Geschmack durch die Kombination von Lavendel und Wacholder, leicht mentholige, frische Note dank Minze, Zitronengras, Zitronen- und Limettenschalen, eingerahmt von den Blüten des Holunders.

Floral, slightly astringent, exceptional taste due to the combination of lavender and juniper, slightly mentholated, fresh note thanks to mint, lemongrass, lemon and lime peel, framed by elderflower.

> „ Great ideas often come from small talks around a gin.

Legacy of a summer evening

They harmonize like gin and tonic: Dennis and Manuel, two buddies from the region of the Ruhr, wrote their own play in 2018. A story marked by ups and downs, learning and maturing, tensions and excitement. A comedy? No. A tragedy? No way! Rather a story about courage and daring. What began on a cozy summer evening with cool drinks and philosophical outpourings now bears the name AMETHYST Gin. The two wanted to create their own spirit, a versatile gin that tastes like summer again and again, whether neat, with tonic or in a cocktail.

The stone of the Ruhr gin

The amethyst is said to have special abilities. It is supposed to have a calming and cleansing effect on the nerves and the heart. A gemstone that increases the ability to concentrate and protects against nightmares when stashed under your pillow. Similar to the lavender that is in this London Dry Gin and whose purple color matches the amethyst so perfectly. It is one of a total of eight botanicals used, most of which can also be found in Dennis and Manuel's home garden in the Ruhr region. The connection to their homeland is important to these friends – after all, the idea for their gin was born here.

> *Proud, Strong & Noble Gin: What success tastes like.*

CATEGORY
New Western Dry Gin

ORIGIN
Germany

ESTABLISHED
2020

SIZE
● ○ ○ ○

TASTING NOTES
Orangen und Zitronen sorgen für ein angenehm frisches und zitrisches Aroma. Im Geschmack vereinen sich Wacholder, Apfel, Kardamom und Zimt.

Oranges and lemons provide a pleasant fresh and citrus aroma. The taste combines juniper, apple, cardamom and cinnamon.

BRENNEREI FRANZ STETTNER

PROUD, STRONG & NOBLE GIN

Ein versilberter Gin

Proud, Strong & Noble Gin: Schon der Name ist eine Ansage – und trifft den Nagel auf den Kopf. Denn auf diesen geschmacklich einzigartigen Gin können die Macher mehr als stolz sein. Der Gründer, Martin Limbeck, hat sich mit Proud, Strong & Noble den Traum vom eigenen Gin letztlich erfüllt. So steht die kompromisslose Qualität dieses exklusiven Dry Gin selbstverständlich außer Frage. Die Herstellung ist durch langjährige Tradition und einen großen Erfahrungsschatz geprägt – so wird der Proud, Strong & Noble Gin in präziser Handarbeit dreifach destilliert. Wirklich einmalig ist die Verwendung einer Silberdestille – dies bedeutet, dass der Auslaufhahn der Destille versilbert ist. So kann der Rohstoff unter Vakuum erhitzt werden und destilliert bereits bei 40 Grad. Zum einen ist diese Art der Destillation besonders schonend – gleichzeitig hat das Silber einen positiven Einfluss auf den Geschmack des Gins.

Auf die besonderen Momente!

Die verwendeten Botanicals – wie zum Beispiel Wacholder, Kardamom, Orangen- und Zitronenzesten und Zimt – stammen ausschließlich aus Deutschland. Getoppt wird das Ganze durch Apfelspalten von einer benachbarten Plantage in Wesel – so steckt im Proud, Strong & Noble Gin ein echtes Stückchen Heimat. Diese unterschiedlichsten Aromen machen ihn zu einem einzigartigen Geschmackserlebnis – und zu einem Gin, der für die ganz besonderen Momente im Leben bestimmt ist. Darauf kann Martin Limbeck voller Stolz ein Glas (oder besser noch einen Silberbecher) Proud, Strong & Noble Gin erheben – und wir mit ihm! Cheers!

Wesel, Germany

A silver-plated gin

Proud, Strong & Noble Gin: The name alone is an announcement – and hits the nail on the head. Because the makers can be more than proud of this unique-tasting gin. The founder, Martin Limbeck, has at last fulfilled his dream of a gin of his own with Proud, Strong & Noble. Thus, the uncompromising quality of this exclusive dry gin is of course beyond question. Its production is characterized by long tradition and a wealth of experience – so Proud, Strong & Noble Gin is distilled precisely by hand three times. Truly unique is the use of a silver still – this means that the outlet tap of the still is silver-plated. This way, the raw ingredients can be heated under vacuum and distilled as low as 40 °C. On the one hand, this type of distillation is particularly gentle – at the same time, the silver has a positive influence on the taste of the gin.

Here's to those special moments!

The botanicals used – such as juniper, cardamom, orange and lemon zest and cinnamon – come exclusively from Germany. The whole thing is topped with apple slices from a neighboring plantation in Wesel – so there is a real piece of home in Proud, Strong & Noble Gin. These diverse flavors make it a unique taste experience – and a gin that is intended for those very special moments in life. Martin Limbeck can proudly raise a glass (or better yet, a silver cup) of Proud, Strong & Noble Gin to this – and we can join him. Cheers!

0,5 L // 44,0 %

129

MICHAEL WITTMANN

MOERSGIN

Spargel und Gin, das passt!

Liebe, Lust und Leidenschaft sind die besten Voraussetzungen, um am Ende das Ergebnis zu bekommen, das man haben möchte. So war es auch beim moersGIN, dem weltweit ersten Spargel-Gin, hergestellt am Niederrhein. Spargel und Gin – das passt zusammen? Und wie! Monatelang wurde am perfekten Rezept getüftelt, mit vielen Aromen und Zutaten experimentiert und die Idee letztendlich mehr als zufriedenstellend umgesetzt. Bei diesem London Dry Gin erwartet den Genießer mit Spargel, Estragon, Knollensellerie, Boskoopäpfeln, Zitronengras, Zimt, Rosa Beeren und natürlich Wacholderbeeren eine feine Komposition mit Zutaten vom Niederrhein sowie aus Asien, Afrika und Südamerika. Diese geben dem moersGIN seinen unverwechselbaren Geschmack.

Moers, Germany

Frische Zubereitung von April bis Juni

Destilliert und abgefüllt wird der Spargel-Gin in liebevoller Handarbeit in kleinen Chargen. Die Besonderheit liegt in der Auswahl: Er ist nicht nur der erste Spargel-Gin. Auch das Zusammenspiel der verschiedenen Aromenträger sowie die unterschiedlichen Dominanzen und Eigenheiten galt es zu berücksichtigen. Weil alle Zutaten frisch zubereitet werden, ist die Produktion dieses speziellen London Dry Gins auch nur während der Spargelsaison von April bis Juni möglich. Die weißen Spargelstangen kommen nämlich erntefrisch direkt von den Feldern am Niederrhein, bevor sie für den moersGIN verarbeitet werden. Insgesamt entsteht somit eine außergewöhnlich aufregende Komposition aus besten, sorgfältig ausgewählten Zutaten. Der moersGIN verbindet präzise Handwerkskunst mit Familientradition und Heimatliebe.

Asparagus and gin, it works!

Love, desire and passion are the best prerequisites for getting the result you ultimately want. This was also the case with moersGIN, the world's first asparagus gin, produced in the Lower Rhine region. Asparagus and gin – do they go together? And how! For months, there was tinkering towards the perfect recipe, experimentation with many flavors and ingredients, and the idea was finally realized in more than satisfactory style. In this London Dry Gin, the connoisseur can expect a fine composition with asparagus, tarragon, celeriac, Boskoop apples, lemongrass, cinnamon, pink pepper and, of course, juniper berries with ingredients from the Lower Rhine as well as from Asia, Africa and South America. These give moersGIN its unmistakable taste.

Fresh preparation from April to June

Distilled and bottled, this asparagus gin is lovingly handcrafted in small batches. What's special is teh matter of selection. It isn't just the first asparagus gin. The interplay of the various conveyors of flavor and the different dominances and peculiarities also had to be taken into account. Because all ingredients are freshly prepared, the production of this special London Dry Gin is also only possible during the asparagus season from April to June. The white asparagus stalks come freshly harvested directly from the fields of the Lower Rhine, before they are processed for moersGIN All in all, this results in an exceptionally exciting composition of the best, carefully selected ingredients. Thus, moersGIN combines precise craftsmanship with family tradition and a love of home.

CATEGORY
London Dry Gin

ORIGIN
Germany

ESTABLISHED
2019

SIZE
● ● ● ○

TASTING NOTES
Runder, aber komplexer Gin, der Spargel als Lead-Botanical sticht deutlich hervor.

Round but complex gin, the asparagus as lead botanical stands out.

MICHAEL WITTMANN // MOERSGIN

0,5 L // 46,0%

GIN

> The Germans' dearest asparagus paired with the cult drink.

131

SAUERLÄNDER EDELBRENNEREI

HERGING

CATEGORY
Barrel Aged Gin

ORIGIN
Germany

ESTABLISHED
2000

SIZE
● ● ○ ○

TASTING NOTES
In der Nase kann man ein mildes Wacholderaroma wahrnehmen, das sich mit einer leichten Zitrusnote und einem maritimen Touch aus Seetang mischt. Im Geschmack überrascht der HerGINg mit einer angenehmen Süße – es folgt eine leichte Salznote, zu der sich das intensive Aroma von Wacholder gesellt. Maritimes Erlebnis pur!

On the nose, a mild juniper aroma is perceptible, mixed with a light citrus note and a maritime touch of seaweed. On the palate, HerGINg surprises with a pleasant sweetness, followed by a slightly salty note, partnered by the intense aroma of juniper. A pure maritime experience!

Der Hering und der HerGINg

Die Sauerländer Edelbrennerei traut sich was! Man überlegt sich etwas ganz Eigenes, um einen Gin zu kreieren, der wirklich heraussticht. So entsteht eine außergewöhnliche Idee: Es werden Virgin-Oak-Fässer mit frischem Hering, Pökelsalz, Wasser und Wein belegt. Über ein halbes Jahr hinweg bleibt der eingelegte Hering in den Fässern, damit er sein Aroma abgeben und das Holz dieses in sich aufnehmen kann. Anschließend werden die Fässer entleert und mit dem Destillat befüllt. So entsteht ein Gin, dessen Geschmack ein harmonisches Zusammenspiel von dem eingelegten Hering, den Aromen der Eichen-Fässer und dem Destillat bildet. Um das Ganze noch perfekt abzurunden, lagern die Fässer auf Rügen an der Ostsee. So kann der Gin während seiner dreimonatigen Reifung die salzige Meeresluft atmen. Das Ergebnis ist ein einzigartiger Gin mit absolutem Wiedererkennungswert: der HerGINg.

Ein Novum in der Gin-Welt – und für den Gaumen

Doch nicht nur die außergewöhnliche Lagerung lässt einen anerkennend nicken. Das Rezept für den Gin hat kein Geringerer als der Starkoch Johann Lafer entwickelt. Ihm war von Anfang an klar, dass er einen Gin kreieren möchte, der auf Lebensmittelbasis aromatisiert wird. Sein Gespür für Zutaten ist es, das den entscheidenden Unterschied macht – denn er legt großen Wert darauf, dass für den HerGINg ausschließlich Wacholderbeeren von höchster Bioqualität verwendet werden. Dieses Zusammenspiel von kompromissloser Qualität und einmaliger Innovation macht den HerGINg zu einem echten Ausnahme-Gin.

> *A gin with the aroma of herring and salty sea air – there's only one.*

Rüthen, Germany

The herring and the HerGINg

The Sauerländer Edelbrennerei distillery has gone out on a limb! They've thought up something altogether unique to create a gin that really stands out. This is how an unusual idea is born: virgin oak barrels are filled with fresh herring, pickling salt, water and wine. The pickled herring remains in the barrels for six months so that it can release its aroma and the wood can absorb it. The barrels are then emptied and filled with the distillate. This creates a gin whose taste is a harmonious interplay of the pickled herring, the aromas of the oak barrels and the distillate. To round off the whole perfectly, the barrels are stored on Rügen island in the Baltic Sea. This allows the gin to breathe the salty sea air during its three-month maturation. The result is a unique gin with absolute recognition value: the HerGINg.

A novelty in the gin world – and for the palate

But it isn't just the extraordinary storage that attracts a nod of approval. The recipe for this gin was developed by none other than celebrity chef Johann Lafer. It was clear to him from the outset that he wanted to create a gin that draws flavor from food. It's his flair for ingredients that makes all the difference – as he places great importance on using only juniper berries of the highest organic quality for HerGINg. This interplay of uncompromising quality and unique innovation makes HerGINg a truly exceptional gin.

KELLER & FRIENDS

KELLER'S GIN

Eslohe, Germany

· 66 BOTANICALS ·
· GRAND CRU ·

Keller's
GIN
· HANDCRAFTED ·
· NATURAL INGREDIENTS ·

DESTILLED IN
DRY GIN
THE BLACK FOREST

Perfekter Gin ist eine Frage des guten Geschmacks

Überwiegend regional angebaute Zutaten, hergestellt im Schwarzwald, eine einmalige Rezeptur und ein schickes Auftreten im edlen Gewand einer poppigen Champagnerflasche oder klassischen Glasflasche – dafür steht Keller's Gin. Für den Dry Gin kommen 66 Botanicals zum Einsatz, dessen Aromen durch Mazeration und Destillation schonend freigesetzt werden, nach Botanical-Gruppen getrennt. Anschließend Lagerung der Einzeldestillate in Steingutgefäßen, bevor es zur finalen Zusammenführung der Komponenten „Blending" kommt. Nur durch hochwertige und sorgfältig ausgewählte Zutaten sowie ein aufwendiges Produktionsverfahren kommt der intensive, weiche und dennoch harmonisch-herbe Geschmack von Keller's Gin zustande. Wie das geht? Alle Zutaten eint die gemeinsame Heimat des Schwarzwaldes, sie wurden in einem langen Prozess ausgewählt und mit Liebe zum Detail aufeinander abgestimmt. Überzeugender kann Gin gar nicht sein.

Das feinaromatische Original aus dem Schwarzwald

Der Wacholder wird mit verschiedenen Zitrusfrüchten kombiniert. Kardamom, Piment und Ingwer runden den Keller's Dry Gin zu einer gelungenen Gesamtkomposition ab. Besonders lecker schmeckt der Dry Gin in Kombination mit zitronig-frischem Tonic Water, das die Zitrusnote des Gins in den Vordergrund stellt, aber auch ein würzig-herbes Tonic Water eignet sich, um die subtilere Gewürznote des Gins zu unterstützen. Durch die Hinzugabe eines Himbeer- bzw. Pflaumenlikörs entstehen aus dem Keller's Dry Gin zwei weitere fruchtige Varianten. Neu im Sortiment ist der erst im Oktober 2021 eingeführte Keller's Gin-Eierlikör.

> 66 botanicals in harmony.

CATEGORY
Dry Gin

ORIGIN
Germany

ESTABLISHED
2019

SIZE
● ○ ○ ○

TASTING NOTES
Ein klassischer Dry Gin von höchster Qualität, gepaart mit einer raffinierten Zitrusnote und einer Schärfe, die für das gewisse Etwas sorgt.

A classic dry gin of the highest quality, paired with a sophisticated citrus note and a spiciness that adds a certain something.

Perfect gin is a matter of good taste

Predominantly regionally grown ingredients, produced in the Black Forest, a unique recipe and chic appearance in the classy garb of a trendy champagne bottle or classic glass bottle – that's what Keller's Gin stands for. For the Dry Gin, 66 botanicals are used, their aromas gently released by maceration and distillation, separately according to botanical group. Subsequently, storage of the individual distillates in earthenware vessels is followed by the final blending of the components. It is only through high-quality and carefully selected ingredients, as well as a complex production process, that the intense, soft and yet harmoniously tart taste of Keller's Gin emerges. How does that work? All ingredients are united by the common home of the Black Forest, selected in a long process and matched with attention to detail. Gin cannot be more convincing.

The fine aromatic original from the Black Forest

Juniper is combined with various citrus fruits. cardamom, allspice and ginger round off Keller's Dry Gin, yielding a successful overall composition. The Dry Gin tastes particularly delicious in combination with lemony-fresh tonic water, which brings the citrus note of the gin to the fore, but a spicy-tart tonic water is also suitable to support the more subtle spicy note of the gin. The addition of a raspberry or plum liqueur creates two more fruity variants of Keller's Dry Gin. A new addition to the range is Keller's Gin Egg Liqueur, launched in October 2021.

SAUERLAND DISTILLERS

WOODLAND SAUERLAND DRY GIN

CATEGORY
New Western Dry Gin

ORIGIN
Germany

ESTABLISHED
2017

SIZE

TASTING NOTES
Das Aroma sanft und frisch, eine Mischung aus Zitrus und leichten Kräuternoten. Fichtenspitzen, Baumpilz und Löwenzahnwurzel sorgen für einen waldig-erdigen Geschmack. Abgerundet durch Botanicals wie Brennnesseln und Sauerampfer.

The aroma gentle and fresh, a mixture of citrus and light herbal notes. Spruce tips, bracket fungi and dandelion root provide an arboreal-earthy flavor. Rounded off by botanicals such as nettles and sorrel.

Lüdenscheid, Germany

Das Land der tausend Berge

Eine wunderschöne Kulisse: Grüne Wiesen, klare Bergseen, dichte Wälder, und am Horizont zeichnet sich die Silhouette der „Tausend Berge" ab. Genau hier ist die Sauerland Distillers GmbH zu Hause: im Land der tausend Berge – im Sauerland. In dieser atemberaubenden Landschaft entsteht ein Gin, der euch nicht minder den Atem rauben wird. Der Woodland Sauerland Dry Gin kommt nicht nur aus dem Sauerland, er ist auch durch und durch ein Sauerländer. Die heimischen Botanicals wie aromatische Fichtenspitzen, Baumpilz oder würzige Löwenzahnwurzel verleihen dem Woodland Sauerland Dry Gin einen waldig-erdigen Geschmack. Für eine spritzig-frische Ergänzung sorgen Brennnesseln, handgepflückter Sauerampfer und Zitrusaromen. Die Mischung aus herben und frischen Geschmacksnoten zeichnet diesen Gin aus – perfekt abgerundet durch mildes Sauerländer Quellwasser.

Regionalität, die man schmecken kann

Kompromisslose Qualität, die Verwendung regionaler Rohstoffe und eine unermüdliche Freude am Experimentieren – genau dafür steht der „Genussbotschafter" des Sauerlands, Olaf Baumeister. Seine Vision: einen Gin kreieren, bei dem man das Sauerland wortwörtlich schmecken kann. Und genau das ist mit dem Woodland Sauerland Dry Gin mehr als geglückt. Der Genuss dieses Gins kommt der Freude gleich, durch das Sauerland zu wandern und den Blick durch die wunderschöne Berglandschaft schweifen zu lassen, während man den würzigen Duft der Wälder einatmet. Dann lasst uns das Glas erheben. Auf das Land der tausend Berge!

> Spruce tips, bracket fungi and dandelion – only the Sauerland tastes like this.

The land of a thousand mountains

Beautiful scenery: green meadows, clear mountain lakes, dense forests, and the silhouette of the "thousand mountains" looming on the horizon. This is precisely where Sauerland Distillers GmbH is at home: in the land of a thousand mountains – the Sauerland. In this breathtaking landscape, a gin is created that will no less than take your breath away. Woodland Sauerland Dry Gin not only comes from the Sauerland, it is also a Sauerland character through and through. Native botanicals such as aromatic spruce tips, bracket fungi and spicy dandelion root give Woodland Sauerland Dry Gin an arboreal-earthy flavor. Nettles, hand-picked sorrel and citrus aromas provide a tangy-fresh addition. The blend of tart and fresh flavors distinguishes this gin – perfectly rounded off by mild Sauerland spring water.

Regionality that you can taste

Uncompromising quality, the use of regional raw materials and a tireless love of experimentation – that's exactly what Sauerland's "pleasure ambassador," Olaf Baumeister, stands for. His vision: to create a gin where you can literally taste the Sauerland. Which is exactly what has more than succeeded with Woodland Sauerland Dry Gin. Enjoying this gin is akin to the joy of hiking through the Sauerland and letting your eyes wander about the beautiful mountain landscape while breathing in the spicy scent of the forests. Let's raise a glass then. To the land of a thousand mountains!

MANUKAT

NATURBUMMLER GIN

Neuss, Germany

Der Ruf des Waldes

Einfach dem Weg folgen, vorbei an leuchtenden Fingerhut-Stauden und mächtigen Farnen, während ein leichter Wind durch die Bäume segelt und die Blätterdächer tanzen lässt. Die Vögel zwitschern, in der Ferne plätschert ein Bach. Ein Baumstamm lädt zum Verweilen ein. Der perfekte Augenblick für einen Schluck Naturbummler Gin. In dem Moment, in dem die Flasche aufploppt, strömt die Natur nach draußen. Ein mildherbes und holziges Bouquet eröffnet sich, das durch den Wacholder und die Süßholzwurzel unterstrichen wird. Koriandersamen, Paradieskörner und Zitronenschalen runden das Ganze ab und harmonisieren dezent miteinander. Fünf Botanicals stecken im Naturbummler Gin aus dem Hause Manukat. Jede einzelne Zutat soll geschmacklich zur Geltung kommen.

Nachhaltigkeit at its best

Gebrannt wird in der Destillerie von Maennerhobby aus Klein Kussewitz bei Rostock. Dort wird neben dem Naturbummler Gin auch die sommerlich frische Schwester Fruchtbrumme gefertigt. Für die Gründer hat der Genuss von Gin eine besondere Bedeutung: Es geht um Geselligkeit und um eine schöne Zeit zusammen und um das Erleben von besonderen Momenten, die in Erinnerung bleiben. Diese Einstellung tragen sie auch in ihr Unternehmen: Nachhaltigkeit, Fairness und Transparenz sind die Säulen des Manukat-Geschäftsmodells. Die Gründer unterstützen Projekte zur Aufforstung von Wäldern oder zur Säuberung von Wasserquellen, die Verpackung besteht aus ökologischer Pappe sowie Bio-Farbe, das Flaschenetikett aus recyceltem Papier.

CATEGORY
Dry Gin

ORIGIN
Germany

ESTABLISHED
2020

SIZE
● ○ ○ ○

TASTING NOTES
Kräftig, erdig und harzig, angenehme Wacholdernote, erfrischende Zitrusaromen harmonieren mit der leichten Würze des Korianders und im Abgang pikant.

Strong, earthy and resinous, pleasant juniper note, refreshing citrus aromas harmonize with the light spiciness of coriander, and in the finish spicy.

„ To the moment!

The call of the forest

Just follow the path, past bright swathes of foxgloves and mighty ferns, while a light wind wafts through the trees and makes the leafy canopies dance. Birds chirp, a brook babbles in the distance. An old log invites you to linger. The perfect moment for a sip of Naturbummler Gin. The moment the bottle pops open, nature pours out. A mildly tart and woody bouquet opens up, highlighted by the juniper and licorice root. Coriander seeds, grains of paradise and lemon zest round out the whole and subtly harmonize with each other. There are five botanicals in Naturbummler Gin from the house of Manukat. Each individual ingredient counts in the ultimate taste.

Sustainability at its best

It's produced in the distillery of Maennerhobby in Klein Kussewitz near Rostock. In addition to Naturbummler Gin, its summery-fresh sister Fruchtbrumme is also produced there. For the founders, the enjoyment of gin has a special meaning. It's about socializing, having a good time together and experiencing special moments forever remembered. They carry this attitude into their company as well: sustainability, fairness and transparency are the pillars of the Manukat business model. The founders support projects to replant forests and clean up water sources, the packaging is made of ecological cardboard as well as organic ink, and the bottle label is made of recycled paper.

FRANGENBERG & FRANGENBERG

GINSAN!TY WHITE TRUFFLE PREMIUM DRY GIN

Der Gin für den puren Genuss

Fast jedermann ist begeisterter Gin Tonic-Trinker. Aber findet man auch Menschen, die Gin gerne pur genießen? Kaum. Grund dafür: Es ist schwierig, einen Gin zu finden, der auch pur schmeckt. Dieser Meinung sind die Gin-Liebhaber Dagmar und Michael Frangenberg ebenfalls. Deshalb entscheiden sie kurzerhand, einen eigenen Gin zu kreieren, der auch pur ein absoluter Genuss ist. Um diesen Plan in die Tat umzusetzen, kaufen die beiden im Jahr 2015 eine kleine Destille und beginnen, zu experimentieren. Doch mit dem ersten Gin im Jahr 2017 geht die Reise erst richtig los – im Laufe der Zeit erblicken verschiedenste Sorten das Licht der Welt. 2021 ist es dann aber so weit: Der GINSAN!TY White Truffle Premium Dry Gin wird zum ersten Mal in eine Flasche abgefüllt.

Insanity is the energy

GINSAN!TY White Truffle Premium Dry Gin ist ein voller Erfolg. Doch was macht diesen Gin so besonders? In erster Linie definitiv die Mazeration von echtem weißen Alba-Trüffel, die pure Handarbeit und die ausschließliche Verwendung hochwertiger und zu 100 % natürlicher Zutaten – dieser Gin kommt gänzlich ohne die Verwendung künstlicher Aromen oder Farbstoffe aus. So entsteht ein Gin, dessen Geschmack den Charakter seiner Macher widerspiegelt: wild, neu, anders, mutig, extravagant. GINSAN!TY White Truffle Premium Dry Gin: ein Wahnsinns- Gin, der auch pur ein wahnsinniger Genuss ist.

> ❝ This is ginsane. Let's do it!

The gin for pure pleasure

Almost everyone is an enthusiastic gin and tonic drinker. But do you also encounter people who enjoy gin neat? Scarcely at all. The reason is that it's difficult to find a gin that also tastes great neat. Gin lovers Dagmar and Michael Frangenberg share this opinion. That's why they decided without further ado to create their own gin, which is also an absolute delight neat. To put this plan into action, the two bought a small distillery in 2015 and began experimenting. But it was with the first gin in 2017 that the journey really began – over time, widely differing variants saw the light of day. But in 2021 the time had come: GINSAN!TY White Truffle Premium Dry Gin was bottled for the first time.

Insanity is the energy

GINSAN!TY White Truffle Premium Dry Gin is a total success. But what makes this gin so special? First and foremost, definitely the maceration of genuine white Alba truffle, the pure handwork and the exclusive use of high-quality and 100 percent natural ingredients – this gin does entirely without any artificial flavors or colorants. The result is a gin whose taste reflects the character of its makers: wild, new, different, bold, extravagant. GINSAN!TY White Truffle Premium Dry Gin: a gin to go crazy for, that's also insanely delightful pure.

CATEGORY
London Dry Gin

ORIGIN
Germany

ESTABLISHED
2021

SIZE
● ● ● ○

TASTING NOTES
Vorherrschend beim GINSAN!TY White Truffle Premium Dry Gin sind Wacholder und Zitrus – und natürlich der weiße Trüffel, der diesen Gin zu etwas ganz Besonderem macht.

Predominant in GINSAN!TY White Truffle Premium Dry Gin are juniper and citrus – and of course the white truffle, which makes this gin something very special.

Colognee, Germany

MATS SPIRITS

MATS DRY GIN

Cologne, Germany

Der Schnaps und die Schnapsidee

Immer schon legte Marcel Tschampel Wert auf gute Gastgeberschaft. Diese war für ihn unweigerlich mit einem guten Drink verbunden – oder auch ein, zwei mehr. Aus seinen 50 verschiedenen Gin-Sorten entstanden mit leidenschaftlicher Hingabe immer wieder interessante Eigenkreationen. Bei einem der gemütlichen Abende im Kreis guter Freunde kam beim Schnaps-trinken auch eine Schnapsidee auf: die Kreation eines eigenen Gins. Dies war nicht weit hergeholt bei einem so begeisterten Gin-Liebhaber. Und auch am nächsten Tag (ein paar Schnäpse nüchterner) war Marcel von der Idee überzeugt. Und so war der Grundstein für den MATS Dry Gin gelegt.

Das Resultat von Leidenschaft und Träumen

MATS Spirits ist ein Ein-Mann-Betrieb. Mit Hingabe führt Marcel jeden einzelnen Handgriff aus. Dabei setzt er sich selbst einen hohen Qualitätsanspruch und kreiert mit viel Hingabe den MATS Dry Gin. Die Handarbeit, die Leidenschaft, die in allem steckt, und die Liebe zum Detail – sie machen den Unterschied, den man schmecken kann. Besonders maßgebend für den Geschmack ist Buddhas Hand – die seltsam anmutende Zitrusfrucht wird in

CATEGORY
Dry Gin

ORIGIN
Germany

ESTABLISHED
2018

SIZE
● ○ ○ ○

TASTING NOTES
Zu Beginn entfalten sich Wacholderaromen, gemischt mit frischen Zitrusnoten und gefolgt von einer leichten Süße der Orangenblüten. Im Abgang rundet pfeffrige Schärfe das Ganze perfekt ab.

Elegant and delicate, markedly complex and soft, confident juniper notes on the palate, accompanied by a pleasant spiciness and the dominant aroma of almonds and citrus.

> ## In the end, it all adds up to a gin… a MATS Dry Gin, to be exact.

The spirit and the spirited idea

Marcel Tschampel has always attached importance to good hospitality. For him, this was invariably linked to a good drink – or even one or two more. Drawing on his 50 different gin varieties, again and again he came up with interesting creations of his own with passionate dedication. On one of many cozy evenings with good friends, while drinking spirits, a spirited idea came up: to create his own gin. Something not far-fetched for such an enthusiastic gin lover. Indeed, the next day too (a few shots soberer), Marcel remained convinced of the idea. So it was that the foundation stone for MATS Dry Gin was laid.

The result of passion and dreams

MATS Spirits is a one-man operation. With dedication, Marcel carries out every single step. In doing so, he sets himself high quality standards and creates MATS Dry Gin with great commitment. The handwork, the passion that goes into everything, and the attention to detail – they make the difference that you can taste. Buddha's hand is particularly instrumental in the taste – this strange-looking citrus fruit is widely used in star-rated kitchens in Germany and gives the gin a very special freshness. Other botanicals blend in seamlessly: a mix of juniper, soft sweet orange blossom and a peppery spiciness. Let's all raise a glass of MATS – here's to good taste!

19 CIRCLE SPIRITS

RASPMARY GIN

CATEGORY
New Western Dry Gin

ORIGIN
Germany

ESTABLISHED
2020

SIZE

TASTING NOTES
Vollmundig mit einer angenehmen Süße, am Gaumen überzeugt eine leichte Wacholdernote, die durch fruchtige Nuancen untermalt wird; Himbeere und Heidelbeere werden von einem Hauch Rosmarin begleitet, Basilikum, Zitrus und Minze versprühen eine wunderbare Frische und Leichtigkeit, im Abgang mit einer feinen Schärfe.

Full-bodied with a pleasant sweetness, a light juniper note convincing on the palate, underlined by fruity nuances; raspberry and blueberry are accompanied by a hint of rosemary; basil, citrus and mint exude a wonderful freshness and lightness, with a fine spiciness in the finish.

Verbunden mit der Natur

19 kleine Kreise ergeben ein großes, vollkommenes, harmonisches Ganzes – als Blume des Lebens. In zahlreichen Kulturen und Religionen steht das Symbol für kosmische Ordnung und den Kreislauf des Seins. Für Ferdinand Zeich und Leon Marco Guaiana ist es weit mehr als das: Es ist der Anfang ihres Gin-Unterfangens 19 Circle Spirits – wiederzufinden im Logo, im Namen und in der Unternehmensphilosophie. All das verkörpert die tiefe Verbundenheit mit der Natur in Form ausgewählter Botanicals. Und diese stecken in dem Raspmary Gin, einer gelungenen Symbiose aus Früchten und Kräutern, bestehend aus Wacholder, Himbeere, Rosmarin, Zitronenschale, Blaubeere, Minze, rosa Pfeffer und Basilikum.

Nicht *micro,* sondern *nano*

Destilliert wird in Eigenregie nach dem Nano-Batch-Prinzip in einer kleinen Kupferdestille bei Niedrigtemperatur bis zu zwölf Stunden. Dadurch können sich die Aromen ausgewogen entfalten und der Geschmack kommt in vollem Umfang zur Geltung. Darüber hinaus wird das Destillat nicht gefiltert, damit die ätherischen Öle der beigefügten Botanicals erhalten bleiben. Dadurch erhält der Raspmary Gin eine leichte Trübung. Das Resultat des Gesamtprozesses ist ein natürlicher und intensiv schmeckender New Western Dry Gin. Die Handarbeit bei der Herstellung des Gins erstreckt sich von der Auswahl der Botanicals über die Mazeration und die Destillation bis hin zur Abfüllung jeder einzelnen Flasche des Batchs. Diese Liebe zum Detail hat die Oma den Gründern mit auf den Weg gegeben. Sie verriet den Jungs, dass eine Sache nur dann gut wird, wenn sie mit Hingabe und Leidenschaft ausgeübt wird.

> *100 % unfiltered,*
> *100 % natural,*
> *100 % handmade.*

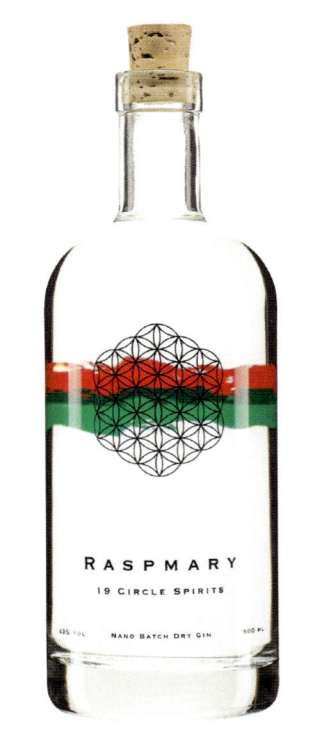

Cologne, Germany

Connected with nature

Nineteen small circles make a large, perfect, harmonious whole – as the flower of life. In numerous cultures and religions, this symbol stands for cosmic order and the cycle of being. For Ferdinand Zeich and Leon Marco Guaiana, it's much more than that. It's the beginning of their gin venture 19 Circle Spirits – to be found again in the logo, the name and the company philosophy. All of this embodies the deep connection with nature in the form of selected botanicals. All to be found in Raspmary Gin, a successful symbiosis of fruits and herbs, consisting of juniper, raspberry, rosemary, lemon zest, blueberry, mint, pink pepper and basil.

Not micro, *but rather* nano

Distilled in-house according to a nano-batch principle in a small copper still at low temperature for up to twelve hours. This allows the aromas to develop in a balanced way and the taste comes into its own to the fullest extent. In addition, the distillate is not filtered, so that the essential oils of the added botanicals are preserved. This gives Raspmary Gin a slight cloudiness. The result of the overall process is a natural and intense tasting New Western Dry Gin. The handwork involved in making the gin extends from the selection of botanicals, through maceration and distillation, to the bottling of each bottle in the batch. This attention to detail is what grandma passed on to the founders. She told the boys that something only becomes good when it is practiced with dedication and passion.

XIII SPIRITS

BIG MOOSE GIN

Much, Germany

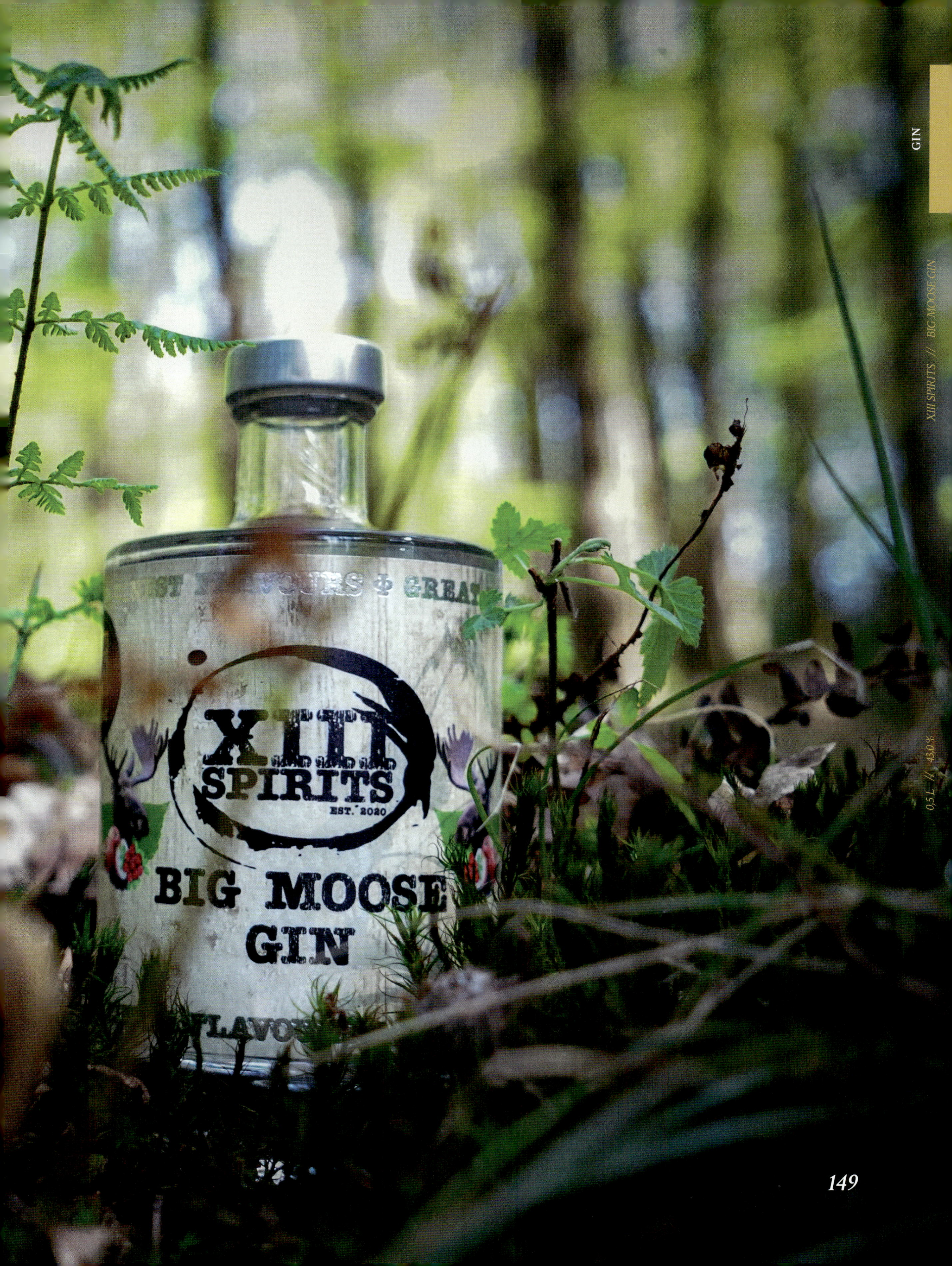

0,5 L // 43,0 %

CATEGORY
Distilled Gin

ORIGIN
Germany

ESTABLISHED
2020

SIZE
● ○ ○ ○

TASTING NOTES
Fruchtig-waldiges Bouquet, zarte Apfelnoten, umschmeichelt vom leicht torfigen Aroma der Birke, hintergründig die Würze des Wacholders mit einer leichten Bitternote von Wildpreiselbeeren.

Fruity-arboreal bouquet, delicate apple notes, caressed by the slightly peaty aroma of birch, background spiciness of juniper with a slight bitter note of wild cranberries.

> # I think I'm being kissed by a moose.

Entdeckungsreise durch Lappland

Hoch oben im Norden gibt es einen Ort, der auch als letzte Wildnis Europas bezeichnet wird. Ein Ort, der sich durch unberührte Natur auszeichnet, durch schier unendliche Weiten, durch kleine Bächlein, moosbewachsene Felsen und duftende skandinavische Wälder. Die Luft ist frisch in Lappland, füllt die Lunge mit Sauerstoff. Ein Ort zum Verweilen, zum Loslassen. Es ist das Lebensgefühl von Freiheit und Wildnis, das Thorsten Rath und Marco Hauser in ihrem Big Moose Gin einfangen wollten. Erfüllt vom Aroma der Birken, der blumigen Note der Beerensträucher, von der erdigen Feuchtigkeit des Bodens und durchsetzt vom zarten Aroma wilden Wacholders.

Wacholder plus vier

Bei der Produktion verfahren Thorsten Rath und Marco Hauser nach dem Motto „Weniger ist mehr" und verwenden neben der Grundzutat Wacholder maximal vier zusätzliche Botanicals. Das Konzept der Gründer: „In einen Gin kommt neben unserem Herzblut nur das hinein, was wir an einer Hand abzählen können." Hergestellt wird der Big Moose Gin nach den strengen Qualitätsmerkmalen eines London Dry Gin. Um die Aromen jedoch zusätzlich zu unterstreichen, wird das Destillat beim Herabsetzen auf Trinkstärke leicht gesüßt. Dies macht ihn zu einem Distilled Gin. Die Herstellung erfolgt im Nano-Batch-Verfahren mit nur rund 100 Flaschen pro Charge.

Journey of discovery through Lapland

High up in the north there's a place that's also called Europe's last wilderness. A place characterized by untouched nature, by seemingly endless expanses, by small streams, moss-covered rocks and fragrant Scandinavian forests. The air is fresh in Lapland, filling the lungs with oxygen. A place where you can linger, let go. It is the feeling of freedom and wilderness that Thorsten Rath and Marco Hauser wanted to capture in their Big Moose Gin. Filled with the aroma of birch trees, the floral note of berry bushes, the earthy moisture of the soil and interspersed with the delicate aroma of wild juniper.

Juniper plus four

Regarding production, Thorsten Rath and Marco Hauser follow the motto "less is more" and use a maximum of four additional botanicals in addition to the basic ingredient juniper. The founders' concept: "Besides our heart and soul, only what we can count on one hand goes into a gin." Big Moose Gin is produced according to the strict quality characteristics of a London Dry Gin. However, to further enhance the flavors, the distillate is lightly sweetened as it is brought down to drinking strength. This makes it a distilled gin. The production takes place in a nano-batch process with only about 100 bottles per batch.

"Carrots – not only good for your eyes, but also in your gin.

WACHOLDAS?! GMBH

MURRE GIN

CATEGORY
London Dry Gin

ORIGIN
Germany

ESTABLISHED
2018

SIZE
● ○ ○ ○

TASTING NOTES
In der Nase Wacholder und Minze, am Gaumen frische Orangen- und Pfefferminznoten, Süße und dezente Schärfe. Mild und ausbalanciert.

In the nose mainly juniper and mint, on the palate some fresh notes of orange and peppermint with a hint of spice. Very mild and well balanced.

Sankt Augustin, Germany

Murre Gin – der Gin mit der Möhre

Ein handgemachter London Dry Gin mit Möhre aus dem Rheinland. Der Murre Gin kommt aus einem kleinen, familiengeführten Betrieb in Sankt Augustin. Soweit es geht, wird auf Regionalität gesetzt. Deshalb wird auf Möhre als Botanical gesetzt, eher ungewöhnlich für einen Gin. Die Möhre ist auch namensgebend für diesen Gin, denn Möhren heißen im Rheinischen Murre. Früher wurden in Hangelar, einem Stadtteil von Sankt Augustin, in unmittelbarer Nähe zu Köln und Bonn, Möhren angebaut. Und so werden die rheinischen Wurzeln auch ins fertige Destillat reflektiert.

Wohlige Süße und dezente Schärfe

Hergestellt wird er in kleinen, handgefertigten Auflagen. Verwendet werden sieben Botanicals, neben Möhre etwa Wacholder, Orangenzeste, Pfefferminze und Zimt, die für ein süßlich-frisches Aroma von Wacholder mit einem Hauch Minze sorgen. Destilliert wird der klassische Wacholdergeist von Frank Ginsberg. Die Nase ist wacholdergeführt, am Gaumen ist zunächst ebenfalls deutlich Wacholder bemerkbar, gleich gefolgt von frischen Orangen- und Pfefferminznoten. Anschließend macht sich wohlige Süße breit und eine dezente Schärfe ist spürbar. Der Abgang ist lang, behält dabei die Frische und die Süße bei und jetzt kommt auch die Möhre geschmacklich zum Vorschein. Es ist ein milder und ausbalancierter Gin, der aber auch im Tonic Water wahrnehmbar bleibt.

Murre Gin – the gin with the carrot

A handmade London Dry Gin with carrots from the Rhineland. Murre Gin comes from a small, family-run business in Sankt Augustin. As far as possible, the focus is on regionality. So, carrot is used as a botanical, rather unusual for gin. The carrot also gives this gin its name, because carrots are called Murre in Rhineland dialect. In the past, carrots were grown in Hangelar, a district of Sankt Augustin, in the immediate vicinity of Cologne and Bonn. And so the Rhenish roots are also reflected in the finished distillate.

Pleasant sweetness and subtle spiciness

It is produced in small, handmade batches. Seven botanicals are used, with carrot joined by juniper, orange zest, peppermint and cinnamon among others, providing a sweet and fresh aroma of juniper with a hint of mint. The classic juniper spirit is distilled by Frank Ginsberg. The nose is juniper-led, on the palate juniper is also clearly noticeable at first, immediately followed by fresh orange and mint notes. Subsequently, a pleasant sweetness spreads and a subtle spiciness is noticeable. The finish is long, maintaining the freshness and sweetness, with the carrot then also making a flavorful appearance. It is a mild and balanced gin, but remains identifiable in tonic water.

SIEBENGEBIRGE DISTILLERS

LITTLE DARLING GIN

> Be my little darling, Darling.

Cheers to the pioneers!

Dieser Gin ist eine Hommage an die Prohibitionszeit. Niemals stehen bleiben und immer neue Wege finden wie die Pioniere der Prohibitionszeit, das ist das Motto des Gründers Tristan Hahne. Dieser liebt es, zwischen diversen Kulturen unterwegs zu sein, und pflegt stets eines seiner Lebensmottos: Das Leben ist zu kurz, um schlecht zu essen oder zu trinken. Durch Wissen und Pioniergeist ist die Rezeptur des Little Darling Gin entstanden und lässt im Geschmack die alte Zeit und ihre Werte wieder aufleben.

Schonende Destillation und reifliche Lagerung

Jedes der elf enthaltenen Botanicals wird gesondert und schonend destilliert. Der Little Darling Gin wird nach Vollendung der Destillation sechs Wochen lang gelagert, um die sogenannte Vermählung der ätherischen Öle zu vollenden. Anschließend wird er lediglich ein einziges Mal gefiltert, damit der besondere Geschmack durch die ätherischen Öle in der Spirituose erhalten bleibt. Gekühlt wird der Gin trüb. Der Little Darling Gin ist in seinem Geschmacksprofil einzigartig, da er sich je nach Trinktemperatur geschmacklich leicht ändert. Wir sagen: Cheers to the pioneers!

CATEGORY
London Dry Gin

ORIGIN
Germany

ESTABLISHED
2018

SIZE
● ○ ○ ○

TASTING NOTES
Der florale Gin wechselt sich am Gaumen zwischen den Hauptbotanicals Kirschblüte, Apfelminze, Tannenspitzen sowie Orange ab. Der Wachholder bleibt im Hintergrund und im Abgang ist eine leichte Note der Tannenspitze zu schmecken. Als Perfect Serve ist die Orange absolut im Vordergrund und lässt den Genießer die Frucht mit allen Sinnen wahrnehmen, eine kleine Erinnerung an den Sommer.

This floral gin alternates on the palate between the main botanicals of cherry blossom, apple mint, fir tips and orange. The juniper remains in the background and a slight note of fir tip can be tasted in the finish. As a perfect serve, the orange is absolutely in the foreground and lets the connoisseur perceive the fruit with all senses, a little reminder of summer.

Bonn,
Germany

Cheers to the pioneers!

This gin is a tribute to the prohibition era. Never stand still and always find new ways like the pioneers of the prohibition era, that is the motto of the founder Tristan Hahne. He loves to travel, experience diverse cultures and always strives to live by one of his life's mottos: life's too short to eat or drink badly. Through knowledge and a pioneering spirit, the recipe of Little Darling Gin has been created, its taste reviving the old days and their values.

Gentle distillation and careful aging

Each of the eleven botanicals contained is distilled separately and gently. Little Darling Gin is stored for six weeks after completion of distillation to complete the so-called marriage of essential oils. It is then filtered just once to preserve the special flavor due to the essential oils in the spirit. Chilled, the gin becomes cloudy. Little Darling Gin is unique in its flavor profile, as it changes slightly in taste depending on the drinking temperature. We say, cheers to the pioneers!

155

Bonn, Germany

Inkognito Way of Life

Würde das Wort „inkognito" als Person visualisiert werden, würde ein Mann mit dunkler Sonnenbrille, unauffälliger Kleidung und einem Basecap auf dem Kopf bei einem Drink in der schattigsten Ecke einer Bar sitzen. Ein Mann mit mystischer Aura, der sich unter dem Deckmantel der Anonymität fortbewegt. Eine Kunstfigur aus Action-Blockbustern made in Hollywood. Mit der Filmindustrie hat der Inkognito Gin made in Bonn nichts gemein, wohl aber mit dem Wunsch, bewusst die eigene Herkunft zu verschleiern. Es ist kein Zufall, dass das Logo in Lautschrift auf dem Flaschenbauch prangt und die Namen der Gründer mit einem dicken schwarzen Balken zensiert werden. Im Vordergrund stehen das Produkt und der Lifestyle, den es verkörpert – den Lifestyle der Feierkultur und des Genusses.

Zwei für alle Geschmäcker

Für die Inkognito-Macher ist Gin nicht nur das vielseitigste Getränk, um jeden Geschmack zu treffen, sondern auch das Getränk einer ganzen Party-Generation. Also haben sie direkt zwei Versionen der beliebten Spirituose entwickelt. Nummer eins widmet sich dem Gin-Urvater Old Tom. In diesem Klassiker erhält die Wacholderbeere den Oscar für ihr Lebenswerk. Koriander, Orangen- und Zitronenschalen sind in der Kategorie „Beste Nebendarsteller" nominiert. Einen Sonderpreis bekommt der Lavendel. Neben dem Gin „Old Tom-Style" ist auch eine London-Dry-Variante erhältlich, die auf den alten, traditionell englischen Rezepten des Gin-Booms aus den Jahren 1720 bis 1751 basiert. Die acht verwendeten Botanicals werden mittels Dampfinfusionsverfahren destilliert. Das Ergebnis ist ein weicher Gin, komplex im Geschmack.

MAENNERHOBBY DESTILLERIE

INKOGNITO GIN

CATEGORY
Old Tom Gin

ORIGIN
Germany

ESTABLISHED
2021

SIZE
● ● ● ●

TASTING NOTES
Vollmundig und rund, lieblich-fruchtig, blumiger Lavendel, frische Zitrusnote, mildes Wacholderaroma, bestens geeignet als Grundlage für Cocktails und Longdrinks.

Full-bodied and round, sweetly fruity, floral lavender, fresh citrus note, mild juniper aroma, ideally suited as a base for cocktails and long drinks.

> The gin scene's Kinder Egg provides excitement, fun and a different perspective.

Way of Life

If the word "incognito" were visualized as a person, then a man with dark sunglasses, inconspicuous clothing and a baseball cap on his head would be sitting with a drink in the shadiest corner of a bar. A man with a mystical aura, moving about under the cloak of anonymity. An artificial figure from action blockbusters made in Hollywood. Inkognito Gin made in Bonn has nothing in common with the film industry, but it does have something in common with the desire to deliberately conceal one's own origins. It is no coincidence that the logo is emblazoned in phonetic script on the bottle's belly and the names of the founders are censored with a thick black bar. The focus is on the product and the lifestyle it embodies – the lifestyle of celebration and enjoyment.

Two for all tastes

For the makers of Inkognito, gin is not only the most versatile drink to suit every taste, but also the drink of an entire party generation. So they have directly developed two versions of the popular spirit. Number one is dedicated to the gin forefather Old Tom. In this classic, the juniper berry receives the Oscar for its life's work. Coriander, orange peel and lemon peel are nominated in the "Best Supporting Actor" category. Lavender gets a special award. In addition to the "Old Tom-Style" gin, a London Dry variant is also available, based on the old, traditional English recipes of the gin boom from 1720 to 1751. The eight botanicals used are distilled using a steam infusion process. The result is a smooth gin, complex in flavor.

GIESSEN SPIRITS

GIESSEN DRY GIN

Apfel und Rhabarber: eine harmonische Fruchtkombination

Mit dem Anspruch, einen Gin mit perfektem Geschmack zu kreieren, begeben sich die beiden Macher von Gießen Spirits auf die Suche – und werden nach über einem Jahr fündig. Bei ihrem vielfach prämierten Gießen Dry Gin entscheiden sie sich für Key-Botanicals, die charakteristisch für ihre mittelhessische Heimat sind. Neben der Gin-typischen Wacholderbeere kommen hier zwei Zutaten in den Destillationsapparat, die beide seit ihrer Kindheit begleiten: Apfel und Rhabarber. Diese harmonische Kombination wird durch elegante Hibiskusblüten verfeinert und durch weitere Zutaten wie Kardamom, rosa Pfeffer, Vanille, Zimt oder auch Zitronenschale ergänzt. Hierdurch entsteht ein wunderbar fruchtig-komplexer Gin, der erfrischend neu und unvergleichlich schmeckt. Insgesamt sind zwölf Botanicals im Gießen Dry Gin enthalten, der sorgfältigst von Hand und mit viel Anspruch in Small Batches hergestellt wird.

Gin mit Geschichte

Den Gießen Dry Gin widmet man keinem Geringeren als dem weltberühmten Chemiker Justus von Liebig. Er hat in Gießen geforscht und innovative Ideen entwickelt, die die Welt nachhaltig verändert haben. Der Gin aus Gi(eße)n ist eine Hommage an seinen Erfindergeist: Sowohl die Form der Flasche als auch diverse Details und „Easter Eggs" nehmen Bezug auf diesen beeindruckenden Mann und sein Schaffen. Der Gießen Gin ist durch diese Geschichte inspiriert – und durch seinen charaktervollen und außergewöhnlichen Geschmack geprägt. So begeistert er Gin-Kenner und absolute Neulinge gleichermaßen. Cheers!

Gießen, Germany

Apple and rhubarb: a harmonious fruit combination

Aspiring to create a gin with the perfect taste, the two makers of Giessen Spirits set out on a search and, after more than a year, they found what they were looking for. For their award-winning Giessen Dry Gin, they chose key botanicals that are characteristic of their home region of central Hesse. In addition to the juniper berry typical for gin, two ingredients come into the distillation setup here that have accompanied both of them since childhood, namely apple and rhubarb. This harmonious combination is refined by elegant hibiscus flowers and complemented by other ingredients such as cardamom, pink pepper, vanilla, cinnamon and lemon peel. This creates a wonderfully fruity-complex gin that tastes refreshingly new and altogether incomparable. In total, twelve botanicals are contained in Giessen Dry Gin, which is produced by hand in small batches with the greatest care and commitment.

Gin with history

Giessen Dry Gin is dedicated to none other than the world-famous chemist Justus von Liebig. He conducted research in Giessen and developed innovative ideas that changed the world forever. The gin from Gi(esse)n is a tribute to his inventive spirit: both the shape of the bottle and various details and "Easter Eggs" refer to this impressive man and his work. Giessen Gin is inspired by this story – and stands out for its extraordinary taste, so full of character. Thus, it inspires both gin connoisseurs and absolute novices alike. Cheers!

> A gin with a fruity complex aroma and the essence of a city.

CATEGORY
New Western Dry Gin

ORIGIN
Germany

ESTABLISHED
2018

SIZE
● ● ○ ○

TASTING NOTES
Fruchtig-komplex, Wacholder mischt sich mit lieblichen Apfel- und Rhabarbernoten in der Nase. Am Gaumen sehr weich und leicht würzig, dazu ein fruchtig-erdiger Geschmack.

Fruity-complex, juniper mixes with sweet apple and rhubarb notes on the nose. On the palate a very soft and slightly spicy, with a fruity earthy flavor

CATEGORY
Coca leaf distillate

ORIGIN
Germany

ESTABLISHED
2021

SIZE

TASTING NOTES
Puristisch, weich, experimentell, intensiv-herbal, ausgeprägte Kokaaromen, frisch durch Zitronengras und Zitronenschalen, würzig durch die Zugabe von Zimt und Anis.

Puristic, soft, experimental, intensely herbal, pronounced coca aromas, lemongrass and lemon peel freshness, spicy through addition of cinnamon and aniseed.

GETRÄNKEWERK GIESSEN

KOKA DESTILLAT

Belebende Wirkung

Manchmal ist es notwendig, bis ans andere Ende der Welt zu fliegen, um neue Inspiration zu finden. Nach Peru zum Beispiel. So wie Julian Hille. Während einer Südamerika-Reise stieß er auf die Kokapflanze und war direkt von deren Wirkung überzeugt. Angebaut auf Plantagen zwischen 300 und 2.000 Metern Höhe, gilt Koka seit Jahrtausenden als Heil- und Kulturpflanze, die die Leistungsfähigkeit steigert, Hunger unterdrückt sowie den Geist wach und den Körper warm hält. Er nahm die Blätter mit nach Deutschland und tüftelte gemeinsam mit seinem Kumpel Tim Schöffmann an der Rezeptur eines Drinks.

25 Gramm in einer Flasche

Das Ergebnis ist das Koka Destillat, die weltweit erste Premium-Spirituose, in der als Hauptzutat destilliertes Kokablatt steckt. Für das Koka Destillat werden ganze 25 Gramm Kokablätter pro Flasche in einem schonenden Herstellverfahren, ähnlich wie bei einem Gin, eingelegt und destilliert. Vier weitere Zutaten runden das Getränk ab: Zitronengras und Zitronenschalen werden mittels Aromakörben im besonders schonenden Dampf-Destillationsverfahren extrahiert, Zimt und Sternanis mindestens 48 Stunden mazeriert und anschließend destilliert. Die Schöpfer des Koka Destillats vertreiben seit 2014 Getränke in Deutschland, Österreich und der Schweiz. An ihrer Spirituose haben sie drei Jahre lang gefeilt.

Invigorating effect

Sometimes it's necessary to fly to the other side of the world to find new inspiration. To Peru, for example. Just like Julian Hille. During a trip to South America, he came across the coca plant and was immediately convinced of its effects. Cultivated on plantations between 300 and 2,000 meters above sea level, coca has been regarded for thousands of years as a medicinal and cultivated plant that increases performance, suppresses hunger, keeps the mind awake and the body warm. He took the leaves back to Germany and, together with his buddy Tim Schöffmann, worked on the recipe for a drink.

25 grams in a bottle

The result is Koka Destillat, the world's first premium spirit containing distilled coca leaf as the main ingredient. For Koka Destillat, a full 25 grams of coca leaves per bottle are macerated and distilled in a gentle manufacturing process similar to that used for gin. Four other ingredients round out the drink: lemongrass and lemon peel are extracted using aroma baskets in a particularly gentle steam distillation process, while cinnamon and star aniseed are macerated for at least 48 hours and then distilled. The creators of Koka Destillat have been distributing beverages in Germany, Austria and Switzerland since 2014. They have been fine-tuning their spirit for three years.

Gießen, Germany

> **Not chewed, but drunk: pure coca flavor in a glass.**

ALEXANDER KAYSER &
CHRISTOPHER SCHUH

LA SU GIN

Altenstadt, Germany

Auf der Reise...

Jeder strebt danach, neue Menschen kennenzulernen, unbekannte Orte zu erkunden, in fremde Kulturen einzutauchen und ständig Neues zu erleben – so auch Alexander Kayser und Christopher Schuh. Angetrieben von dieser Sehnsucht machen sie sich auf die Reise. Zurück kehren sie mit jeder Menge aufregender Erlebnisse und einer Idee: Sie wollen ihren eigenen Gin kreieren – die Botanicals haben sie bereits im Gepäck.

Ein Gin, der einen an fremde Orte entführt

Der Gin steht für alles, was die Macher auf ihrer Reise in sich aufgesogen haben. So kreieren sie mit viel Liebe eine exotische Rezeptur: den LA SU Gin. Dieser Premium Handcrafted Gin wird in einer der ältesten Destillerien Europas in kleinen Chargen gebrannt. Es werden ausschließlich natürliche Aromastoffe verwendet und bei der Auswahl der feinen Botanicals wird viel Wert auf Qualität gelegt. So entsteht ein Gin, der einem geschmacklichen Abenteuer gleichkommt: Wacholder mischt sich mit fruchtiger Mango, Sternanis, Lavendel, Kardamom, Chili, ergänzt durch Orangen- und Zitronenzesten. Das aufwendige Flaschendesign ist im Travelstyle gehalten und passt zu der geschmacklichen Reise, auf die einen der LA SU Gin entführt. Bereits der erste Schluck dieses absoluten Qualitätsprodukts lässt einen von fernen Orten träumen. Also: Cheers – auf das Abenteuer!

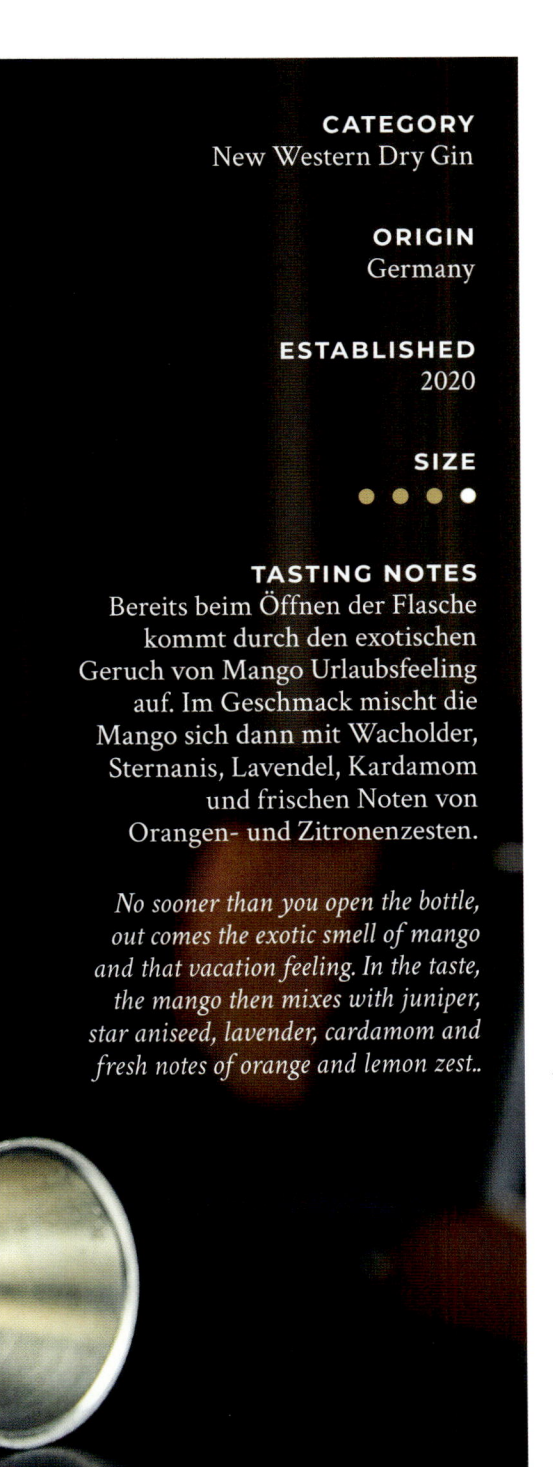

CATEGORY
New Western Dry Gin

ORIGIN
Germany

ESTABLISHED
2020

SIZE
● ● ● ○

TASTING NOTES
Bereits beim Öffnen der Flasche kommt durch den exotischen Geruch von Mango Urlaubsfeeling auf. Im Geschmack mischt die Mango sich dann mit Wacholder, Sternanis, Lavendel, Kardamom und frischen Noten von Orangen- und Zitronenzesten.

No sooner than you open the bottle, out comes the exotic smell of mango and that vacation feeling. In the taste, the mango then mixes with juniper, star aniseed, lavender, cardamom and fresh notes of orange and lemon zest..

> LA SU – for your taste experience, your moment, your adventure and your journey.

On the journey...

We all want to meet new people, explore unknown places, immerse ourselves in foreign cultures and constantly experience something new – and so do Alexander Kayser and Christopher Schuh. Driven by this longing, they set off on their journey. They returned with lots of exciting experiences and an idea. They wanted to create their own gin, and they already had the botanicals in their luggage.

A gin that takes you to foreign places

The gin represents everything that the creators had absorbed on their journey. So, with much love, they created an exotic recipe: the LA SU Gin. This premium handcrafted gin is distilled in small batches in one of the oldest distilleries in Europe. Only natural flavorings are used and a lot of emphasis is placed on quality when selecting the fine botanicals. The result is a gin that is like a taste adventure: juniper mixes with fruity mango, star aniseed, lavender, cardamom, chili, complemented by orange and lemon zest. The elaborate bottle design reflects travel styling and fits the flavorful journey on which LA SU Gin takes you. Even the first sip of this absolute quality product makes you dream of faraway places. So, cheers! To adventure!

BRENNEREI HENRICH

MANDARINA DRY GIN

Kriftel, Germany

Der Duft der Kindheit

Wer kennt ihn nicht? Diesen erfrischenden Duft von Mandarinen, der einem schon beim Schälen in die Nase steigt und sofort die Erinnerung an Kindertage aufleben lässt. Die Obstbrenner Ralf und Holger Henrich haben einen Gin entwickelt, der genau dieses Gefühl verinnerlicht hat. Der Mandarina ist ein New Western Dry Gin, der auf frischen Mandarinen basiert, wie der Name schon sagt. Aber nicht nur: Insgesamt werden elf Botanicals verarbeitet. Neben Wacholder finden sich Thymian, Ingwer, Süßholzwurzel, weitere Zitrusfrüchte sowie Zitronenmelisse und Zitronengras im Rezept wieder. In der Nase findet man fruchtige Noten der Mandarine und die Würze aus Thymian und Süßholzwurzel.

Mandarine in allen Facetten

Das Aroma wird bestimmt von Zesten der Mandarine, gefolgt von Limette und etwas Orangen, Mandarinenkuchen mit Mandeln, Fruchtdrops mit Puderzucker bestäubt, sehr dezente Wacholdernoten, Zitronenmelisse, später folgen Anklänge von Kräutern der Provence. Der Geschmack beginnt mit dem ausgeprägten Aroma frischer Mandarinen, eingebettet in ein Potpourri von hesperiden Aromen und herbe Fruchtsüße mit leichten Bittertönen. Er führt über leichte Kräuternoten zu einem herb-süßen Abgang mit kräutrig-floralen Tönen. Die Mandarine ist Programm und präsentiert sich wunderbar balanciert in jeder Facette, ohne die anderen Aromen zu übertönen. Die Wacholderaromen spielen hierbei eine untergeordnete Rolle, der Star ist hierbei eindeutig der gelungene Mix aus Zitrusfrüchten der Extraklasse.

The scent of childhood

Who could fail to recognize it? That refreshing scent of mandarins that hits your nose as soon as you peel it and immediately brings back memories of childhood days. The fruit distillers Ralf and Holger Henrich have developed a gin that has internalized exactly this feeling. Mandarina is a New Western Dry Gin based on fresh mandarins, as the name suggests. But not only them; a total of eleven botanicals are processed. In addition to juniper, thyme, ginger, licorice root, other citrus fruits as well as lemon balm and lemongrass contribute to the recipe. On the nose, you'll find fruity notes of mandarin and the spice from thyme and licorice root.

Mandarin in all its facets

The aroma is determined by zests of mandarin, followed by lime and some orange, mandarin cake with almonds, fruit drops dusted with powdered sugar, very subtle notes of juniper, lemon balm, later followed by hints of herbs of Provence. The taste starts with the distinct aroma of fresh mandarins, embedded in a potpourri of hesperidic aromas and tart fruit sweetness with slight bitter tones. It leads through light herbal notes to a tart-sweet finish with herbal-floral tones. The mandarin is the star and presents itself wonderfully balanced in every facet, without drowning out the other flavors. The juniper flavors play a subordinate role here; the lead role is clearly played by the successful mix of citrus fruits in a class of its own. Mandarina tastes wonderful after long summer nights.

> Mandarina tastes wonderful after long summer nights.

CATEGORY
New Western Dry Gin

ORIGIN
Germany

ESTABLISHED
2020

SIZE
● ○ ○ ○

TASTING NOTES
Ein Aroma von Zesten von Mandarine, gefolgt von Limette und etwas Orangen, Mandarinenkuchen mit Mandeln, Fruchtdrops mit Puderzucker bestäubt, sehr dezente Wacholdernoten, Zitronenmelisse, später Anklänge von Kräutern der Provence. Im Geschmack ausgeprägte Aromen von Mandarine, eingebettet in ein Potpourri von hesperiden Aromen, herbe Fruchtsüße mit leichten Bittertönen. Im Abgang herb-süß mit kräutrig-floralen Tönen.

An aroma of mandarin zest followed by lime and some orange, mandarin cake with almonds, fruit drops dusted with powdered sugar, very subtle juniper notes, lemon balm, later hints of herbs de Provence. On the palate, pronounced aromas of mandarin embedded in a potpourri of hesperidic flavors, tart fruit sweetness with slight bitter tones. Finishes tartly sweet with herbaceous floral tones.

GIANFRANCO AMATO

AMATO MEDITERRANEAN DRY GIN

Wiesbaden, Germany

CATEGORY
Dry Gin

ORIGIN
Germany

ESTABLISHED
2014

SIZE
● ○ ○ ○

TASTING NOTES
Ausbalanciert, mild und leicht, sanft und aromatisch, mit einem fruchtigen Charakter, bestärkt durch Quitte und Aprikose, ergänzt durch den leicht würzigen Geschmack der Tomate; der Wacholder zeigt sich zurückhaltend, die Gurke erzeugt eine frische Leichtigkeit, die Kräuter sorgen für das mediterrane Flair.

Balanced, mild and light, gentle and aromatic, with a fruity character, strengthened by quince and apricot, complemented by the slightly spicy taste of tomato; the juniper shows restraint, the cucumber creates a fresh lightness, the herbs provide that Mediterranean flair.

" Tomato and thyme aren't just perfect on pizza, but also perfect in this gin.

Da ist Liebe drin

„Amato" ist italienisch und heißt übersetzt „die Geliebte". Amato ist auch der Nachname von Barkeeper Gianfranco, ebenfalls Italiener, aber auch Deutscher – zumindest wuchs er in Wiesbaden auf. Dort verwarf er seinen Plan, Fotograf zu werden, und wechselte stattdessen in die Gastronomie und ging als Restaurantfachmann nach Italien, Österreich, Spanien, in die Schweiz und kam wieder zurück nach Deutschland. Er arbeitete als Barkeeper, eröffnete schließlich seine eigene Bar und schenkt dort seit 2014 seinen eigenen Gin aus, seinen Amato. Was könnte in einem Gin stecken, der mit dem Begriff der Liebe jongliert? Eben genau diese: Liebe zur Handarbeit und Liebe zu den Zutaten aus der Natur.

Ein Abstecher ans Mittelmeer

Unter Verwendung von ausgewählten Botanicals aus der Region entsteht ein einzigartiger Gin, der die Aromen des Rhein-Main-Gebiets in sich bündelt. Neben Klassikern wie Wacholder, Zitrus und Koriander finden sich im Amato Gin handverlesene Akzente von frischer Gurke, Tomate und Quitte wieder. Dazu gesellt sich der würzige Geschmack von Thymian, der sich während der Destillation zu einer feinen, subtil auftretenden Note entwickelt. Um die geschmackliche Balance der frisch mazerierten Botanicals optimal auszutarieren, wird der Alkoholgehalt im letzten Arbeitsschritt mit frischem Quellwasser auf Trinkstärke herabgesetzt. Der mediterranean Dry Gin wird im Small-Batch-Verfahren produziert. Nur wenige hundert Flaschen werden jeweils in einem Rutsch gefertigt.

There's love in it

"Amato" is Italian and translates as "beloved". Amato is also the surname of bartender Gianfranco, also Italian but also German – well, he grew up in Wiesbaden. There he discarded his plan to become a photographer and instead switched to catering, going to Italy, Austria, Spain, Switzerland and coming back to Germany as a restaurant professional. He worked as a bartender, eventually opened his own bar and has been serving his own gin there since 2014, his Amato. What could be in a gin that juggles the concept of love? Precisely this: love of manual work and love of ingredients from nature.

A detour to the Mediterranean

Using selected botanicals from the region, a unique gin is created, which brings together the flavors of the Rhine-Main region. In addition to classics such as juniper, citrus and coriander, hand-picked accents of fresh cucumber, tomato and quince can be found in Amato Gin. These are joined by the spicy flavor of thyme, which develops into a fine, subtle note during distillation. In order to optimally balance the taste of the freshly macerated botanicals, the alcohol content is reduced to drinking strength with fresh spring water in the final production step. This Dry Gin from Wiesbaden is produced in a small-batch process. Only a few hundred bottles are produced in one go.

SCHLOSS JOHANNISBERG

SCHLOSS GIN

Ein moderner Gin mit Geschichte

Zu einem Schloss gehört immer auch ein Schatz. So lag auch auf der Fürst von Metternich-Winneburg'schen Domäne Schloss Johannisberg im Rheingau, dem ältesten Riesling-Weingut der Welt, ein echter Schatz vergraben. Bei Umbauarbeiten des Schlosses stößt man ganz zufällig auf alte Dokumente des Kellermeisters Odo Staab von 1805. In diesem verborgenen Schatz befinden sich Aufzeichnungen zur Herstellung von Wacholderwasser und Bitterorangenlikör – fast schon schicksalhaft, dass man diese nun über 200 Jahre später wieder ausgräbt. So wird der Grundstein für einen Gin gelegt, der einem das Gefühl gibt, im Märchen zu sein. Denn der Schloss Gin schmeckt einfach zu gut, um wahr zu sein.

Wacholder meets Bitterorange

Doch als wäre die verzaubernde Entstehungsgeschichte nicht beeindruckend genug, ist der Schloss Gin ein wahrlich edler Tropfen: ein zugleich handwerkliches und geschmackvolles Meisterwerk. Sonnengereifte Bitterorangen aus dem schlosseigenen Garten verleihen ihm eine fruchtige Frische. Diese trifft auf ein feines Wacholderaroma und mischt sich mit floralen Lavendelnoten. Für den Schloss Gin werden diese mit Bedacht ausgewählten Botanicals von Stefan Doktor destilliert – so wird er in kleinen Chargen produziert und von Hand in Flaschen abgefüllt. Das macht den Schloss Gin zu einem richtigen Sammlerstück – sozusagen zu einem echten Schatz!

Geisenheim, Germany

CATEGORY
London Dry Gin

ORIGIN
Germany

ESTABLISHED
2018

SIZE
● ○ ○ ○

TASTING NOTES
Zu dem typischen Wacholder gesellen sich feine Bitterorangen- und erfrischende Zitrusnoten. Piment und Ingwerwurzel verleihen ihm Würze und leichte Schärfe, während Lavendel und Rosenblüten für angenehm florale Noten sorgen. Aromenvielfalt und beeindruckende Komplexität.

The typical juniper is partnered by fine bitter orange and refreshing citrus notes. Allspice and ginger root add spice and slight spiciness, while lavender and rose petals provide pleasant floral notes. Aromatic diversity and impressive complexity.

0,5 L // 44,0 %

SCHLOSS JOHANNISBERG // SCHLOSS GIN

A modern gin with history

Every castle has associated treasure. So it was that real treasure was buried at Fürst von Metternich-Winneburg'sche Domäne Schloss Johannisberg castle in the Rheingau, the oldest Riesling winery in the world. During renovation work on the castle, old documents of cellar master Odo Staab from 1805 were discovered by chance. This hidden treasure contained records on the production of juniper water and bitter orange liqueur – perhaps fate that these have been unearthed again over 200 years later. This lays the foundation for a gin that makes you feel like you're in a fairy tale. Because Schloss Gin simply tastes too good to be true.

Juniper meets bitter orange

But as if the enchanting story of its origin were not impressive enough, Schloss Gin is a truly noble spirit, a masterpiece of craftsmanship and taste in one. Sun-ripened bitter oranges from the castle's own garden give it a fruity freshness. This partners a fine juniper aroma and mixes with floral lavender notes. For Schloss Gin, these botanicals are carefully selected and distilled by Stefan Doktor, then to be produced in small batches and bottled by hand. This makes Schloss Gin a real collector's item – a real treasure, so to speak!

> **With regal botanicals from the palace's own garden.**

BRENNEREI VALLENDAR

PURE GIN

Kail, Germany

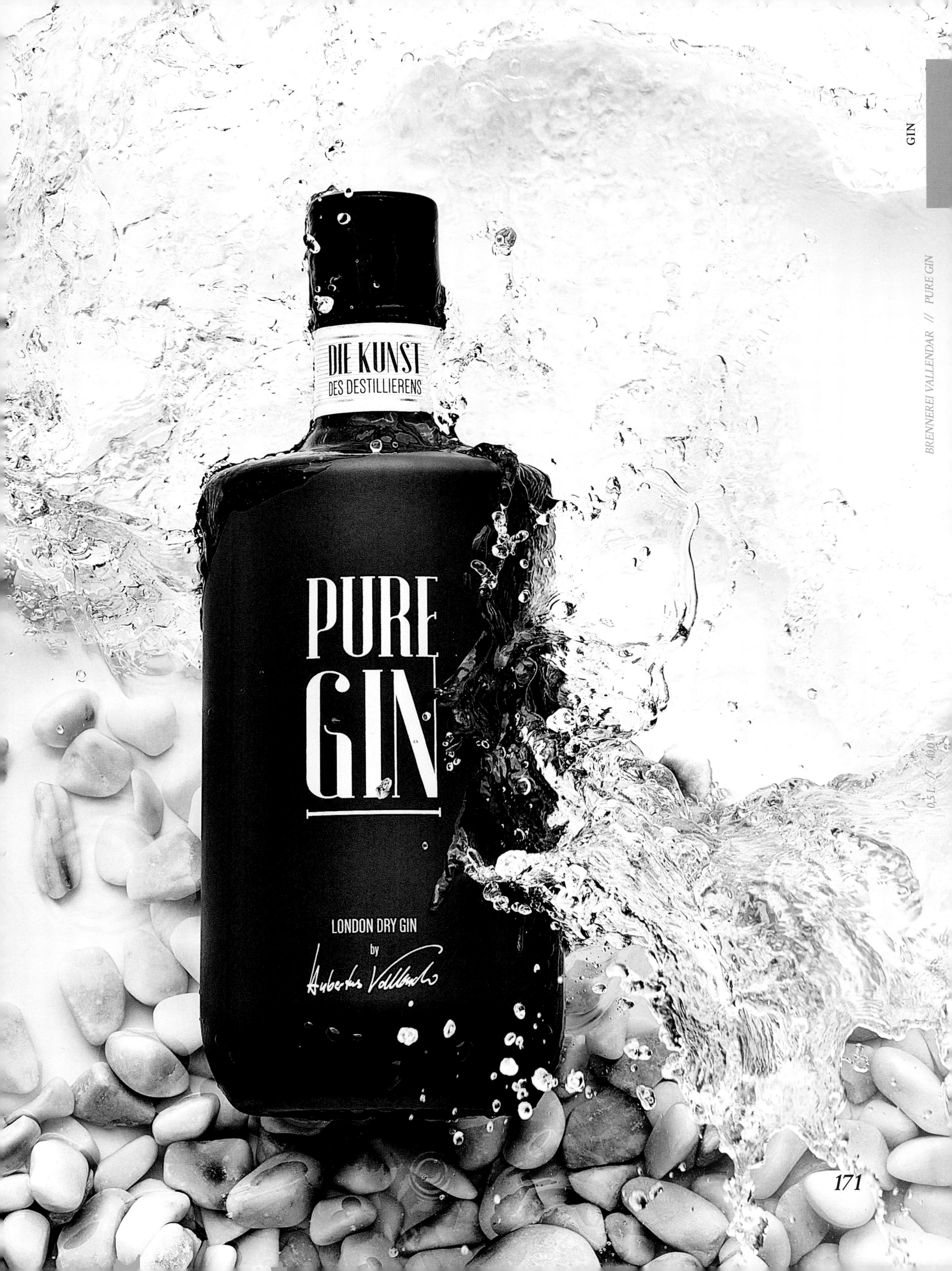

0,5 L // 40,0 %

Pure Gin – Hier wird nichts dem Zufall überlassen

Pure Gin vereint bestes Wasser, ausgewählte Wacholderbeeren und eine dezente Auswahl gintypischer Kräuter in einer einzigartigen, puren Rezeptur. Ein handwerkliches Rezept, das aus dem Gin ein Gesamtkunstwerk macht. Wer die Destillerie Vallendar in Kail in der Nähe der Mosel kennt, der weiß, dass hier Perfektionisten am Werk sind. Nichts wird dem Zufall überlassen, um das Beste aus der Natur in die Spirituose zu bringen. Seit mehr als 30 Jahren kreiert Hubertus Vallendar Destillate von außergewöhnlicher Qualität, für die er mehrfach ausgezeichnet wurde. Von Beginn an standen der Wille und das Qualitätsbestreben im Vordergrund, sie werden von Sohn Mario weitergelebt, der für Innovationen und die siegreichen Produkte ebenfalls verantwortlich ist. Der Familienbetrieb trägt seit 2003 die Auszeichnung World Class Distillery und agiert nach einer kompromisslosen Qualitätsphilosophie.

Nicht irgendein Wasser, sondern reines *Norder Wasser*

So ist es nicht verwunderlich, dass für den Pure Gin nicht irgendein Wasser als Basis dient, sondern „Norder Wasser", bekannt durch seine Reinheit und seinen unvergleichlichen Geschmack. Die Reaktion beim Herabsetzen trägt entscheidend zur Klarheit des Gins bei.

Der Pure Gin wartet aromatisch auf mit sehr dichten Wacholdernoten mit Anklängen von Angelikawurzel, Zitrus und Süßholz. Geschmacklich erwartet den Genießer ein intensives etherisches Wacholder-Zitrus-Aroma sowie Orange, Zitronenmelisse, Minze und Kamille. Der Pure Gin schmeckt fruchtig-beerig, erdig-moosig, hat eine feine Süße und einen lang anhaltenden Abgang.

> ## A gin with very dense juniper notes based on purity and incomparable taste

Pure Gin – Nothing is left to chance here

Pure Gin combines the best water, selected juniper berries and a discreet selection of herbs typical of gin in a unique, pure recipe. An artisanal recipe that makes the gin a total work of art. Anyone familiar with the Vallendar distillery in Kail near the Moselle knows that perfectionists are at work here. Nothing is left to chance when bringing the best of nature into the spirit. For more than 30 years, Hubertus Vallendar has been creating distillates of exceptional quality, for which he has received several awards. From the beginning, a real will and the pursuit of quality have been in the foreground, now perpetuated by son Mario, who is also responsible for innovation and the winning products. The family business has earned the World Class Distillery award since 2003 and operates according to an uncompromising philosophy of quality.

Not just any water, but pure Norder Wasser

So it's no surprise that, for Pure Gin, not just any water serves as a basis, but rather "Norder Wasser", known for its purity and incomparable taste. The reaction during dilution contributes decisively to the clarity of the gin. Pure Gin presents itself aromatically with very dense juniper notes with hints of angelica root, citrus and licorice. Taste-wise, the connoisseur can expect an intense ethereal juniper-citrus aroma as well as orange, lemon balm, mint and chamomile. The Pure Gin tastes fruity-berry, earthy-mossy, has a fine sweetness and a long-lasting finish.

CATEGORY
London Dry Gin

ORIGIN
Germany

ESTABLISHED
1987

SIZE
● ● ○ ○

TASTING NOTES
Zarte und sehr dichte Wacholdernoten, mit Anklängen von Angelikawurzel, Bittermandel sowie Zitrus und Süßholz in der Nase. Im Gaumen breit, klar, trocken, zitrusartig, erdig, moosig mit großer Frische.

Delicate and very dense juniper notes, with hints of angelica root, bitter almond and citrus and licorice on the nose. The palate is broad, clear, dry, citrusy, earthy, mossy with great freshness.

BRENNEREI VALLENDAR // PURE GIN

0,5 L // 40,0 %

173

RESTAURANT KIRSCHWEILER BRÜCKE

AQUAMARIN GIN

Botanicals aus dem heimischen Kräutergarten

Der Aquamarin Gin ist eng mit der Edelsteinstadt Idar-Oberstein verbunden. Durch eine bedachte Auswahl an Zutaten ist ein Gin entstanden, dessen Geschmack für die Region Idar-Oberstein steht. Die Botanicals wachsen in den heimischen Kräutergärten der Kirschweiler Brücke. Hier werden die besten Kräuter sorgfältig ausgewählt, um anschließend einzeln destilliert zu werden. Eine Vielzahl an Botanicals sorgt für den unverwechselbaren Geschmack des Aquamarin Gin. Wacholderbeere mischt sich mit Kaskadenthymian und Zitronenmelisse – abgerundet durch das intensiv-fruchtige Aroma von Orangen, die in der Sonne Italiens reifen durften. Ein Schluck Aquamarin Gin und man steht inmitten einer blühenden Kräuterwiese und kann den intensiven Duft der vielseitigen Aromen in sich aufnehmen.

Benannt nach dem kostbaren Aquamarin

Entwickelt wurde dieser einzigartige Tropfen von Hans-Werner Veek. Daher schmücken seine Initialen jede Flasche Aquamarin Gin. Sie hat ein besonderes Design – und nicht minder exklusiv: In jeder einzelnen befindet sich ein echter Aquamarin, der dem Gin seinen Namen gibt. Diesem macht er mit seinem extravaganten Geschmack alle Ehre. Der Aquamarin Gin ist vielfältig und facettenreich: Ein Gin, den man nicht einfach nur genießen, sondern mit allen Sinnen erleben kann. Aquamarin Gin – ein flüssiges Juwel.

Kirschweiler, Germany

Botanicals from the local herb garden

Aquamarin Gin is closely associated with the gemstone city of Idar-Oberstein. Through a thoughtful selection of ingredients, a gin has been created whose taste stands for the Idar-Oberstein region. The botanicals grow in the local herb gardens of Kirschweiler Brücke. Here, the best herbs are carefully selected for subsequent individual distillation. A variety of botanicals provides the distinctive taste of Aquamarin Gin. Juniper berry mixes with cascade thyme and lemon balm – rounded off by the intensely fruity aroma of oranges that have been allowed to ripen in the Italian sun. One sip of Aquamarin Gin and you stand in the middle of a blooming, herb-rich meadow and can absorb the intense fragrance of the wide-ranging scents.

Named after precious aquamarine

This unique spirit was developed by Hans-Werner Veek. Therefore, his initials adorn each bottle of Aquamarin Gin. It has a special design and, no less exclusively, each one contains a real aquamarine, which gives the gin its name; an appropriate homage to its extravagant taste. Aquamarin Gin is diverse and multifaceted: a gin that you can not merely enjoy, but also experience with all your senses. Aquamarin Gin – a liquid jewel.

> Aquamarin Gin:
> As noble as the stone whose name it bears.

CATEGORY
London Dry Gin

ORIGIN
Germany

ESTABLISHED
2014

SIZE

TASTING NOTES
Der Geschmack ist durch verschiedenste Aromen geprägt: Wacholder mischt sich mit Zitronenmelisse, Kaskadenthymian, Bergbohnenkraut, Mandarinen-Minze und angenehm leichten Noten von Zitrus und Kräutern.

The taste is characterized by a wide variety of aromas: juniper blends with lemon balm, cascade thyme, mountain savory, mandarin mint and pleasantly light notes of citrus and herbs..

*DESTILLERIE UND
LIKÖRMANUFAKTUR DEHECK*

LITTLE BIG HILL

*Gau-Odenheim,
Germany*

GIN

DESTILLERIE UND LIKÖRMANUFAKTUR DEHECK // LITTLE BIG HILL

0,5 L // 42,0 %

CATEGORY
Dry Gin

ORIGIN
Germany

ESTABLISHED
2015

SIZE
● ● ● ●

TASTING NOTES
Gin-typisches Wacholderaroma, eine frische Zitrusnote von Orange, Limette und Zitrone sowie weitere Gewürze wie Melisse, Koriander, Ingwer und Pfeffer bilden hierbei den Rahmen und Hintergrund, dazu kommen Lavendel, Majoran, Angelikawurzel und Enzian.

Gin-typical juniper aroma, a fresh citrus note of orange, lime and lemon and other spices such as lemon balm, coriander, ginger and pepper form the framework and background here, plus lavender, marjoram, angelica and gentian.

Aus dem Land der Tausend Hügel

Produzenten, die ihr Handwerk verstehen. So beschreiben sich Brennermeister Karl-Peter und seine Tochter Barbara Deheck. Das Streben, die traditionelle Brennerkunst mit innovativen Ideen aufzuwerten, motiviert sie tagtäglich, hochwertige Rohstoffe in Hochprozentiges zu verwandeln. Hinter ihrer Destillerie und Likörmanufaktur steckt keine Marketingfirma mit großer Story, sie stellen einfach gute Produkte her.

Der Little Big Hill ist nun der erste gemeinsame Gin von Vater und Tochter. Dabei geht es back to the roots – dieser Dry Gin ist sehr wacholderbetont und orientiert sich an alten Rezepturen. Hier wird keine Massenware produziert, sondern kleine Chargen, denn Vater und Tochter stellen den Gin in Handarbeit her.

Der Fokus auf Regionalität und Natürlichkeit

Little Big Hill erhält seine regionale Note durch den weitgehenden Verzicht auf exotische Zutaten und die überwiegende Verwendung heimischer Kräuter und Gewürze. Der Fokus bei der Auswahl der Botanicals liegt klar auf Regionalität und Natürlichkeit. Das macht diesen Gin bodenständig und regionstypisch. Auch der Name gibt Rückschlüsse darauf, woher er kommt. Rheinhessen wird das Land der Tausend Hügel genannt, worauf Little Big Hill eine Anspielung ist. Dieser Gin vereint die Tradition der Ginherstellung mit dem Charme und der Persönlichkeit seiner Herkunft.

> ## From the land of the Thousand Hills.

From the land of a thousand hills

Producers who know their craft. This is how master distiller Karl-Peter and his daughter Barbara Deheck describe themselves. The ambition to enhance the traditional art of distilling with innovative ideas motivates them each and every day to transform high-quality raw materials into high-proof spirits. There isn't a marketing company with a big story behind their distillery and liqueur operation; they simply make good products.

Little Big Hill is now the first gin jointly produced by father and daughter. It goes back to the roots, this dry gin being very juniper-accentuated and oriented to old recipes. This is no mass-production, rather it's about small batches, because father and daughter make the gin by hand.

Focus on regionality and naturalness

Little Big Hill gets its regional flavor by largely avoiding exotic ingredients, instead mainly using local herbs and spices. The focus in the selection of botanicals is clearly on regionality and naturalness. This makes this gin down-to-earth and typical of the region. The name also gives clues as to where it comes from. Rheinhessen is called the land of a thousand hills, to which Little Big Hill is an allusion. This gin combines the tradition of gin-making with the charm and personality of its origin.

Gau-Odernheim, Germany

WEINGUT DANIEL MATTERN

NATURAL DRY GIN

CATEGORY
Natural Dry Gin

ORIGIN
Germany

ESTABLISHED
2011

SIZE

TASTING NOTES
Neben klassischen Botanicals wie Wacholder und Zitrus ist der Geschmack von diesem Natural Dry Gin besonders durch Noten von frischer Gurke und sonnengetrockneten Tomaten geprägt.

In addition to classic botanicals such as juniper and citrus, the flavor of this Natural Dry Gin is particularly characterized by notes of fresh cucumber and sun-dried tomatoes.

> A gin with a soft, smoky and strong whiskey note.

Mettenheim, Germany

Natural Dry Gin vom Winzer

Der Winzer Daniel Mattern kann nicht nur guten Wein, er kann auch guten Gin. Sein erst 2011 gegründetes Weingut hat zwar keine Tradition, aber dafür viel Potenzial. Es ist jung, frisch und anders. Das Ziel, das er Jahr für Jahr verfolgt? Den besten Tropfen aus seinen Trauben zu pressen. Der Winzermeister arbeitet im Einklang mit der Natur und legt dabei den eigenen Charakter der Rebsorten, Böden und Lagen frei. Zu seinen Eigenschaften zählen der Mut zu Neuem und keine Angst, gegen den Strom zu schwimmen.

Frische Gurke und sonnengetrocknete Tomaten

So kam es, dass er nun neben Wein auch noch Gin produziert. Der Schnaps und der Tresterbrand kommen dabei aus der Edelobstbrennerei seines Vaters. Seine ausgewogene Balance erhält der Natural Dry Gin durch einen letzten Arbeitsschritt, bei dem er mit frischem Quellwasser auf milde 42 % vol. herabgesetzt wird. Wer es lieber kräftiger haben möchte: Daniel Mattern stellt auch den Natural Dry Gin Whiskey Barrels her. Als Basis dient der Natural Dry Gin. Dieser lagert, wie der Name schon sagt, in kleinen, bloß 38 Liter fassenden Whisky-Fässern aus New York von Millers Whisky. Das gibt diesem Gin eine weiche, rauchige und kräftige Whisky-Note mit 55 % Alkoholgehalt.

Natural Dry Gin from the winemaker

Winemaker Daniel Mattern not only makes good wine, he also makes good gin. His winery, founded as recently as 2011, may not have a tradition, but it has a lot of potential. It's young, fresh and different. As to the goal he pursues year after year? To produce the best from his grapes. This master winemaker works in harmony with nature, revealing the unique character of the grape varieties, soils and slopes. His qualities include the courage to try new things and not being afraid to swim against the current.

Fresh cucumber and sun-dried tomatoes

Circumstances led to his producing gin as well as wine. The schnapps and grape marc spirit come from his father's fine fruit distillery. This Natural Dry Gin gets its balance from a final step in which it is diluted to a mild 42 % ABV with fresh spring water. For those who prefer it stronger, Daniel Mattern also makes the Natural Dry Gin Whiskey Barrels. The Natural Dry Gin serves as the basis. This is stored, as the name suggests, in small, just 38-liter whiskey barrels from Miller's Whiskey in New York. This gives this gin a soft, smoky and strong whiskey note with 55 % alcohol content.

DESTILLE KALTENTHALER

MOMOTARŌ GIN

Westhofen, Germany

500 ML

MOMOTARŌ

Japanisch inspirierter Craft Gin mit erle...
Momo-Pfirsich, Yuzu-Zitrone, Saku...
und Sencha-Tee

DESTILLE KALTENTHALER // MOMOTARŌ GIN

GIN

0,5 L // 42,0 %

183

CATEGORY
New Western Dry Gin

ORIGIN
Germany

ESTABLISHED
2021

SIZE
● ● ● ○

TASTING NOTES
In der Nase zeigt er sich von seiner fruchtigen Seite. Besonders die Noten des Momo-Pfirsich und der Sakura-Kirschblüte machen Lust auf mehr. Zu diesen Aromen gesellt sich die Frische der Yuzu-Zitrone, die durch den würzigen Wacholder und den Sencha-Tee perfekt abgerundet werden. Am Gaumen überzeugt er besonders durch seinen samtig weichen Abgang.

Shows a fruity side on the nose with notes of Momo peach and Sakura cherryblossom particularly making you crave more. These fruity aromas partner up with the fresh notes of yuzu lemon, which are perfectly rounded off by spicy juniper and sencha tea. On the palate it is especially remarkable for its velvety soft finish.

Ein Gin, der für Leidenschaft steht

Die japanische Sage des Momotarōs handelt von einem kinderlosen Ehepaar, das eines Tages an einem Fluss vorüberspaziert und einen wunderschönen Pfirsich im Wasser treiben sieht. Die Frau holt den Pfirsich aus dem Wasser und möchte ihn mit ihrem Mann teilen. In dem Moment springt daraus das Kind hervor, das die beiden sich immer gewünscht haben. Momotarō – der Pfirsichjunge. Das Ehepaar hatte von nun an einen Sohn, den es von ganzem Herzen liebte. Gleichermaßen inspiriert von dieser Liebe und der japanischen Sage entsteht mitten in Deutschland in einer kleinen Craft-Destille der Momotarō Gin.

Eintauchen in die Genusswelt Japans

Bei der Auswahl der Botanicals für den Momotarō Gin hat man sich von der traditionsreichen japanischen Sage inspirieren lassen. So werden Zutaten wie Momo-Pfirsich, Yuzu-Zitrone, Sakura-Kirschblüten und Sencha-Tee handverlesen und sorgfältig in bester Craft-Manier destilliert. Sowohl die Mazeration als auch die Destillation werden besonders langsam und schonend durchgeführt, damit die Botanicals ihr volles Aroma entfalten können. So entwickeln sich elegante Zitrus-Noten, perfekt ergänzt durch den fruchtig-süßen Momo-Pfirsich. Mit diesen unverwechselbar frisch-fruchtigen Aromen entführt der Momotarō Gin in die japanische Genusswelt und lässt vom Land der aufgehenden Sonne träumen.

A gin that stands for passion.

The Japanese saga of Momotarō is about a childless couple who one day walk by a river and see a beautiful peach floating along in the water. The woman takes the peach out of the water and wants to share it with her husband. At that moment, the child that the two of them have always wanted springs out of it. Momotarō – the peach boy. From that moment on, the couple had a son whom they loved with all their heart. Inspired equally by this love and the Japanese legend, Momotarō Gin is created in the middle of Germany in a small craft distillery.

Immerse yourself in the world of delight of Japan

The selection of botanicals for Momotarō Gin has been inspired by that traditional Japanese saga. Thus, ingredients such as momo peach, yuzu lemon, sakura cherry blossoms as well as sencha and sencha tea are handpicked and carefully distilled in the best craft manner. Both maceration and distillation are carried out particularly slowly and gently, so that the botanicals can develop their full aroma. Thus, elegant citrus notes develop, perfectly complemented by the fruity-sweet momo peach. With these unmistakably fresh and fruity aromas, Momotarō Gin transports you to the world of Japanese delight and lets you dream of the land of the rising sun.

> „
> **Momotarō Gin is a tribute to the Japanese saga of Momotarō."
> A gin that stands for passion.**

WEINGUT SCHREIECK

GIN DRY – PFÄLZER EDELGIN

St. Martin, Germany

Ein Klassiker vom Weingut

Inmitten des malerischen Luftkurortes St. Martin, zwischen liebevoll restaurierten Fachwerkhäusern und romantischen Gassen, hat sich die Familie Schreieck ein kleines Imperium aufgebaut. Der Blick über das grüne Rebenmeer, das sich vor den Burgen und Schlössern am Rande des Pfälzer Waldes verbeugt, lässt erahnen, dass das Steckenpferd der Schreiecks eigentlich nicht im Gin-Destillieren, sondern im Weinanbau liegt. Auf rund 27 Hektar hegt und pflegt die Familie Dutzende Rebsorten. Wolfgang Schreieck, der seit 2020 die Betriebsleitung innehat, hat dies jedoch nicht davon abgehalten, die Produktpalette zu erweitern. Herausgekommen ist ein Winzer-Gin, der Weinlieber für Gin begeistern soll.

Von Grund auf ehrlich

Ganz ohne eine Assoziation zum Wein kommt der London Dry Gin dennoch nicht aus. Die Namensgebung „Gin dry" wurde in Anlehnung an das Hauptprodukt des Weinguts gewählt. Dabei wird erst die Rebsorte und dann der Geschmack angegeben, zum Beispiel „Riesling trocken". Für den Winzer-Gin setzt Wolfgang Schreieck auf ein klassisches, geradliniges Geschmackserlebnis. Im Glas dominiert der Wacholder, gefolgt von einer fruchtigen Ingwer- und einer frischen Zitrusnote. Mehr braucht der Gin nicht. Drei Zutaten. Von Grund auf ehrlich. Ohne viel Schnickschnack und Gedöns. Dazu serviert Wolfgang Schreieck sein hauseigenes, gezielt für den Gin dry komponiertes Tonic.

CATEGORY
London Dry Gin

ORIGIN
Germany

ESTABLISHED
1698

SIZE
● ○ ○ ○

TASTING NOTES
Ausgeprägte, schön bittere, leicht süße Wacholdernote in Kombination mit einer fruchtigen Ingwernote, die sich auf der Zunge ablegt, und zarten, frischen Zitrusaromen.

Pronounced, nicely bitter, slightly sweet juniper note combined with a fruity ginger note that lingers on the tongue, and delicate, fresh citrus aromas.

> Jesus turned water into wine. Gin dry turns wine lovers into gin drinkers.

A classic from the winery

In the midst of the picturesque climatic health resort of St. Martin, between lovingly restored half-timbered houses and romantic alleys, the Schreieck family has built up a small empire. The view over the green expanse of vines that bow to the castles and palaces on the edge of the Pfälzer Forest suggests that the Schreiecks' hobbyhorse might not actually be distilling gin, but rather growing grapes. The family cultivates dozens of grape varieties on around 27 hectares. Wolfgang Schreieck, who has been managing the business since 2020, has not let this stop him from expanding the product range. The result is a vintner's gin that should get wine lovers excited about gin.

Honest from the ground up

But the London Dry Gin doesn't completely escape an association with wine. The name "Gin dry" was chosen in reference to the winery's main product. Wine is named first by grape variety and then the flavor, for example "Riesling dry". For the vintner's gin, Wolfgang Schreieck goes for a classic, straightforward taste experience. Juniper dominates in the glass, followed by a fruity ginger and a fresh citrus note. That's all the gin needs. Three ingredients. Honest from the ground up. Without a lot of frills and fuss. Wolfgang Schreieck serves his own tonic, composed specifically for Gin dry.

WEINGUT PETER STÜBINGER

GIN 24/7 – STÜBINGER'S DRY GIN

CATEGORY
Dry Gin

ORIGIN
Germany

ESTABLISHED
2021

SIZE
● ● ● ●

TASTING NOTES
Kräuterig-herb, ausgeprägt würzig, mit einer vordergründigen Wacholdernote und einem intensiven fruchtigen Aroma – geprägt durch Zitronen, Grapefruits und Hibiskus.

Herbaceous-tart, distinctly spicy, with a foreground juniper note and an intense fruity aroma – characterized by lemons, grapefruit and hibiscus.

Sieben Tage im Dornröschenschlaf

Traditionen zu bewahren steht auf dem Stübinger Weingut an oberster Stelle. Dass diese Strategie hervorragend mit innovativen Ideen vereinbar ist, beweisen die Mitglieder des Familienbetriebes unter anderem bei der Auswahl ihrer angebotenen Weine und Sekte. Seit inzwischen drei Generationen werden im beschaulichen pfälzischen Leinsweiler vielfältige Rebsorten angebaut und im eigenen Keller sorgfältig mit modernster Technik veredelt. In der hauseigenen Edelobstbrennerei werden darüber hinaus Branntweine hergestellt und seit Januar 2021 auch der erste Stübinger's Dry Gin. Entsprechend den 24 hinzugefügten Botanicals, die sieben Tage lang in Alkohol eingelegt und erst im Anschluss sorgfältig gebrannt werden, trägt er den Namen "Gin 24/7".

Wie der Vater, so der Sohn

Ergänzt wird das 24/7-Konzept durch die nicht ganz ernst gemeinte Empfehlung, dass die Spirituose an 24 Stunden und an sieben Tagen in der Woche perfekt zu genießen ist. Sein dominierendes Aroma nach Kräutern erhält der Gin durch die Zugabe von Thymian, Rosmarin, Kardamom und Basilikum. Für die fruchtig-süße Säure sorgen Grapefruitschalen und verschiedene Zitrusfrüchte. Diverse Pfefferarten und Ingwer verleihen dem Stübinger's Gin, der in Tonflaschen erhältlich ist, zudem eine angenehme Schärfe. Die Gin-Produktion ist das Ergebnis der Zusammenarbeit von Peter und Daniel Stübinger – von Vater und Sohn. Während Peter Stübinger als Chef des Hauses die Brennerei bedient, liefert Daniel Stübinger den kreativen Input mit dem gemeinsamen Ziel, den bestmöglichen Gin zu produzieren.

> **24 hours/7 days absolutely delightful.**

Seven days as Sleeping Beauty

Preserving traditions is a top priority at the Stübinger winery. The fact that this strategy is perfectly compatible with innovative ideas is demonstrated by the members of the family business in the selection of their wines and sparkling wines, among other things. For three generations now, a wide variety of grape varieties have been cultivated in the tranquil Palatinate town of Leinsweiler and carefully refined in the winery's own cellar using state-of-the-art technology. In addition, brandies are produced in the in-house fine fruit spirit distillery and, since January 2021, the first Stübinger's Dry Gin too. In keeping with the 24 added botanicals, which are steeped in alcohol for seven days and only then carefully distilled, it bears the name "Gin 24/7".

Like father, like son

The 24/7 concept is complemented by the not entirely serious recommendation that the spirit is perfect to enjoy 24 hours a day, seven days a week. The gin gets its dominant aroma of herbs from the addition of thyme, rosemary, cardamom and basil. Grapefruit zest and various citrus fruits provide the fruity-sweet acidity. Various types of pepper and ginger also lend a pleasant spiciness to Stübinger's gin, which is available in clay bottles. The gin production is the result of collaboration between Peter and Daniel Stübinger – father and son. While Peter Stübinger operates the distillery as head of the house, Daniel Stübinger provides the creative input with the common goal of producing the best possible gin.

Leinsweiler, Germany

AVADIS DISTILLERY

FERDINAND'S GIN

CATEGORY
New Western Dry Gin

ORIGIN
Germany

ESTABLISHED
2013

SIZE
● ● ● ●

TASTING NOTES
Frisch und komplex, schöne florale Noten, zum Wacholder gesellen sich fruchtige Aromen, im Gaumen sehr mild und vollmundig, im angenehm langen Abgang dominiert Lavendel.

Fresh and complex, beautiful floral notes, juniper is partnered by fruity aromas, very mild and full-bodied on the palate, lavender dominates in the pleasantly long finish.

Von einer Königin umgarnt

Im Dreiländereck zwischen Deutschland, Luxemburg und Frankreich, dort, wo die Saar auf die Mosel trifft, liegt die Heimat eines der größten Weinanbaugebiete Deutschlands. Hier, in der Saar-Region, in der sich die renommiertesten Riesling-Produzenten des Landes auf engstem Raum begegnen, beginnt 2013 die Geschichte von Ferdinand's Saar Dry Gin. Ein Gin, dessen Besonderheit darin besteht, dass er mit einem Riesling aus dem Haus des VDP-Weinguts Forstmeister Geltz-Zilliken, verfeinert wird. Namensgebend für den Ferdinand's ist der preußische Forstmeister Ferdinand Geltz. Er war Mitbegründer des Verbandes Deutscher Prädikatsweingüter (VDP) Mosel-Saar-Ruwer und steigerte durch sein Engagement die Bekanntheit der Weine aus der Region im In- und Ausland.

Das Beste der Saar-Mosel-Region

Die ursprüngliche Idee für den "Riesling infused Gin" hatten die Brüder Denis Reinhardt und Erik Wimmers. Für die Umsetzung holten sie keinen Geringeren als Andreas Vallendar, Master Distiller der Avadis Distillery, mit ins Boot. Seine Familie destilliert bereits seit mehreren Generationen Obstbrände auf dem 1824 in Wincheringen-Bilzingen gegründeten Gutshof. Die Basis des Ferdinand's ist ein eigens destillierter Rohbrand aus Getreide, das von den umliegenden Feldern der Brennerei stammt. Dieser wird durch eine Dampfinfusion mit anderen Botanicals zuerst mazeriert und dann destilliert wird. Mehr als 34 Botanicals stecken in dem edlen Tropfen, von denen rund zwei Drittel aus eigenem Anbau stammen: Direkt hinter der Brennerei wachsen Pfirsich, Quitten- und Apfelbäume, der Lavendel stammt von brachliegenden Weinbergen im Konzer Tälchen und das Gros der Kräuter aus dem eigenen Garten.

> Uncork the flavor of the Saar.

Embraced by a queen

In the border triangle between Germany, Luxembourg and France, where the Saar meets the Moselle, lies the home of one of Germany's largest wine-growing regions. Here, in the Saar region, where the country's most renowned Riesling producers cluster in a very small space, the story of Ferdinand's Saar Dry Gin began in 2013. A gin whose special feature is that it is refined with a Riesling from the house of the VDP winery Forstmeister Geltz-Zilliken. Ferdinand's is named after the Prussian forester Ferdinand Geltz. He was one of the founders of the Association of German Prädikat Wine Estates (VDP) Mosel-Saar-Ruwer and, through his commitment, he increased awareness of wines from the region at home and abroad.

The best of the Saar-Moselle region

The original idea for this "Riesling-infused gin" came from the brothers Denis Reinhardt and Erik Wimmers. For the implementation, they brought on board none other than Andreas Vallendar, Master Distiller of Avadis Distillery. His family has been distilling fruit brandies for several generations on the estate founded in Wincheringen-Bilzingen in 1824. The basis of Ferdinand's is a self-distilled raw spirit made from grain sourced from the distillery's surrounding fields. This is first macerated and then distilled by steam infusion with other botanicals. More than 34 botanicals are used in this fine spirit, around two-thirds of which come from the distillery's own cultivation. Peach, quince, and apple trees grow directly behind the distillery, the lavender comes from fallow vineyard slopes of the Konzer Valley, and the bulk of the herbs come from the distillery's own garden.

Wincheringen, Germany

HEIKO HOOS

HOOS LONDON GIN

CATEGORY
London Dry Gin

ORIGIN
Germany

ESTABLISHED
2014

SIZE
● ● ○ ○

TASTING NOTES
Bodenständig, waldige Noten, blumiger Lavendel, frische Kamille, kräftiger Wacholder, nuancierte Kiefernknospen.

Down-to-earth, arboreal notes, floral lavender, fresh chamomile, strong juniper, nuanced pine buds.

Ein Gründer, ein Gedanke, ein Gin

In der Ruhe liegt die Kraft. Pflanzen brauchen Nährstoffe, Wasser, Zeit und Platz zum Wachsen. Wer die Natur schätzt und mit ihr sorgsam umgeht, kann aus ihr fabelhafte Produkte herstellen, so der Leitgedanke von Heiko Hoos, Entwickler des Hoos London Gin. Dabei beginnt seine Gin-Geschichte gar nicht so philosophisch. Der Pfälzer hatte seine kleine Gin-Produktion aus einer Behauptung heraus gestartet. An einem Bar-Abend versicherte er, er könne selbst einen als Gin erkennbaren Schnaps brennen. Die Arbeit begann am nächsten Morgen. Heiko Hoos fand sich zwischen alten Rezepturen und Dokumenten aus dem 19. Jahrhundert wieder, dachte akribisch über die Auswahl von Botanicals nach und unternahm an einer Arnold-Holstein-Kupferbrennblase erste Brennversuche. Das Ergebnis kann sich schmecken lassen.

Small Batch mit 120 Flaschen

Seit 2014 ist Heiko Hoos als Ein-Mann-Unternehmen in der Gin-Welt unterwegs. Sein nach ihm benannter London Gin entsteht im Small-Batch-Verfahren. Nur etwa 120 Flaschen werden pro Destillation von Hand abgefüllt. Süßfenchel, Kiefernsprossen, Zitronenmelisse, Majoran, Orangen- und Zitronenzeste, Koriander, Wacholder, Kamille und Kardamom werden 36 Stunden mazeriert und bei niedrigen Temperaturen destilliert. Wie für einen London Gin typisch, wird nach der Destillation kein Zucker zugesetzt und auf eine abschließende Kältefiltration verzichtet. Nach einer mehrwöchigen Ruhephase in einem Glasballon wird das Destillat mit Quellwasser aus dem Pfälzer Wald auf die Alkoholstärke von 44,4 % herabgesetzt und in schlichte, dunkle, handsignierte Flaschen abgefüllt.

Karlsruhe, Germany

> **Dry and aromatic at the same time, with that certain something resinous.**

One founder, one thought, one gin

Still waters run deep. Plants need nutrients, water, time and space to grow. If you appreciate nature and treat it with care, you can make fabulous products from it, according to the guiding principle of Heiko Hoos, developer of Hoos London Gin. Yet his gin story does not begin so philosophically. A native of the Palatinate region, he started his small gin operation based on an assertion. One evening at a bar, he assured people he could distill a spirit recognizable as gin. Work began the next morning. Heiko Hoos found himself among old recipes and documents from the 19th century, thought meticulously about the selection of botanicals, and made his first distilling attempts using an Arnold Holstein copper still. The result is something to be proud of.

Small batch with 120 bottles

Heiko Hoos has been a one-man operation in the gin world since 2014. His London Gin, named after him, is produced in a small-batch process. Only about 120 bottles are filled by hand from each distillation. Sweet fennel, pine shoots, lemon balm, marjoram, orange and lemon zest, coriander, juniper, chamomile and cardamom are macerated for 36 hours and distilled at low temperatures. As is typical for a London Gin, no sugar is added after distillation and final cold filtration is omitted. After a resting phase of several weeks in a glass flask, the distillate is reduced to a strength of 44.4 % alcohol by volume using spring water from the Palatinate forest, and bottled in plain, dark, hand-signed bottles.

CATEGORY
Infused Gin

ORIGIN
Germany

ESTABLISHED
2021

SIZE

TASTING NOTES
Mild und sehr weich, blumig, fruchtig, mit Noten von Holunder und Cranberrys; Empfehlung: mit Fever Tree Mediterranean Tonic genießen.

Mild and very smooth, floral, fruity, with notes of elderberry and cranberry; recommendation: enjoy with tonic.

EDELOBSTBRENNEREI SCHLEIHAUF

BÖSER KATER TWO FACED GIN

> # This cat can be evil,
> # but he also has another side.

Der ikonische Rüdiger

Miau und ganz viel schnurr. Ein bisschen kraulen hier, ein bisschen kraulen dort, aber bitte nicht am Bauch. Nicht, dass der Schmusetiger noch ungnädig wird. Eigentlich ist es genau das, was niemand nach einem geselligen Abend haben will, an dem auch Alkohol ausgeschenkt wurde: einen kratzbürstigen flauschigen Mitbewohner oder einen brummenden Schädel. Doch "Böser Kater" bekommt eine ganz neue Bedeutung, wenn er in Zusammenhang mit der Edelobstbrennerei Schleihauf steht. Denn genau so heißen die außergewöhnlichen Spirituosen, welche die Gin-Landschaft Deutschlands beleben – gewidmet dem Familienkater Rüdiger. Natürlich ist seine Laune nicht immer gleich und so hat sein Besitzer Adrian Clausing einen Two Faced Gin entwickelt, der diese Wechselhaftigkeit unterstreicht.

Das Spiel mit den Farben

Der Gin verdankt seine bläuliche Farbe einer natürlichen Zutat. Bei Zugabe von Tonic Water verändert sich der pH-Wert des Gins, wodurch sich seine Farbe in ein dezentes Violett verwandelt. Doch der Böser Kater Two Faced Gin ist nicht nur etwas für die Augen. Geschmacklich punktet die samtigweiche Spirituose mit ihrem floral-fruchtigen Bouquet. Und weil nicht alle Katzen so ein wohlbehütetes Zuhause haben wie Rüdiger, unterstützt das Familienunternehmen on top seit mehr als 15 Jahren den Katzenschutzverein Karlsruhe sowie den Tierschutzverein Pfötchenhilfe Österreich. In diesem Sinne: Miau und ganz viel schnurr.

The iconic Rüdiger

Plenty of meowing and purring. A little scratching here, a little scratching there, but please not on the belly. Not that the cuddly tiger will still be ungracious. The name means angry tom cat, German slang for a hangover, exactly what no one wants to have after a social evening involving alcohol: a scratchy fluffy roommate or a bad headache. But it takes on a whole new meaning when it's associated with the Schleihauf fine fruit distillery. Because that's exactly the name of the exceptional spirits that enliven Germany's gin landscape – dedicated to the family cat, Rüdiger. Of course, his mood is not always the same and so his owner, Adrian Clausing, has developed a two-faced gin that underlines this changeability.

Playing with colors

The gin owes its blue coloration to a natural ingredient. When tonic water is added, the gin's pH changes, turning its color a subtle purple. But Böser Kater Two Faced Gin is not just eye candy. In terms of taste, this velvety-smooth spirit scores with its floral-fruity bouquet. Moreover, because not all cats have such a well-protected home as Rüdiger, the family business has been supporting the Karlsruhe Cat Protection Association, as well as the Pfötchenhilfe Österreich animal protection association, for more than 15 years. With this in mind: plenty of meowing and purring.

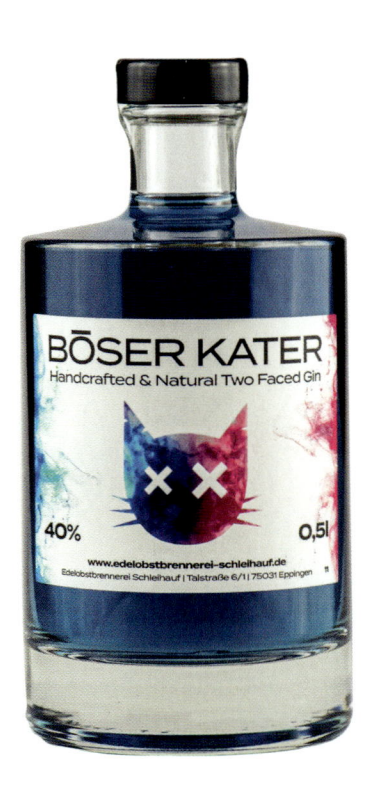

Eppingen, Germany

> "A gin like a walk from the orangery to the pine forest.

CATEGORY
London Dry Gin

ORIGIN
Germany

ESTABLISHED
2018

SIZE
● ● ○ ○

TASTING NOTES
Komplexer Charakter, vordergründig bestimmt durch den Geschmack der Blutorange, begleitet durch Zitrone, Pfeffer und eine dezente Wacholdernote, umrahmt von Koriander, Lavendel und Muskat, edle Bitternoten, fruchtig und würzig im Abgang.

Complex character, determined by the taste of blood orange in the foreground, accompanied by lemon, pepper and a subtle note of juniper, framed by coriander, lavender and nutmeg, noble bitter notes, fruity and spicy finish.

SATOSHI SPIRITS DESTILLERIE

SATOSHI GIN

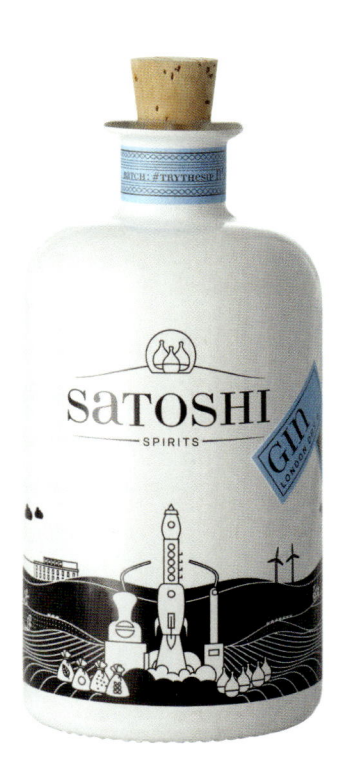

Von Bitcoins zu Destillaten

Satoshi ist ein typisch japanischer Vorname und den meisten in Kombination mit Nakamoto bekannt als das Pseudonym des sagenumwobenen Bitcoin-Erfinders. Dabei stehen die drei ersten Buchstaben in Satoshi Gin für drei Jungs aus Deutschland. Gemeint sind Sebastian, Alessandro und Thomas – der Logistiker, der Feinkosthändler und der Filmemacher – mit der gemeinsamen Hingabe für exquisite Destillate und eben auch für Bitcoins. Letztere tauschten sie jedoch in Euro und letztlich in Flaschen ein, um ihren Traum vom selbst kreierten London Dry Gin zu verwirklichen. Und so stecken in jeder Flasche der ersten Charge Satoshi Gin viele echte Satoshi, die kleinste Einheit des Bitcoins.

Im Herzen pulsieren Blutorangen

Feuerrot ist die wichtigste Zutat im Satoshi Gin: Die Königin der Blutorangen, die wundervolle Moro, beziehen die Gründer direkt von Giuseppe, ihrem Orangenbauern auf Sizilien. Schon beim Öffnen der Flasche strömt ihr Durft dominant aus dem Flaschenhals. Sie schenkt dem klassischen London Dry Gin eine extravagante, unverkennbar fruchtige Note. Abgerundet wird das Aroma der sizilianischen Lady durch acht weitere Botanicals. Feinwürzige Muskatblüten und wild wachsender Pfeffer aus den tropischen Wäldern Madagaskars verleihen dem Destillat seinen extravaganten Charakter. Und weil eine Gin-Exposition für drei Jungs zwei zu wenig sind, haben sie den Brennkessel noch einmal angeworfen. Herausgekommen sind der Satoshi Geist Toskana Wacholder und der Satoshi Geist Blutorange Moro.

Ludwigsburg, Germany

From Bitcoins to distillates

Satoshi is a typical Japanese first name and is better known to most people in combination with Nakamoto as the pseudonym of the legendary Bitcoin inventor. However, the first three letters in Satoshi Gin stand for three guys from Germany. They are Sebastian, Alessandro and Thomas – the logistician, the delicatessen owner and the filmmaker – who share a passion for exquisite distillates and indeed Bitcoin. However, they exchanged the latter for euros and ultimately for bottles in order to realize their dream of creating their own London Dry Gin. And so each bottle of the first batch of Satoshi Gin contains many genuine Satoshis, the smallest unit of Bitcoin.

Blood oranges pulsate in the heart

The most important ingredient of Satoshi Gin is fire red: the queen of blood oranges, the wonderful Moro, which the founders obtain directly from Giuseppe, their orange farmer in Sicily. As soon as the bottle is opened, its scent pours dominantly from the neck of the bottle. It gives the classic London Dry Gin an extravagant, unmistakably fruity note. The aroma of that lady of Sicily is rounded off by eight other botanicals. Finely spicy nutmeg flowers and wild pepper from the tropical forests of Madagascar give the distillate its extravagant character. And because one gin exhibit is two too few for three guys, they fired up the still again. The results are Satoshi Spirit Tuscany Juniper and Satoshi Spirit Blood Orange Moro.

SWABIANGINDISTILLERS

ERICH SCHWÄBISCHER DRY GIN

Berglen, Germany

Der Opa, der das Brennen lehrte

Erich war ein fleißiger Mann, ein liebender Vater, ein fürsorglicher Großvater. Ein Schwabe, der in seiner Brennerei aus dem Jahr 1993 Obstbrände herstellte und daran die ganze Familie teilhaben ließ. In Erinnerung an Opa Erich und sein Handwerk hatte Tim Andrä die Idee, die alte Destillerie wiederaufzubauen und dort einen Gin zu kreieren, den auch sein Großvater gern getrunken hätte. 2019 schließlich fand der erste Dry Gin den Weg aus der Brennerei in die Flasche. Verwendet werden insgesamt 13 Botanicals, allesamt aus nachhaltigem Anbau.

Ein familiäres Herzensprojekt

Als Grundbrand wird ein milder vierfach gefilterter Neutralalkohol verwendet. Über einen Zeitraum von fünf bis sieben Tagen werden die Botanicals darin mazeriert. Nach dem Filterprozess wird der Gin mit schwäbischem Quellwasser auf Trinkstärke gebracht. Jeder Schritt ist Handarbeit. Selbst die Brennblase wird noch mit Feuer angeheizt. Tim Andrä betont, der Erich Gin sei ein Herzensprojekt der Familie, eine Hommage an Opa Erich, der alle inspirierte. Nicht zuletzt deshalb zeigt das Flaschenetikett, das übrigens zu 100 Prozent aus recyclebarem Graspapier besteht, eine selbst entworfene Zeichnung des Großvaters.

The grandpa who taught how to distill

Erich was a hardworking man, a loving father, a caring grandfather. A Swabian who made fruit spirits in his distillery dating back to 1993 and shared them with the whole family. In memory of Grandpa Erich and his craft, Tim Andrä had the idea of rebuilding the old distillery and creating a gin there that his grandfather would also have loved to drink. Finally, in 2019, the first Dry Gin found its way from the distillery into the bottle. A total of 13 botanicals are used, all from sustainable cultivation.

A family project of the heart

A mild quadruple-filtered neutral alcohol is used as the base spirit. Over a period of five to seven days, the botanicals are macerated in it. After the filtering process, the gin is brought to drinking strength with Swabian spring water. Every step is hand craft. The still is stoked with fire even now. Tim Andrä emphasizes that Erich Gin is a project of the family's heart, a tribute to Grandpa Erich, who inspired them all. Not least for this reason, the bottle label – which, by the way, is made of 100 percent recyclable grass paper – features a drawing of his grandfather that he designed himself.

> " A uniquely refreshing gin as a tribute to grandpa Erich.

CATEGORY
London Dry Gin

ORIGIN
Germany

ESTABLISHED
2019

SIZE
● ● ● ○

TASTING NOTES
Rund und ausgewogen, mit einem souveränen Wacholder-Anteil, florale Aromen sorgen für einen weichen Geschmack, spritzig-frisch dank Kardamom und spanischen Biozitronen, Ingwer und roter Pfeffer verleihen dem Gin eine angenehme Schärfe.

Round and balanced, with a superior juniper content, floral aromas provide a smooth taste, tangy-fresh thanks to cardamom and Spanish organic lemons, ginger and red pepper give the gin a pleasant spiciness.

GIN-WERKSTATT

GIN UNDER CONSTRUCTION

CATEGORY
London Dry Gin

ORIGIN
Germany

ESTABLISHED
2021

SIZE
● ○ ○ ○

TASTING NOTES
Fruchtige-süße Erdbeeren trifft auf die leicht herben Eigenschaften des Basilikums. Elegant ausbalanciert spielen sie mit ihren gegensätzlichen Noten eine ganz eigene Symphonie. Als Basis schmeckt man wunderbar den herben Wacholder, Koriander und im Hintergrund frische Zitrusnoten. Der Gin überzeugt mit komplexer Tiefe und fruchtiger Frische sowie einer soliden kräuterigen Basis.

Fruity-sweet strawberries meets the slightly tart properties of basil. Elegantly balanced, with their contrasting notes they play their very own symphony. As the basis, you taste the tart juniper, coriander and fresh citrus notes in the background, which complete the flavor picture. With complex depth, this gin convinces with fruity freshness and a solid herbal base.

Esslingen at the Neckar, Germany

Manchmal ist der Weg das Ziel.

So kamen Steffi Katzenmaier und Matthias Holzäpfel auf jedem Fall zu ihrem Gin under Construction. Während der London Dry Gin sein gewünschtes Endergebnis erreicht hat, erinnert der Name an den spannenden Weg, den die beiden Gründer gegangen sind. Ebenso symbolisiert er, dass der Weg noch lange nicht zu Ende ist. Während Matthias bei einem privaten Tasting vom Gin-Fieber ergriffen wurde, wuchs Steffi hinter verschiedenen Tresen zur Barkeeperin heran. Beide haben ihre unterschiedlichen Erfahrungen zu einem Projekt vereint und seit 2020 geben sie Brennkurse in ihrer eigenen „Gin-Werkstatt". Ihr Ziel ist es, dem geneigten Genießer die Materie Gin noch näherzubringen, als nur die Nase ins Glas zu halten.

Erdbeere trifft Basilikum

Nach so vielen Kursen und Tastings gab es genug Input, um die brennende Leidenschaft in einem eigenen Produkt zu vereinen. Der Gin under Construction wird im London Dry Gin-Verfahren in kleinen Batches in der Esslinger „Gin-Werkstatt" am Neckar hergestellt. Seine Hauptzutaten sind frische Erdbeeren und Basilikum, die sich auf die klassischen Gin-Zutaten wie Wacholder, Koriander oder Zitronen stützen können. Ziel war es, einen fruchtigen Gin zu kreieren, der in frischen Drinks besticht, aber auch pur überzeugt. Ein harmonisches Zusammenspiel zweier spannender Zutaten, die für uns ein wenig den Sommer symbolisieren, aber im Gin zeigen, was sie wirklich können.

Sometimes the path is the goal.

So it was that Steffi Katzenmaier and Matthias Holzäpfel arrived at their "Gin under Construction". While this London Dry Gin has reached its desired end result, the name is a reminder of the exciting path the two founders took. Likewise, it symbolizes the fact that the journey is far from over. While Matthias was seized by gin fever at a private tasting, Steffi spent time behind various bars developing to become a bartender. Both have combined their different experiences into one project and, since 2020, they have been giving distilling courses in their own "gin workshop". Their goal is to acquaint avid connoisseurs with the matter of gin beyond merely holding their noses to the glass.

Strawberry meets basil

After so many courses and tastings, there was enough input to combine that burning passion into a product of their own. "Gin under Construction" is produced according to the London Dry Gin process in small batches in the Esslingen "Gin Workshop" on the Neckar River. Its main ingredients are fresh strawberries and basil, founded on classic gin ingredients like juniper, coriander and lemons. The goal was to create a fruity gin that is captivating in fresh drinks, but also convincing pure. A harmonious interplay of two exciting ingredients that symbolize summertime somewhat for us, but show what they can really do in gin.

> A perfect gin under construction.

MÄDCHEN&JUNGS DISTILLERS
MÄDCHEN & JUNGS GIN

CATEGORY
London Dry Gin

ORIGIN
Germany

ESTABLISHED
2021

SIZE
● ○ ○ ○

TASTING NOTES
Ein klassischer London Dry Gin mit dominierender Wacholder-Note und spritzigen Anklängen, durch Zitrusfrüchte und eine feinherbe Kaffee-Aromatik unterstrichen, am besten pur ohne Eis oder im Cold Brew mit zwei Espressobohnen genießen.

A classic London Dry Gin with a dominant juniper note and tangy overtones, underlined by citrus fruits and a fine tart coffee aroma, best enjoyed neat without ice or in a cold brew with two espresso beans.

Gin trifft Kaffee

Was mögen Mädchen? Was mögen Jungs? Genussvolle Getränke! Mandy Frey und André Sirocks, Gründer der Marke mädchenundjungskram, haben 2021 den mädchenundjungsgin auf den Markt gebracht. Eine Spirituose, die einen Ausflug in die Welt des mädchenundjungskaffees unternimmt. Im Vordergrund steht die typische Wacholdernote mit unterstützenden Gin-Botanical-Aromen und dem feinen Geschmack der Espressobohne. Der hierbei zugrunde liegende Espresso Strong Organic kommt aus Südamerika und Indien. Dort wurde der aus biologisch gewachsenen Arabica- und Robustabohnen komponierte Espresso im perfekt abgestimmten Mischverhältnis zusammengestellt und geröstet.

Filderstadt, Germany

Ideen leben

Neben Kaffee und Wacholder finden Kardamom, Koriander, Rosenblüten, Lavendel, Bitterorangenschalen, Zitronenschalen und Zimt den Weg in das Destillat. Hergestellt wird der mädchenundjungsgin in der kleinen, feinen Boutique-Brennerei in Gussenstadt auf der schwäbischen Alb von Dr. Klaus Hagmann, der an der Rezeptentwicklung maßgeblich beteiligt war. Der Gin basiert auf hochwertigem, aus Weizen gewonnenem Alkohol. Durch die langsame und mehrfache Destillation in einer klassischen Kupferdestillationsanlage mit Verstärkerkolonne wird eine ganz besondere Reinheit erreicht und die individuelle Note des Gins unterstrichen. Am Ende wird jede Flasche per Hand abgefüllt und etikettiert, anschließend mit einer handgeschriebenen Charge versehen sowie einzeln und von Hand in Wachs getaucht. Für die Gründer ist der mädchenundjungsgin nicht einfach nur ein Gin, sondern die Verwirklichung ihres Mottos: Ideen leben!

Gin meets coffee

What do girls like? What do boys like? Enjoyable drinks! Mandy Frey and André Sirocks, founders of the mädchenundjungskram brand, launched mädchenundjungsgin in 2021. A spirit that takes a trip into the world of their coffee, mädchenundjungskaffee. The focus is on the typical juniper note with supporting gin botanical flavors and the subtle taste of the espresso bean. The underlying espresso strong organic comes from South America and India. There the espresso, composed of organically grown Arabica and Robusta beans, was blended and roasted in a perfectly balanced ratio.

Live your ideas

In addition to coffee and juniper, cardamom, coriander, rose petals, lavender, bitter orange zest, lemon zest and cinnamon find their way into the distillate. Mädchenundjungsgin is produced in the small, fine boutique distillery in Gussenstadt in the Swabian Alb by Dr. Klaus Hagmann, who was instrumental in developing the recipe. The gin is based on high-quality alcohol extracted from wheat. Through slow and multiple distillation in a classic copper still with a rectifying column, a very special purity is achieved and the individual note of the gin is emphasized. At the end, each bottle is filled and labeled by hand, then provided with a handwritten batch and dipped individually by hand in wax. For the founders, mädchenundjungsgin is not just a gin, but the realization of their motto: Live your ideas!

> Our espresso says gin gin.

BLACK FOREST DISTILLERS

MONKEY 47 SCHWARZWALD DRY GIN

Loßburg, Germany

BLACK FOREST DISTILLERS // MONKEY 47 SCHWARZWALD DRY GIN

0,5 L // 47,0 %

> # The monkey tale from the Black Forest.

Zum wilden Affen

Sie waren unter den Ersten: Alexander Stein und Christoph Keller haben dem Gin in Deutschland Auftrieb verschafft – und zwar bereits 2010, als die erste Flasche ihres Monkey 47 den Weg ins Regal fand. Inzwischen gehört das Unternehmen zu den Gin-Imperialisten. Dabei fing alles ganz beschaulich an: 1945 mit der Patenschaft für einen Affen aus dem Berliner Zoo, übernommen von Montgomery Collins. Als Collins im Schwarzwald einen Gasthof eröffnete, nannte er diesen aus Liebe zu seinem tierischen Adoptivkind „Gasthof zum wilden Affen". Jahrzehnte später wurde im Gasthof eine Kiste mit der Aufschrift „Max the Monkey – Schwarzwald Dry Gin" entdeckt. Darin behütet: Das Grundrezept für den Monkey 47.

47 Botanicals für den besonderen Geschmack

Die Zahl im Namen des Gins steht für den Alkoholgehalt in Höhe von 47 % sowie für die Anzahl der 47 Zutaten, davon ein Drittel aus dem Schwarzwald, die dem Getränk zu seinem Geschmack verhelfen. Dabei sind frische Preiselbeeren das Pièce de Résistance. Die Botanicals werden vor der Destillation 36 Stunden mit Basisalkohol und Quellwasser eingelegt und mazeriert. Nach dem Brennvorgang reift der Monkey 47 für drei Monate in Steingutbehältern, bevor er mit Schwarzwälder Quellwasser auf die Trinkstärke von 47 % gebracht wird.

CATEGORY
Dry Gin

ORIGIN
Germany

ESTABLISHED
2008

SIZE
● ● ● ○

TASTING NOTES
Harmonisch komplexer Gin mit klarem Wacholderaroma, frischer Zitrusnote, leichtem Pfefferaroma und subtil bitterer Fruchtnote.

Harmoniously complex gin with clear juniper aroma, fresh citrus note, light pepper aroma and subtly bitter fruit note.

To the wild monkey

They were among the first: Alexander Stein and Christoph Keller gave gin a boost in Germany – back in 2010, when the first bottle of their Monkey 47 found its way onto the shelves. Since then, the company has become one of the gin heavyweights. But it all began quite modestly; in 1945, Montgomery Collins sponsored a monkey from Berlin Zoo. When Collins opened an inn in the Black Forest, he named it "Gasthof zum wilden Affen" [Wild Monkey Inn] out of love for his adopted animal. Decades later, a crate labeled "Max the Monkey – Schwarzwald Dry Gin" was discovered in the inn. Carefully stored away inside was the basic recipe for Monkey 47.

47 botanicals for that special taste

The number in the name of the gin stands for the alcohol content of 47 % as well as for the total of 47 ingredients, one third of which come from the Black Forest, helping to deliver that special taste. Here, fresh cranberries are the pièce de résistance. The botanicals are macerated with base alcohol and spring water for 36 hours before distillation. After the distillation process, Monkey 47 is aged for three months in stoneware containers before being brought to the drinking strength of 47 % with Black Forest spring water.

CATEGORY
London Dry Gin

ORIGIN
Germany

ESTABLISHED
2021

SIZE
● ○ ○ ○

TASTING NOTES
Mediterrane Aromen wie Lavendel, Rosmarin und Zitrone treffen auf selbst gepflückte Kräuter aus dem Schwarzwald, abgerundet wird der Geschmack durch Beeren und Nuancen von Pfeffer.

Mediterranean aromas such as lavender, rosemary and lemon meet self-picked herbs from the Black Forest, the taste being rounded off by berries and nuances of pepper.

HERSTELLPROZESS VON EINEM BATCH CRYPTO-GIN – REALE WELT –

MAZERATION — DESTILLATION — LAGERUNG — ABFÜLLUNG — ETIKETTIERUNG

SPEICHERUNG DES DESTILLATIONSDATUMS AUF DER BLOCKCHAIN

SPEICHERUNG DES ABFÜLLDATUMS AUF DER BLOCKCHAIN

LINK ZWISCHEN „REALER" UND „DIGITALER WELT": QR-CODE AUF RÜCKETIKETT

DIGITALER ZWILLING AUF DER BLOCKCHAIN GESPEICHERT – DIGITALE WELT –

BLOCKCHAIN

CRYPTO-GIN DESTILLERIE
CRYPTO-GIN

Der digitale Zwilling

Zwei Freunde, zwei Leidenschaften – Andreas Krüger und Tom-Oliver Welle trinken nicht nur gern Gin, sondern haben auch ein Faible für Kryptowährungen. Gut, dass sie auf die familieneigene Brennerei zurückgreifen können. Während der Gin dort in traditioneller Handarbeit hergestellt wird, tüfteln die beiden bereits an seinem digitalen Zwilling. Das Produktions- und das Abfülldatum werden als virtuelles Abbild fälschungssicher auf einer Blockchain gespeichert. Aufrufbar sind die Produktionsdaten mittels eines QR-Codes auf der Flasche. Für die Gründer hat diese unverfälschbare Methode einen entscheidenden Vorteil: Jede Flasche ist eindeutig und für den Verbraucher transparent zurückzuverfolgen. Dabei liegt auf der Hand, dass das Unikat der Freunde nur den Namen Crypto-Gin bekommen konnte.

Im Dunkeln ist gut reifen

Mindestens sechs Wochen wird der Gin in Glasballons gelagert, bevor er abgefüllt wird. Hierbei wird das Licht ausgeknipst. Die Lagerung im Dunkeln schützt die empfindlichen Aromen vor schädlichem UV-Licht. Dies ist auch der Grund, weshalb der Crypto-Gin in schwarzen Apothekerflaschen erhältlich ist. Auf dem Crypto-Gin, der 2021 gelauncht wurde und aktuell in kleinen Batches von rund 200 Flaschen abgefüllt wird, steht nicht nur Schwarzwald drauf, es ist auch Schwarzwald drin – und zwar doppelt. Unter den Botanicals finden sich heimische Kräuter, die während des Herstellungsprozesses von weichem Schwarzwälder Quellwasser umschlossen werden.

Bühl im Schwarzwald, Germany

The digital twin

Two friends, two passions – Andreas Krüger and Tom-Oliver Welle not only like to drink gin, but also have a soft spot for crypto-currencies. It's a good thing they can fall back on their family's own distillery. While the gin is produced there traditionally by hand, the two are already tinkering with its digital twin. The production and bottling dates are stored as a virtual image in a tamper-proof block chain. The production data can be accessed via a QR code on the bottle. For the founders, this forgery-proof method has a decisive advantage: each bottle can be unequivocally and clearly traced by the consumer. So obviously the friends' unique product could only be assigned the name Crypto-Gin.

It's good to mature in darkness

The gin is stored in glass carboys for at least six weeks before it is bottled. Here, the light is switched off. Storage in the dark protects the sensitive flavors from harmful UV light. This is also the reason why Crypto-Gin is available in black apothecary bottles. Crypto-Gin, which was launched in 2021 and is currently bottled in small batches of around 200 bottles, not only has the Black Forest on it, there's also Black Forest in it – twice indeed. The botanicals include native herbs that are steeped in soft Black Forest spring water during the production process.

> **Something as authentic and genuine as the Black Forest meets block chain.**

0,5 L // 45,0 %

SALAMANSAR – BRENNEREI AM FEUERGRABEN

DELICIUM GIN

CATEGORY
New Western Dry Gin

ORIGIN
Germany

ESTABLISHED
2021

SIZE
● ○ ○ ○

TASTING NOTES

Wie ein Atemzug aus den Feldern der Provence zum Höhepunkt ihrer Blütezeit. Hier finden sich verschiedene florale Noten zu einer eleganten Komposition zusammen, die von der warmen Sonne und einem angenehmen Luftzug in die Nase getragen werden. Lavendel und andere blumige Noten sind im Geschmack präsent und werden von einer eleganten Fruchtnote aus Orangen und Zitronen getragen. Leicht vermerkt man eine Kräuternote, die dem Gin innewohnt, aber eher als tragender Begleiter im Hintergrund.

Like a breath from the fields of Provence at the height of flowering. Here, various floral notes come together in an elegant composition, carried to the nose by the warm sun and a pleasant breeze. Lavender and other floral notes are present in the taste and are carried by an elegant fruity note of oranges and lemons. There's a gentle hint of a herbal note inherent in the gin, but rather as a supporting companion in the background.

Achern, Germany

Wie Phönix aus der Asche

Der Delicium Gin ist nur einer von vielen Bränden aus der kleinen Edelbrennerei am Feuergraben aus dem lieblichen Schwarzwald. Aus der Region stammen mittlerweile viele gute Gin-Sorten und der Delicium Gin kann sich hier problemlos einordnen. Gegründet wurde die Destillerie 1966 von der Oma Luise. Während hier im kleinen Stil gebrannt wurde, wuchsen über die Jahre hinweg Erfahrung, Portfolio und Gerätschaft an. Heute wird die Brennerei am Feuergraben von Josef Kurz in der 3. Generation weitergeführt und ausgebaut. Klassisch absolvierte er mehrere Ausbildungen und Studiengänge und kombinierte das vergangene Wissen seiner Vorgänger mit den Entwicklungen und Möglichkeiten von heute. Ebenso spannend ist, dass Josef mit der Brennerei einen eigenen Obstgarten und Waldabschnitt besitzt, aus denen er nicht nur Zutaten bezieht, sondern auch Inspiration.

Eine Hommage an die Parfümregion Provence

Der Delicium Gin ist eine Hommage an die Parfümregion Provence und ihre Düfte, die über den dortigen Feldern liegen wie ein sinnlicher Traum. In ihm kommen Eindrücke aus den Wäldern, aber vor allem dem Obstgarten von Josef zur vollen Geltung. Seine Spaziergänge finden Anklang in den verschiedenen Bränden und werden aufwändig von Hand hergestellt. Hierbei spielen der richtige Reifezeitpunkt, eine perfektionierte Maischeführung sowie eine handwerklich und meisterlich geführte Destillation eine besonders große Rolle und Josef hat sie zweifellos verinnerlicht und perfektioniert. Vor allem aber nimmt sich Josef Kurz Zeit für seine Produkte, etwas, das man zweifelsohne in seinen Produkten herausschmeckt.

> Craftsmanship, patience, and time.

Like a phoenix from the ashes

Delicium Gin is just one of many spirits from the small, fine spirit Feuergraben distillery in the delightful Black Forest. Many good gins now come from the region, and Delicium Gin can easily hold its own here. The distillery was founded in 1966 by grandma Luise. As distillation went on here on a small scale, experience, range and equipment grew over the years. Today, the Feuergraben distillery continues to be run and expanded by Josef Kurz, now in the 3rd generation. Classically, he completed several apprenticeships and courses of study, combining the accumulated knowledge of his predecessors with the developments and possibilities of today. Equally exciting is that, along with the distillery, Josef owns an orchard and forest section, from which he draws not only ingredients, but also inspiration.

A tribute to the perfume region

Delicium Gin is a tribute to the perfume region of Provence and its scents, which float above the fields there like a sensual dream. In it, impressions from the forests, but especially from Josef's orchard, come to full fruition. His walks are reflected in the various brandies and are elaborately produced by hand. Here, the right time of ripening, a perfected management of the mash, as well as the handcraft and mastery of distillation, all play particularly important roles, and Josef has undoubtedly internalized and perfected them. Above all, Josef Kurz takes time for his products, without question something that you can taste in his products.

CATEGORY
Distilled Dry Gin

ORIGIN
Germany

ESTABLISHED
2016

SIZE

BIMMERLE PRIVATE DISTILLERY

NEEDLE BLACKFOREST MASTERPIECE

All you need is Needle

Bekanntlich ist es ein Ding der Unmöglichkeit, die Nadel im Heuhaufen zu finden. Doch mit dem Needle Blackforest Masterpiece wird das Unmögliche möglich. Das Masterpiece – bekannt als großer Bruder des klassischen Needle Gin – ist die Nadel im Heuhaufen der Gin-Welt. Ein Gin, in dem sich Qualität, Aromenvielfalt und bester Geschmack vereinen. Dafür sorgen die Brenner der Bimmerle Private Distillery. Um dem Qualitätsanspruch gerecht zu werden, wird der Needle Blackforest Masterpiece auf einer Schwarzwälder Kupferbrennblase im selten angewandten Single-Batch-Verfahren destilliert. Damit wird sichergestellt, dass ein Gin von echter Spitzenklasse entsteht. Und die Macher des Needle Blackforest Masterpiece füllen das pure Schwarzwald-Erlebnis in der Flasche ab.

Schwarzwald in der Flasche

Der würzige Duft des Schwarzwaldes wird im Needle Blackforest Masterpiece perfekt eingefangen – und mischt sich mit den Aromen der harmonischen Botanicals, die für diesen Gin verwendet werden. Die Basis aus handverlesenen Wacholderbeeren wird durch Lavendel und Ingwer bereichert, wodurch der Gin eine blumige und zugleich gewollt leicht scharfe Note erhält. Gewürze wie Zimt und Piment sorgen für einen orientalischen Touch, während Orangen und Zitronen dieses Aromenspektrum um frische Zitrustöne ergänzen. Gekrönt wird diese Vielfalt an Botanicals durch würzig-frische Fichtennadeln, die im Schwarzwald von Hand gepflückt werden und sich deutlich im Geschmack widerspiegeln. Sie sind es, die dem Needle Blackforest Masterpiece seine charakteristische Würze verleihen und zu einem unverfälschten Schwarzwald-Erlebnis machen. Diesen Gin genießt man am besten pur – so können sich die vielfältigen Aromen des Schwarzwaldes in ihrer ganzen Intensität entfalten.

Achern, Germany

TASTING NOTES

In die vorherrschende Präsenz von Wacholder mischt sich eine bunte Vielfalt von Botanicals. Handgepflückte Fichtennadeln sorgen für kräftige Würze, eine fruchtige Note durch Orangen- und Zitronenschalen, dazu Piment, Koriander, Zimt, Ingwer und floraler Geschmack von Lavendel.

The predominant presence of juniper is mixed with a colorful variety of botanicals. Hand-picked spruce needles provide strong spice, a fruity note from orange and lemon peel, plus allspice, coriander, cinnamon, ginger and floral flavor of lavender.

> **Hand-picked Black Forest spruce needles make Needle Blackforest Masterpiece an inimitable Black Forest experience.**

All you need is Needle

Everyone knows it's impossible to find a needle in a haystack. But, with Needle Blackforest Masterpiece, the impossible becomes possible. The Masterpiece – known as the classic Needle Gin's big brother – can be seen as the needle in the haystack of the gin world. A gin that combines quality, aromatic diversity and the best taste. This is ensured by the distillers of the Bimmerle Private Distillery.

To achieve the required quality, Needle Blackforest Masterpiece is distilled in a Black Forest copper still in the rarely used single-batch process. This ensures that a gin of true excellence is created, and the makers of Needle Blackforest Masterpiece capture a pure Black Forest experience in the bottle.

Black Forest in the bottle

The aromatic scent of the Black Forest is perfectly captured in Needle Blackforest Masterpiece – blending with the flavors of the harmonious botanicals used in this gin. The base of hand-picked juniper berries is enriched by lavender and ginger, giving the gin a floral and slightly spicy note. Spices such as cinnamon and allspice provide an oriental touch, while oranges and lemons add fresh citrus tones to this spectrum of flavors. This variety of botanicals is crowned by aromatically fresh spruce needles, which are hand-picked in the Black Forest and give the gin its unique taste. They are what give Needle Blackforest Masterpiece its characteristic aroma and make it an unadulterated Black Forest experience. This gin is best enjoyed neat – allowing the diverse flavors of the Black Forest to unfold in all their intensity.

> "Because you can also distill homeland.

CATEGORY
New Western Dry Gin

ORIGIN
Germany

ESTABLISHED
2018

SIZE
● ○ ○ ○

TASTING NOTES
Komplex und vielschichtig, würzig-herb und nussig, kräuterig und floral mit Duftrosen und weißer Schafgarbe, dazu die Frische von Pfefferminze und ein Hauch von Schwarzwälder Kirsche.

Complex and multilayered, spicy-tart and nutty, herbal and floral with fragrant roses and white yarrow, plus the freshness of peppermint and a hint of Black Forest cherry.

ROSENHOF WEISS

WEISSBART GIN

Offenburg, Germany

Zu Hause ist's auch ganz schön

Wenn Heimat kein Ort ist, sondern ein wärmendes, vertrautes Gefühl. Für jeden anders, aber immer herzlich und willkommen heißend. Wie schmeckt denn dann diese Heimat? Diese Frage haben sich Ulf Tietge und Stephan Fuhrer, die Macher des Weissbart Gins vom team tietge in Offenburg, gestellt und ihre Heimat, den Schwarzwald, in Flaschen gegossen – nicht so, wie er auf den ersten Blick in touristischen Broschüren erscheint, sondern so, wie sie ihn sehen: reich an Wacholder und Zibärtle, Schafgarbe, Rose, Haselnuss, Pfefferminze, Kirsche und mit einer Handvoll Hopfen – vollgepackt mit all den Essenzen der Region. Aus Baden. Vom Kaiserstuhl. Vollgepackt mit Heimat.

Überall sind weiße Bärte

Gebrannt wird in der Rosenhof-Destillerie von Marcel Weiß in dessen kleiner kupferner Brennblase. Er ist auch einer der Namensgeber für den Gin – zumindest ist er ein Plus in der Gleichung. Zunächst tragen nämlich die Gründer Bärte, keine übermäßig langen, aber immerhin Bärte. Und einer der Hauptbestandteile des Gins, das Zibärtle, trägt einen Bart im Namen. Das Weiß liefern die Blüten der Schafgarbe sowie der Nachname des Brennmeisters. In der Summe ist dieser Gin also ein Weissbart. Wie passend, dass den Jungs dann auch noch zufällig ein Schwarzwald-Rocker mit Weihnachtsmann-Vollbart auf der Suche nach dem Gin des Lebens über den Weg lief, der prompt das Etikett des edlen Tropfens schmücken durfte.

It's nice at home too

When home is not a place, but a warming, familiar feeling. Different for everyone, but always warm and welcoming. What then does this home taste like? This is the question that Ulf Tietge and Stephan Fuhrer, the makers of Weissbart Gin from team tietge in Offenburg, asked themselves, and then poured their homeland, the Black Forest, into bottles – not as it appears at first glance in tourist brochures, but as they see it: rich in juniper and zibarte plum, yarrow, rose, hazelnut, peppermint, cherry and with a handful of hops – packed with all the essences of the region. From Baden. From the Kaiserstuhl. Packed with homeland.

White beards everywhere

It's distilled in Marcel Weiß's Rosenhof distillery in his small copper still. He is also one of the namesakes for the gin – at least he is a plus in the equation. Additionally, the founders wear beards, not excessively long ones, but beards nonetheless, and one of the gin's main ingredients, "Zibärtle" plum, has a beard (German 'Bart') in its name. The white (German 'Weiß') is provided by the flowers of the yarrow and the surname of the master distiller. In sum, then, this gin translates as "white beard". How fitting that the guys then also happened to run into a Black Forest rocker with a full Santa Claus beard in search of the ideal gin, who was promptly invited to adorn the label of the noble spirit.

MARKUS WURTH EDELBRENNEREI

LIQUID EMOTIONS & LEVIATHAN GIN

CATEGORY
Dry Gin

ORIGIN
Germany

ESTABLISHED
1919, takeover Markus Wurth 1995

SIZE

TASTING NOTES
Ausgewogenes Aromenspektrum; für jeden etwas dabei, von typisch Wacholder über pfeffrig-würzig bis zu frischen, fruchtigen Zitrusnoten.

Balanced aroma spectrum, something for everyone, from typical juniper on through peppery-spicy to fresh, fruity citrus notes.

Pimp your Gin Tonic

Mitten im Corona-Lockdown hat der Edelbrenner Markus Wurth eine Idee: Wie wäre es mit Extrakten? Gemeinhin als Wundermittel der Natur beschrieben, können sie auch in der Küche oder in der Bar vielseitig genutzt werden. Sei es für atemberaubende Gin Tonics, intensive Aromen oder verfeinerte Gerichte. Oder wie wäre es mit einem alkoholfreien Gin Tonic?

Mit Extrakten die Geschmackssinne verzaubern

Die Idee wurde mit hochwertigsten Zutaten umgesetzt. Mit wenigen Sprühstößen finden sich die Aromen der fünf verschiedenen Extrakte-Linien von Liquid Emotions im Glas oder auf dem Teller. Die „Dark Spirits" sind mit dunklen Aromen wie Wacholder genau das Richtige für extravagante Geschmackserlebnisse. Die „Black Forest Spirits" verzaubern die Geschmackssinne mit Aromen von wilden Beeren. Bei den „Citrus Spirits" ist mit der Hand Buddhas eine Rarität unter den Zitrusfrüchten vertreten. Die „Herbal Spirits" trumpfen mit der australischen Lemonmyrte auf. Geschmacklich in den Süden geht es mit den „Special Spirits". Sie erinnern an einen warmen Sommerabend mit Freunden.

Auf Entdeckungsreise mit Extrakten und Gin

Nicht nur mit den Extrakten begibt man sich auf eine Entdeckungsreise, sondern auch mit dem Leviathan Gin. Das Zusammenspiel von 37 Botanicals macht diesen Gin unverwechselbar. Ein kleiner Auszug gefällig? Wilder Urwaldpfeffer aus Madagaskar sowie drei weitere Pfeffersorten, Ceylon-Zimt, Ingwer, Kardamom, Piment, Nelken, Wacholderbeeren, Kaffirlimette, mehrere Zitrusfrüchte wie Buddhas Hand oder Lavendelblüten sowie Zitronenverbene. Pur getrunken wie einen edlen Obstbrand trinkt man sich durch Zeiten und Kontinente, auch im Mixgetränk ist er ein Genuss.

Pimp your gin tonic

In the midst of Corona lockdown, fine distiller Markus Wurth has an idea: how about extracts? Commonly described as nature's miracle cure, they can also be used in a variety of ways in the kitchen or bar. Be it for stunning gin and tonic creations, intense flavors or refined dishes. Or how about an alcohol-free gin and tonic?

Enchanting the taste buds with extracts

The idea was implemented with the highest quality ingredients. With just a few sprays, the flavors of Liquid Emotions' five different extract lines can be applied to the glass or plate. "Dark Spirits" are just right for extravagant taste experiences with dark flavors like juniper. "Black Forest Spirits" enchant the taste buds with aromas of wild berries. "Citrus Spirits" include the Buddha's Hand, a rarity among citrus fruits. "Herbal Spirits" come up trumps with Australian lemon myrtle. "Special Spirits" take the taste to the south, being reminiscent of a warm summer evening with friends.

On a voyage of discovery with extracts and gin

Not only with the extracts do you embark on a voyage of discovery, but also with Leviathan Gin. The interplay of 37 botanicals makes this gin unmistakable. A small excerpt perhaps? Wild jungle pepper from Madagascar as well as three other types of pepper, Ceylon cinnamon, ginger, cardamom, allspice, cloves, juniper berries, kaffir lime, several citrus fruits such as Buddha's hand along with lavender flowers and lemon verbena. Drunk neat like a fine fruit spirit, enjoy a trip through times and continents, but also a delight in mixed drinks.

> Pure emotions.

Neuried, Germany

0,7 L // 44,0 %

BUCHHOLZENHOF

GIN FICHTE | ZITRONE

Klar. Fokussiert. Reduziert.

Der ökologisch bewirtschaftete Buchholzenhof, der bereits in 13. Generation betrieben wird, ist im malerischen Bärenbach in Mühlenbach zu Hause. Dieses idyllische kleine Tal liegt mitten im Schwarzwald – und ist umgeben von saftig-grünen Wiesen und dichten Wäldern. Neben der eigenen Forstwirtschaft betreibt der Familienbetrieb eine eigene kleine Hof-Brennerei. Seit jeher beruft man sich hier auf die gleichen Werte. So auch Inhaber Augustin Schmider, der die Brennerei mit Leidenschaft betreibt. Das Motto lautet: „Klar. Fokussiert. Reduziert." Man besinnt sich auf das Wesentliche. Die Zutaten werden mit Bedacht ausgewählt und dann sorgfältig destilliert. Die Verwendung regionaler Botanicals und die Heimatverbundenheit sind genauso Grundsätze der Brennerei wie höchste Qualität und ein nachhaltiger Umgang mit der Natur.

Heimatgefühl in der Flasche

Der GIN FICHTE | ZITRONE bringt den Geschmack einfach auf den Punkt. Es werden fünf ausgewählte Botanicals verwendet: Neben der klassischen Wacholderbeere spielen vor allem Fichtensprossen und Zitrone eine wichtige Rolle. Durch den Fokus auf einige wenige Zutaten kann man jedes einzelne Aroma intensiv wahrnehmen. Die Fichtensprossen werden im eigenen Fichtenwald nahe der Brennerei handgepflückt und bilden so die Grundlage für einen Gin, der echtes Heimatgefühl in Flaschen abfüllt. Das frische, belebende Zitrusaroma sonnengeküsster Zitronen ist eine perfekte Ergänzung der herb-würzigen Fichte. GIN FICHTE | ZITRONE ist der perfekte Gin für Liebhaber – und all jene, die es noch werden wollen. Ein spritzig-frischer Gin, der den Geist belebt und die Seele durchatmen lässt.

> **Hand-picked spruce shoots from the local forest meet an invigorating citrus note from sun-kissed lemons.**

Clear. Focused. Reduced.

The ecologically managed Buchholzenhof farm, now in its 13th generation, nestles in picturesque Bärenbach in Mühlenbach. This idyllic little valley lies in the middle of the Black Forest – and is surrounded by lush green meadows and dense forests. In addition to its own forestry operations, the family business also runs its own small farm distillery. The same values have always been invoked here, continued by owner Augustin Schmider, who runs the distillery with passion. The motto is: "Clear. Focused. Reduced." The focus is on the essentials. The ingredients are carefully selected and then carefully distilled. The use of regional botanicals and a close connection to the local area are just as much principles of the distillery as the highest quality and sustainable dealings with nature.

Home feeling in the bottle

GIN FICHTE | ZITRONE simply has taste at its heart. Five selected botanicals are used: In addition to the classic juniper berry, spruce shoots and lemon play important roles. By focusing on just a few ingredients, you can perceive every single aroma intensively. The spruce shoots are hand-picked in the distillery's own spruce forest near the distillery and thus form the basis for a gin that bottles genuine homeland feeling. The fresh, invigorating citrus aroma of sun-kissed lemons is a perfect complement to the tart, spicy spruce. GIN FICHTE I ZITRONE is the perfect gin for connoisseurs – and all with the wish to become one. A tangy, fresh gin that invigorates your spirit and lets your soul breathe deeply.

CATEGORY
Dry Gin

ORIGIN
Germany

ESTABLISHED
2019

SIZE
● ● ○ ○

TASTING NOTES
Die Wacholdernote ist sehr ausgewogen, dazu kommen sanfte Nuancen von Zitrone und Fichtensprossen.

The juniper note is very well balanced, accompanied by gentle nuances of lemon and spruce shoots.

Mühlenbach, Germany

0,5 L // 42,0 %

MUNDART DESTILLERIE

MUNDART – KAISERSTUHL DRY GIN

CATEGORY
Dry Gin

ORIGIN
Germany

ESTABLISHED
2015

SIZE
● ● ● ●

TASTING NOTES
Ein Schluck – und der Gin verteilt sich mild und ölig auf der Zunge. Geschmacklich tun sich vor allem die dezente Wacholdernote und die frischen Zitrus- und Orangenaromen hervor.

One sip – and the gin spreads as a mild, pleasantly oily texture on the tongue. On the palate, the subtle juniper note and the fresh citrus and orange aromas stand out.

> A small distillery creates a gin with flavorful greatness.

Die ehrliche Destillerie vom Kaiserstuhl

Ein Gin aus DER Genussregion in Deutschland – das spricht schon für sich. Die MUNDART Destillerie liegt im Herzen des malerischen Kaiserstuhls. In dieser Idylle, umgeben von der endlosen Weite der wunderschönen Weinberge, entsteht der MUNDART – KAISERSTUHL DRY GIN. Man destilliert mit dem Erfahrungsschatz, der noch vom Großvater Franz mitgegeben wurde. Schon er brannte für das und nach dem Motto: einfach, bodenständig und mit Liebe zum Detail. Er prägte außerdem die Verbundenheit mit der Region und die Wertschätzung für die Natur und ihre Rohstoffe. Diese besondere Form der Verbundenheit und Wertschätzung lebt in der Familie bis heute fort. Um dem Ausdruck zu verleihen, wird das gebrannt, was direkt vor der eigenen Haustür wächst – oder auf

den Feldern der Landwirte aus der Region. Im MUNDART – KAISERSTUHL DRY GIN vereinen sich insgesamt 17 Botanicals, unter anderem Wacholder, Anis, Koriander sowie Orangen- und Zitronenschalen für eine fruchtig-frische Note.

Liebe und Sorgfalt, die man schmecken kann

Guter Geschmack und beste Qualität sind keine Frage von Größe. Die MUNDART Destillerie ist dafür das beste Beispiel, denn sie ist eine der kleinsten ihrer Art. Doch das hält diese kleine Destillerie nicht davon ab, einen Gin zu produzieren, der geschmacklich ganz groß ist. Die Verwendung regionaler Zutaten, die echte Handarbeit und die nachhaltige Produktion machen den MUNDART – KAISERSTUHL DRY GIN zu dem, was er ist: zu einem echten Qualitätsprodukt, das ausnahmslos begeistert.

The honest distillery from the Kaiserstuhl

A gin from THE region of delights in Germany – that speaks for itself. The MUNDART distillery is located in the heart of the picturesque Kaiserstuhl hills. It is in this idyll, surrounded by the endless expanse of beautiful vineyards, that MUNDART – KAISERSTUHL DRY GIN is created. Distillation based on a wealth of experience, passed on by grandfather Franz, who worked with spirited passion back then according to the motto "simple, down-to-earth and with a love for detail". He also helped to define the gin's attachment to the region, accompanied by an appreciation of nature and its raw materials. This special form of attachment and appreciation lives on in the family to this day. To express this, they distill what grows right on their own doorstep – or in farmers' fields in the region. MUNDART – KAISERSTUHL DRY GIN combines a total of 17 botanicals, including juniper, aniseed, coriander and orange and lemon zest for a fruity-fresh note.

Love and care that you can taste

Good taste and best quality are not a question of scale. The MUNDART distillery is the best example of this, as it is one of the smallest of its kind. But that doesn't stop this small distillery from producing a gin that is big on taste. The use of regional ingredients, genuine working by hand and sustainable production make MUNDART – KAISERSTUHL DRY GIN what it is: a real quality product that inspires without exception.

Vogtsburg im Kaiserstuhl, Germany

WEINGUT RINKLINS
GEISTIGES AUS DER BRENNEREI

GINKLIN

Ginklin aus dem Hause Rinklin

Das idyllische Eichstetten befindet sich im sonnigen Weinbaugebiet östlich des Kaiserstuhls in Baden-Württemberg. Hier liegt auch das Weingut Rinklin. Der historische Hof mit alter Tradition entstand bereits im Jahre 1713. Die Initialen auf dem „Schwibbogen" – eine Rundbogen-Torart – weisen noch heute darauf hin. Hier bauten bereits ab 1955 Lydia und Wilhelm Rinklin auf dem fruchtbaren Boden Trauben, Obst und Gemüse an. Somit gehört der Betrieb zu den Gründungsbetrieben des Bioanbaus in Deutschland. Inzwischen ist Friedhelm Rinklin Chef des Hauses.

Feinster Muskatellerbrand aus eigener Herstellung

Doch hier werden nicht nur ökologische Weine hergestellt: Der GINklin ist eine weitere Spezialität des Hauses, die sich bereits durch die Zubereitung von anderen Destillaten unterscheidet. Denn für diesen Winzer-Gin wird kein Neutralalkohol verwendet, sondern ausschließlich Muskatellerbrand aus der eigenen Brennerei. Außerdem wird alles handgemacht und über dem Holzfeuer gebrannt. Für den GINklin werden nur feinste Trester der Eichstetter Muskateller-Trauben selektiert, übrigens eine der ältesten Weißweinsorten. Diese geben dem Brand seinen unvergleichlich floralen Duft und zarten Geschmack. Verfeinert mit klassischen Gin-Botanicals wie Koriander und Wacholder, natürlich aus biologischem Anbau, vereinen sich blütiges Aroma und subtile Würze. So entsteht ein Gin, der perfekt geeignet für Cocktails, aber auch pur ein Hochgenuss ist. Geschmacklich mit Nuancen von Wacholder, Citrus und natürlich Muskateller. Unbedingt mit Gurke zu genießen, empfehlen die Hersteller.

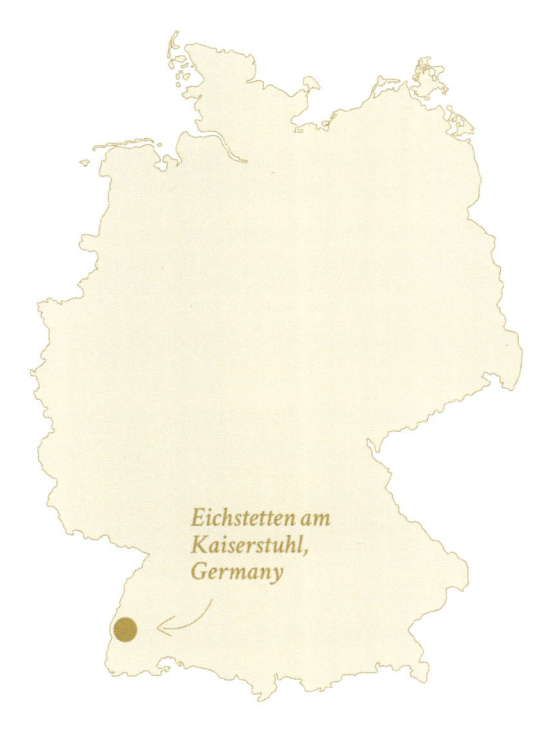

Eichstetten am Kaiserstuhl, Germany

Ginklin from the house of Rinklin

The idyllic town of Eichstetten is located in the sunny wine-growing region east of the Kaiserstuhl in Baden-Württemberg. The Rinklin winery is also located here. The historic farm, steeped in tradition, was established back in 1713. The initials on the "Schwibbogen" – a type of round arch gate – still display this today. Lydia and Wilhelm Rinklin started cultivating grapes, fruit and vegetables on the fertile soil in 1955. Thus the farm became one of the founding farms of organic cultivation in Germany. Now, Friedhelm Rinklin has become head of the house.

Finest muscatel brandy from our own production

It isn't only ecological wines that are produced here. GINklin is another specialty of the house, which differs from other distillates due to its preparation, in that no neutral alcohol is used for this vintner's gin, but only muscatel brandy from the company's own distillery. In addition, everything is handmade and distilled over a wood fire. For GINklin, only the finest marc from the Eichstetter Muskateller grapes are selected, incidentally one of the oldest white wine varieties. These give the brandy its incomparable floral fragrance and delicate taste. Refining with classic gin botanicals such as coriander and juniper, organically cultivated of course, combines a floral aroma with subtle spiciness. The result is a gin that's perfectly suited for cocktails, but also a delight neat. Flavorful with nuances of juniper, citrus and, of course, muscatel. Be sure to enjoy with cucumber, recommend the producers.

> Gin made from the oldest white wine species.

CATEGORY
Dry Gin

ORIGIN
Germany

ESTABLISHED
2021

SIZE
● ○ ○ ○

TASTING NOTES
Blütiges Aroma mit subtiler Würze durch die Kombination von Muskatellertrauben mit klassischen Botanicals wie Koriander und Wacholder.

Floral aroma with subtle spice from the combination of muscat grapes with classic botanicals like coriander and juniper.

LONGITUDE GIN GBR

LONGITUDE LONDON DRY GIN

CATEGORY
London Dry Gin

ORIGIN
Germany

ESTABLISHED
2015

SIZE
● ○ ○

TASTING NOTES
Zu der klassischen Wacholdernote gesellt sich ein intensiv fruchtiger Körper: Pink Grapefruit, Granatapfel, australische Zitronenmyrte und ein intensives Aroma von Tasmanischen Pfefferbeeren.

The classic juniper note is partnered by an intense fruity body: pink grapefruit, pomegranate, Australian lemon myrtle and an intense aroma of Tasmanian pepper berries.

Weil am Rhein, Germany

A bond of friendship

Stefan und Pete verbindet eine jahrelange Freundschaft. Warum diese nicht mit einem gemeinsam entwickelten Gin begießen? Die Voraussetzungen könnten nicht besser sein: Die beiden verfügen bereits über eine kleine Kupferdestille und Stefan hat durch die Produktion seiner eigenen Obstbrände schon über viele Jahre hinweg Erfahrung im Brennen gesammelt. Das Ganze ist von Anfang an ein Herzensprojekt. Die Idee der beiden ist es, einen Gin für ihre Freunde und ihre Familie zu kreieren. Ein guter Tropfen nur für die Liebsten – ausschließlich mit Zutaten von bester Qualität. Diese sorgen – in Kombination mit der Handarbeit und der sorgfältigen Destillation in einer Kupferbrennblase – für den herausragenden Geschmack des Longitude London Dry Gin.

Aromen aus Australien

Als Inspirationsquelle dient den beiden Gin-Brüdern eine Reise nach Australien. Beim Besuch ihrer australischen Freunde sitzen sie beim gemeinsamen Abendessen zusammen und der Küchenchef lässt Stefan und Pete Früchte und Gewürze des Landes probieren. Sofort ist klar, dass diese Aromen zukünftig den Charakter des Longitude Gin prägen sollen. Doch nicht nur der Geschmack des Gins ist auf der gemeinsamen Reise geboren. Während ihres Aufenthalts übernachten die beiden Freunde in einem Hotel namens Longitude. Longitude London Dry Gin ist eine Hommage an die Freundschaft und soll all jene miteinander verbinden, die auf den verschiedenen Längen- und Breitengraden dieser Welt verteilt sind. So lädt jede Flasche Longitude dazu ein, an all die besonderen Menschen zu denken, die im Herzen immer nah sind, so weit entfernt sie auch sein mögen. Lasst uns gemeinsam das Glas erheben: Auf die Freundschaft!

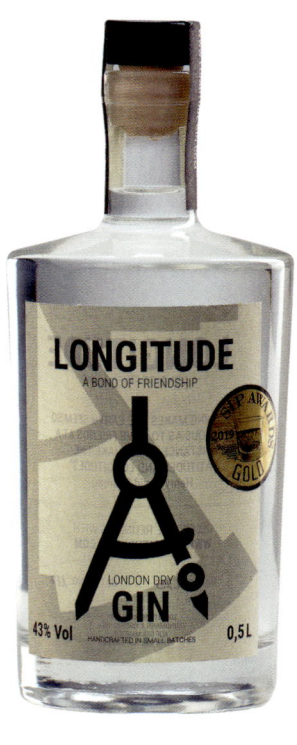

A bond of friendship

Stefan and Pete have been friends for years. So why not celebrate this with a jointly developed gin? The prerequisite conditions couldn't be better: they already have a small copper still and Stefan has already gained many years' experience in distilling by producing his own fruit spirits. The whole thing has been a work of love from the very beginning. Their shared idea was to create a gin for their friends and family. A great drink just for their loved ones – using only ingredients of the very best quality. These, in combination with skilled handwork and careful distillation in a copper still, ensure the outstanding taste of Longitude London Dry Gin.

Flavors from Australia

It was a trip to Australia that served as inspiration for the two gin-buddies. During a visit to their Australian friends, as they sat together at dinner, the chef let Stefan and Pete taste the fruits and spices of the country. Immediately it was clear that these flavors were to shape the character of Longitude Gin. But it wasn't just the gin's taste that was born on their journey together. During their stay, the two friends stayed at a hotel called Longitude. Longitude London Dry Gin is a tribute to friendship, with the intention of connecting all who are spread across the different longitudes and latitudes of this world. Thus, each bottle of Longitude invites us to think of all those special people who are always close to our hearts, however far away they may be. Let's raise a glass together: to friendship!

> Nothing makes the earth seem so spacious as to have friends at a distance; they make the latitudes and longitudes.
> – Henry David Thoreau

FLORIAN GOROLL

RED BEARD GIN

Das Allgäu im Geiste

Saftig-grüne Wiesen, ein weiter Blick auf die Gipfel der Alpen und die Ursprünglichkeit des Allgäus – dazu ein Getränk in der Hand, das eben diese Region widerspiegelt. Das macht den Red Beard London Dry Gin aus. Destillateur Florian Goroll widmet seinen Gin all jenen, die das Allgäu lieben und welche die große Gin-Tradition schätzen. Der Red Beard Gin steht für erstklassige Qualität und Reinheit, die sich wie ein roter Faden durch die Herstellung dieses außergewöhnlichen Erzeugnisses zieht. Das beginnt mit der sorgfältigen Auswahl der hochwertigen Botanicals und zieht sich hin bis zur äußerst schonenden Destillation. Destilliert wird nämlich ganz ursprünglich in alter Handwerkstradition und in kleinen Chargen.

Wie die Reinheit einer Bergquelle

So entsteht in einer Kupferblase ein exzellenter Gin, der wirklich seinesgleichen sucht. Er entsteht so rein wie eine Bergquelle des Allgäus. Durch das Allgäu inspiriert, werden 24 erlesene Kräuter, Blüten und Beeren zur perfekten Symbiose miteinander vereint. Und wo wir schon beim roten Faden waren: Name und Design der Flasche des Red Beard Gin gehen auf den Destillateur Florian Goroll zurück, der mit seinem roten Bart unverwechselbar ist. Sein Gin verwöhnt den Genießer mit seinem vollmundigen Geschmack. Unterstrichen wird er durch ein blumiges und fruchtiges Wesen. Neben dem Red Beard Gin kann die Brennerei – die übrigens auch besucht werden kann – auch mit zwei weiteren spannenden Sorten aufwarten: dem SimsalaGin sowie RevoluGin. Darauf ein „Cheers, Allgäu im Geiste!"

Urlau in Allgäu, Germany

The Allgäu in spirit

Lush green meadows, a panoramic view of the peaks of the Alps and the originality of the Allgäu area – plus a drink in your hand that reflects this very region. That's what makes Red Beard London Dry Gin. Distiller Florian Goroll dedicates his gin to all those who love the Allgäu and who appreciate the great gin tradition. Red Beard Gin stands for first-class quality and purity, running like a red thread through the production of this exceptional product. This begins with the careful selection of high-quality botanicals and extends to the extremely gentle distillation. It's distilled altogether in the old craft tradition and in small batches.

Like the purity of a mountain spring

This way, created in a copper vessel is an excellent gin, truly without compare. It arises as pure as a mountain spring of the Allgäu. Inspired by the Allgäu, 24 exquisite herbs, flowers and berries are combined to form the perfect symbiosis. And while we were on the subject of that common red thread: The name and design of the bottle of Red Beard Gin go back to the distiller, Florian Goroll, who is unmistakable with his red beard. His gin indulges the connoisseur with its full-bodied taste. It's underlined by a floral and fruity nature. The distillery – which by the way can also be visited – has produced also another couple of interesting gins: the SimsalaGin as also the RevoluGin. Here's to "Cheers, Allgäu in spirit!"

„

Cheers, Allgäu in spirit!

CATEGORY
London Dry Gin

ORIGIN
Germany

ESTABLISHED
2019

SIZE
● ● ● ●

TASTING NOTES
Vollmundiger Geschmack, die Kräuter dominieren, dann blumig und fruchtig.

Moderate, subtle, classic and elegant, fruity, fine citrus notes, distinctive spicy juniper flavor, subtle finish.

FLORIAN GOROLL // RED BEARD GIN

0,5 L // 44,0 %

GIN

UNITED BOS DEUTSCHLAND GMBH & CO. KG

BERNSTEIN BROTHERS PROHIBITED DRY GIN

Damals verboten, heute ein Klassiker

Detroit in den 1920er-Jahren: Abe Bernstein und seine Brüder, bekannt als die Purple Gang, versetzen die USA in Aufruhr. Während der Alkoholprohibition schmuggeln sie schwarzgebrannte Spirituosen von Kanada über den Detroit River in die USA. Das Vorgehen der Bande ist rücksichtslos, kaltblütig und originell. Kriminelle wie der berüchtigte Boss der Chicagoer Unterwelt, Al Capone, gehören zu den Vertrauten der Brüder. Illegal gebrannt wurde in dieser Zeit mit allen Mitteln, die zur Verfügung standen. In Anlehnung daran konzentriert sich dieser Gin auf das Wesentliche, insbesondere im Geschmack. Er überzeugt durch Klarheit, durch seine vornehme Zurückhaltung und hält die Balance zwischen Frische und Aroma. Eine klassische Spirituose, die im Schwarzwald gebrannt, aber längst nicht als Schmuggelware gehandelt wird.

> **The Gin Al Capone would have loved!**

Ein elegantes Erbe

Die Rezeptur des Bernstein Brothers Prohibited Dry Gin folgt einer klaren, ausbalancierten Linie, als Gin in seiner reinsten Form, vornehm zurückhaltend, bestehend aus Zitrusfrüchten und Wacholder, ergänzt durch weiches, mineralhaltiges Wasser aus dem Schwarzwald. Passend zu diesem klassischen Dry Gin ist auch die Anmutung des Flaschendesigns im Stil der Goldenen Zwanziger gewählt, auf dessen rückseitigem Etikett die Schmuggler-Route der Bernstein Brüder abgebildet ist. Mit dem Bernstein Brothers Prohibited Dry Gin landen die gleichnamigen Geschwister also auch noch in der heutigen Zeit einen großen Coup.

Prohibited then, a classic today

Detroit in the 1920s: Abe Bernstein and his brothers, known as the Purple Gang, put the USA in turmoil. During alcohol prohibition, they smuggled moonshine from Canada across the Detroit River into the USA. The gang's actions were ruthless, cold-blooded and original. Criminals like the notorious boss of the Chicago underworld, Al Capone, were among the brothers' confidants. Illegal distilling was done in this period with whatever means at hand. As a consequence, this gin focuses on the essentials, especially regarding taste. Convincing by virtue of its clarity, its distinguished restraint and the balance it achieves between freshness and aroma. A classic spirit, distilled in the Black Forest, but far from being contraband.

An elegant heritage

The recipe of Bernstein Brothers Prohibited Dry Gin follows a clear, balanced line, as a gin in its purest form, finely restrained, consisting of citrus and juniper, complemented by soft, mineral-rich water from the Black Forest. In keeping with this classic Dry Gin, the look of the bottle design is also chosen in the style of the roaring twenties, with the Bernstein Brothers' smuggler's route depicted on the back label. With Bernstein Brothers Prohibited Dry Gin, the eponymous siblings have thus made hit even in modern times.

Aschaffenburg, Germany

CATEGORY
Dry Gin

ORIGIN
Germany

ESTABLISHED
2006

SIZE

TASTING NOTES
Maßvoll, subtil, klassisch und elegant, fruchtig, feine Zitrusnoten, markant würziger Wacholder-Geschmack, dezent im Abgang.

Moderate, subtle, classic and elegant, fruity, fine citrus notes, distinctive spicy juniper flavor, subtle finish.

KULTUR.GUT DESTILLERIE

KULTUR.GUT LONDON DRY GIN

Aura im Sinngrund, Germany

Aromatische Früchtchen

Magdalena Jeckel ist an einem Sehnsuchtsort für Genießer aufgewachsen. Seit mehr als zehn Jahren führt sie gemeinsam mit ihrer Familie ein Hofgut in Aura im Sinngrund – den Spessarthof, ein Idyll inmitten einer waldreichen, hügeligen Landschaft im Herzen Deutschlands. Teil des Hofes ist von Anfang an eine Schaubrennerei von Arnold Holstein, in der unter anderem die aromatischen Früchte der örtlichen Streuobstwiesen veredelt werden. Magdalena Jeckel entschied sich schon früh für den Einstieg in den elterlichen Betrieb: Mit gerade einmal 24 Jahren schloss sie eine Brennerausbildung an der Bayerischen Landesanstalt für Weinbau und Gartenbau ab. Mit ihrem ersten Produkt KULTUR.GUT teilt die junge Brennerin ein Stück ihrer einzigartigen Heimat und liefert damit umfangreiche Einblicke in das Brennerhandwerk.

Ein Naturprodukt als KULTUR.GUT

KULTUR.GUT verbindet etwas, das als kultureller Wert Bestand hat und bewahrt wird. Etwas, das vielfältig und besonders ist. Im Mittelpunkt steht der London Dry Gin als zeitloser, ausdauernder und prägender Klassiker, persönlich und vor allem nachhaltig kreiert. Die Grundlage bilden die Botanicals aus eigenem Anbau: Zitrusfrüchte aus der Tannenspitze, Beeren wie Himbeeren und Brombeeren, reife Äpfel und Schokominze. Für ihre neu gegründete Spirituosenlinie hat Magdalena Jeckel bereits das passende Setting konstruiert: getrunken in einer lauen Sommernacht, begleitet von guten Gesprächen mit Freunden und leckerem Essen. Ihr Gin wird zum Bestandteil eines unvergesslichen Abends, zum Hauptdarsteller eines Moments, den alle Anwesenden für immer bewahren wollen – er wird zum KULTUR.GUT.

> *As sparkling, carefree and light as an unforgettable summer evening.*

Aromatic fruitlets

Magdalena Jeckel grew up in a place gourmets long for. For more than ten years, she and her family have been running a farmstead in Aura im Sinngrund – the Spessarthof, an idyll in the middle of a wooded, hilly landscape in the heart of Germany. From the very beginning, part of the farm has been a show distillery run by Arnold Holstein where, among other things, the aromatic fruits of the local orchards are distilled. Magdalena Jeckel decided to join her parents' farm at an early age. At just 24, she completed a distiller's apprenticeship at the Bavarian State Institute for Viticulture and Horticulture. With her first product KULTUR.GUT, the young distiller shared a piece of her unique homeland and thus provided comprehensive insights into the craft of distilling.

A natural product – KULTUR.GUT

KULTUR.GUT connects with something that endures and is preserved as cultural heritage. Something that is diverse and special. At the center is this London Dry Gin as a timeless, enduring and characteristic classic, personally and, above all, sustainably created. Botanicals from proprietary cultivation form the basis: citrus fruits from fir-tree buds, berries like raspberries and blackberries, ripe apples and chocolate mint. Magdalena Jeckel has already constructed the appropriate setting for her newly founded line of spirits; to be enjoyed on a balmy summer night, accompanied by good conversation with friends and delicious food. Her gin as a component of an unforgettable evening, the lead character in a moment that everyone present wants to preserve forever – it becomes KULTUR.GUT, cultural heritage

CATEGORY
London Dry Gin

ORIGIN
Germany

ESTABLISHED
2021

SIZE
● ● ● ●

TASTING NOTES
Lebendig, lässig und facettenreich, natürlich und unverfälscht, spritzig-frisch dank Zitrusfrüchten aus der Tannenspitze, gepaart mit einer aromatischen Beerensüße, reifem Apfel und Schokominze – diese Aromen dominieren am Gaumen.

Lively, casual and multi-faceted, natural and genuine, tangy-fresh thanks to limonene overtones from fir buds, paired with an aromatic berry sweetness, ripe apple and chocolate mint – these flavors dominate the impression on the palate..

SACK'S DESTILLE

ILLEGAL GIN OUTLAW

CATEGORY
Dry Gin

ORIGIN
Germany

ESTABLISHED
1864

SIZE

TASTING NOTES
Runder, weicher, unverfälschter und natürlicher Gin, würziger Wacholder mit einem Hauch von Zitrone, Orangenschalen, Angelikawurzel und Anis.

Round, smooth, genuine and natural gin, spicy juniper with hints of lemon, orange peel, angelica root and aniseed.

Von guten Geistern besessen

Er ist nicht von allen guten Geistern verlassen, sondern von einem besessen. Doch der ist ein „Outlaw", ein Gesetzloser, eine Schlange, die schneller den Revolver zückt, als es Lucky Luke je konnte. Er verstellt sich nicht, sein Charakter ist herb, doch er hat auch eine milde Seite – und die kommt immer dann zur Geltung, wenn er in Sack's Destille auf seine aromatischen Botanicals trifft. Der Outlaw ist Bestandteil der Illegal Gin-Reihe, die in dem Traditionsunternehmen inmitten des Naturparks Fichtelgebirge produziert wird. Seit 1864 werden die Ressourcen des umliegenden Gebirges genutzt, um Schnaps herzustellen – ganz frei von Aromazusätzen oder Farbstoffen und basierend auf alten Rezepturen und dem Wissen verschiedener Generationen.

Ein fantastisches Trio

Der ungefilterte Illegal Outlaw Gin bricht die Gesetze der Massenproduktion. Die Devise lautet Small Batches mit maximal 200 Flaschen pro Charge. Jede Flasche wird per Hand abgefüllt, gekorkt und etikettiert. Der Gesetzlose hat auch etwas gegen Massengeschmack. Ein kleiner Zusatz erlesener Kräuter und Extras wie Anis, Angelikakraut, Zitrone und Orangenschalen verleihen ihm seinen aromatischen Charakter. Damit steht der Gin seinen beiden Gangsterkollegen in nichts nach: Der Illegal Gin Bandit mit einem Zigarre rauchenden Waschbären auf dem Flaschenbauch überzeugt durch die Zugabe von einem Hauch Bourbonvanille aus Madagaskar und der tätowierte Wolf aka Illegal Gin Rebel vereint Waldmeister und Zitrone zu einer einmaligen Kombination..

> Every sip is a culinary greeting from the Fichtelgebirge mountains.

Possessed by good spirits

He isn't abandoned by all good spirits, but rather possessed by one. He is indeed an "outlaw", a lawbreaker who pulls out his revolver faster than Lucky Luke ever could. He's no pretender, there's a bitterness to him, but he also has a mild side – and it always comes to the fore when he meets his aromatic botanicals in Sack's Distillery. Outlaw is part of the Illegal Gin series produced at this traditional business in the middle of the Fichtelgebirge Nature Park. Since 1864, the resources of the surrounding mountains have been used to produce schnapps – completely free of flavoring additives or colorants and based on old recipes and the knowledge of different generations.

A fantastic trio

Unfiltered Illegal Outlaw Gin breaks the laws of mass production. The motto is small batches with a maximum of 200 bottles per batch. Each bottle is filled, corked and labeled by hand. The Outlaw also has something against mass tastes. A small addition of select herbs and extras, such as aniseed, angelica, lemon and orange peel, give it its aromatic character. Thus, this gin is in no way inferior to its two gangster colleagues: The Illegal Gin Bandit with a cigar smoking raccoon on the belly of the bottle convinces with the addition of a touch of bourbon vanilla from Madagascar and the tattooed wolf aka Illegal Gin Rebel combines woodruff and lemon to yield a unique combination.

Weißenstadt, Germany

233

CATEGORY
London Dry Gin

ORIGIN
Germany

ESTABLISHED
1818

SIZE
● ● ●

TASTING NOTES
Texturreich, weich und ausgeglichen, vordergründig Wacholder, unterlegt mit einer feinen Zitrus-Frische und einer leichten Ingwernote, ergänzt durch einen Hauch Nelke und Koriander.

Rich in texture, soft and balanced, primarily juniper, underpinned with a fine citrus freshness and a light ginger note, complemented by a hint of clove and coriander.

SCHRAML – DIE STEINWALD-BRENNEREI

KAISER HILL 16

Ein Experiment aus den 50ern

Wo einst Benediktinermönche und katholische Pfarrer lebten, wird heute Gin gebrannt. Im beschaulichen Oberbayern pflegt die Familie Schraml seit 1818 – und inzwischen in sechster Generation – ein traditionelles Handwerk: die Herstellung hochprozentiger Spirituosen. Was mit Whisky begann – die Brennerei gilt als älteste Whisky-Destillerie in Deutschland – wurde 1957 um einen Dry Gin ergänzt. Weil Wacholderstauden traditionell in der Oberpfalz an (fast) jeder Ecke zu finden waren, lag es nahe, dass ein Schraml auf die damals in Deutschland noch experimentelle Idee kam, einen Gin auf den Markt zu bringen. Allerdings hieß dieser zunächst „Krammelbeer Dry Gin", denn Krammelbeer bedeutet auf Nordbayerisch Wacholderbeere.

Mia san Gin

Der heutige Name Kaiser Hill 16 ist als eine Reminiszenz an die Herkunft des Gins zu verstehen: Der „Kaiserberg 16" ist die Adresse des Familien-Stammhauses in Erbendorf, wo er erstmals destilliert wurde. Seit nunmehr 60 Jahren wird er ganz klassisch und dem Leitspruch "Mia san Gin" folgend nach der Urrezeptur und dem Verfahren von damals hergestellt und orientiert sich damit ganz strikt an dem klassischen London Dry Gin. Das prägnante Aroma des Wacholders dominiert. Dieser wird ummantelt von zehn sorgsam ausgewählten und zusammenkomponierten Botanicals wie der Pappelknospe oder dem Ysopkraut, die dem Destillat letztlich seine breite und füllige Struktur geben.

> A gin as classic as the juniper berry.

An experiment from the 50's

Where Benedictine monks and Catholic priests once lived, gin is now distilled. In tranquil Upper Bavaria, the Schraml family has been cultivating a traditional craft since 1818 – and now in its sixth generation: the production of high-strength spirits. What began with whiskey – the distillery is considered the oldest whiskey distillery in Germany – was supplemented by a dry gin in 1957. Because juniper shrubs were traditionally found on (almost) every corner in the Upper Palatinate, it was only natural that a Schraml should come up with the idea, still experimental in Germany at the time, of launching a gin on the market. However, this was initially called "Krammelbeer Dry Gin", because Krammelbeer means juniper berry in northern Bavarian.

Mia san Gin

The present-day name, Kaiser Hill 16, is reminiscent of the origin of the gin: "Kaiserberg 16" is the address of the family's ancestral home in Erbendorf, where it was first distilled. For 60 years now, it has been produced quite classically and following the motto "Mia san Gin", meaning "we're gin" in the local dialect, according to the original recipe and the process of yesteryear, thus being strictly oriented to classic London Dry Gin. The concise aroma of juniper dominates. This is surrounded by ten carefully selected and composed botanicals including poplar bud and hyssop herb, which ultimately give the distillate its broad and full-bodied structure.

Erbendorf, Germany

LUEBKE & SOHN DISTILLERS

SHADOWS FRANCONIAN DRY GIN CLASSIC

Fränkischer Gin von Vater und Sohn

Was passiert, wenn Vater und Sohn sich aufmachen, um zu lernen, wie man Gin herstellt? Im Falle von Gerhard und Patrick Lübke: Sie gründen ihre eigene Manufaktur. Seit 2019 destillieren und vertreiben sie ihren eigenen Gin. Für den Wiedererkennungswert der Marke steht ein Uhu, der in der Fränkischen Schweiz zwischen Wäldern, Höhlen und Burgruinen anzutreffen ist. Ihr SHADOWS Franconian Dry Gin classic bildet den Grundstein und entsteht in der kleinen familiengeführten Manufaktur, die auf Nachhaltigkeit Wert legt. Aromahopfen aus der Fränkischen Schweiz, denn Franken ist die Heimat der Biere, und weitere Botanicals wie Hibiskusblüten, Koriandersamen, Muskatnuss sowie schwarzer Pfeffer werden in einer traditionellen Kupferbrennblase zu einem einzigartigen Destillat zusammengeführt und im Anschluss zwölf Wochen gelagert. Jeder Arbeitsschritt, von der 24-stündigen Mazeration bis zur Abfüllung, erfolgt in sorgfältiger Handarbeit. Selbst die Gewürze werden per Hand im Mörser zerkleinert. Hergestellt wird im Small-Batch-Verfahren von etwa 100 Flaschen.

In der Nase ist dieser London Dry Gin würzig-fruchtig mit erfrischenden Zitrusaromen und dezenten blumigen Noten. Er hat ein kräftiges Wacholderaroma, Aromahopfen und Koriandersamen geben ihm eine fruchtig-herbe Note. Außerdem hat er eine milde Schärfe durch Pfeffer und Ingwer, wohingegen Orangen, Zitronen und Lavendel den fruchtig-blumigen Geschmack prägen. Dieser Gin ist sehr geschmacksintensiv und wurde 2021 mit der Goldmedaille bei der Frankfurt International Trophy in der Kategorie London Dry Gin ausgezeichnet.

> **In the shadow of the night a gin awakens.**

Franconian gin from father and son

What happens when father and son set out to learn how to make gin? In the case of Gerhard and Patrick Lübke, they founded their own operation. Since 2019, they've been distilling and distributing their very own gin. The brand is recognizable for its eagle owl, which can be found in Franconian Switzerland among forests, caves and castle ruins. Their SHADOWS Franconian Dry Gin classic is the cornerstone and is created in the small, family-run operation with an emphasis on sustainability. Aromatic hops from Franconian Switzerland, because Franconia is the home of beers, and other botanicals, such as hibiscus flowers, coriander seeds, nutmeg as well as black pepper, are combined in a traditional copper still to create a unique distillate then stored for twelve weeks. Every step of the process, from 24-hour maceration to bottling, is carefully done by hand. Even the spices are crushed by hand in a mortar. It's produced in a small batch process of about 100 bottles.

On the nose, this London Dry Gin is spicy fruity with refreshing citrus aromas and subtle floral notes. It has a strong juniper aroma, aromatic hops and coriander seeds give it a fruity-tart note. It also has a mild spiciness from pepper and ginger, whilst oranges, lemons and lavender shape the fruity-floral flavor. This gin is very flavorful and was awarded the gold medal at the Frankfurt International Trophy in 2021 in the category of London Dry Gin.

Heroldsbach, Germany

CATEGORY
London Dry Gin

ORIGIN
Germany

ESTABLISHED
2019

SIZE

TASTING NOTES
Fruchtig-herb durch das kräftige Wacholderaroma, Aromahopfen und Koriandersamen. Milde Schärfe durch Pfeffer und Ingwer. Fruchtig-blumig durch Orangen, Zitronen und Lavendel.

Fruity-tart due to the strong juniper aroma, aromatic hops and coriander seeds. Mild spiciness from pepper and ginger. Fruity-floral from oranges, lemons and lavender.

CATEGORY
London Dry Gin

ORIGIN
Germany

ESTABLISHED
2017

SIZE

TASTING NOTES
Kräftiger Wacholder, frische Zitrusaromen, gepaart mit fruchtig-würziger Note des Kubeben- und Szechuan-Pfeffers.

Strong juniper, fresh citrus aromas, paired with fruity-spicy notes of cubeb and Szechuan pepper.

EISVÔGEL GIN DESTILLERIE
EISVÔGEL GIN

100 % handmade

Die Eisvôgel Gin Destillerie kann man als echte Kreativwerkstatt bezeichnen. Experimentierfreudig werden hier Ideen umgesetzt, es wird getestet, mit verschiedenen Aromen herumgespielt und immer wieder Neues ausprobiert. Es werden jährliche Sondereditionen kreiert – auf dem Trockenen sitzt hier keiner. Diesen ganz besonderen Manufakturbetrieb haben die Gründer Florian Herlinger und Florian Friedl komplett alleine auf die Beine gestellt. Von Anfang an machen die beiden alles selbst, sei es die Entwicklung des Gin-Rezepts oder die Gestaltung des Designs. Diesem Konzept sind sie treu geblieben. Auch bei der Herstellung ihres Eisvôgel Gins setzt das dynamische Duo auf 100-prozentige Handarbeit: von der Mazeration über die Destillation bis hin zur Abfüllung und der händischen Beschriftung jeder einzelnen Flasche.

> **Every drop of this gin is a guarantee of the best taste.**

Qualität statt Quantität

Durch die Handarbeit wird der Eisvôgel Gin nur stark limitiert hergestellt. Man setzt auf Qualität, nicht Quantität. Um diese zu garantieren, werden selbstverständlich nur beste Zutaten verwendet. Zudem verzichten die beiden Destillateure auf eine Kälte- oder Eisfiltration. Stattdessen wird der Gin ausschließlich bei Raumtemperatur gefiltert. Dies hat zur Folge, dass die ätherischen Öle der verschiedenen Botanicals beim Filtrationsprozess nicht verloren gehen und im Gin enthalten bleiben. So entsteht ein extrem intensiver, polarisierender Geschmack. Wir garantieren: Nach einem Schluck Eisvôgel Gin werdet ihr vor Begeisterung abheben.

100 % handmade

The Eisvôgel gin distillery can be described as a real creative workshop. Here they realize ideas with an eagerness to experiment, test them, play around with different flavors and try new things out over and over. Special editions are created every year – no way is this spirit drying out. The founders Florian Herlinger and Florian Friedl have set up this very special operation completely on their own. From the very beginning, the two have done everything themselves, be it developing the gin recipe or creating the design. They have remained true to this concept. The dynamic duo also relies on 100 percent manual work in the production of their Eisvôgel Gin: from maceration and distillation to bottling and the manual labeling of each individual bottle.

Quality instead of quantity

Working by hand means Eisvôgel Gin is produced only in very limited quantities. The focus is on quality, not quantity. To guarantee this, of course, only the best ingredients are used. In addition, the two distillers don't use cold or ice filtration. Instead, the gin is filtered exclusively at room temperature. As a result, the essential oils of the various botanicals are not lost during the filtration process, instead being preserved in the gin. This results in an extremely intense, polarizing flavor. We guarantee that after one sip of Eisvôgel Gin, you'll take off with delight.

Regensburg, Germany

0,5 L // 46,0 %

HUUBERT GMBH & CO.KG

HUMULUS DRY GIN

Neuburg an der Donau, Germany

GIN // HUUBERT GMBH & CO. KG // HUMULUS DRY GIN // 0,5 L // 41,0 %

Ein Stück Hallertau in der Flasche

Benjamin Vogt, Robert Pfab und Rupert Schwarzbauer kennen sich seit Kindheitstagen und leben gemeinsam einen wahr gewordenen Traum. Sie gründeten 2014 in ihrer wunderschönen Heimat Hallertau, Bayern, ihre eigene Firma und gingen mit den heute sehr bekannten HUUBERT-Weinschorlen und den belebenden Spritz-Getränken an den Markt. Es folgten weitere spannende Produkte, bis 2020 der HUMULUS Dry Gin den bisherigen Weg krönte und mit einer regionalen Traditionszutat überzeugt: dem Hallertauer Mandarina Bavaria Hopfen.
Für diesen speziellen Hopfen ist die Region besonders bei Craft-Beer-Fans bekannt, denn der Geschmack gilt als fruchtige, an Mandarine erinnernde Sorte mit eleganter Frische und dem Herben des Hopfens.

Bayern trifft Mittelmeer

Insgesamt kommen im HUMULUS Dry Gin 30 Botanicals aus Mittel- und Südeuropa zum Einsatz, aber gerade die Basis aus Wacholder und dem speziellen Hopfen ermöglicht ein spannendes Geschmackserlebnis. Weitere Früchte und elegante Kräuter runden den Charakter des London Dry Gins zusätzlich ab und schaffen ein harmonisches Aromaprofil mit der Persönlichkeit

CATEGORY
London Dry Gin

ORIGIN
Germany

ESTABLISHED
2014

SIZE
● ○ ○ ○

TASTING NOTES

Bei diesem Gin spielen zwei Hauptakteure ihre verführerische und elegante Rolle: Herbe, harzige Noten tanzen mit den würzig-mandarinenartigen Nuancen des Hopfens. Dazu gesellen sich verschiedene Zitrusnoten und eine zart-blumige Finesse von Holunder. Gepaart mit verschiedenen Wurzeln und Gewürzen ergibt das einen spannenden und tiefen Charakter.

In this gin, two main actors play their seductive and elegant roles: astringent, resinous notes dance with the spicy-tangerine nuances of the hops. These are joined by various citrus notes and a delicate floral finesse of elderberry. Paired with various roots and spices, this makes for an exciting and deep character.

> # A piece of Hallertau homeland.

A little Hallertau in a bottle

Benjamin Vogt, Robert Pfab and Rupert Schwarzbauer have known each other since childhood and are living a dream come true together. They founded their own company in 2014 in their beautiful home of Hallertau, Bavaria, and went to market with the now very well-known HUUBERT wine spritzers and invigorating spritz drinks. Other exciting products followed till, in 2020, HUMULUS Dry Gin crowned the glory of their path to date, distinguished by a traditional regional ingredient: Hallertau Mandarina Bavaria hops. The region is particularly well known among craft beer fans for this special hop, as the flavor is considered a fruity variety reminiscent of tangerine with elegant freshness and the tartness of hops.

Bavaria meets Mediterranean

A total of 30 botanicals from Central and Southern Europe are used in HUMULUS Dry Gin, but it is the base of juniper and the special hops that make for an exciting taste experience. Additional fruits and elegant herbs further round out the character of this London Dry Gin and create a harmonious flavor profile with the personality of two worlds. Bottled in a beautiful earthenware bottle, the gin is produced in the heart of the Hallertau region at the Lutzenburger distillery in Mainburg, a distillery that can look back on a history of over 200 years. Tradition, but also the courage to try new ways, particularly characterize this family business and are therefore a perfect fit for the three guys and their crazy ideas.

[German text continuation:] zweier Welten. Abgefüllt in eine wunderschöne Steingutflasche, wird der Gin im Herzen der Hallertau bei der Brennerei Lutzenburger in Mainburg hergestellt, eine Brennerei, die auf eine über 200 Jahre alte Geschichte zurückblicken kann. Tradition, aber auch Mut zu neuen Wegen zeichnen den Familienbetrieb besonders aus und passen daher perfekt zu den drei Jungs mit ihren verrückten Ideen.

KONKANI DISTILLERY

KONKANI GOA INSPIRED GIN

Munich, Germany

KONKANI DISTILLERY // KONKANI GOA INSPIRED GIN

0,5 L // 42,0%

GIN

CATEGORY
New Western Dry Gin

ORIGIN
Germany

ESTABLISHED
2019

SIZE
● ● ○ ○

TASTING NOTES
Komplex und abwechslungsreich, intensive, fruchtige Aromen, betont mango- und zitruslastig, Litsea cubeba, Tamarinde und Kurkuma verleihen dem Gin eine außergewöhnliche Aromatik, milder Wachholdergeschmack, leichte Angelika-Würze.

Complex and varied, intense, fruity aromas, emphasis on mango and citrus, litsea cubeba, tamarind and turmeric give the gin an extraordinary aroma, mild juniper flavor, light angelica spice.

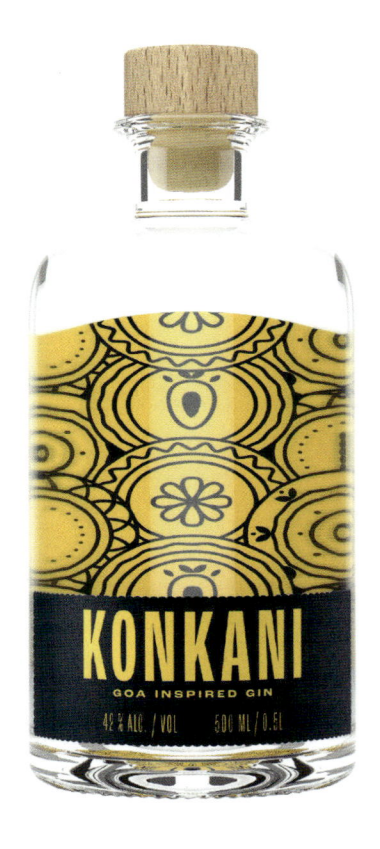

Die Seele Goas

An der mittleren Westküste Indiens liegt Goa – ein einstiges Hippieparadies, bekannt für palmengesäumte Strände, kitschig-schöne Sonnenuntergänge und Früchte, die nach Wärme schmecken. Für die Gründer von KONKANI war es eben genau dieses Eldorado, das ihnen als Inspiration für ihren Gin diente. Die Leichtigkeit des Lebens erlebten sie dort – fernab des Alltagsstresses in der Heimat. Während sie in einladend bunten Bars fruchtige Mango-Drinks schlürften, wollten sie das Gefühl der Entschleunigung mit nach Hause nehmen. Sie wollten es konservieren, in Stein meißeln – oder besser gesagt: in Flaschen gießen. Die Idee war geboren, einen Gin zu kreieren, der die bunte, leichte und zugleich gelassene Seele Goas einfängt.

Mango, Mango, Mango

Rundum exotisch ist dieser Gin. Er schreit förmlich nach Mango. Sie nimmt den Front Seat ein und lässt auf ihrem Beifahrersitz Platz für frische Limetten und herbe Grapefruit. Der Wacholder sowie indische Kräuter wie die Tamarinde finden auf der Rückbank Platz. Gemeinsam fahren die Botanicals zur nächsten Sommerparty, verkleidet als Geschmackswelt Goas. Doch nicht nur die fruchtig-frischen Nuancen dieses Gins erinnern an Indien, auch sein Name und das Design. Konkani ist die meistgesprochene Sprache in Goa und die Mandalas, die das Etikett zieren, sind das Sinnbild für das Menschsein. Der KONKANI Goa Inspired Gin wurde nicht nur von Goa inspiriert. KONKANI ist Goa.

The soul of Goa

On the mid-west coast of India lies Goa – a former hippie paradise known for palm-fringed beaches, kitschy sunsets, and fruits that taste of warmth. For the founders of KONKANI, it was precisely this Eldorado that served as the inspiration for their gin. They experienced the lightness of life there – far away from the day-to-day stress of home life. While they sipped fruity mango drinks in invitingly colorful bars, they wanted to take that feeling of slowing down home with them. They wanted to

preserve it, carve it in stone – or rather, pour it into bottles. The idea was born to create a gin that captures the colorful, light, and at the same time serene soul of Goa.

Mango, mango, mango

This gin is all-round exotic. It practically screams mango. That takes the front seat, leaving room on the passenger seat for fresh limes and tart grapefruit. The juniper, as well as Indian herbs like tamarind, find room on the back seat. Together, the botanicals drive to the next summer party, dressed up as Goa's world of flavors. But it isn't just the fruity-fresh nuances of this gin that remind us of India, but also its name and design. Konkani is the most widely-spoken language in Goa, and the mandalas that adorn the label are emblematic of being human. KONKANI Goa Inspired Gin was not only inspired by Goa. KONKANI is Goa

> Taking a KONKANI break. Rest your soul.

BAVARIAN FINEST GMBH

LINDWURM GIN – SOMMER EDITION

Munich, Germany

BAVARIAN FINEST GMBH // LINDWURM GIN – SOMMER EDITION // 0,5 L // 42,0 %

Drachen-Power

Das gusseiserne Geländer der um 1900 errichteten Eisenbahnbrücke über der Lindwurmstraße in München ziert ein kleiner Drache mit einer wichtigen Aufgabe: Erzählungen zufolge soll dieser „Lindwurm" das „Tor nach Sendling" im Auge behalten und über sein Viertel wachen. Inspiriert von diesem Fabelwesen und dessen Bedeutung, hatten zwei zu Freunden gewordene Nachbarn aus dem Lindwurmhof die Idee, die Mythologie in einem Gin zu verpacken. Auch wenn der Lindwurm Gin kein Feuer spuckt, so hat die Sommer-Edition Feuer in ihrer DNA. Insgesamt 30 mit Bedacht ausgesuchte und fein abgestimmte Gewürze verleihen diesem Gin den besonderen Touch. Dazu zählen diverse Pfefferarten, schwarze Johannisbeere, Muskatblüte sowie Orangen- und Zitronenschalen.

Mehr als Freundschaft

Eigentlich sollte die Sommer-Edition gar nicht released werden, war sie doch als Probebrand für Freunde und Familie gedacht. Weil diese den fruchtig-frischen Drink für rundum gut befanden, sollte er schließlich doch Gin-Liebhabern zugänglich gemacht werden. Der Lindwurm Gin wird traditionell auf einer kleinen, handgefertigten 180-Liter-Destille gebrannt, ganz langsam und gleichmäßig. Daher werden pro Brennvorgang lediglich 135 Flaschen produziert, die für weitere vier bis sechs Wochen in Glasballons direkt in der Destillerie ruhen, bis sie letztlich gefiltert und in Flaschen abgefüllt werden. Der sommerliche Lindwurm Gin hat übrigens noch einen Bruder: die Lindwurm Dry Gin Winter-Edition.

> *Fruity on the nose, spicy on the palate, with a hint of summer.*

CATEGORY
New Western Dry Gin

ORIGIN
Germany

ESTABLISHED
2021

SIZE
● ○ ○ ○

TASTING NOTES
Besonders mild, frisch und fruchtig, am Gaumen tanzen der Pfeffer, Cranberrys, Kardamom und Tonkabohnen.

Particularly mild, fresh and fruity, whilst the pepper, cranberries, cardamom and tonka beans dance on the palate.

Munich, Germany

Dragon Power

The cast-iron railing of the railroad bridge over Lindwurmstraße in Munich, built around 1900, is adorned with a small dragon with an important task. The story goes that this "Lindwurm" keeps an eye on the "gateway to Sendling" and watches over its neighborhood. Inspired by this mythical creature and its significance, two creatives from the neighboring Lindwurmhof operation, having become friends, had the idea of packaging the mythology in a gin. Even though Lindwurm Gin doesn't breathe fire, the Summer Edition has fire in its DNA. A total of 30 carefully selected and finely tuned spices give this gin its special touch. These include various types of pepper, black currant, mace and orange and lemon zests.

More than friendship

In reality, the summer edition should not have been released. It was intended as a test spirit for friends and family. But because they liked the fruity-fresh drink, the ultimate decision was to make it accessible to all gin lovers. Lindwurm Gin is traditionally distilled on a small, handmade 180-liter still, very slowly and steadily. So only 135 bottles are produced per distillation, which rest for another four to six weeks in glass carboys directly in the distillery, until they are ultimately filtered and bottled. By the way, the summer Lindwurm Gin has another brother: Lindwurm Dry Gin Winter Edition.

JOCHEN ZEYHER & THOMAS KURZENBERGER

MUNIG – MUNICH PREMIUM GIN

CATEGORY
London Dry Gin

ORIGIN
Germany

ESTABLISHED
2018

SIZE

TASTING NOTES
Dank des Roggens ist der Gin würziger und vollmundiger. Trotzdem schön mild, weich, ungewöhnlich mit den Botanicals Sanddorn, Cranberrys, Birkenblättern und Mädesüß – absolut eindrucksvoll.

The gin is spicier and more full-bodied owing to the rye. Beautifully mild nevertheless, soft, unusual with the botanicals sea buckthorn, cranberries, birch leaves and meadowsweet – absolutely impressive.

Aus Liebe zu München und aus Liebe zum Gin!

Der MUNiG Gin vereint all die Facetten, die das Münchener Leben so lebenswert machen. Dort, wo der Duft des Wacholders an heiße Wandertage über trockene Weiden erinnert und Blaubeeren an süße Kindheitstage, an denen man sich pfadfinderisch an der Natur bediente. Dort, wo einem samstags im geschäftigen Trubel des Viktualienmarkts fruchtig-rote Granatäpfel entgegenstrahlen, italienische Zitronen und Orangen Sehnsucht nach einem weiteren Wochenende am Gardasee wecken und frische Kräuter und Gewürze die Sinne verzaubern – dort ist dieser London Dry Gin zu Hause.

Aus dem Herzen der pulsierenden Großstadt

Bei der Gin-Manufaktur im Herzen Münchens wird alles von Hand gemacht. Pro Brand werden 150 Flaschen hergestellt, jede wird von Hand signiert und somit zu einem Unikat. Destilliert wird mit 12.000-jährigem Münchener Wasser aus dem Giesinger Tiefbrunnen. Verwendet werden 22 Botanicals, unter anderem regionale Kräuter, sizilianische Zitrusfrüchte sowie Granatapfelkerne und -blüten. Was ist es, das München so besonders macht? Der Reiz einer pulsierenden Großstadt? Das Angebot an Kultur und Arbeitsmöglichkeiten? Oder ist es doch die Lage Münchens? Um diese Gefühle im MUNiG Gin widerzuspiegeln, wurde in mehr als 50 Brenngängen am schließlich perfekten Ergebnis getüftelt: Die klassische Wacholdernote harmoniert hervorragend sowohl mit der herben Süße des Granatapfels als auch mit den feinen Pfeffernoten und der wunderbaren Frische italienischer Zitrusfrüchte.

> Gin MUNiG – aus München, für München und den Rest der Welt!

For the love of Munich and for the love of gin!

MUNiG Gin combines all the facets that make Munich life so worth living. A place where the scent of juniper reminds you of hot hiking days over dry pastures, with blueberries reminiscent of sweet childhood days when you helped yourself to nature like a scout. Where, on Saturdays in the bustle of the Viktualienmarkt, fruity-red pomegranates seem to glow, Italian lemons and oranges make you long for another weekend at Lake Garda and fresh herbs and spices enchant the senses – that's where this London Dry Gin is at home.

From the heart of the pulsating metropolis

At this gin operation in the heart of Munich, everything is done by hand. Just 150 bottles are produced from each distillation, each is signed by hand, a unique specimen. Distilled with 12,000-year-old Munich water from the Giesinger deep well. There are 22 botanicals used, including regional herbs, Sicilian citrus fruits and pomegranate seeds and blossoms. What is it that makes Munich so special? The allure of a vibrant metropolis? The range of cultural and employment opportunities? Or is it Munich's location actually? In order to reflect these feelings in MUNiG Gin, more than 50 distillation cycles were used to create the perfect result. The classic juniper note harmonizes perfectly with the tart sweetness of the pomegranate as well as with the fine pepper notes and the wonderful freshness of Italian citrus fruits.

Munich, Germany

SUSANNE STRAUBINGER MEILLER

ORO IBIZA GIN

Gern gesehener Partygast

Wenn die Sonne am Horizont langsam untergeht und mit ihren letzten Strahlen sanft die Küste küsst, erwacht „The Spirit of Ibiza" zu neuem Leben. Die Insel ist ein Inbegriff sonniger Tage und wilder Nächte. Der Freigeist der Hippiebewegung, der in den 1960er-Jahren durch ein kleines Partyvölkchen auf die ehemalige Pirateninsel gelangte, ist allgegenwärtig, wenn die bekanntesten DJs der Welt in den Klubs an den Turntables stehen. Bei diesen legendären Partys steht einer auffällig oft auf der Gästeliste: der ORO IBIZA GIN. Über ihn wacht Tanit, die Schutzgöttin der Fruchtbarkeit, die regelmäßig in der Abendsonne erscheint und alles segnet, was die goldenen Sonnenstrahlen berühren.

Gold und Tanit

Die eisenhaltige rote Erde Ibizas hat einen magischen Ruf. Zwischen den schroffen Felsen, auf den offenen Feldern und in den stillen Wäldern wächst nur, was gut für die Menschen ist: Wacholdersträucher, Zitronen- und Orangenbäume, Kamille, Holunderblüten und Rosmarin. Zwölf dieser wundersamen Botanicals finden ihren Weg in den ORO IBIZA GIN, so auch eine ganz besondere Zutat: Johannisbrot, dessen Schoten gleichzeitig nach Kaffee und Kakao schmecken. Die Fruchtkerne wurden in der Antike als Maßeinheit verwendet. Von ihnen kommt der Begriff Karat, abgeleitet vom arabischen al-carob. Noch heute wird Gold in Karat gemessen. So entstand ORO IBIZA – ein Gin, der geschmacklich wie optisch eine Symbiose aus Gold, Ibiza und der Göttin Tanit eingeht.

> „ Ibiza, how drunk with happiness you are.

Gern/Eggenfelden, Germany

A welcome party guest

When the sun slowly sets on the horizon, gently kissing the coast with its last rays, "The Spirit of Ibiza" comes to life. The island is synonymous with sunny days and wild nights. The free spirit of the hippie movement, brought to the former pirate island in the 1960s by a small party crowd, is omnipresent when the world's most famous DJs stand on the decks in the clubs. At these legendary parties, one guest is conspicuously often on the list: ORO IBIZA GIN. It's watched over by Tanit, the patron goddess of fertility, who regularly appears in the evening sun and blesses everything touched by the golden rays of the sun.

Gold and Tanit

Ibiza's iron-rich red earth has a magical reputation. Among the rugged rocks, in the open fields and in the quiet forests, only what is good for people grows: juniper bushes, lemon and orange trees, chamomile, elderflower and rosemary. Twelve of these wondrous botanicals find their way into ORO IBIZA GIN, including a very special ingredient: carob, whose pods taste like coffee and cocoa at the same time. The fruit seeds were used in ancient times as a unit of measurement. From them comes the term carat, derived from the Arabic al-carob. Even today, gold is measured in carats. This is how ORO IBIZA came into being – a gin that is a symbiosis of gold, Ibiza and the goddess Tanit, in terms of both taste and appearance.

CATEGORY
London Dry Gin

ORIGIN
Germany

ESTABLISHED
2015

SIZE

TASTING NOTES
Deutlich blumig, angenehme Würze, am Gaumen frischer Wacholder, feine Zitrusaromen, Noten von Alpenhonig und Bienenwachs, ein Hauch Zedernholz, leicht ölig, hoch aromatisch mit langem, weichem Abgang.

Distinctly floral, pleasant spiciness, fresh juniper on the palate, fine citrus aromas, notes of alpine honey and beeswax, a touch of cedar, slight oiliness, highly aromatic with a long, soft finish.

BRENNEREI STOCKER

LORBÄR GIN

> " Spicy, strong, truly like a bear!

Der Lorbär

Keine Angst, beim Lorbär Gin müsst ihr kein Tänzchen mit einem Bären wagen oder Omas eingestaubten Lorbeerkranz neu flechten. Hier ist alles schon fertig, harmonisch ins Glas gebracht worden und durch seine goldgelbe Farbe leuchtet euch der Lorbär Gin aus dem Regal regelrecht an. Eine weitere Errungenschaft in Sachen Gin aus dem Hause Stocker, denn mit dem Clitoria Gin und weiteren spannenden Kreationen begann Brennmeister Christian Stocker seine persönliche Gin-Reise. Natürlich kann die Destillerie viel mehr und schaut auf eine „brennreiche" Geschichte zurück. Seit 1946 ist die Brennerei in der 3. Generation und im Voralpenraum – genauer gesagt in Tattenhausen – zu Hause.

Bärenstarke Noten

Im Lorbär Gin kommen genau sieben Botanicals zum Einsatz. Diese werden vorab einige Zeit in einem Weizenfeindestillat mazeriert und anschließend sehr schonend und langsam destilliert, um das Beste aus den Aromen herauszuholen. Hier beginnen die Protagonisten Wacholder und Lorbeerblätter ihren Auftritt. Zusammen mit Angelikasamen, Zitronenschalen, Kardamom, Koriander und einer weiteren geheimen Zutat ergeben sie ein einzigartiges Destillat, in dem auf die Verwendung von Aromastoffen verzichtet wird. Durch das Lorbeerblatt im Inneren des Gins erhält der Dry Gin seine zarte goldgelbe Farbe. Oma würde nach ein paar Gläschen den Kranz in Windeseile neu geflochten haben und nebenbei noch ein paar nette Geschichten von damals zum Besten geben – Da sind wir uns bärensicher!

Tattenhausen, Germany

Bear with laurel?

No worries, with Lorbär Gin you don't have to risk dancing with a bear or to reweave grandma's dusty laurel wreath. Here, everything is already complete, harmoniously brought into the glass and, through its golden yellow color, Lorbär Gin verily beams at you from the shelf. Another achievement in terms of gin from the house of Stocker, because it was with Clitoria Gin and other exciting creations that master distiller Christian Stocker began his personal gin journey. Of course, the distillery can do much more and looks back on a "spiritually rich" history. Since 1946, the distillery has been in 3rd-generation hands, located in the foothills of the Alps – more precisely in Tattenhausen.

The strength of a bear

In Lorbär Gin precisely seven botanicals are used. These are macerated in advance for some time in a wheat fine spirit, then distilled very gently and slowly to get the best out of the flavors. This is where juniper and bay leaves make their appearance on stage. Together with angelica seeds, lemon zest, cardamom, coriander and another secret ingredient, they create a unique distillate in which the use of flavorings is avoided. The bay leaf in the bottle gives this Dry Gin its delicate golden yellow color. After a few glasses, Granny would have that wreath rewoven in no time, alongside top renditions of a few nice tales of yesteryear – sure proof of the bear.

CATEGORY
Dry Gin

ORIGIN
Germany

ESTABLISHED
1946

SIZE
● ● ● ○

TASTING NOTES
Ein bärenstarke Note von Wacholder, eine ausgeprägte komplexe Würze und eine leichte pfeffrige Schärfe machen den Anfang. Es folgt nahtlos eine dezente Zitrusfrische, während sich eine ausgeprägte Lorbeernote aufbaut. Der Abgang hält lange an und verbleibt mit spezieller Intensität trocken, würzig und warm in Erinnerung.

Juniper note as strong as a bear, a pronounced complex spiciness and a slight peppery edge get things started. This is followed seamlessly by a subtle citrus freshness, while a pronounced bay leaf note builds. The finish lingers long and with special intensity; dry, spicy and warm in your memory.

LANTENHAMMER DESTILLERIE

JOSEF BAVARIAN GIN

> Perfection takes time and calmness.

Griaß Gott!

"Griaß eich, liabe Leut'. I bin da Sepp, da Lantenhammer Josef. Grad hab i meine Buam a paar Wachholderbrand ins Bergwerk vorbeibracht. Sollten einen griabigen Feierabend habn, neda?

Hab g'hört, dass da 'Grundstein von meim Erbe' jetzt a pfundige Destille is! Sogar an Rum habt's ihr g'macht, und no andre interessante Spirituosen, die i no nie ned gehört und probiert hab. Einen eigenen Gin, habt ihr auch noch g'macht. Respekt! Dafür a 'Vergelt's Gott' und i bin scho ganz schee stolz, was aus meinen Sachen und der Familie gwoan is. Aber jetzt, lasst's euch den Gin schmegga. Prost!!" Wir sind sicher, dass Josef etwas Ähnliches sagen würde, wenn er wüsste, was aus der Brennerei, die er 1928 gründete, geworden ist.

Bayerische Liebeserklärung

Die LANTENHAMMER Destillerie, tief im Süden Bayerns gelegen, beherbergt die bunte Gin-Serie JOSEF (Blue Edition, den Raspberry Infused, Alpine Botanicals und Sloe Gin) und stellt verschiedene Rum-Sorten, Liköre, Geiste, den SILD Whisky und weitere Raritäten in ihrer Erlebnis-Brennerei her. Stolz können sie allemal sein, denn neben dem Fortführen der Familienbrennerei ist die LANTENHAMMER Destillerie eine der modernsten Brennereien Deutschlands. Trotz aller Moderne blieb man hier dennoch dem wahren Charakter der Brennkunst treu und das mit Zeit und Geduld. Das schmeckt man auch in den edlen Produkten.

CATEGORY
BIO Dry Gin

ORIGIN
Germany

ESTABLISHED
1928

SIZE
● ● ● ○

TASTING NOTES
Beim JOSEF Bavarian Gin überrascht euch ein Potpourri an wilden Zutaten. So findet ihr im Dry Gin einen kräftigen Wacholder kombiniert mit waldigen Noten und dezentem Holzaroma. Fruchtiges Bouquet aus Hagebutte und anderen Beeren werden von zarter Zitrusfrische umgarnt. Diese Zitrusfrische bildet zusammen mit einer aromatisch-intensiven Würze den Nachgang. Ein kernig-kräftiger Gin mit Power unterm Korken.

JOSEF Bavarian Gin surprises you with a potpourri of wild ingredients. So you will find in this Dry Gin a strong juniper combined with arboreal notes and a subtle wood aroma. Fruity bouquet of rosehip and other berries is ensnared by delicate citrus freshness. This citrus freshness, together with an aromatically intense spiciness, forms the aftertaste. A pithy gin with power under the cork.

Greetings!

"Greetings, one and all. I'm Sepp, or Josef Lantenhammer. Just brought some juniper spirit for my boys down the mine. Should have a nice evening, I'll be bound.

I heard that the 'cornerstone of my heritage' is now a fine distillery! You've even made rum, and other interesting spirits that I've never heard of or tasted. You've also made your own gin. Respect! For this 'thanks be to God' and I'm well and truly proud of what has come of my things and the family. But now, let's enjoy the gin. Cheers!" We are sure that Josef would say something like that if he knew what has become of the distillery he founded in 1928.

Bavarian declaration of love

The LANTENHAMMER distillery, located deep in the south of Bavaria, is home to the colorful JOSEF gin series (Blue Edition, Raspberry Infused, Alpine Botanicals and Sloe Gin) and produces various rums, liqueurs, spirits, SILD whisky and other rarities in their show distillery. They can certainly be proud because, in addition to continuing the family distillery, the LANTENHAMMER distillery is one of the most modern distilleries in Germany. Despite all the modernity, they still remained faithful to the true character of the art of distilling, giving it plenty of time and patience. You can taste that in the exquisite products.

Hausham, Germany

AUSTRIAN GIN DISTILLERIES

Vorarlberg

Bregenzerwald

1. *Löwen Green Gin*

Hirschegg

2. *Elfer-Gin*

Tyrol

Innsbruck

3. *Zirbin Dry Gin*

Salzburg

Salzburg

4. *5020 London Dry Gin*

Upper Austria

Salzkammergut

5. *Fior Gin*

Styria

Kalwang

6. *GIN.milla Magic Distilled Gin*

Graz

7. *The Good Gin – essence of life*

Gamlitz

8. *Skoff oriGINal*

Ehrenhausen a. d. Weinstraße

9. *STIN Classic Proof*

Burgenland

Weichselbaum

10. *GIN_Uh!*

GIN

AUSTRIAN GIN DISTILLERIES

261

BERGBRENNEREI LÖWEN

LÖWEN GREEN GIN

Bregenzerwald, Austria

BERGBRENNEREI LÖWEN // LÖWEN GREEN GIN

0,7 L // 40,0 %

CATEGORY
London Dry Gin

ORIGIN
Austria

ESTABLISHED
2011

SIZE
● ● ○ ○

TASTING NOTES
Umfangreich und angenehm mild, üppiger Kräutergeschmack, abgerundet durch blumige Akzente und der markanten Ästhetik der Holunderblüten.

Extensive and pleasantly mild, lush herbal flavor rounded off by floral accents and the striking esthetics of elderflower.

Ein Spaziergang durch die Alpen

Wie würde sich wohl eine Liebeserklärung an das Alpenvorland lesen? Eine Liebeserklärung an die facettenreiche Landschaft, die sich durch saftig-grüne Felder, kühle Wälder, zart-plätschernde Bächlein und steile Berghänge auszeichnet. An die Magerwiesen, die unberührt und schön in den Tälern ruhen und die dank ihrer artenreichen Gräser- und Kräuterwelt so wunderbar riechen. Wer die Antwort wissen möchte, braucht lediglich die Zutatenliste des Löwen Green Gins studieren. Die Bergbrennerei Löwen, aus deren Feder die Rezeptur für diese flüssige Liebeserklärung stammt, hat ihren Firmensitz im Herzen dieser vielfältigen Natur. Es liegt also nahe, dass sich die Destillateure für die Herstellung ihres Kräutergins der wunderbaren Blumenwelt bedienen. Ausgewählte Wiesenblumen, gepflückt von ungedüngten Magerwiesen, sorgen für den besonderen Geschmack des Löwen Green Gins.

Die Magie der Bergkräuter

Die enthaltenen Kräuter und Wiesenblumen werden im hauseigenen Basisalkohol maceriert und erst nach ausreichend Zeit doppelt im Feinbrandverfahren destilliert. Als 1890 das Löwen-Wirtshaus erbaut wurde, konnte niemand ahnen, dass es rund 120 Jahre später als Destillerie genutzt werden würde. 2013 wurde die Liegenschaft umgebaut, aus dem Wirts- wurde ein Gutshaus und der hintere Teil zur Brennerei und Lager. Hier werden inzwischen mehr als 40 Kräuterspezialitäten hergestellt, darunter gesellen sich vier feine Gin-Sorten. Als Basis der Kollektion dient der klassische Löwen Dry Gin, ergänzt durch den Löwen Green Gin sowie den fassgereiften Löwen Wood Gin und den durch Safran verfeinerten Leo Nobile Gin.

A walk through the Alps

How might a declaration of love to the Alpine foothills indeed read? A declaration of love for the multifaceted landscape, so outstanding for its lush green meadows, cool forests, gently babbling brooks and steep mountain slopes. To the rough pasture resting untouched and beautiful in the valleys, so wonderfully scented thanks to the rich variety of grass and herb species. Those who want to know the answer need only study the list of ingredients of Löwen Green Gin. The Bergbrennerei Löwen mountain distillery, which penned the recipe for this liquid declaration of love, has its headquarters in the heart of this region of natural diversity. So it stands to reason that the distillers would draw on the wonderful world of flowers to create their herbal gin. Selected meadow flowers, picked from unfertilized natural meadows, provide the special taste of Löwen Green Gin.

The magic of mountain herbs

The herbs and meadow flowers within are macerated in the distillery's own base alcohol and, only once sufficient time has passed, are they then distilled twice in the fine distillation process. When the Löwen inn was built in 1890, no one could have guessed that it would be used as a distillery some 120 years later. In 2013, the property was rebuilt, the inn became a manor house and the rear part was converted into a distillery and warehouse. More than 40 herbal specialties are now produced here, joined by four fine gin varieties. The classic Löwen Dry Gin serves as the basis of the collection, supplemented by Löwen Green Gin as well as barrel-aged Löwen Wood Gin and Leo Nobile Gin refined with saffron.

> **This gin embodies like no other the meadow world at the foot of the Alps.**

KWT-GIN

ELFER-GIN

Angelehnt an den Elfer-Berg

Raik Strassas hat fast schon sein ganzes Leben mit Gin zu tun. Durch seine langjährige Arbeit als Barkeeper hat er seine Liebe zu dieser Spirituose entdeckt – und möchte ihr mit einem eigenen Gin Ausdruck verleihen: dem Elfer-Gin. Der Name steht für alles, was diesen Gin ausmacht: für Leidenschaft, Hingabe und die Liebe zum Detail. Der namensgebende Elferkopf (auch „Elferköpfle" genannt) ist ein Berg im österreichischen Kleinwalsertal. Als Raik Strassas eines Tages diesen Berg erklimmt, verliebt er sich in die weitläufige Alpenlandschaft und das wunderschöne Kleinwalsertal. Als Hommage an diese Landschaft und die dort entfachte Leidenschaft entsteht der Elfer-Gin.

Aromen, die überzeugen

Der Elfer-Gin wird in reiner Handarbeit und im Zeichen traditionellen Handwerks produziert. Dabei führt Raik Strassas jeden Handgriff selbst durch – vom Ansatz bis zum Verkauf. Er handelt ganz nach dem Grundsatz: Qualität statt Quantität. So brennt er in seinem kleinen Ein-Mann-Betrieb den Elfer-Gin ausschließlich im Small-Batch-Verfahren. Der Elfer-Gin ist ein dreifach destillierter Dry Gin, in dem sich elf verschiedene Botanicals zu einem harmonischen Ganzen vereinen. Zu den vorrangig aus der näheren Umgebung stammenden Zutaten zählen Wacholderbeeren, Enzian, Holunderblüten und auch Blutwurz, aber auch Reisende wie die Pink Grapefruit, Zimt oder Kardamom. Die Mischung dieser unterschiedlichsten Aromen prägt den Charakter des Elfer-Gins und macht ihn zu einem einmaligen Geschmackserlebnis.

Honoring Elfer mountain

Raik Strassas has been involved with gin almost all his life. Through his many years of work as a bartender, he has discovered his love for this spirit – and wants to express it with his own gin: Elfer Gin. The name stands for everything that distinguishes this gin: for passion, dedication and attention to detail. The eponymous Elferkopf (also called "Elferköpfle") is a mountain in Austria's Kleinwalsertal valley. When Raik Strassas climbed this mountain one day, he fell in love with the vast alpine landscape and the beautiful Kleinwalsertal valley. As a tribute to this landscape and the passion it ignited, Elfer Gin was born.

Flavors that convince

Elfer Gin is produced purely by hand in the spirit of traditional craftsmanship. Raik Strassas carries out every step himself – from preparation to sale. In all he does, the principle is the same: quality instead of quantity. In his small one-man operation, he distills Elfer Gin in a small-batch process exclusively. Elfer Gin is a triple-distilled dry gin in which eleven different botanicals are combined to form a harmonious whole. The ingredients, which come primarily from the local area, include juniper berries, gentian, elderflower and bloodroot, but also „wayfarers" such as the pink grapefruit, cinnamon or cardamom. The mixture of these diverse flavors shapes the character of Elfer Gin and makes it a unique taste experience.

Hirschegg, Austria

> **Elfer Gin:**
> A tribute to the beautiful alpine landscape of the Allgäu.

CATEGORY
Dry Gin

ORIGIN
Austria

ESTABLISHED
2019

SIZE

TASTING NOTES
Das Aroma ist eine Mischung aus frischem Zitrus und würzigem Wacholder, ergänzt durch einen Hauch von blumigen Noten. Im Geschmack weich, es dominiert bitter-frische Grapefruit, dazu kommen Wacholder und ein Hauch von Blutwurz und Enzian.

The aroma is a mixture of fresh citrus and spicy juniper, complemented by a touch of floral notes. The taste is soft, dominated by bitter-fresh grapefruit, joined by juniper and hints of bloodroot and gentian.

FLORIAN STERN

ZIRBIN DRY GIN

CATEGORY
Dry Gin

ORIGIN
Austria

ESTABLISHED
2019

SIZE

TASTING NOTES
Eine elegante Komposition aus Wacholder und Zirbe, ergänzt durch Botanicals wie Lavendelblüten, Ingwerwurzeln und Angelikasamen.

An elegant composition of juniper and stone pine, complemented by botanicals such as lavender flowers, ginger root and angelica seeds.

Gin aus den Bergen

Hoch im Gebirge, umgeben von rauen Winden und einer wunderschönen Berglandschaft, ist die „Königin der Alpen" zu Hause: die Zirbe. Ein durchaus passender Name für diesen majestätischen Baum, der würdevoll über allem thront und eng mit Tirol verbunden ist. Davon inspiriert entsteht ein Gin, bei dem bereits der Name den Geschmack klar benennt und transportiert: ZIRBIN Dry Gin. Für diesen Gin werden die Besonderheiten des Landes aufgegriffen, sorgfältig destilliert und in einer Flasche abgefüllt. Der ZIRBIN Dry Gin ist wie ein Schluck Tirol.

Eine harmonische Komposition

ZIRBIN Dry Gin spiegelt so zum einen den einzigartigen Geschmack der Zirbe wider und steht zum anderen für die Region Tirol, geprägt durch ihre wunderschönen Berge und Täler. Der tragende Geschmack des Gins ist der unverkennbare Charakter des Zirbenzapfens. Dieser vermischt sich mit der Wacholderbeere, die das grundlegende Botanical für jeden Gin bildet. Hinzu kommen neun weitere Botanicals, unter anderem Lavendelblüten, Ingwerwurzeln und Angelikasamen. Diese harmonische Komposition verschiedenster Zutaten bildet die Grundlage, auf der sich die Zirbe als wichtigstes Botanical majestätisch entfalten kann. ZIRBIN Dry Gin – ein Gin, vor dem man sich nur verneigen kann.

Gin from the mountains

High in the mountains, surrounded by brisk winds and a beautiful mountain landscape, the "Queen of the Alps" is at home: the stone pine. A thoroughly fitting name for this majestic tree, which towers gracefully above everything and is closely associated with Tyrol. Inspired by this, a gin has been created whose name alone clearly conveys the taste: ZIRBIN Dry Gin. For this gin, the treasures of the landscape are collected, carefully distilled and bottled. ZIRBIN Dry Gin is like a sip of Tyrol.

A harmonious composition

ZIRBIN Dry Gin thus reflects, on the one hand, the unique taste of stone pine and, on the other, stands for the region of Tyrol, characterized by its beautiful mountains and valleys. The founding flavor of this gin is the unmistakable character of stone pine cone. This blends with juniper berry, constituting the essential botanical of every gin. In addition, there are nine other botanicals, including lavender flowers, ginger root and angelica seeds. This harmonious composition of diverse ingredients forms the basis on which the stone pine, as the most important botanical, can majestically unfold. ZIRBIN Dry Gin – a gin to which one can only bow.

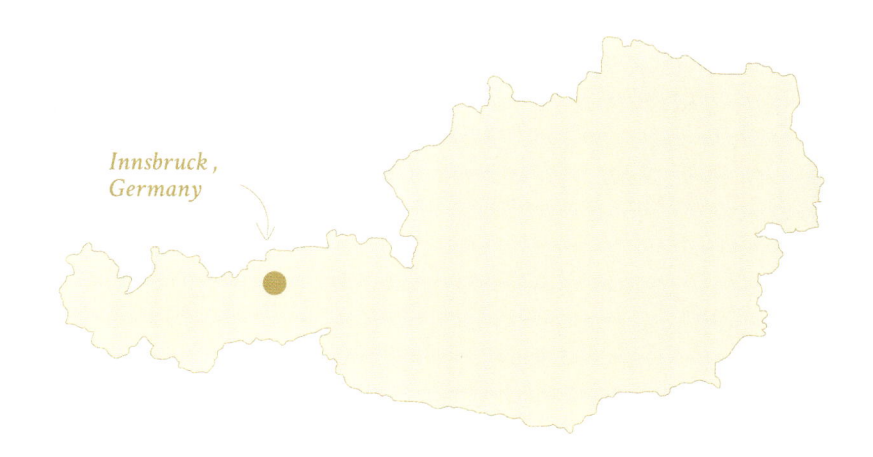

Innsbruck, Germany

> ZIRBIN Dry Gin – (y)our sip of Tyrol!

5020 DISTILLERY

5020 LONDON DRY GIN

> The all new London Dry Gin.
> Handcrafted in Salzburg.

CATEGORY
London Dry Gin

ORIGIN
Austria

ESTABLISHED
2014

SIZE
● ○ ○ ○

TASTING NOTES
Insgesamt ausgewogen, komplex im Geruch, mit herb-grasigen Anklängen und fruchtigen Akzenten, am Gaumen spielen Galgant und Sternanis, dazu die klassisch harzige Wacholderstruktur, umgarnt von feinen Zitrusnoten, mit einem würzigen Abgang.

Overall balanced, complex aroma, with tart grassy hints and fruity accents, galangal and star anise play on the palate, along with the classic resinous juniper structure, ensnared by subtle citrus notes, with a spicy finish.

Zurück zu den Wurzeln

5020 lautet die Postleitzahl der Stadt Salzburg. Eine Stadt, in der sich Tradition und Moderne auf kleinstem Raum begegnen und in der Architektur, Kunst und Kultur eine übergeordnete Rolle spielen. Nicht nur Wolfgang Amadeus Mozart zählt zu den Söhnen der UNESCO-Weltkulturerbestadt, auch Stephan Koudelka hat hier ein Business aufgebaut – zwar nicht in der Musikbranche, dafür aber in der Genusswelt. Er hat einen Gin gezaubert, der ganz deutlich macht, worin seine Prioritäten liegen: Klassik und das Hervorheben der eigenen Wurzeln, zusammengefasst verkörpert in dem Namen 5020 London Dry Gin. Drei Jahre lang feilte Stephan Koudelka an der Rezeptur.

Trial and Error

Die zwischenzeitigen Brennversuche, deren Ergebnis von Gin-Kennern als "ganz nett" abgetan wurden, kann er heute als learning by doing abhaken. Der 5020 Gin, der 2017 gelauncht wurde, ist mehr als nett, er ist Feinkost. Die hohe Qualität wird unter anderem durch das Brennverfahren einerseits und die sorgfältig ausgewählten Botanicals anderseits erzielt. Der 5020 Gin wird ausschließlich in einem kleinen Kupferkessel mit einem Fassungsvermögen von rund 100 Litern destilliert und schrittweise mit biozertifizierten Zutaten verfeinert. Das Einhängen eines Aromakorbs direkt in die Brennblase ermöglicht, dass auch die feinen und empfindlichen Botanicals ihr Aroma optimal entfalten können. Durch eine langsame Steigerung der Temperatur, laufende Kontrollen sowie eine zehn- bis zwölfwöchige Lagerung im Glasballon kommt der 5020er zu dem Geschmack, den Liebhaber des London Dry Gin so lieben.

Back to the roots

5020 is the postal code of the city of Salzburg. A city where tradition and modernity meet in the smallest of spaces and where architecture, art and culture play an overriding role. Wolfgang Amadeus Mozart is not the only son of this UNESCO World Heritage City. Stephan Koudelka has also built up a business here – not in the music industry, but in the world of gourmet food. He has conjured up a gin that makes it quite clear where his priorities lie: classical music and highlighting his own roots, summed up in the name 5020 London Dry Gin. Stephan Koudelka spent three years fine-tuning the recipe.

Trial and error

His interim distillation experiments, with results dismissed by gin connoisseurs as "quite nice", can now be checked off as learning by doing. 5020 Gin, which was launched in 2017, is more than nice, it is haute cuisine. The high quality is achieved, among other things, by the distillation process on the one hand and the carefully selected botanicals on the other. 5020 Gin is distilled exclusively in a small copper pot still with a capacity of about 100 liters and gradually refined with certified organic ingredients. Hanging an aroma basket directly in the still allows even the delicate and sensitive botanicals to develop their aroma to the fullest. A slow increase in temperature, ongoing controls and ten to twelve weeks of storage in a glass carboy give 5020 the taste that lovers of London Dry Gin love so much.

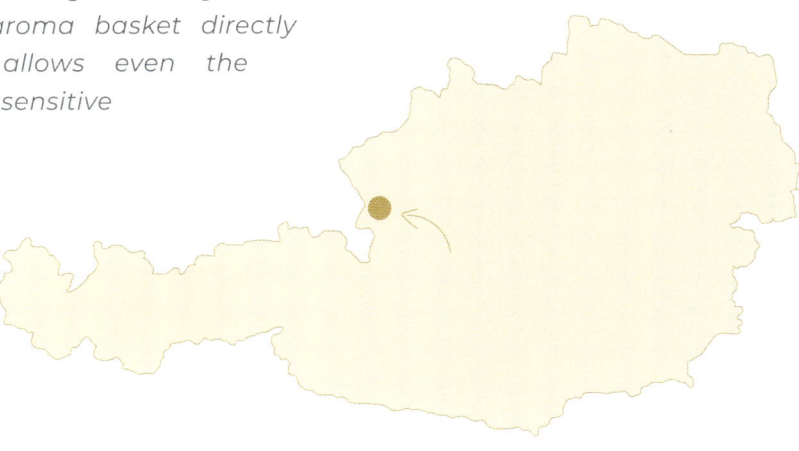

GIN FIOR

GIN *FIOR*

CATEGORY
London Dry Gin

ORIGIN
Austria

ESTABLISHED
2020

SIZE

TASTING NOTES
Elegant, ausbalanciert, vielfältig aromatisch, typischer Wacholdergeschmack, spritzige Zitrusnuancen, fruchtige Apfelnoten, floral durch einen Hauch von Lavendel, überaus mild im Abgang.

Elegant, well-balanced, aromatic complexity, typical juniper taste, tangy citrus nuances, fruity apple notes, floral due to a hint of lavender, very mild finish.

Vier Kumpels, ein Gin

Die Geschichte hinter dem "Gin FIOR" ist simpel und schön. Eine Geschichte von Freundschaft und der entscheidenden Botschaft, das Leben zu feiern, wie es ist. "Fior" ist Althochdeutsch und steht für die Zahl Vier. Ein konsequenter Name in Anbetracht dessen, dass die Vier die Entstehung des edlen Tropfens von Beginn an begleitete. Zunächst sind da vier Jungs, die sich regelmäßig trafen, austauschten und dabei Gin aus aller Herren Länder tranken. Dabei kamen sie auf die Idee, ihren eigenen Gin herzustellen. Prompt war eine kleine Tischbrennerei angeschafft. Bereits der 4. Versuch – wie könnte es auch anders sein – war ein Glückstreffer, der nicht nur das Quartett vergnügte. Der Gin gefiel auch anderen – für die Freunde ein Ansporn, mehr zu produzieren.

Und der Fünfte folgt sogleich

Doch das funktionierte nicht im eigenen Wohnzimmer. Die Suche nach einer verlässlichen Destillerie führte die Vier nach Oberösterreich an den Sammerhof. Dort begegneten sie ihrem Brenner des Vertrauens und fanden einen neuen Freund, den fünften im Bunde. Zehn Botanicals stecken in dem Gin FIOR: feine Noten aus Lavendel, Zitrus und Apfel, gepaart mit dem typischen Wacholdergeschmack sowie einem Hauch von Rosmarin, Kardamom, Zimt und Ingwer. Unterstrichen wird dieser Trinkgenuss durch die Aufmachung des Gins. Elegant stechen die Botanicals als eine filigrane silbrige Gravur auf der weißgrauen Flasche hervor und vermitteln eine Botschaft: Hier steckt drin, was draufsteht.

Salzkammergut, Austria

Four buddies, one gin

The story behind Gin FIOR is simple and beautiful. A story of friendship and the crucial message of celebrating life as it is. "Fior" is Old High German and stands for the number four. An appropriate name considering that the four accompanied the creation of this fine spirit from the very beginning. It began with four guys who met regularly, exchanged ideas and drank gin from all over the world. In the process, they came up with the idea of making their own gin. In no time, a small table distillery had been purchased. As soon as the 4th attempt – how could it be otherwise – came a lucky hit, which didn't just amuse the quartet. This gin also pleased others – for the buddies an incentive to produce more.

And the fifth immediately followed

But that didn't work in their own living room. The search for a reliable distillery led the four to Sammerhof in Upper Austria. There they met their trusted distiller and found a new friend, the fifth in the bunch. Ten botanicals go into Gin FIOR: subtle notes of lavender, citrus and apple, paired with the typical juniper flavor and a hint of rosemary, cardamom, cinnamon and ginger. The pleasure of imbibing is underlined by the presentation of the gin. Elegantly, the botanicals stand out as a delicate silvery engraving on the white-gray bottle and convey a message: what you see is what you get.

> ❝ Makes life more beautiful – just like good friends.

MANNA'S SPIRITS MANUFAKTUR

GIN.MILLA MAGIC DISTILLED GIN

CATEGORY
Distilled Gin

ORIGIN
Austria

ESTABLISHED
2019

SIZE
● ● ● ●

TASTING NOTES
Sehr würzige Komposition mit einem Hauch von Zimt – langanhaltender Abgang.

Very spicy composition with a hint of cinnamon – long-lasting finish.

Ein Gin von höchster Qualität

Die Idee von Edelbrandsommelier Mario Angerer war es, einen Gin von höchster Qualität zu erzeugen. Nach mehreren Versuchen wurde die perfekte Rezeptur gefunden – ein klares Wacholderaroma, abgerundet durch Zitronennoten. Das klassische Verfahren der Gin-Herstellung wird durchgeführt: Das beginnt mit der Mazeation und anschließender Destillation. Hierbei wird besonders darauf geachtet, die komplexen Aromen der Botanicals zu bewahren, indem sie von der kupfernen Brennblase langsam und schonend in den Kühler geleitet werden. Nach dem Brennvorgang wird der Gin einige Zeit gelagert, bevor er schließlich abgefüllt und verköstigt wird.

Geheimnisvolle Blüte sorgt für blaue Farbe

Insbesondere Wacholder und ein frischer Zitrusduft stechen heraus. Man riecht direkt kandierte Blüten, Maraschino und exotische Früchte. Dieser Gin schmeckt recht elegant, der Frucht wird Zimt und Pfeffer beigefügt. Das oberste Gebot: höchste Qualität bei der Auswahl der Gewürze sowie die Reinheit des Alkohols. Dieser besondere Gin zeichnet sich durch seine azurblaue Farbe und ein blumiges und weiches Aroma aus. Eine geheimnisvolle Blüte gibt ihm eine unverwechselbare und einmalige blaue Farbe. Wird nun noch Tonic Water hinzugefügt, wird es wirklich interessant: Beim GIN .milla Magic erlebt man ein echtes Farbenspiel, denn durch die Säure des Tonics verfärbt sich der Gin von Blau auf Lila. Überrascht eure Gäste mit diesem Farbwechsler und einem unvergleichbaren Geschmackserlebnis.

Kalwang, Austria

A gin of the highest quality

The idea of fine spirits sommelier Mario Angerer was to create a gin of the highest quality. After several attempts, the perfect recipe was found – a clear juniper aroma, rounded off with lemon notes. The classic process of gin production is used, beginning with maceration and then subsequent distillation. Here, special care is taken to preserve the complex aromas of the botanicals by passing them slowly and gently from the copper pot into the condenser. After the distillation process, the gin is stored for some time before it is finally bottled and tasted.

Mysterious blossom provides blue color

Juniper and a fresh citrus scent particularly stand out. You can directly smell candied flowers, maraschino and exotic fruits. This gin tastes altogether elegant, the fruit complemented by cinnamon and pepper. Top priorities are the highest quality in the selection of spices, as well as the purity of the alcohol. This special gin is characterized by its azure color and a floral and soft aroma. A mysterious blossom gives it a distinctive and unique blue color. If tonic water is now added, it gets really interesting. With the GIN .milla Magic, you experience a real play of colors, because the acidity of the tonic turns the gin from blue to lilac. Surprise your guests with this color shifter and its incomparable taste experience.

> **A little bit of magic from beautiful Austria.**

275

EVA SUSANNE BAUMANN-COX

THE GOOD GIN

CATEGORY
London Dry Gin

ORIGIN
Austria

ESTABLISHED
2019

SIZE

TASTING NOTES
Vorherrschend sind
Kräuter und leichter
Kakao, Minze ergänz
mit einer frischen Note
Geschmacklich seh
smooth, dazu leicht herb
Der Rohkakao sorg
für einen besonder
weichen Abgang

*Predominant are herb
and light cocoa, min
complementing with
fresh note. Very smooth
taste, also slightly tar
The raw cocoa provides
particularly soft finish*

© Mària Rosselló

Die Verbindung von Genuss und Wohlbefinden

Eva Susanne Baumann-Cox ist Yoga-Lehrerin, Journalistin (unter anderem eines Gesundheits-Magazins) – und natürlich leidenschaftliche Gin-Trinkerin. Doch als der abendliche Aperitif immer mehr zum Wohlfühlritual wird, fragt sie sich, wie gesund der Genuss von Gin wohl sein kann. So findet sie heraus, dass Gin in seiner Urform „Genever" ursprünglich als Medizin verwendet wurde, da er bei der Verdauung hilft und das allgemeine Wohlbefinden steigert. Durch den Ursprung inspiriert möchte sie diese Tradition wieder aufleben lassen und will einen Gin kreieren, der Genuss und Wohlbefinden verbindet.

Auf die Gesundheit!

Damit diese Idee Wirklichkeit werden kann, verbringt Susanne viele Monate mit Recherchen über Nährstoffe, der Entwicklung von Rezepturen und verschiedenen Probeläufen. Als die perfekte Rezeptur endlich gefunden ist, beauftragt sie Wolfgang Thomann – Gin-Experte und Eigentümer der Aeijst-Brennerei –, den Gin für sie herzustellen. Das Besondere: die Botanicals, die verwendet werden.

Diese wählt sie alle nach ihren gesundheitsunterstützenden Eigenschaften aus. Die typische Wacholderbeere ist bei ihrem Gin eher subtil, während Botanicals wie Ashwagandha, eine ayurvedische Heilpflanze, Kurkuma oder auch Rohkakao den Charakter prägen. Diese eher ungewöhnlichen Botanicals werden durch bekanntere Zutaten wie Ingwer, Kardamom, Zitrusschale und Apfel ergänzt. So entsteht: The Good Gin. Mit diesem Gin wird nicht nur ihr eigener, sondern auch der Traum eines jeden Genussmenschen wahr. The Good Gin – essence of life ist ein Gin, der wahrlich genossen werden kann. Und mit dem man am besten auf die Gesundheit anstößt!

> "A gin that warms the body and the soul.

Graz, Austria

The combination of pleasure and well-being

Eva Susanne Baumann-Cox is a yoga teacher, a journalist (for a health magazine, among others) – and, of course, a passionate gin drinker. But as the evening aperitif became more and more of a feel-good ritual, she wondered how healthy drinking gin might potentially be. She found out that gin in its original form, "genever", was originally used as a medicine, as it aids digestion and increases general well-being. Inspired by this origin, she wanted to revive this tradition and create a gin that combined pleasure and well-being.

To health!

To make this idea a reality, Susanne spent many months researching nutrients, developing recipes and conducting various trial runs. When the perfect recipe was finally found, she commissioned Wolfgang Thomann – gin expert and owner of the Aeijst distillery – to produce the gin for her. What makes it special is the choice of botanicals. She selects all of these according to their health-supporting properties. The typical juniper berry is rather subtle in her gin, while botanicals such as ashwagandha, an Ayurvedic medicinal plant, turmeric and raw cocoa shape the character. These rather unusual botanicals are complemented by more familiar ingredients such as ginger, cardamom, citrus zest and apple. The result: The Good Gin. With this gin, not only her own dream but also those of every epicurean have come true. The Good Gin – essence of life is a gin that can truly be enjoyed, and one best suited to a toast to health.

CATEGORY
New Western
Dry Gin

ORIGIN
Austria

ESTABLISHED
1983

SIZE
● ● ● ●

TASTING NOTES
Aromatisch und finessenreich, im Geschmack sehr intensiv mit einem langen Abgang. Wacholder sehr dezent, die Sauvignonnoten werden nicht überdeckt.

Rich in aroma and finesse, very intense on the palate with a long finish. Juniper very discreet, the Sauvignon notes are not masked.

WALTER SKOFF WEIN GMBH

SKOFF ORIGINAL

Der Gin vom *Mr. Sauvignon*

Walter Skoff ist Winzer in vierter Generation und ausgezeichnet als „Mr. Sauvignon" in Österreich. Das Wissen und das Gespür für die Natur, die Böden und für das Klima rund um das familieneigene Weingut in Gamlitz sind gut behütete Geheimnisse. Von Generation zu Generation weitergegeben, verwurzelt es mit der Tradition des steirischen Weins.

Neben Wein wird ein geschmacklich komplexer, fruchtiger New Western Dry Gin produziert, der aromatisch und finessenreich ist, im Geschmack sehr intensiv mit einem langen Abgang. Anders als bei üblichen Gins, die herkömmlicherweise auf Basis von Getreide oder Kartoffeln hergestellt werden, destillierte Walter Skoff für den Skoff oriGINal Sauvignon Blanc aus seinen besten Rieden in der Südsteiermark. Dies macht den Gin einzigartig. In der hauseigenen Brennerei werden die Früchte aus eigenem Anbau zu herausragenden Edelbränden verarbeitet.

Diese Rebsorte hat nicht nur in der Steiermark eine besondere Bedeutung, sondern genießt auch international hohes Ansehen. Sie verleiht dem Basisdestillat eine frische Aromatik und unterstützt die Stilistik zusammen mit verschiedenen Botanicals und Wacholder. Diese Geschmacksgeber vermischte Walter Skoff mit dem Destillat von Sauvignon Blanc, um eine Fülle von Aromen zu erhalten. Der Wacholder ist hierbei nur sehr dezent enthalten, um die zarten Sauvignon-Noten nicht zu überdecken. Der Skoff oriGINal besticht durch seine klare Farbe, seinen komplexen und fruchtigen Geruch sowie nicht zuletzt seine große aromatische Intensität.

The gin from Mr. Sauvignon

Walter Skoff is a fourth generation winemaker and acknowledged as "Mr. Sauvignon" in Austria. The knowledge and feel for nature, the soils and for the climate around the family winery in Gamlitz, are well-kept secrets, passed down from generation to generation, rooted in the tradition of Styrian wine.

In addition to wine, he produces a flavorful, complex, fruity New Western Dry Gin, rich in aroma and finesse, very intense in taste with a long finish. Unlike common gins, which are traditionally made on the basis of grain or potatoes, for Skoff oriGINal Walter Skoff distilled Sauvignon blanc from his best vineyards in southern Styria. This makes the gin unique. At the in-house distillery, the fruits from own cultivation are processed into outstanding, fine spirits.

This grape variety has a special significance not only in Styria, but also enjoys a great reputation internationally. It gives the base distillate a fresh aroma and supports the style together with various botanicals and juniper. Walter Skoff blended these flavoring agents with the distillate of Sauvignon blanc to obtain a richness of aromas. The juniper is only very subtly included here, so as not to overpower the delicate Sauvignon notes. Skoff oriGINal impresses with its clear color, complex and fruity aroma and, last but not least, its great aromatic intensity.

> **Sauvignon blanc meets Gin.**

Gamlitz, Austria

> "In Styria, the apple falls not far from the elder.

CATEGORY
London Dry Gin

ORIGIN
Austria

ESTABLISHED
2017

SIZE
● ● ○ ○

TASTING NOTES
Aromatisch und facettenreich, sehr warm, langanhaltend und würzig-maskulin, mild und fruchtig in der Kopfnote, leicht scharf und intensiv im Abgang.

Aromatic and multifaceted, very warm, long-lasting and spicy-masculine, mild and fruity top notes, slightly spicy and intense finish.

THE STIN – STYRIAN GIN

STIN CLASSIC PROOF

Destillieren geht über Studieren

Wer viel Zeit hat, kommt auf absurde Ideen. Manchmal stellt sich dann heraus, dass die Ideen doch gar nicht so absurd sind. Johannes Firmenich und Reinhard Jagerhofer haben sich beim Studium in Wien kennengelernt. Sie kommen beide aus der Steiermark und haben beide ein Faible für Gin. Eines Abends stellten sie sich dann die Frage, deren Antwort ihre Zukunft dominieren sollte: Wie kommt die Steiermark in einen Gin? Geboren war die Idee für STIN. Die beiden wichtigsten Zutaten wachsen bei den Freunden daheim praktischerweise direkt vor der Hoftür: südsteirische Äpfel und oststeirischer Holunder. Wie gut, dass ihre Väter ihnen auch noch die Handwerkskunst des Destillierens mit in die Wiege gelegt haben.

Der Klassiker bekommt Geschwister

Insgesamt 28 Botanicals gehören in den STIN Classic Proof. Für die Aromaentfaltung werden diese zuerst in Alkohol eingelegt. Anschließend wird das Mazerat destilliert und mithilfe steirischen Quellwassers auf Trinkstärke herabgesetzt – ein klassisches Verfahren, wie es der London Dry Gin verlangt. Neben Wacholder, Äpfeln und Holunder sind es erfrischende Zitronen und fruchtige Orangen, die den Weg in die Spirituose finden. Dazu gesellen sich unter anderem Kümmel, Koriander, Ingwer, Kardamom und Pfeffer. Inzwischen haben die Freunde drei weitere Varianten ihres STINs auf den Markt gebracht: den Overproof mit einem Alkoholgehalt von 57 %, den auf 999 Flaschen limitierten Distiller's Cut, der lieber Birnen als Äpfel nascht, und den fruchtigen Schlehen-Gin Sloeberry.

Distilling through studying

If you have time on your hands, you come up with absurd ideas. Sometimes it turns out that the ideas aren't so absurd after all. Johannes Firmenich and Reinhard Jagerhofer met while studying in Vienna. They both come from Styria and both have a soft spot for gin. Then, one evening, they asked themselves a question, the answer to which would dominate their future: How can Styria get itself a gin? The idea for STIN was born. The two most important ingredients grow at the friends' home, conveniently right on the farm's doorstep: apples from southern Styria and elderberries from eastern Styria. How fortunate that their fathers also passed on to them the craft of distilling.

The classic gets siblings

A total of 28 botanicals belong in STIN Classic Proof. To develop the aroma, they are first macerated in alcohol. The macerate is then distilled and reduced to drinking strength with the help of Styrian spring water – a classic process as required for London Dry Gin. In addition to juniper, apples and elderberries, refreshing lemons and fruity oranges find their way into the spirit. They are joined by cumin, coriander, ginger, cardamom and pepper, among others. In the meantime, these friends have launched three more variants of their STIN: Overproof, with an alcohol content of 57 % ABV; Distiller's Cut, limited to 999 bottles and with a preference for snacking on pears rather than apples; Sloeberry, the fruity sloe gin.

Ehrenhausen a. d. Weinstraße, Austria

281

WEINGUT FAMILIE GRATL

GIN_UH!

> The first Uhudler gin from Southern Burgenland.

CATEGORY
Dry Gin

ORIGIN
Austria

ESTABLISHED
2019

SIZE
● ● ○ ○

TASTING NOTES
Im Geschmack überrascht der GIN_Uh! mit Komplexität und Tiefe. In der Nase überwiegt im ersten Eindruck natürlich Wacholder, frische Zitrus- und Orangennoten, kombiniert mit fruchtiger Walderdbeere und intensiven Kräuternuancen. Am Gaumen erkennt man zusätzlich noch den würzigen Kardamom, Veilchen und Sternanis. Im Abgang entfaltet sich unverkennbar das unverwechselbare Aroma der Uhudler-Trauben.

On the palate, GIN_Uh! surprises with complexity and depth. Prevailing in the nose initially of course are juniper, fresh citrus and orange notes, combined with fruity wild strawberry and intense herbal nuances. On the palate, one additionally recognizes spicy cardamom, violet and star anise. The unmistakable aroma of the Uhudler grapes unfolds in the finish.

Der Uhu und der Wein

Nein, beim GIN_Uh! ist kein Uhu mit dem Gin ausgebüxt. In dieser Geschichte handelt es sich um in der Weinwelt eher mit kritischen Augen betrachtete Weinreben, die auf eine lange Historie, spezielle Eigenheiten und starke Wurzeln zurückblicken können. Hier, in der „heutigen Toskana Österreichs", herrschen lange Sonnentage und ein mildes Klima. Im Südburgenland, nahe der ungarischen Grenze, avancierte ein ganz besonderer Wein in den letzten Jahren zum Kultgetränk: Der Uhudler.

Außer den sehr robusten Eigenschaften der Reben verdanken sie ihren Namen den Frauen des Dorfes. Wenn die Winzer erst nach Tagen von der Arbeit in den Weinbergen zurückkehrten, kamen ihre Frauen nicht umhin zu bemerken „Der hat schon wieder Augen wie ein Uhu". Der Charakter der Traube ist süß, fruchtig und erinnert an frische Walderdbeernoten – da drücken wir doch mal ein Auge zuhu.

Wein und Gin, das macht Sinn

In dieser Region ist Weinbauer Christoph Gratl mit seinen Qualitätsreben sehr bekannt. Das Repertoire an Weinen kann sich sehen lassen, er produziert aber ebenso edle Feinbrände und Grappas. So kam er auf die Idee, zwei Kultgetränke miteinander zu kombinieren: Uhudler und Gin.

Wacholder, exotische Aromen und die Uhudler Weintrauben werden hierbei zu einem spannenden Dry Gin kombiniert, der durch klassische Noten und dem Fruchtigen der Traube einen ganz eigenen Charakter erhält. Da braucht man nicht mehr in die Weinberge, sondern kann den Uhu-Blick gleich an Ort und Stelle ertesten.

Uhu and wine

No, GIN_Uh! has nothing to do with glue but with „Uhu", the German word for eagle owl and the famous Uhudler wine. This story is about grapes viewed through critical, viticultural eyes, which can look back on a long history, special peculiarities and strong roots. Here, in the "present-day Tuscany of Austria", long sunny days and a mild climate prevail. In Southern Burgenland, near the Hungarian border, a very special wine has become a cult drink in recent years, called Uhudler.

Apart from the very robust characteristics of the grape, it owes its name to the women of the village. When the vintners returned from days of working in the vineyards, their wives couldn't help but remark "He has eyes like an owl again". The character of the grape is sweet, fruity and reminiscent of fresh wild strawberry notes – keep an eye on it.

Gin and wine, that's just fine

In this region, winemaker Christoph Gratl is very well known for his quality vines. The repertoire of wines is impressive, but he also produces fine brandies and grappas. So he came up with the idea to combine two cult drinks: Uhudler and gin.

Juniper, exotic aromas and Uhudler grapes are combined to create an exciting Dry Gin, which is given its unique character by classic notes and the fruity essence of the grape. So you don't need to go to the vineyard slopes; you can get eyes like an owl wherever you drink GIN_Uh!

Weichselbaum, Austria

SWISS GIN DISTILLERIES

Berne
Bern
1. *Chameleon Gin*

Lucerne
Entlebuch
2. *Edelwhite Gin*

Zurich
Opfikon
3. *Deux Frères Gin*

Zurich
4. *Dr. Becker's Gin*

Thurgovia
Strohwilen in Thurgau
5. *Sir Dry Gin*

Gottlieben
6. *Porto Sofie Gin*

Appenzell Inner Rhodes
Appenzell
7. *Gin 27*

SWISS GIN DISTILLERIES

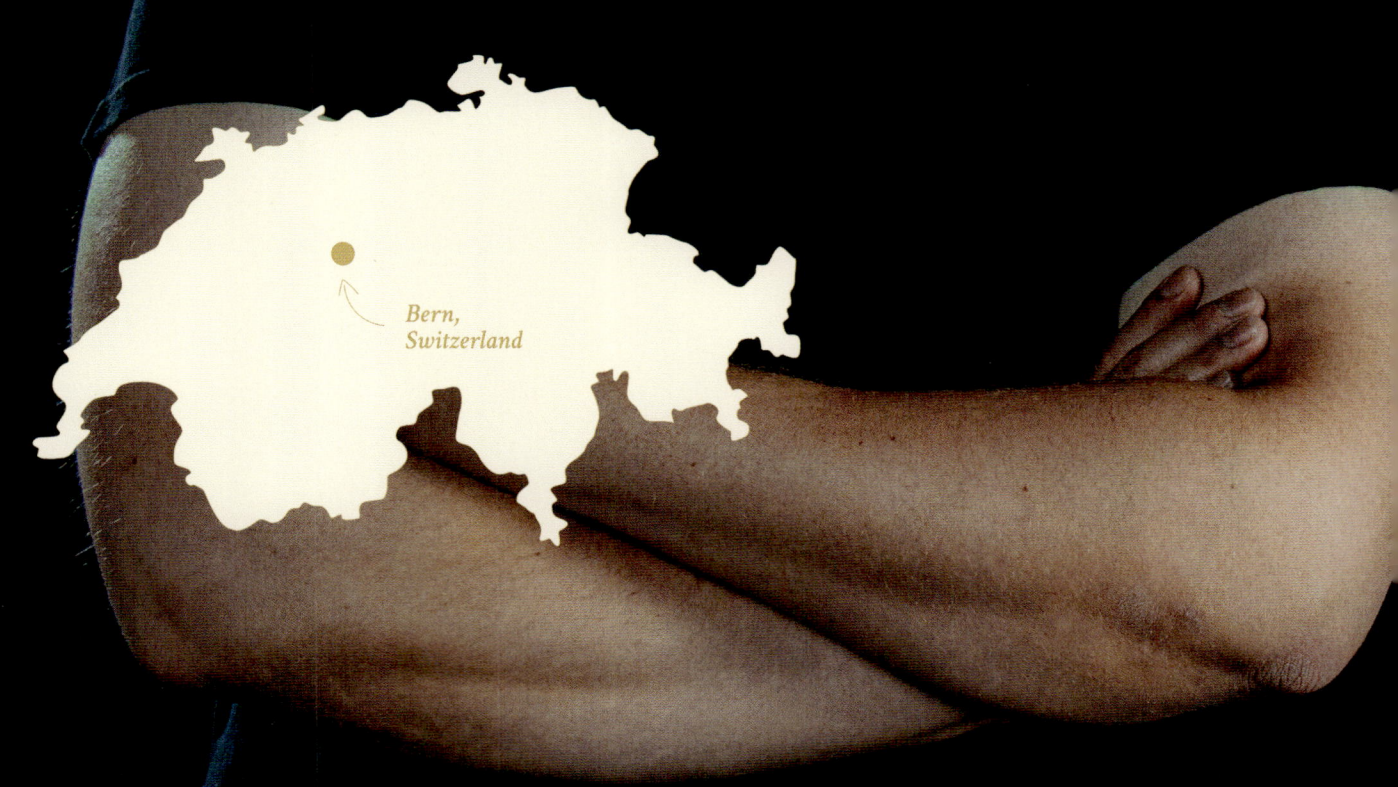

CHAMELEON LIQUIDS

CHAMELEON GIN

Bern, Switzerland

CHAMELEON LIQUIDS // CHAMELEON GIN

0,5 L // 42,0 %

GIN

CATEGORY
Dry Gin

ORIGIN
Switzerland

ESTABLISHED
2019

SIZE
● ○ ○ ○

TASTING NOTES
Angenehm milde florale Noten geben dem Gin eine gewisse Leichtigkeit – durch den Ingwer dezent scharf im Abgang.

Pleasantly mild floral notes give the gin a certain lightness – due to the ginger a little bit spicy in the finish.

Der Farbwechsler: Chameleon Gin

Zwei Männer, die sich im Studium kennenlernen und das Ziel haben, unverwechselbare Erlebnisse zu schaffen, die man mit Freunden teilen und genießen kann. Sandro Batoni und Lukas Trautweiler hat die Ausbildung zusammengebracht, ihre Leidenschaft für guten Geschmack verbindet sie. Aus einem Studienprojekt der Lebensmittelwissenschaften entwickelt sich ein Start-up in Bern. Herausgebracht wird ein besonderer Gin, der von Hand in kleinen Mengen abgefüllt und veredelt wird.

Der Chameleon Gin bietet ein rundes Geschmackserlebnis mit Noten von Rosenblüten, Kardamom, Zitronengras und Ingwer und einem speziellen optischen Effekt. Denn bei der Zugabe eines säurehaltigen Erfrischungsgetränkes, wie zum Beispiel Tonic Water, wechselt der Gin seine Farbe von einem runden Königsblau in ein verspieltes Violett. Dieser Effekt entsteht durch den Farbstoff der Clitoria ternatea, der aus der Blüte in den Gin übergeht. Die Hauptaromen sind Kardamom und Rose, dazu kommen Nuancen von Orange und Fenchelsamen.

Mystische Farbe und einzigartiges aromatisches Profil

Der Chameleon Gin besteht aus reinstem Quellwasser, hochwertigem Alkohol und den besten natürlichen Zutaten. Die einzigartige Zusammensetzung wird sowohl erfahrene Gin-Liebhaber als auch -Neulinge ansprechen und begeistern. Durch die Mischung von Kräutern, Samen und Blüten wurde ein einzigartiges aromatisches Profil entwickelt, das durch seine mystische, für Gin unübliche Farbe unterstrichen wird. Der Chameleon Dry Gin: mit seinem optischen Spezialeffekt ein Erlebnis für alle Sinne!

> *A gin as variable as a chameleon.*

The color changer: Chameleon Gin

Two men who met at college and shared the goal of creating distinctive experiences to share and enjoy with friends. Sandro Batoni and Lukas Trautweiler were brought together by their education, and their passion for good taste unites them. A start-up in Bern developed from a study project in food science. The result is a special gin that is bottled and refined by hand in small batches.

Chameleon Gin offers a round taste experience with notes of rose petals, cardamom, lemongrass and ginger and a special optical effect. This is because when an acidic soft drink, such as tonic water, is added, the gin changes color from a round royal blue to a playful violet. This effect is created by the Clitoria ternatea pigment that passes from the flower into the gin. The main aromas are cardamom and rose, with nuances of orange and fennel seed.

Mystic color and unique aromatic profile

Chameleon Gin is made from the purest spring water, high quality alcohol and the best natural ingredients. The unique composition will appeal to and delight both experienced gin connoisseurs and novices. The blend of herbs, seeds and flowers has developed a unique aromatic profile, which is emphasized by its cryptic color, unusual for gin. Chameleon Dry Gin: with its special optical effect, an experience for all the senses.

BARB GROSSENBACHER

EDELWHITE GIN

Entlebuch, Switzerland

In der Höhle der Löwen

Wenn gleich zwei Investoren aus der „Höhle der Löwen" investieren möchten, könnte man selbst vor Freude brüllen. Jedoch nicht die liebe Barb Grossenbacher, die mit äußerer Ruhe und Coolness handelte und den Sieg nach Hause brachte. Gebrüllt vor Freude hat sie vielleicht im Auto, das weiß nur sie. Aber was überzeugte die Löwen? Der Edelwhite Gin von Barb Grossenbacher war ursprünglich als Diplomarbeit gedacht. Was als „Hausaufgabe" mit 300 Flaschen begann, wurde eine eigene Firma mit Brennanlage, Lager und einem Investor als Mentor im Hintergrund. Seit 2018 sammelt der Edelwhite Gin weltweit Medaillen ein und lebt seine ganz eigene Erfolgsgeschichte.

Gin aus dem Entlebuch

Die kleine Gemeinde Entlebuch mitten in den Bergen der alpinen Schweiz ist die Heimat der gebürtigen Kanadierin und ihrer kleinen Manufaktur. Zusammen mit einer Freundin entwickelte sie den Edelwhite Gin, der die vielfältige Natur der UNESCO-Biosphäre um Entlebuch und der Schweiz widerspiegeln sollte. Dabei bezieht sie von den insgesamt 27 Botanicals 14 aus der Umgebung. Der eigene Garten und Gärten von Freunden sowie ein lokaler Händler versorgen sie mit dem, was die Region hergibt. Zum Edelwhite Gin kamen der Edelwhite 57 (Navy Strength Gin) und der Edelwhite Vodka dazu. Barb Grossenbacher ist jedoch noch lange nicht fertig. Bei allen Produkten möchte sie die Qualität und Regionalität bewahren. Die Geschichte des Edelwhite Gin geht weiter.

CATEGORY
London Dry Gin

ORIGIN
Switzerland

ESTABLISHED
2018

SIZE
● ○ ○ ○

TASTING NOTES

Der Edelwhite Gin ist vom Beginn bis zum Abgang eine abenteuerliche Wanderung durch einen üppigen Garten. Am Anfang spielt eine zarte Süße, die anschließend vom kernig-waldigen Wacholder eingeholt wird. Was dann folgt, ist eine Explosion der Botanicals. Blumig, würzig, kräuterig und frisch geben die Zutaten ihr Bestes. Der Abgang bleibt blumig, mit einem Hauch von eleganter Süße. Eine Wanderung für die Sinne.

From start to finish, Edelwhite Gin is an adventurous trek through a lush garden. A delicate sweetness plays at the beginning, pursued by the pithy, arboreal juniper. What follows is an explosion of botanicals. Floral, spicy, herbal and fresh, the ingredients deliver their best. The finish remains floral, with a hint of elegant sweetness. A trek for the senses.

In the Shark Tank

If two investors from the Swiss version of that TV show want to invest simultaneously, your job might be difficult to suppress. But not dear Barb Grossenbacher, who acted with outward calm and coolness as she brought her victory home. Maybe she released her happiness on the car ride home, only she knows. But what convinced the sharks? Edelwhite Gin by Barb Grossenbacher began as a diploma thesis. What started as a "homework assignment" involving 300 bottles became a company of its own with a distillation plant, warehouse and an investor as a mentor in the background. Since 2018, Edelwhite Gin has been collecting medals worldwide and experiencing its very own success story.

Gin from Entlebuch

The small community of Entlebuch, in the midst of the mountains of alpine Switzerland, is the home of this native Canadian and her small operation. Together with a friend, she developed Edelwhite Gin to reflect the diverse nature of the UNESCO biosphere around Entlebuch and Switzerland. Consequently, she sources 14 of the total 27 botanicals from the surrounding area. Her own garden and the gardens of friends, as well as a local trader, supply her with what the region has to offer. Edelwhite Gin was joined by Edelwhite 57 (Navy Strength Gin) and Edelwhite Vodka. Barb Grossenbacher is far from finished, however. She wants to preserve quality and regionality in all her products. The story of Edelwhite Gin continues.

> From botanicals to the bottle.

DEUX FRÈRES GMBH

DEUX FRÈRES GIN

Opfikon, Switzerland

DEUX FRÈRES

DRY GIN

25 BOTANICALS · HANDCRAFTED

Bis idem non est idem

43% VOL { 500 ML

DEUX FRÈRES GMBH // DEUX FRÈRES GIN

0,5 L // 43,0%

Aus 11 mach 25

Es waren einmal zwei Brüder. Sie lebten glücklich und zufrieden auf dem Bauernhof ihrer Eltern nahe Zürich. Doch eines Tages wollten sie eine neue Welt kennenlernen. Eine Welt voller Aromen und chemischer Prozesse. Sie wollten einen eigenen Gin kreieren. Fernab großer Brennereien entstand im Heimlabor die erste Rezeptur ihres Deux Frères. Der L1000T1 wurde mit elf Botanicals mit einer Destillationsanlage Marke Eigenbau hergestellt. Nach zahlreichen weiteren Destillationen und Rezepturanpassungen fanden Gian und Florian Grundböck eineinhalb Jahre später die entscheidende Rezeptur mit 25 Botanicals. Inzwischen ist Deux Frères die größte Schweizer Gin-Marke im In- und Ausland.

Ein netter Show-Effekt

Im Purzustand leuchtet der Gin in einem kräftigen Blau. Ändert sich der Charakter des Getränks, zum Beispiel durch die Zugabe von Tonic Water, verfärbt sich die Spirituose rosa. Für den Zaubertrick im Glas sind die Farbpigmente einer sagenumwobenen Blume verantwortlich – die 25. Zutat im Deux Frères. Je nach pH-Wert wechseln die darin enthaltenen Anthocyanen ihre Farbe, erscheinen also im sauren und im basischen Bereich in unterschiedlichen Tönen. Als die Brüder 2015 mit Deux Frères auf den Markt kamen, war der Farbeffekt ein Alleinstellungsmerkmal im deutschsprachigen Raum. Inzwischen haben auch andere Produzenten verstanden, wie der Zaubertrick funktioniert. Gian und Florian Grundböck haben das geahnt und ihren Fokus deshalb von Anfang an auf die Qualität ihres Gins gelegt und den Farbwechsel immer als unterhaltsamen Showeffekt verstanden.

> The blue one from Zurich, who also likes pink.

From 11 make 25

Once upon a time there were two brothers. They lived happily on their parents' farm near Zurich. But one day they wanted to get to know a new world. A world full of aromas and chemical processes. They wanted to create their own gin. Far away from large distilleries, the first recipe of their Deux Frères gin was created in their home laboratory. The L1000T1 was made with eleven botanicals using a homemade distillation system. After numerous further distillations and recipe adjustments, Gian and Florian Grundböck found the ultimate recipe with 25 botanicals one and a half years later. Since then, Deux Frères has become the largest gin brand in Switzerland and abroad.

A nice show effect

When neat, the gin glows a vibrant blue. If the character of the drink changes, for example by adding tonic water, the spirit turns pink. The color pigments of a legendary flower are responsible for the magic trick in the glass – the 25th ingredient in Deux Frères. Depending on the pH value, the anthocyanins contained in it change color, thus exhibiting different shades across the acid-alkali range. When the brothers launched Deux Frères in 2015, the color effect was a unique selling point in the German-speaking world. In the meantime other producers have also understood how the magic trick works. Gian and Florian Grundböck suspected this and therefore put their focus on the quality of their gin from the very beginning, having always seen the color change as an entertaining show effect.

CATEGORY
Dry Gin

ORIGIN
Switzerland

ESTABLISHED
2015

SIZE

TASTING NOTES

Blumig und frisch in der Nase, weich und harmonisch, komplexe Aromen, abgerundet durch eine feine Würze, klare Wacholdernote, lang anhaltender Abgang.

Flowery and fresh in the nose, soft and harmonious, complex aromas, rounded by a fine spiciness, clear juniper note, long-lasting finish.

HIGH CLASS DENTISTRY GMBH

DR. BECKER'S GIN

Zurich, Switzerland

Bewegte Geschichte

Als junger Mann war Hans-Jörg Becker auf einem Schüleraustausch in England. Neben den musikalisch hinterlegten Pub-Besuchen blieb ihm eine Sache ganz besonders im Gedächtnis. Im nahe gelegenen Altersheim untergebracht, wurde er einem Phänomen Zeuge, das junge Leute in seinem Alter zum Umdenken bewegt. Die alten Damen und Herren schwangen hier das Tanzbein und zelebrierten das Leben, als gäbe es kein Morgen. Wie er später erfuhr, waren das die besten Partys in der Gegend. Hier machte er das erste Mal Bekanntschaft mit dem Gin als Jungbrunnen. Heute, viele Jahre später, unterhalten Dr. Hans-Jörg Becker und seine Frau Ursula eine florierende Zahnarztpraxis und können in den Jahren auf weitere spannende Begegnungen und Abenteuer zurückblicken. Das Bedürfnis, etwas zurückzugeben, war groß. Es kam die verrückte Idee auf, einen eigenen Gin zu produzieren, der eine Hommage an die kleinen und großen Ereignisse darstellen sollte: den Dr. Becker's Gin.

Gute Worte, guter Gin

Die heilende Wirkung von Wacholder ist vielen bekannt. Ebenso die Macht eines gut gemeinten Wortes. Kombiniert ergibt das eine Idee, deren Ergebnis sich sehen lassen kann. „Liebe und Dankbarkeit" ist nicht nur den vielen Menschen gewidmet, die der Familie Becker im Leben halfen, sondern ebenso all jenen, die diese Worte einfach mal wieder brauchen (oder ein guten Schluck Gin). Wenn man das Ehepaar über ihren kleinen Traum reden hört, hat man Lust, den Gin auf der Stelle zu probieren. In kleinen Chargen von der Brennerei Penth hergestellt, ist der klassische London Dry ein wohltuender und angenehmer Begleiter. Seit 2018 gibt der Gin gute gemeinte Worte sowie ein warmes Gefühl weiter und animiert bestimmt auch das ein oder andere Tanzbein hier und da zu später Stunde. Wohl bekomms!

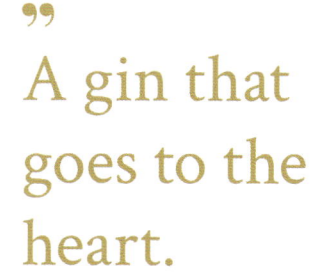

> **A gin that goes to the heart.**

Moving history

As a young man, Hans-Jörg Becker was on a student exchange in England. In addition to pub visits with musical backing, one thing in particular remained in his memory. Staying in a nearby retirement home, he witnessed a phenomenon that made young people his age change their minds. Here, the old ladies and gentlemen were dancing and celebrating life like there's no tomorrow. As he later learned, these were the best parties in the area. It was here that he first became acquainted with gin as a fountain of youth. Today, many years later, Dr. Hans-Jörg Becker and his wife Ursula maintain a thriving dental practice and can look back on other exciting encounters and adventures over the years. The need to give something back was great. The crazy idea came up to produce their own gin, which should be a tribute to events big and small: Dr. Becker's Gin.

Good words, good gin

The healing properties of juniper are known to many. So is the power of a well-intentioned word. Combined, this results in an idea the outcome of which is a source of pride. "Love and Gratitude" is dedicated not only to the many people who helped the Becker family in life, but equally to all those who simply need those words again (or a good sip of gin). Hearing the couple talk about their little dream makes you want to taste the gin right then and there. Made in small batches by Penth Distillery, this classic London Dry is a soothing and enjoyable companion. Since 2018, the gin has been passing on well-meant words as well as a warm feeling and is sure to animate the odd dancing leg here and there late at night. Good cheer!

CATEGORY
London Dry Gin

ORIGIN
Germany

ESTABLISHED
2018

SIZE
● ● ● ●

TASTING NOTES
Ein überraschend aromatischer und fruchtiger Start. Eine sehr angenehme Note nach Orangen macht hier den ersten Schritt, bevor frische Zitronen und herbe Kräuter den ersten Eindruck schnell übernehmen. Ein milder Gin mit ausbalancierten, angenehmen Aromen, die einen eleganten London Dry mit fruchtigem Charakter wiedergeben.

Starts off surprisingly aromatic and fruity. A very pleasant note of oranges makes the first step here, before fresh lemons and tart herbs quickly take over the first impression. A mild gin with balanced, pleasant flavors that reflect an elegant London Dry with a fruity character.

0,5 L // 48,0 %

MACARDO SWISS DISTILLERY

SIR DRY GIN

Komplexer Gin mit einzigartigem Geschmack

Die Rezeptur des mit 18 auserwählten regionalen Bio-Botanicals bereicherten Schweizer Dry Gin ist geheim. Am Gaumen hat er eine milde Würze sowie eine zarte Säure und im Abgang eine raffinierte Schärfe. Der Sir Dry Gin ist sehr komplex, herrlich parfümiert, mit Minze, Anis, Kokos, Limette, Schwarztee und Heu. Er ist körperreich, facettenreich und angenehm herb, mit anderen Worten: Sein Geschmack ist einzigartig. In der Nase hat er einen aromatischen Wacholderduft, riecht angenehm frisch mit Röst- und Getreidenoten sowie einem finessenreichen Spiel von Zitrusaromen. Optisch ist er glasklar, funkelnd und hat einen leichten Blaustich.

Tradition, Destillierhandwerk und Genuss

Der Sir Dry Gin wird in der Schweiz nach einem Rezept aus dem London des 18. Jahrhunderts hergestellt und mehrfach destilliert. Es werden keine Farbstoffe oder Zucker verwendet. Die Macardo Swiss Distillery steht für Tradition, Innovation, Handwerk, Small-Batch, Premiumqualität und Nachhaltigkeit. Mit dieser Philosophie hat es das Schweizer Unternehmen in wenigen Jahren zu internationaler Beachtung gebracht. Gegründet im Jahr 2007 in Strohwilen im Thurgau, galten sowohl der beschauliche Ort als auch die Distillery als Geheimtipp. Hier wollen die Macher den Genuss zelebrieren und für ihre Kunden einzigartige Erlebnisse schaffen. Der Ort steht für Tradition, Destillierhandwerk und Genuss, hier gibt es die besten Voraussetzungen, um das Handwerk zu pflegen und weiterzuentwickeln.

Complex gin with unique taste

The recipe of this Swiss Dry Gin enriched with 18 selected regional organic botanicals is secret. On the palate it has a mild spiciness as well as a delicate acidity and a refined edge in the finish. Sir Dry Gin is very complex, wonderfully perfumed, with mint, anise, coconut, lime, black tea and hay. It's full-bodied, multi-faceted and pleasantly tart, in other words, its flavor is unique. On the nose, it has an aromatic juniper scent, smelling pleasantly fresh with toasty and cereal notes and a fine play of citrus aromas. Visually, it's crystal clear, sparkling and has a slight blue tint.

Tradition, distilling craft and pleasure

Sir Dry Gin is made in Switzerland according to a recipe from 18th century London and distilled several times. No colorants or sugar are used. Macardo Swiss Distillery stands for tradition, innovation, craftsmanship, small-batch, premium quality and sustainability. With this philosophy, the Swiss company has made it to international recognition in just a few years. Founded in 2007 in Strohwilen in Thurgau, both the tranquil village and the distillery were considered insider tips. Here, the makers want to celebrate pleasure and create unique experiences for their customers. The place stands for tradition, distillery craft and enjoyment; here are the best conditions for cultivating and further developing the craft.

> **Juniper and citrus aromas, delicate acidity and refined spiciness.**

Strohwilen in Thurgau, Switzerland

CATEGORY
Dry Gin

ORIGIN
Switzerland

ESTABLISHED
2007

SIZE
● ○ ○ ○

TASTING NOTES
Am Gaumen eine milde Würze mit einer zarten Säure und im Abgang eine raffinierte Schärfe. Körperreich, facettenreich und angenehm herb. In der Nase hat er einen aromatischen Wacholderduft, riecht angenehm frisch mit Röst- und Getreidenoten sowie einem finessenreichen Spiel von Zitrusaromen.

Mild spice on the palate with a delicate acidity and a refined spiciness on the finish. Full-bodied, multi-faceted and pleasantly tart. The nose has an aromatic juniper scent, smelling pleasantly fresh with toasty and cereal notes and a fine play of citrus aromas.

FAUDE FEINE BRÄNDE

PORTO SOFIE DRY GIN

Gottlieben, Switzerland

Zeit für neue Traditionen

Im Osten der Schweiz liegt, ganz idyllisch an der Uferpromenade des Seerheins als Teil des Bodensees, das pittoreske Dorf Gottlieben. In die kleine Gemeinde mit Baudenkmälern aus dem 17. Jahrhundert und in die bewegte Vergangenheit des sogenannten Steinhauses verliebte sich das Unternehmerpaar Sophie Schreiber und Jürgen Seifert sofort – und erfüllte sich mit der Eröffnung seines Hotels im antiken Stil von Louis-seize bis Art déco im April 2021 einen Traum. Mit Liebe zum Detail gestalteten sie jedes Zimmer individuell, mit geschmackvoll aufeinander abgestimmten Antiquitäten aus dem Alpenraum. Direkt gegenüber der alten Gottlieber Schiffsanlegestelle gelegen, wollen die beiden Entrepreneurs auch das „Porto Sofie" sinnbildlich zu einem Ort des Ankommens machen, an dem sich Kaffeehaus- mit Bar-Kultur, aber auch Spezialitäten und Spirituosen aus der ganzen Welt stimmig vereinen. Herzstück dieses Vorhabens ist die hufeisenförmige, in edlem Gold, Grün und Schwarz gehaltene Bar: Sie beherbergt neben vielen anderen hochwertigen Spirituosen einen hauseigenen Gin – komponiert vom Spirituosen-Sommelier und Mitglied der internationalen Gin-Gilde Patrick Braun.

Freie Entfaltung im Steingut

Der Trend in der Spirituosen-Welt entfernt sich immer mehr weg von schnell zusammengemixten Getränken hin zu einer Rückbesinnung auf alte Werte und hochwertige Spirituosen, die mit frischen Zutaten komponiert werden: Mit Kräutern wie Basilikum, Rosmarin, Chili oder Zitronengras werden die Klassiker wieder lebendig. Dem folgt auch der Porto Sofie Dry Gin. Im Vordergrund seiner traditionellen Rezeptur steht eine ausgewogene, dominante Wacholdernote: Durch die Botanicals Angelikawurzel und Koriander, vor allem aber durch die Frische der Zitrone wird er gekonnt in Szene gesetzt. Gebrannt wird der Gin im Pot-Still-Verfahren von Florian Faude in Zusammenarbeit mit Patrick Braun. Nach der Destillation geben Steingut-Gefäße dem Porto Sofie Dry Gin die Ruhe und dem Aromenspiel die notwendige Zeit, sich zu verbinden und zu entfalten.

> With its traditional recipe and production, 'Porto Sofie Dry Gin' reflects the expertise in spirits of the in-house bar.

Time for new traditions

In the east of Switzerland, lying quite idyllically on the shore promenade of the Seerhein as part of Lake Constance, is the picturesque village of Gottlieben. The entrepreneurial couple Sophie Schreiber and Jürgen Seifert immediately fell in love with this small community, with its architectural monuments dating back to the 17th century and the eventful past of the so-called stone house – and fulfilled a dream by opening their hotel in the antique style ranging from Louis-seize to Art déco in April 2021. With attention to detail, they designed each room individually, with tastefully coordinated antiques from the Alpine region. Situated directly opposite the old Gottlieber landing stage, the two entrepreneurs also wanted to make "Porto Sofie" symbolically a place of arrival, where coffee house and bar culture, but also specialties and spirits from all over the world, harmoniously combine. The heart of this project is the horseshoe-shaped bar, decorated in noble gold, green and black. Alongside many other high-quality spirits, it is home to an in-house gin – composed by spirits sommelier and member of the international gin guild Patrick Braun.

Unfettered development in earthenware

The trend in the world of spirits is increasingly away from quickly mixed drinks and back to old values and high-quality spirits composed with fresh ingredients. With herbs like basil, rosemary, chili or lemongrass, classics are coming back to life. Porto Sofie Dry Gin also follows this trend. In the foreground of its traditional recipe is a balanced, dominant juniper note. Then, through the botanicals angelica and coriander, but especially through the freshness of lemon, it is skillfully set in scene. The gin is distilled in the pot still process by Florian Faude in collaboration with Patrick Braun. After distillation, earthenware vessels give Porto Sofie Dry Gin peace and the necessary time for the play of aromas to combine and unfold.

CATEGORY
London Dry Gin

ORIGIN
Switzerland

ESTABLISHED
2021

SIZE
● ○ ○ ○

TASTING NOTES
Klassischer Dry Gin mit einer klaren Rückbesinnung auf Wacholder, weich, rund und vollmundig am Gaumen, Anklänge von Zitrone, Angelikawurzel und Koriander, dezente Kräuternoten.

Classic Dry Gin with a clear return to juniper, soft, round and full-bodied on the palate, hints of lemon, angelica and coriander, subtle herbal notes.

APPENZELLER ALPENBITTER AG

GIN 27

CATEGORY
Dry Gin

ORIGIN
Switzerland

ESTABLISHED
2013

SIZE
● ● ●

TASTING NOTES
In der Nase komplex und facettenreich. Koriander, Kardamom, , Veilchen, Zimt und Sternanis lassen sich erahnen. Weich und rund am Gaumen. Den langen Abgang begleitet ein Hauch Pfeffrigkeit.

Complex and multi-faceted on the nose. Coriander, cardamom, licorice, violet, cinnamon and star anise are evident. Soft and round on the palate. The long finish is accompanied by a touch of pepperiness.

Ein Schweizer Qualitätsprodukt

Im Jahr 1902 legten die beiden Appenzeller Emil Ebneter und Beat Kölbener den Grundstein für die Appenzeller Alpenbitter AG. Sie entwickelten ein Naturprodukt von hervorragender Qualität und unvergleichlichem Aroma: den Appenzeller Alpenbitter mit 42 auserlesenen Kräutern. Das Originalrezept des beliebtesten Bitters der Schweiz ist bis heute ein gut gehütetes Geheimnis der Gründerfamilie.

Der Tradition verbunden

Wie die beiden Gründer pflegen auch die Nachkommen das Brennhandwerk mit großer Sorgfalt. Sie leben die Tradition und legen gleichzeitig Wert auf Innovation. Qualität steht stets an erster Stelle. Der GIN 27 wird von den Brennmeistern in Appenzell nach eigenem Rezept und nur mit feinsten Zutaten destilliert und abgefüllt. Er vereint Tradition, Bodenständigkeit und eine über Generationen gepflegte Kräuterkompetenz. Das Zusammenspiel von warmen Gewürzaromen, Orange und Wacholder verleiht diesem Edeldestillat seinen frischen und würzigen Charakter.

Wunderbar für exzellente Drinks

Wesentlich an der Entwicklung des GIN 27 beteiligt waren die Barfachleute Peter Roth, Christian Heiss und Markus Blattner. Zusammen mit den Brennmeistern der Appenzeller Alpenbitter AG ließen sie diesen Premium Dry Gin zu dem wachsen, was er ist: ein Meisterwerk mit Herkunft und Tradition und mit einem unverkennbaren Charakter. Der GIN 27 eignet sich ganz wunderbar für exzellente Drinks.

Appenzell, Switzerland

A Swiss quality product

In 1902, Emil Ebneter and Beat Kölbener from Appenzell laid the foundation for Appenzeller Alpenbitter AG. They developed a natural product of outstanding quality and incomparable aroma, namely Appenzeller Alpenbitter, based on 42 selected herbs. The original recipe of Switzerland's most popular bitters has remained a well-kept secret of the founding family to this day.

Connected to tradition

Like the two founders, their descendants also maintain the distilling craft with great care. They live by tradition and, at the same time, attach importance to innovation. Quality always comes first. GIN 27 is distilled and bottled by the master distillers in Appenzell according to their own recipe and only with the finest ingredients. It combines tradition with a down-to-earth nature and herbal expertise developed over generations. The interplay of warm spicy aromas, orange and juniper gives this fine spirit its fresh and spicy character.

Wonderful for excellent drinks

Bar experts Peter Roth, Christian Heiss and Markus Blattner played key roles in the development of GIN 27. Together with the master distillers of Appenzeller Alpenbitter AG, they allowed this premium dry gin to grow into what it is: a masterpiece with background and tradition, along with an unmistakable character. GIN 27 is altogether wonderful for excellent drinks.

> GIN 27: A Swiss quality product.

BRITISH GIN DISTILLERIES

Scotland

Leven, Cameronbridge

1. *Tanqueray London Dry Gin*
2. *Tanqueray Flor de Sevilla Distilled Gin*
3. *Tanqueray Blackcurrant Royale Distilled Gin*

Edinburgh

4. *Lind & Lime Gin*

England

Hampshire

5. *Bombay Sapphire Premiere Cru*

London

6. *Beefeater Dry Gin*
7. *BROCKMANS Gin*
8. *Hayman's Old Tom Gin*
9. *Oxley Gin*
10. *Sipsmith London Dry*

St. Erwan

11. *Tarquin's Cornish Dry Gin*

GIN

BRITISH GIN DISTILLERIES

1-3
4
5
6-10
11

305

DIAGEO CAMERONBRIDGE DISTILLERY

TANQUERAY

*Leven, Cameronbridge,
Great Britain*

DIAGEO CAMERONBRIDGE DISTILLERY // TANQUERAY

0,7 L // 43,1 % (EXPORT STRENGTH 47,3 %)

Auf der Suche nach dem feinsten Gin der Welt

Der Name Tanqueray steht für Perfektion und Geschmack. Charles Tanqueray wollte den feinsten Gin der Welt herstellen. Deshalb verbrachte er viele Jahre auf Reisen damit, mit den erlesensten Botanicals aus aller Welt zu experimentieren. Durch seine unkonventionellen Ideen fand er zu seinem ganz eigenen Stil. Dieser zahlte sich nach sechs Jahren und unzähligen Versuchen aus: Er kreierte den perfekt ausbalancierten Gin – Tanqueray London Dry. Das war 1830. Im gleichen Jahr begann Charles Tanqueray zusammen mit seinem Bruder Edward in der Vine Street Distillery in Bloomsbury, London zu arbeiten. Er übernahm die Destillerie und machte sie zu einer der besten seiner Zeit. Später stieg sein Sohn, Charles Waugh Tanqueray, mit ein und führte die Marke hin zu wirtschaftlichem Erfolg.

Beste Qualität an Botanicals

Das Rezept für diesen London Dry Gin ist seit 1830 unverändert. Wichtig ist ein im Vorfeld aufwändiges selektives Verfahren. So muss der Wacholder mindestens zwei Jahre gereift sein. Verarbeitet werden nur Botanicals bester Qualität: Wacholder, Angelikawurzel, Süßholz und Koriandersamen. Sie bilden die Basis dieses Gins, bei dessen Herstellung insgesamt vierfach destilliert wird. Das Aroma ist vielseitig und klassisch. Die Würze von Wacholder und Koriander wird um eine frische zitronige Note ergänzt. Der Tanqueray London Dry Gin schmeckt intensiv nach Wacholder und Pinie, dazu kommen eine leichte Zitrusnote und Pfeffer. Eine Gin-Ikone!

In search of the finest gin in the world

The name Tanqueray stands for perfection and taste. Charles Tanqueray wanted to produce the finest gin in the world. That's why he spent many years traveling experimenting with the most exquisite botanicals from around the world. Through his unconventional ideas, he found his very own style. This paid off after six years and

> Unchanged since 1830 – a true gin icon!

countless experiments, when he created the perfectly balanced gin – Tanqueray London Dry. That was in 1830, the same year Charles Tanqueray began working with his brother Edward at the Vine Street Distillery in Bloomsbury, London. He took over the distillery and made it one of the best of its time. Later, his son, Charles Waugh Tanqueray, joined in and led the brand to commercial success.

Best quality botanicals

The recipe for this London Dry Gin has remained unchanged since 1830. An important aspect is a prior elaborate process of selection. Thus, the juniper must be matured for at least two years. Only the best quality botanicals are processed: juniper, angelica root, licorice and coriander seeds. They form the basis of this gin, which is distilled a total of four times during its production. The aroma is versatile and classic. The spice of juniper and coriander is complemented by a fresh lemony note. Tanqueray London Dry Gin tastes intensely of juniper and pine, plus a light citrus note and pepper. A gin icon!

CATEGORY
London Dry Gin

ORIGIN
Great Britain

ESTABLISHED
1830

SIZE
● ● ● ●

TASTING NOTES
Würziger Wacholder und Koriander mit einer frischen Zitrusnote. Im Geschmack intensiver Wacholder und Pinie, dazu kommen eine leichte Zitrusnote und Pfeffer.

An aroma of spicy juniper and coriander in combination with a fresh lemony note. A taste intensely of juniper and pine, plus a light citrus note and pepper.

309

DIAGEO CAMERONBRIDGE DISTILLERY

TANQUERAY FLOR DE SEVILLA DISTILLED GIN

CATEGORY
Distilled Flavored Gin

ORIGIN
Great Britain

ESTABLISHED
2018

SIZE
● ● ● ●

TASTING NOTES
Wacholder, Angelikawurzel, Süßholz und Koriandersamen – auf die bittere Süße der spanischen Orangen.

Juniper, angelica root, licorice and coriander seeds – meet the bitter sweetness of Spanish oranges.

> A fruity, spicy combination reminiscent of warm summer nights and the sunny south of Spain.

Fruchtig und pikant

Sonne, Hitze und der Geruch von Wäldern und Früchten: Der Geschmack des sonnendurchfluteten Mittelmeerraumes resultiert in einem einzigartig genussvollen und doch komplexen Gin: dem Tanqueray Flor de Sevilla Distilled Gin. Er schmeckt intensiv nach bittersüßen Sevilla-Orangen und hat eine leichte florale Note von Orangenblüten und einem Hauch Allspice. So schmeckt der Sommer! Tanqueray-Gründer Charles Tanqueray war ein Innovator und Pionier, seine Marke steht für Perfektion und Eleganz. Das Portfolio bietet die passende Variante für jeden Geschmack und jede Gelegenheit.

Experimentieren macht den Meister

Das hängt damit zusammen, dass Charles Tanqueray viele Jahre damit verbrachte, mit den erlesensten Botanicals aus aller Welt zu experimentieren. Sein Ziel war kein Geringeres, als den feinsten Gin der Welt herzustellen. Im Laufe der Zeit hat er Pflanzenextrakte aus der ganzen Welt herangezogen und mit ihnen über 300 Rezepte kreiert. Inspiriert von seinen Reisen zu den sonnenverwöhnten Wäldern Spaniens entstand in den 1860er Jahren ein ganz besonderer, einzigartiger Gin-Likör mit bittersüßen Orangen aus Sevilla: der Tanqueray Flor de Sevilla mit seinem einzigartigen Aroma von Zitrus- und Orangenschale sowie einem Hauch von Wacholder, Vanille und Gewürzen.

Fruity and spicy

Sun, heat and the scent of forests and fruits; the taste of the sun-drenched Mediterranean results in a uniquely enjoyable yet complex gin – Tanqueray Flor de Sevilla Distilled Gin. It tastes intensely of bittersweet Seville oranges and has a light floral note of orange blossom and a hint of allspice. This is what summer tastes like! Tanqueray founder Charles Tanqueray was an innovator and pioneer, his brand stands for perfection and style. The portfolio offers the right variant for every taste and every occasion.

Experimenting makes perfect

This is due to Charles Tanqueray's spending many years experimenting with the most exquisite botanicals from around the world. His goal was no less than to produce the finest gin in the world. Over the years, he sourced botanicals from around the world and used them to create over 300 recipes. Inspired by his travels to the sun-drenched forests of Spain, a very special, one-of-a-kind gin liqueur was created in the 1860s with bittersweet oranges from Seville. Tanqueray Flor de Sevilla, with its unique aroma of citrus and orange peel, as well as hints of juniper, vanilla and spices.

CATEGORY
Distilled Flavored Gin

ORIGIN
Great Britain

ESTABLISHED
2021

SIZE
● ● ● ● ○

TASTING NOTES
Eine Komposition aus
frischer Johannisbeere
und zarter Vanille
– abgerundet durch
florale Noten.

*A composition of fruity
blackcurrant and a touch
of vanilla – complemented
by floral notes.*

DIAGEO CAMERONBRIDGE DISTILLERY

TANQUERAY BLACKCURRANT ROYALE DISTILLED GIN

Ein Flavored Gin der Premiumklasse

Der Tanqueray Blackcurrant Royale ist ein Flavored Gin der Premiumklasse, wie man es von der erfolgreichen Traditionsmarke Tanqueray gewohnt ist. Der Name der Marke steht für Perfektion und Geschmack, das Portfolio bietet die passende Variante für jeden Geschmack und jede Gelegenheit. Mit seiner eleganten violetten Farbe und dem französischen, floralen Design ist dieser Gin ein wahrer Blickfang und macht Lust auf einen fruchtigen Drink. Ob als Getränk am frühen Abend oder als Sundowner: Der Tanqueray Blackcurrant Royale Distilled Gin eignet sich ideal als Mix-Drink.

Dunkle Früchte und ein Hauch Orchidee

Inspiriert durch die Reisen von Charles Tanqueray in den 1840er-Jahren nach Paris basiert das Rezept des Tanqueray Blackcurrant Royale Distilled Gin auf dem klassischen Tanqueray London Dry Gin. In zusätzlichen Destillationen werden Mazerate der Schwarzen Johannisbeere und Vanille sowie weitere Extrakte – inspiriert durch Schwarze Orchideen – weiterverarbeitet. Dadurch bekommt er ein einzigartiges Geschmacksprofil. Die typischen Botanicals im Tanqueray London Dry Gin treffen auf eine komplexe und fruchtige Nase. Das Aroma saftiger, reifer Schwarzer Johannisbeeren vermischt sich mit einer subtilen Süße und endet mit den zarten Noten von Vanille. Hinzu kommen Aromen, die von Schwarzen Orchideen inspiriert sind. So entsteht ein intensiver Geschmack von Schwarzer Johannisbeere mit einem exotischen, geheimnisvollen Hauch von floralen Noten. Ein abschließender Touch von Vanille und Blumen rundet das Gaumengefühl ab.

A flavored gin of the premium class

Tanqueray Blackcurrant Royale is a flavored gin of the premium class, as is familiar coming from the successful traditional brand, Tanqueray. The name of the brand stands for perfection and taste, with the portfolio offering the right variant for every taste and every occasion. With its elegant purple color and French floral design, this gin is a real eye-catcher and makes you fancy a fruity drink. Whether as an early-evening drink or a sundowner, Tanqueray Blackcurrant Royale Distilled Gin is ideal as a mixing drink.

Dark fruit and a touch of orchid

Inspired by Charles Tanqueray's travels to Paris in the 1840s, the recipe of Tanqueray Blackcurrant Royale Distilled Gin is based on classic Tanqueray London Dry Gin. In additional distillations, macerates of blackcurrant and vanilla as well as other extracts – inspired by black orchids – are further processed. This gives it a unique flavor profile. The typical botanicals in Tanqueray London Dry Gin meet a complex and fruity nose. The aroma of juicy, ripe blackcurrants mingles with a subtle sweetness and finishes with the delicate notes of vanilla. In addition, there are aromas reminiscent of black orchids. This creates an intense taste of blackcurrant with an exotic, mysterious touch of floral notes. A final touch of vanilla and flowers completes the palate sensation.

> „ The fruity alternative to the gin icon as an ideal sundowner.

0,7 L // 41,3 %

THE TOWER STREET STILLHOUSE

LIND & LIME GIN

Historische Hinterlassenschaften

Was haben ein schottischer Chirurg, Vitamin-C-Mangel und London Dry Gin gemeinsam? Limetten! 1747 bemerkte Dr. James Lind, dass Zitrusfrüchte Skorbut vorbeugen – eine medizinische Sensation, denn Lind gelangte zu der Erkenntnis, weil er sich nicht wie seine Kollegen an der Theorie festklammerte, sondern weil er seiner Beobachtung – einer medizinischen Studie – vertraute. Eben diesem renommierten Schiffsarzt aus dem 18. Jahrhundert ist der Lind & Lime Gin aus der Tower Street-Brennerei, einer kleinen Destillerie in Leith im Hafenbezirk von Edinburgh, gewidmet. Wie könnte

CATEGORY
London Dry Gin

ORIGIN
Scotland

ESTABLISHED
2017

SIZE
● ● ○ ○

TASTING NOTES
Weich und puristisch, harmonisch und ausbalanciert, Wacholderbeeren und Rosa Pfeffer dominieren im Aroma, dazu gesellen sich süßlich-spritzige Limette und ein Hauch von Lakritze.

Smooth with purity, harmonious and balanced, juniper berries and pink pepper dominate the aroma, joined by sweet tangy lime and a hint of licorice.

„

A gin with outstanding inner values and a beautiful exterior.

Historical legacies

What do a Scottish surgeon, vitamin C deficiency and London Dry Gin have in common? Limes! In 1747, Dr. James Lind noticed that citrus fruits prevented scurvy – a medical sensation because Lind came to the realization not by clinging to theory like his colleagues, but by trusting his observation – a medical study. It is to this renowned 18th-century ship's doctor that Lind & Lime Gin, from Tower Street Distillery, a small distillery in Leith in Edinburgh's waterfront district, is dedicated. So what, other than limes, could possibly lead the seven botanicals in Lind & Lime London Dry Gin?

Filled into wine bottles

Four days pass before a batch of this fine spirit is ready. During those 96 hours, the alcohol first enters into a liaison with juniper berries, pink pepper, coriander seeds as well as iris, angelica and licorice root, before lime peels find their way into the distillation rig, powered by renewable energy, and distillation begins. After the water-infused gin settles for 48 hours and stabilizes, it is filled into a wine bottle. That's right! A wine bottle – and there's a good reason for that. For Leith was a major center of glassmaking during the Industrial Revolution – a historical legacy to which the makers of Lind & Lime Gin are happy to pay homage with the "Leith Glass Works" certificate embossed on the bottom of the bottle.

LAVERSTOKE MILL DISTILLERY

BOMBAY SAPPHIRE PREMIER CRU

Hampshire, Great Britain

LAVERSTOKE MILL DISTILLERY // BOMBAY SAPPHIRE PREMIER CRU

0,7 L // 47,0 %

ORIGIN
Great Britain

ESTABLISHED
1986 as Bombay Sapphire,
Premier Cru introduced 2021

SIZE
● ● ● ●

TASTING NOTES
Von Beginn an begleitet einen deutlich das Zitrusaroma im Bombay Sapphire Premier Cru. Mit einer sanften, aber bestimmenden Explosion breitet sich dieses im Mundraum aus. Dennoch weist der Gin eine angenehme Milde auf. Dezent im Hintergrund vernimmt man erst im Nachhinein die Wacholderaromen und eine leichte Schärfe von Pfeffer. Im Ganzen harmoniert die Zitrusfrische perfekt mit den Kräuterauszügen und sorgt für einen angenehmen Abgang.

From the beginning, the citrus aroma is your clear companion in Bombay Sapphire Premier Cru. With a gentle but decisive explosion, this spreads in the mouth. Nevertheless, the gin has a pleasant mildness. Discreetly in the background, one notices the juniper aromas and a slight spiciness of pepper only in retrospect. Overall, the citrus freshness harmonizes perfectly with the herbal extracts and provides a pleasant finish.

Der Bombay Sapphire Premier Cru Murcian Lemon

Die 1986 eingeführte Marke Bombay Sapphire ist allen ein Begriff. Es gab sie bereits vor dem Gin-Hype und es wird sie auch noch danach geben. Die blauen patentierten Flaschen stehen schon immer majestätisch für Bombay. So groß die Marke, die seit 1997 zur Bacardi Group gehört, auch ist, sie weiß sich des Ursprungs zu erinnern. Im ländlichen Laverstoke Mill in Hampshire, süd-westlich von London, liegt die 2014 eröffnete Destillerie. Wo früher Banknoten für das britische Empire hergestellt wurden, entwickelten Masterdestillerin Dr. Anne Brock und Master of Botanicals Ivano Tonutti den Bombay Sapphire Premier Cru, der auf einem Rezept aus dem Jahr 1761 basiert. Alle Botanicals stammen aus zertifizierter, nachhaltig betriebener Landwirtschaft, allen voran eine aromatisch starke Zitrusfrucht, die dem Bombay Sapphire Premier Cru seinen deutlichen Zitruscharakter verleiht. Somit wird beim Super Premium Gin besonders auf Nachhaltigkeit geachtet.

Qualität und Besinnung

Wer Bombay Sapphire kennt, weiß, dass sie keine halben Sachen machen. In direkter Zusammenarbeit mit den murcianischen Landwirten werden die Zutaten von Master of Botanicals Ivano Tonutti strengstens auf ihre Qualität kontrolliert. Masterdestillerin Dr. Anne Brock destilliert unter strenger Aufsicht mittels hundertprozentiger Dampfinfusion besonders schonend. Die für den Bombay Sapphire Premier Cru ausschlaggebenden Zitrusfrüchte stammen von einem Hof aus der Region Murcia und werden nur einmal im Jahr zur Frühernte von Hand gepflückt. Nicht nur die Zutaten sind somit in der Menge limitiert, auch der Gin selbst wird in begrenzter Stückzahl, im sogenannten Small Batch-Verfahren, hergestellt. Mit der Zielsetzung, einen Gin möglichst nachhaltig und liebevoll herzustellen, zeigt Bombay wieder deutlich, dass er nicht grundlos an der Weltspitze anzutreffen ist.

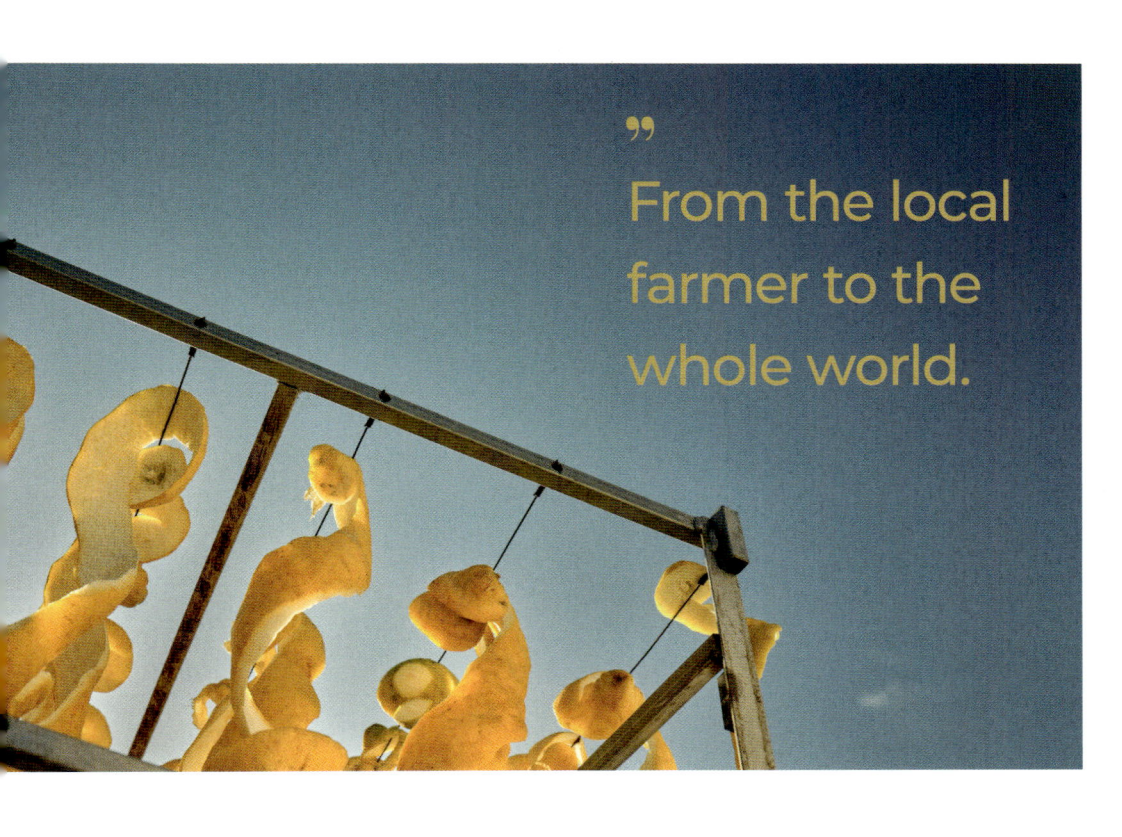

> "From the local farmer to the whole world.

Bombay Sapphire Premier Cru Murcian Lemon

The Bombay Sapphire brand, launched in 1986, is a household name to everyone. It existed before the gin hype and it will continue to exist afterwards. The blue patented bottles have always stood majestically for Bombay. Notwithstanding the size of the brand, which has been part of the Bacardi Group since 1997, it's perfectly capable of remembering its origins. Located in rural Laverstoke Mill in Hampshire, southwest of London, the distillery opened in 2014. Where banknotes were once produced for the British Empire, master distiller Dr. Anne Brock and Master of Botanicals Ivano Tonutti developed Bombay Sapphire Premier Cru, based on a recipe dating back to 1761. All botanicals are sourced from certified, sustainably farmed sources, led by an aromatically strong citrus fruit that gives Bombay Sapphire Premier Cru its distinct citrus character. Thus, the Super Premium Gin pays particular attention to sustainability.

Quality and contemplation

Anyone who knows Bombay Sapphire knows that they don't do things by halves. In direct collaboration with Murcian farmers, the ingredients are strictly controlled for quality by Master of Botanicals Ivano Tonutti. Master distiller Dr. Anne Brock distills under strict supervision using hundred-strength steam infusion in a particularly gentle manner. The citrus fruits that are crucial for Bombay Sapphire Premier Cru come from a farm in the Murcia region and are hand-picked just once a year for the early harvest. Thus, not only are the ingredients limited in quantity, but also the gin itself is produced in limited quantities, in the so-called small batch process. With the objective of producing a gin as sustainably and lovingly as possible, Bombay again have clearly shown there's good reason why they're world-leading.

Desmond Payne –
Master Distiller Beefeater

CATEGORY
London Dry Gin

ORIGIN
Great Britain

ESTABLISHED
1863

SIZE
● ● ● ●

TASTING NOTES
Klassisch und bodenständig, intensiv und mild, mit einer feinen Würze und Süße, kräftiger Wacholder, am Gaumen pikante Zitronen- und Orangennoten, zusammen mit dem dezenten Aroma von Parma-Veilchen und Koriandersamen, pfeffrig-korianderartiges Finale.

Classic and down-to-earth, intense and mild, with a subtle spiciness and sweetness, strong juniper, zesty lemon and orange notes on the palate, together with the subtle aroma of Parma violets and coriander seeds, peppery-coriander finish.

BEEFEATER GIN DISTILLERY LONDON

BEEFEATER DRY GIN

James Burroughs Flaggschiff

Er gleicht einem Fels in der Brandung. Seit mehr als 150 Jahren stellt er sich mit stolz geschwellter Brust mutig gegen alle Jungpioniere. Er weiß um seine Fertigkeiten, um seine traditionsreiche Geschichte, die ihm zu diesem kühnen, unverwechselbaren Beefeater Gin werden ließen, der er ist. Alles begann im Jahr 1862, als James Burrough die Brennerei Chelsea von Rectifier & Compounder für 400 Pfund kaufte und ein Jahr später anfing, seinen eigenen Gin herzustellen. Er verbrachte viel Zeit damit, zu experimentieren und neue Verfahren aufzuspüren, und brachte so einen kräftigen Gin hervor, der direkt zum Flaggschiffprodukt der James Burrough Company wurde.

Das Herz schlägt in London

Das Originalrezept aus dem Jahr 1895 sieht vor, dass die Verwendung von neun Botanicals unerlässlich ist, um den vollmundigen Geschmack des Beefeaters zu erzeugen: Wacholder, Angelikawurzel, Angelikasamen, Koriandersamen, Süßholz, Mandeln, Iriswurzel, Sevilla-Orangen und Zitronenschalen. Die Zutaten für jede Charge werden jeden Morgen per Hand gewogen. Destilliert wird jede einzelne Flasche Beefeater inzwischen im Londoner Stadtteil Kensington. 1985 zog die Destillerie hierher, nachdem die ursprüngliche Produktionsstätte in Chelsea zu klein geworden war. Der Name für den Gin entstand übrigens durch eine Beobachtung. Die als Yeoman Warders bezeichneten Wächter des London Towers trugen den Spitznamen Beefeater. Für James Burrough die ideale Bezeichnung für seinen herzhaften und körperreichen Gin, die darüber hinaus die starke Verbindung zu London hervorhebt.

James Burrough's flagship

He is like a rock in the breakers. For more than 150 years, he has bravely stood up to all the young pioneers with a proudly swollen chest. He knows his skills, his history steeped in tradition, have allowed him to become the bold, distinctive Beefeater Gin that he is. It all began in 1862, when James Burrough bought the Chelsea distillery from Rectifier & Compounder for £400 and started making his own gin a year later. He spent a lot of time experimenting and seeking out new processes, producing a powerful gin that went straight to becoming the flagship product of the James Burrough Company.

The heart beats in London

The original recipe, dating back to 1895, calls for the use of nine botanicals essential to creating Beefeater's full-bodied flavor: juniper, angelica root, angelica seed, coriander seed, licorice, almonds, orris root, Seville oranges and lemon peel. The ingredients for each batch are weighed by hand each morning. Meanwhile, every single bottle of Beefeater is distilled in the London borough of Kensington. In 1985, the distillery moved here after the original production facility in Chelsea had become too small. Incidentally, the name for the gin came from an observation. The guards of the Tower of London, known as Yeoman Warders, were nicknamed Beefeaters. For James Burrough it was the ideal name for his hearty and full-bodied gin, further emphasizing its strong connection to London.

London, Great Britain

" A meat eater who's also suitable for vegetarians.

321

LANGLEY DISTILLERY

BROCKMANS GIN

CATEGORY
New Western Dry Gin

ORIGIN
Great Britain

ESTABLISHED
2008

SIZE
● ● ● ○

TASTING NOTES
Primär fruchtig: Blaubeere und Brombeere sorgen für ein intensives Aroma reifer Beeren. Ergänzt wird dieses durch Anklänge von Angelikawurzel, Koriander, Wacholder und Zitrusfrüchten. Sehr intensiv fruchtig und gleichzeitig angenehm mild im Geschmack. Perfekte Balance!

Primarily fruity: blueberry and blackberry provide an intense aroma of ripe berries. This is complemented by hints of angelica root, coriander, juniper and citrus. Very intensely fruity and, at the same time, pleasantly mild in taste. Perfect balance!

" The properly improper gin

Der Gin für Freigeister

Dieser Gin kombiniert außergewöhnliche Noten von Blaubeere und Brombeere mit klassischem Wacholder – das Ganze in einer tiefschwarzen Flasche mit edlem Design. Bereits nach dem ersten Schluck ist klar: Der BROCKMANS Gin ist ein Gin wie kein anderer. Ein geschmeidiger Tropfen – beerig, mild und herrlich unangepasst.

With the unique character of dark berries

Die Vision von vier Freunden war der Grundstein für diesen faszinierenden Gin. Mit ihrem gebündelten Wissen wollten sie einen Gin kreieren, der so angenehm weich und unvergleichlich mild ist, dass man ihn am liebsten pur genießen möchte. Ob sie das geschafft haben? Keine Frage. Denn genau so möchte man diesen Ausnahme-Gin intuitiv am liebsten trinken: pur und unverfälscht. Um dieses einmalige Geschmackserlebnis zu garantieren, wird der BROCKMANS Gin in traditionellen kupfernen Destillationsapparaten hergestellt. Vor der Destillation werden die Botanicals für 24 Stunden in 100-prozentigem Getreide-Neutralalkohol eingelegt. So können sich die einzelnen Aromen besonders gut entfalten, und es entsteht ein Gin, dessen geschmackliche Nuancen kaum zu übertreffen sind. Zu den klassischen Botanicals wie Angelikawurzel, Zitrus- und Orangenschalen, Koriander und Wacholder mischen sich Blaubeeren und Brombeeren. Diese fruchtigen Aromen sind es, die den BROCKMANS Gin zu einer komplett neuen Erfahrung machen. Ein Gin für Freigeister, Genussmenschen und Geschmacks-Abenteurer – und für jeden, der sich gerne begeistern lässt. Cheers!

The gin for free spirits

This gin combines exceptional notes of blueberry and blackberry with classic juniper – the whole in a jet black bottle with a noble design. One sip and it's clear: BROCKMANS Gin is a gin like no other. A smooth taste – berries, mild and wonderfully unadjusted.

With the unique character of dark berries

The vision of four friends was the cornerstone for this fascinating gin. With their combined knowledge, they wanted to create a gin that is so pleasantly smooth and incomparably mild that you'd prefer to enjoy it neat. Did they succeed? No question about it. Because that's exactly how you intuitively want to drink this exceptional gin: pure and unadulterated. To guarantee this unique taste experience, BROCKMANS Gin is produced in traditional copper stills. Before distillation, the botanicals are steeped for 24 hours in 100 % grain-neutral alcohol. This allows the individual aromas to develop particularly well, resulting in a gin whose flavor nuances are hard to beat. The classic botanicals such as angelica root, citrus and orange peel, coriander and juniper are mixed with blueberries and blackberries. These fruity flavors are what make BROCKMANS Gin a completely new experience. A gin for free spirits, epicureans and taste adventurers – and for anyone who likes to be inspired. Cheers!

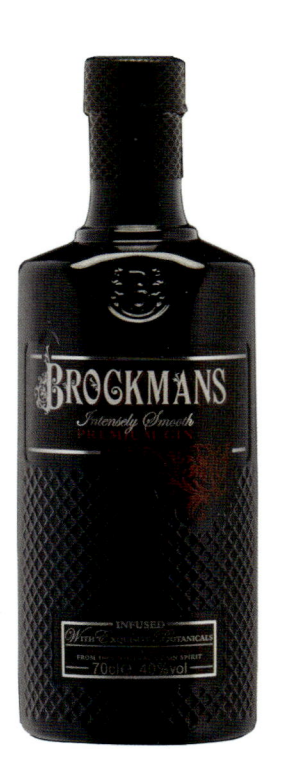

London, Great Britain

HAYMAN'S DISTILLERY

HAYMAN'S OLD TOM GIN

CATEGORY
Old Tom

ORIGIN
Great Britain

ESTABLISHED
1863

SIZE
● ● ○ ○

TASTING NOTES
Wärmend und mild, lieblich und blumig, leicht süß, breite Aromen von Kandis, Orange, Lavendel und Süßholz, delikat mit einem Hauch von Zitrusfrucht, Gewürzkuchennoten und Honig, im Abgang erdig

Warming and mild, mellow and floral, slightly sweet, broad aromas of rock candy, orange, lavender and licorice, delicate with hints of citrus, spice cake notes and honey, earthy finish

London, Great Britain

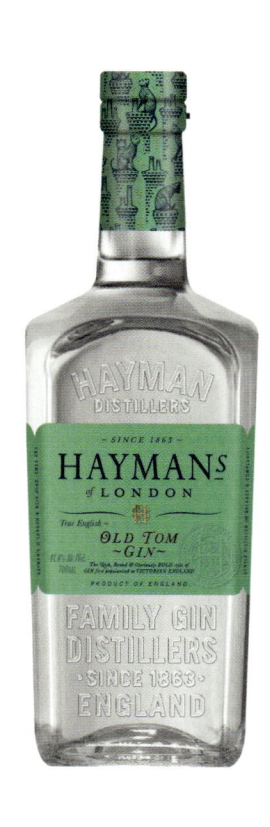

Behütetes Familiengeheimnis

Seit Beginn des 19. Jahrhunderts befasst sich das britische Familienunternehmen Hayman's Original English Gin Makers intensiv mit der Herstellung von Gin. Heute ist die Hayman's Distillery die älteste im gesamten Vereinigten Königreich. Für die Produktion verlässt sich Hayman's auf den englischen Weizen. Dieser wird mit zehn Zutaten und Wasser aromatisiert, bevor es an die Destillation geht. Die Botanical-Lieferanten stammen aus denselben Ländern, die schon im 19. Jahrhundert die Destillerie belieferten. Wie bei allen Gins von Hayman's werden für den Old Tom Wacholder, Koriander, Muskatnuss, Zimt, Orangenschale, Angelikawurzel, Deutsche Schwertlilie, Kassiarinde, Lakritz und Zitronenschale verwendet, allerdings in einer anderen Intensität und in einem anderen Arrangement als beispielsweise beim London Dry Gin.

Gefeiertes Comeback

Das entsprechend gut gehütete Familienrezept stammt aus den 1860er-Jahren, also aus einer Zeit, als der Old Tom Gin aufgrund des "Gin Acts" quasi beim Vorbeigehen an Kneipen und Bars aus hölzernen "Automaten" getrunken wurde. Mit Aufhebung der steuerlichen Repressionen verschwand der Old Tom aus den Gassen Großbritanniens, abgelöst durch den London Dry Gin. 2007 nahm die Hayman's Distillery ihren gesüßten Ur-Gin Old Tom wieder ins Portfolio auf. Mit Erfolg: Heute wie damals funktioniert dieser vollmundige Gin ausgezeichnet für Cocktails wie den Tom Collins oder den Martinez.

> *A true English gin that lets the past become the present.*

Guarded family secret

Since the beginning of the 19th century, the British family business, Hayman's Original English Gin Makers, has been deeply involved in the production of gin. Today, Hayman's Distillery is the oldest in the entire United Kingdom. For production, Hayman's relies on English wheat. This is flavored with ten ingredients and water before it goes to distillation. The botanical suppliers come from the same countries that supplied the distillery back in the 19th century. As with all Hayman's gins, Old Tom uses juniper, coriander, nutmeg, cinnamon, orange zest, angelica root, German iris, cassia bark, licorice and lemon zest, but in a different intensity and arrangement from, say, London Dry Gin.

Celebrated comeback

The appropriately well-guarded family recipe dates back to the 1860s, a time when, due to the "Gin Act", the Old Tom category of gin was drunk from wooden "vending machines" practically while passing pubs and bars. With the lifting of fiscal repression, Old Tom disappeared from the alleys of Great Britain, replaced by London Dry Gin. In 2007, Hayman's Distillery reintroduced its sweetened original gin, Old Tom, to its portfolio. Indeed, with success; today, as then, this full-bodied gin serves excellently in cocktails like Tom Collins or Martinez.

THAMES DISTILLERY

OXLEY GIN

> This gin will catch you cold, ice-cold.

Kalt geht es her

Der Oxley Gin ist ein London Dry Gin und du denkst sicherlich, was soll dich hier jetzt noch überraschen. Dann sagen wir einfach, dieser Gin wird dich eiskalt erwischen. Denn an diesem Gin wurde knapp acht Jahre gebastelt, allerdings nicht an der Rezeptur. Eigens für den Oxley Gin wurde ein originelles Herstellungsverfahren entwickelt, bei dem es kalt hergeht. Die sogenannte Vakuumdestillation, ein Verfahren, bei dem Temperaturen unter 0 °C für die Destillation sorgen, bildet hierbei nur die Spitze des Eisbergs. Innovativ und definitiv ein Nischenprodukt, sorgt der stark aromatische Oxley Gin für ein weiteres unerwartetes Gin-Abenteuer – wobei doch jeder von uns dachte, er hätte schon alles gesehen.

Intensität neu erleben

Bewusst geht man den anderen Weg. Statt zu erhitzen wird der Gin bei -5 °C hergestellt. Für alle, die mit Infos angeben möchten: Alkohol destilliert genau ab dieser Temperatur unter Vakuum. Verwendet werden Wacholder, verschiedene Zitrusfrüchte, Koriander, Lakritze, Mandeln, Kakao, Vanille und weitere Zutaten. Die Botanicals werden frisch gepflückt und schockgefrostet, um anschließend in kaltem Ethanol eingelegt zu werden. Das Ganze wird dann bei bis zu minus 120 °C kältedestilliert, ein Verfahren, bei dem die Aromen regelrecht konserviert werden. Das ermöglicht es, die Aromen in einer ungeahnten Intensität zu erleben. Wer die Zutatenliste noch einmal liest, stellt fest, dass er ein Erlebnis für die Sinne erwarten kann.

Cold process

Oxley Gin is a London Dry Gin and, for sure, you're thinking what is there to surprise you here now. Then let's just say, this gin will catch you ice cold. Because this gin was tinkered with for almost eight years, but not the recipe. Just for Oxley Gin, an original manufacturing process was developed, involving cold. So-called vacuum distillation, a process in which temperatures below 0°C drive distillation, is here just the tip of the iceberg. Innovative and definitely a niche product, this strongly aromatic Oxley Gin provides another unexpected gin adventure – even though we all thought we'd seen everything.

Experience intensity anew

Deliberately heading the other way. Instead of heating, the gin is produced at -5 °C. For those who want to show what they know: alcohol distilled exactly from this temperature under a vacuum. Juniper, various citrus fruits, coriander, licorice, almonds, cocoa, vanilla and other ingredients are used. The botanicals are freshly picked and flash frozen, then steeped in cold ethanol. The whole thing is then cold distilled as low as minus 120°C, a process that absolutely preserves the flavors. This makes it possible to experience the flavors with an unimagined intensity. Anyone re-reading the list of ingredients can expect a sensorial experience.

London, Great Britain

CATEGORY
London Dry Gin

ORIGIN
England

ESTABLISHED
2009

SIZE
● ● ● ○

TASTING NOTES
Der Gin ist klassisch, wie ein London Dry sein sollte, aber noch mehr. Kräftig beginnt der Wacholder zusammen mit den Zitrusfrüchten. Obschon der Gin mit dem Bitteren und der Süße der Grapefruit und des Kakaos spielt, bleibt er dennoch bis zum Schluss ein London Dry, der durch zusätzliche Raffinesse und unter Verwendung der Botanicals einen überzeugenden Spirit offenbart. Perfekt für Cocktails und den puren Genuss.

This gin is a classic, as any London Dry should be, but even more so. The juniper launches powerfully with the citrus fruits. Even though this gin plays with the bitterness and sweetness of grapefruit and cocoa, it still remains a London Dry till the end, which reveals a convincing spirit through additional refinement and use of the botanicals. Perfect for cocktails and pure enjoyment.

SIPSMITH DISTILLERY

SIPSMITH LONDON DRY GIN

London, Great Britain

Drei Ritter stellen sich gegen das Gesetz

Drei ehemalige Manager hängen ihren Anzug an den Nagel und wollen einen Dienst an der Gesellschaft leisten. Drei Musketiere, ohne Muskete, aber dafür mit der Idee für einen Gin. Eine angemietete Garage im Londoner Stadtteil Hammersmith und den Ankauf der Kupfer-Destille "Prudence" später konnten die Ritter, die ihr Unterfangen "Sipsmith" tauften, fast schon loslegen. Aber eben auch nur fast. Weil in London zuletzt 1820 eine Kupferbrennerei gegründet wurde, standen sie vor einem alten Gesetz, das nicht vorsah, eine Lizenz für eine Destille unter 1800 Liter zu erteilen. Die Männer wollten aber lediglich 300 Liter brennen. Sie bewirkten, dass das Gesetz 2008 geändert wurde, und brachten mit ihrem Sipsmith London Dry Gin direkt einen geradlinigen britischen Klassiker in die Bars.

Die Kluge mit dem schönen Hals

Der Gin wird nach der "One Shot"-Methode produziert, bei der auf die Zugabe von Konzentrat verzichtet wird. Das Resultat ist ein voller Erfolg, sodass der Sipsmith London Dry mit dem würzig-pikanten Lemon Drizzle und dem fruchtig-frischen Zesty Orange inzwischen Nachwuchs bekommen hat. Und weil eine Garage und eine Destille für die Großfamilie zu klein geworden sind, hat Prudence in der neuen Umgebung von Chiswick ihre Geschwister Patience und Constance begrüßt. Das Besondere an den Pot Stills ist ihr Swans Neck. So entstanden auch das Logo von Sipsmith – ein Schwanenkopf – sowie der Leitspruch "Cygnus inter anates – Ein Schwan unter Enten".

CATEGORY
London Dry Gin

ORIGIN
England

ESTABLISHED
2009

SIZE
● ● ● ●

TASTING NOTES
Klassisch und weich, angeführt von trockenen Wacholdernoten, harmonierend mit Zitrone und Orange sowie Süßholz und Zimt, leicht würzig-pfeffriger Ton, florale Nuancen.

Classic and soft, led by dry juniper notes, harmonizing with lemon and orange as well as licorice and cinnamon, slightly spicy-peppery tone, floral nuances.

Drei Ritter stellen sich gegen das Gesetz

Drei ehemalige Manager hängen ihren Anzug an den Nagel und wollen einen Dienst an der Gesellschaft leisten. Drei Musketiere, ohne Muskete, aber dafür mit der Idee für einen Gin. Eine angemietete Garage im Londoner Stadtteil Hammersmith und den Ankauf der Kupfer-Destille "Prudence" später konnten die Ritter, die ihr Unterfangen "Sipsmith" tauften, fast schon loslegen. Aber eben auch nur fast. Weil in London zuletzt 1820 eine Kupferbrennerei gegründet wurde, standen sie vor einem alten Gesetz, das nicht vorsah, eine Lizenz für eine Destille unter 1800 Liter zu erteilen. Die Männer wollten aber lediglich 300 Liter brennen. Sie bewirkten, dass das Gesetz 2008 geändert wurde, und brachten mit ihrem Sipsmith London Dry Gin direkt einen geradlinigen britischen Klassiker in die Bars.

Die Kluge mit dem schönen Hals

Der Gin wird nach der "One Shot"-Methode produziert, bei der auf die Zugabe von Konzentrat verzichtet wird. Das Resultat ist ein voller Erfolg, sodass der Sipsmith London Dry mit dem würzig-pikanten Lemon Drizzle und dem fruchtig-frischen Zesty Orange inzwischen Nachwuchs bekommen hat. Und weil eine Garage und eine Destille für die Großfamilie zu klein geworden sind, hat Prudence in der neuen Umgebung von Chiswick ihre Geschwister Patience und Constance begrüßt. Das Besondere an den Pot Stills ist ihr Swans Neck. So entstanden auch das Logo von Sipsmith – ein Schwanenkopf – sowie der Leitspruch "Cygnus inter anates – Ein Schwan unter Enten".

> **Sleek and elegant – truly a swan among ducks.**

SOUTHWESTERN DISTILLERY

TARQUIN'S CORNISH DRY GIN

Ein Klassiker zeitgenössisch interpretiert

Rau fegt der Wind über die Küste Nordcornwalls. Am Horizont zeichnen sich Regenwolken. Der Ozean peitscht gegen die Klippen, hinterlässt Gischt auf den massiven Felsen. In der Southwestern Distillery macht Tarquin Leadbetter seinen kupfernen Ladies Feuer unter dem Hintern. Tamara, Senara, Tressa und Ferarra sind seine treusten Gefährtinnen. Während der Brennmeister aufs offene Meer schaut, ist er sich sicher: Als er unglücklich in seinem Londoner Büro seine Kündigung schrieb, war es die Verwirklichung seiner Leidenschaft, die er im Sinn hatte, genau hier, fernab jeglichen Großstadtgetümmels. Er wollte kreativ sein, etwas Neues schaffen, eine zeitgenössische Variante des klassischen London Dry Gin komponieren.

Cornwall als wichtigstes Aroma

Gesagt, getan. In der Nähe von Padstow stellt Tarquin Leadbetter auf traditionelle Weise seit 2012 seinen nach ihm und der Ortschaft benannten Tarquin's Cornish Dry Gin in Chargen von 300 Flaschen her. Die zwölf Botanicals für diesen Gin, eine Mischung aus Wurzeln, Gewürzen, Nüssen, Samen, Früchten und Blumen, stammen aus allen Teilen der Welt: Kardamon aus Guatemala, Iriswurzel aus Marokko, Wacholder aus dem Kosovo, Veilchenblätter aus dem kornischen Garten. Während des gesamten Destillationsprozesses überwacht Tarquin jede einzelne Variable, er optimiert, riecht und schmeckt ab. Am Ende wird jede einzelne Flasche von Hand gelabelt, mit Wachs verschlossen, gestempelt und signiert.

St. Ervan, Great Britain

CATEGORY
London Dry Gin

ORIGIN
Great Britain

ESTABLISHED
2012

SIZE
● ● ● ○

TASTING NOTES
Knackig, klar und kräftig, cremig, trocken, floralkomplex, kiefriger Wacholder, duftende Veilchen, frische Orangenzeste, leicht marzipanig, kombiniert mit der Wärme fernöstlicher Gewürze.

Crisp, clear and powerful, creamy, dry, florally complex, piney juniper, fragrant violets, fresh orange zest, slightly marzipan, combined with the warmth of far-eastern spices.

> This gin is a mix of science and art, of an understanding of ingredients and of the subtleties of distilling.

A classic interpreted in a contemporary way

A raw wind sweeps over the coast of North Cornwall. Rain clouds appear on the horizon. The ocean lashes against the cliffs, leaving spray on the massive rocks. At the Southwestern Distillery, Tarquin Leadbetter lights a fire under the butts of his copper ladies. Tamara, Senara, Tressa and Ferarra are his most loyal companions. As the master distiller gazes out to sea, he's sure of one thing; when, unhappy in his London office, he wrote his resignation, it was the realization of his passion that he had in mind, right here, far from any big-city hustle and bustle. He wanted to be creative, to accomplish something new, to compose a contemporary variation on the classic London Dry Gin theme.

Cornwall as the main aroma

No sooner said than done. Near Padstow, Tarquin Leadbetter has been making his Tarquin's Cornish Dry Gin, named after him and his location, in the traditional way since 2012, in batches of 300 bottles. The twelve botanicals for this gin, a blend of roots, spices, nuts, seeds, fruits and flowers, come from all parts of the world: cardamom from Guatemala, orris root from Morocco, juniper from Kosovo, violet leaves from the Cornish garden. Throughout the distillation process, Tarquin monitors each variable, tweaking, smelling and tasting. At the end, each bottle is labeled by hand, sealed with wax, stamped and signed.

DISTILLERIES FROM AROUND THE GLOBE

United States of America

Cambridge, Wisconsin
1. *Death's Door*

New York City, New York
2. *Brooklyn Gin*

Venezuela

Amazon
3. *Canaïma*

The Netherlands

Schiedam
4. *Bobby's Schiedam Dry Gin*
5. *Sir Edmond Gin*

Soest
6. *Hanami Dry Gin*

Hulst
7. *Solar Gin*

France

Cognac region
8. *Citadelle Jardin d'Été*
9. *Citadelle*

Forcalquier
10. *MistralGin*

Spain

Barcelona
11. *Le Tribute*

Italy

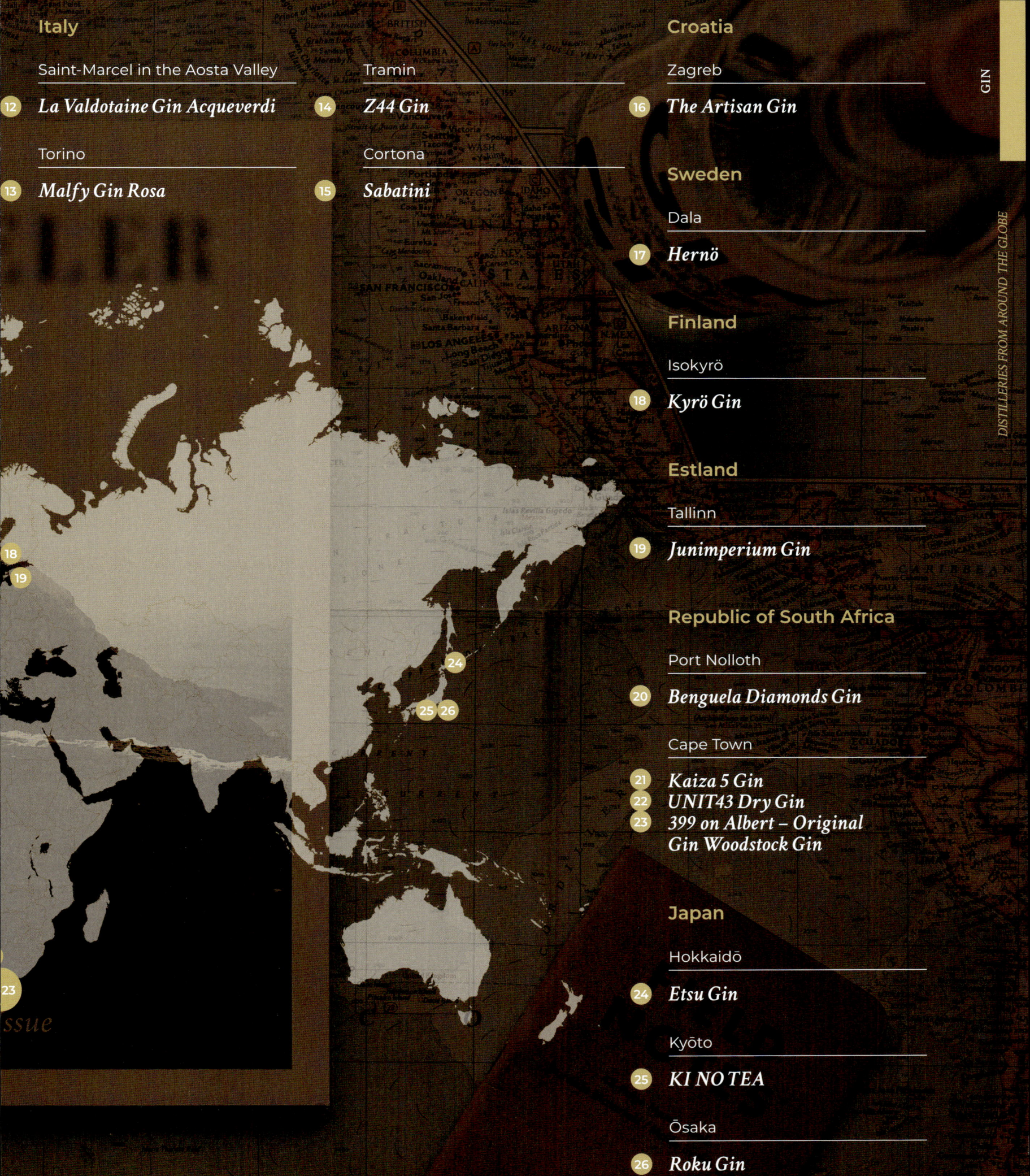

Saint-Marcel in the Aosta Valley

12 *La Valdotaine Gin Acqueverdi*

Torino

13 *Malfy Gin Rosa*

Tramin

14 *Z44 Gin*

Cortona

15 *Sabatini*

Croatia

Zagreb

16 *The Artisan Gin*

Sweden

Dala

17 *Hernö*

Finland

Isokyrö

18 *Kyrö Gin*

Estland

Tallinn

19 *Junimperium Gin*

Republic of South Africa

Port Nolloth

20 *Benguela Diamonds Gin*

Cape Town

21 *Kaiza 5 Gin*
22 *UNIT43 Dry Gin*
23 *399 on Albert – Original Gin Woodstock Gin*

Japan

Hokkaidō

24 *Etsu Gin*

Kyōto

25 *KI NO TEA*

Ōsaka

26 *Roku Gin*

DANCING GOAT DISTILLERY

DEATH'S DOOR GIN

Alles andere als ein Todestrip

Wer den Namen Death's Door liest, könnte auf die Idee kommen, nach einem Glas des gleichnamigen London Dry Gins in Lebensgefahr zu sein. Doch weit gefehlt. Der Death's Door Gin sucht die Harmonie und findet sie in der geschmacklich einzigartigen Zusammensetzung seiner Zutaten. Dabei ist Death's Door lediglich die Bezeichnung für die Wasserstraße, die der Weizen und die Gerste, die für die Ginproduktion benötigt werden, überqueren müssen, um in der Brennerei anzukommen.

Hergestellt wird der Death's Door Gin in kleinen Chargen von der familiengeführten Dancing Goat Distillery im amerikanischen Bundesstaat Wisconsin.

Drei sorgen für Harmonie

Der für den Basisalkohol genutzte Weizen stammt von der nur 22 km² großen Insel Washington Island. Die Insel war zunächst für den Anbau von Kartoffeln bekannt. Nachdem der Industriezweig in den 1970er-Jahren zusammenbrach, lag das Ackerland brach – bis zum Jahr 2005. Die ungenutzten Ackerflächen wurden für den Weizenanbau reaktiviert. Dieser hochwertige lokale rote Winterweizen vermählt sich für den Death's Door Gin mit gemälzter Gerste. Bei der anschließenden Mazeration kommen lediglich drei Botanicals zum Einsatz: Wacholder, Koriander und Fenchel, allesamt wild auf der Insel gewachsen. Durch den gezielten Einsatz dieser drei Zutaten wird eine Überladung mit Aromen verhindert. Das Resultat ist ein ausgewogener London Dry Gin-Geschmack. Anything but a death trip.

> „This isn't Death knocking at the door, but rather excellent taste.

Anything but a death trip

Anyone reading the name Death's Door might surmise they're in mortal danger after a glass of the eponymous London Dry Gin. But far from it. Death's Door Gin seeks harmony and finds it in the unique flavor composition of its ingredients. Yet Death's Door is simply the name for the waterway that the wheat and barley needed for gin production must cross to arrive at the distillery. Death's Door Gin is produced in small batches by the family-run Dancing Goat Distillery in the American state of Wisconsin.

Three provide harmony

The wheat used for the base alcohol comes from Washington Island, which is only 22 km² in size. The island was initially known for growing potatoes. After that industry collapsed in the 1970s, the farmland lay fallow – until 2005. The unused farmland was reactivated for wheat cultivation. This high-quality local red winter wheat marries with malted barley for Death's Door Gin. Only three botanicals are used in the subsequent maceration: juniper, coriander and fennel, all growing wild on the island. The selective use of these three ingredients prevents aroma overload. The result is a balanced London Dry Gin flavor.

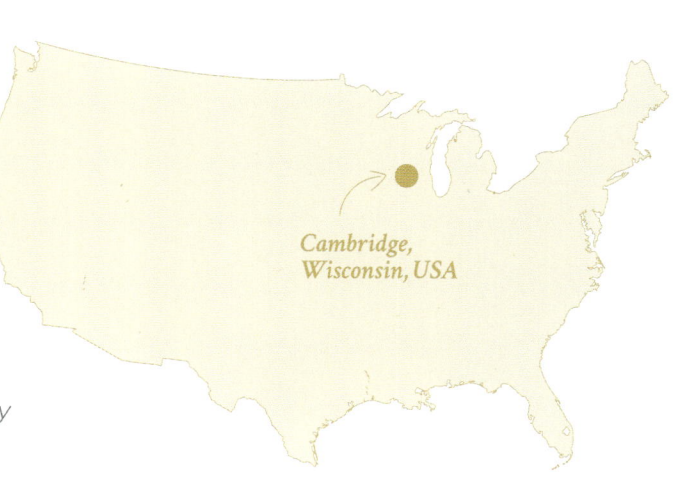

Cambridge, Wisconsin, USA

CATEGORY
London Dry Gin

ORIGIN
Cambridge, Wisconsin, USA

ESTABLISHED
2005

SIZE
● ● ● ●

TASTING NOTES
Klar, weich und ausbalanciert, einzigartig komplex trotz weniger Zutaten, süßlich-fruchtig im Geschmack, kühlend, lakritzähnliche Aromen durch Fenchel, lang anhaltend und sanft im Abgang.

Clear, soft and balanced, uniquely complex despite few ingredients, sweetish-fruity taste, cooling, licorice-like aromas due to fennel, long-lasting and smooth finish.

CATEGORY
Distilled Gin

ORIGIN
New York, USA

ESTABLISHED
2010

SIZE
● ● ○ ○

TASTING NOTES
Weich und komplex, mit einem satten, runden, klassischen Wacholderaroma und der bleibenden Präsenz von Zitrusfrüchten und dezenten Lavendelanklängen.

Smooth and complex, with a rich, round, classic juniper aroma and the lingering presence of citrus and subtle hints of lavender.

BROOKLYN GIN DISTILLERY

BROOKLYN GIN

Aus dem Herzen New Yorks

Schon Frank Sinatra sang über sein New York: Wenn ich es hier schaffe, dann schaffe ich es überall. Eine Stadt, in der Tellerwäscher zu Millionären werden. Eine Stadt, die niemals schläft. Hier, in dem berühmten Borough Brooklyn, sind Emil Jättne and Joe Santos zu Hause. In dieser multikulturellen, bunten Welt, zwischen all den erstklassigen Restaurants und Bars, hatten sie die Idee, einen Gin zu kreieren, der das Feeling des Szeneviertels auf einzigartige Weise verkörpert. Ehemals angestellt bei einem amerikanischen Spirituosenkonzern, inspiriert von der New Yorker DIY-Mentalität nutzten sie ihr Wissen, um einen qualitativ hochwertigen Gin auf den Markt zu bringen, dessen Inhaltsstoffe und Botanicals frisch von Hand verarbeitet werden.

Erinnerung an einen Freund

Elf Botanicals stecken im Brooklyn Gin: allen voran handgeknackte Wacholderbeeren sowie Kakaobohnenspitzen, Lavendel, Koriander, Veilchenwurzeln, aber auch frisch geschnittene Zitrusschalen von vier verschiedenen Zitrusfrüchten. Der zugrunde liegende Neutralalkohol wird aus Mais hergestellt. Destilliert wird in der Warwick Valley Winery & Distillery, der ältesten Destille im Hudson Valley. Die geschmackliche Individualität des Gins wird durch seine mächtige Aufmachung untermauert. Das unverwechselbare Design der Flasche ist von der Brooklyn Bridge inspiriert und mit echten Kupferbeschlägen versehen. Der Verschluss kann als Eiswürfelstempel verwendet werden und muss durch die chemische Reaktion von Kupfer mit Eis nicht einmal zuvor erhitzt werden. In Gedenken an ein noch während der Gründungsphase verstorbenes Team-Mitglied wurde ein Steinchen auf dem Kupfer-Verschluss entfernt. Es verkörpert die Lücke, die hinterlassen wurde.

*New York City
New York, USA*

From the heart of New York

Frank Sinatra sang about his New York: "If I can make it there, I'll make it anywhere". A city where dishwashers become millionaires. A city that never sleeps. Here, in the famous borough of Brooklyn, Emil Jättne and Joe Santos are at home. In this multicultural, colorful world, among all the first-class restaurants and bars, they had the idea of creating a gin that embodies the feeling of the trendy neighborhood in a unique way. Formerly employed by an American spirits company, inspired by New York's DIY mentality, they used their knowledge to launch a high-quality gin with ingredients and botanicals freshly processed by hand.

Memory of a friend

Eleven botanicals are in Brooklyn Gin: first and foremost, hand-cracked juniper berries, as well as cocoa nibs, lavender, coriander, violet root, and freshly cut citrus peels from four different citrus fruits. The underlying neutral alcohol is made from corn. Distilled at Warwick Valley Winery & Distillery, the oldest distillery in the Hudson Valley, this gin's flavorful individuality is underpinned by its powerful presentation. The bottle's distinctive design is inspired by the Brooklyn Bridge and features real copper hardware. The cap can be used as an ice cube punch and doesn't even need to be heated beforehand, due to the chemical reaction of copper with ice. In memory of a team member who passed away while the company was still in its formative stages, a small stone on the copper cap was removed. It embodies the gap that was left behind.

> **An American juniper bomb – as imposing as the Brooklyn Bridge.**

DESTILERÍAS UNIDAS S. A.

CANAÏMA

Amazon, Venezuela

Aus der Mitte des Regenwaldes

Im Südosten Venezuales, an der Grenze zu Guyana und Brasilien ergießen sich zwischen den uralten Tepui-Tafelbergen Wasserfälle in malerische Lagunen. Hier, im durch die Einheimischen bezeichneten "mystischen Land", gedeihen unter dem immer grünen Blätterdach des Amazona-Regenwaldes die besonderen Botanicals für den exotischen Canaïma Gin. Açai, die Palmenfrucht Seje, das aus den Blättern des Cashew-Baumes gewonnene Harz Merey, die Tupiro-Frucht, Copoazú und die „Liebesfrucht" der Moriche-Palme sind Teil des Zutatenportfolios dieses unkonventionellen Gins. In Canaïma treffen sie auf acht traditionelle Gin-Gewürze, auf Wacholder, Zitronen-, Grapefruit- und Orangenschalen, auf Angelikawurzel, Koriander und auf Kümmel. Die schwer zugänglichen Rohstoffe werden mithilfe der beheimateten Penóm-Indigenen in den Tiefen des Regenwaldes von Hand gepflückt.

Für eine bessere Welt

Jedes Botanical wird einzeln maseriert und separat in Kupferbrennblasen zu der einzigartigen Canaïma-Mischung destilliert. Kein Wunder also, dass dieser Gin im Small Batch-Verfahren gewonnen wird. Das Ergebnis ist ein Blend mit einem Anteil von 65 % amazonischen Ursprungs – ein Getränk aus der Lunge der

CATEGORY
Dry Gin

ORIGIN
Venezuela

ESTABLISHED
2019

SIZE
● ● ● ○

TASTING NOTES
Mild und weich, tropisch und komplex, intensiv, fruchtig und floral, kräuterige, leicht bittere Noten, untermalt von frischen Zitrusfrüchten.

Mild and mellow, tropical and complex, intense, fruity and floral, herbal, slightly bitter notes, underlined by fresh citrus fruits.

From the middle of the rain forest

In southeastern Venezuela, on the border with Guyana and Brazil, waterfalls pour into picturesque lagoons between the ancient Tepui Table Mountains. Here, in what the locals call the "mystical land", the special botanicals for exotic Canaïma Gin thrive under the evergreen canopy of the Amazona rainforest. Açai, the palm fruit Seje, the resin Merey extracted from the leaves of the cashew tree, the Tupiro fruit, Copoazú and the "love fruit" of the Moriche palm form part of the portfolio of ingredients of this unconventional gin. In Canaïma they meet eight traditional gin spices, juniper, lemon, grapefruit and orange peel, angelica root, coriander and cumin. The raw materials, which are difficult to access, are hand-picked in the depths of the rainforest with the help of the indigenous Penóm people.

For a better world

Each botanical is individually macerated and separately distilled in copper stills to create the unique Canaïma blend. It's no wonder, then, that this gin is made in a small batch process. The result is a blend with a 65 % Amazonian origin – a drink from the lungs of the world. Diseased lungs threatened by forest fires, so Canaïma's makers are committed to its recovery by supporting the Saving the Amazon Foundation and local organizations working to reforest and improve the quality of life for indigenous communities in the Amazon.

> **A taste born in the Amazon.**

HERMAN JANSEN BEVERAGES NEDERLAND B.V.

BOBBY'S SCHIEDAM DRY GIN

Schiedam, The Netherlands

CATEGORY
New Western Dry Gin

ORIGIN
The Netherlands

ESTABLISHED
1777

SIZE
● ● ● ●

TASTING NOTES
Sehr weicher zitrusartiger Geschmack mit kräuterigen Tönen, unverkennbare Gewürznelke, lauter, klarer Wacholder im Abgang, lang anhaltend mit pfeffrigen Noten.

Very soft, citrusy taste with herbal tones, unmistakable clove, loud, clear juniper in the finish, long-lasting with peppery notes.

Opa Bobby und sein Genever

1950 wanderte Jacobus Alfons, von Familie und Freunden liebevoll Bobby genannt, vom indonesischen Naku in die Niederlande aus. Bobby zelebrtierte niederländischen Genever, vermisste aber den Geschmack seiner Heimat und so begann er damit, seinen Genever mit vertrauten indonesischen Gewürzen und Kräutern zu verfeinern. 2012 entdeckte Bobbys Enkel Sebastiaan eine alte Flasche im Haus seiner Mutter. Inspiriert durch die Geschichte über seinen Großvater und sein einzigartiges indonesisches Rezept, besuchte er Schiedam, die Stadt, aus der das Rezept stammt. Dort lernte er den Meisterbrenner Ad van der Leer der traditionsbewussten Herman Jansen Destillerie kennen und kreierte mit ihm gemeinsam in Anlehnung an Opas alten Genever den Bobby's.

Indonesisch-europäisch

Im Bobby's treffen die Geschmackswelten zweier Kulturkreise aufeinander, ganz ohne Zusatzstoffe, Zucker und irgendwelche Extrakte. Hochwertige Nelken, Koriander, Zitronengras und Kubeben-Pfeffer treten in Verbindung mit Wachdolder, Orangenschale und Hagebutte. In harmonischem Einklang mit einer weiteren geheimen Familienzutat vereinen die Botanicals den indonesischen Spirit mit niederländischer Courage. Die Wurzeln in Schiedam und der indonesische Einfluss werden zusätzlich unterstrichen durch das Flaschendesign dieses Gins. Er wird abgefüllt in klassische Genever-Flaschen, in die sogenannte Kruik, verziert durch ein im Siebdruckverfahren hergestelltes Ikat-Muster. Anlässlich des fünften Geburtstages des Gins wurde übrigens eine auf Genever basierende Sonderedition des Bobby's herausgebracht, ein zweifach im Bourbon-Eichenfass gereifter Gin, der durch sein intensives Vanillearoma aufwartet.

Grandpa Bobby and his genever

In 1950, Jacobus Alfons, affectionately known as Bobby to family and friends, emigrated from Naku, Indonesia, to the Netherlands. Bobby celebrated Dutch genever, but missed the taste of his homeland, so he began to refine his genever with familiar Indonesian spices and herbs. In 2012, Bobby's grandson Sebastiaan discovered an old bottle in his mother's house. Inspired by the story about his grandfather and his unique Indonesian recipe, he visited Schiedam, the city where the recipe originated. There, he met master distiller Ad van der Leer of the tradition-conscious Herman Jansen Distillery, and together they created Bobby's in the style of Grandpa's old genever.

Indonesian-European

In Bobby's, the taste-worlds of two cultures meet, completely free of additives, sugar or any extracts. High-quality cloves, coriander, lemongrass and cubeb pepper join forces with juniper, orange zest and rosehip. In harmony with another secret family ingredient, the botanicals combine Indonesian spirit with Dutch courage. The Schiedam roots and Indonesian influence are further emphasized by the bottle design of this gin. It is bottled in classic genever bottles, the so-called Kruik, decorated by a screen-printed ikat pattern. Incidentally, to mark the fifth birthday of the gin, a special edition of Bobby's, based on genever, was released, a gin aged twice in bourbon oak barrels, which stands out for its intense vanilla aroma.

> **East meets west – Dutch courage, Indonesian spirit.**

HERMAN JANSEN BEVERAGES NEDERLAND B.V. // BOBBY'S SCHIEDAM DRY GIN

0,7 L // 42,0 %

HERMAN JANSEN DESTILLERIE

SIR EDMOND GIN

Schiedam, The Netherlands

Eine Hommage an die beliebteste Zutat der Welt

Die Geschichte des Sir Edmond Gins beginnt bereits im Jahr 1841 auf der Insel La Réunion. Edmond Albius entdeckt im zarten Alter von zwölf Jahren ganz zufällig ein Verfahren zur manuellen Bestäubung der bis dato aus Mexiko eingeführten Gewürzvanille. Dabei benutzte er für das Öffnen des männlichen Staubbeutels und der weiblichen Narbe einen dünnen Stock. Anschließend strich er mit dem Daumen den klebrigen Pollen vom Staubbeutel über die Narbe. Die Entdeckung von Edmond Albius erlaubte die industrielle Entwicklung und Kultivierung der Bourbon Vanille, der geschmacksgebenden wertvollen Hauptzutat des Sir Edmond Gins und zugleich beste sowie aromatischste Vanillesorte der Welt. Noch heute wird die Handbestäubung von Vanillepflanzen à la Edmond Albius überall auf dem Globus angewendet.

Flamingos auf der Vanilleplantage

In dem aus fünf Botanicals erzeugten Destillat wird etwa sechs Wochen lang mit Bourbon Vanille aus La Réunion infundiert. Hierdurch entsteht nicht nur der einprägsame Vanillegeschmack, sondern auch die leicht goldene Farbe des Gins. Und noch etwas erinnert an Sir Edmond: Das vordere Flaschenetikett ist beidseitig bedruckt, zeigt einen Flamingo mit Hut und Monokel auf der Vorder- und auf der Rückseite, den Hauptdarsteller dieser Geschichte.

CATEGORY
New Western Dry Gin

ORIGIN
The Netherlands

ESTABLISHED
2016

SIZE
● ● ● ○

TASTING NOTES
Süß und komplex, mild im Gaumen, wärmende Nuancen von Zimt und Kardamom, dominant-kräftige Würze durch Ingwer und Wacholder, ausgeprägte Vanillenote, die Angelikawurzel sorgt zusätzlich für eine erdige Note.

Sweet and complex, mild on the palate, warming nuances of cinnamon and cardamom, dominant spiciness from ginger and juniper, pronounced vanilla note, the angelica root provides an additional earthy note.

Edmond Albius, vor dem Vulkan Piton de la Fournaise auf einer Plantage der Insel La Réunion. Die Vanille vom anderen Ende der Welt streichelt beim Trinkgenuss zart den Gaumen und erinnert in Kombination mit dem verwendeten Zimt an ein leckeres Stück Kuchen, von dem ein zweites Stück unbedingt gereicht werden muss.

> ## A bourbon vanilla explosion on the palate.

A tribute to the most popular ingredient in the world

The story of Sir Edmond Gin begins back in 1841 on the island of La Réunion. At the tender age of twelve, Edmond Albius accidentally discovered a method of manually pollinating vanilla spice which, to date, had been imported from Mexico. He used a thin stick to open the male anther and the female stigma. He then stroked the sticky pollen from the anther over the stigma with his thumb. Edmond Albius's discovery allowed the industrial development and cultivation of Bourbon vanilla, the valuable main ingredient influencing the flavor of Sir Edmond Gin and, at the same time, the best as well as the most aromatic vanilla variety in the world. Even today, the hand-pollination of vanilla plants à la Edmond Albius is used all over the globe.

Flamingos on the vanilla plantation

The distillate produced from five botanicals is infused with bourbon vanilla from La Réunion for around six weeks. This creates not only the memorable vanilla flavor, but also the light golden color of the gin. And there is something else reminiscent of Sir Edmond. The bottle's front label is printed on both sides, showing a flamingo with hat and monocle on the front and on the back, the main character of this story, Edmond Albius, in front of the Piton de la Fournaise volcano on a plantation on the island of La Réunion. The vanilla from the other side of the world delicately caresses the palate when drinking and, in combination with the cinnamon used, reminds us of a delicious piece of cake, a second piece of which must inevitably be served.

PRIVATBRENNEREI BOENTE

HANAMI DRY GIN

CATEGORY
Dry Gin

ORIGIN
The Netherlands

ESTABLISHED
2016

SIZE
● ● ○ ○

TASTING NOTES
Blumige Noten, dazu fruchtig-aromatisch und im Geschmack kräftig.

Floral notes, also fruity aromatic and strong on the palate.

Soest, The Netherlands

Zu Ehren des Kirschblütenfests

Jährlich wird in Japan das Kirschblütenfest „Hanami" gefeiert und die Schönheit der in Blüte stehenden Kirschbäume zelebriert. Sakura, die japanische Kirschblüte, blüht je nach Gegend von Ende März bis Anfang Mai für etwa zehn Tage. Fast alle Bewohner Japans feiern mit Freunden, Familien oder Kollegen. Man trifft sich unter der wunderschönen rosafarbenen und weißen Pracht der blühenden Kirschbäume, freut sich über die wärmer werdenden Temperaturen und fühlt die Kräfte der Natur erwachen. Inzwischen wird auch dieses Fest immer mehr in Deutschland begangen.

Weicher Gin mit floralem Hauch

Der Hanami Dry Gin kam zu Ehren eben dieses Festes auf den Markt. So ist es nur logisch, dass natürliche Essenzen der Kirschblüte verwendet werden. Sein Cherry Blossom-Destillat verleiht diesem Qualitätsprodukt neben der vierfachen Destillation seinen einzigartigen Geschmack. Außerdem enthält er die neun Botanicals Koriander, Wacholder, Angelikawurzel, Pfefferminze, Bitterorange, Fenchel, Kümmel, Dianthus und Muskatnuss Myristica. So entsteht ein weicher Gin mit floralem Hauch. Man kann gar nicht anders, als an die Blüten des japanischen Kirschbaumes zu denken. Neben den blumigen Noten ist er fruchtig-aromatisch und im Geschmack kräftig. Nicht nur geschmacklich macht dieser Dry Gin viel her: Die Flasche ist mit einer unverwechselbaren rosafarbenen Kirschblütenoptik gestaltet. Das macht den Gin zur perfekten Kombination von Destillier- und Designkunst. Die ausgezeichnete Qualität ist wortwörtlich zu nehmen, hat doch der Hanami Dry Gin eine Medaillenflut an internationalen Preisen eingeheimst.

> A gin as soft as cherry blossoms on a spring morning.

In honor of the cherry blossom festival

Every year in Japan sees the marking of the "Hanami" cherry blossom festival, when the beauty of the cherry trees in bloom is celebrated. Sakura, the Japanese cherry blossom, blooms from late March to early May for about ten days, depending on the area. Almost all residents of Japan celebrate with friends, family or colleagues. People gather under the beautiful pink and white splendor of the blossoming cherry trees, rejoice in the warmer temperatures and feel the forces of nature awakening. Nowadays this festival is also increasingly celebrated in Germany.

Soft gin with a floral touch

Hanami Dry Gin came on the market in honor of this very festival. So it is only logical that natural essences of cherry blossom are used. Its cherry blossom distillate, in addition to the quadruple distillation, gives this quality product its unique flavor. It also contains these nine botanicals: coriander, juniper, angelica, peppermint, bitter orange, fennel, caraway, dianthus and Myristica nutmeg. The result is a smooth gin with a floral touch. One can't help but think of the blossoms of the Japanese cherry tree. In addition to the floral notes, it's fruity-aromatic and strong on the palate. It's not just the taste that makes this Dry Gin stand out: the bottle is designed with a distinctive pink cherry blossom look. This makes the gin the perfect combination of distilling and design art. Its excellent quality has to be taken literally, as Hanami Dry Gin has won copious medals at international competitions.

THE SOLAR GIN DISTILLERY

SOLAR GIN

Hulst,
The Netherlands

Mit der Kraft der Sonne

Die Solarenergie zählt zu den saubersten, leisesten und umweltschonendsten Methoden der Energiegewinnung. Sie gilt als eine der Schlüsselindustrien, um energiebedingte Treibhausgase zu reduzieren. In der Theorie liefert die Sonne der Weltbevölkerung mehr Energie, als verbraucht wird. Das Problem: Um die kostenlose Energie nutzen zu können, braucht es teure Systeme, die die Sonnenstrahlen einfangen und in elektrische Energie und Wärme umwandeln. Glück dem, der ein talentiertes Händchen beweist und dieses Problem smart löst sowie es gleichzeitig noch auf die Herstellung von Gin übertragen kann. So wie der Gründer des Solar Gin Kevin van de Merlen. Der Solar Gin überzeugt neben seinem harmonisch-milden Geschmack vor allem durch sein innovatives und nachhaltiges Destillationskonzept. Der Brennvorgang erfolgt bei vergleichsweise niedrigen Temperaturen im Kupferkessel einer solarbetriebenen, selbstentwickelten Destille.

Kleine Besonderheiten

Damit ist Solar Gin der erste Gin der Welt, der zu 100 % klimaneutral durch Sonnenkraft hergestellt wird. Destilliert wird in den Frühlings- und Sommermonaten in den Niederlanden, an dem Ort, wo der Gin einst als Genever seinen Ursprung fand. Da die Destille frei beweglich ist, kann sie der Sonne hinterherreisen. Innovativ ist an dem Solar Gin jedoch nicht nur sein Herstellungsprozess, sondern auch die farbenfrohe exotische Flasche. Diese wird durch ein LED-Licht am Flaschenboden sonnig beleuchtet und muss nach Verbrauch ihres Inhalts nicht im Glascontainer landen, sondern kann als Lampe genutzt werden. Der Solar Gin holt den Sommer ins Glas und die Sonne ins Haus, unterstrichen durch die spritzige, fruchtig-florale Aromenvielfalt von Zitronen, Orangen und Kamille.

> # Taste the sun in your gin.

With the power of the sun

Solar power is one of the cleanest, quietest and most environmentally friendly methods of energy generation. It is considered one of the key industries for reducing energy-related greenhouse gases. In theory, the sun provides more energy to the world's population than is consumed. The problem is that to use the free energy, expensive systems are needed to capture the sun's rays and convert them into electrical energy and heat. So all credit to anyone proving their talents and solving this problem smartly whilst, at the same time, applying it to the production of gin. Like the founder of Solar Gin, Kevin van de Merlen. In addition to its harmonious, mild taste, Solar Gin is particularly impressive for its innovative and sustainable distillation concept. This process takes place at comparatively low temperatures in the copper pot of a solar-powered distillery developed by himself.

Special little features

This makes Solar Gin the first gin in the world to be produced 100 % climate-neutrally by solar power. Distilling takes place in the spring and summer months in the Netherlands, in the place where gin once originated as genever. Because the still is freely movable, it can follow the sun. But what is innovative about Solar Gin is not just its production process, but also the colorful exotic bottle. This is sunnily lit by an LED light at the bottom of the bottle which, once emptied, isn't condemned to glass recycling but can instead be used as a lamp. Solar Gin brings the summer into your glass and the sun into your house, its taste underlined by the tangy, fruity-floral range of aromas from lemons, oranges and chamomile.

CATEGORY
Contemporary Gin

ORIGIN
The Netherlands

ESTABLISHED
2018

SIZE
● ● ● ●

TASTING NOTES
Wacholder und Kardamom dominieren im Geschmack, ergänzt durch die fruchtig-süße Note frischer Zitrusfrüchte, Orangenblüten und Süßholz, im Nachgang leicht pfeffrig, mit dem bestimmenden Aroma von Koriander und der Ausgewogenheit der Kamille.

Juniper and cardamom dominate the taste, complemented by the fruity-sweet notes of fresh citrus, orange blossom and licorice, slightly peppery in the finish, with the defining aroma of coriander and the balance of chamomile.

DISTILLERIE DE BONBONNET

CITADELLE GIN ORIGINAL

CATEGORY
London Dry Gin

ORIGIN
France

ESTABLISHED
1996

SIZE
● ● ● ○

TASTING NOTES
Elegant und delikat, ausgesprochen komplex und selbstbewusste Wacholderanklänge im Geschmack, begleitet von einer angenehmen Schärfe und der dominierenden Aromatik von Mandeln und Zitrusfrüchten.

Elegant and delicate, markedly complex and confident juniper notes on the palate, accompanied by a pleasant spiciness and the dominant aroma of almonds and citrus.

Zu neuem Leben erweckt

Die Zitadelle ist eine Festung, der letzte Widerstandskern einer Stadt. Die Wurzeln des Citadelle Gin Original reichen Jahrhunderte zurück: Im Jahr 1775 erhielt eine in einer Zitadelle angesiedelte Destillerie in Dünkirchen die königliche Lizenz, Gin für das britische Königshaus herzustellen. Durch die Teilnahme Frankreichs am Unabhängigkeitskrieg der Vereinigten Staaten von Amerika erstarben die Handelsbeziehungen mit den Briten und die Destillerie erhielt die Erlaubnis, ihren Gin fortan auch an französische Kunden zu verkaufen. Eine schöne Geschichte, die auch Alexandre Gabriel, dem Gründer und Inhaber von Maison Ferrand, gefiel. Hiervon angespornt, erweckte er die Gin-Marke Citadelle zu neuem Leben.

Progressive Infusion

Der Citadelle Gin Original ist seit 1998 eine feste Größe in der Welt der Spirituosen. Die Destillation erfolgt in direkt befeuerten Kupferbrennkesseln nach der Cognac-Methode entsprechend der sogenannten progressiven Infusion, einem patentierten Konzept von Maison Ferrand. Die Grundzutat bildet hochwertiger französischer Bio-Weizen, der mit Quellwasser aus der Region Cognac vermischt wird. Jedes der 19, vorrangig aus der Region des Château de Bonbonnet stammenden zu ergänzenden Botanicals wird für einen individuellen Zeitraum in ein Weizen-Destillat infundiert, um so ein einzigartiges Geschmacksprofil zu erzeugen. Drei Mal brennt der Destillateur den Gin, um ihn so geschmeidig zu machen, wie er ist. Anschließend gibt er zu diesem neutralen, sehr reinen Alkohol das Mazerat der aromatischen Kräuter und Gewürze hinzu und destilliert ein viertes Mal. Danach wird das aromatische Destillat in die typischen blauen Flaschen abgefüllt.

Cognac region, France

Brought to new life

The citadel is a fortress, the last core of resistance of a city. The roots of Citadelle Gin Original go back centuries. In 1775, a distillery in Dunkirk, located in a citadel, received a royal license to produce gin for the British royal family. France's participation in the War of Independence of the United States of America caused trade relations with the British to cease, and the distillery received permission to sell its gin to French customers from then on. A nice story that also pleased Alexandre Gabriel, the founder and owner of Maison Ferrand. Spurred on by this, he revived the Citadelle gin brand.

Progressive Infusion

Citadelle Gin Original has been an established name in the world of spirits since 1998. Distillation takes place in direct-fired copper stills using the Cognac method involving so-called progressive infusion, a patented concept of Maison Ferrand. The basic ingredient is high-quality organic French wheat blended with spring water from the Cognac region. Each of the 19 botanicals to be added, primarily from the Château de Bonbonnet region, is infused into a wheat distillate for an individual period of time to create a unique flavor profile. The gin is distilled three times to make it as smooth as it is. Then the macerate of aromatic herbs and spices are added to this neutral, very pure alcohol and distilled a fourth time. Finally, the aromatic distillate is bottled in the characteristic blue bottles.

> **Extravagant seasoning from the garden of France.**

DISTILLERIE DE BONBONNET

CITADELLE GIN JARDIN D'ÉTÉ

Ein betörend fruchtiger Sommer

Die Orangen- und Zitronenbäume werden in den frühen Morgenstunden zart von der Sonne geküsst. Bienen summen durch die Äste. Ein lauer Wind wiegt die Blätter aus ihrem Schlaf. In diesem Sommergarten namens "Citadelle Gin Jardin d´Été" riecht und schmeckt alles nach der warmen Jahreszeit, nach reifen Früchten, floral und fruchtig. Kopf der Marke ist Alexandre Gabriel. Er gilt als innovativer Pionier, ein Macher, ein Künstler, dessen besondere Energie, Experementierfreudigkeit und Lebensfreude in außergewöhnlichen Bränden ihren Ausdruck finden. Einer Erzählung nach soll Debbie Gabriel, die Ehefrau von Citadelle-Schöpfer Alexandre Gabriel einen Sommergarten in einem kleinen französischen Dorf gepflegt haben. Dort baute sie Früchte und Blumen an. Beeindruckt von deren wunderschöner Optik und betörendem Duft sowie von den Ernte-Erträgen verewigte Gabriel seine Impressionen in einem Gin.

> **French joie de vivre in every single drop.**

Cognac region, France

Die Melone im Herzen

Destilliert wird der "Citadelle Gin Jardin d´Été" auf Château de Bonbonnet in Ars im Herzen der französischen Region Cognac. Hierfür kommen neun rund 50 Jahre alte Pot-Still-Destillierapparate mit einem Fassungsvermögen von je 25 Hektoliter zum Einsatz. Grundlage bildet ein dreifach destillierter französischer Weizen, der seinen unverwechselbaren Geschmack durch die Infusion von 22 Früchten und Botanicals erhält, die dem Destillat vor dem vierten und damit letzten Brennvorgang zugegeben werden. Neben für die Gin-Produktion klassischen Zutaten wie Kardamom, Koriander, Zimt und Süßholz, bilden beim "Citadelle Jardin d'Été" Zitrone, Yuzu- und Orangenzesten sowie das Fruchtfleisch reifer Melonen das Herzstück des Bouquets.

A beguiling fruity summer

The orange and lemon trees are delicately kissed by the sun in the early morning hours. Bees buzz through the branches. A balmy breeze lulls the leaves from their slumber. In this summer garden called "Citadelle Gin Jardin d'Été" everything smells and tastes of the warm season, of ripe fruit, floral and fruity. The mastermind of the brand is Alexandre Gabriel. He is considered an innovative pioneer, a go-getter, an artist, whose special energy, eagerness to experiment and joie de vivre find expression in exceptional spirits. According to a tale, Debbie Gabriel, the wife of Citadelle creator Alexandre Gabriel tended a summer garden in a small French village. There she grew fruits and flowers. Impressed by their beautiful appearance and beguiling fragrance, as well as by the harvest yields, Gabriel immortalized his impressions in a gin.

The melon at its heart

Citadelle Gin Jardin d'Été" is distilled at Château de Bonbonnet in Ars in the heart of the French region of Cognac. Nine 50-year-old pot stills with a capacity of 25 hectoliters each are used. The basis is a triple-distilled French wheat, which gets its unmistakable taste from the infusion of 22 fruits and botanicals, which are added to the distillate before the fourth and thus final distillation process. In addition to classic ingredients such as cardamom, coriander, cinnamon and licorice, lemon, yuzu and orange zest as well as the pulp of ripe melons form the heart of the bouquet in the "Citadelle Jardin d'Été".

CATEGORY
Dry Gin

ORIGIN
France

ESTABLISHED
2021

SIZE
● ● ● ○

TASTING NOTES
Mild, harmonisch, elegant, delikat, vielschichtig und sommerlich frisch, mit anfänglich floralen Noten, im Verlauf ein deutlich fruchtiges Aroma mit würzigen Anklängen, Aromen von Melone, Tangerine, Muskatnuss, Sternanis, Iriswurzel und der dominierenden Zitrone.

Mild, harmonious, elegant, delicate, complex and pleasantly fresh, with initial floral notes, in the course a distinctly fruity aroma with spicy hints, flavors of melon, tangerine, nutmeg, star angelica, orris root and the dominant lemon.

BOUTIQUE DISTILLERIES
ET DOMAINES DE PROVENCE

MISTRALGIN

"A gin for the sunny side of life.

CATEGORY
Dry Gin

ORIGIN
France

ESTABLISHED
1879

SIZE
● ○ ○ ○

TASTING NOTES
Vielseitig und intensiv im Aroma. Eine Mischung aus Fenchel, Wacholder, Kardamom, rosa Pfeffer, Grapefruit und Basilikum. Die Wacholderbeeren sorgen für eine würzige Note, es gesellt sich Iris und ein frischer Hauch von Zitrusfrüchten hinzu. Abgerundet wird das Ganze durch eine subtile Fenchel-Note. Reichhaltig und gleichzeitig elegant.

Versatile and intense aroma. A blend of fennel, juniper, cardamom, pink pepper, grapefruit and basil. The juniper berries provide a spicy note, partnered by iris and a fresh touch of citrus. The whole is rounded off by a subtle note of fennel. Rich and elegant at the same time.

Der Spirit Südfrankreichs

Der Ursprung dieses Gins ist die unbändige Leidenschaft für die Provence. Gründer des Mistral-Gin, Guillaume Bonnefoi, liebt diese Region: Hier kann man sich die südfranzösische Sonne ins Gesicht scheinen lassen und den unverwechselbaren Duft der mediterranen Landschaft einatmen, während man das Zirpen der Zikaden im Ohr hat. Weite Felder mit Weinreben, Olivenbäumen, Kräutern – und natürlich dem typischen Lavendel, dessen intensives Lila man noch in weiter Ferne leuchten sieht – erstrecken sich über das Terrain. Genau dieses Lebensgefühl, das die Provence in einem weckt, gibt es jetzt in Flaschen abgefüllt: Ein Schluck MistralGin – und man fühlt sich in diese einzigartige und wunderschöne Landschaft versetzt.

Botanicals aus der Provence

Doch nicht nur aufgrund ihrer atemberaubenden Landschaft ist die Provence der Entstehungsort dieses einzigartigen Gins. Hier, im Süden Frankreichs, wachsen auch die verschiedensten Gewürze und Kräuter. Thymian, Basilikum, Fenchel, Grapefruit, Eukalyptus und Minze vereinen sich zu einem einzigartigen Gin, dessen Genuss dem Lebensgefühl der Provence gleichkommt. Der MistralGin beeindruckt jedoch nicht nur mit seinem frischen, unverwechselbaren Aroma, sondern fasziniert gleichzeitig mit seiner rosa Farbe. Als erster Rosé Dry Gin aus der Provence steht er für einen exquisiten Lebensstil und erinnert uns daran, das Leben in vollen Zügen zu genießen. So ist dieser raffinierte, handwerklich hergestellte Gin der perfekte Tropfen für jeden Genussmenschen. Mit dem MistralGin stößt man am besten auf glückliche Momente an. À votre santé!

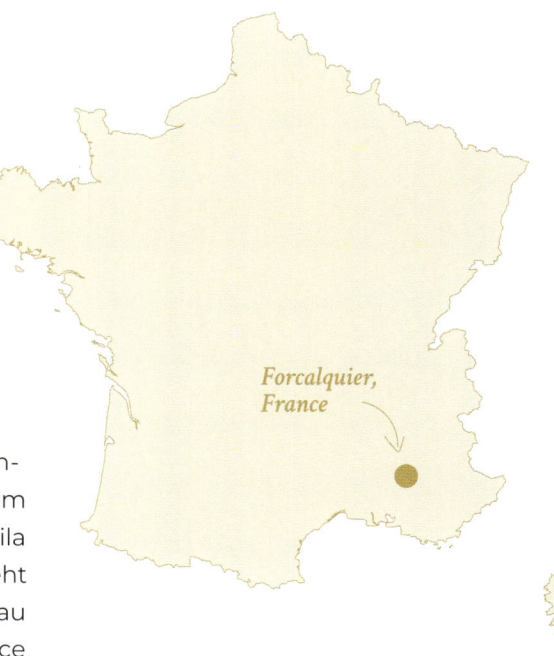

Forcalquier, France

The Spirit of the South of France

The origin of this gin is an irrepressible passion for Provence. The founder of MistralGin, Guillaume Bonnefoi, loves this region. Here you can let the southern French sun shine on your face and breathe in the unmistakable scent of the Mediterranean landscape, while listening to the chirping of the cicadas. Vast fields of vines, olive trees, herbs – and of course that typical lavender, with its intense purple visible glowing even in the far distance – all stretch across the terrain. It's precisely this living feeling that Provence awakens in you that is now available bottled. One sip of MistralGin and you feel transported to this unique and beautiful landscape.

Botanicals from Provence

But it isn't just because of its breathtaking landscape that Provence is the place of origin of this unique gin. Southern France is also home of the most diverse spices and herbs. Thyme, basil, fennel, grapefruit, eucalyptus and mint combine to create a unique gin, the enjoyment of which equals the lifestyle of Provence. However, MistralGin is not only impressive for its fresh, distinctive aroma but also, at the same time, fascinating because of its pink color. As the first Rosé Dry Gin from Provence, it stands for an exquisite lifestyle and reminds us to enjoy life to the fullest. Thus, this refined, artisanal gin is the perfect treat for any epicurean. MistralGin is the best way to toast happy moments. À votre santé!

MG DESTILERIAS S.L.

LE TRIBUTE GIN

Barcelona, Spain

Wenn dir das Leben Zitronen reicht

Erfrischend weht der Wind in der spanischen Stadt Vilanova i la Geltrú in der Nähe von Barcelona. Eine willkommene Abkühlung an einem heißen Sommertag, dessen perfekter Ausklang mit einem Glas des in der örtlichen Destillerie der Familie Giró Ribot hergestellten Le Tribute Gins endet. Sieben unterschiedliche natürliche Botanicals, die in einem besonders schonenden Destillationsverfahren getrennt extrahiert werden, um den facettenreichen puren Geschmack jeder einzelnen Zutat herauszukitzeln, beschreiben die Ästhetik dieses Dry Gins. Als wichtigster Bestandteil kommen nur die besten reifen Wacholderbeeren vom Giro-Landgut in der Provinz Teruel im Nordosten Spaniens in den Le Tribute. Zu ihnen gesellen sich Orangen aus Valencia, Zitronen aus Sevilla, Kumquat aus China, süße Mandarinen von der Mittelmeerküste, drei verschiedene Sorten Grapefruit, Zitronengras, Koriandersamen und Limette.

Erfrischend wie das Mittelmeer

"Alt, aber neu" ist der Leitgedanke, der die Konzeption des Le Tribute Gins angetrieben hat. In ihm steckt die Anerkennung für die Pioniere, die Prozesse und das Erbe der Destillation als Handwerkskunst. Er ehrt die Tradition als das Alte und setzt auf die Innovation als das Neue, die ihn zu einem Unikat werden lässt. Das macht Le Tribute zu einem zeitgenössischen Gin mit Seele und Charakter, hübsch umhüllt von einer an den Jugendstil angelehnten prachtvollen, exklusiven türkisblauen Karaffe, die ein wenig an die Farbe des Atlantiks vor der Küste Spaniens erinnert.

CATEGORY
Dry Gin

ORIGIN
Spain

ESTABLISHED
1835

SIZE
● ● ● ●

TASTING NOTES
Weich und mild, maximal aromatisch, erfrischend sommerlich, belebend, dennoch überraschend trocken, komplex fruchtig dank der Orangen, Grapefruits und Mandarinen, zitruslastig durch Zitronen, Limetten und Zitronengras.

Soft and mild, maximally aromatic, refreshingly summery, invigorating, yet surprisingly dry, complex fruitiness thanks to orange, grapefruit and tangerine, citrus-heavy due to lemons, limes and lemongrass.

> " A tribute to life, summer, the fruits of Spain and gin.

When life hands you lemons

A refreshing wind blows in the Spanish town of Vilanova i la Geltrú, near Barcelona. A welcome cooling on a hot summer day, the perfect end to which is a glass of Le Tribute Gin, produced in the local distillery of the Giró Ribot family. Seven different natural botanicals, extracted separately in a particularly gentle distillation process to tease out the multi-faceted pure flavor of each ingredient, describe the aesthetic of this dry gin. As the most important ingredient, only the best ripe juniper berries from the Giro estate in the province of Teruel in northeastern Spain go into Le Tribute. They are joined by oranges from Valencia, lemons from Seville, kumquat from China, sweet tangerines from the Mediterranean coast, three different varieties of grapefruit, lemongrass, coriander seeds and lime.

Refreshing like the Mediterranean Sea

"Old but new" is the guiding principle that has driven the concept of Le Tribute Gin, embodying recognition for the pioneers, the processes and the heritage of distillation as a craft. It honors tradition as the old and embraces innovation as the new, rendering it unique. This makes Le Tribute a contemporary gin with soul and character, handsomely packaged in a magnificent exclusive turquoise blue decanter inspired by the Art Nouveau style, somewhat reminiscent of the color of the Atlantic Ocean off the coast of Spain.

LA VALDÔTAINE S.R.L.

LA VALDÔTAINE ACQUEVERDI GIN DELLE ALPI

Saint-Marcel in the Aosta valley, Italy

CATEGORY
Distilled Gin

ORIGIN
Italy

ESTABLISHED
1947

SIZE
● ● ○ ○

TASTING NOTES
Trocken, aromatisch, blumig. Ausgeprägte Wacholdernote, dazu intensive Aromen von Orangenblüten, Koriander und Rosmarin.

Mild, soft and full-bodied, with resinous and floral nuances and an elegant, earthy-arboreal format, juniper dominant, conifers in a skillful interplay with citrus, fresh and harmonious finish.

In luftigen Höhen

Türkisblau und klar glitzert das Wasser, das in 1.400 Metern Höhe in den Bergen des Aostatals im Norden Italiens seinen Ursprung hat. Seltene Mineralien lassen die darunter vorschimmernden Steine wie Smaragde erscheinen. Die Acqueverdi-Quelle mit dem magischen und mineralreichen Wasser ist die besondere, einmalige Zutat, die dem La Valdôtaine Acqueverdi Gin delle Alpi zu seiner unvergleichlichen Reinheit verhilft. Um zu dem Wasser zu gelangen, ist ein zweistündiger Fußmarsch notwendig. Genau von dort bezieht die in dem kleinen Dorf Saint-Marcel gelegene Brennerei La Valdôtaine das Wasser für die Herstellung ihres Acqueverdi Gins. Wie gut, dass die darüber hinaus verwendeten Zutaten in Hülle und Fülle am Ufer des Baches wachsen. Alpine Botanicals wie Enzian, Wacholder, Holunderblüten, Malve, Alpenrosenknospen, Tannennadeln, Schwarze Edelraute, Kiefernsprossen und Latschenkiefer veredeln das Profil dieses Gins.

Kräutergrüße aus den Alpen

La Valdôtaine ist eine kleine Destillerie in den Bergen, die von den alten Traditionen des Aostatals inspiriert ist und dort in Handarbeit Gin in kleinen Chargen produziert. Die Brennerei wurde 1947 gegründet. Bereits seit 1978 werden mit modernen Destillationstechniken exquisite Brände mit seltenen Bergkräutern und Früchten des Tales auf Basis des sehr mineralischen Quellwassers

produziert. Mit Einführung der Vakuumdestillationsanlage gelang es der Destillerie, noch effektiver zu brennen und die Aromen noch besser zu extrahieren. Das Ergebnis ist ein üppiger, alpinwürziger Kräuterstrauß mit dem belebenden Charakter der Acqueverdi-Quelle.

> **Water is the life and the soul of Acqueverdi gin.**

In lofty heights

Turquoise blue and clear, the water glistens, originating at an altitude of 1,400 meters in the mountains of the Aosta Valley in northern Italy. Rare minerals make the stones glimmering underneath appear like emeralds. The Acqueverdi spring, with its magical and mineral-rich water, is the special, unique ingredient that helps La Valdôtaine Acqueverdi Gin delle Alpi achieve its incomparable purity. To get to the water source, you have to walk for two hours from the distillery. It is precisely from here that the distillery La Valdôtaine, located in the small village of Saint-Marcel, obtains the water for production of its Acqueverdi Gin. How good that the ingredients used also grow in abundance on the banks of the stream. Alpine botanicals such as gentian, juniper, elderflower, mallow, alpine rosebuds, fir needles, black rue, pine shoots and mountain pine refine the profile of this gin.

Herbal greetings from the Alps

La Valdôtaine is a small distillery in the mountains, inspired by the ancient traditions of the Aosta Valley, where it produces gin by hand in small batches. The distillery was founded in 1947. Ever since 1978, modern distillation techniques have been used to produce exquisite spirits with rare mountain herbs and fruits of the valley, based on the mineral-rich spring water. With the introduction of vacuum distillation equipment, the distillery was able to distill even more effectively and extract the flavors even better. The result is a lush, alpine-rich bouquet of herbs with the invigorating character of the Acqueverdi spring.

357

CATEGORY
Flavored Gin

ORIGIN
Italy

ESTABLISHED
1906

SIZE
● ● ● ●

TASTING NOTES
Weich, frisch, herb-fruchtig, florale Nuancen, Bitternoten, sattes, frisches Zitrusaroma, Grapefruit mit einem reichen und lang anhaltenden Wacholdergeschmack, leicht pfeffrige Schärfe.

Soft, fresh, tart-fruity, floral nuances, bitter notes, rich, fresh citrus aroma, grapefruit with a rich and long-lasting juniper flavor, slightly peppery spiciness.

TORINO DISTILLATI

MALFY GIN ROSA

Zitronen von der Amalfiküste

Südlich der romantisch-chaotischen Stadt Neapel liegt im Sorrent in der Region Kampanien die wunderschöne Amalfiküste. Sie zählt zu den sonnenreichsten Gegenden Italiens und als Geburtsort der angeblich besten Zitrusfrüchte der Welt. Was also tun, wenn einem das Leben frische Zitronen reicht? Gin daraus zaubern! So oder so ähnlich könnte das Motto der Familie Vergnano lauten, die aus den aromatischen Limonen d'Amalfi in der Torino Distillati ihren Malfy Gin Rosa herstellt. In diesem saftig-frischen Drink treffen italienische Wacholderbeeren auf italienische Pink Grapefruits, die unweit des Meeres an der mediterranen Küste reifen und dem Gin seinen Namen und seine schöne Farbe verleihen. Hinzu stoßen aromatischer Rhabarber, Pfeffer und Zitronen, die für den herb-fruchtigen Geschmack sorgen.

Wasser vom Monte Viso

Die 1906 gegründete Brennerei der Familie Vergnano befindet sich in Moncalieri, nahe der Stadt Turin, einem Gebiet, das für erlesene Weine und Spirituosen bekannt ist. Der Malfy Gin Rosa reiht sich in diese Welt ein. Hergestellt wird er mittels Vakuumdestillation, auch Kaltdestillation genannt. Auf diese Weise bleiben die Aromen der insgesamt neun verwendeten, ausschließlich italienischen Botanicals fast unverändert erhalten. Die ausgewählten Zutaten werden separiert und getrennt voneinander destilliert. Das Wasser, das den Gin schließlich auf Trinkstärke bringt, stammt aus einer Quelle vom Monte Viso, einem mehr als 3500 Meter hohen Berg der Alpen, der sich in unmittelbarer Nähe der Destillerie befindet.

Torino, Italy

Lemons from the Amalfi Coast

South of the romantic and chaotic city of Naples, in Sorrento, in the Campania region, lies the beautiful Amalfi Coast. It counts as one of the sunniest areas of Italy and as the birthplace of what is said to be the best citrus fruit in the world. So what to do when life hands you fresh lemons? Conjure gin out of them! That, or something like it, could be the motto of the Vergnano family, which produces its Malfy Gin Rosa from aromatic Amalfi lemons at Torino Distillati. In this juicy, fresh drink, Italian juniper berries meet Italian pink grapefruit, which ripen not far from the sea on the Mediterranean coast and give the gin its name and beautiful color. Aromatic rhubarb, pepper and lemons are added to provide the tart, fruity taste.

Water from Monte Viso

Founded in 1906, the distillery of the Vergnano family is located in Moncalieri, near the city of Turin, an area known for fine wines and spirits. Malfy Gin Rosa fits into this world. It is produced by vacuum distillation, also called cold distillation. In this way, the flavors of the total of nine exclusively Italian botanicals used are preserved almost unchanged. The selected ingredients are separated and distilled separately. The water that finally brings the gin to drinking strength comes from a spring on Monte Viso, a mountain in the Alps more than 3500 meters high and located in the immediate vicinity of the distillery.

> When life hands you grapefruits & lemons, make Malfy Gin Rosa.

RONER AG BRENNEREIEN

Z44 DISTILLED DRY GIN

CATEGORY
Dry Gin

ORIGIN
Italy

ESTABLISHED
1946

SIZE
● ● ○ ○

TASTING NOTES

Sanft und geschmeidig, süßlich-herbes, komplexes Aroma, würzig, fruchtig sowie leicht blumig, mit Kräuter- und Kiefernaromen aus Südtirol und einer angenehmen Schärfe.

Soft and smooth, sweet-tart, complex aroma, spicy, fruity as well as slightly floral, with herbal and pine aromas from South Tyrol and a pleasant spiciness.

Ein risikoreiches Unterfangen

Wenn sich der Sommer langsam verabschiedet und dem Herbst die Bühne überlässt, dann hat die Königin der Alpen ihren großen Auftritt: Die Zirbe erlebte in den vergangenen Jahren eine wahre Renaissance, nicht nur als Mittel in der Naturheilkunde, sondern auch in Speisen und Getränken. Zu den Highlights dieser Feinkost-Produktpalette zählt der Z44 Gin der Qualitätsbrennerei Roner. Die Zirben vom Berg Weisshorn werden mühevoll nach dreijähriger Reifung in Handarbeit von den harzigen Bäumen in luftiger Höhe geerntet. Das Pflücken ist eine riskante Angelegenheit, da die Zapfen der Zirbe nur an den äußersten Ästen hängen. Doch der Geschmack ist es wert.

Fescher Wacholderbub aus der Zallinger Straße

Verwendet wird die mentholige Essenz der Zirben. Im Z44 Gin wird diese durch frische Limettennuancen, eine Vielzahl alpiner und mediterraner Kräuter sowie Blüten ergänzt. Schafgarbe, Veilchenwurzel und Enzianwurzel umrahmen die typischen Noten des Wacholders. Die Tiroler Brennerei Roner stellt seit 1946 und inzwischen in dritter Generation hochwertige Brände her. Was mit einer Brennblase in Gottfried Roners Elternhaus begann, weitete sich auf die Mazeration von Wurzeln, Beeren und Obst aus. Der Z44 Distilled Dry Gin gehört zu den Vorzeigeprodukten Roners. Das zeigt sich auch in der Wahl des Namens. Z44 heißt der Südtiroler, weil der Firmensitz in der Zallinger Straße 44 liegt – und natürlich, weil es sich um einen Zirbenschnaps mit einem Alkoholgehalt von 44 % handelt.

> Pine reasons to drink the Alps.

A risky venture

When summer slowly says goodbye and leaves the stage to the fall, the queen of the Alps makes her grand entrance. The stone pine has experienced a true renaissance in recent years, not only as a remedy in naturopathy, but also in food and beverages. One of the highlights of this delicate product range is the Z44 Gin from Roner. The stone pines from Mount Weisshorn are painstakingly harvested by hand from the resinous trees at lofty heights after three years of ripening. Picking is a risky business, as the cones of the stone pine hang only on the outermost branches. But the taste is worth it.

Dashing juniper guy from Zallinger Straße

The menthol essence of stone pines is used in distillation. The Z44 Gin then is complemented by fresh lime nuances as well as a variety of.... alpine and Mediterranean herbs and flowers. Yarrow, violet root and gentian root frame the typical notes of juniper. The Roner distillery in the Tyrolean region has been producing high-quality spirits since 1946 and is now family-led in third generation. What began with a still in Gottfried Roner's childhood home expanded to the maceration of roots, berries and fruit. Z44 Distilled Dry Gin is one of Roner's flagship products. This is also reflected in the choice of name. The gin from South Tyrol is called Z44 because the company headquarters are located at Zallinger Straße 44 – and, of course, because it is a stone pine schnapps with an alcohol content of 44,0 % ABV.

Tramin, Italy

THAMES DISTILLERS LTD.

SABATINI LONDON DRY GIN

Bella Italia

Das gute Eis und leckere Pasta, die wunderschönen Landschaften, gesäumt von Olivenhainen, Zypressenalleen und Pinienbäumen, die kleinen Städte mit ihren wunderbar schönen Steinhäusern und verträumten Gassen – es gibt zahlreiche Gründe, die Toskana zu lieben. Seit 2015 gibt es einen weiteren und dieser trägt den Namen Sabatini Gin. Jeder Schluck Sabatini schmeckt nach der toskanischen Landschaft, er ist ein flüssiges Abbild der Region rund um die Provinz Arezzo. Hier, in Teccognane, nahe der Stadt Cortona, ist die Geburtsstätte dieses London Dry Gins. Die stolzen Eltern heißen Enrico, Filippo, Niccolò und Ugo – allesamt Mitglieder der Familie Sabatini.

Toskanischer Reiz der Sinne

Für ihre Komposition haben sie mit zwei Hochkarätern der Gin-Szene zusammmengearbeitet: Sie baten Charles Maxwell von Thames Distillers, seines Zeichens Erbe der 11. Generation von Londoner Gin-Herstellern, sowie Alessandro Palazzi, den Manager einer der renommiertesten Cocktailbars in London, um Rat. Gemeinsam wählten sie neun Botanicals aus. Die besten Wacholderbeeren kommen aus Südosteuropa, die Königsklasse aus Italien, heißt es. Und so wird diese unerlässliche Komponente im Sabatini Gin ergänzt durch Koriander, Iris, Fenchel, Lavendel, Olivenblätter, Thymian, Zitronenverbene und Salbei, gewachsen auf den Ländereien der Familie. Das Ergebnis ist eine perfekte Mischung aus Geschichte, Aromen und einem Reiz der Sinne.

Cortona, Italy

CATEGORY
London Dry Gin

ORIGIN
Italy

ESTABLISHED
2015

SIZE
● ● ● ○

TASTING NOTES

Mediterran, trocken und komplex, eindrucksvoll kräftig und würzig, florales Aroma von Iris, Frische dank Zitrus-Verbene, am Gaumen vollmundig, im Nachgang fein und lang wirkend.

Mediterranean, dry and complex, impressively strong and spicy, floral aroma of iris, freshness thanks to citrus verbena, full-bodied on the palate, fine and long-lasting aftertaste.

Bella Italia

The good ice cream and delicious pasta, the beautiful landscapes lined with olive groves, cypress avenues and pine trees, the small towns with their delightfully beautiful stone houses and sleepy alleys – there are so many reasons to love Tuscany. Since 2015, there has been one more, and it's called Sabatini Gin. Every sip of Sabatini tastes of the Tuscan countryside; it is a liquid reflection of the region around the province of Arezzo. Here, in Teccognane, near the town of Cortona, is the birthplace of this London Dry Gin. The proud parents are Enrico, Filippo, Niccolò and Ugo – all members of the Sabatini family.

Tuscan appeal to the senses

For their composition, they collaborated with two top names in the gin scene. They asked Charles Maxwell of Thames Distillers, heir to the 11th generation of London gin makers, and Alessandro Palazzi, manager of one of London's most prestigious cocktail bars, for advice. Together, they selected nine botanicals. The best juniper berries come from southeastern Europe, with the top grade from Italy, they say. And so this indispensable component in Sabatini Gin is complemented by coriander, iris, fennel, lavender, olive leaves, thyme, lemon verbena and sage, grown on the family's estates. The result is a perfect blend of history, flavors and appeal to the senses.

> A gin like a trip to Italy: tasty, aromatic & emotional.

THE ARTISAN D.O.O.

THE ARTISAN GIN

CATEGORY
London Dry Gin

ORIGIN
Croatia

ESTABLISHED
2019

SIZE
● ● ● ●

TASTING NOTES
Einladend, reichhaltig, harmonisch, floral durch einen Hauch von Lavendel, Rose und Holunderblüte, sanft, komplex, samtig, mit Mandel- und Pfeffernoten, eine Prise Zimt und Wacholder, mit einem Touch Olive, langes Finish, trocken und ein wenig süß.

Inviting, rich, harmonious, floral through hints of lavender, rose and elderflower, soft, complex, velvety, with notes of almond and pepper, a pinch of cinnamon and juniper, with a touch of olive, long finish – dry and a little sweet.

Völkerverständigung auf Kroatisch

Die blaue Iris, auch Schwertlilie genannt, ist ein Symbol für Hoffnung und Glauben. Einer Überlieferung zufolge hinterließen die Blitze des Donnergottes Perun beim Einschlag in die Erde überall verschiedenfarbige Schwertlilien. In ihrer Bedeutung als Blume des Völkerfriedens hat Kroatien die blaue Iris im Jahr 2000 zur Nationalblume ernannt. Wen wundert also, dass ein waschechter Kroate wie der Artisan Gin die Schwertlilie honoriert. Ihr Wurzelpulver verfeinert den Premium London Dry Gin als ganz besondere Zutat. Daneben stecken in der überaus elegant daherkommenden schwarzen Designer-Flasche lokale Früchte und Kräuter. Zu den Zutaten zählen Koriandersamen, Angelikawurzel, Zitronen- und Orangenschalen, Mandeln, Olivenbaumblätter, Holunderblüten und Lavendel.

29 Grad und es wird nicht heißer

Das Besondere des Artisan Gins liegt jedoch nicht allein in den Zutaten und der schönen Hülle. Kern des Produktes ist sein überaus aufwendiger Fertigungsprozess, der sich durch Extravaganz, Fingerspitzengefühl, Komplexität und jede Menge Geduld auszeichnet. Die 14 verwendeten Botanicals werden pulverisiert, anschließend mit Ultraschall behandelt, vermengt und drei Tage lang in 42 %igem Alkohol gelagert, bevor sie schließlich den Weg in die Destillationsanlage finden. Ist das Mazerat filtriert, durchläuft es eine niedrig temperierte Vakuumdestillation mit einem Siedepunkt von 29 Grad Celsius. Nach einer vierwöchigen Ruhephase wird das Alkoholvolumen des Destillats bei 44 % eingestellt, bevor es erneut vier Wochen ruht und abschließend abgefüllt wird. Auf diese Weise entsteht ein milder Gin und die feinen floralen Aromen der Botanicals bleiben vollständig erhalten.

> *A craftsman in noble garb who strikes like lightning.*

Intercultural understanding in Croatian

Blue iris, also called spurious iris, is a symbol of hope and faith. According to tradition, the thunderbolts of the thunder god Perun left irises of different colors everywhere when they struck the earth. In its significance as a flower of peace among nations, Croatia named the blue iris its national flower in 2000. So it's no surprise that a true Croatian like Artisan Gin honors the iris. As a very special ingredient, its root powder refines this premium London Dry Gin. In addition, local fruits and herbs reside in the exceedingly elegant black designer bottle. The ingredients include coriander seeds, angelica root, lemon and orange zest, almonds, olive tree leaves, elderflower and lavender.

29 degrees and no hotter

However, what makes Artisan Gin so special is not just the ingredients and the beautiful vessel. The core of the product is its extremely elaborate manufacturing process, which is characterized by extravagance, finesse, complexity and a lot of patience. The 14 botanicals used are pulverized, then treated with ultrasound, blended and stored in 42 % alcohol for three days before finally finding their way into the distillation facilities. Once the macerate is filtered, it passes through a low-temperature vacuum distillation process with a boiling point of 29 degrees Celsius. After a four-week rest period, the alcohol concentration of the distillate is adjusted to 44 % before it rests again for four weeks and is finally bottled. In this way, a mild gin is created and the fine floral aromas of the botanicals are fully preserved.

Zagreb, Croatia

CATEGORY
London Dry Gin

ORIGIN
Sweden

ESTABLISHED
2012

SIZE
● ● ○ ○

TASTING NOTES
Satter Wacholder-Charakter, gepaart mit einer feinen Note von frischem Zitrus, komplexe florale Noten, Vanille und Cassia-Ringe zaubern eine sanfte Süße, im Abgang bleibt ein Hauch von schwarzem Pfeffer.

A round juniper character, fresh citrus notes and a floral complexity. Fresh crunchy green and spicy notes of coriander. A mellow sweetness combined with vanilla and cassia bark lingers on with a long-lasting citrus and juniper finished with a hint of black pepper..

HERNÖ GIN DISTILLERY

HERNÖ DRY GIN

Träume werden wahr

Gin hat im Gegensatz zu Fleischbällchen und Zimtschnecken in Schweden wenig Tradition. Doch inzwischen bekommen die Leckereien flüssige hochprozentige Konkurrenz. Zu verdanken ist das Jon Hillgren. 1999 kam dieser als Bartender nach London und verliebte sich prompt in Gin. Er träumte davon, in seiner Heimat eine Destillerie aufzubauen, bereiste die Welt, um Ginspiration zu finden und traf 2011 eine Kaufentscheidung. Im schwedischen Dörfchen Dala erwarben er und seine Frau eine Farm aus dem 17. Jahrhundert – die Entstehungsschmiede des Hernö Gins und damit der ersten Gin-Brennerei Schwedens. Ein Jahr später wurde bereits das erste Produkt auf den Markt gebracht, gebrannt im handgeschmiedeten Kupferkessel "Kierstin", benannt nach der ersten bekannten Dame, die einst auf der Farm lebte.

Die Welt in einem Glas

Obwohl dieser Gin aus Schweden stammt, ist er in Sachen Geschmack international unterwegs. Denn er vereint insgesamt acht Botanicals aus der gesamten Welt: Wacholder, Koriander, Zitronen, Preiselbeeren, Mädesüße, Pfeffer, Kassien und Vanille. Haben sich die Aromen während der Destillation entfaltet, wird der Gin mit nicht kältefiltriertem Wasser aus dem eigenen Brunnen auf Trinkestärke gebracht. Inzwischen wird der Hernö Gin in der Destillerie als Basis-Gin für die Herstellung einiger weiterer Flaggschiffe genutzt: der leicht gesüßte Hernö Old Tom Gin, den Hernö Navy Strength Gin mit einem Alkoholgehalt von 57 % und den im Wachholder-Fass gereiften Hernö Juniper Cask Gin.

Dala, Sweden

Dreams come true

Unlike meatballs and cinnamon rolls, there is little tradition behind gin in Sweden. But, today, the former delicious treats have had high-proof, liquid competition. Thanks to Jon Hillgren who started the first gin distillery in Sweden 2011. It all began more than a decade earlier in London. Jon was working as a bartender and promptly fell in love with gin. Dreaming of starting his own distillery in his home country, he travelled the world to find inspiration. In 2011 he and his wife bought the 17th century farm in the Swedish village of Dala, where Hernö Gin distillery today is located. A year later, the first product was launched, distilled in the first copper still, "Kierstin", bearing the name of the first woman known to have lived on the farm.

The world in a glass

Although this gin comes from Sweden, it has an international taste. Eight organic botanicals from all over the world brings the very best in taste and quality: juniper, coriander seeds, lemon zest, lingonberries, meadowsweet, black pepper, cassia and vanilla. Once the aromas have unfolded during distillation, using organic spirit made from Swedish wheat, the gin is diluted to the desired drinking strength with water from Hernö Gins own well. The first product, Hernö Dry Gin, has come to be used in the distillery as a base gin for the production of several other flagship gins, for example: Hernö Old Tom Gin that is slightly sweetened, Hernö Navy Strength Gin with an alcohol strength of 57 %, and Hernö Juniper Cask Gin aged in juniper casks.

> # Hernö Gin, Dala, Home of Swedish Gin.

KYRÖ DISTILLERY

KYRÖ GIN

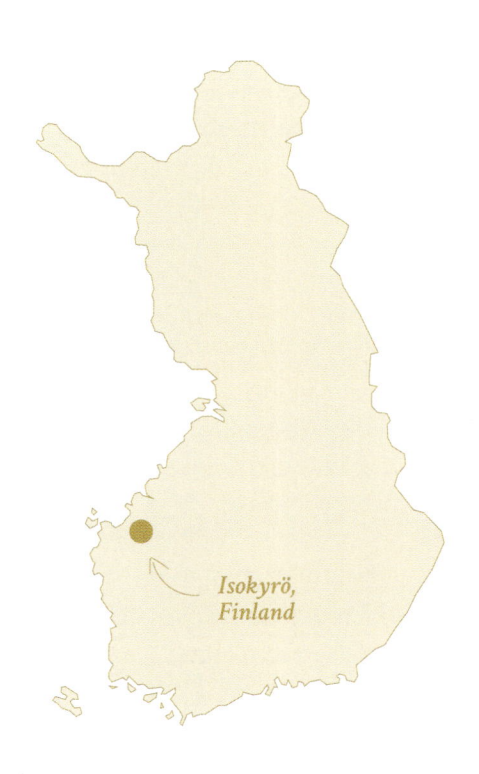

CATEGORY
Rye Gin

ORIGIN
Finland

ESTABLISHED
2014

SIZE
● ● ● ○

TASTING NOTES
Erfrischend kühl, würzig, kräftig, ein harmonisches Zusammenspiel von einer angenehmen Wacholdernote, der herben Roggenbasis, den leichten Beeren- und Kräuteraromen sowie einem Hauch Zitrusnoten und würzigem Pfeffer.

Refreshingly cool, spicy, strong, a harmonious interplay of pleasant juniper note, tart rye base, light berry and herbal aromas along with a hint of citrus notes and spicy pepper.

Isokyrö, Finland

Mit den Finnen in die Sauna

Sauna ist das einzige finnische Wort, das international in andere Sprachen übernommen wurde. Zu Recht, denn der Begriff beschreibt eine gesamte Kultur. In Finnland gibt es so viele Saunen, dass alle Bewohnerinnen und Bewohner zeitgleich darin Platz fänden. Dass hier die Geschichte zu einem international gefeierten Gin beginnt, ist folglich wenig verwunderlich. Eine Gruppe von Freunden ging in die Sauna, trank dabei Roggenwhisky und sinnierte darüber, wieso in Finnland niemand Roggenwhisky herstellt. Wieso also nicht eine eigene Destillerie gründen? Im Wohnzimmer der Eltern nahm das Abenteuer seinen Anfang und mündete schließlich in einer alten Molkerei, in der 2014 erstmals der Destillierapparat aufgeheizt wurde.

Im Sonnenaufgang Beeren pflücken

Als die erste Charge Whisky ruhig in ihren Fässern lagerte, stellten die Freunde fest, dass sie noch etwas anderes produzieren sollten: Gin zum Beispiel. Wie alle Spirituosen aus der Kyrö Distillery basiert diese zu 100 % auf finnischem Vollkornroggen. Veredelt wird dieser mit einer Vielzahl regionaler Zutaten sowie 13 traditionellen Gin-Ingredienzien. Die genaue Zusammensetzung der Botanicals bleibt unter Verschluss. Bekannt ist, dass der Kyrö Gin unter anderem Birkenblätter, Cranberrys, Mädesüß, Schwertlilie, Moosbeeren, Engelwurz und Sanddorn enthält. In ihrem Zusammenspiel sollen die Botanicals das Gefühl vermitteln, mit seinen besten Freunden morgens um 3 Uhr nach einem Saunagang durch ein Roggenfeld zu rennen und auf einer nebligen Wiese Beeren zu pflücken – ganz finnisch eben.

" **The catchers in the rye encounter forest, mist and morning dew.**

To the sauna with the Finns

Sauna is the only Finnish word that has been adopted internationally in other languages. And rightly so, because the term describes an entire culture. There are so many saunas in Finland that all the inhabitants could fit into them at once. So it's hardly surprising that the story of an internationally celebrated gin begins here. A group of friends went to the sauna, drank rye whiskey and pondered why no one in Finland was making rye whiskey. So why not start their own distillery? The adventure began in their parents' living room and eventually led to an old dairy, where the still was fired up for the first time in 2014.

Picking berries at sunrise

When the first batch of whiskey was gently maturing in their barrels, the friends realized they should produce something else – gin, for example. Like all spirits from the Kyrö Distillery, this one is based 100 % on whole-grain Finnish rye. This is refined with a variety of regional ingredients, as well as 13 traditional gin ingredients. The exact composition of the botanicals remains under lock and key. What is known is that Kyrö Gin contains birch leaves, cranberries, meadowsweet, iris, cranberries, angelica and sea buckthorn, among others. In their interaction, the intention is that the botanicals should convey the feeling of running through a rye field with your best friends at 3 o'clock in the morning after a sauna session, whilst picking berries in a misty meadow – altogether very Finnish.

JUNIMPERIUM DISTILLERY

JUNIMPERIUM BLENDED DRY GIN

Tallinn, Estland

JUNIMPERIUM DISTILLERY // JUNIMPERIUM BLENDED DRY GIN

0,7 L // 45,0 %

371

Made in Estonia

Die Geschichte der Junimperium Distillery im angesagten Telliskivi-Viertel mitten in Estlands Hauptstadt Tallin beginnt mit dem Mitgründer Tarvo Jaansoo. Durch seine Liebe zu handgefertigten Gins in Premiumqualität kam ihm die Idee, selbst einen solchen Gin zu kreieren. Er sollte etwas ganz Besonderes, Einzigartiges werden. Zusammen mit dem Destillateur Aare Ormus legte er los, sie experimentierten fast anderthalb Jahre mit verschiedenen Wacholderbeeren aus der Welt und anderen Botanicals, bis sie mit ihrem Ergebnis zufrieden waren: Heraus kam der Junimperium Blended Dry Gin. Dieser unter anderem meistausgezeichnete estnische London Dry Gin ist sehr wacholderbetont, mit einer Zitrusnote im Hintergrund und einem Tick Pfeffer. Der Junimperium Blended Dry Gin hat einen puren, trockenen Wacholdergeschmack mit einem Hauch von Pfeffer. Im Abgang kommt die Zitrusnote durch, die sich auf süße Noten ausdehnt.

Weltweit einzigartig

Die Destillerie ist die einzige der Welt, die eine natürliche und einzigartige Wacholderholzkappe verwendet. Ebenfalls weltweit einzigartig für den Junimperium Gin ist, dass vier Wacholderbeeren aus vier verschiedenen Orten in Europa beigemischt und verwendet werden, darunter lokale Wacholderbeeren aus Estland. Auf diese Weise kommt der einzigartige Geschmack zustande. Insgesamt werden nur sieben verschiedene Botanicals verwendet. Neben Wacholder sind es Koriandersamen, Angelikawurzel, Kubebenpfeffer und Thymian, außerdem zwei geheime lokale Botanicals aus Estland. Alle Zutaten werden separat destilliert und später nach Rezept zusammengemischt.

Co-founder Tarvo Jaansoo with his Master Distiller Aare Ormus (on the left)

CATEGORY
London Dry Gin

ORIGIN
Estonia

ESTABLISHED
2019

SIZE
● ● ○ ○

TASTING NOTES
Purer, trockener Wacholdergeschmack mit einem Hauch von Pfeffer. Im Abgang kommt die Zitrusnote durch, die sich auf süße Noten ausdehnt.

Pure, dry juniper flavor with a hint of pepper. Citrus notes come through in the finish, extending to sweet notes.

> The most awarded Estonian London Dry Gin.

Keep it Made in Estonia

The history of the Junimperium Distillery, located in the trendy Telliskivi district in the heart of Estonia's capital, Tallinn, begins with co-founder Tarvo Jaansoo. His love for handcrafted premium quality gins gave him the idea of creating such a gin himself. He wanted it to be something very special, unique. Together with the distiller, Aare Ormus, he got started; they experimented for almost one and a half years with various juniper berries from around the world and with other botanicals until they were satisfied with their result, namely Junimperium Blended Dry Gin. This gin, winner of many prizes – among other things it is the most awarded Estonian London Dry Gin – is very juniper accented, with a touch of pepper and citrus. Junimperium Blended Dry Gin has a pure, dry taste of juniper with a hint of pepper. The citrus note comes through in the finish, which expands to sweet notes.

Unique throughout the world

The Distillery produces the only gin brand in the world that uses a natural and unique juniper wood cap. Adding to the uniqueness, Junimperium Gin mixes and uses four juniper berries from four different locations in Europe, including local juniper berries from Estonia. That creates the unique taste. A total of only seven distinct botanicals are used. In addition to juniper, there are coriander seeds, angelica root, cubeb pepper and thyme, as well as two secret, local botanicals from Estonia. All ingredients are distilled separately and later mixed together according to the recipe.

*BENGUELA DIAMONDS EUROPE –
A BRAND OF YOUNG TERRITORIES AG*

BENGUELA DIAMONDS GIN

Die raue Küste Südafrikas

Vor dem Atlantikhafen Port Nolloth im Westen Südafrikas liegt auf dem Meeresboden, versteckt zwischen Sand und Kieseln, ein hochkarätiges Vermögen: edle Diamanten, die hier über die Jahrtausende aus dem Herzen Afrikas durch Regen und den Orange River in den Südatlantik gespült wurden. An rund 80 Tagen im Jahr suchen professionelle Taucher nach den kostbaren Steinen – immer dann, wenn die raue See es zulässt. Dieses schwierige, teils gefährliche Unterfangen faszinierte auch Brennmeister Florian Faude und Spirituosen-Sommelier Patrick Braun. Auf einer gemeinsamen Reise in die Küstenregion gingen sie auf Tuchfühlung mit den Benguela Diamonds und fanden so den kreativen Input für ihren Gin.

Port Nolloth, South Africa

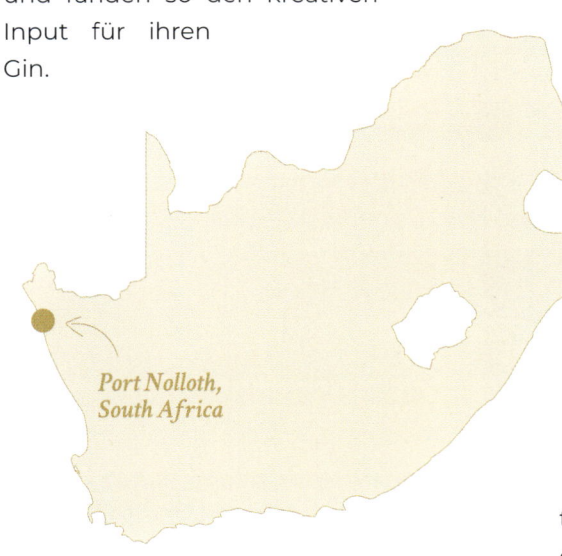

Unten im Meer

Die Rezeptur für den Benguela Diamonds Gin wurde vor Ort unter Verwendung der heimischen Pflanzenvielfalt entwickelt und ist eine Hommage an die Schönheit der Landschaft sowie an den Benguela-Strom, der entlang der Küste fließt und als Namensgeber für den Gin fungiert. Für das außergewöhnliche Aroma spielt Zuckertang eine wesentliche Rolle. Dieser wird von den Diamantentauchern gepflückt und getrocknet. Die Algenart ist mit ihrer besonderen, maritimen Note Spiegelbild des Ozeans. Neben wilder afrikanischer Wacholderbeere fließen zudem frische Zitronenzeste, afrikanischer Lavendel, Kardamom und afrikanischer Wermut in die Kreation ein. Die Verbindung zum Cape kommt auch im Flaschendesign zur Geltung. Auf dem bläulich-maritimen Rückenetikett sind die geografischen Koordinaten von Port Nolloth zu erkennen, dem Zentrum der Förderung von Meeresdiamanten in Südafrika.

> Diamonds are a gin's best friend.

CATEGORY
London Dry Gin

ORIGIN
South Africa

ESTABLISHED
2006

SIZE
● ○ ○ ○

TASTING NOTES
Gut eingebundene Wacholdernote mit intensiven mediterranen Kräuternoten und floralem Bouquet, Assoziationen von Kiefernnadeln und einer Idee Meersalz, äußerst subtile Mentholanklänge, kräftig, vollmundig mit langem intensivem Abgang.

Well-integrated juniper taste with intense Mediterranean herbal notes and floral bouquet, associations of pine needles and a hint of sea salt, extremely subtle menthol tones, powerful, full-bodied with a long intense finish.

The rugged coast of South Africa

Off the Atlantic port of Port Nolloth in western South Africa, hidden among sand and pebbles on the seabed, lies a high-carat fortune: precious diamonds that have been washed into the South Atlantic from the heart of Africa by rain and the Orange River over the millennia. Professional divers search for the precious stones around 80 days a year – whenever the rough seas permit. This difficult, sometimes dangerous undertaking also fascinated master distiller Florian Faude and spirits sommelier Patrick Braun. On a joint trip to the coastal region, they got up close and personal with the Benguela Diamonds and thus found the creative input for their gin.

Down in the sea

The recipe for Benguela Diamonds Gin was developed locally using the native plant diversity and is a tribute to the beauty of the landscape as well as to the Benguela River, which flows along the coast and has given the gin its name. Sugar kelp plays an essential role in the exceptional aroma. This is picked and dried by diamond divers. With its special, maritime note, this type of seaweed is a reflection of the ocean. In addition to wild African juniper berry, also flowing into the creation are fresh lemon zest, African lavender, cardamom and African wormwood. The connection to the Cape also comes through in the bottle design. The bluish maritime back label features the geographical coordinates of Port Nolloth, the center of marine diamond mining in South Africa.

CATEGORY
New Western Dry Gin

ORIGIN
Republic of South Africa

ESTABLISHED
2013

SIZE
● ● ○ ○

TASTING NOTES
Trotz seiner starken Zutaten angenehm mild und fruchtig. Frische Komponenten von Koriander und Wacholder dominieren den ersten Eindruck Exotisch, vollmundig, rund und mit der leichten Süße der Schwarzen Johannisbeere wird das Geschmacksprofil deutlich definiert. Zum Ende hin bescheren die elegante Zitrusfrische der Grapefruit und eine zarte Kräuternuance dem Gin einen gehaltvollen Abgang.

Pleasantly mild and fruity despite its strong ingredients. Fresh components of coriander and juniper dominate the first impression. Exotic, full-bodied, round and with the slight sweetness of blackcurrant, these clearly define the flavor profile. To close, the elegant citrus freshness of grapefruit and a delicate herbal nuance give the gin a full-bodied finish..

AGNES BERNRIEDER GMBH GETRÄNKEVERTRIEB

KAIZA 5 GIN

> „ I want the one with the tiger.

Cape Town, Republic of South Africa

Eine Reise, die alles veränderte

Ja, es gibt ihn, den einen Moment, der alles verändert. Für Julia und Ulrich Bernrieder war es ein lauer Sommerabend in Südafrika, an dem die 'Sommeliers' auf einer Geschäftsreise zu ihren Winzern am Fuße des Tafelbergs eine geschmackliche Alternative zu den wild anmutenden Sauvignon Blancs, Chardonnays, Sémillons, Cabernet Sauvignons und Pinotages rund um den Tafelberg suchten – und fanden. „Ich will den mit dem Tiger". Julia bestand auf diese eine Gin-Flasche unter knapp 100 im Regal, die sie fast magisch in den Bann zog: mit forschen Tigeraugen, die nahezu spürbar aus dem Etikett heraus zu ihr „sprachen". Der Rest war „life changing": Das Unternehmerpaar war wie verzaubert von dem „outstanding taste" des Gins, dem hohen künstlerischen Wert der Verpackung – und der einzigartigen Story, die sie von nun an als Vertriebspartner für Europa fortschreiben wollten. Ihr eigener Wein- und Getränkefachhandel nahe München, den sie in 40-jähriger Familientradition bislang führten? Geschichte!

Free your senses

Ihre Botschaft: „Mach dein Ding". Natürlich hätten sie auch weiterhin umsatzstarke Weine und Spirituosen eruieren und verkaufen können. Das Gespür dafür haben sie ja, die Vertriebskontakte und das unternehmerische Know-how auch. Doch der Ruf nach Unabhängigkeit wurde immer lauter. „KAIZA 5 hat den Tiger in uns geweckt." Und so steht KAIZA 5 nicht nur für die fünf charakterstarken Botanicals Wacholder, Schwarze Johannisbeere, Grapefruit, Angelikawurzel und Koriander, sondern für Unabhängigkeit. Destilliert wird der New Western Dry Gin von Master-Distiller Keegan Cook in Kapstadt. Dort trägt er den Namen „Blind Tiger". Für den Weltmarkt wurde er umbenannt. KAIZA bedeutet übersetzt „unabhängiger König". Ein sehr passendes Synonym für das Label, die Story und die Botschaft: Befrei dich und deine Sinne. Sei mutig und geh deinen Weg!

A journey that changed everything

Yes, it exists, that single moment that changes everything. For Julia and Ulrich Bernrieder, it was a balmy summer evening in South Africa when, on a business trip to their winemakers at the foot of Table Mountain, the 'sommeliers' sought – and found – a flavorful alternative to the wild-looking Sauvignon Blancs, Chardonnays, Sémillons, Cabernet Sauvignons and Pinotages around Table Mountain. "I want the one with the tiger." Julia insisted on this one gin bottle among nearly 100 on the shelf that almost magically captivated her, with brash tiger eyes that almost palpably "spoke" to her from the label. The rest was "life-changing": the entrepreneurial couple were enchanted by the "outstanding taste" of the gin, the high artistic value of the packaging – and the unique story, which they wanted to extend from that moment on as sales partners for Europe. As for their own wine and beverage specialty store near Munich, which they had run in a 40-year family tradition? History!

Free your senses

Their message: "Do your thing". Of course, they could have continued to identify and retail top-selling wines and spirits. They have the flair for it, the sales contacts and the entrepreneurial know-how, too. But the call for independence grew louder and louder. "KAIZA 5 awakened the tiger in us." And so KAIZA 5 stands not only for the five botanicals of strong character – juniper, black currant, grapefruit, angelica root and coriander – but for independence. This New Western Dry Gin is distilled by Master Distiller Keegan Cook in Cape Town. There it bears the name "Blind Tiger". For the world market, it was renamed. KAIZA translated means "independent king". A very fitting synonym for the label, the story and the message: Free yourself and your senses. Be brave and go your own way!

UNIT 43 DISTILLING COMPANY

UNIT 43 ORIGINAL

Heilende Kräfte

In der Westkap-Provinz Südafrikas liegt der kleinste floristische Landstrich der Welt: Das zum Weltkulturerbe erklärte Cape Floral Kingdom beherbergt zirka 9.500 Pflanzenarten, von denen etwa drei Viertel nirgendwo sonst auf dem Globus zu finden sind. In dieser Vielfalt wachsen die besonderen Botanicals für den Unit 43 Original Gin, darunter der „feine Busch" (Fynbos), dessen eigener Artenreichtum mit mehr als 7.000 Farn- und Blütenpflanzen schier gigantisch ist, sowie das Strauchgewächs Buchu, dem entzündungshemmende und entgiftende Eigenschaften zugesprochen werden. Kein Wunder also, dass die Gründer dieses Dry Gin in der facettenreichen Landschaft vor ihrer Haustür alles gefunden haben, was sie benötigen, um ihren Traum zu verwirklichen. Ihr Motto dabei: „Find and refine", zu Deutsch „finde und verfeinere".

Recycelt & Handcrafted

Jason und Bruno – das sind Onkel und Neffe – haben viel gemeinsam: ein Faible für Motorräder und alte Autos, für vermeintlichen Schrott – und für Gin. Ihre Destillerie liegt in einem Industrie-Suburb von Kapstadt. Dieses Gebiet ist in Units, also Einheiten, unterteilt. Für ihre Produktion mieteten die Gründer die Unit 43 an – wie passend, dass der Unit 43 Gin als Resultat ihrer Zusammenarbeit einen Alkoholgehalt von genau 43 % hat. In dem familiengeführten Unternehmen wird „self-made" großgeschrieben: Die Brennerei, die Abfüllanlage, die Möbel und die Bar wurden von den beiden Besitzern aus recycelten Materialien eigenständig angefertigt, so auch die Kupferdestille „Sylvia", benannt nach ihrer Mutter bzw. Großmutter.

Cape Town, Republic of South Africa

Healing powers

The Western Cape Province of South Africa is home to the smallest floristic region in the world. The Cape Floral Kingdom, which has been declared a World Heritage Site, is home to around 9,500 plant species, around three quarters of which are found nowhere else on the globe. The special botanicals for Unit 43 Original Gin grow in this diversity, including the "fine bush" (fynbos), whose own species richness is essentially huge, with more than 7,000 ferns and flowering plants, as well as the bush plant buchu, which is said to have anti-inflammatory and detoxifying properties. No wonder, then, that the founders of this dry gin found everything they needed to realize their dream in the multifaceted landscape on their doorstep. Their motto: "Find and refine".

Recycled & Handcrafted

Jason and Bruno – actually uncle and nephew – have a lot in common: a soft spot for motorcycles and old cars, for supposed scrap metal – and for gin. Their distillery is located in an industrial suburb of Cape Town. This area is divided into Units. For their production, the founders rented Unit 43 – how fitting that Unit 43 gin, as a result of their collaboration, has an alcohol content of exactly 43 % by volume. In the family-run company "self-made" is writ-large. The distillery, the bottling plant, the furniture and the bar were made independently by the two owners from recycled materials, as was the copper still "Sylvia," named after their mother and grandmother, respectively.

CATEGORY
Dry Gin

ORIGIN
Republic of South Africa

ESTABLISHED
2018

SIZE
● ○ ○ ○

TASTING NOTES
Seidig weich, mit Kiefern- und Wacholdernoten, süßlich-würzig durch den Einsatz von Paradieskörnern und Zitrusfrüchten, mit einem Hauch von Kardamom, Koriander und einer blumigen Fynbos-Präsenz.

Silky smooth, with pine and juniper notes, sweetly spicy from the use of grains of paradise and citrus, with hints of cardamom, coriander and a floral fynbos presence.

UNIT 43 DISTILLING COMPANY // UNIT 43 ORIGINAL

0,7 L // 43,0 %

" An African gin safari through the flora of the Cape.

WOODSTOCK GIN COMPANY

399 ON ALBERT – ORIGINAL GIN WOODSTOCK GIN

Cape Town, South Africa

Das Soho der Mother City

Die Fassaden sind bunt, unkonventionell gestaltet von den Kreativen, die sich an ihnen verewigt haben. In den ehemaligen Fabrikhallen fertigen Designer, Möbelschreiner und Dekorateure einzigartige Unikate an. Restaurants reihen sich an Feinschmeckergeschäfte und trendige Cafés. Was Soho für New York ist, ist Woodstock für Kapstadt. Die bekannteste Straße ist die Albert Road. Zwischen Handwerks-Shops, Möbeln, Klamotten und Secondhandläden befindet sich im Haus mit der Nummer 999 ein kleines Geschäft mit der Aufschrift Woodstock Gin. In der Brennerei gibt es das, was draufsteht: einen Gin, der den Way of Life Woodstocks verkörpert, hergestellt in kleinen Chargen mit handverlesenen Botanicals, nach einem Rezept, das von einem Brenner zum nächsten weitergegeben wird.

Mythos oder Wahrheit?

Die Straßen Woodstocks haben alles gesehen, Geschichte(n) geschrieben. Eine dieser Geschichten diente als Inspiration für den Woodstock Gin – und zwar die Legende von einem gerissenen Dieb, der versuchte Diamanten zu verstecken und entdeckt wurde, als er seine Beute unter einem Baum vergrub. Als er zurückkam, fand er Dreck, der zu Asphalt wurde, und Bäume, die zu Laternenpfählen wurden. Die Straßen warten auf niemanden. Und die Diamanten? Nun, sie könnten immer noch da sein, irgendwo unter den Straßen der Albert Road. Wo Mythos und Wahrheit aufeinandertreffen und Traditionen von Rebellen gebrochen werden, findet sich immer ein Schatz – zum Beispiel einer, der nach Gin schmeckt.

> „
> Woodstock's streets tell a thousand stories, manifested in every drop of this gin.

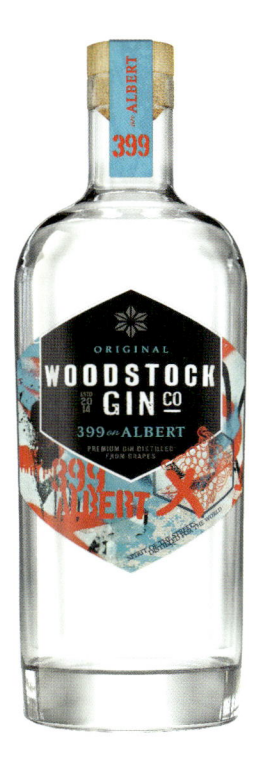

The Soho of the Mother City

The façades are colorful, unconventionally designed by the creative people who have immortalized themselves on them. In the former factory halls, designers, cabinet makers and decorators make unique one-of-a-kind pieces. Restaurants line up with gourmet stores and trendy cafés. What Soho is to New York, Woodstock is to Cape Town. The most famous street is Albert Road. Among craft stores, furniture, clothes and secondhand stores, there is a small store labeled Woodstock Gin in the house with the number 999. The distillery delivers what it says: a gin that embodies Woodstock's way of life, made in small batches with hand-selected botanicals, following a recipe passed down from one distiller to the next.

Myth or truth?

The streets of Woodstock have seen it all, tale(s) written. One of those tales served as the inspiration for Woodstock Gin – namely, the legend of a wily thief who tried to hide diamonds and was discovered burying his loot under a tree. When he returned, he found dirt that became asphalt and trees that became lampposts. The streets wait for no one. And the diamonds? Well, they might still be there, somewhere under the streets of Albert Road. Where myth and truth collide and traditions are broken by rebels, there's always a treasure to be found – one that tastes like gin, for example.

CATEGORY
New Western Dry Gin

ORIGIN
South Africa

ESTABLISHED
2014

SIZE
● ● ○ ○

TASTING NOTES
Sehr weich, elegant und vollmundig, floral und würzig, mit starken Wacholderaromen und einem Hauch von Rosengeranie und Wildem Rosmarin sowie anhaltenden Noten von Buchu und Zitrusfrüchten.

Very soft, elegant and full-bodied, floral and spicy, with strong juniper aromas and hints of rose geranium and wild rosemary, as well as lingering notes of buchu and citrus.

ASAHIKAWA DISTILLERY

ETSU HANDCRAFTED JAPANESE GIN

CATEGORY
Dry Gin

ORIGIN
Japan

ESTABLISHED
2017

SIZE

TASTING NOTES
Ausdrucksstark, mild und angenehm würzig, frisch und glatt strukturiert, leicht bitter mit floralen Noten, am Gaumen etwas pfeffrig, aber ausbalanciert mit Noten von Yuzu, grünem Tee, Beeren und Paprika.

Expressive, mild and pleasantly spicy, fresh and smooth-structured, slightly bitter with floral notes, slightly peppery on the palate but balanced with notes of yuzu, green tea, berries and peppers.

Mit Vergnügen aus Fernost

Etsu bedeutet auf Japanisch Genuss und Vergnügen. Genau dafür steht der gleichnamige Gin, der in erster Linie durch seine fernöstliche Aromatik überzeugt, die vornehmlich durch die Yuzu-Frucht und den Sancho-Pfeffer hervorgerufen wird. Gelber Yuzu wird wegen seiner anmutenden Früchte primär in der Parfümindustrie genutzt. Insbesondere die Schale enthält wertvolle Öle. Der leicht saure Saft hingegen findet Anwendung in der gehobeneren Küche, da er ein komplexeres Aroma als die Zitrone bietet. Der japanische Bergpfeffer Sansho verströmt einen intensiven, reinen Zitrusgeruch und wird zumeist als Würzmittel für Fisch, Geflügel, Suppen und Nachspeisen verwendet. Dass er auch für Spirituosen steht, beweist der Etsu Gin, der als zusätzliches Highlight auch noch eine geheime Grünteemischung enthält.

Das Auge trinkt mit

Der Etsu Japanese Gin wird auf der Insel Hokkaido nach einem alten asiatischen Rezept in der Asahikawa Distillery gebrannt. Die Botanicals mazerieren mindestens 24 Stunden lang in neutralem Zuckerrohrbrand. Die Destillation erfolgt in Copper Stills mit Schwanenhals. Das Destillat mit einem Alkoholgehalt von 83 % wird mit Wasser aus dem Taisetsu-Gebirge auf Trinkstärke gebracht und für optimale Reinheit durch Holzkohle filtriert. Seine japanische Herkunft verschweigt der Etsu Gin keinesfalls. Diese wird nicht nur anhand der verwendeten Botanicals deutlich. Mit seinem dekorativen Etikett samt Geisha, die einer Lotusblüte entspringt, und seiner Kalligrafie lässt er das Auge am Genuss teilhaben.

Hokkaidō, Japan

A flavorful delight from the Far East

Etsu means pleasure and enjoyment in Japanese. This is exactly what the gin of the same name stands for, particularly appealing for its Far Eastern aroma, which is primarily conferred by yuzu fruit and Sancho pepper. Yellow yuzu is primarily used in the perfume industry because of its lemon-like fruit. The peel in particular contains valuable oils. The slightly sour juice, on the other hand, is used in more upscale cuisine because it offers a more complex aroma than lemon. The Japanese mountain pepper Sansho exudes an intense, pure citrus smell and is mostly used as a seasoning for fish, poultry, soups and desserts. That it also serves well in spirits is proven by Etsu Gin, which also contains a secret green tea blend as an additional highlight.

The eye imbibes too

Etsu Japanese Gin is distilled on the island of Hokkaido according to an old Asian recipe at the Asahikawa Distillery. The botanicals macerate for at least 24 hours in neutral sugarcane spirit. Distillation takes place in copper stills with goosenecks. The distillate, with an alcohol content of 83 %, is brought to drinking strength with water from the Taisetsu Mountains and filtered through charcoal for optimal purity. Etsu Gin does not conceal its Japanese origin. This is clear not only given the botanicals used. With its decorative label, including a Geisha springing from a lotus blossom, and calligraphy, it makes no secret of the fact that it comes from Japan, it lets the eye share in the pleasure.

> Etsu stands for pleasure.

THE KYOTO DISTILLERY

KI NO TEA
KYOTO DRY GIN

> „It's tea time! But in a Japanese-wow way.

Ein Fest der Sinne

Wenn die hochwertigsten Zutaten, die Japan zu bieten hat, aufeinander treffen, um ein geschmackliches Feuerwerk auszulösen, dann haben die Meister der Kyoto Distillery ihre Brennkessel angeschmissen, um den KI NO TEA Gin zu produzieren. Für dieses Fest der Sinne wurde mit dem traditionellen Teehersteller Hori-Shichimeien zusammengearbeitet, der Tee anbaut und auch selbst zu aromatischen Kombinationen vermengt. Das Herz des KI NO TEA Kyoto Dry Gin bilden die beiden aromatisch-süßen Teesorten Tencha und Gyokuro. Letzterer entwickelt durch die Aufzucht im Vollschatten weniger Bitterstoffe und zählt deshalb zu den hochwertigsten Grüntees. Bei der Destillation besteht die Herausforderung darin, den erstaunlichen und wertvollen Charakter des Tees zu extrahieren, ohne ihn zu verbrennen oder schwere, grasige oder überkochte Aromen zu erhalten.

Drei Destillate für die Exklusivität

KI NO TEA besteht aus insgesamt drei Destillaten, die unter strengen Proportionen zusammengemischt werden. Die Grundlage bilden Wacholder, Orris und Hinoki, dazu gesellen sich frische Yuzu- und Zitronenschalen für die Ausgewogenheit und zu guter Letzt, aber als größter Anteil, der Gyokuro- und Tencha-Tee. Als Basisalkohol wird Reisschnaps verwendet. Dieser sorgt für die sanfte und fast vanillig-süße Qualität des Gins. Ergänzt wird das Destillat mit Fushimi-Wasser aus einem Brunnen der 1675 gegründeten Tsuki no Katsura Sake-Brauerei. Unterstrichen wird die Exklusivität des KI NO TEA Gins durch seine Aufmachung. Die nach Karakami-Methode designten und mit einem alten traditionellen Edo-Muster aus dem 17. Jahrhundert verzierten dunkelgrünen Glasflaschen werden von Akihiko Toto, einem Kunsthandwerker in der 12. Generation, ausgewählt und produziert.

CATEGORY
Dry Gin

ORIGIN
Japan

ESTABLISHED
2014

SIZE
● ● ● ●

TASTING NOTES
Ausbalanciert, seidig-weich, dezent blumig, mit süßer Textur, einer delikaten Würze, einem Hauch von Zitrusfrüchten und Anklängen weißer Schokolade, am besten pur genießen.

Balanced, silky-soft, subtly floral, with a sweet texture, a delicate spiciness, hints of citrus and hints of white chocolate, best enjoyed neat.

A feast for the senses

When the highest quality ingredients Japan has to offer come together to unleash flavorful fireworks, that's when the masters at Kyoto Distillery have fired up their stills to produce KI NO TEA Gin. For this feast for the senses, they collaborated with the traditional tea producer Hori-Shichimeien, which grows tea and also blends it itself into aromatic combinations. At the heart of KI NO TEA Kyoto Dry Gin are the two aromatic-sweet tea varieties Tencha and Gyokuro. The latter develops less bitter content due to its cultivation in full shade, and is therefore one of the highest quality green teas. During distillation, the challenge is to extract the amazing and valuable character of the tea without either singeing it or preserving heavy, grassy or overcooked flavors.

Three distillates for exclusivity

KI NO TEA consists of a total of three distillates blended together under strict proportions. The basis is juniper, orris and hinoki, joined by fresh yuzu and lemon zest for balance and, last but most rather than least, the Gyokuro and Tencha tea. Rice liquor is used as the base alcohol. This provides the gentle and almost vanilla-sweet quality of the gin. The distillate is supplemented with Fushimi water from a well of the Tsuki no Katsura sake brewery, founded in 1675. The exclusivity of the KI NO TEA gin is underlined by its presentation. Designed using the Karakami method and decorated with an old traditional Edo pattern from the 17th century, the dark green glass bottles are selected and produced by Akihiko Toto, a 12th generation artisan.

385

SUNTORY SPIRITUOSEN ATELIER OSAKA, JAPAN

ROKU GIN

CATEGORY
New Western Dry Gin

ORIGIN
Japan

ESTABLISHED
1919

SIZE
● ● ● ●

TASTING NOTES
Samtig-weich, komplex, harmonisch und vielschichtig, perfekte Harmonie zwischen klassischem Gin-Geschmack und den speziellen Noten japanischer Botanicals, mit Yuzu als Hauptaroma und blumig-süßen Anklängen.

Velvety-smooth, complex, harmonious and multilayered, perfect harmony between classic gin taste and the special notes of Japanese botanicals, with yuzu as the main aroma and floral-sweet hints.

Ōsaka, Japan

Über sechs Ecken musst du gehen...

Die Theorie "Six Degrees of Seperation" beschreibt, dass jeder Mensch mit jedem anderen beliebigen Menschen über maximal sechs Ecken persönlich bekannt ist. Sechs Ecken hat auch jene Flasche, welche die Essenzen Japans sanft umhüllt und deren Inhalt die Kraft hat, Menschen auf der ganzen Welt zu verbinden. Der Roku Gin ist das Ergebnis langjähriger Erfahrung und ein Abbild fernöstlicher Tradition. 1923 träumte Shinjiro Torii davon, Spirituosen herzustellen, welche die Essenz der japanischen Natur einfangen. Er verfolgte seinen Traum und investierte in den Bau einer Destillerie. Bereits seine zweite Kreation, der Suntory Kakubin, wurde zum meistverkauften Whisky des Landes. Doch Shinjiro wollte mehr: 1936 kreierte er erstmals einen Gin.

... um Traditionen zu verstehen

„Roku" bedeutet „sechs" und diese Anzahl an Zutaten wurde dem gleichnamigen Gin, neben acht grundlegenden Aromagebern, beigefügt. Yuzu-Schale, Sakura-Blume und -Blätter, Sencha- und Gyokuro-Tee sowie Sansho-Pfeffer bilden die Eckpfeiler der Spirituose. Sie werden nach dem Shun-Prinzip über das gesamte Jahr hinweg geerntet. Dabei bezieht sich Shun auf die Tradition, jede Speise und jedes Getränk nur dann zu genießen, wenn die Zutaten auf dem Höhepunkt ihres Geschmacks sind. Hergestellt im Spirituosen-Atelier von Beam Suntory in Osaka, werden die japanischen

> **Big in Japan.
> Big in taste.**

You have to go via six corners…

The theory of "six degrees of separation" suggests that any person is personally known to any other person via turns at a maximum of six corners. Six corners are also to be found on the bottle, which gently envelops the essences of Japan, contents that have the power to connect people around the world. Roku Gin is the result of many years' experience and a reflection of far eastern tradition. In 1923, Shinjiro Torii dreamed of producing spirits that captured the essence of Japanese nature. He pursued his dream and invested in the construction of a distillery. Already his second creation, Suntory Kakubin, became the country's best-selling whiskey. But Shinjiro wanted more: in 1936, he created a gin for the first time.

… to understand traditions

"Roku" means "six" and this number of ingredients was added to the eponymous gin, along with eight basic flavoring agents. Yuzu peel, sakura flower and leaves, sencha and gyokuro tea, and sansho pepper are the cornerstones of the spirit. They are harvested according to the Shun principle throughout the year. Here, Shun refers to the tradition of enjoying any food or drink only when the ingredients are at the peak of their flavor. Produced at Beam Suntory's spirits atelier in Osaka, the Japanese botanicals are distilled individually, according to their characteristics; the cherry blossoms through a careful vacuum distillation in stainless steel stills, the yuzu fruit through a distillation in copper pot stills. This precision in handling the botanicals led to Roku becoming a Japanese favorite.

"Friends forever,
Through Thick
& Gin.

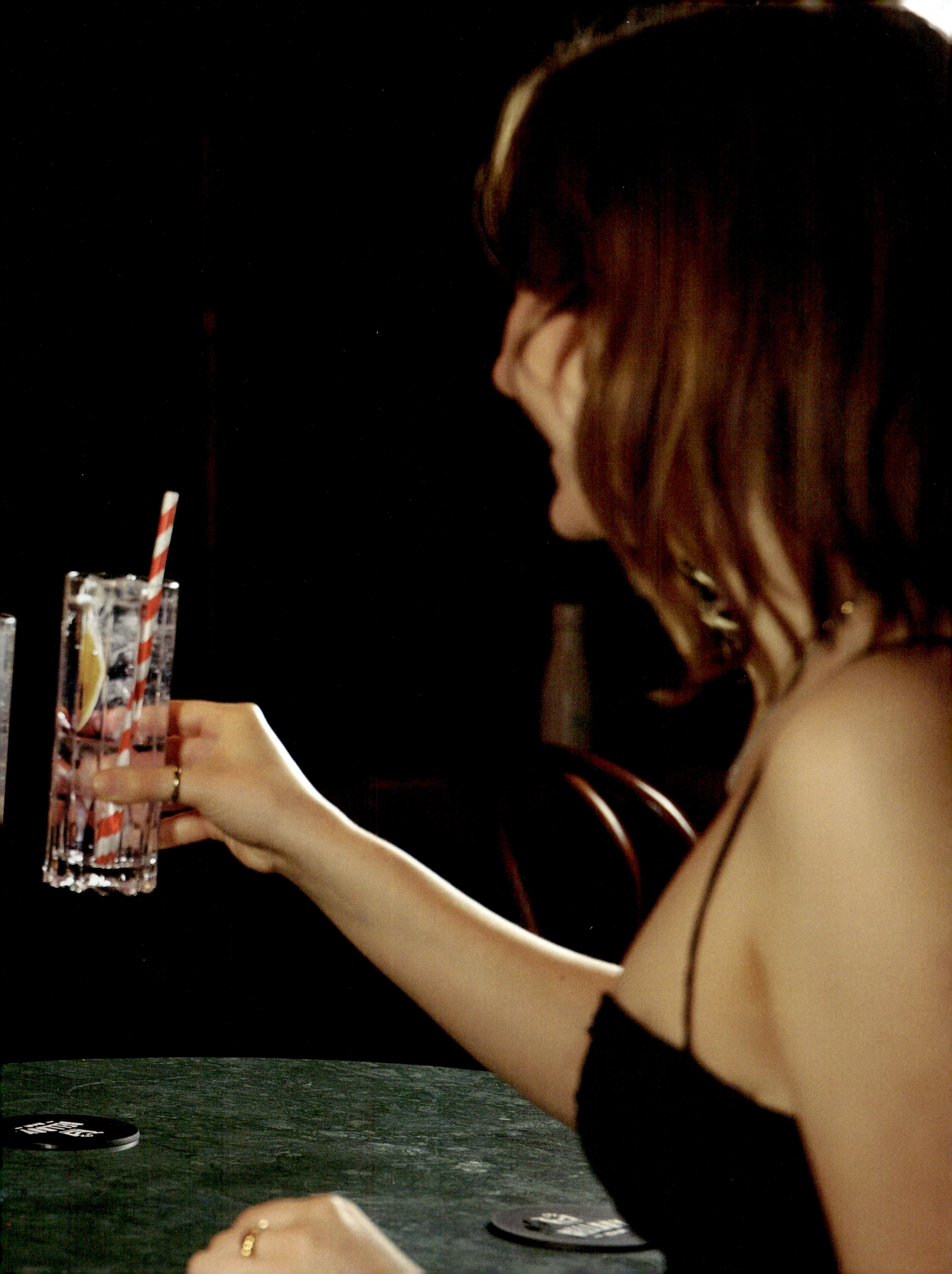

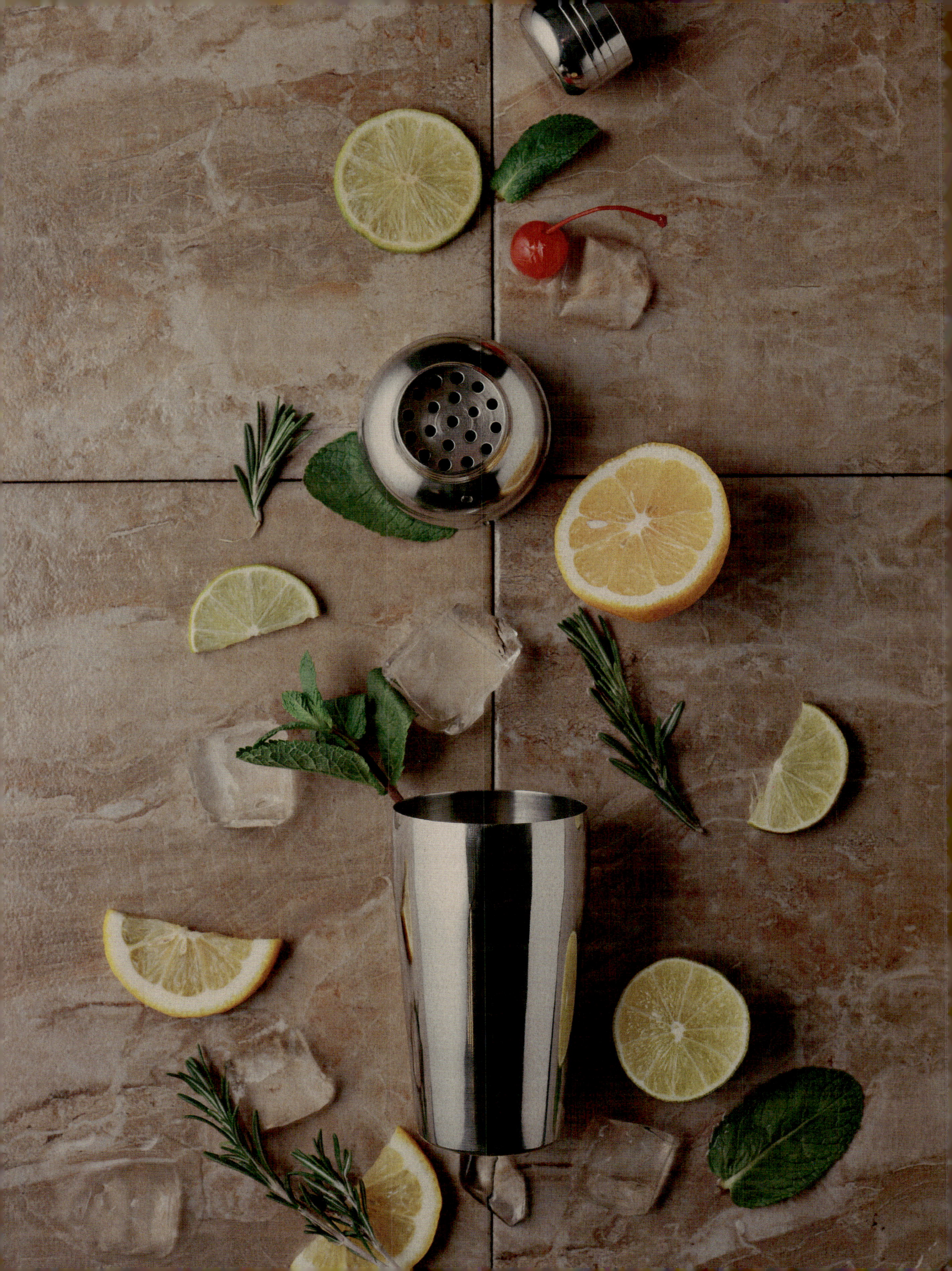

4
FILLER

HARIOLF SPROLL

ROSEBOTTEL TONIC ESSENCES

„
An Ulm Original

Nicht zu bitter, sondern fruchtig

Eine Essenz, die, mit Sodawasser aufgegossen, entweder pur oder als Filler in Cocktails eingesetzt werden kann. Diese Idee kam Hariolf Sproll im Jahr 2012. Und so legte er, zusammen mit seiner Partnerin Anna Reccia, los. Entstanden ist dabei unter anderem die Rosebottel Tonic Essence, ein sehr fruchtiges und komplexes Tonic mit einer leichten Bitternote aus natürlicher Chinarinde. Der Geschmack ist fruchtig-herb und nicht zu bitter mit Noten frischer Zitrusfrüchte. Die Ulmer Tonic Essence kann mit regionalen Kräutern und Bio-Bergamotten direkt aus Kalabrien aufwarten, während die Enzian-Variante sogar ganz ohne Chinin auskommt.

Aus der Bar in die Flasche

Hergestellt werden die Essenzen in Ulm. Hariolf Sproll betreibt hier zwei Bars, die Blaupause und die Rosebottel-Bar. Letztere, eine klassische Cocktailbar ähnlich einer American Bar, wurde im Jahr 2012 eröffnet. Die Herausforderung bestand für den Unternehmer darin, eine Bar zu etablieren, die ziemlich abseits vom Ausgehzentrum Ulms liegt. Das Problem löste er, indem er seine eigenen Essenzen herstellte, die er seitdem für seine Cocktails verwendet. Nachdem die Nachfrage danach immer weiter anstieg, wurde 2014 damit begonnen, die Essenzen auch in Flaschen abzufüllen. Doch egal, ob für die Verwendung in der Bar oder den Verkauf in Flaschen: Gekocht werden seine verschiedenen Essenzen bis heute in nur sehr kleinen Chargen. Wichtig ist hierbei, dass ausschließlich natürliche Zutaten verwendet werden und die Essenzen ebenso schmecken.

Not too bitter, but fruity

An essence that, diluted with soda water, can be used either neat or as a filler in cocktails. This idea came to Hariolf Sproll in 2012, and so he set to work with his partner Anna Reccia. One of the results was Rosebottel Tonic Essence, a very fruity and complex tonic with a slight bitter note from natural cinchona bark. The taste is fruity-tart and not too bitter with lots of fresh citrus. The Ulmer Tonic Essence can put forward with regional herbs and bergamot straight from Calabria, while the Enzian Tonic Essence is made entirely without quinine.

From the bar into the bottle

It is produced in Ulm. Hariolf Sproll runs two bars here, the Blaupause and the Rosebottel Bar. The latter, a classic cocktail bar similar to an American Bar, opened in 2012. The challenge for the entrepreneur was to establish a bar that was fairly remote from Ulm's nightlife center. He solved the problem by making his own essences – since then used in his cocktails. After demand rose more and more, he started bottling his essences in 2014. But whether for use in his own bars or selling bottles elsewhere: Up to this day, his various essences are still cooked up in very small batches. The important thing here is that only natural ingredients are used and that the essences' taste reflects that.

ÖSELSTUFF OÜ

ÖSELBIRCH MIXERS

Der Birke sei Dank

Es wirkt wie eine längst vergessene traditionelle Heilmethode, die Essenz lang vergessener Kräuterkundler, dabei wird die Gewinnung des Birkensaftes in Skandinavien seit Jahrhunderten betrieben. Kinder berichten mit einem Leuchten in den Augen, wenn die Oma den im Frühling gewonnenen Saft der Birken zubereitet hatte und er als wohltuende Erfrischung den heißen Sommer milder werden ließ. So erging es auch den Geschwistern Katri, Anne-Liis, Mirjam und Ardon, die sich von ihrer Oma zu genau dieser Geschäftsidee inspirieren ließen. Was mit einer Kindheitsschwärmerei begann, ist heute ein florierendes Business. Mittlerweile sind die verschiedenen Geschmacks-Birkensäfte und Tonics – entsprechend der wachsenden Begeisterung – in ganz Europa erhältlich.

Vom Birkensaft zum Tonic

Die verschiedenen ÖselBirch BIO Mixers und Tonic basieren auf dem fermentierten Birkenwasser, das es schon vorher in verschiedenen Geschmacksrichtungen gab. Die Mixers und Tonic enthalten keine Konservierungsstoffe und wenig bis gar keinen Zucker. Die Mixers sind außerdem ganz ohne Chinin. Ein Teil des Gewinns wird in die Wiederaufforstung investiert. Das Sprudel-Tonic gibt es bisher in drei verschiedenen Geschmacksvarianten: Rhabarber, Mojito und Fichte. Durch das Birkenwasser erhalten sie in diesem Zusammenspiel ein einzigartiges Geschmacksprofil. Birkensaft hat ein erfrischendes, waldiges und kerniges Erlebnisprofil. Etwas bitter, leicht fruchtig und dennoch mit Würze und belebender Frische, ist es mit keinem anderen Geschmack vergleichbar. Verbindet man dieses Profil mit verschiedenen Geschmacksaromen wie Limette, Pfefferminze oder Fichte, kreiert man ebenso einzigartige Formate an Erfrischungsgetränken und Fillern, die so manchen Cocktail auf eine neue waldige Ebene heben und nebenbei vitalisierend und belebend auf das Verdauungssystem wirken.

Thanks to the birch

It seems like a long forgotten traditional healing method, the essence of long forgotten herbalists, yet the extraction of birch sap has been practiced in Scandinavia for centuries. Children lined up with a gleam in their eyes when their grandmother prepared the birch sap obtained in spring and, as a pleasant refreshment, it made the hot summer seem milder. So it was for siblings Katri, Anne-Liis, Mirjam and Ardon, who were inspired by their grandmother to create precisely this business idea. What began as a childhood relish is now a thriving business. In the meantime, the various flavored birch juices and tonics – responding to growing enthusiasm – are available throughout Europe.

From birch sap to tonic

The various ÖselBirch BIO Mixers and Tonic are based on fermented birch water, which gives it a unique flavour bouquet. All ÖselBirch mixers and tonic contain no preservatives and have very low sugar. In addition, the mixers are also completely quinine-free. A portion of the profits is invested in reforestation. So far, the fizzy tonic is available in three different flavors: rhubarb, mojito and spruce. The birch water gives them a unique flavor profile in this interplay. Birch sap has a refreshing, arboreal and pithy experience profile. Somewhat bitter, slightly fruity, yet with spice and invigorating freshness, it is unlike any other flavor. Combine this profile with different flavor aromas such as lime, peppermint or spruce, and you create equally unique formats of refreshing drinks and fillers that take many a cocktail to forest canopy level and, by the way, have a vitalizing and invigorating effect on the digestive system.

> „ With birch sap a taste adventure unlike any other.

MG DESTILERIAS S.L.

LE TRIBUTE TONIC WATER & LEMONADE

It's a match!

Der Le Tribute Gin gehört zu den beliebtesten Spirituosen Spaniens. Verständlich, dass hierfür das passende fruchtige, leicht herbe Tonic Water entwickelt wurde. Der Gin und das Tonic sind wie füreinander gemacht, das perfekte Paar deren gemeinsamer Nenner im Zitronengras-Destillat liegt. Das Tonic Water wird mit natürlichem Chinin hergestellt, das aus Loja in Ecuador stammt. Dass das Chinin die Reise aus Südamerika antritt, liegt in einer Erzählung aus dem Jahr 1639 begründet: Die Gräfin von Chinchón wurde dank eines Aufgusses aus der Rinde des Chinchonabaums aus der Region Loja von einem Fieber geheilt. Fortan half dieses wunderbare Mittel unter anderem verschiedenen europäischen Königen auf ihrem Weg der Genesung.

Freundschaft Plus

Weil der Le Tribute Gin nichts von Monogamie hält, gehören auch Bitterlimonade, Ginger Ale und Ginger Beer in seinen näheren Bekanntenkreis. Den Status Freundschaft Plus hegt er unter anderem mit der natürlich zitrischen Le Tribute Olive Lemonade. Hierfür werden Zitronenschalen in Wasser einer natürlichen hauseigenen Quelle mit einer kleinen Menge Oliven destilliert, um der Limonade ihre subtile Olivennote zu verleihen. Der Geschmack der Oliven und der Zitronen wird zusätzlich durch Zugabe von Meerwasser hervorgehoben. Obwohl jedes Mitglied der Le Tribute-Familie auf Individualität besteht, haben alle eine hübsche Gemeinsamkeit: Sie werden in quadratische, geriffelte Glasflaschen abgefüllt, die an die Ursprünge der Destillerie als Arzneimittelproduzent erinnern

It's a match!

Le Tribute Gin is one of the most popular spirits in Spain. Understandable then that this matching fruity, slightly tart tonic water was developed for it. The gin and tonic are made for each other, the perfect couple whose common denominator is a lemongrass distillate. The tonic water is made with natural quinine, sourced from Loja in Ecuador. That the quinine makes the journey from South America is rooted in a tale from 1639: The Countess of Chinchón was cured of a fever thanks to an infusion made from the bark of the cinchona tree from the Loja region. From then on, this miraculous remedy helped, among others, various European kings on their road to recovery.

Friendship plus

Because Le Tribute Gin doesn't think much of monogamy, bitter lemonade, ginger ale und ginger beer are is also part of its circle of immediate acquaintances. Among others, it has friendship plus status with the naturally citrusy Le Tribute Olive Lemonade. Lemon zest is distilled in water from a natural in-house source with a small amount of olives to give the lemonade its subtle olive note. The flavor of the olives and lemons is further enhanced by the addition of seawater. Although each member of the Le Tribute family insists on individuality, they all have one pretty feature in common: they're bottled in square-section, fluted glass bottles that recall the distillery's origins as a producer of medicines.

"
Young Spaniard seeks fresh tonic for serious relationship.

WEINGUT SCHREIECK

SCHREIECK INDIAN TONIC

„One into two, two into one, that's the gin-tonic-101.

Geeignet für komplexe Gins

Eine beliebte Zugabe zum Gin ist Tonic. Dass beide harmonieren müssen, liegt auf der Hand. Immerhin macht das Tonic im Mischverhältnis rund zwei Drittel des Getränks aus. Zahlreiche Hersteller entwickeln daher die passenden Filler zu ihren Spirituosen – so auch die Familie Schreieck, die das gleichnamige Weingut betreibt und als idealen Partner zu ihrem Pfälzer Edelgin bereits 2018 ein Indian Tonic Water herausgebracht hat. Durch den reduzierten Zuckeranteil ist das Tonic mit einem angenehmen Kohlensäureanteil besonders gut für komplexere Gins mit feinen Aromen geeignet. Es überzeugt durch eine leichte, zurückhaltende Süße, kombiniert mit einer angenehmen Frische und den Bitterstoffen des Chinins, die hier wie üblich weniger stark ausgeprägt sind als beispielsweise bei einem Dry Tonic Water. Die „Indian"-Bezeichnung stammt übrigens von den Briten, die um 1870 in Indien lebten und das Getränk wegen seines Geschmacks und zur Malariavorbeugung bevorzugten.

Suited to complex gins

A popular addition to gin is tonic. It's obvious that the pairing must harmonize. After all, the tonic makes up around two-thirds of the drink in the mixing ratio. Numerous manufacturers are therefore developing suitable fillers for their spirits – including the Schreieck family, which runs the winery of the same name and had already launched an Indian tonic water in 2018 as the ideal partner for its Pfälzer Edelgin. Due to its reduced sugar content and pleasant carbonic acid content, this tonic is particularly well suited to more complex gins with fine aromas. It's a winner with its light, restrained sweetness, combined with a pleasant freshness and the bitter effect of quinine which, as usual, are less pronounced here than in a dry tonic water, for example. Incidentally, the "Indian" designation comes from the British, who lived in India around 1870 and preferred the drink for its taste and to prevent malaria.

> Appreciation towards food.

Transparent und ehrlich

Als leidenschaftlicher Barkeeper mixt Tim von Herzen gern mit den verschiedensten Zutaten und Ingredienzien. Dabei fiel ihm auf, dass es zu jedem Produkt eine hochwertige Alternative gibt: bio, regional, fairtrade. Gerade in Sachen Ingwer ließ das Angebot zu wünschen übrig und er fand bis dahin kein hochwertiges und ebenso liebevolles wie handwerklich hergestelltes Ginger Ale für sich. Das war der Beginn von Ginger & Fred. Heute steht Ginger & Fred für 100 % natürliches Ginger Ale-Sirup aus echten Früchten und Wurzeln. In seiner kleinen Manufaktur produziert Tim so 100 % natürliche Essenzen aus regionalen veganen und natürlichen Rohstoffen. Mit der Sirup-Serie von Ginger and Fred bist du der nächste Barkeeper.

100 % natürlich

Ob alkoholfrei oder in einem speziellen Cocktail: Die Essenzen auf Ingwer-Basis, die in vielen verschiedenen Geschmacksrichtungen erhältlich sind, verleihen dir die Möglichkeit, als Barkeeper zu glänzen. Dabei sind die Drinks schnell zubereitet und das vielseitig, gesund und harmonisch. Im Handumdrehen lässt sich hier ein Moscow Mule oder ein Ginger Ale ins Glas zaubern. In seiner kleinen Manufaktur stellt Tim die Essenzen her. Die Qualität der Zutaten entscheidet in erster Linie über den Geschmack eines Drinks und so war es dem Team besonders wichtig, jedem Filler nur das Beste zukommen zu lassen. Überzeugen könnt ihr euch selbst, denn neben der Produktion steht Tim gern mit seiner mobilen Bar auf eurem nächsten Event und verzaubert mit seinen Kreationen, die er gern an eure Wünsche anpasst.

Alles dreht sich um die Basis

Was haben Sanddorn, Spicy und Limette gemeinsam? Eine angenehme Schärfe von Bio-Ingwer als Basis, ein Spiel mit leichter Süße sowie einen würzigen Charakter. Zu den Ginger & Fred-Sorten gesellen sich jeweils verschiedene Zutaten, die harmonisch mit dem Ingwer abgestimmt sind. Euch erwartet ein gehaltvoller, natürlicher und belebender Geschmack, wie er für jeden Drink sein sollte.

TIM ANDREAS FAHRION

GINGER & FRED SYRUPS

Transparent and honest

As a passionate bartender, Tim loves to mix using a wide variety of ingredients. He noticed that there is a high-quality alternative for every product: organic, regional, fair trade. But especially when it came to ginger, what was on offer left a lot to be desired and, to date, he'd been unable to find a high-quality and equally lovingly and handcrafted ginger ale. That was the beginning of Ginger & Fred. Today, Ginger & Fred stands for 100% natural ginger ale syrup made from real fruit and roots. In his small operation, Tim produces 100% natural essences from regional vegan and natural raw materials. With the "Ginger and Fred" syrup range you are the next bartender.

100 % natural

Whether alcohol-free or in a special cocktail, the ginger-based essences, which are available in many different flavors, give you the opportunity to shine as a bartender. The drinks are quickly prepared and are versatile, healthy and harmonious. In a jiffy, a Moscow Mule or a ginger ale can be conjured up in the glass. In his small operation Tim produces the essences. The quality of the ingredients is primarily what determines the taste of a drink, and so it was especially important to the team to give each filler only the best. You can see for yourself because, in addition to production, Tim is happy to stand with his mobile bar at your next event and enchant you with his creations, adapted to your wishes.

It's all about that base

What do sea buckthorn, spicy and lime have in common? A pleasant spiciness of organic ginger as a base, an interplay with subtle sweetness as well as a spicy character. The Ginger & Fred essences are each combined with different ingredients that are harmoniously coordinated with the ginger. You can expect a rich, natural and invigorating taste, as it should be for every drink.

HITCHCOCK GMBH

HITCHCOCK JUICE COLLECTION

HITCHCOCK
DEEPDARK
CRANBERRY
Premium Nektar

SINCE 1966

HITCHCOCK
ROYAL
PINEAPPLE
Premium Direktsaft

SINCE 1966

HITCHCOCK
IMPERIAL
ORANGE
Premium Direktsaft

SINCE 1966

HITCHCOCK
ULTIMATE
MANGO
Premium Nektar

SINCE 1966

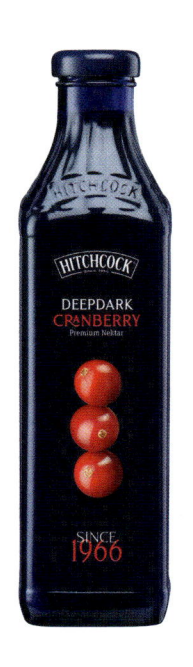

For juice drinkers with the highest demands

The exterior excludes all doubt: no ordinary juice looks like this. An iconic blue glass bottle with a design award and the highest quality contents: this is what unites the four varieties comprising the Juice Collection. The world-famous fruit from Valencia, Spain, is used in Imperial Orange. The multi-faceted interplay between complex sweetness and filigree acidity is unparalleled. The exotic taste of the Alphonso mango from southern India enchants with the purest magic. It makes the Ultimate Mango intense, complex, delicate and sweet. The "Millie Dillard" pineapple from Costa Rica tastes like a Caribbean night, lush and sweet. And so does the Royal Pineapple. Not for beginners is the Deepdark Cranberry. The fruit from Canada is bitter, sour and impresses with complex tannins.

The cranberries used come from the best growing areas in the world for incomparable juice quality. Only the best fruits are used for the production. A conscious decision was made to use mono-fruit varieties in order to capture the pure, full flavor of each respective fruit. These guarantee a particularly fruity and aromatic taste. But these blue highlights are juices for that special moment; the Juice Collection is aimed at adult and trend-conscious connoisseurs who are only satisfied with the best – whether for pure juice enjoyment, on ice, or for mixing into drinks and cocktails.

> ❝ No ordinary juice looks like this.

Für Safttrinker mit höchsten Ansprüchen

Das Äußere lässt keine Zweifel offen: So sieht kein gewöhnlicher Saft aus. Ikonische Blauglasflasche mit Design-Auszeichnung und hochwertigster Inhalt: Das verbindet die vier Sorten der Juice Collection.

Im Imperial Orange werden die weltbekannten Früchte aus dem spanischen Valencia verwendet. Das facettenreiche Spiel zwischen komplexer Süße und filigraner Säure sucht seinesgleichen. Die Geschmacks-Exotik der Alphonso-Mango aus dem Süden Indiens bezaubert durch reinste Magie. Sie macht den Ultimate Mango intensiv, vielschichtig, zart und süß. Wie eine karibische Nacht, üppig und süß, schmeckt die „Millie Dillard"-Ananas aus Costa Rica. Und dadurch auch der Royal Pineapple. Nichts für Anfänger ist der Deepdark Cranberry. Die Früchte aus Kanada sind bitter, sauer und bestechen durch komplexe Tannine.

Die verwendeten Cranberrys stammen aus den weltweit besten Anbaugebieten für unvergleichbare Saftqualität. Nur die besten Früchte werden für die Herstellung verwendet. Dabei hat man sich bewusst für Monofruchtsorten entschieden, um den reinen, vollen Geschmack der jeweiligen Frucht einzufangen. Diese garantieren einen besonders fruchtig-aromatischen Genuss. Doch die blauen Highlights sind Säfte für den besonderen Moment: Die Juice Collection richtet sich an erwachsene und trendbewusste Genießer, die sich nur mit dem Besten zufriedengeben – egal, ob für den puren Saftgenuss, auf Eis oder zum Mixen für Drinks und Cocktails.

Grüße aus München

Richtig gelesen: Das klassische Aqua Monaco Tonic stammt aus der bayerischen Hauptstadt und nicht aus dem Stadtstaat Monaco und hat auch wenig damit zu tun. Wusstest ihr, dass das Wort „Monaco" aus dem Italienischen übersetzt München heißt? Jetzt wisst ihr es. Das ist aber nicht alles, was die Marke so besonders macht. Schon mit ihrem Mineralwasser erreichte sie Kultstatus in der Landeshauptstadt. Denn Aqua Monaco bedient sich eines unterirdisch liegenden Wasservorkommens aus einem uralten Gletscher. Hier in 150 Meter Tiefe gewinnen die Macher ein reines und sehr weiches Wasser, das als perfekte Basis für die verschiedensten Produkte dient. Mit dem aufkommenden Gin-Hype legte die Marke mit ihrem klassischen Tonic Water die Messlatte hoch an und katapultierte sich nach weit oben in der Szene.

Noch mehr Grüße aus München

Nicht nur geschmacklich trifft das Aqua Monaco Tonic Water das Herz der Gin-Fans, auch optisch signalisiert das Design deutlich seine Qualität. Der Schwan symbolisiert die Reinheit und die Elemente, in denen er sich bewegt. Aber die Marke steht für so viel mehr, denn sie umfasst – Achtung, festhalten! – mittlerweile mehr als 20 verschiedene Produkte. Vegane Filler für deine Drinks, zuckerreduzierte Produkte, eine Bio-Mixer-Serie – und alle werden klimaneutral hergestellt. Auch das soziale Engagement hat man sich auf die Fahne geschrieben und so unterstützt Aqua Monaco kulturelle, soziale und ökologische Projekte.

Ein Tonic Water der kräftigen Sorte

Die Bitter- und Zitrusnoten sind gut ausgeprägt und zeigen deutlich, dass es hier klassisch zugeht. Die Kohlensäure ist intensiv und dominiert zu Beginn mit starkem Auftritt. Ein „sauguates" Tonic Water, das zu vielen Gins passt.

AQUA MONACO GMBH

AQUA MONACO TONICS

> " Purity in the glass.

Greetings from Munich

Correctly read, the classic Aqua Monaco Tonic comes from the Bavarian state capital, not the city-state of Monaco, and it has little to do with the latter. Did you know that the word "Monaco" translated from Italian means Munich? Now you know. But that's not all that makes the brand so special. It had already achieved cult status in the state capital with its mineral water. Aqua Monaco draws on a subterranean aquifer from an ancient glacier. Here, at a depth of 150 meters, the makers extract pure, very soft water that serves as the perfect base for a wide variety of products. Leaping with the emerging gin hype, the brand set the bar high with its classic tonic water and catapulted itself to the top of the scene.

Even more greetings from Munich

It isn't just in terms of taste that Aqua Monaco Tonic appeals to gin fans' hearts; the design clearly signals its quality visually too. The swan symbolizes purity and the elements in which it moves. But the brand stands for so much more, as it covers – brace yourself – more than 20 different products now. Vegan fillers for your drinks, reduced-sugar products, an organic mixer range – and all through carbon-neutral production. The company is also committed to social responsibility, and Aqua Monaco supports cultural, social, and ecological projects.

A tonic water of the strong variety

The bitter and citrus notes are well pronounced and clearly show that things are classic here. The carbonation is intense and dominates at the beginning with a strong presence. A brilliant tonic water that goes well with many gins.

SÜDAFRIKA GENUSS | OBELISK AG

FITCH & LEEDES – PREMIUM MIXERS

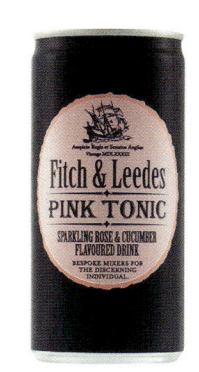

Prickelnde Tonics, handgemacht in Südafrika

Im Jahr 1583 machten sich die Kaufmänner Ralph Fitch und Williams Leedes von London aus auf die Reise gen Osten. Sie stachen in See, um in Indien neue, exotische Geschmäcker zu finden. Und sie wurden fündig! Die Marke Fitch & Leedes der Chill Beverages ist eine Hommage an sie. Ihr Indian Tonic Water ist ein Klassiker unter den Tonics. Es kombiniert das Bittere des Chinins wunderbar mit feinen Gewürzen und Zitrusnoten. Das Tonic unterstreicht die Aromen des Gins, anstatt sie zu erschlagen. Das Pink Grapefruit Tonic aus Südafrika ist extravagant angelegt. Bitter trifft hier den Geschmack frischer Grapefruit. Es gibt dem Gin genug Raum. Bereits die leuchtend blaue Farbe des Blue Tonic begeistert und gibt die Identität des „Blueberry-Infused Tonic" preis. Es verwandelt jeden Drink in einen Genuss für alle Sinne und bringt dabei fruchtige Blaubeeraromen sowie eine elegante Kardamom-Note mit. Trotz all der Frische bleibt es ein Tonic Water mit der notwendigen Bitternis und interagiert perfekt mit den Botanicals des Gins. Extravagant ist das Pink Tonic Water, verfeinert mit einem Hauch von Rosenblättern und dezenter Gurkennote. Perfekt zu feinen Gins. Besonders für all diejenigen, für die ein Gin Tonic etwas Gurke als Garnitur enthalten muss oder die der Hommage des „Klassikers" mit Gurkengeschmack frönen, der perfekte Filler.

Sparkling tonics, handmade in South Africa

In 1583, merchants Ralph Fitch and Williams Leedes set out from London on a journey to the East. They set sail to find new, exotic tastes in India, and they found what they were looking for! Chill Beverages' Fitch & Leedes brand is a tribute to them. Their Indian Tonic Water is a classic tonic. It beautifully combines the bitterness of quinine with subtle spices and citrus notes. The tonic underscores the flavors of the gin instead of overpowering them. The Pink Grapefruit Tonic from South Africa is extravagantly created. Bitter meets the taste of fresh grapefruit here. It gives the gin enough space. The bright blue color of the Blue Tonic inspires and reveals the identity of the "Blueberry-Infused Tonic". It transforms any drink into a treat for all the senses, bringing with it fruity blueberry aromas and an elegant note of cardamom. Despite all the freshness, it remains a tonic water with the necessary bitterness and interacts perfectly with a gin's botanicals. Extravagant in character is the Pink Tonic Water, refined with a touch of rose petals and a subtle cucumber note. Perfect with fine gins, especially for all requiring a gin and tonic to contain some cucumber as a garnish or indulging in that homage of the "classic" with cucumber flavor, the perfect filler.

> " Handmade mixers from the finest ingredients from Stellenbosch, South Africa.

Ein Papagei und ein Foxterrier auf Reisen

Papagei Barker und Foxterrier Quin waren auf dem Segelschiff, das nach Delagoa Bay reiste, um die Medizin und Vorräte der Gestrandeten des Segelschiffs „Mary" zu erkunden. Dabei wurde der Überlieferung nach das Tonikum entdeckt. Angelehnt an diese Anekdote produziert die promovierte Ökologin Hanneli van der Merwe in Paarl außergewöhnliche Tonic Water und Filler.

Fünf Tonics für jeden Geschmack

Das Indian Tonic ist ein hervorragendes, handwerklich erzeugtes Tonikum aus Südafrika. Es besteht aus Bergquellwasser mit der Bitternis von natürlichem Chinin, gesüßt mit Rohrzucker von höchster Qualität. Dazu kommt die Frische und Säure aus Grapefruit, Zitrone und Orange. Abgerundet wird es mit Noten von Kardamom, Sternanis und Wacholderbeeren. Diese verleihen dem Tonic seine angenehme Würze und einen leicht scharfen Twist. Beim Marula Tonic wird das klassische Tonic Water um ein African Botanical erweitert, nämlich die Früchte des Elefantenbaums (Marula-Baum). Das Tonic schmeckt saftig, fruchtig und hat eine tolle Bitternis. Das Honeybush & Orange Tonic ist ein weiterer Signatur-Filler, der mit afrikanischen Pflanzen spielt. Angelegt wie ein klassisches Tonic Water kommen Honeybush, eine südafrikanische Wildpflanze, und frische Orangenzeste dazu. Das Aroma ist herb, mit der typischen Note von Orangenschale, kombiniert mit dem honig- und teeartigen Geschmack des Honeybush. Das Light at Heart Tonic ist eine konsequente Light- oder Dry-Version des Indian Tonic. Es werden keine Zuckerersatzstoffe verwendet. Das Hibiscus Tonic bringt ein Bouquet aus Hibiskusblüten, Himbeeren und Rosenblättern mit.

A fox terrier and a parrot on a journey

Fox terrier Barker and parrot Quin were on the sailing ship that undertook a voyage to Delagoa Bay to explore the medicine and supplies of the stranded crew of the sailing ship "Mary". In the process, tonic was discovered, so the story goes. In the spirit of this anecdote, Hanneli van der Merwe, who holds a doctorate in ecology, produces exceptional tonic water and fillers in Paarl.

Five tonics to suit every taste

The Indian Tonic is an excellent artisanal tonic from South Africa. It consists of mountain spring water with the bitterness of natural quinine, sweetened with cane sugar of the highest quality. To this is added freshness and acidity from grapefruit, lemon and orange. It's rounded off with notes of cardamom, star anise and juniper berries. These give the tonic its pleasant flavor and a slightly spicy twist. In the Marula Tonic, an African botanical is added to the classic tonic water, namely the fruit of the elephant tree (marula tree). The tonic tastes juicy, fruity and has a pleasing bitterness. The Honeybush & Orange Tonic is another signature filler that plays with African botanicals. Created like a classic tonic water, honeybush, a South African wild plant, and fresh orange zest are added. The aroma is tart, with the typical note of orange peel combined with the honey and tea-like flavor of honeybush. The Light at Heart Tonic is a strictly light or dry version of the Indian Tonic. No sugar substitutes are used. The Hibiscus Tonic brings a bouquet of hibiscus flowers, raspberries and rose petals.

> A South African tonic, artisanal and with a unique history.

SÜDAFRIKA GENUSS | OBELISK AG

BARKER & QUIN TONIC WATERS

AVADIS DISTILLERY

DOCTOR POLIDORI FINE TONIC WATERS

Der Arzt mit alchemistischem Geschick

Das im Hause des Familienunternehmens, die sich unter anderem für den Ferdinand's Saar Dry Gin verantwortlich zeichnet, hergestellte spritzige Polidori Dry Tonic wird nach einer geheimen Rezeptur hergestellt, als Hommage an John William Polidori. Dieser war Leibarzt des britischen Dichters Lord Byron. Als solcher experimentierte er mit diversen Essenzen, Tinkturen und Kräutern. Eines Tages kam er mit einem „Tonikum" in Berührung, das gegen Malaria half und nur in Verbindung mit Gin wirklich genießbar war, und legte mit seinen Aufzeichnungen die Basis für das heutige Doctor Polidori Fine Tonic Water, dessen Bestandteile sich an der Reiseroute von Doctor Polidori orientieren und verschiedene Kräuteressenzen aufgreifen.

> An ode to the doctor, who mixed tonic with gin.

Zucker(zusätze) adé

Das Doctor Polidori Fine Tonic Water ist der Inbegriff eines klassischen Fillers, der kreiert wurde, um die botanische Vielfalt eines Gins zu untermalen. Neben Basilikum, Kubebenpfeffer und Thymian tritt am Gaumen vor allem eine erfrischende Zitrusnote hervor. Ergänzt wird die Mixtur durch Quellwasser aus einem nahe gelegenen Naturpark. Doctor Polidori ist ein Tonic mit reduziertem Zuckeranteil, wodurch der Gin im Rampenlicht steht. Wer in Sachen Tonic Water experimentierfreudiger ist, wird ebenfalls bei Capulet & Montague fündig. Doctor Polidori Cucumber Tonic überzeugt geschmacklich mit Anklängen von Wacholder, Thymian und Basilikum und durch sein frisches Gurkenaroma, Doctor Polidori Grape Tonic hingegen mit seinem fruchtigen und frischen Geschmack nach saftigen und vollmundigen Weintrauben.

The doctor with alchemical skill

Produced in-house by family-owned distillery, which is responsible, among other things, for Ferdinand's Saar Dry Gin, sparkling Polidori Dry Tonic is made according to a secret recipe, as a tribute to John William Polidori. The latter was personal physician to the British poet Lord Byron. As such, he experimented with various essences, tinctures and herbs. One day he came into contact with a "tonic" that helped against malaria, whilst only really being enjoyable in combination with gin. With his notes, he laid the foundation for today's Doctor Polidori Fine Tonic Water, the ingredients of which are based on the itinerary of Doctor Polidori's travels and incorporate various herbal essences.

Goodbye (added) sugar

Doctor Polidori Fine Tonic Water is the epitome of classic fillers, created to underscore the botanical diversity of a gin. In addition to basil, cubeb pepper and thyme, a refreshing citrus note stands out on the palate. The mixture is complemented by spring water from a nearby natural park. Doctor Polidori is a tonic with reduced sugar content, which puts the gin in the spotlight. People who tend to more experimentation when it comes to tonic water will also find what they are looking for at Capulet & Montague. Doctor Polidori Cucumber Tonic has a convincing taste with hints of juniper, thyme and basil and by virtue of its fresh cucumber aroma, while Doctor Polidori Grape Tonic, on the other hand, achieves this with its fruity and fresh taste of juicy and full-bodied grapes.

SWABIANGINDISTILLERS

ERICH BEE TONIC WATER

> "A snappy "Bee" for gin, that kisses lemons.

Zwei Freunde aus dem Schwabenland

Ob Opa Erich seinen Gin auch mit einem Tonic getrunken oder diesen lieber pur genossen hätte? Die Entwickler des Erich Schwäbischer Dry GIN, der zulieb des benannten Großvaters hergestellt wird, sind sich einig: Das zum Erich Gin passende Tonic Water namens Gin Bee rundet das Geschmacksprofil des Wacholder-Destillats ab. Das Tonic Water wird in Zusammenarbeit mit der Firma Iceergy hergestellt und kommt in einem modernen, schlichten Design daher. Der Schriftzug des Logos knüpft an das elegante Etikett des Erich-Gins an. Wie bereits die Rezeptur des Gins wird auch das Tonic Water in eigener Zusammenstellung produziert.

Geheime Zitruswürze

Die Basis des veganen und kalorienarmen Gin Bee bildet Chinin, umgarnt von einem unter Verschluss gehaltenen Zitrusgewürz. Die perfekte Balance beider Bestandteile macht das Tonic zum perfekten Begleiter für Gins, deren dominierendes Aroma von Zitrusfrüchten bestimmt wird. Seine erfrischende und spritzige Süße kommt am besten gut gekühlt zur Geltung. Das Erich Tonic und der Erich Gin – die besten Freunde aus dem Schwabenland – sind auch im direkten Mix erhältlich als Gin Bee Gin & Tonic und in der sommerlich-fruchtigen Version Gin Bee Gin & Himbeer.

Two friends from Swabia

Would Grandpa Erich have drunk his gin with a tonic or would he have preferred it neat? The developers of Erich Schwäbischer Dry GIN, which is produced in honor of that very grandfather, agree that Gin Bee tonic water, which partners Erich Gin, rounds off the flavor profile of the juniper distillate. This tonic water is created in collaboration with the company Iceergy and comes in a modern, simple design. The logo lettering ties in with Erich Gin's elegant label. Like the gin recipe, that of the tonic water is also our own composition.

Secret citrus seasoning

The basis of this vegan and low-calorie Gin Bee is quinine, wrapped up with a secret citrus spice. The perfect balance of both ingredients makes this tonic the perfect companion for gins whose dominant aroma is determined by citrus fruits. Its refreshing and tangy sweetness is best enjoyed well chilled. Erich Tonic and Erich Gin – best friends from Swabia – are also available in a direct mix as Gin Bee Gin & Tonic and in the summery, fruity version Gin Bee Gin & Raspberry.

FILLER

SWABIAN GIN DISTILLERS // ERICH BEE TONIC

413

FEVER-TREE TONIC WATERS

FEVER-TREE LTD.

> If ¾ of your drink is the mixer, mix with the best.

Eine Reise mit Ansprüchen

Fever-Tree wurde im Zuge des Gin-Hypes zu Beginn der 2000er-Jahre eine der bekanntesten Marken in Sachen Tonic Water – und das nicht ohne Grund. Am Anfang gab es in der Tat wenige Filler und zudem eine Vielzahl an unterschiedlichen Konservierungsstoffen, künstlichen Süßungsmitteln und einfachem Fruchtzusatz. Charles Rolls und Tim Warrillow kamen beide zu dem Entschluss, dass sich das Angebot und die Leidenschaft zu Fillern so ändern mussten, wie es der Gin bereits vermochte. Eine Reise, die zunächst in Bibliotheken ihren Anfang nahm, wurde bald zu einem Abenteuer auf der Suche nach den weltweit besten Zutaten. Im Jahre 2005 rollten die ersten Flaschen vom Band und eroberten vorerst England – doch der weltweite Boom ließ nicht lange auf sich warten.

Qualität für deinen Drink

Wenn schon die Menge an Premium-Spirituosen zunahm, musste ein ebenso passender Filler mit mindestens den gleichen Ansprüchen her. Qualität und ein breites Sortiment, um den Anforderungen der verschiedenen Spirituosen zu entsprechen, waren ambitionierte Ziele. Beispielsweise stammt das hochwertige Chinin von einer Plantage aus dem Kongo, Zitronenthymian von der Mittelmeerküste, Ingwer aus Indien und Nigeria und die Bitterorangen aus Mexiko. Das Portfolio von Fever-Tree umfasst mittlerweile eine große Anzahl an Fillern und Limonaden, Mediterranean Tonic Water, Premium Dry Tonic Water, Ginger Ale, Premium Wild Berry oder sogar Distillers Cola sind nur einige beliebte Beispiele. Hier findet ihr wirklich für jeden Drink euren passenden hochwertigen Begleiter.

So schmeckt's

Mit einem wirklich ausgeglichenen Indian Tonic Water beginnt die Reise der Marke Fever-Tree. Schnell eroberte das kräuterige Mediterranean Tonic Water im Anschluss die Welt, während das Premium Dry Tonic Water mit seinen speziellen Chininnoten es in vielen Gläsern trockener werden lässt. Weitere spannende Filler mit Ingwer, Holunder, Zitronen oder schottischen Himbeeren folgten als geschmacklich hochwertige Erweiterung.

A journey with aspirations

Fever-Tree became one of the best-known brands of tonic water in the course of the gin hype at the beginning of the 2000s – and not without reason. At the beginning, there were indeed few fillers and also numerous different preservatives, artificial sweeteners, and simple fruit additions. Charles Rolls and Tim Warrillow both came to the conclusion that the range of and passion for fillers had to change in the same way that gin had already managed to do. A journey that initially began in libraries soon became an adventure in search of the world's finest ingredients. In 2005, the first bottles rolled off the production line and conquered England initially – but the worldwide boom was not long in coming.

Quality for your drink

Given the choice of premium spirits was already increasing, the need arose for an equally suitable filler with at least the same aspirations. Quality and a wide range of products to meet the requirements of the various spirits were ambitious goals. For example, the high-quality quinine comes from a plantation in the Congo, lemon thyme from the Mediterranean coast, ginger from India and Nigeria, and the bitter oranges from Mexico. Fever-Tree's portfolio now includes a large number of fillers and sodas, Mediterranean Tonic Water, Premium Dry Tonic Water, Ginger Ale, Premium Wild Berry and even Distillers Cola being just a few popular examples. Here you can really find the right high-quality accompaniment to every drink.

How it tastes

The journey of the Fever-Tree brand began with a truly balanced Indian Tonic Water. Quickly, the herbal Mediterranean Tonic Water subsequently conquered the world, while the Premium Dry Tonic Water, with its special quinine notes, has made for many a drier glass. Other exciting fillers with ginger, elderberry, lemons or Scottish raspberries followed as flavorful extensions.

KROMBACHER

SCHWEPPES TONIC WATERS

Der Pionier der Limonadenindustrie

Die Markenhistorie von Schweppes beginnt mit Jacob Schweppe, einem deutschen Juwelier. Er perfektioniert den Prozess zur industriellen Herstellung von mit Kohlensäure versetztem Sodawasser, auch Genever-Verfahren genannt. Im Jahr 1783 lässt er sich sein Verfahren patentieren: Die Marke Schweppes ist geboren. Knapp 100 Jahre später entsteht mit dem Schweppes Indian Tonic Water der unbestrittene Klassiker des Gin Tonics. Seit der Gründung steht Schweppes weltweit für Lifestyle und Frische sowie Tradition und Qualität. Rund 50 verschiedene Geschmacksrichtungen werden inzwischen angeboten, die außergewöhnliche Geschmackskreationen für Erwachsene bieten.

Die bittersüße Vielfalt

Der unumstrittene Klassiker Schweppes Indian Tonic ist prickelnd und unverwechselbar. Mit einem hohen Chiningehalt und basierend auf natürlichen Rohstoffen und feinperliger Kohlensäure ist es von höchster Qualität und Frische. Der besondere, süßlich-bittere und erfrischende Geschmack macht das älteste Tonic der Welt zum perfekten Filler. Weniger Süße und dafür mehr Chinin gibt es beim Schweppes Dry Tonic Water. Das macht es erfrischend bitter. Verfeinert mit Kohlensäure und natürlichen Aromen von Zitrone, Orange und Grapefruit bietet es noch mehr Vielfalt. Der neueste Zugang bei Schweppes ist das Schweppes Herbal Tonic. Dabei handelt es sich um ein herbes Tonic mit einem Hauch spritziger Zitrone und feinen Kräuternoten von Rosmarin, Thymian, Oregano und Majoran. Ein richtiger Allrounder.

> **The original since 1783.**

The pioneer of the lemonade industry

The brand history of Schweppes begins with Jacob Schweppe, a German jeweler. He perfected the process for the industrial production of carbonated soda water, also known as the Geneva process. In 1783, he patented his process, and the Schweppes brand was born. Almost 100 years later, Schweppes Indian Tonic Water was created, the undisputed classic for gin and tonic. Since its founding, Schweppes has stood for lifestyle and freshness as well as tradition and quality worldwide. Around 50 different flavors are now offered, providing exceptional taste creations for adults.

The bittersweet diversity

The undisputed classic Schweppes Indian Tonic is sparkling and distinctive. With a high quinine content and based on natural raw materials and fine bubbly carbonic acid, it features the highest quality and freshness. The special, sweetly bitter and refreshing taste makes the oldest tonic in the world the perfect filler. Schweppes Zero Indian Tonic Water has less sugar. Schweppes Dry Tonic Water has less sweetness and more quinine. This makes it refreshingly bitter. Refined through carbonation and natural flavors of lemon, orange and grapefruit, it offers even more variety. The newest addition to Schweppes is Schweppes Herbal Tonic. This is a tart tonic with a hint of tangy lemon and subtle herbal notes of rosemary, thyme, oregano and marjoram. A real all-rounder.

> **Gincident:**
> An event that happened due to too many gins.

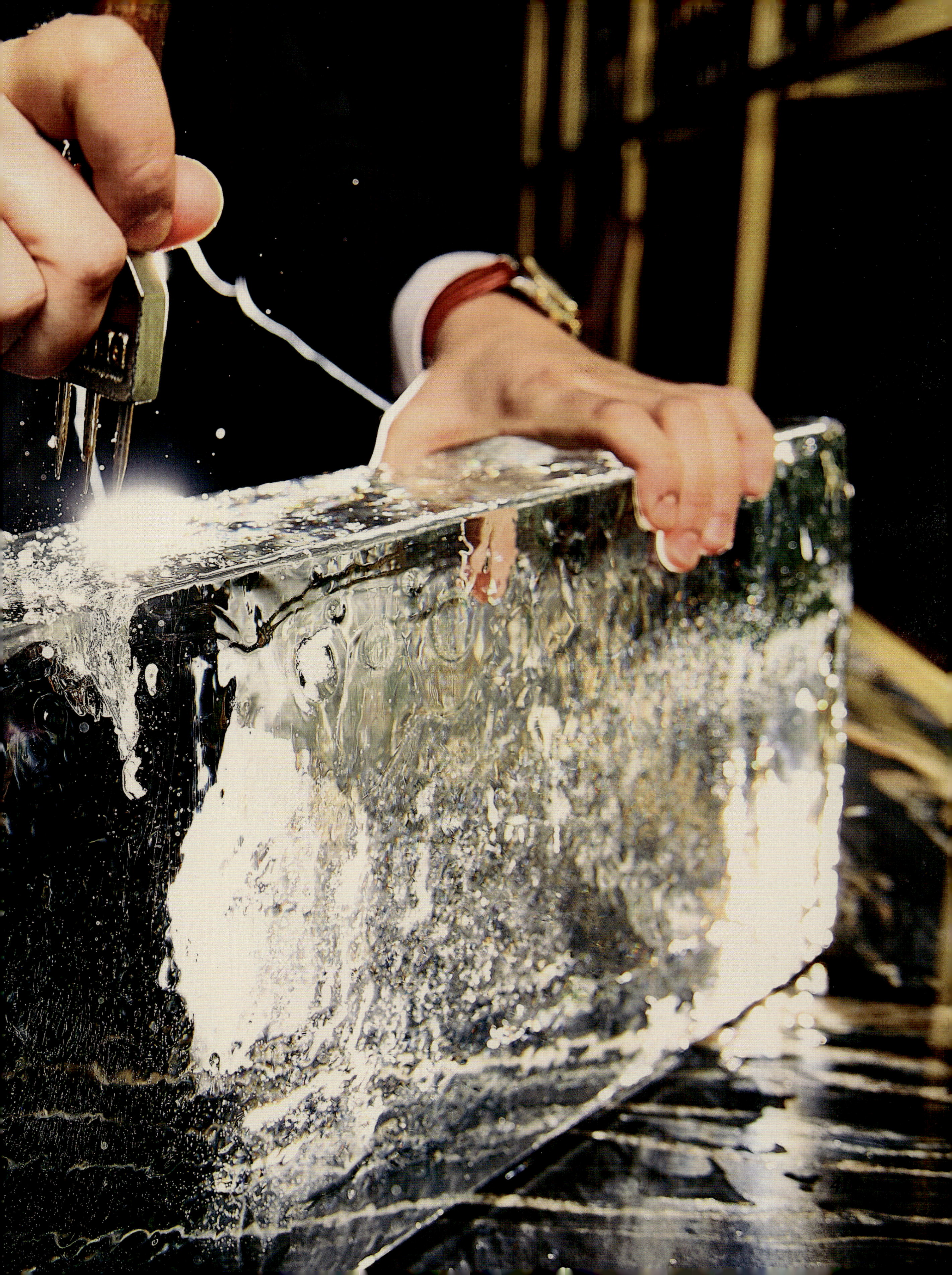

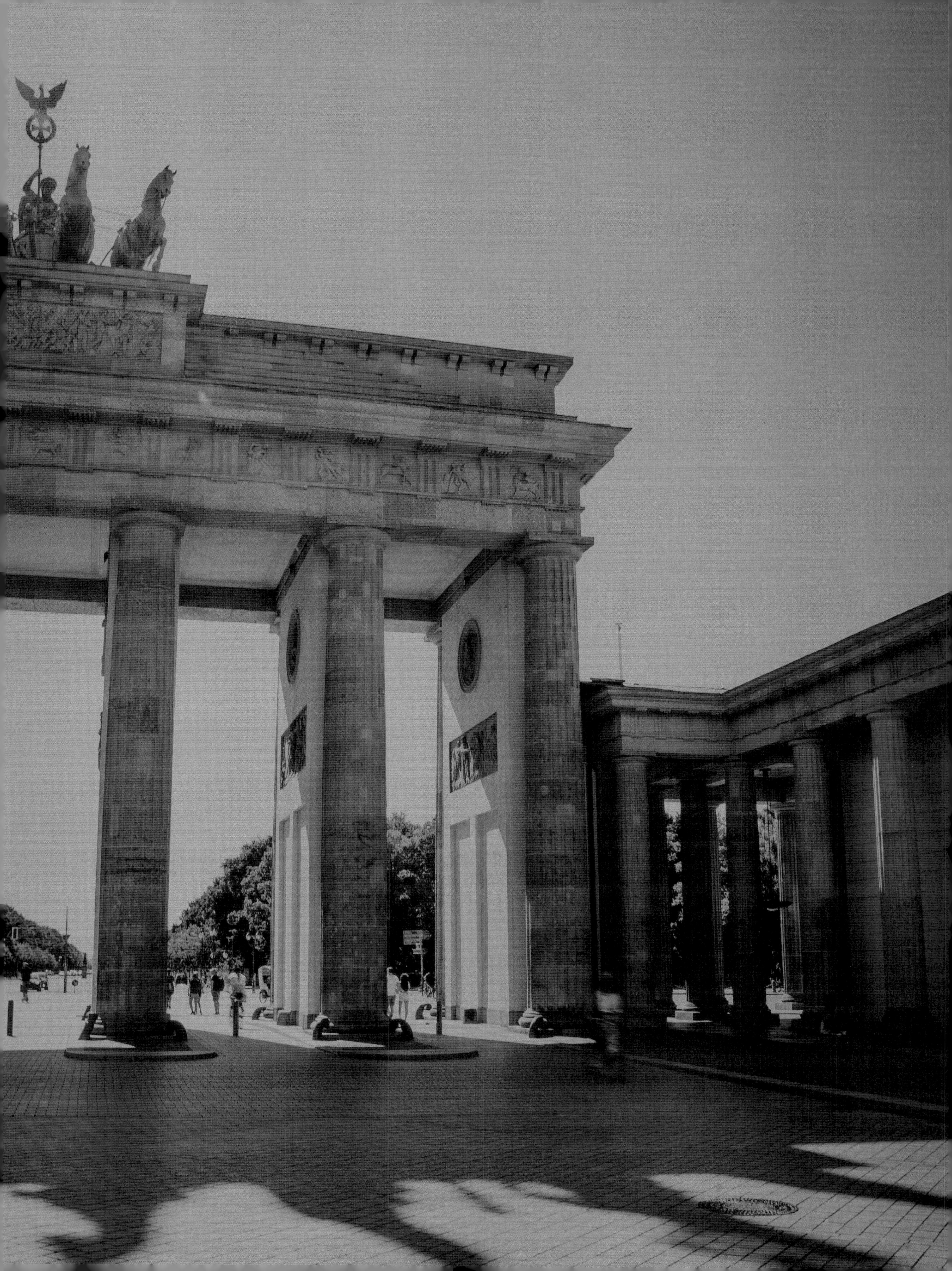

5
BARS

Darf's ein bisschen mehr sein?

Funkelnde Kronleuchter, ein weißer Marmortresen, schwere Polstermöbel und allerlei skurrile Antiquitäten – wenn Tel Avivs Gastropfeil das pulsierende Herz Berlins trifft, schreit die Opulenz. Wer das Besondere sucht, wird im Bellboy fündig. Das Konzept setzt auf Extravaganz, auf das ganzheitliche Genusserlebnis. Das harmonische Zusammenspiel von Ästhetik, Textur und Aromen findet im Bellboy seinen Höhepunkt. Die Karte ist ein aufregender Mix aus nah- und fernöstlichen Speisen, im Arrangement mit bekannten Klassikern. Dazu gibt es Cocktails, immer extravagant serviert, immer mit hausgemachten Zutaten kreiert. Jeder Drink erinnert an ein kleines Kunstwerk mit seiner ganz eigenen Geschichte. Manche erzählen ein Märchen von rauschenden Nächten, andere eine Kurzgeschichte mit knallharter Superhelden-Action. In Kombination mit der angebotenen Fusionsküche vervollständigt sich das meisterhafte Geschmacksabenteuer.

Willkommen im Pink Room

Die Bellboy Group betreibt in Israel weitere Cocktailbars und Restaurants, unter anderem das namensgebende Stammhaus, das zur festen Größe im Nachtleben Tel Avivs gehört. In Berlin dominiert die Exzentrik, das Bar-Erleben – immer mit einem dezenten Augenzwinkern, versteht sich. Dafür darf es von allem ruhig ein bisschen mehr sein: Vielseitigkeit, Opulenz, ausgezeichnete Zutaten. Der Gast wird immer etwas Neues entdecken, egal ob er das Bellboy regelmäßig oder das erste Mal betritt. Und auch Tagschwärmer können sich demnächst überraschen lassen: Im wunderbar plüschigen Pink Room des Bellboy lässt es sich ab Sommer 2022 ausgezeichnet brunchen.

WHEN TEL AVIV HITS THE BEATING HEART OF BERLIN, THE OPULENCE SCREAMS:

BELLBOY BERLIN

Would you like a little more?

Sparkling chandeliers, a white marble counter, heavy upholstered furniture and all manner of whimsical antiques – when Tel Aviv's gastronomic arrow hits the beating heart of Berlin, opulence screams. Those looking for something special will find it at Bellboy. The concept focuses on extravagance, on the holistic experience of pleasure. The harmonious interplay of aesthetics, texture and flavors achieves its zenith at Bellboy. The menu is an exciting mix of Middle Eastern and Far Eastern dishes, arranged alongside well-known classics. It is accompanied by cocktails, always served extravagantly, always created with homemade ingredients. Each drink is reminiscent of a small work of art with its own unique story. Some tell a tale of roaring nights, others a short story with tough-guy superhero action. Combined with the fusion cuisine on offer, the masterful taste adventure is complete.

Welcome to the Pink Room

The Bellboy Group operates other cocktail bars and restaurants in Israel, including the eponymous parent company, which is a fixture in Tel Aviv's nightlife. In Berlin, eccentricity dominates the bar experience – always with a subtle wink, of course. In return, there can be a bit more of everything: versatility, opulence, excellent ingredients. Guests will always discover something new, whether they visit Bellboy regularly or for the first time. Daytime diners will soon be in for a surprise, too. The Bellboy's wonderfully plush Pink Room will be the perfect place for brunch from summer 2022.

ADDRESS TORBAR
Bellboy Berlin
Mohrenstraße 30
10117 Berlin

CONTACT
+49 (0) 30 20077070
info@bellboyberlin.com
www.bellboybar.com

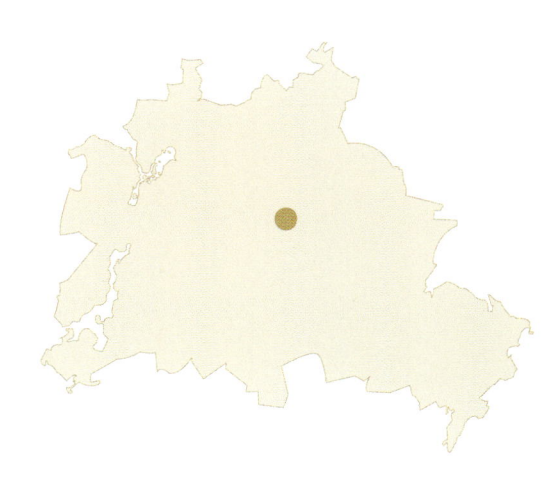

ITALIAN DESIGN MEETS THE CAPITAL'S COCKTAIL CULTURE:

BELLUCCI BAR

Nackte Haut und jede Menge Champagner

Flanieren, shoppen, ausgehen. Der Kurfürstendamm im Herzen Berlins hat auf rund 3,5 Kilometer zu bieten, wovon andere Städte in Sachen Unterhaltung nur träumen. Hier reiht sich eine Top-Location an die nächste. Seit dem 3. Januar 2022 gehört die Bellucci Bar dazu – der neue Stern am Berliner Nightlife-Himmel. In der Bellucci Bar trifft italienisches Design auf die Cocktail-Kultur der Hauptstadt. Die großformatigen obszön anmutenden Schwarz-Weiß-Fotografien an den Wänden, auf denen nackte Haut durchaus eine Rolle spielt, inszenieren das Ambiente und harmonieren mit samtenen roten Sitzbänken und pinken Neonlicht-Röhren. Eigens gefertigte Marmortische, elegante Glaskronleuchter, von Hand bemalte Mosaik-Fliesen, goldene Deko-Elemente und Dschungel-Tapeten unterstreichen den extravaganten, eleganten Charme der Bellucci Bar.

Das Who is Who der Musik-Szene

Dabei ist „Bellucci" kein unbekannter Name auf dem Ku'damm. Die neue angesagte Bar gehört zum gleichnamigen Edel-Restaurant, das in schickem Ambiente mit hochkarätigen, authentisch mediterranen Speisen aufwartet und regelmäßig prominente Gäste empfängt. Wie das Restaurant verfolgt die Bellucci Bar vor allem zwei Attribute: Qualität und Lifestyle. Auf der einzigartigen Sonnen-Terrasse lässt sich bei einem Aperitif ein entspannter Sommerabend einläuten oder das gehobene Berliner Nachtleben feiern.

Serviert wird am liebsten guter Champagner – passend zu den erstklassigen Events, bei denen sich donnerstags bis sonnabends das Who is Who der Berliner Musik-Szene die Hände reicht.

Naked skin and lots of champagne

Stroll, shop, go out. The Kurfürstendamm street in the heart of Berlin has around 3.5 kilometers offering what other cities can only dream of in terms of entertainment. Here, one top location follows the next. Since January 3, 2022, Bellucci Bar has been one of them – the new star in Berlin's nightlife sky. At Bellucci Bar, Italian design meets the capital's cocktail culture. The large-format, obscene-looking black-and-white photographs on the walls, in which naked skin definitely plays a role, set the stage for the ambience and harmonize with velvety red benches and pink fluorescent lighting. Custom-made marble tables, elegant glass chandeliers, hand-painted mosaic tiles, gold decorative elements and jungle wallpaper underscore the extravagant, elegant charm of Bellucci Bar.

The Who's Who of the music scene

"Bellucci" is not an unknown name on the Ku'damm. The new hip bar is part of the classy restaurant of the same name, which serves top-class, authentic Mediterranean food in a chic ambience and regularly welcomes celebrity guests. Like the restaurant, the Bellucci Bar follows two attributes above all: quality and lifestyle. On the unique sun terrace, you can embark on a relaxed summer evening with an aperitif or celebrate Berlin's classy nightlife.
They prefer to serve good champagne – in-keeping with those first-class events, where the Who's Who of Berlin's music scene party from Thursday to Saturday.

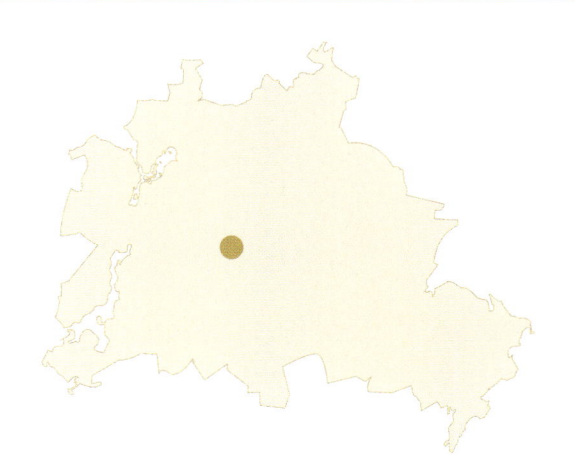

ADDRESS
Bellucci Bar
Kurfürstendamm 63
10707 Berlin

CONTACT
+49 (0) 162 3009925
kontakt@belluccis.de
www.bellucci-bar.de

BELLUCCI BAR // KURFÜRSTENDAMM 63, 10707 BERLIN

WITH MORE THAN 150 VARIETIES OF GIN, THE NAME SAYS IT ALL:

HOUSE OF GIN

Glamour, Gold und Gin

Mitten in der City-West, zwischen dem Ku'damm und dem Zoologischen Garten Berlin, werden Wünsche waschechter Gin-Liebhaber wahr: Im House of Gin warten mehr als 150 Sorten Gin teils aus limitierten Abfüllungen, teils von kleinen unbekannten Herstellern darauf, verköstigt zu werden. Nachdem die „alte" Bar 2017 aus dem Hinterhof des „Hotels Palace" Berlin von einem Wasserschaden fortgespült wurde, präsentiert sie sich seit 2018 in neuer Aufmachung an einem neuen Standort. Das bisherige 1980er-Jahre-Holzoptikgewand ist Geschichte und wurde gegen ein glamouröses transparentes Abendkleid getauscht. Bodentiefe Glasfronten eröffnen den Blick auf den goldenen Tresen, auf bequeme Lounge-Ecken, auf goldglänzende Lampenstäbe, die dekorativ von der Decke hängen, und auf das prall gefüllte Rückbuffet.

Drei gibt es nur hier

Das House of Gin hat sich das Motto „STAY GOLD!" auf die Haut tätowiert, sichtbar als leuchtender Schriftzug über dem Eingang zur Bar. Offensiv spiegelt sich das Gold im Interieur wider. Defensiv versteckt sich dahinter die tiefere Botschaft, sich selbst treu zu bleiben, ohne die Neugierde und Offenheit gegenüber Unbekanntem zu verlieren. Umgesetzt wird das Credo unter anderem bei der Interpretation der angebotenen Cocktails, die sowohl geschmacklich als auch optisch auf einen Wow-Effekt setzen und mit den unterschiedlichsten Gins zubereitet werden. Aus Liebe zum Gin hat das Team drei eigene Gins mitentwickelt, die ausschließlich im House of Gin auf der Karte stehen. Daneben gibt es Gin Tonics in allen möglichen Geschmacksvarianten und natürlich auch den klassischen Gin Tonic – „STAY GOLD!" eben.

ADDRESS
House of Gin
Budapester Str. 45
10787 Berlin

CONTACT
+49 (0) 30 25021080
hotel@palace.de
www.houseofgin.de

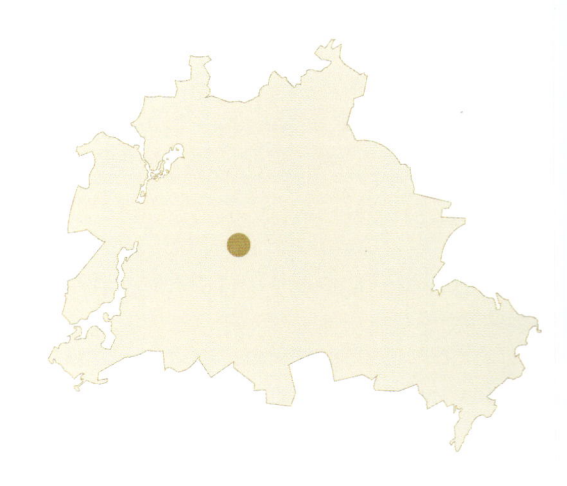

Glamour, gold and gin

In the middle of City-West, between Ku'damm and the Zoological Gardens of Berlin, the dreams of genuine gin lovers come true. At the House of Gin more than 150 varieties of gin, some from limited batches, some from small, unknown producers, are waiting to be tasted. After the "old" bar was swept from the backyard of the Hotel Palace Berlin in 2017 by flood water, since 2018 it has presented itself in a new look at a new location. The previous 1980s wood-look garb is history and has been swapped for a glamorous see-through evening dress. Floor-to-ceiling glass fronts open up views of the golden counter, comfortable lounge areas, gleaming gold lamp rods hanging decoratively from the ceiling, and the well-stacked back bar.

Three only available here

The House of Gin has the motto "STAY GOLD!" tattooed on its skin, visible as luminous lettering above the entrance to the bar. Projecting, the gold is reflected in the interior. Defending, it conceals the deeper message of remaining true to oneself without losing curiosity or openness to the unknown. The credo is implemented, among other things, in the interpretation of the cocktails on offer, which focus on a wow effect, both in terms of taste and appearance, and are prepared with a wide variety of gins. Out of love for gin, the team has co-developed three of its own gins, available exclusively on the menu at the House of Gin. In addition, there are gin tonic options in all possible flavors and, of course, the classic gin tonic – "STAY GOLD!" indeed.

Gemütliche Wohnzimmeratmosphäre

Ein moderner Casual-Lifestyle, gepaart mit exklusivem Interior-Design und cooler Lounge-Musik sorgen in der Stue Bar für den so geschätzten Wohlfühlfaktor. Nicht ohne Grund, denn „Stue" bedeutet auf Dänisch „Wohnstube". Die Bar ist Bestandteil des gleichnamigen SO/ Berlin Das Stue, das sich einen exzellenten Ruf in der Kategorie „Luxury Boutique Hotels" erarbeitet hat. In dem historischen Gebäude der ehemaligen Dänischen Gesandtschaft im Berliner Stadtteil Tiergarten gelingt die perfekte Symbiose aus modernem Stil, avantgardistischer Atmosphäre und hochklassigem Service. Dieser Leitgedanke spiegelt sich auch in der einzigartigen Gestaltung des Hauses wider, das in den 1930er-Jahren von dem KaDeWe-Architekten Johann Emil Schaudt entworfen wurde. Seit der Hoteleröffnung 2012 werden hier fabelhafte Kulinarik, Kunst, Kultur und ausgezeichnete Drinks miteinander vereint.

Erstklassiger Ausblick inklusive

Für eine tierische Überraschung sorgt der Blick aus dem großen Fenster der Stue Bar Neben imposanten Straußenvögeln zeigen sich muntere Antilopen in den angrenzenden Gehegen des Berliner Zoos. Das Bar-Team mixt neben den geschätzten Klassikern auch ausgefallene Kreationen, wobei die Verwendung saisonaler Produkte im Fokus steht. Raffinierte Food-Highlights runden das Angebot ab und sorgen dafür, dass aus einem After-Work-Meeting schnell ein langer Abend wird. Veredelt wird das Barerlebnis durch musikalische Live-Events. Für laue Sommernächte bietet die üppig begrünte Terrasse die perfekte Kulisse.

Cozy living-room atmosphere

A modern casual lifestyle, paired with exclusive interior design and cool lounge music provide the much appreciated feel-good factor at the Stue Bar Not without reason, because "Stue" means "living room" in Danish. The bar is part of the eponymous hotel SO/ Berlin Das Stue, which has earned an excellent reputation in the "Luxury Boutique Hotels" category. In the historic building of the former Danish legation in Berlin's Tiergarten district, the perfect symbiosis of modern style, avant-garde atmosphere and high-class service is achieved. This guiding principle is also reflected in the unique design of the hotel, which was designed in the 1930s by KaDeWe architect Johann Emil Schaudt. Since the hotel opened in 2012, fabulous cuisine, art, culture and excellent drinks have come together here.

First class view included

The view from the large window of the Stue Bar provides a wild surprise. In addition to imposing ostriches, lively antelopes can be seen in the adjacent enclosures of Berlin Zoo. The bar team mixes not only those cherished classics but also unusual creations, focusing on the use of seasonal products. Sophisticated food highlights round out the offerings and ensure that an after-work meeting quickly turns into a long evening. The bar experience is enhanced by live music events. For balmy summer nights, the lush green terrace provides the perfect backdrop.

MODERN CASUAL LIFESTYLE PAIRED WITH EXCLUSIVE INTERIOR DESIGN:

STUE BAR

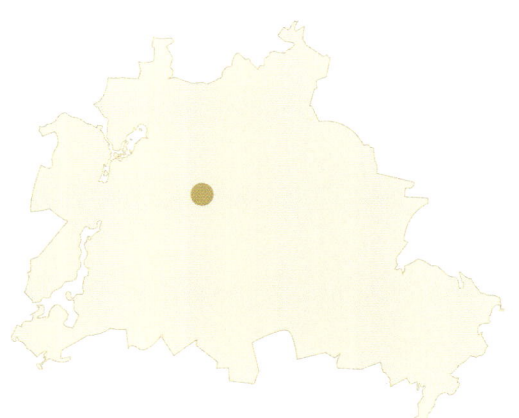

ADDRESS
Stue Bar
Drakestraße 1
10787 Berlin

CONTACT
+49 (0) 30 3117220
stay@das-stue.com
www.so-berlin-das-stue.com

" Berlin... where else would you find a bar dedicated to Gin!?

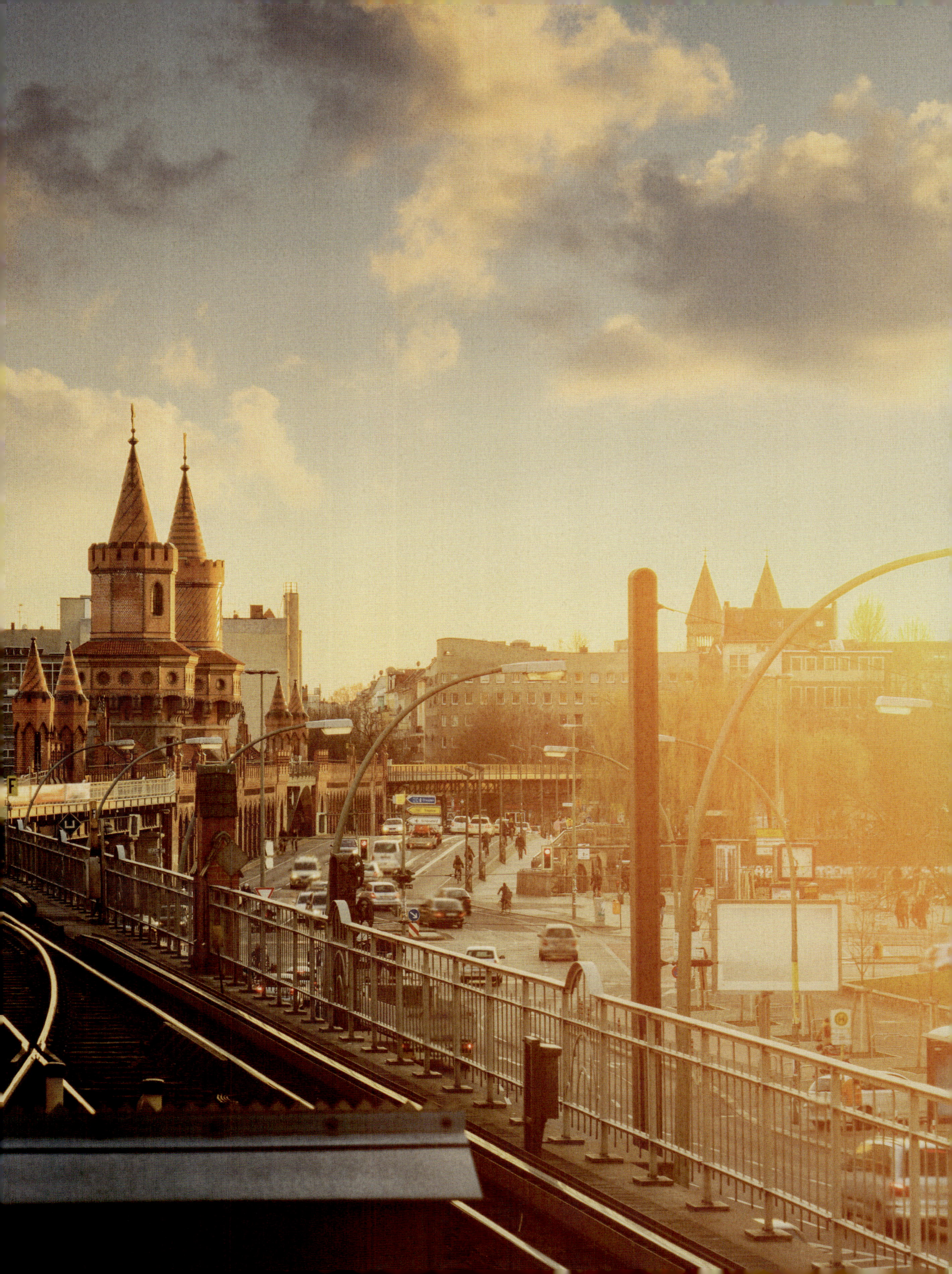

"
It's not about how much you know – it's about what you know

6

GIN INSIDER

© Rankin

EXPERT INTERVIEW WITH MARTIN THIBAULT

WITH SMALL AND BIG IDEAS, MAKING THE WORLD A LITTLE BIT BETTER

His Instagram bio should read: entrepreneur, world traveler, sneaker-fan and pizza-lover. But Martin Thibault is much more than that. A Berlin native, he has worked in Europe's big cities, most recently as Food & Beverage Manager at the Design-Hotel Provocateur, before Bombay Sapphire knocked on his door. He has been a brand ambassador at Bacardi GmbH since 2018 and represented Bombay Gins in Germany, Austria and Switzerland till February 2021. Now he heads that same company's advocacy department for the three locations, where he faces the issue of sustainability. He spoke with VT-Verlag about gin, the power of the individual and the responsibility of companies in the global climate conflict.

VT-Verlag: Martin, please tell us about your first encounter with gin.

MARTIN THIBAULT: *That was in my first year of training in 2003. I was having dinner with my flat mate in a good restaurant. When the waitress offered an aperitif, my buddy chose champagne, which we couldn't really afford at all. We saved up for a long time for this evening, which was going to cost us about 70 euros per person. I wanted to drink a gin, because I had already observed at that time that people who had a touch more self-respect and a bit more money in their pockets drank gin. Of course, aged just 18 I had no idea in this regard. The waitress asked how I liked my gin. I remembered that the cool people always ordered the drink neat, so I did the same. I wanted my gin neat, on the rocks, with a bit of lemon. I toasted my buddy, took a sip, and thought, "No one can drink this. It's way too strong. It tastes like woods and meadows." I didn't learn to appreciate gin another way, to really appreciate it, till I went to the Ritz-Carlton in 2006. That's when the gin trend had arrived in society-central with Hendrick's, Beefeater 24 und Tanqueray. People came up to me at the bar and didn't just order a gin tonic any more, but rather a Hendrick's tonic with a piece of cucumber as a topping.*

nicht mehr nur einen Gin Tonic, sondern einen Hendrick's Tonic mit einem Stück Gurke als Topping.

Die Welt dreht sich weiter. Inzwischen hat der Gast mehr Auswahl, muss nicht mehr nur zwischen Gurke und Zitrone wählen, sondern sich auch entscheiden, ob sein Gin glitzert oder die Farbe ändern soll. Wie stehst du dazu?

Wer als Produzent über seine Landesgrenze hinweg wahrgenommen werden möchte, zeigt sich meist überaus kreativ. Es gibt zum Beispiel einen „Bayerischen Wurstgin", der mit Sauerkraut destilliert wird. Das ist definitiv Geschmackssache. Da geht es darum, mit allen Mitteln mutig zu sein und Flagge zu zeigen. Das muss nicht sein. Von dem aufgeblähten Gin-Universum bleibt immer weniger übrig. Das zeigt sich in den Bars, an den Back Shelfs, dass dort wieder ausgewählte Flaschen stehen. Die Bars stellen sich vielleicht 20 Gins ins Regal, darunter meist die großen Player in Kombination mit ein paar lokalen Herstellern.

Inzwischen arbeitest du an keiner Bar mehr und hast einen ganz anderen Blick auf die Entwicklung des Spirituosenmarktes. Wie bist du bei Bacardi gelandet?

Letztlich über Vitamin B. Ein Kollege hat die Abteilung gegründet, das Team neu besetzt und dafür Leute gesucht. Eines Abends schaute er mich aufgrund meiner Expertise mit einem Augenzwinkern an und fragte, ob ich noch jemanden kennen würde, der als Markenbotschafter für Bombay Sapphire geeignet wäre. Ich hatte im Vorfeld bereits hin und wieder für Bombay gearbeitet und kannte die Marke ganz gut. Als er mir den entsprechenden Arbeitsvertrag vorlegte, musste ich nicht lange überlegen. Das Arbeiten in der Gastronomie macht Spaß, wirtschaftet dich aber körperlich irgendwann kaputt. Mein Sozialleben hat sich seit meinem Jobwechsel enorm verbessert, ich habe inzwischen geheiratet und eine Tochter. Das Cocktailmixen habe ich an den Nagel gehängt und mich um den Aufbau nachhaltiger Geschäftsbeziehungen gekümmert. Ich nehme potenzielle Geschäftspartner mit in unsere Destillen oder zu anderen Veranstaltungen, mit dem Ziel, eine freundschaftliche Beziehung aufzubauen. Für den Vertrieb bin ich aber nicht verantwortlich. Ein Verkaufsgedanke in einer Freundschaft ist grundsätzlich ungesund.

Du hast das Thema Nachhaltigkeit gerade schon angerissen. Nachhaltigkeit im Sinne des Aufbaus einer harmonischen, lange währenden Geschäftsbeziehung. Doch Nachhaltigkeit hat viele Gesichter. Eine Geschäftsbeziehung ist nicht das Erste, was einem in den Kopf kommt, wenn das Wort Nachhaltigkeit im Spiel ist. Seit wann ist Nachhaltigkeit bei euch im Konzern relevant und wie setzt ihr eure Vorstellungen davon um?

Man muss beim Thema Nachhaltigkeit immer sehr weit ausholen. Ich habe lange darüber referiert. Nachhaltigkeit ist ein riesiger Regenschirm als Oberbegriff. Im klassischen Sinn meint Nachhaltigkeit, dass der Verbrauch von Rohstoffen nicht größer sein darf als die erforderliche Nachbeschaffungsmenge. Dazu gehören natürlich der Anbau von Rohstoffen, die Vertriebswege, Gebindegrößen und vieles mehr. Aber um das zu gewährleisten,

The world keeps turning. In the meantime, guests have more choice, no longer only have to choose between cucumber and lemon, but can also decide whether their gin should sparkle or change color. What's your take on that?

Those who want to be perceived as producers beyond their national borders usually show themselves to be extremely creative. For example, there is a "Bavarian sausage gin" that is distilled with sauerkraut. That's definitely a matter of taste. It's all about being bold and showing the flag by any means necessary. It doesn't have to be. There's less and less of the inflated gin universe left. This is evident in the bars, at the back shelves, that there are selected bottles again. The bars put maybe 20 gins on the shelves, including usually the big players in combination with a few local producers.

You now no longer work at any bar and have a completely different view of the development of the spirits market. How did you end up at Bacardi?

Ultimately through connections. A colleague founded the department, re-staffed the team and was looking for people for it. One evening, he looked at me with a twinkle in his eye because of my expertise and asked if I knew anyone else who would be suitable as a brand ambassador for Bombay Sapphire. I had already worked for Bombay from time to time beforehand and knew the brand quite well. When he presented me with the corresponding employment contract, I didn't need to think twice. Working in the restaurant business is fun, but ultimately it wears you out physically. My social life has improved enormously since I changed jobs; I'm now married and have a daughter. I've given up mixing cocktails and focused on building enduring business relationships. I take potential business partners to our distilleries or to other events, with the goal of building a friendly relationship. However, I am not responsible for sales. A sales mindset in a friendship is fundamentally unhealthy.

You've just touched on the subject of sustainability. Sustainability in the sense of building a harmonious, long-lasting business relationship. But sustainability has many faces. A business relationship is not the first thing that comes to mind when the word sustainability is mentioned. Since when has sustainability been relevant to you in the Group and how do you implement your ideas about it?

When it comes to sustainability, you always have to reach a long way out. I have lectured on this for a long time. Sustainability is a huge umbrella term. In the classic sense, sustainability means that the consumption of raw materials must not be greater than the required replenishment quantity. Of course, this includes the cultivation of raw materials, distribution distances, packaging sizes and much more. But to ensure this, I need people as a resource. When we talk about sustainability, we always talk about resources, and when we talk about resources, we always talk about money. Let me break this down to the microcosm of the bar as an example. If I treat my employees badly because I make them work 16 hours a day, they will never give a thought to how to most effectively separate trash. But if I treat my employees well

MURCIAN LEMON
BOMBAY SAPPHIRE
PREMIER Cru
Distilled
LONDON
DRY GIN
Vapour
INFUSED
Hand selected exotic botanicals
MURCIAN LEMON
LEMON, MANDARIN & SWEET ORANGE
FROM A 1761 RECIPE

brauche ich den Menschen als Ressource. Wenn wir über Nachhaltigkeit sprechen, sprechen wir immer über Ressourcen und wenn wir über Ressourcen sprechen, sprechen wir immer über Geld. Ich breche das beispielhaft auf den Mikrokosmos der Bar herunter: Wenn ich mit meinen Mitarbeitern schlecht umgehe, weil ich sie täglich 16 Stunden arbeiten lasse, werden sie niemals einen Gedanken daran verschwenden, wie sie am effektivsten Müll trennen. Wenn ich meine Mitarbeiter aber nachhaltig gut und fair behandle, haben sie ganz andere eigene innere Ressourcen, um sich mit dem Thema Nachhaltigkeit auseinanderzusetzen. Deshalb ist mir die Ressource Mensch als Manipulator der Nachhaltigkeit am wichtigsten.

Nur weil ein Mensch Zeit hat, sich mit Nachhaltigkeit zu beschäftigen, heißt es nicht, dass er nachhaltig lebt oder die Weitläufigkeit des Themas erfasst. Was muss also passieren, damit sich ein Nachhaltigkeits-Bewusstsein entwickelt?
Es gibt verschiedene Auslöser. Seit unsere Tochter auf der Welt ist, denken meine Frau und ich zum Beispiel viel mehr darüber nach, wie wir uns in unserem Umkreis engagieren können, damit unser Kind, das hoffentlich die nächsten 90 Jahre auf diesem Planeten wandeln darf, eine wunderbare Zukunft hat. Aber wir waren vor der Geburt unserer Tochter auch schon fokussiert darauf, nachhaltig zu leben. Wir haben uns für Bio-Strom entschieden, wir trennen Müll, alle Lichter im Haushalt sind LEDs und wir wissen, dass das alles nur die Spitze des Eisbergs ist. Grundsätzlich kehre ich zunächst

and fairly in a sustainable way, they have completely different inner resources of their own to deal with the issue of sustainability. That's why the human resource is most important to me as a manipulator of sustainability.

Just because a person has time to think about sustainability doesn't mean they live sustainably or grasp the vastness of the topic. So what has to happen for sustainability awareness to develop?

There are several triggers. For example, since our daughter was born, my wife and I have been thinking much more about how we can get involved in our communities to ensure that our child, who will hopefully be allowed to walk this planet for the next 90 years, has a wonderful future. But we were also focused on living sustainably before our daughter was born. We chose bioenergy, we separate trash, all the lights in the house are LEDs, and we know that all of this is just the tip of the iceberg. Basically, I take the first steps at home. What can I do with my means, with my time and monetary resources, to live more sustainably? This includes purchasing. Do I buy regionally? Do I buy seasonally? Do I buy organic? Or do I prefer Angus beef from Australia? It's important to make a start yourself whilst, at the same time, not pointing a finger at others. We always try to find out what others are doing wrong and then expose them. That's an absolute disaster and unfortunately also a German phenomenon. People who live on welfare can't necessarily buy organic, they make sure they buy

vor meiner eigenen Haustür. Was kann ich mit meinen Mitteln, mit meinen zeitlichen und monetären Ressourcen anstellen, um nachhaltiger zu leben? Dazu gehört auch der Einkauf. Kaufe ich regional? Kaufe ich saisonal? Kaufe ich bio? Oder doch lieber das Angus Beef aus Australien? Wichtig ist, selber anzufangen und zeitgleich aufzuhören, mit dem Finger auf andere zu zeigen. Wir versuchen immer herauszufinden, was der andere falsch macht, und diesen dann bloßzustellen. Das ist eine absolute Katastrophe und leider auch ein deutsches Phänomen. Menschen, die von Sozialhilfe leben, können nicht unbedingt bio kaufen, die achten darauf, dass sie günstig kaufen, damit alle zu Hause satt werden. Auch das ist nachvollziehbar. Ich muss in den Spiegel schauen können, ohne mich zu schämen. Zur Bewusstseinsentwicklung gehört auch das Hinterfragen, zum Beispiel: „Woher kommen meine Turnschuhe, die ich heute trage?" Gemeint ist das Schauen über den Tellerrand, und zwar mit einem 360-Grad-Blick. Das ist nicht immer einfach.

Aber steht neben der Säule „Bewusstsein" nicht auch die Säule „Bildung", wenn wir über Nachhaltigkeit sprechen?
Beide Säulen sind verknüpft. Mein Opa sagt immer: Was Hänschen nicht lernt, lernt Hans nimmermehr. Nachhaltigkeit ist auf keinem Lehrplan in der Sekundarstufe 1. Ich bin dankbar für kostenfreie Bildung, dass ich in Frieden aufgewachsen bin und dass ich über sauberes Wasser verfüge, dass ich reisen und meine Meinung frei äußern kann, aber mir hat nie jemand gesagt, dass das nicht selbstverständlich ist. Schaut in andere Länder, guckt euch die Ozeane an, guckt euch die Bildungssysteme an und dann seid froh über das, was ihr habt, und pflegt und hegt es, damit ihr es der nächsten Generation weitergeben könnt.

Der Vergleich nach unten erfordert Disziplin, und zwar nicht nur, wenn große Fernsehsender zum Spendenmarathon aufrufen. Besteht nicht das grundsätzliche Problem darin, dass sich der Mensch selten nach unten vergleicht?
Wenn du zwei Euro im Monat an Greenpeace überweist und sonst nichts unternimmst, ist das dein eigenes Greenwashing, weil ja jeder Euro hilft. Es ist einfacher und günstiger, nicht nachhaltig zu leben. Ausreden ändern aber die Relevanz der Thematik nicht. Am Ende bleibt die Quintessenz: Fang bei dir selber an, Schritt für Schritt. Vergleiche bringen wenig. Heute ist es vielleicht die Mülltrennung, morgen die Energieeffizienz A+ bei der neuen Waschmaschine.

Wir haben über die Möglichkeiten gesprochen, die jeder Einzelne hat, um nachhaltig zu leben, doch schauen wir mal eine Etage darüber: Was können Konzerne unternehmen, um beim Thema Nachhaltigkeit zu punkten? Immerhin haben diese in der Vorbildrolle eine übergeordnete Verantwortung…
Absolut. Der Begriff Nachhaltigkeit wird meist sehr inflationär für Marketingzwecke genutzt und leider meist nicht für das große Ganze. Wenn wir beim Gin bleiben, geht es um Ressourcen-, also Botanical-Beschaffung. Große Hersteller kaufen ihre Botanicals in der Regel auf dem Großmarkt. Hier stellt sich die Frage, ob diese immer fair gehandelt werden. Aus der Expertise von Bombay Sapphire kann ich sagen, dass wir seit Jahrzehnten immer mit den

cheap so that everyone at home is full. That is also understandable. I have to be able to look in the mirror without feeling ashamed. Developing awareness also involves questioning, for example, "Where did the sneakers I'm wearing today come from?" What I mean is looking outside the box, and with a 360-degree view. This isn't always easy.

But isn't the pillar of "education" next to the pillar of "awareness" when we talk about sustainability?
Both pillars are linked. My grandpa always says, "One must break a horse in young." Sustainability isn't on any curriculum in secondary school. I am grateful for free education, that I grew up in peace and that I have clean water, that I can travel and express my opinion freely, but no one has ever told me that this is not a matter of course. Look at other countries, look at the oceans, look at the education systems and then be happy for what you have and nurture and cherish it so that you can pass it on to the next generation.

Comparing downward requires discipline, and not only when major TV stations stage a telethon. Isn't the fundamental problem that people rarely compare themselves downward?

439

gleichen Bauern zusammenarbeiten. Wir wissen also ganz genau, wo unsere Botanicals herkommen. Das ist nicht nur gut für die Nachhaltigkeit, sondern auch für die Qualitätssicherung. Es sind keine Nichtregierungsorganisationen dazwischen, die die Hand aufhalten. Für jeden Farmer, mit dem wir zusammenarbeiten, gibt es Jahrespläne, nicht nur in Bezug auf die Abnahme der Rohstoffe, sondern auch in Bezug auf unvorhersehbare Ereignisse. Was passiert zum Beispiel bei Ernteausfällen durch Naturkatastrophen? Die Sicherstellung, dass es der Familie und allen Feldarbeitern gut geht, wird immer durch uns gewährleistet. Der Anbau wird überwacht, alle zehn Botanicals, die im Bombay Sapphire verwendet werden, sind als nachhaltig zertifiziert. Natürlich geht es auch darum, wie in der Destille gearbeitet wird. Auch dort wurden wir 2015 erstmals mit einer Nachhaltigkeitsurkunde ausgezeichnet.

Autark funktioniert die Destille aber noch nicht?

Das wird leider auch nicht zu 100 Prozent möglich sein. Wir brauchen sehr viel Energie, wenn wir destillieren. Wir heizen die Stills auf über 80 Grad Celsius auf, aus einer Raumtemperatur von 17 Grad heraus. Bei vier riesigen Pot Stills sind das Unmengen an Energie. Deshalb haben die Kessel einen zweiten Mantel, der Wärme isoliert. Die Wärme aus dem Mantel wird in einen Wärmespeicher zurückgeführt, der durch die überschüssige Energie permanent auf 60 Grad erhitzt ist. Die Wärme wird entsprechend einem Kreislaufprinzip zurückgeführt und verwendet, wenn wir die Pot Stills wieder erhitzen müssen. Wir heizen also nicht mehr von 17 Grad Raumtemperatur auf 80 Grad hoch, sondern von 60 Grad. Dadurch sparen wir jede Menge Energie. Darüber hinaus haben wir eigene Verbrennungsöfen, die mit unserem organischen Müll befüllt werden und ebenfalls Energie zurückspeisen. Die Asche, die dabei entsteht, erhalten die Farmer in der Umgebung, die wiederum ihre Felder damit düngen. Im Gegenzug bekommen die Kollegen in der Destille Wurst und Käse von den Farmern. Unterhalb der Destille gibt es ein großes Wasserrad in einem Fluss. Das Wasserrad erzeugt durch die Flussbewegung genug Energie,

If you give two euros a month to Greenpeace and do nothing else, that's your own greenwashing, because every euro helps. It's easier and cheaper to live unsustainably. But excuses do not change the relevance of the issue. In the end, the bottom line remains: start with yourself, step by step. Comparisons are of little use. Today it may be waste separation, tomorrow it may be the A+ energy efficiency of the new washing machine.

We've talked about what individuals can do to live sustainably, but let's take it up a notch. What can corporations do to earn sustainability points? After all, as role models, they have an overriding responsibility...

But the distillery is not yet self-sufficient?

Unfortunately, this will not be possible to the 100 percent level. We need a lot of energy when we distill. We heat the stills to over 80 degrees Celsius from a room temperature of 17 degrees. With four

um jede Lampe in der Destille zu betreiben. Es gibt also keine externe Stromzufuhr für Licht.

Du hast die Botanicals genannt und den Betrieb der Destille erläutert. Wie nachhaltig seid ihr ab dem Zeitpunkt, an dem sich der Gin auf seinen Weg in die Welt macht?
Dann stellen sich zum Beispiel Verpackungsfragen: Muss ich alles in vierfach verstärkter Pappe verschicken oder reicht auch zweifach verstärkte Pappe? Muss ich alles in Frischhaltefolie einwickeln, wenn ich es auf Europaletten staple? Nein, muss ich nicht. Tatsächlich reichen zwei Streifen. Hierfür haben wir ein patentiertes System entwickelt. Wir nutzen die größtmöglichen Transportmethoden, um insgesamt seltener den Transportweg anzutreten. Beim Kalkulieren der Produktionsmengen schöpfen wir aus Erfahrungswerten und aus Trendanalysen.

Wo könnt ihr noch besser werden?
Derzeit wird die Zukunft der Flasche diskutiert. Bacardi Rum und Bombay Sapphire werden ab 2030 nicht mehr in einer Glasflasche, sondern in einer nachhaltig hergestellten natürlichen Plastik-Pappe-Gemisch-Flasche abgefüllt. Diese ausgefuchste Hightech-Flasche ist komplett recyclebar. Die bisherige Flaschenherstellung ist alles andere als nachhaltig, weil die dafür benötigte Hitze unfassbar viel Energie verbraucht. Nachhaltig zu arbeiten, ist immer eine perspektivische Arbeit. Der Erfolg ist nicht sofort, sondern erst später sichtbar. Es gibt viele Fragezeichen in meinem Kopf, aber die haben nicht unbedingt etwas mit Bacardi zu tun.

Wie sehen diese Fragezeichen aus?
Warum müssen so viele exotische Produkte zu uns kommen? Dass die keiner herträgt, ist doch klar. Wir haben uns daran gewöhnt, dass alles immer verfügbar ist, egal wo und wann es wächst. Die Transportwege sind ein großes Thema. Fliegen wird teurer, die Frachtkosten für die Schiffe ebenfalls. Das zwingt zum Umdenken. Wir gucken in keine perfekte Welt. Aber gerade in Deutschland

huge pot stills, that's a lot of energy. That's why the boilers have a second jacket that insulates heat. The heat from the jacket is returned to a heat accumulator, which is permanently heated to 60 degrees by the excess energy. The heat is recycled, based on a circulation principle, and used when we need to heat the pot stills again. So we no longer heat up from 17 degrees room temperature to 80 degrees, but from 60 degrees. This saves us a lot of energy. In addition, we have our own incinerators, which are filled with our organic waste and also feed energy back. The ash produced in the process is given to the farmers in the surrounding area, who in turn use it to fertilize their fields. In return, our colleagues in the distillery get sausage and cheese from the farmers. Below the distillery there is a large water wheel in a river. The water wheel generates enough energy from the river's movement to power every lamp in the distillery. So there is no external power for lights.

You mentioned the botanicals and explained the operation of the distillery. How sustainable are you from the moment the gin makes its way into the world?
Then, for example, packaging questions arise. Do I have to ship everything in 4-layer reinforced cardboard or is 2-layer enough? Do I have to wrap everything in cling film when I stack it on Euro pallets? No, I don't. In fact, two strips are enough. We have developed a patented system for this. We use the largest possible transportation methods to reduce the total number of journeys. When calculating production quantities, we draw on empirical values and trend analyses.

Where can you still improve?
The future of the bottle is currently being discussed. From 2030, Bacardi Rum and Bombay Sapphire will no longer be bottled in a glass bottle, but in a sustainably produced natural plastic-paperboard mix bottle. This sophisticated high-tech bottle is completely recyclable. The previous bottle production process is anything but sustainable because the heat required for it

tun wir vieles, um Dinge zu optimieren. Manchmal sind wir noch zu langsam. Wir sind aber auf einem guten Weg. Nicht zuletzt, weil der Druck seitens des Konsumenten steigt, der daran interessiert ist, nachhaltigere Produkte zu kaufen. Die Industrie denkt um, wenn es der Konsument einfordert. Das lässt sich auch auf dem Spirituosenmarkt beobachten. Die Leute kaufen inzwischen lieber zertifizierte Premiumprodukte.

Beobachtest du eine ähnliche Entwicklung nur in Deutschland oder auch in Österreich und der Schweiz?
Vom Prinzip liegen alle Länder gleichauf. Aber alle schauen immer darauf, ob sich Deutschland traut. Selbst wenn wir unser Klimaziel erreichen, haben wir global betrachtet wenig Einfluss. Aber der inspirative Effekt für andere Staaten ist gigantisch. Veränderung erfordert Mut. Mut kostet Geld. Geld haben die wenigsten Länder. Deutschland kann sich das meist noch leisten und deshalb schauen so viele auf uns.

Wie können wir unsere Klimaziele erreichen?
Ich glaube an die Weisheit der Masse. Je mehr Leute mitmachen, desto besser wird es auch. Selbst wenn die ganzen Klimawarnungen für die nächsten Jahrzehnte nicht eintreffen – was haben wir dann im schlimmsten Fall gemacht, wenn wir nachhaltig gelebt haben? Dann haben wir uns um unseren Planeten und dessen Gesundung gekümmert.

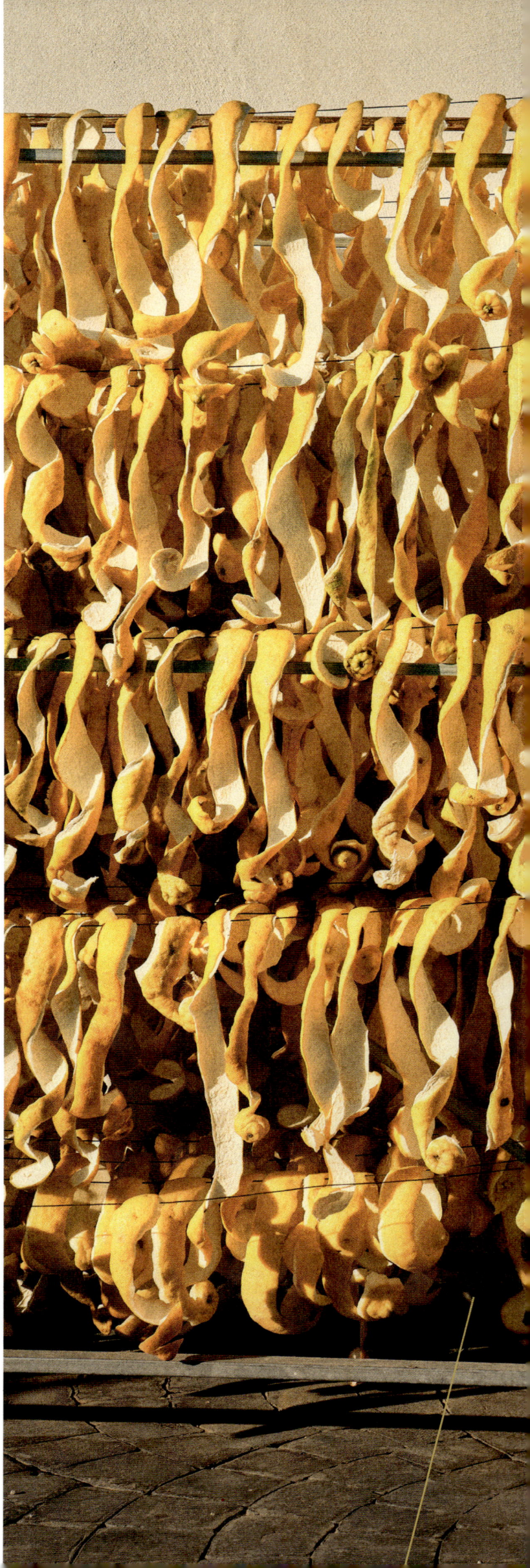

consumes an incredible amount of energy. Working sustainably always means taking perspectives. Success is not visible immediately, but only later. There are many question marks in my head, but they don't necessarily have anything to do with Bacardi.

What do these question marks look like?
Why do so many exotic products have to come to us? It's clear that no one brings them here. We have become accustomed to everything always being available, no matter where and when it grows. Transportation distances are a big issue. Flying is becoming more expensive, as are freight costs for ships. This forces us to rethink. We are not looking at a perfect world. But in Germany in particular, we are doing a lot to optimize things. Sometimes we are still too slow. But we are on the right track. Not least because there is increasing pressure from consumers who are interested in buying more sustainable products. The industry is rethinking when the consumer demands it. This can also be observed in the spirits market. People now prefer to buy certified premium products.

Do you see a similar development only in Germany or also in Austria and Switzerland?
In principle, all countries are on an equal footing. But everyone is always looking to see whether Germany dares. Even if we achieve our climate target, we have little influence globally. But the inspirational effect for other countries is gigantic. Change requires courage. Courage costs money. Very few countries have money. Germany can usually afford it still, and that's why so many look to us.

How can we achieve our climate goals?
I believe in the wisdom of crowds. The more people join in, the better things will be. Even if all the climate warnings for the next decades don't come true – what will we have done in the worst case if we've lived sustainably? We'll have taken care of our planet and its health.

443

"
The first cocktail listed in the first British cocktail book... *was a gin cocktail with ginger syrup, orange curaçao and bitters.* It features in William Terrington's Cooling Cups and Dainty Drinks.

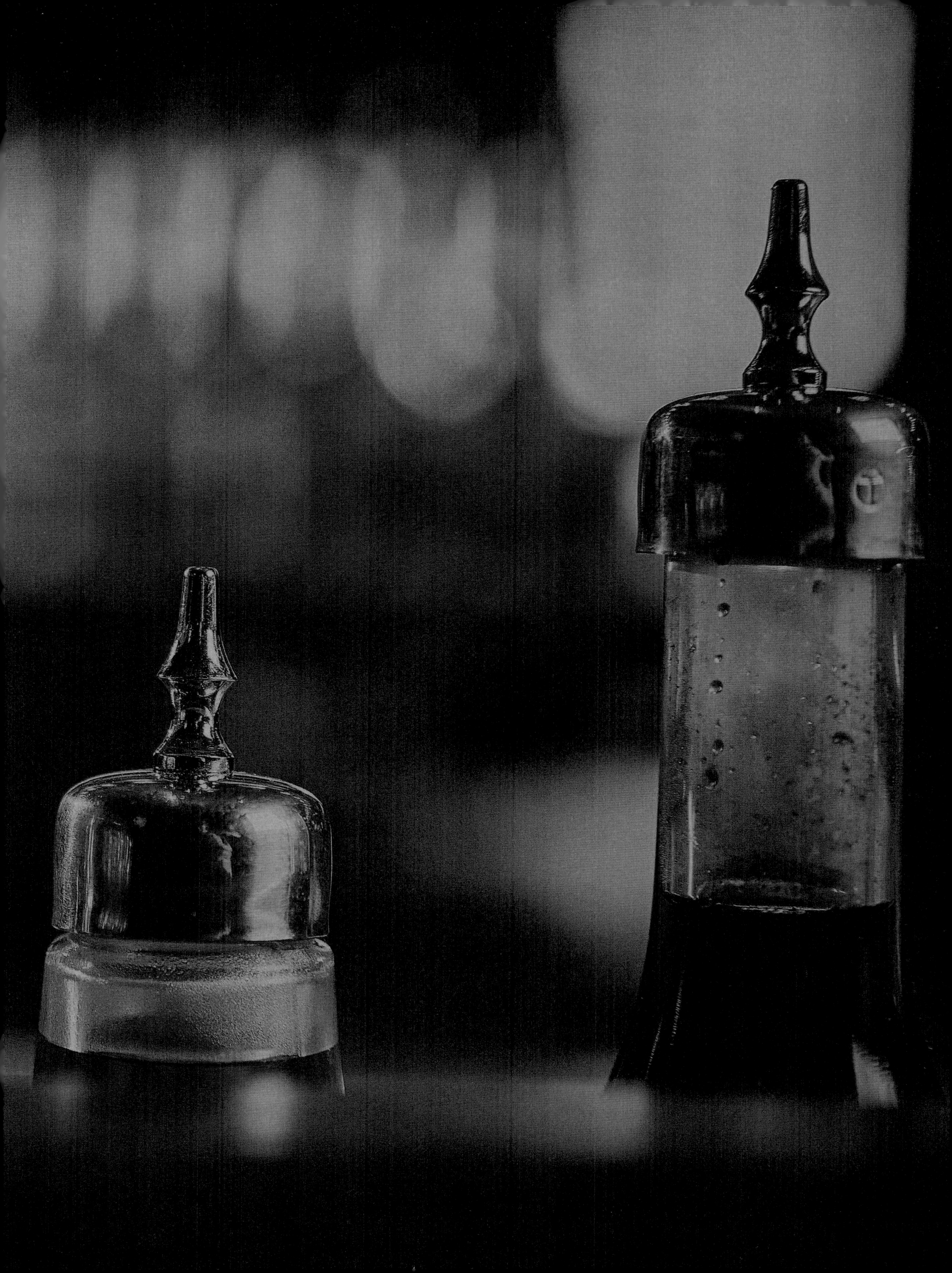

EXPERT CONTRIBUTION BY FRANK THELEN

BLOODY MARY FOR BREAKFAST? NOT QUITE!

Or even: What brand ambassadors really do.

Der Bartender des schnieken Fünf-Sterne-Hotels kündigt die letzte Runde an. Er stellt das Glas, gefüllt mit einem Champagner, auf den Tresen. Die Uhr schlägt eins, der Beginn eines prall gefüllten Tages, noch bevor der alte überhaupt aufgehört hat. Die Bässe aus dem nächstliegenden Club dringen auf die Straße. Die freudigen Gäste warten auf die angekündigten Drinks. Na dann. Das Hemd sitzt, die Frisur auch. Vier Stunden später schreit das Hotelbett nach Nähe. „Morgen dasselbe", sinniert Frank Thelen, Brand Ambassador aus dem Hause Diageo. „Nur eben doch ganz anders", sagt er. „Die meisten Menschen denken, dass mein Alltag als Markenbotschafter so aussieht: Partys, Drinks, zu wenig Schlaf. Woche für Woche. Vielleicht wurde der Job einmal so ausgeübt, aber was heute zählt, sind Fachwissen, Leidenschaft für seine Marke und ein hohes Maß an Selbstdisziplin. Als Markenbotschafter betrittst du keine hübsch vorbereitete Bühne. Du baust diese Bühne selber auf."

The bartender of the swanky five-star hotel calls the last round. He places the glass, filled with champagne, on the counter. The clock strikes one, the start of a packed day before the old one has even ended. The bass from the nearest club pours out onto the street. The excited guests are waiting for the announced drinks. Well then. The shirt fits, the hairstyle too. Four hours later, the hotel bed craves closeness. "Same again tomorrow," muses Frank Thelen, Brand Ambassador from Diageo. "Just very different," he says. "Most people think that my day-to day life as a brand ambassador goes like this: parties drinks, too little sleep. Week in, week out. Maybe that's how the job was once done, but what matters today is expertise, passion for your brand and a high level of self discipline. As a brand ambassador, you don't walk onto a nicely prepared stage. You build that stage yourself."

Lang lebe der König

Frank Thelen ist ein Kind der Gastro. Er ist zwischen den Kochtöpfen aufgewachsen. Seine Eltern betreiben ein mediterranes Restaurant. Er lebte in Deutschland, Spanien und wieder in Deutschland. In beiden Ländern ist er verwurzelt, beide Länder sind seine Heimat. Er arbeitete als Tellerwäscher, Kellner, absolvierte eine Ausbildung in einem Luxushotel, war Bartender und schließlich Barmanager – und das alles in Zeiten einer neuen aufstrebenden Cocktailära. „Es wurden klassische Rezepturen hervorgekramt und frische Zutaten verwendet. Die Gäste bekamen nur noch hochwertige Spirituosen serviert und die Bars schrieben sich das Siegel absoluter Qualität auf die Fahne. Ich selbst hatte einige Cocktailwettbewerbe bestritten, mal mehr, mal weniger erfolgreich. Doch ich war gelangweilt. Für meine persönliche Weiterentwicklung brauchte ich dringend eine neue Herausforderung." Wie schön, dass es das Schicksal manchmal gut meint. Just zu diesem Zeitpunkt bekam Frank Thelen die Position als Brand Ambassador in der global agierenden Firma Diageo angeboten. Der Spirituosenhersteller vertreibt mehr als 150 Marken, unter anderem Smirnoff

Everyday life as brand ambassador: Fizz, the clock strikes one, the night turns into day... #repeat

Spain and Germany:
He has roots in both countries, both countries are his home.

Vodka, Johnnie Walker Whisky, Baileys-Likör, Don Julio Tequila und Tanqueray Gin. Für Letzteren sollte Frank Thelen ab Januar 2019 die Schirmherrschaft übernehmen: „Das war ein aufregendes Gefühl, eine so renommierte Marke vertreten zu dürfen." Das erste Meeting fand in Polen statt, international aufgestellt, mit einer dezent überheblichen Begrüßung der neuen Markenbotschafter als die Könige der Brands. „Mir war das sehr unangenehm. Ich hatte einfach eine andere Wahrnehmung von meiner Position. Ich musste mich erst einmal im Unternehmen orientieren, die Arbeitsbereiche und Verantwortungen kennenlernen und meinen eigenen Platz finden." Geduld und Durchhaltevermögen waren in diesem Lernprozess seine ständigen Begleiter. „Natürlich gehört es dazu, bestens über die eigenen Marken Bescheid zu wissen: In welche Sparte gehören die Produkte? Welche Zielgruppe sprechen sie an? Welche Botschaften und Geschichten liegen in ihnen verpackt? Insbesondere bei Events ist es wichtig, mit den relevanten Informationen punkten zu können." Ihm wurde viel Spielraum gelassen, verdeutlicht der Kölner und so konzentrierte er sich 2019 direkt darauf, eine Tanqueray-Unit, bestehend aus den besten Bartendern Deutschlands, aufzubauen. Die Idee dahinter: Die Bartender entwickeln die Marke Tanqueray weiter, generieren und geben Workshops und kreieren in den Bars, in denen sie tätig sind, Drinks mit dem Produkt.

Zum Start des Unit-Abenteuers organisierte Frank Thelen eine Reise – und zwar dorthin, wo er selbst einst Wurzeln schlug. Es ging in die spanische Küstenstadt Barcelona. „Das war für mich sehr emo-

Long live the king

Frank Thelen is a child of the catering industry. He grew up between the cooking pots. His parents ran a Mediterranean restaurant. He has lived in Germany, Spain and back in Germany. He has roots in both countries, both countries are his home. He worked as a dishwasher, a waiter, trained in a luxury hotel, was a bartender and finally a bar manager – all during a new emerging cocktail era. "Classic recipes were dug up and fresh ingredients were used. Guests were served only high-end spirits, and bars flew flags of absolute quality. I myself competed in a few cocktail competitions, sometimes more, sometimes less successfully. But I was bored. For my personal development, I desperately needed a new challenge." How nice it is that fate sometimes means well. Just right then, Frank Thelen was offered the position of Brand Ambassador at the global company Diageo. This spirits manufacturer distributes more than 150 brands, including Smirnoff vodka, Johnnie Walker whisky, Baileys liqueur, Don Julio tequila and Tanqueray gin. For the latter, Frank Thelen was to take over as patron from January 2019: "That was an exciting feeling, to be able to represent such a renowned brand." The first meeting took place in Poland, set up internationally, with a discreetly pretentious welcome to the new brand ambassadors as the kings of the brands. "I was very uncomfortable with that. I simply had a different perception of my position. I first had to find my way around the company, learn about the work areas and responsibilities, and find my own place." Patience and perseverance were his constant companions in this

tional. Ich bin Halb-Spanier und wir verbrachten zwei wundervolle Tage in dieser bezaubernden Metropole. Ich konnte der Unit zeigen, wo ich aufgewachsen bin, wo sich die schönsten Ecken verstecken. Wir haben den Spirit Barcelonas aufgesogen und in der Unit-Identität manifestiert." Ein besseres Kick-off-Event hätte es nicht geben können. „Wir erzählen auch heute noch gerne davon und tauschen Erinnerungen aus. Der damals neu erschienene Tanqueray Flor de Sevilla stand im Mittelpunkt dieser Reise." Veranstaltungen zu organisieren, gehöre zu den Hauptaufgaben eines Brand Ambassador, sowohl im kleineren Rahmen als auch im großen Stil. Dabei haben alle Events neben der Markenplatzierung eine zentrale Gemeinsamkeit: das Erlebbarmachen der Spirituosen. Dies geschieht in Form von Workshops, bei denen die Teilnehmenden zum Beispiel in das wilde Berlin der 1920er- und 1930er-Jahre abtauchen und Cocktails aus der Ära verkosten, oder bei kulinarischen Treffen, wo Bartender gemeinsam mit Köchen ein aufeinander abgestimmtes Tanqueray-Menü, inklusive Getränk, zaubern.

Ein Stelldichein mit Ikonen

Eine Marke, die bereits international gefeiert wird, weiter in der Beliebtheits-Skala gen Himmel zu katapultieren, bedarf Kreativität und Einfallsreichtum. Tanqueray wird bereits seit 1830 hergestellt und seit 1847 exportiert, damals aus dem Herzen Londons, inzwischen aus Schottland. An der Rezeptur hat sich bis heute nichts verändert, auch das Flaschendesign ist seit 1948 gleich geblieben. Was sich verändert hat, ist jedoch die Geschwindigkeit, in der immer neue Gin-Varianten von immer neuen Herstellern auf den Markt gebracht werden. Der Konkurrenzdruck ist groß. An diesem Punkt kommen die Markenbotschafter ins Spiel: Sie müssen innovativ sein, ihre „Brand" breit ausspielen und dürfen dabei weder Traditionen brechen noch Erwartungshaltungen enttäuschen. Eine ikonische Marke wie Tanqueray angemessen und würdevoll zu vertreten, hat Frank Thelen am Anfang vor viele Fragen gestellt. Er habe einen Weg finden müssen, die Marke bestmöglich am Markt zu präsentieren und sich dabei selbst gerecht zu werden. Die Lösung bestehe darin, die besten Eigenschaften beider Welten zu verknüpfen. Natürlichkeit und Authentizität seien die Hauptakteure. Nur wer im Kern vollends von seinen Aufgaben überzeugt sei, werde mit Anerkennung belohnt. Dazu gehöre auch, sich intensiv mit dem Produkt auseinanderzusetzen. „Charles Tanqueray und Charles Waugh Tanqueray sind die Protagonisten in der Geschichte des Tanqueray-Imperiums. Beide verfolgten die Philosophie, die Konsumenten einerseits und diejenigen, die mit dem Produkt arbeiten, andererseits in den Mittelpunkt zu stellen. Es wurden unter anderem erfolgreiche Werbekampagnen mit Legenden wie Frank Sinatra und Sammy Davis jr. in den USA umgesetzt, um mögliche Konsumenten für den Gin zu interessieren. Die Flaschenform eines Cobbler-Shakers entstand hingegen in Anlehnung an die unzähligen Bartender, die aus dem Tanqueray wunderbare Drinks in die Gläser zaubern. In der Unternehmensphilosophie ist der Erfolg unmittelbar mit dem Menschen verbunden. Diesen Geist wollte ich aufgreifen und weiterentwickeln", erzählt Frank Thelen. Wer heutzutage auffallen will, muss sich jedoch etwas einfallen lassen und über den eigenen Tellerrand hinausschauen. „Das, was wir riechen, bestimmt das, was wir schmecken, zu mehr als 90 Prozent.

learning process. "Of course, knowing the best about your own brands is part of it. What sector do the products belong in? Which target group do they appeal to? What messages and stories are packed into them? Especially at events, it's important to be able to score points with the relevant information." Our guy from Cologne explains he was given a lot of leeway and so, in 2019, he focused directly on building up a Tanqueray unit consisting of Germany's best bartenders. The idea was that the bartenders should further develop the Tanqueray brand, generate and give workshops, and create drinks with the product in the bars where they work.

To kick off the unit adventure, Frank Thelen organized a trip – to the place where he himself once put down roots. It was to the Spanish coastal city of Barcelona. "That was very emotional for me. I am half-Spanish and we spent two wonderful days in this charming metropolis. I was able to show the unit where I grew up, where the most beautiful little corners are hidden away. We soaked up the spirit of Barcelona and expressed it in the unit identity." There could not have been a better kick-off event. "We still like to talk about it today and share memories. The then newly released Tanqueray Flor de Sevilla was the focus of that trip." Organizing events, he says, is one of the main tasks of a Brand Ambassador, both on a smaller scale and on a grand scale. In addition to brand placement, all events have one central theme in common: helping people experience the spirits. This takes place in the form of workshops, where participants immerse themselves in the wild Berlin of the 1920s and 1930s, for example, and taste cocktails

449

In London gibt es Aroma-Bars, in denen ein subtiler Wacholdergeruch versprüht wird, damit Gäste Lust auf einen Gin bekommen. Die Sinne potenzieller Konsumenten anzusprechen, ist hierbei der Schlüssel", gibt der Markenbotschafter zu bedenken und konkretisiert: „In Kooperation mit dem Parfümhersteller AER haben wir vier Duftkerzen-Varianten entwickelt, die nach den vier im Tanqueray verwendeten Botanicals riechen." Das Konzept dahinter verfolge die Strategie, den Gin auf vielfältige Weise in die Haushalte zu bringen. Es gehe darum, das Genusserlebnis zu perfektionieren, sozusagen die Kirsche auf der Sahne anzubieten, mit dem Ziel, den

from that era, or at culinary meetings, where bartenders work together with chefs to conjure up a coordinated Tanqueray menu including drinks.

A rendezvous with icons

To catapult a brand that is already internationally acclaimed further up the popularity scale requires creativity and ingenuity. Tanqueray has been produced since 1830 and exported since 1847, originally from the heart of London, now from Scotland. Nothing has changed in the recipe to this day, even the bottle

Geschmacks- mit dem Geruchssinn nachhaltig zu verknüpfen und auf diesem Weg positive Assoziationen und Gefühle in Verbindung mit der Marke zu erzeugen. Die Unit sei in diesem Zusammenhang eine stützende Säule. „Innerhalb der Community geben wir uns Ratschläge und konstruktiven Input. Auf diese Weise gibt es keinen Stillstand. Wir entwickeln uns mit der Marke weiter und sind zeitgleich auch abseits der beruflichen Bedürfnisse füreinander da. Das macht den Beruf als Brand Ambassador nicht nur vielschichtig, sondern auch besonders schön."

Brand Passion

Wer als Markenbotschafter arbeitet, ist viel unterwegs. Heute Berlin, morgen München, übermorgen mit dem Flieger in die Schweiz. Hier ein Tasting, dort ein Netzwerktreffen, am darauffolgenden Tag die Weiterbildung. Die vermeintlichen Pausen in den heimischen vier Wänden werden vom Homeoffice touchiert. Wir reisen viel. Wir leben viel. Wir treffen viele Menschen. Wir sind gesellig. Das ist alles sehr erstrebenswert und ich bin dankbar für jede einzelne Erfahrung, die ich im und mit dem Diageo-Konzern erleben darf. Nur mache ich das alles beruflich. Allein weil ich in Zürich bin, heißt das nicht, dass ich die Stadt besichtige, in einer Luxus-Suite residiere oder die Nacht zum Tag mache. Wenn ich dann irgendwann wieder nach Hause komme, ist da mein Büro. Ich arbeite dort, wo ich auch Feierabend mache." Für Frank Thelen ist sein Beruf in den vergangenen Jahren zur Berufung geworden. Der Kontakt mit Kunden und Konsumenten habe ihn bestärkt. Als Markenbotschafter bespielt er nicht nur die Unit. Er ist auch im Direktkontakt mit Bar- und Restaurantbesitzern. „Wer jetzt denkt, man nimmt ein paar Flaschen mit in eine Location und legt los, liegt falsch. Erst einmal kann ich nicht voraussetzen, dass mein Gegenüber alles über unsere Marke weiß. Zeitgleich muss ich für mich definieren, welche Informationen ich vermitteln möchte. Meistens ist ein Tasting auch wie eine Schulung, bei der es darum geht, die Leidenschaft für die eigenen Produkte zu vermitteln. Wir nennen das Brand Passion." Der Erstkontakt mit einem Kunden sei der wichtigste. Letztlich ginge es darum, eine langfristige und gute Geschäftsbeziehung aufzubauen, die auf Vertrauen basiert. Hierfür übernimmt der Brand Ambassador auch schon einmal selbst eine Schicht hinter dem Tresen. Manchmal stellt er sich sogar einen bekannten Barkeeper an seine Seite, mit dem er dann selbstkreierte Cocktails zur Verkostung anbietet. „Im Vorfeld rühren wir kräftig die Werbetrommel. Schließlich wollen alle Beteiligten, dass der Abend ein voller Erfolg wird. So ist das mit allen Veranstaltungen, die ich plane. Bei anderen, größeren Events liegt dann zusätzlich noch die Organisation eines Caterings, eines DJs und eines Fotografen auf meinem Tisch. Das muss gut werden." Die Erfahrungen, die Frank Thelen dabei sammelt, teilt er mit seinen Kolleginnen und Kollegen aus anderen Abteilungen im Unternehmen. Mit ihnen entwickelt er einen Fahrplan, um auch den letzten Konsumenten von Tanqueray zu überzeugen. Anders als noch vor zwanzig Jahren spielen soziale Medien dabei eine relevante Rolle. Wer jüngere Zielgruppen ansprechen will, kommt an Instagram und Co. nicht vorbei. Die Markenbotschafter werden zur Marke innerhalb ihrer Marke. Als Franqueray postet Thelen regelmäßig Beiträge rund um Tanqueray. „Natürlich sind wir dane-

design has remained the same since 1948. What has changed, however, is the speed at which ever newer gin variants are being brought to market by ever newer manufacturers. The competitive pressure is great. This is where brand ambassadors come in: they have to innovate, play their "brand" broadly, and not break with tradition or disappoint expectations. Representing an iconic brand like Tanqueray appropriately and with dignity presented Frank Thelen with many questions at the outset. He had to find a way to present the brand in the best possible way on the market while doing himself justice. The solution, he said, was to combine the best qualities of both worlds. Naturalness and authenticity were the key characteristics. Only those who are completely convinced of their tasks will be rewarded with recognition. This, he says, also includes dealing with the product at an intense level. "Charles Tanqueray and Charles Waugh Tanqueray are the lead characters in the history of the Tanqueray empire. Both pursued the philosophy of focusing on consumers on the one hand and those who work with the product on the other. Among other things, successful advertising campaigns, featuring legends such as Frank Sinatra and Sammy Davis Jr., were run in the USA to interest potential consumers in the gin. The bottle shape of a cobbler shaker, on the other hand, was created by way of reference to the countless bartenders who use Tanqueray to conjure up glasses of wonderful drinks. In the company's philosophy, success is directly linked to people. I wanted to pick up on this spirit and develop it further," says Frank Thelen.

But if you want to stand out these days, you have to come up with something and think outside the box. "What we smell determines what we taste by more than 90 percent. In London, there are aroma bars that spray a subtle smell of juniper to make guests want a gin. Appealing to the senses of potential consumers is the key here," the brand ambassador points out, adding, "In cooperation with perfume manufacturer AER, we have developed four scented candle variants that smell like the four botanicals used in Tanqueray." The concept behind this, he said, follows the strategy of bringing gin into homes in a variety of ways. The idea, he says, is to perfect the enjoyment experience, to offer the cherry to top off the whipped cream, so to speak, with the aim of creating

451

ben auch in klassischen (Print-)Medien unterwegs. Das Bestreben bleibt gleich: Ich möchte dasselbe Feuer für die Marke entfachen, das auch in mir brennt." Ein Markenbotschafter sei zeitgleich auch indirekt ein Verkäufer. Alle Maßnahmen müssen am Ende auch einen kommerziellen Mehrwert für das Unternehmen aufwerfen. „Markenbotschafter sind vielseitig einsetzbar. Das macht die Arbeit so spannend und gleichzeitig auch wertvoll für eine Firma, ähnlich wie ein Schweizer Taschenmesser."

In Deutschland gibt es lediglich eine Handvoll Markenbotschafter, die für verschiedene Spirituosenfirmen im Einsatz sind. Letztlich ginge es darum, das Genießen als Erlebnis zu vermitteln. Frank Thelen liebt die Komplexität seines Berufes. Er liebt es, kreativ zu sein, seine Marke immer wieder neu zu inszenieren. „Das Wichtigste ist aber, das Bewusstsein zu entwickeln, für und mit Menschen zu arbeiten. Nur so ist es möglich, aus voller Überzeugung ein Markenbotschafter zu sein, der bestrebt ist, voranzukommen – immer angepasst an die Bedürfnisse einer Zeit im Wandel." Und das ganz ohne Fünf-Sterne-Hotels und wilde Partynächte.

an enduring link between the sense of taste and the sense of smell, and in this way creating positive associations and feelings in connection with the brand. The unit is a supporting pillar in this context, he said. "Within the community, we give each other advice and constructive input. In this way, there is no stagnation. We continue to develop with the brand and, at the same time, we're there for each other away from professional needs. That makes the job as a Brand Ambassador not only particularly multi-facetted, but also particularly enjoyable."

Brand Passion

Those who work as brand ambassadors are on the road a lot. Today Berlin, tomorrow Munich, the day after tomorrow by plane to Switzerland. Here a tasting, there a networking meeting, the next day further training. The supposed breaks within the four walls at home brush with home office. "We travel a lot. We live a lot. We meet a lot of people. We're social. It's all very worthwhile, and I'm grateful for every single experience I get to have in and with the Diageo Group. It's just that I do all of this professionally. Just because I'm in Zurich doesn't mean I'm visiting the city, residing in a luxury suite, or turning night into day. When I come back home at some point, that's where my office is. I work where I also finish my workday." For Frank Thelen, his profession has become his calling in recent years. The contact with customers and consumers has brought him strength, he says. As a brand ambassador, he doesn't just play the unit. He is also in direct contact with bar and restaurant owners. "Anyone who now thinks you take a few bottles to a location and get started is wrong. First of all, I can't assume that my counterpart knows everything about our brand. At the same time, I have to define for myself what information I want to convey. Most of the time, a tasting is also like a training session which is about conveying passion for your own products. We call that brand passion." The initial contact with a customer is the most important, he said. Ultimately, he says, it's about building a long-term, good business relationship based on trust. To this end, the brand ambassador sometimes takes on a shift behind the counter himself. Sometimes he even sets up a well-known bartender at his side, with whom he then offers self-created cocktails for tasting. "In the run-up, we bang the advertising drum real hard. After all, everyone involved wants the evening to be a complete success. That's the way it is with all the events I plan. For other, larger events, there is then the additional organization of catering, a DJ and a photographer on my table. It has to turn out well." Frank Thelen shares the experience he gains with his colleagues from other departments in the company. With them he develops a roadmap to convince even the very last Tanqueray consumer. Unlike twenty years ago, social media play a relevant role in this. If you want to appeal to younger target groups, you can't get around Instagram and the like. Brand ambassadors are becoming the brand within their brand. As "Franqueray", Thelen regularly posts about Tanqueray. "Of course, we're also active in classic (print) media alongside this. The aspiration remains the same: I want to ignite the same fire for the brand that burns inside me." A brand ambassador is also indirectly a salesperson. In the end, all measures taken must also raise a commercial added

value for the company. "Brand ambassadors are versatile. That's what makes the work so exciting and at the same time valuable for a company, a bit like a Swiss Army knife."

In Germany, there are only a handful of brand ambassadors working for various distillers. Ultimately, all these measures are about conveying enjoyment as an experience. Frank Thelen loves the complexity of his job. He loves being creative, staging his brand anew time and again. "But the most important thing is to develop the awareness of working for and with people. Only in this way is it possible to be a brand ambassador with full conviction, striving to move forward – always adapted to the needs of a time in flux"; and all this without five-star hotels and wild party nights.

Brand ambassadors through the ages: With an awareness of brand and people, all without bar and five-star hotels.

WL201 WL202 WL203 WL204 WL205

ve you!
you or the gin talking?
me talking to the gin.

WL207 WL208 WL209 WL2 WL211 BP601 BP602 BP603

SIPSMITH
London
Zesty Orange
GIN
SIPSMITH
London
London
DRY GIN
SIPSMITH
London
Lemon Drizzle
GIN

EXPERT CONTRIBUTION BY MAGNUS TOBLER

TALKING FAIRY DUST & GLITTER CONFETTI:

Why not every trend is successful

Ein Blick auf die Gin-Weltkarte zeigt: Es gibt kaum eine Nation, die sich nicht im Destillieren versucht. Dem Gin-Universum wird ein jährliches Umsatzwachstum von mehr als 7 % Prozent prognostiziert. Großbritannien präsentiert sich dabei als Marktführer, dicht gefolgt von Deutschland. Die beiden Staaten blicken inzwischen auf eine Liste mit mehr als 1000 Gin-Sorten, darunter experimentelle Varianten, die mit ihrer zauberhaften, glitzerbehafteten Wirkung werben und damit nicht auf einen Rausch anspielen. Zu den Global Playern am Weltmarkt gehört Beam Suntory als Anbieter von Premium-Spirituosen, deren Gin-Sparte in Deutschland durch Markenbotschafter Magnus Tobler in die Öffentlichkeit getragen wird.

Magnus Tobler ist 1985 in der Schweiz geboren und in jungen Jahren nach Schleswig-Holstein gezogen. Dort besuchte er die Realschule, früh mit dem Bewusstsein, in einem Job arbeiten zu wollen, auf dem er zu 100 Prozent Lust hat. Er wagte als Teenager einen Ausflug in die Schauspielerei, wirkte in verschiedenen Komparsen-Rollen, fand Spaß daran und musste sich schließlich doch eingestehen, dass nur die Wenigsten damit gutes Geld verdienen. Er zog mit 17 von zu Hause aus, suchte sich einen Job in der Gastronomie, absolvierte eine Ausbildung zum Restaurantfachmann, ging nach Flensburg und arbeitete bereits mit Anfang 20 als Restaurantleiter in einem kleinen Gasthof – bis er abgeworben wurde, nach Glücksburg ging und dort gleich mehrere Leitungspositionen bekleidete. Hals über Kopf brach er drei Jahre später alle Zelte ab. Dem Ruf der wilden Hauptstadt folgend, strandete er in Berlin. Irgendwann sagte mir ein Kumpel, dass Beam Suntory jemanden für den Vertrieb suche. Ich konnte mir darunter wenig vorstellen. Und genau das sagte ich dann auch meinem zukünftigen Chef im Vorstellungsgespräch. Allerdings erzählte ich ihm auch von meinen Stärken. Mit diesen konnte ich punkten."

Sipsmith geht unter die Haut

Inzwischen ist Magnus Tobler als Ginfluencer, Brand Ambassador und Community Manager in ganz Deutschland unterwegs und

A quick look at the gin world map demonstrates: there's barely a single nation that doesn't dabble in distilling. Annual sales growth of more than 7 % is forecast for the gin universe. Great Britain is the market leader, closely followed by Germany. These two countries now boast a list of more than 1000 gin varieties, including experimental variants that advertise their enchanting, glittery effects, thus not alluding to intoxication. One of the global players on the world market is Beam Suntory as a supplier of premium spirits, whose gin spate is

vertritt als solcher Sipsmith und Roku Gin für Beam Suntory. Dass sein Werdegang diesen Lauf nehmen würde, war mehr Zufall als bewusste Wahl. „Man kann sich nicht zum Ziel setzen, das Gesicht einer Marke zu werden." Und dennoch ist er als Lobbyist für die Marken unterwegs, als Magnus, als cooler Typ, der an einem Tag im Achselhemd und kurzer Jogger beim Tischtennisturnier von Thomas Henry Spaß versprüht und am nächsten eine seriöse Masterclass für das Who-is-Who der Getränke-Industrie auf die Beine stellt. „People follow people, people do not follow brands." Dafür braucht es keinen Hochglanzauftritt. Dafür braucht es Authentizität. Ich muss meine Oma genauso überzeugen können wie einen professionellen Bartender." Als Ginfluencer ist Magnus Tobler ein Trendbeobachter. Die (sozialen) Medien helfen ihm dabei. Aus erster Hand erhält er von Instagram und Co. sowie aus der Fachpresse wichtige Informationen zur Entwicklung des globalen Gin-Marktes. Dabei hat er den Hype um Gin erst 2017 richtig bewusst wahrgenommen. „Im Endeffekt gehört Gin seit 2008 zu den beliebtesten Getränken. Aber nicht für mich, der aus Norddeutschland kam und bei Partys lieber zu einer Rum-Cola-Mische griff. Ich habe nicht verstanden, warum alle so darauf abgehen", erinnert er sich. „Im Januar 2017 wollte Beam Suntory den Gin von Sipsmith ins Portfolio aufnehmen. Mein Gedanke damals: Bitte nicht! Ein halbes Jahr später flog ich mit nach Großbritannien, um den Gin vor Ort kennenzulernen. Das war mein erstes Mal im UK und mein erstes Mal, dass ich eine Gin-Destillerie besucht habe. Zur Begrüßung gab es einen Welcome-Gin-Tonic, einen Sipsmith London Dry Gin mit Fever Tree Indian Tonic. Das war das erste Mal, dass mir ein Gin geschmeckt hat und ich sogar noch einen zweiten bestellt habe." Die London-Reise hat Eindruck hinterlassen, auch heute noch sichtbar auf der Haut von Magnus Tobler. „Beim abendlichen Bankett saß ich neben einem US-Kollegen, der am ganzen Körper tätowiert war. Nur eine Stelle war noch frei. Ich sagte, dass dort der Sipsmith Schwan hinpasst und ich mir diesen aus Solidarität auch stechen lasse, sofern Master Distiller Jared Brown zustimmt. Dieser hatte nur eine Bedingung: Er sucht den Tätowierer aus. Eineinhalb Tage später flogen wir wieder nach Hause. Mit einem Tattoo von Paul, dem Tätowierer, der Sipsmith Gin als Zugabe in seiner Farbe verwendete." Seit Mai 2018 ist Magnus Tobler als Brand Ambassador für Beam Suntory tätig, seit September 2018 in vollem Umfang. 2020 kreierte er innerhalb einer Woche gemeinsam mit seinen internationalen Kolleginnen und Kollegen einen Markenbotschafter-Gin. Der Lerneffekt dahinter: Gut Ding will Weile haben. „Derzeit kommen so viele Gins auf den Markt, die teilweise noch gar nicht ausgereift sind. Bei den Trend-Gins geht es häufig nicht mehr um die Qualität, sondern um Marketing." Bereits bei der Herstellung gäbe es signifikante Unterschiede, die letztlich den Trinkgenuss beeinflussen. „Derzeit werden primär zwei Herstellungsverfahren angewandt: Die One-Shot-Methode und die Concentrate-Technik. Bei der One-Shot-Methode kommt das Produkt nach dem Destillieren mit einem hohen Alkoholgehalt aus dem Kessel und wird nur noch mit Wasser auf Trinkstärke gebracht. Mehr als 80 Prozent der Produzenten nutzen jedoch die Concentrate-Technik. Dabei gewinnen sie ein Konzentrat, das sie mit Wasser und Neutralalkohol auffüllen. Die One-Shot-Methode ist die teurere, dafür geschmacklich intensivere Methode", verdeutlicht Magnus Tobler.

promoted in Germany by brand ambassador Magnus Tobler

Magnus Tobler was born in Switzerland in 1985 and moved to Schleswig-Holstein at a young age. There he attended secondary school, aware early on that he wanted to work in a job he was 100 percent passionate about. As a teenager, he ventured into acting, appeared in various roles as an extra, enjoyed it and, finally, had to admit to himself that only very few people earn good money doing it. He left home at 17, looked for a job in the restaurant business, trained as a restaurant manager, went to Flensburg and was already working as a restaurant manager in a small inn in his early 20s – till he was then headhunted, went to Glücksburg and held several management positions there. Head over heels he broke all ties three years later. Following the call of the wild capital, he landed up in Berlin. "At some point, a buddy told me that Beam Suntory was looking for someone for sales. I couldn't imagine what that meant really. Indeed, that's exactly what I told my future boss at the job interview. But I told him about my strengths, and I was able to score points there."

Sipsmith gets under your skin

Magnus Tobler now travels throughout Germany as a ginfluencer, brand ambassador, and community manager, representing Sipsmith and Roku Gin for Beam Suntory. That his career would take this course was more of a coincidence than a conscious choice. "You can't set yourself the goal of becoming the face of a brand." And yet he's out lobbying for brands as Magnus, a

Die London-Reise hat Eindruck hinterlassen…

Aus dem Abgrund an die Spitze

Gin war nicht immer ein hippes Trendgetränk, gab es doch eine Zeit, in der ihm sogar der Beiname „Mother's ruin", also Mutters Elend, verliehen wurde. Gin galt als billiger Fusel, eine Droge, die für den schnellen Rausch sorgte, getrunken von den Ärmsten der Ärmsten, die mit jedem Schluck des giftigen Elixiers ihrem Leben den Rücken zukehrten. Den Umhang der Verwahrlosung hat der Gin längst abgelegt, nicht zuletzt wegen der inzwischen strengen Herstellungsprozesse. Mittlerweile werden die Batches nach strengen Qualitätsstandards teils geprüft. Abweichungen vom Grundgerüst fallen sofort auf. Wer beispielsweise einen London Dry Gin produzieren möchte, muss nicht in das Herz des Vereinigten Königreichs reisen, sondern sich schlichtweg an Gesetzesvorgaben der Europäischen Union halten. Die Regeln sind deutlich und auf das Wesentliche reduziert: reiner Ethylalkohol wird mehrfach destilliert, ohne dass ihm dabei Farbstoffe und mehr als 0,1 Gramm Zucker pro Liter zugegeben werden. Die aromagebenden Botanicals dürfen lediglich während des Destillationsprozesses ihren Weg in die Spirituose finden, wobei sich der Wacholder im Geschmack deutlich abzeichnen soll. Der London Dry Gin ist klassisch, verzichtet auf Exotik und Experimente. Dabei ist er beinahe selbst zum Exoten

cool guy who one day turns up emanating pure fun at Thomas Henry's table tennis tournament in a skimpy shirt and jogging shorts, and puts on a serious master class for the who's who of the beverage industry the next. "People following people"; people aren't following brands. You don't need a glossy appearance for that. You need authenticity. I need to be able to convince my grandma just as much as a professional bartender." As a ginfluencer, Magnus Tobler is a trend observer. The (social) media help him with this. He gets important first-hand information on the development of the global gin market from Instagram and co. as well as from the trade press. Yet he only really became aware of the hype surrounding gin in 2017. "The bottom line is that gin has been one of the most popular drinks since 2008. But not for me; I came from northern Germany and preferred to reach for a rum and cola mix at parties. I didn't understand why everyone was so into it," he recalls. "In January 2017, Beam Suntory wanted to add Sipsmith's gin to its portfolio. What I thought at the time was please don't! Six months later, I flew along to the UK to get to know the gin right there. This was my first time in the UK and my first time visiting a gin distillery. To welcome us, we had a welcome gin tonic, a Sipsmith London Dry Gin with Fever Tree

geworden, in einem Gin-Universum zwischen New Western Gins und New Eastern Gins, in dem Glitzerstaub, Farbeffekte und extravagante Zutaten die Aufmerksamkeit des Verbrauchers auf sich lenken sollen. Abgefahrene Gin-Varianten wurden im Laufe des vergangenen Jahrzehnts an die Bartresen gespült, den Fokus auf die zwingende Wacholder-Zutat setzen diese schon lange nicht mehr. „Es gibt keine Vorgabe, die besagt, wie viel Wacholder im Gin sein muss, nur dass Wacholder drin sein muss. Insofern haben die Hersteller sehr viel Spielraum. Die unterschiedlichen Formen, Farben und Etiketten verfolgen in der Regel das Ziel, in dem Haifischbecken der Gins Aufmerksamkeit zu generieren. Gin gehört zu den am schnellsten herzustellenden Spirituosen. Deshalb ist der Markt so rasch überflutet worden. Dem Endverbraucher hilft in diesem Zusammenhang nur, sich ein bisschen schlau zu machen", betont Magnus Tobler und ergänzt: „Gin ist anders als beispielsweise ein fassgereifter Whisky, ein ungelagertes Produkt, das für seine Eigenschaften recht hochpreisig ist. Dies wird zunehmend auch von den Konsumenten wahrgenommen. Nur weil etwas teuer ist, muss es nicht gut sein. Der Verbraucher ist informierter, er weiß mehr über Gin, kann die Spielereien identifizieren, die einfach nur neugierig machen sollen. Die Produktpalette im Gin-Segment ist unfassbar vielfältig, allein in Bezug auf die Botanicals. Gin wird deshalb aber auch immer am Markt bestehen: Weil er so viele verschiedene Geschmäcker bedient." Insbesondere Sammler freut das. „Es gibt Foren, in denen Gin-Liebhaber ihre vollen Regale präsentieren. Sie werden die Spirituosen niemals trinken. Darum geht es ihnen auch nicht. Ihnen geht es um das Besitzen. Und sie zahlen liebend

Indian Tonic. That was the first time I enjoyed a gin and even ordered a second one." The London trip left an impression, still visible on Magnus Tobler's skin today. "At the evening banquet, I sat next to a US colleague who had tattoos all over his body. Only one spot was still free. I said that the Sipsmith Swan would fit there and that I would also have it engraved out of solidarity, provided Master Distiller Jared Brown agreed. The latter had only one condition: He chooses the tattoo artist. One and a half days later we flew back home. With a tattoo from Paul, the tattoo artist who used Sipsmith Gin as an addition in his paint." Magnus Tobler has been a Brand Ambassador for Beam Suntory since May 2018, and full time since September 2018. In 2020, he created a brand ambassador gin together with his international colleagues within one week. The learning effect behind it: good things take time. "There are currently so many gins coming onto the market, some of which are not even mature yet". With trendy gins, it's often no longer about quality, but about marketing. Even in the production process, there are significant differences that ultimately influence drinking enjoyment, he said. "Currently, two production methods are primarily used: The one-shot method and the concentrate technique. In the one-shot method, the product comes out of the kettle after distillation with a high alcohol content and is diluted to drinking strength with water only. However, more than 80 percent of producers use the concentrate technique. In this process, they obtain a concentrate that they top up with water and neutral alcohol. The one-shot method is more expensive but has a more intense taste," explains Magnus Tobler.

gern einige Euro mehr für schicke Tonflaschen oder aufregendes Marketing." Wem es ums Genießen gehe, müsse bedenken, dass sich der Geschmack nach etwa drei bis fünf Jahren verflüchtige. Danach sehe schlichtweg nur noch die Flasche gut aus. Erfolg versprechend sei, das Design eines Gins und seinen Geschmack in harmonischen Einklang zu bringen – so wie bei dem sechseckigen Roku Gin. „Das Produkt gibt es seit den 1920er-Jahren, hieß damals aber Hermes Gin und wurde in einer Flachmann-Flasche in Japan verkauft. Mit der Fusion von Suntory und Beam Global im Jahr 2016 bekam die Ginproduktion in Fernost einen neuen Stellenwert. Das Design der Flasche und der Name des Gins wurden mit Blick auf die Identität des Gins überarbeitet. Die sechs Ecken der Flasche stehen für die sechs typisch japanischen Botanicals, die in dem Gin stecken. Der Name Roku, der übersetzt sechs bedeutet, rundet das Profil ab. Inzwischen gehört der Roku Gin zu den weltweit bekanntesten und erfolgreichsten japanischen Spirituosen."

Fassgereifte Orangenhaut

Zu den Tendenzen in der Spirituosen-Welt gehören zunehmend auch alkoholfreie Getränke-Varianten bekannter Marken – als Alternative für all diejenigen, die nicht so gern Alkohol konsumieren oder keinen Alkohol trinken dürfen. „Ein Trend ist das noch nicht. Es passt zur jetzigen Zeit und hat mit Sicherheit auch jede Menge Fans. Alkoholfreier Gin oder Low ABV Drinks mit weniger Alkoholgehalt werden sich mit hoher Wahrscheinlichkeit etablieren, aber niemals klassische Spirituosen in Gänze ablösen." Tatsächlich beobachtet Magnus Tobler einen ganz anderen Trend und dieser konzentriert sich auf die Rückbesinnung auf das Weniger-ist-mehr-Prinzip. Neue Produkte haben es schwer, auf dem übersättigten Gin-Markt zu bestehen. „Es wird langsam weniger mit neuen Pro-

From the abyss to the top

Gin wasn't always a hip trendy drink; there was a time when it was even given the nickname "Mother's ruin." Gin was considered cheap booze, a drug that provided a quick high, drunk by the poorest of the poor, who turned their backs on life with every sip of the poisonous elixir. The cloak of neglect has long since been shed by gin, not least because of the now stringent manufacturing processes. Now, the batches are partly tested according to strict quality standards. Deviations from the basic framework are immediately noticeable. Anyone who wants to produce a London Dry Gin, for example, does not have to travel to the heart of the United Kingdom, but simply adhere to legal requirements of the European Union. The rules are clear and reduced to the essentials: pure ethyl alcohol is distilled several times without adding any colorants or more than 0.1 grams of sugar per liter. The aroma-giving botanicals are only allowed to find their way into the spirit during the distillation process, and the juniper should stand out clearly in the taste. London Dry Gin is a classic, renouncing exoticism and experimentation. In the process, it has almost become exotic itself, in a gin universe between New Western Gins and New Eastern Gins, where glitter dust, color effects and extravagant ingredients are meant to attract the consumer's attention. Offbeat gin variants have washed up at bar counters over the past decade, but the focus on the compelling juniper ingredient has long since disappeared. "There is no specification that says how much juniper has to be in the gin, only that juniper has to be in it. In this respect, manufacturers have a lot of leeway. The different shapes, colors and labels usually pursue the goal of generating attention in the shark tank of gins. Gin is one of the fastest spirits to be produced. That is why the market has been

flooded so quickly. In this context, the only thing that helps the end consumer is to get a bit smart," emphasizes Magnus Tobler adding, "Gin, unlike barrel-aged whiskey, for example, is an unaged product that is quite highly priced for its characteristics." This is also increasingly how consumers see it. Just because something is expensive doesn't mean it has to be good. Consumers are more informed, they know more about gin, they can identify the gimmicks that are simply intended to arouse curiosity. The product range in the gin segment is incredibly diverse, even just in terms of botanicals. But gin will always exist on the market because of this; because it serves so many different tastes." Gin collectors in particular are happy about this. "There are forums where gin lovers present their full shelves. They will never drink the spirits. That's not what they're about either. For them, it's about owning, and they're happy to pay a few euros more for fancy clay bottles or exciting marketing." Those who want to enjoy it must remember that the taste dissipates after about three to five years. After that, it's simply the bottle that looks good. He says it's promising to bring the design of a gin and its taste into harmonious harmony – as is the case with that hexagonal Roku Gin. "The product has been around since the 1920s but, at the time, it was called Hermes Gin and was sold in a hip flask in Japan. With the merger of Suntory and Beam Global in 2016, gin production in the Far East took on a new significance. The design of the bottle and the name of the gin were revised with the identity of the gin in mind. The six corners of the bottle represent the six typical Japanese botanicals that are in the gin. The name Roku, which translates to six, rounds out the profile. Now, Roku Gin has become one of the world's best-known and most successful Japanese spirits."

Barrel-aged orange peel

Increasingly, trends in the spirits world include non-alcoholic beverage variants of well-known brands – as an alternative for those who are not so fond of alcohol or are not allowed to drink alcohol. "It's not a trend yet. It fits in with current times and certainly has plenty of fans. Alcohol-free gin or low ABV drinks with less alcohol content will most likely establish themselves, but will never replace classic spirits entirely." In fact, Magnus Tobler is observing a very different trend, and it focuses on a return to the less-is-more principle. New products are having a hard time competing in the oversaturated gin market. "It's getting less with new products. Also because there are many gins that you would rather not have bought on looks. They have a nice look, but the core is not right. They are then bought once and never again. But manufacturers want consistency, they want regular customers. That's the only way they can build up a business in the long term. Of course, those who have succeeded must not rest on their laurels." The challenge here, he says, is to move with the times without violating one's own values. The customer should experience an "aha" moment without being put off by the changes. Currently, many producers are focusing on the use of citrus fruits such as oranges. The oils and aromas can be easily extracted from the skin. With a strawberry or raspberry, he said, it's much more complicated. "Other producers are starting to subsequently store their gin in a sherry or whiskey barrel for two

dukten. Auch weil es viele Gins gibt, die man lieber nicht nach dem Aussehen gekauft hätte. Die haben eine schöne Optik, aber der Kern stimmt nicht. Die werden dann einmal und nie wieder gekauft. Die Hersteller wollen aber eine Konstanz, sie wollen den Stammkunden. Nur so können sie langfristig ein Business aufbauen. Wer es geschafft hat, darf sich natürlich auch nicht auf dem Erfolg ausruhen." Hier bestehe die Herausforderung darin, mit der Zeit zu gehen, ohne die eigenen Werte zu verletzen. Der Kunde soll einen Aha-Moment erleben, ohne von den Veränderungen abgeschreckt zu werden. Aktuell würden zahlreiche Produzenten ihren Fokus auf die Verwendung von Zitrusfrüchten wie Orangen setzen. Aus der Haut ließen sich die Öle und Aromastoffe leicht herauslösen. Bei einer Erdbeere oder einer Himbeere sei das wesentlich komplizierter. „Andere Produzenten fangen an, ihren Gin nachträglich für zwei bis drei Monate in einem Sherry- oder Whisky-Fass zu lagern. Dadurch bekommt der Gin ein wenig Farbe und eine leicht rauchige Note. Mit Gin hat das meiner Ansicht nach nicht mehr viel zu tun. Dahinter steckt der Versuch, die Cognac- oder die

Whiskytrinker einzufangen. Ein Versuch, der wahrscheinlich nicht gelingen wird. Cognac-Trinker sind Cognac-Trinker, weil sie den Geschmack mögen und nicht, weil sie an Gin interessiert sind, der in einem Cognac-Fass gelagert wurde." Magnus Tobler betrachtet diese Entwicklung mit einem Augenzwinkern. „Es wird vielmehr dabei bleiben, dass hochwertige, ausgewählte Gins Bestand haben. Das schließt auch kleinere, regionale Hersteller ein. Das harmoniert mit dem zunehmenden Bewusstsein, lokal und regional einkaufen zu wollen. Die höheren Preise werden akzeptiert. Die Produktionsmengen sind geringer, sodass die Kleinen anders kalkulieren müssen als die Giganten."

Magnus Tobler trinkt keinen Rum mehr – so wie damals, als er noch jung und wild auf Partys in Schleswig-Holstein herumhüpfte. Sipsmith hat seine Vorlieben verändert und auch seine Optik. Inzwischen schmücken mehr als 30 Tattoos seinen Körper. Das Letzte ist ein Schriftzug: „It's all about money". Dabei ist das Wort „money" durchgestrichen und durch „passion" ersetzt. Seine Leidenschaft führt ihn hinaus in die Welt mit dem Ziel, Gin-Trinker emotional von Roku Gin und Co. zu überzeugen – vielleicht auch bald als internationaler Brand Ambassador für Sipsmith.

to three months. This gives the gin a little color and a slightly smoky note. In my opinion, this no longer has much to do with gin. Behind this is an attempt to ensnare cognac or whiskey drinkers. An attempt that will probably not succeed. Cognac drinkers are cognac drinkers because they like the taste, not because they're interested in gin that's been aged in a cognac barrel." Magnus Tobler views this development with a twinkle in his eye. "What will rather endure are high-quality, selected gins. That also includes smaller, regional producers. This harmonizes with the increasing awareness of wanting to buy locally and regionally. Higher prices are accepted. Production volumes are lower, so the small players have to calculate differently from the giants."

Magnus Tobler no longer drinks rum – as he did when he was young and wild, hopping around parties in Schleswig-Holstein. Sipsmith has changed his preferences, and his look, too. Now more than 30 tattoos adorn his body. The latest states: "It's all about money", with the word "money" crossed out and replaced by "passion". His passion leads him out into the world with the goal of emotionally convincing gin drinkers of Roku Gin and Co. – perhaps soon as an international brand ambassador for Sipsmith.

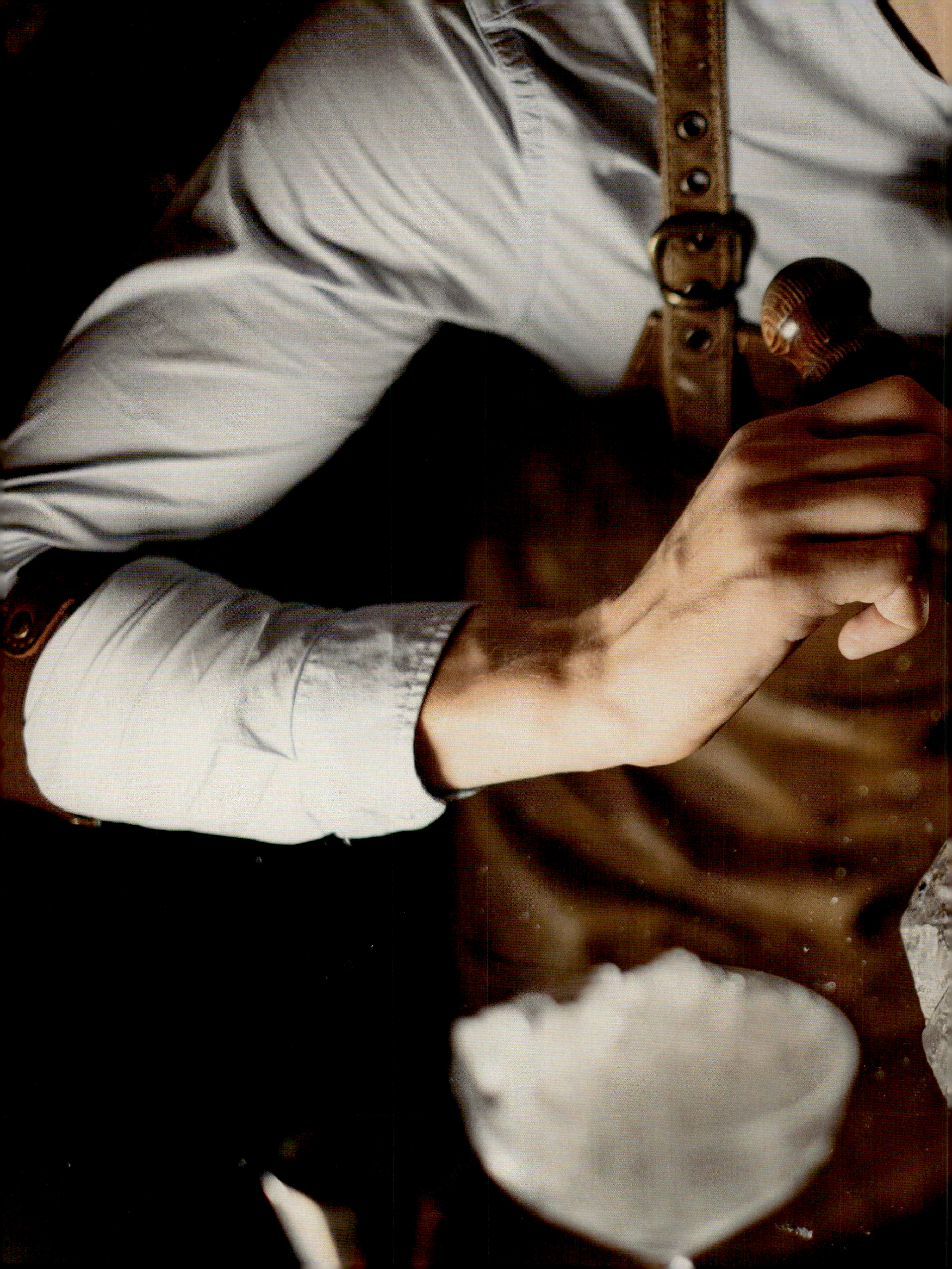

> "I don't know what reception I'm at, but for God's sake give me a gin tonic.
> – Denis Thatcher

EXPERT CONTRIBUTION BY LU GEIPEL

LU ALONE IN THE BAR

– how a Berlin woman stirs up a scene that is (still) dominated by men

Es gibt sie noch, die Ur-Berliner, born and raised in der deutschen Hauptstadt, deren DNA aus Schrippen, Pfannkuchen und Currywurst besteht und deren schnörkellose, direkte und oft auch ein wenig spöttisch-süffisante, saloppe Mundart international als „Berliner Schnauze" von sich reden macht. „Dit heißt immer Du oder du, aber niemals Sie!", gehört zu den festen Regeln im Sprachgebrauch. In Berlin ist alles möglich: Hier werden Sneaker zu den schönsten Kleidern getragen, die U-Bahnen sind Auffangbecken skurriler Gestalten, Spätis sind die eigentlichen Wahrzeichen der Stadt und gute Partys beginnen niemals vor Mitternacht. Eine feste Größe in der Kulturszene ist eine Ur-Berlinerin mit dem wohlklingenden Namen Lu Geipel. Als Bartenderin macht sie regelmäßig mit ausgefallenen Cocktailkreationen auf sich aufmerksam. Ihr Leben spielt sich vor allem nachts ab: Wenn das Licht der Sonne durch Straßenlaternen abgelöst wird, steht sie hinterm Tresen und serviert Drinks.

They still exist, the original Berliners, born and raised in the German capital, whose DNA is made of traditional "Schrippen" bread rolls, "Pfannkuchen" pancakes and "Currywurst" sausages, and whose straightforward, direct and often slightly mocking-smug manner of casual dialect is internationally known as "Berliner Schnauze". "Dit is always the informal, never the formal version of 'you'!" is one of the fixed rules in linguistic usage. In Berlin, anything is possible. Here, sneakers are worn with the most beautiful clothes, the subways are catch basins for bizarre characters, "Späti" late-night shops are the real landmarks of the city and good parties never start before midnight. A permanent fixture on the cultural scene is a woman, long resident in Berlin, by the melodic name of Lu Geipel. As a bartender, she regularly gets noticed for her unusual cocktail creations. Her life takes place mainly at night; when the light of the sun yields to street lighting, she gets behind the bar and serves up drinks.

Den Wunsch, Soziale Arbeit und Psychologie zu studieren, hat sie vor langer Zeit über Bord geworfen. Sozial, das ist ihr Job dennoch. Irgendwie. „In meinem Alltag bin jetzt eine bessere Psychologin, als ich es jemals hätte sein können", gibt sie augenzwinkernd zu bedenken. Tatsächlich habe es nie etwas anderes in ihrem Leben gegeben als die Gastronomie. „Meine Mutter hat viel in und mit Restaurants gearbeitet und so habe ich schon als kleines Mädchen mitgeholfen, beginnend beim Aschenbecherleeren. Ich war immer das Lieblingskind von allen, habe mittags meine Pancakes mit Gummibärchen aus der Küche bekommen und nachmittags meine Hausaufgaben am Tresen erledigt", erinnert sich Lu Geipel. „Als ich 14 Jahre alt war, hat meine Mum gesagt, sie wird jetzt langsam zu alt, und hat mich zu all ihren Saisonjobs geschickt. Natürlich ist das nicht erlaubt als Teenie, aber ich wollte Geld verdienen. Damit fing alles an. Irgendwann habe ich mir dann meine eigenen Jobs gesucht." Sie wurde schnell zum rebellischen Kind, das früh von zu Hause auszog und bereits zu Fachabi-Zeiten 40-Stunden-Schichten pro Woche schob. Sie fand Spaß daran, suchte sich einen

She abandoned her desire to study social work and psychology a long time ago. Yet social work is still her job. Kind of. "In my everyday life, I'm a better psychologist now than I ever could have been," she admits with a wink. In fact, she says, there has never been anything else in her life but the catering business. "My mother worked a lot in and with restaurants, so I helped out as a little girl, starting with emptying ashtrays. I was always everyone's favorite kid, getting my pancakes with gummy bears from the kitchen at lunch and doing my homework on the counter in the afternoon," Lu Geipel recalls. "When I was 14, my mom said she was getting too old now and sent me to all her seasonal jobs. Of course, that's not allowed as a teen, but I wanted to make money. That's where it all started. Eventually, I started getting my own jobs." She quickly became a rebellious kid, leaving home early and working 40-hour weeks even in her technical school days. She had fun doing it, looked for an apprenticeship as a restaurant specialist in a store in Prenzlauer Berg, and there she encountered "every tourist Berlin had ever seen." She moved to

GIN INSIDER

LU ALONE IN THE BAR – HOW A BERLIN WOMAN STIRS UP A SCENE THAT IS (STILL) DOMINATED BY MEN

Ausbildungsplatz zur Restaurantfachfrau in einem Laden in Prenzlauer Berg und begegnete dort „jedem Touri, den Berlin gesehen hat". Sie wechselte in das Palace Hotel, wurde zum Bar-Azubi und Marcus Wolff ihr Mentor. „Zusammen haben wir damals das erste House of Gin aufgemacht. Nach der Ausbildung bin ich Marcus Wolff nach Stuttgart gefolgt, um da eine neue Bar für jemanden aufzumachen, der eine Menge Geld hatte. Das wurde aber nicht realisiert und so bin ich zurück nach Berlin. Stuttgart taugte mir nichts."

Zu Gast als Quotenfrau

Lu Geipel ist in Berlin geblieben. Inzwischen hat sie sich einen eigenen Namen in der Branche gemacht und gehört damit zu den wenigen Frauen in dieser immer noch weitgehend männerdominierten Barwelt, die darin ihre Verwirklichung finden. Sie arbeitete in der Kantine Kohlmann, in der Torbar, im Schloss Neuschweinsteiger. „Ich bin immer in leitende Positionen gerutscht, weil niemand anderes mehr da war. Dabei hat sich irgendwann herausgestellt, dass ich im Consulting ganz gut bin. Ich wurde also angeheuert, um Bars ökonomischer zu machen." Doch Lu Geipel sah sich im Laufe ihrer bisherigen Karriere auch mit anderen Situationen konfrontiert, Situationen, in denen ihr aufgrund ihres Geschlechts nicht zugetraut wurde, den Job hinter der Bar zu erledigen. „Ich bin Männern begegnet, die mich nicht eingestellt haben, weil sie nicht wollten, dass ich abends den Laden abschließe. Die hatten kein Vertrauen in mich", erinnert sie sich. „Als ich damals in meinem Job anfing, gab es nicht sehr viele Frauen in einer ähnlichen Position wie meiner. Weil wir etwas Besonderes waren, wurden wir dann irgendwann viele, doch letztlich sind nur ein paar von uns geblieben." Um hinter dem Tresen einer Bar zu stehen, bedarf es des Selbstvertrauens und der Stärke, für sich selbst einstehen zu können. Eigenschaften, mit denen Lu Geipel seit ihrer Kindheit dienen kann. Sie ist 1990 geboren, emanzipiert aufgewachsen, mutig, willensstark, strebsam. Inzwischen ist sie Mitglied in der Liga der außergewöhnlichen Frauen, ein von Lillet ins Leben gerufenes Bartenderinnen-Netzwerk mit Mitgliedern aus Deutschland, Österreich und der Schweiz. Die Community wurde ins Leben gerufen, damit Frauen aus der Bar-Szene die Möglichkeit haben, sich adäquat auszutauschen. Zudem ginge es darum, die Popularität des Jobs zu steigern. „Es gab Events, zu denen ich nur eingeladen wurde, um die Quotenfrau zu spielen. Das habe ich auch eine Weile mitgemacht, um mich zu positionieren. Das muss ich jetzt nicht mehr."

Innerhalb ihrer bisherigen Laufbahn habe es verschiedene Situationen gegeben, die eine besondere Entschlossenheit erfordert hätten, zum Beispiel zu kündigen, weil eine Position an einen Mann mit weniger Talent und einer wechselhaften Vita vergeben worden sei. Sowohl auf Arbeitgeberseite als auch vonseiten des Gastes habe Lu Geipel gute wie schlechte Erfahrungen gesammelt: Sie habe zuvorkommende Herren erlebt und Chauvinisten getroffen. Sie habe in einem Gentlemen's Club gearbeitet, bei dem sie mit fünf Frauen hinter dem Tresen stand und gelernt habe, Tequila zu trinken, zwischen samtenen Vorhängen und braunen Ledersesseln. Sie wurde „Mäuschen" getauft und als Bedienung in kurze

the "Palace Hotel," became a bar apprentice, and Marcus Wolff became her mentor. "Together we opened the first House of Gin back then. After the apprenticeship, I followed Marcus Wolff to Stuttgart to open a new bar there for someone who had a lot of money. But that didn't come to fruition, so I went back to Berlin. Stuttgart didn't suit me."

Guesting as a token woman

Lu Geipel stayed in Berlin. She has since made her own name in the industry, making her one of the few women in this still largely male-dominated bar world to find fulfillment in it. She has worked at the Kohlmann Canteen, the Torbar, the Neuschweinsteiger Castle. "I always slipped into managerial positions because there was no one else. At some point, it turned out that I was quite good at consulting. So I was hired to make bars more commercial." But Lu Geipel has also faced other situations during her career so far, situations where she wasn't trusted to do the job behind the bar because of her gender. "I've encountered men who didn't hire me because they didn't want me to close up store at night. They didn't have confidence in me," she recalls. "When I started in my job back then, there weren't very many women in a position similar to mine. Then, because we were special, eventually there were a lot of us, but ultimately only a few of us stayed." Being behind the counter of a bar requires confidence and the strength to stand

Röckchen und Nylons gesteckt. Sie wurde gefragt, ob sie mal den Chef holen könne, weil es sich nur mit diesem lohne, über den Schnaps in den prallgefüllten Bar-Regalen zu sprechen. Sie habe indiskrete Angebote ausgeschlagen und sich für andere Frauen eingesetzt, die sich brenzligen Situationen ausgesetzt sahen. Der Tresen sei ihr Beschützer, ihre Barriere. Dahinter fühle sie sich groß und stark. „Andere brauchen dafür eine Nase Koks", sagt sie. Sie wisse ganz genau, dass Alkohol Hemmungen löst und dass nicht jeder gut damit umgehen kann. „Ich kann mich an einen Samstagabend in der Kantine Kohlmann erinnern. Der Laden war brechend voll. Lediglich am Tresen waren noch zwei Plätze frei. Ein großer, breitschultriger Mann setzte sich in Begleitung einer jungen Dame genau vor unsere Nase. Meine Barchefin und ich dachten damals, die beiden wären ein Paar – bis der Typ seiner Begleitung immer mehr auf den Schoß kletterte. Das Mädchen stand auf, suchte Hilfe. Wir haben sie zu uns hinter die Bar geholt. Dem Kerl habe ich die Rechnung hingelegt, ihn gebeten zu zahlen und den Laden zu verlassen. Er hat über mich hinweggeguckt und angefangen, mit meinen männlichen Kollegen zu diskutieren. Also wurde ich laut. Am Ende entgegnete mir mein Chef, ich solle mich nicht so verhalten hinterm Tresen. Dass der Typ uns nach unserer Schicht aufgelauert hat, war egal." Die Frage, die im Gedächtnis bleibt: „Was mache ich, wenn ich alleine in einem

up for yourself. Qualities that Lu Geipel has been able to exhibit since childhood. She was born in 1990, grew up emancipated, courageous, strong-willed, ambitious. She is now a member of the League of Extraordinary Women, a network of female bartenders launched by Lillet with members from Germany, Austria and Switzerland. The community was founded so that women from the bar scene would have the right opportunity to exchange ideas. In addition, she said, the goal was to increase the popularity of the job. "There were events to which I was invited only to play the token woman. I went along with that for a while, too, to position myself, but I don't have to do that anymore."

During her career so far, she says, there have been various situations that have required a special determination, for example to resign because a position was given to a man with less talent and a shaky resume. Both on the employer side and on the guest side, Lu Geipel has had a mix of good and bad experiences. She encountered courteous gentlemen and chauvinists. She worked in a gentlemen's club, where she stood behind the counter with five women and learned to drink tequila between velvet curtains and brown leather armchairs. She was given the moniker "Mäuschen" [little mouse] and put in short skirts and stockings as a waitress. She was asked if she could fetch the boss sometime, because it was only worth talking to him about the liquor on the bulging bar shelves. She rebutted indiscreet offers and stood up for other women who found themselves in dicey situations. The bar, she said, was her protector, her barrier. Behind it, she felt big and strong. "Others need a nose of coke for that," she says. She knows full well that alcohol releases inhibitions and that not everyone handles it well. "I remember one Saturday night at the Kohlmann Canteen. The place was packed. Only two seats were still free at the counter. A tall, broad-shouldered man sat down right in front of us, accompanied by a young lady. My bar manager and I thought at the time that the two were a couple – till the guy kept climbing on her lap. The girl stood up, looking for help. We got her to join us behind the bar. I laid the bill on the guy, asked him to pay and leave the place. He looked right past me and started arguing with my male colleagues. So I turned up the volume. In the end, my boss replied that I shouldn't behave like that behind the counter. The fact that the guy ambushed us after our shift didn't matter." The question that sticks in mind: "What do I do when I'm alone in a store? When I'm the last one, the one locking up?" She works in the multicultural Neukölln, a place with an image that wavers between hip trendy neighborhood and scary clan atmosphere. She has no fears, she says. Most of the guests are "sweet as sugar," she says. Lu Geipel likes the Berlin mentality and she likes what Berlin does to others. Berlin triggers a feeling of freedom, of independence and friendly rebelliousness, she says. All the things women need to bring with them if they want to succeed as bartenders. "I fought for a long time to be noticed not for my breasts, but for my smart head. I showed backbone, didn't let it get me down, had balls like a man. Of course, I also had some fantastic bosses who recognized that." Having women on the team basically has advantages, she said. "I ended up being able to do better than men more often in job interviews. A lot

Laden bin? Wenn ich die Letzte bin, diejenige, die abschließt?" Sie arbeitet im multikulturellen Neukölln, dessen Image zwischen hippen Szene-Viertel und beängstigender Clan-Atmosphäre wandelt. Angst habe sie keine. Die meisten Gäste seien „zuckersüß". Lu Geipel mag die Berliner Mentalität und sie mag das, was Berlin mit anderen macht. Berlin löse ein Gefühl von Freiheit aus, von Unabhängigkeit und freundlichem Rebellentum. All das, was Frauen mitbringen müssten, wenn sie als Bartenderinnen erfolgreich sein wollen. „Ich habe lange dafür gekämpft, dass ich nicht wegen meiner Brüste, sondern wegen meines klugen Kopfes wahrgenommen werde. Ich habe Rückgrat bewiesen, mich nicht kleinkriegen lassen, Eier wie ein Mann gehabt. Natürlich hatte ich auch einige fantastische Chefs, die das erkannt haben." Frauen im Team zu haben, habe grundsätzlich Vorteile. „Am Ende konnte ich mich in Vorstellungsgesprächen häufiger gegen Männer durchsetzen. Viele Barbesitzer merken, dass die sozialen Fähigkeiten einer Frau, die Empathie, die sie ausstrahlt, wirklich praktisch sind und dass das oft den Jungs fehlt. Frauen denken, bevor sie die Faust benutzen, schätzen die Situationen oftmals besser und bewusster ein."

Der gelbe Mexikaner

Lu Geipel habe schon das ein oder andere Mal darüber nachgedacht, selbst eine Bar zu führen. Das Personal würde sie fifty-fifty aufteilen, die eine Hälfte Männer, die andere Hälfte Frauen. In der Torbar habe sie bereits weitreichende Management-Aufgaben übernommen, als Schlüsselfigur zwischen dem Personal und der Leitung. Ihr gefällt der Kontakt mit den Gästen, das Zwischenmenschliche, und dass ihrer Kreativität am Tresen keine Grenzen gesetzt sind. „Ich würde kein Eigenkapital in eine Bar stecken, ich würde aber eine Bar aufbauen und führen, sofern mir das jemand anbieten würde, der ein gutes Konzept und ehrliche Absichten hat", sagt sie. Die Corona-Pandemie habe das Barleben verlangsamt und dann wieder aufgepeitscht, abhängig von der Intensität und den Inhalten des gerade währenden Lockdowns. Für Lu Geipel bleibt die Gelegenheit, sich hinter der Bar weiter auszuprobieren, sich wild auszutoben. Privat brenne sie Liköre selbst – im Winter den Bratapfel-, ganzjährig den Kaffee-Likör –, die sie dann in ihre Kompositionen einfließen lässt. „Viele Drinks behalte ich und verbessere sie einfach nur. Andere denke ich um." Wie den Mexikaner, den der Gast bei ihr nicht als getarnten Italiener, sondern als gelben Salsa-Freund bekommt, vollgepackt mit gelber Tomate, Ananas, gelber Paprika, Koriander, Tequila und Mezcal. „Was mir in den Kopf kommt, wird probiert. Wenn es gut schmeckt, dann bleibt es." Es gehe darum, den Studenten, der einfach nur ein Bier trinken wollte, von einem Negroni zu überzeugen, also um eine Art Umerziehung des Gastes, etwas Neues probieren zu wollen. „Es gibt Gäste, die sich entschuldigen, dass sie ein Bier bestellen. Das ist natürlich Quatsch. Bars verdienen mehr an Bier- als an Cocktailtrinkern. Wir waren aber schon so weit, dass wir mehr Cocktails als Bier verkauft haben." Mit Gin könne Lu Geipel aus dem Stegreif die meisten Mixgetränke ins Glas bringen. Gin ist ihr Flagship-Produkt, geschuldet ihrer Zeit im House of Gin. „Mein persönlicher Liebling ist die ‚Ginny Bitch', die aus Gin, Limette und Soda besteht und wie eine leckere Wacholderlimonade schmeckt.

of bar owners realize that a woman's social skills, the empathy she exudes, really comes in handy, and that's often something guys lack. Women think before they use their fists, often assess situations better and more sensibly."

The yellow Mexican

Lu Geipel had already thought once or twice about running a bar herself. She would split the staff fifty-fifty, half men, half women. It was already at the Torbar that she took on far-reaching management tasks as a key figure between staff and management. She liked the interaction with guests, the interpersonal aspect, and that there were no limits to her creativity at the counter. "I wouldn't put equity of my own into a bar, but would build and run a bar if it was offered to me by someone who had a good concept and honest intentions," she says. The Corona pandemic, she says, has slowed bar life down and then whipped it back up, depending on the intensity and content of the lockdown prevailing at the time. For Lu Geipel, the opportunity remains to keep trying things out behind the bar, to go wild. In her private life, she distills liqueurs herself – baked apple liqueur in winter, coffee liqueur year-round – which she then incorporates into her compositions. "A lot of drinks I hold onto and just improve them. Others I rethink." Like the Mexican, which diners get from her not as a disguised Italian but as a yellow salsa friend, packed with yellow tomato, pineapple, yellow bell pepper, cilantro, tequila and mezcal. "Whatever pops into my head gets tasted. If it tastes good, it stays." For her it's a matter of convincing the student who just wanted a beer to try a Negroni, in other words, a kind of re-education of the guest to want to try something new. "There are guests who apologize for ordering a beer. That's nonsense of course. Bars earn more from beer drinkers than from cocktail

Ich liebe Gin, würde aber niemals einen eigenen destillieren. Es wäre vergebliche Liebesmüh, ein Stück von diesem viel zu kleinen Gin-Kuchen abzubekommen."

Wenn die Berlinerin ausgeht, dann überwiegend in andere Bars. Meist sind es Männer, denen sie dort begegnet. „Ein Großteil meiner Lieblingsgastgeber sind tatsächlich Männer. Das spiegelt sich aber auch in meinem Freundeskreis wider, in dem es auch mehr Männer als Frauen gibt. Ich bin sehr vielen Kollegen begegnet, die sehr sympathisch sind und einen ganz tollen Job machen", sagt sie. „Natürlich wünsche ich mir, dass es selbstverständlich wird, dass das auch über Frauen gesagt wird. In der Welt, in der wir leben, können Frauen alles. Und das sogar richtig gut, egal, ob sie spezialisierte Ärztinnen sind oder hervorragende Cocktails aus dem Ärmel schütteln."

Plötzlich ist alles vorbei

Lu Geipel wisse aber auch, dass es große Barrieren gibt, den Beruf als Bartenderin zu wählen und diesem treu zu bleiben. Die wohl größte liegt in der schwierigen Vereinbarkeit des Jobs mit der Gründung einer Familie. „Der Gedanke, Kinder in die Welt zu setzen, kommt für mich selbst aus ethischen und moralischen Gründen und in Anbetracht der politischen Weltlage nicht in Frage. Aber wenn ich jetzt schwanger würde, wäre mein Job eigentlich vorbei." Bartenderinnen werden sofort aus dem Beruf genommen, da sie nachts arbeiten, häufig schwer tragen sowie Rauch und Alkohol ausgesetzt sind. Die Gefahr für das ungeborene Kind ist zu groß. Der Job beinhaltet zu viele Risiken. „Ich stelle mir den Wiedereinstieg auch sehr schwer vor. Du bist mindestens zwei Jahre raus und in dieser Zeit einfach kurz mal vergessen. Die Schwangerschaft, die Geburt, das Muttersein, das kann den Frauen keiner abnehmen. Welche Mutter geht direkt nach der Geburt zurück ins Bar-Business? Wer lässt sein Kind nachts bei seinem Partner und füllt dafür Leute ab?" Lu Geipel kennt niemanden. Keine einzige Kollegin. Wenn doch, dann gingen die Frauen in die Industrie. „Ich habe mich ja quasi entschieden, Alkoholikerin zu sein, so wie das zum Beispiel auch jeder Sommelier tut. Es gibt Tage, an denen ich nichts trinke, aber ich trinke gelegentlich regelmäßig. Definitionsgemäß bin ich damit Alkoholikerin. Für mich passt das mit der Verantwortung, Mutter zu sein, schwer zusammen. Ich glaube, dass meine Karriere vorbei wäre, wenn ich Mama wäre."

Eigentlich ist die Frage nach der Familienplanung in Vorstellungsgesprächen tabu. Lu Geipel habe sie dennoch jedes einzelne Mal gestellt bekommen. Sie hoffe, dass die Politik die Rechte von Frauen weiter stärkt, dass Frauen das gleiche Gehalt wie ihre männlichen Kollegen in denselben Positionen bekommen, dass es Frauen einfacher gemacht wird, ihre beruflichen Kompetenzen mit ihren persönlichen Verpflichtungen in Einklang zu bringen. „Ich habe Glück, dass ich eine große Klappe habe und mich durchsetzen kann. Unser Job wird aufgrund einer Leidenschaft gemacht, nicht wegen der Brüste einer Frau oder des großen Bizeps eines Mannes. Ich wünsche mir, dass es normal ist. Dass Gäste nicht mehr überrascht sind, wenn eine Frau in der Leitung steht." Bis dahin geht Lu Geipel gerne als Vorbild voran.

drinkers. But we've gotten to the point where we've sold more cocktails than beer." With gin, Lu Geipel says she can put most mixed drinks in a glass simply off the cuff. Gin is her flagship product, down to her time at House of Gin. "My personal favorite is the 'Ginny Bitch,' which is gin, lime and soda and tastes like a delicious juniper lemonade. I love gin, but would never distill my own. It would be a wasted labor of love just to get a slice of that way-too-small gin pie."

When the Berlin woman goes out, it's mostly to other bars. Mostly it's men she meets there. "The majority of my favorite hosts are actually men. But that is also reflected in my circle of friends, in which there are also more men than women. I've met a lot of colleagues who are very personable and do a really great job," she says. "Of course, I wish it might become natural to say the same about women. In the world we live in, women can do anything, and they do it really well, whether they're medical specialists or conjuring up outstanding cocktails."

Suddenly everything is over

However, Lu Geipel also knows that there are major barriers to choosing a career as a bartender and sticking with it. Probably the biggest lies in the difficulty of reconciling the job with starting a family. "The thought of bringing children into the world is out of the question for myself for ethical and moral reasons and in view of the world political situation. But if I got pregnant now, my job would actually be over." Female bartenders are immediately taken out of the profession because they work at night, often have heavy stuff to carry, and are exposed to smoke and alcohol. The risk to the unborn child is too great. The job involves too many risks. "I imagine the re-entry is also very difficult. You're out for at least two years, and during that time you just forget about it for a minute. The pregnancy, the birth, being a mother, no one can take that away from women. What mother would go back into the bar business right after giving birth? Who would leave her child with her partner at night, then to go and fill people up?" Lu Geipel doesn't know anyone. Not a single female colleague. Any that did went into the industry. "After all, I sort of chose to be an alcoholic, just like any sommelier does, for example. There are days when I don't drink, but I do drink regularly from time to time. By definition, that makes me an alcoholic. For me, it's hard to reconcile that with the responsibility of being a mother. I think my career would be over if I were a mom."

Any question about family planning is actually taboo in job interviews. But Lu Geipel has been asked it every single time. She hopes that politics will continue to strengthen women's rights, that women will receive the same salary as their male colleagues in the same positions, that it will be made easier for women to balance their professional skills with their personal commitments. "I'm lucky that I have a big mouth and can assert myself. We do our job because of passion, not because of a woman's breasts or a man's big biceps. I wish it was normal. That guests are no longer surprised when a woman is in charge." Until then, Lu Geipel is happy to lead by example.

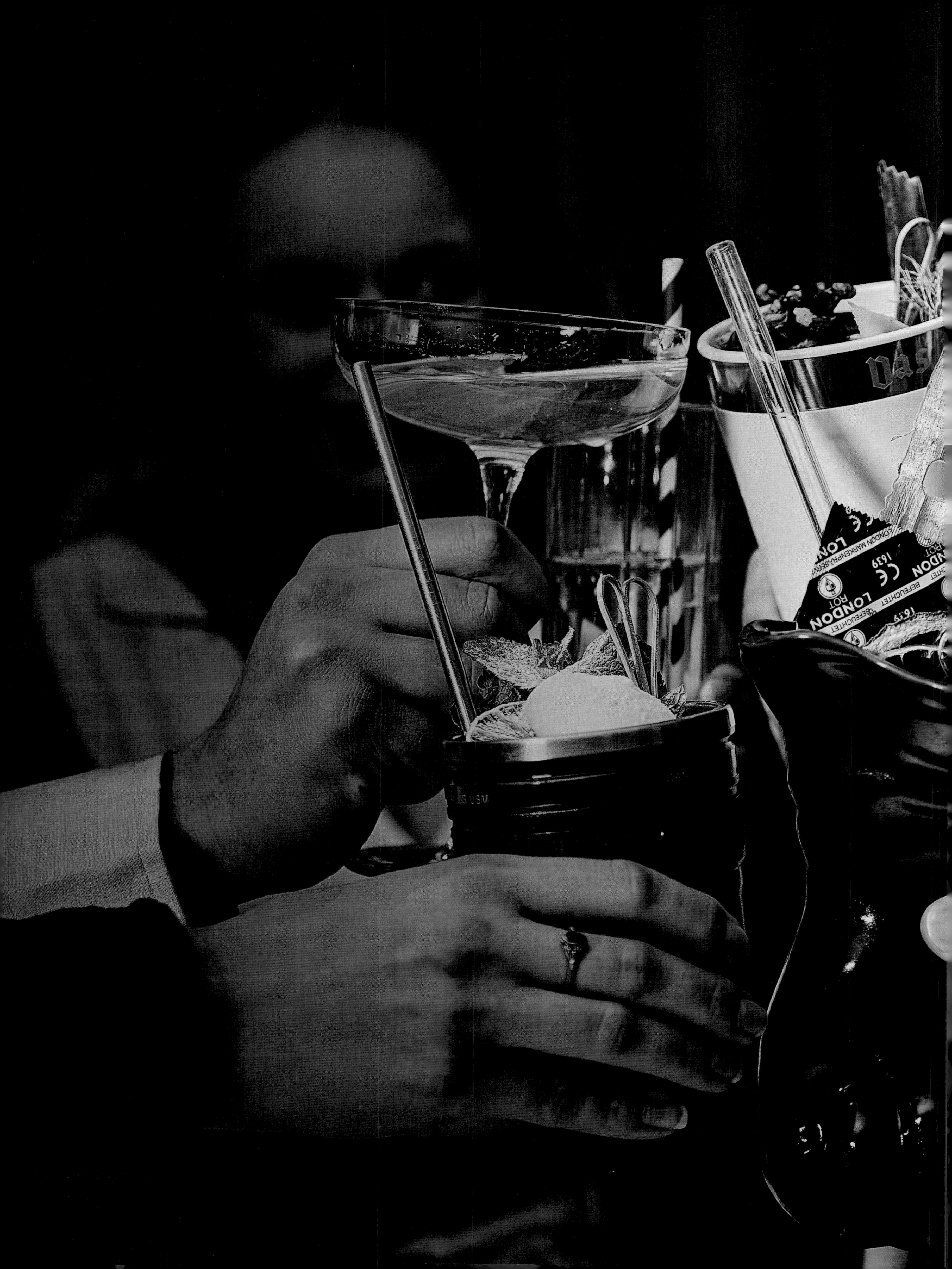
LONDON
ROT
BEFEUCHTET
1639

> "Trust me:
> You can dance.
> – Gin

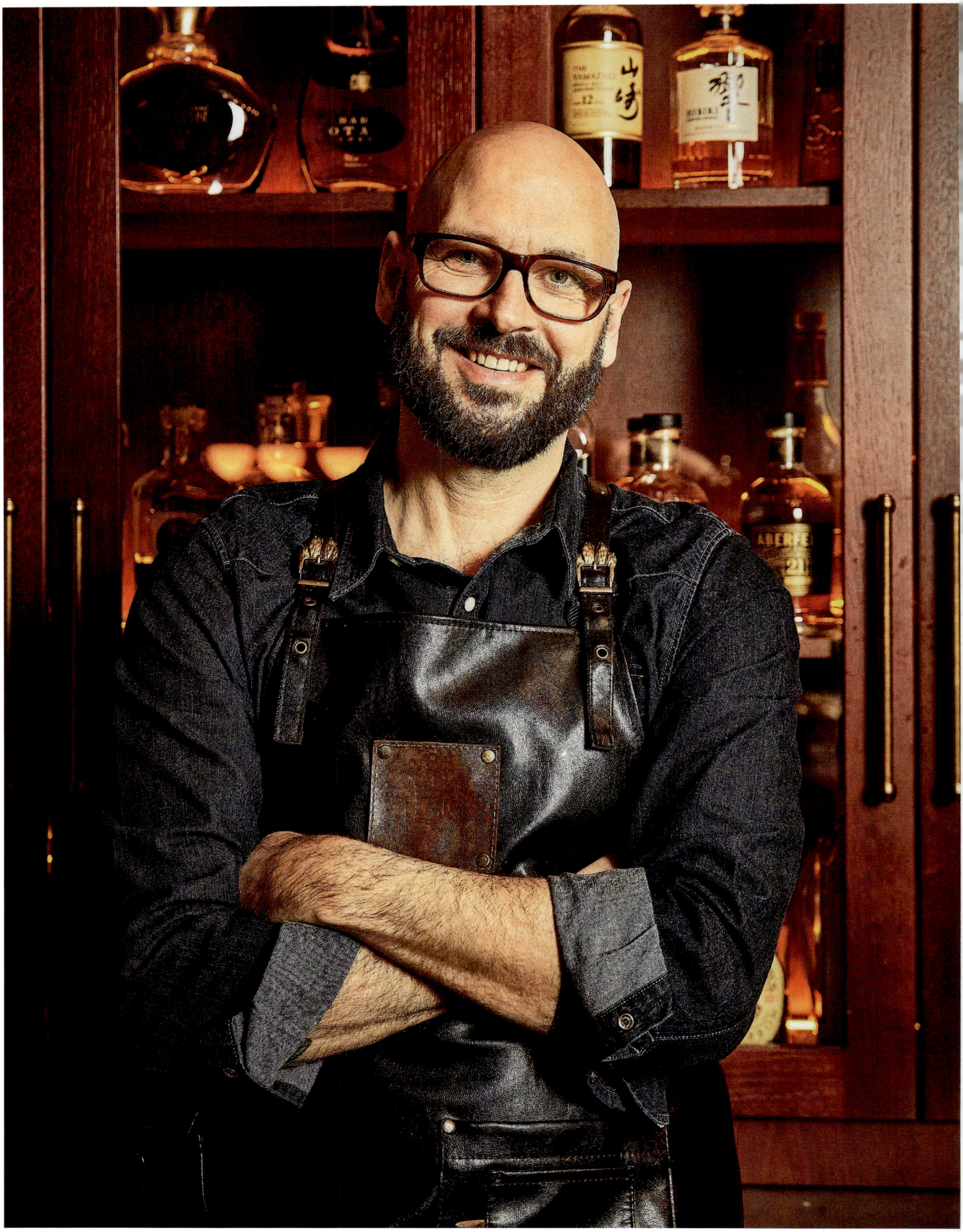

EXPERT CONTRIBUTION BY STEFFEN ZIMMERMANN:

PRETTY MUCH BEST FRIENDS

– how Steffen Zimmermann found his way to gin tonic

Die besten Freundschaften beginnen nicht selten mit einem „Eigentlich" – so auch die von Steffen Zimmermann zu Gin und Tonic. Dieses „Eigentlich" trägt den Zusatz „mochten wir uns nicht". Von Liebe auf den ersten Blick kann keineswegs die Rede sein, nicht einmal von Sympathie. „Mein erster Gin Tonic ist eine Weile her. Damals gab es in deutschen Bars maximal eine Auswahl von vier bis fünf Gins, die mit genau einem Tonic gemixt wurden. Für meinen zu dieser Zeit sehr unerfahren Spirituosen- und Mischgetränke-Gaumen war der Longdrink, der zu stark nach Wacholder und der durchdringenden Bitterkeit des Chinins schmeckte, nur schwer zu ertragen. Ein Rum mit Cola oder der damals beliebte Wodka Lemon war da wesentlich zugänglicher", sagt Steffen Zimmermann. Eigentlich. Denn der Reiz, die ideale Gin- und Tonic-Kombination zu finden, blieb. „Der Drink übte eine gewisse Attraktion auf mich aus. Es musste einen Grund geben, weshalb er sich als beliebtestes Feierabendgetränk unserer Zunft etablierte."

The best friendships not infrequently begin with an "actually" – including Steffen Zimmermann's with gin tonic. This "actually" was followed by "we didn't like each other". No question of love at first sight, not even of sympathy. "My first gin tonic was a while ago. Back then, German bars had a maximum selection of four to five gins mixed with precisely one tonic. For my palate, which was very inexperienced with spirits and mixed drinks at the time, the long drink, which tasted too strongly of juniper and the pervasive bitterness of quinine, was difficult to bear. A rum and cola or the then-popular vodka lemon was much more approachable," says Steffen Zimmermann. Actually. Because the appeal of finding the ideal gin tonic combination persisted. "The drink exerted a certain attraction for me. There had to be a reason why it had established itself as the most popular after-work drink in our set."

Steffen Zimmermann war viele Jahre Bartender in den angesagten Clubs und Bars Berlins. Zu seinen Stationen gehörten unter anderem der Sage Club, Spindler & Klatt, die Amano Bar und die Bar Tausend. Parallel dazu spielte er professionell Schlagzeug in einer Band und studierte erfolgreich Landschaftsarchitektur. Trotz oder gerade wegen der zahlreichen beruflichen Optionen in seinem Leben verstärkte sich Anfang der 2000er-Jahre sein Interesse für die Welt der Drinks. Er arbeitete als Kreativ-Barkeeper, als Event-Planer, eröffnete Bars, gab Workshops. Inzwischen ist er Brand Ambassador für Schweppes und als solcher dem perfekten Gin Tonic auf die Schliche gekommen. Tatsächlich war es aber zunächst der Gin Fizz-Cocktail, der Steffen Zimmermanns Skepsis gegenüber Gin den Garaus machte. „Ich folgte dem Tipp des Bartenders meines Vertrauens, das mit dem Chinin erst mal zu lassen und mich zunächst dem Wacholder zu nähern. Er schlug vor, einen Gin Fizz zu trinken. Die Kombination aus Süße und Säure, die Würze des Gins, entschärft durch einen guten Schuss Soda, war für mich der perfekte Einstieg." Und so wurde aus einem „eigentlich mögen

Steffen Zimmermann was a bartender in Berlin's trendy clubs and bars for many years. Places he worked included the Sage Club, Spindler & Klatt, the Amano Bar and Bar Tausend. At the same time, he played drums professionally in a band and completed his studies of landscape architecture. Despite, or perhaps because of, the numerous career options in his life, his interest in the world of drinks intensified in the early 2000s. He worked as a creative bartender, as an event planner, opened bars, gave workshops. Since then, he's become a brand ambassador for Schweppes and, as such, has discovered the perfect gin tonic. In fact, however, it was initially the gin fizz cocktail that put an end to Steffen Zimmermann's skepticism about gin. "I followed the tip of a trusted bartender to leave the quinine for now and approach juniper first. He suggested drinking a gin fizz. The combination of sweetness and acidity, the spiciness of the gin, defused by a good shot of soda, was the perfect introduction for me." So "actually, we don't like each other" turned into "actually, we quite like each other" pretty quickly. Steffen Zimmermann

wir uns nicht" ziemlich schnell ein „eigentlich mögen wir uns ganz gern". Dieses Mögen teilt Steffen Zimmermann, indem er eigene oder adaptierte Variationen bekannter Cocktail-Klassiker vorstellt und gleichzeitig sein persönliches Lieblingsrezept hinaus in die Welt trägt, beginnend mit dem Gin Fizz.

In der Geschichte wurde der Gin Fizz als Limonade gereicht – als Erfrischungsgetränk für Erwachsene, das im 19. Jahrhundert gern bereits zum Frühstück konsumiert wurde. Grundlage bildet ein Sour. „Es gab und gibt zahlreiche Diskussionen zum Thema Gin Fizz: Was ist der Unterschied zum Tom Collins? Mit Eis oder ohne Eis? Mit Eiweiß oder ohne? In welchem Glas soll er serviert werden? Ich mag den Gin Fizz leicht, modern und doch klassisch. Schließlich symbolisiert der Drink für mich den Beginn einer wunderbaren Freundschaft."

> **Ein Toast auf gute Freunde:**
> 5 cl London Dry Gin
> 3 cl frischer Zitronensaft
> 2 cl Zuckersirup
> 1 dash Schweppes Soda
>
> Shaken und anschließend mit Soda toppen. Im Highball-Glas auf Eis servieren und mit Zitronenzeste garnieren.

Fruchtiges Abenteuer aus Fernost

Zum Gin Fizz gesellte sich für Steffen Zimmermann schnell ein naher Verwandter: der Singapore Sling, 1915 kreiert von Ngiam Tong Boon, serviert in der zur Jahrhundertwende besten Adresse in Singapur – der Long Bar des Raffles Hotels. Das Hotel ist nach dem Gründer Singapurs, Sir Thomas Stamford Raffles, benannt, der zur Kolonialzeit im Namen der East India Company südlich von Malaysia einen Handelsposten eröffnete. Das Gebiet gehörte zu den „Straits Settlements". Schon lange bevor der erste Singapore Sling gereicht wurde, rutschte der Straits Sling über die Bartresen, wobei sich beide Varianten in ihrer Zusammensetzung weit von einem klassischen Sling, der lediglich aus den vier Zutaten Basis-Alkohol, Zucker, Wasser und Muskat besteht, entfernt haben. Der Straits Sling und der Singapore Sling teilen sich die DNS aus Gin, Kirsche und Bénédictine, gehen ansonsten aber getrennte Wege. Der Straits Sling gehört zu den trockenen Cocktails, der Singapore Sling zu den fruchtigen. Doch gerade letzterer erfreute sich Anfang des 20. Jahrhunderts überschwänglicher Beliebtheit. Schnell etablierte sich der Singapore Sling zum Nationalgetränk, insbesondere deshalb, weil er auch von den Damen ohne Probleme genossen werden durfte. Während die Gentlemen Gin und Whisky bestellten, war es den Frauen moralisch untersagt, in der Öffentlichkeit Alkohol zu konsumieren, sodass diese normalerweise Tees und Fruchtsäfte tranken. Ein Cocktail, der wie ein Fruchtsaft aussah, unauffällig feminin rosa, eröffnete der weiblichen Zunft neue Welten. Die Basis des Singapore Sling bildet Gin, in fruchtiger Gesellschaft von Ananas- und Limettensaft, Gre-

You can call me: Gin Fizz

shares this liking by presenting his own or adapted variations of well-known cocktail classics and, at the same time, taking his personal favorite recipe out into the world, starting with gin fizz.

Historically, gin fizz was served as a lemonade – a refreshing drink for adults which, in the 19th century, was gladly consumed as early as breakfast. The basis is a sour. "There were and are numerous discussions on the subject of gin fizz. How does it differ from a Tom Collins? With ice or without? With egg white or without? What glass should it be served in? I like gin fizz light, modern, yet classic. After all, for me, the drink symbolizes the beginning of a wonderful friendship."

> ***A toast to good friends:***
> *5 cl London Dry Gin*
> *3 cl fresh lemon juice*
> *2 cl sugar syrup*
> *1 dash of Schweppes soda*
>
> *Shake and then top with soda. Serve in a highball glass on ice and garnish with lemon zest.*

nadine und Kirschlikör. Die beiden letzteren erzeugen den rosigen Farbton des Drinks. Curaçao und Bénédictine runden den Geschmack der ursprünglichen Cocktailvariante ab. „Für mich ist diese Version zu saftig. Ich bevorzuge die Alternative mit Soda", gesteht Steffen Zimmermann.

> **Weniger (süß) ist mehr:**
> 4 cl London Dry Gin
> 2 cl Cherry Heering
> 2 bl DOM Bénédictine
> 3 dash Angostura
> 2 cl Zitronensaft
> Schweppes Soda
>
> Alle Zutaten zusammen shaken und mit Soda toppen. Im Highball-Glas auf Eis servieren und mit Zitronenzeste garnieren.

Wundersames Heilmittel

Die Weiterentwicklung in Zusammenhang mit der Erprobung neuer abenteuerlicher Gin-Reisen führte Steffen Zimmermann zu den Short Drinks. „Auch hier zeigte mir mein Lieblingsbartender,

Nice to meet you: Singapore Sling

Fruity adventure from the Far East

For Steffen Zimmermann, gin fizz was quickly joined by a close relative, Singapore Sling, created in 1915 by Ngiam Tong Boon, served at the best address in Singapore at the turn of the century – the Long Bar of the Raffles Hotel. That hotel is named after Singapore's founder, Sir Thomas Stamford Raffles, who opened a trading post south of Malaysia on behalf of the East India Company during colonial times. The area formed part of the "Straits Settlements". Long before the first Singapore Sling was served, the Straits Sling was slipping across bar counters, with both variants moving far away in their composition from a classic sling consisting simply of the four ingredients of base alcohol, sugar, water and nutmeg. The Straits Sling and the Singapore Sling share the DNA of gin, cherry and Bénédictine, but otherwise go their separate ways. The Straits Sling belongs to the dry cocktails, the Singapore Sling to the fruity ones. But it was the latter that enjoyed exuberant popularity at the beginning of the 20th century. The Singapore Sling quickly established itself as the national drink, especially because it could also be enjoyed by the ladies without any problems. While gentlemen ordered gin and whiskey, women were morally forbidden to consume alcohol in public, so they usually drank teas and fruit juices. A cocktail that looked like a fruit juice, inconspicuously feminine pink, opened up new worlds for the female guild. The base of the Singapore Sling is gin, in the fruity company of pineapple and lime juice, grenadine and cherry liqueur. The latter two create the drink's rosy hue. Curaçao and Bénédictine round out the flavor of the original cocktail version. "For me, this version is too juicy. I prefer the alternative with soda," admits Steffen Zimmermann.

> ***Less (sweet) is more:***
> *4 cl London Dry Gin*
> *2 cl Cherry Heering*
> *2 bsp DOM Bénédictine*
> *3 dashes Angostura*
> *2 cl lemon juice*
> *Schweppes soda*
>
> *Shake all ingredients together and top with soda. Serve in a highball glass on ice and garnish with lemon zest.*

Miracle cure

Further developments in connection with testing new adventurous gin trips led Steffen Zimmermann to short drinks. "Here, too, my favorite bartender showed me what was possible. In order not to overwhelm me initially with high intensity and too much alcohol, he put a gimlet on the bar for me: gin, lime cordial and a touch of fresh lime, served in a cocktail bowl."

Gimlet is simple and does not require many ingredients – or, to be more precise, just the two basic components of gin and lime cordial, the quality of which should be of the highest grade.

was möglich war. Um mich zunächst nicht mit hoher Intensität und zu viel Alkohol zu überfordern, stellte er mir einen Gimlet auf den Tresen: Gin, Lime Cordial und ein Hauch frische Limette, serviert in einer Cocktailschale."

Der Gimlet ist simpel und benötigt nicht viele Zutaten – genauer gesagt: lediglich die beiden Grundkomponenten Gin und Lime Cordial, deren Qualität von höchster Güte sein sollte. Der erste Lime Cordial, ein mit Zucker konservierter Limettensaft, wurde 1867 von Lauchlin Rose in Schottland zum Patent angemeldet. Im selben Jahr wurde der Merchant Shipping Act verabschiedet, der die Royal Navy und alle britischen Handelsschiffe dazu verpflichtete, täglich Limettensaft an die Mannschaft auszuschenken, um Skorbut vorzubeugen. Gleichzeitig wurde zunehmend Gin auf den Schiffen ausgegeben und verzehrt. Die Crew führte mit dem Lime Juice jedoch einen ähnlichen Konflikt wie mit dem chininhaltigen Tonic, das seit Mitte des 19. Jahrhunderts verstärkt zur Malaria-Prophylaxe verwendet wurde. Die „Heilmittel" glitten die Kehle besser herunter, wenn ihnen Gin hinzugefügt wurde. Aus der Liebe zum Gin und der Verpflichtung der Limette gegenüber wurde der Gimlet geboren. Als Namenspate des Drinks wird Sir Thomas Desmond Gimlette gehandelt, seit 1879 General der Sanitätsabteilung der Kriegsmarine des Vereinigten Königreichs und noch heute von der Royal Navy als Urheber des Getränks benannt. In den Bars erschien der Gimlet allerdings erst in den 1920er-Jahren. „Die Kombination aus

Gimlet my name, Sir!

The first lime cordial, a lime juice preserved with sugar, was patented in 1867 by Lauchlin Rose in Scotland. That same year, the Merchant Shipping Act was passed, requiring the Royal Navy and all British merchant ships to serve lime juice to the crew daily to prevent scurvy. At the same time, gin was increasingly served and consumed on ships. The crew, however, had a similar conflict with lime juice as they had with tonic containing quinine, which had been increasingly used for malaria prophylaxis since the mid-19th century. The "cures" slid down the throat better when gin was added to them. From the love of gin and the commitment to the lime, the gimlet was born. The drink's namesake is Sir Thomas Desmond Gimlette, Surgeon General of the Medical Department of the British Navy since 1879 and still named by the Royal Navy as the originator of the drink. However, the gimlet didn't appear in bars until the 1920s. "The combination of the English national spirit and vitamin C still works today, although the Royal Navy probably served the drink in a less balanced and less elegant way. The Gimlet accompanied me for some time as my favorite drink," admits Steffen Zimmermann.

> **Against vitamin C deficiency:**
> 6 cl London Dry Gin
> 3 cl Lime Cordial
> ¼ squeeze of lime.
> Stir ingredients over ice and serve in a cocktail bowl without garnish.

A liquid legend

He has a license to kill – and a penchant for good drinks. Secret agent 007, James Bond, is famous for daring maneuvers, hot love affairs and for ordering martinis at hotel bars around the world. "Shaken, not stirred," of course. British author Ian Lancaster Fleming, who penned the iconic spy character Bond and who himself loved to drink martinis, created the Martini à la Bond in his 1953 novel "Casino Royal", a vodka martini consisting of "three measures of Gordon's gin, one measure of vodka and half a measure of Kina Lillet" served with a slice of lemon. "Sophisticated gin drinkers would forgo the gin-vodka marriage in this classic," Steffen Zimmermann says jokingly. In addition, he says, Martini is not usually shaken or served with a slice of lemon these days. Bond breaks conventions – as befits a true action hero. His cocktail creation is listed by the International Bartenders Association as Vesper Martini – in honor of Bond's mistress Vesper Lynd – but without Kina Lillet, whose production was discontinued decades ago and is now replaced by Lillet Blanc, for example. "The story surrounding James Bond is a myth in its own right and shows once again that it's impossible to find a definition for the perfect martini. Every martini drinker has his own detailed ideas about how his drink should be served," emphasizes Steffen Zimmermann. He adds, "Anyone who enters into a liaison with the martini cocktail must first understand that this drink has no connection whatsoever with the wine

der englischen Nationalspirituose und Vitamin C funktioniert auch heute noch, auch wenn die Royal Navy den Drink vermutlich weniger ausbalanciert und weniger elegant serviert hat. Der Gimlet hat mich einige Zeit als mein liebster Drink begleitet", gesteht Steffen Zimmermann.

> **Gegen den Vitamin-C-Mangel:**
> 6 cl London Dry Gin
> 3 cl Lime Cordial
> ¼ gepresste Limette pressen
>
> Die Zutaten auf Eis rühren und in einer Cocktailschale ohne Garnitur servieren.

Eine liquide Legende

Er hat die Lizenz zum Töten – und den Hang zu guten Drinks. 007-Geheimagent James Bond ist für waghalsige Manöver, heiße Liebschaften und dafür berühmt, dass er an den Hotel-Bars dieser Welt Martini bestellt. „Geschüttelt, nicht gerührt" natürlich. Der britische Schriftsteller Ian Lancaster Fleming, aus dessen Feder die Spionage-Kultfigur Bond stammt und der selbst gern Martini trank, erschuf in seinem 1953 erschienenen Roman „Casino Royal" den Martini à la Bond, einen Wodka Martini, bestehend aus „drei Maß Gordon's Gin, ein Maß Wodka und einem halben Maß Kina Lillet", serviert mit einer Scheibe Zitrone. „Kultivierte Gin-Trinker würden auf die Gin-Wodka-Vermählung in diesem Klassiker verzichten", sagt Steffen Zimmermann scherzhaft. Hinzu käme, dass Martini heutzutage normalerweise weder geschüttelt noch mit einer Zitronenscheibe serviert wird. Bond bricht Konventionen – so wie es sich für einen wahren Action-Helden gehört. Seine Cocktail-Kreation wird vom Internationalen Bartender-Verband als Vesper Martini geführt – zu Ehren Bonds Geliebter Vesper Lynd –, allerdings ohne Kina Lillet, dessen Produktion bereits vor Jahrzehnten eingestellt wurde und heute beispielsweise durch Lillet Blanc ersetzt wird. „Die Geschichte um James Bond ist ein eigener Mythos und zeigt einmal mehr, dass es unmöglich ist, eine Definition für den perfekten Martini zu finden. Jeder Martini-Trinker hat seine eigenen detaillierten Vorstellungen, wie sein Drink serviert werden sollte", betont Steffen Zimmermann. Er ergänzt: „Wer eine Liaison mit dem Martini Cocktail eingeht, muss zunächst verstehen, dass dieses Getränk keinerlei Verbindungen zu den Weinaperitif-Produkten von 'Martini' hat. Aufgrund dieser Namensverwechslung gab es im Laufe meiner Bartender-Karriere doch den ein oder anderen überraschten Gast."

Der Martini gilt als König unter den Cocktail-Legenden, um dessen Herkunft sich zahlreiche Geschichten ranken. Nachdem im Mai 1906 erstmals der Begriff „Cocktail" in einer US-amerikanischen Zeitschrift als belebendes, zucker- und spirituosenhaltiges Mixgetränk auftrat, eroberten in den folgenden Jahrzehnten berühmte Bartender wie Jerry Thomas und Harry Johnson die Ratgeber-Bühne. Sie brachten Mitte des 19. Jahrhunderts Hand-

I am legend: Martini

aperitif products of 'Martini'. Because of this name confusion, there has indeed been the odd surprised guest in the course of my bartending career."

The martini is considered the king among cocktail legends, with numerous stories surrounding its origins. After the term "cocktail" first appeared in a U.S. magazine in May 1806 as an invigorating mixed drink containing sugar and spirits, famous bartenders such as Jerry Thomas and Harry Johnson conquered the market for guide publications over succeeding decades. They published manuals on cocktail creations in the mid-19th century. In the 1880s, the "Martinez" or "Martini" also made its first appearance in them. Jerry Thomas's Martinez cocktail called for vermouth and Old Tom gin, among other things, and was shaken, strained and then garnished with a slice of lemon. Harry Johnson's martini cocktail called for additional absinthe and curaçao . Any connection with the old recipes is vague, also considering that the taste of the martini has matured over the past 150 years. The martini cocktail has shed its sweetness; rather, it embodies freshness, is delicate, high-proof at the same time, and has grown into a cultural entity. "There's an incredible number of recipes. Personally, I'm just too weak for this drink – but that's my problem. But I remember how my father liked his martini: lots of gin, a touch of vermouth, two olives – very cold, alternatively also as a Gibson variant with pearl onions," recalls Steffen Zimmermann.

bücher über Cocktail-Kreationen heraus. In den 1880er-Jahren hatte darin auch erstmals der „Martinez" bzw. der „Martini" seinen Auftritt. Der Martinez-Cocktail von Jerry Thomas verlangte neben Wermut unter anderem einen Old Tom Gin, wurde geschüttelt, abgeseiht und anschließend mit einer Zitronenscheibe garniert. Der Martini-Cocktail von Harry Johnson verlangte zusätzlich Absinth und Curaçao. Der Zusammenhang mit den alten Rezepturen ist vage, auch in Anbetracht dessen, dass der Geschmack des Martinis in den vergangenen 150 Jahren gereift ist. Der Martini-Cocktail hat seine Süße abgeworfen, vielmehr verkörpert er Frische, ist filigran, hochprozentig zugleich und zu einer kulturellen Instanz gewachsen. „Es gibt unfassbar viele Rezepturen. Persönlich bin ich einfach zu schwach für diesen Drink – aber das ist ja mein Problem. Ich erinnere mich aber, wie mein Vater seinen Martini mochte: viel Gin, ein Hauch Wermut, zwei Oliven – sehr kalt, alternativ auch als Gibson-Variante mit Perlzwiebeln", erinnert sich Steffen Zimmermann.

> **Gerührt, nicht geschüttelt:**
> 7 cl London Dry Gin
> Eis mit Wermut
> 2 Oliven
>
> 2 cl Wermut auf Eis rühren und dann abgießen. Anschließend mit Gin kalt rühren und mit zwei Oliven in einem Martini-Glas servieren.

Zu gleichen Teilen

Der Martini-Cocktail hat die Höhen und Tiefen der Trinkkultur miterlebt – und vor allem überlebt. Nicht zuletzt, weil die Kombination aus Gin und Wermut unter Bartendern als fundamental beschrieben wird. „Ich bin vielen Gin-Klassikern begegnet – Aviation, Negroni, Vesper, Clover Club, Gin & Juice – kaum ein Drink hat wirklich einen Eindruck bei mir hinterlassen. Für mich waren das alles kurze, maximal mittelfristige Affären, niemals etwas Ernstes", verrät Steffen Zimmermann. Dem Martini zollt er Respekt – wie der Drink dort oben eisern auf seinem Thron sitzt. „Einen bleibenden Eindruck hat bei mir auch der Last Word hinterlassen." Die Geschichte des Cocktails aus Gin, Limette, Chartreuse Verte und dem besonders um 1900 beliebten Maraschino beginnt in Detroit, genauer: im Detroit Athletic Club. Dort stand der Drink im Sommer 1916 erstmals auf der Karte. Doch sein Siegeszug hielt nicht lange an. Die Prohibition und das damit verbundene landesweite Alkoholverbot ließ den Last Word als Rezeptaufzeichnung im Keller verschwinden. Erst 1951 tauchte der Cocktail wieder auf – in Ted Sauciers erschienenem Buch „Bottoms Up". Saucier beschreibt, dass Entertainer Frank Fogarty den Drink in den 1920er-Jahren nach New York brachte. Wie Fogarty an das Rezept kam und weshalb der Last Word auch nach 1951 wieder in Vergessenheit geriet, ist unklar. Es ist der Bartender Murray Stenson, der rund 50 Jahre später den Drink auf die Karte des Zig Zag Cafés in Seattle brachte, nachdem er Ted Sauciers Buch studierte, der damit eine ungewöhnliche

> *Stirred, not shaken:*
> *7 cl London Dry Gin*
> *Ice with vermouth*
> *2 olives*
>
> *Stir 2 cl vermouth over ice and then pour off. Then stir cold with gin and serve with two olives in a martini glass.*

In equal parts

The martini cocktail has experienced the ups and downs of drinking culture and, above all, survived. Not least because the combination of gin and vermouth is described among bartenders as fundamental. "I've encountered many gin classics – Aviation, Negroni, Vesper, Clover Club, Gin & Juice – hardly any drinks have really left an impression on me. For me, they were all short, at most medium-term affairs, never anything serious," reveals Steffen Zimmermann. He pays respect to the martini – as the drink sits resolutely on its throne up there. "The Last Word also left a lasting impression on me." The story of this cocktail, made from gin, lime, Chartreuse Verte and Maraschino, which was particularly popular around 1900, begins in Detroit, or more

Let's have a word: A Last Word

Gin Basil Smash – best-known neo-classic cocktail

Wiederentdeckung feierte, die sich schnell zum Bartender-Liebling in den USA und Europa entwickelte. „Ich entdeckte den Drink während meiner Zeit bei einem Hamburger Spirituosenvertrieb, der damals mit einem grünen – oder alternativ: gelben – französischen Kräuterlikör in der nationalen Barszene für den einen oder anderen Kopfschmerz sorgte. Der Last Word war für mich der perfekte Absacker, der seinem Namen alle Ehre machte", erinnert sich Steffen Zimmermann. Das Grundrezept sieht vor, dass alle vier Zutaten – Gin, Chartreuse Verte, Maraschino und Limettensaft – zu gleichen Teilen im Drink vorkommen. Dies lässt ihn zu einem hochprozentigem Gesamterlebnis heranwachsen. „Auch für mich war der Last Word häufig das Letzte, was ich an einem Abend an der Bar bestellte."

> **Auf ein letztes Wort:**
> 2 cl Celery Gin
> 2 cl Chartreuse grün
> 2 cl frischer Limettensaft
> 2 cl Maraschino
>
> Alle Zutaten auf Eis shaken und anschließend in einer Cocktailschale servieren.

precisely, at the Detroit Athletic Club. The drink first appeared on the menu there in the summer of 1916. But its triumphal march didn't last long. Prohibition and the associated nationwide ban on alcohol caused the Last Word to vanish into a recipe record in the cellar. It wasn't till 1951 that the cocktail resurfaced – in Ted Saucier's published book "Bottoms Up". Saucier relates that entertainer Frank Fogarty brought the drink to New York in the 1920s. How Fogarty got the recipe and why the Last Word was forgotten again after 1951 is unclear. It was bartender Murray Stenson who, some 50 years later after studying Ted Saucier's book, put the drink on the menu at Seattle's Zig Zag Café, celebrating an unusual rediscovery that quickly became a bartender favorite in the U.S. and Europe. "I discovered the drink while working for a Hamburg-based liquor distributor, which at the time was causing a headache or two on the national bar scene with a green – or alternatively, yellow – French herbal liqueur. For me, the Last Word was the perfect nightcap that lived up to its name," recalls Steffen Zimmermann. The basic recipe calls for all four ingredients – gin, Chartreuse Verte, maraschino, and lime juice – to be present in equal parts in the drink. This allows it to grow into a high-proof overall experience. "For me, too, the Last Word was often the last thing I ordered at the bar on any given night."

> **To a last word:**
> 2 cl Celery gin
> 2 cl green Chartreuse
> 2 cl fresh lime juice
> 2 cl Maraschino
>
> Shake all ingredients on ice and then serve in a cocktail bowl.

From Hamburg to the world

At the same time, Steffen Zimmermann spent a lot of time in Hamburg's Le Lion bar. It was there that he met the owner, Jörg Meyer. The latter served him his own sparkling-fruity Gin Basil Smash, developed in 2008. "With that, he created what is probably the best-known neo-classic in today's gin world," Steffen Zimmermann explains. This involved Basil Smash being born out of necessity. Meyer opened his bar and was looking for new summer drinks. During a previous trip to New York, he tasted his way through a series of whiskey smashes. Based on that, he wanted to develop a gin smash – in search of his own bar profile. After getting his hands on a recipe book that used basil as a drink garnish, he came up with the idea of placing basil as the main player in his drink. So he combined gin with basil, lemon juice and sugar syrup. The juniper flavor of the gin harmonized perfectly with the grassy freshness of the basil, as well as the acidity of the lemon. "Gin Basil Smash initially had a somewhat bumpy start in its first version as 'Gin Pesto'. But, with the name change, the success story was then unstoppable," Steffen Zimmermann confirms. Le Lion is now one of the most renowned bars in the

Von Hamburg in die Welt

Zur selben Zeit verbrachte Steffen Zimmermann viel Zeit in der Hamburger Bar Le Lion. Dort lernte er den Besitzer Jörg Meyer kennen. Dieser servierte ihm seinen eigenen 2008 entwickelten prickelnd-fruchtigen Gin Basil Smash. „Damit hat er den wohl bekanntesten Neo-Klassiker der heutigen Gin-Welt kreiert", verdeutlicht Steffen Zimmermann. Dabei entstand der Basil Smash aus einer Not heraus. Meyer eröffnete seine Bar und suchte nach neuen sommerlichen Drinks. Während einer vorangegangenen New York-Reise probierte er sich durch eine Reihe Whisky Smashes. Auf dieser Grundlage wollte er – auf der Suche nach einem eigenen Bar-Profil – einen Gin Smash entwickeln. Nachdem ihm ein Rezeptbuch in die Hände fiel, in dem Basilikum als Drink-Garnitur genutzt wurde, kam ihm die Idee, den Basilikum als Hauptakteur in seinem Drink zu platzieren. Er kombinierte also Gin mit Basilikum, Zitronensaft und Zuckersirup. Das Wacholderaroma des Gins harmonierte ideal mit der grasigen Frische des Basilikum sowie der Säure der Zitrone. „Der Gin Basil Smash hatte in seiner ersten Version als ‚Gin Pesto' zunächst einen etwas holprigen Start. Mit der Namensänderung war die Erfolgsgeschichte dann aber nicht mehr zu stoppen", weiß Steffen Zimmermann. Das Le Lion gehört inzwischen zu den renommiertesten Bars weltweit und auch der Gin Basil Smash hat es in die internationalen Barkarten geschafft.

> **Das Original:**
> 7 cl London Dry Gin
> 3 cl frischer Zitronensaft
> 2 cl Zuckersirup
> Eine große Handvoll Basilikum
>
> Den Basilikum kräftig muddeln. Alle Zutaten zusammen shaken. Anschließend doppelt auf Eiswürfel abseihen. Mit Basilikum garnieren.

Steffen Zimmermann hat mit Gin in kleinen Cocktail-Schritten eine loyale Verbindung aufgebaut. Insbesondere in den Jahren als Gin Brand Ambassador habe er sich intensiv mit der Gin-Historie, mit der Herstellung von Gin und den in den unterschiedlichen Gin-Sorten verwendeten Botanicals beschäftigt.

„Ich habe meine Beziehung zu Gin vertieft. Circa 30 Jahre nach meinem ersten Gin Tonic sitze ich wieder vor einem Gin Tonic und kann sagen: Wir sind seit vielen Jahren sehr glücklich miteinander."

world, and Gin Basil Smash has also made it onto international bar menus.

> *The original:*
> *7 cl London Dry Gin*
> *3 cl fresh lemon juice*
> *2 cl sugar syrup*
> *A large handful of basil*
>
> *Vigorously muddle the basil. Shake all ingredients together. Then double strain onto ice cubes. Garnish with basil.*

Steffen Zimmermann has built up a loyal connection with gin in small cocktail steps. Particularly in his years as a gin brand ambassador, he says he has intensively studied gin history, how gin is made, and the botanicals used in the different types of gin.

"I deepened my relationship with gin. Around 30 years after my first gin tonic, I'm sitting in front of a gin tonic again and I can say we've been very happy together for many years now."

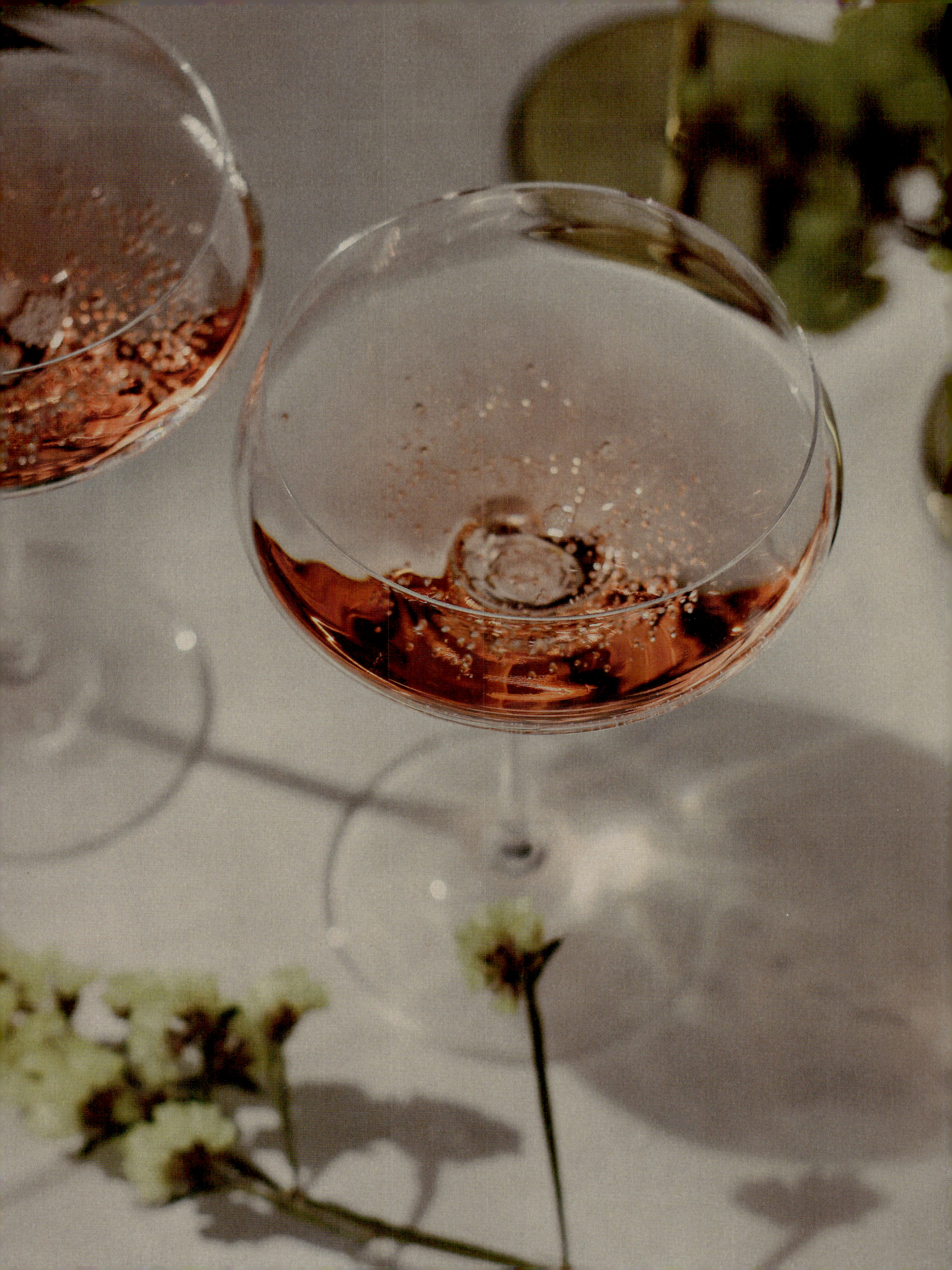

7

COCKTAILS & THEIR CREATORS

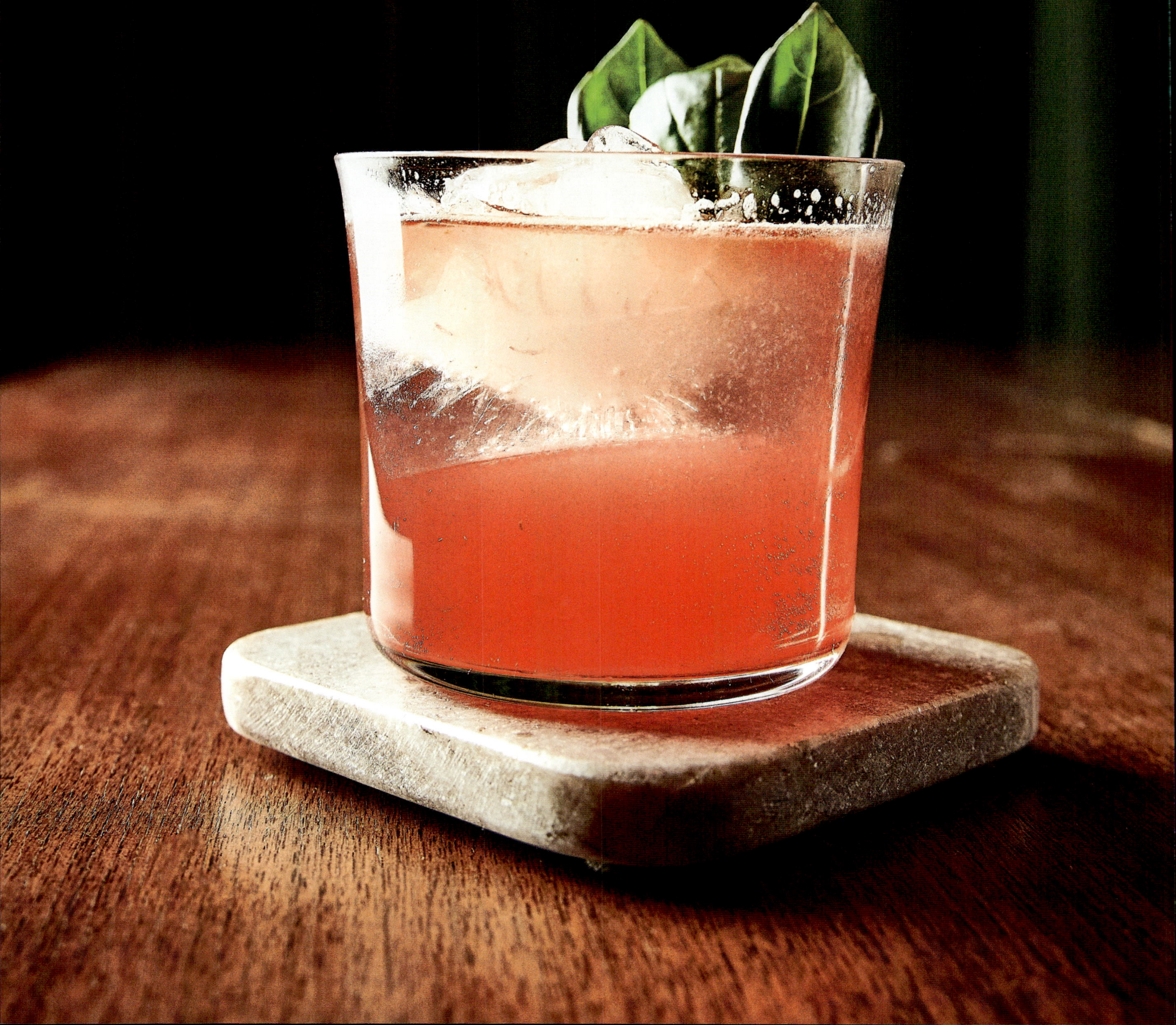

ANNE RUSCH RECOMMENDS:

KATE

Anne Rusch

... ist eigentlich eine Weltenbummlerin, die ihre Leidenschaft fürs Reisen in ihren Cocktailkreationen auslebt. Drei Jahre trudelte sie mit der MS Europa in internationale Häfen ein, bevor sie im Jahr 2016 in der Bar Lebensstern ihren Ankerplatz fand. Seit 2017 ist die gelernte Hotelfachfrau dort die Barchefin.

... is actually a globetrotter who lives out her passion for travel in her cocktail creations. For three years, she cruised into international ports with the MS Europa before finding her anchorage at Bar Lebensstern in 2016. Having trained as a hotel manageress, since 2017 she's been the bar manager there.

Temperament:
Pleasantly sweet, spicy & feisty.

Recommended glass:
Mixing glass

Ingredients:
5 cl	**Dry Gin**
2 cl	**eingelegte Preiselbeeren** *preserved cranberries*
3 cl	**frischer Limettensaft** *fresh lime juice*
1 cl	**Chili-Likör**
	Sodawasser *soda water*
3	**Basilikumzweige** *sprigs of basil*

Instructions for a „Kate":

1. **Alle Zutaten** – bis auf das Sodawasser – in einen Shaker geben, diesen mit Eiswürfeln füllen und kräftig shaken.
2. Doppelt in das Gästeglas auf drei Eiswürfel abseihen.
3. Mit **Sodawasser** auffüllen und einem **Basilikumzweig** garnieren.

1. *Add **all ingredients** except the soda water to a shaker, fill with ice cubes and shake vigorously.*
2. *Double strain into the mixing glass over three ice cubes*
3. *Top up with **soda water** and garnish with **a sprig of basil.***

YANNIK WALTER RECOMMENDS:

HOTTIE

Yannik Walter

… unternahm seine ersten Bartender-Versuche im Jahr 2008, damals noch in einem kleinen Club in Hannover. Er wurde ein Kind der Gastronomie, probierte sich aus, wurde besser, besuchte deutschlandweit Bars. 2015 stand sein Entschluss fest, endgültig an die klassische Bar zu wechseln. Das tat er dann auch – in der „Bukowski's Bar" in Hannover. Der Reiz nach Mehr und der Kontakt zu Roberto Di Pasquali führten ihn schließlich in die AMANO Bar nach Berlin. Inzwischen ist er in der Golvet Bar der Kopf eines kreativen Bar-Teams und als solcher kreiert er regelmäßig unkonventionelle Drinks mit extravaganten und vor allem selbst hergestellten Zutaten.

… made his first bartending attempts in 2008, back then in a small club in Hanover. He became a child of the catering world, tested himself, got better, visited bars all over Germany. In 2015, he made his decision to switch to the classic bar for good. And so he did – at "Bukowski's Bar" in Hanover. The desire for more, and contact made with Roberto Di Pasquali, finally led him to the AMANO Bar in Berlin. Now he's the head of a creative bar team at Golvet Bar and, as such, he regularly creates unconventional drinks with extravagant and, above all, home-made ingredients.

Temperament:
Dominating sweetness & acidity, slightly bitter.

Recommended glass:
Champagne glass

Ingredients:

1,5 cl	**Lindenblütenhonig**
	lime blossom honey
4 cl	**London Dry Gin**
1 cl	**Williams Birne**
	williams pear
2,5 cl	**Zitronenwasser**
	lemon water
	Champagner
	Zitronenzeste
	lemon peel

Instructions for a „Hottie":

1. Den **Honig** 1:1 mit heißem Wasser unter stetigem Rühren verdünnen.
2. **Alle Zutaten,** abgesehen vom Champagner, in einen Shaker geben.
3. Auf viel Eis kalt shaken.
4. Doppelt in ein Champagner-Glas abseihen.
5. Mit **Champagner** aufgießen und mit **Zitrone** abzesten.

1. Dilute the **honey** 1:1 with hot water, stirring constantly.
2. Put **all the ingredients,** except the champagne, in a shaker.
3. Shake cold on plenty of ice.
4. Double strain into a champagne glass.
5. Top with **champagne** and decorate with **lemon peel.**

YANNIK WALTER RECOMMENDS: HOTTIE

COCKTAILS

489

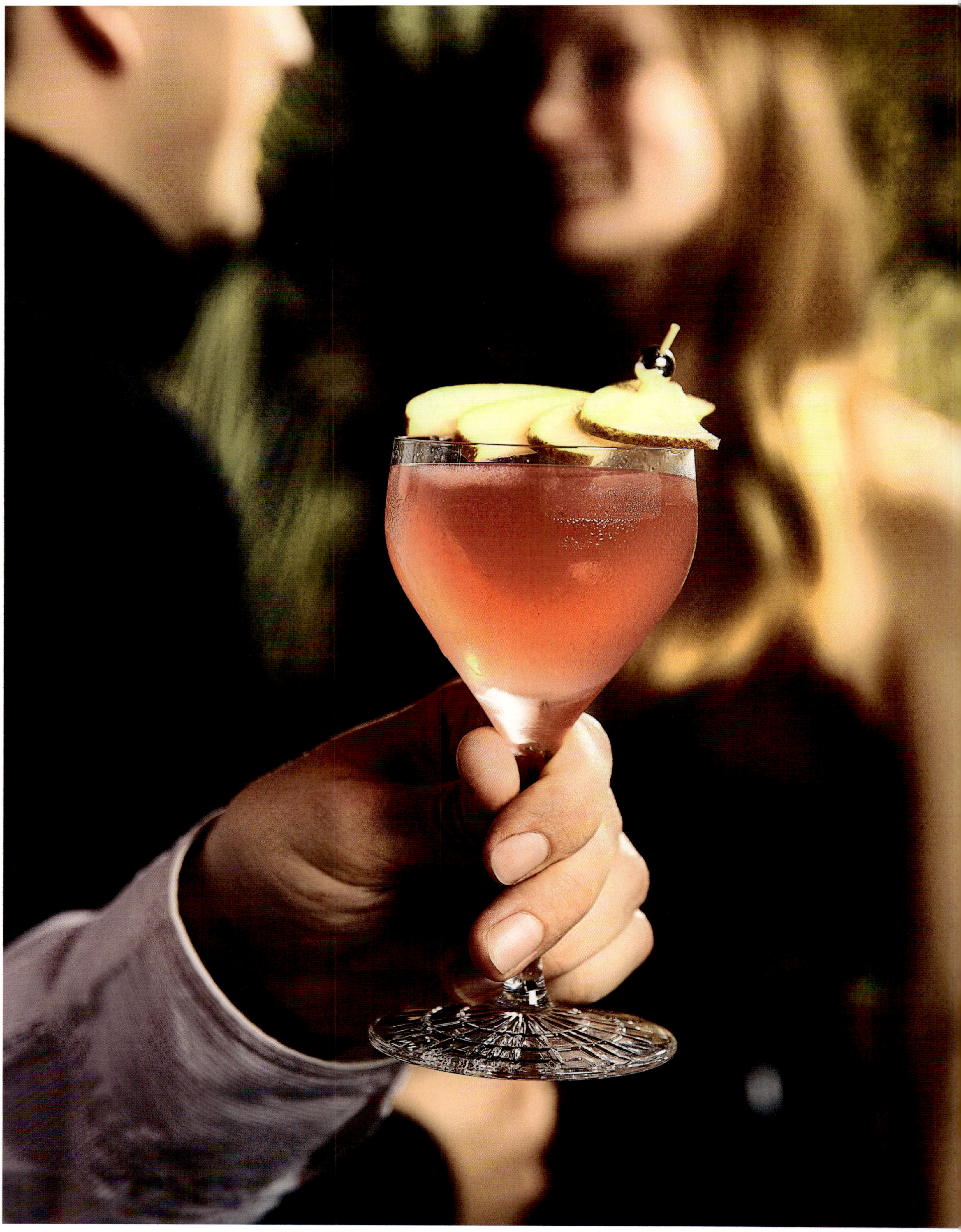

DIEGO ASPRA RECOMMENDS:

DEVIL'S TEARS

Diego Aspra

... mit Wurzeln in Mexiko ist ein Newcomer in der Berliner Cocktail-Szene. Mit viel Liebe für Geschmack und Texturen komponiert er ausgefallene Getränke-Kreationen. Bevor er im House of Gin zum Stammpersonal zählte, arbeitete er in der Getränkeindustrie. Inzwischen nennt er The Gin Room Bar sein berufliches Zuhause.

... with roots in Mexico, is a newcomer to the Berlin cocktail scene. With a great love for flavors and textures, he composes unusual drink creations. Before becoming a regular staffer at the House of Gin, he worked in the beverage industry. Now he nominates The Gin Room Bar as his professional home.

Temperament:
Bitter, tart, slightly acidic & discreetly salty.

Recommended glass:
„Nick & Nora" glass

Ingredients

4 cl	**Barrel Aged Gin**
1,5 cl	**Chartreuse Jaune**
1 cl	**Italicus**
2 cl	**Tomatenwasser** *tomato water*
1 cl	**Oregano-Himbeer-Shrub** *oregano-raspberry shrub*
2 dashes	**Chipotle Bitter** *of chipotle bitters*
	Apfel oder Chili zur Garnitur *apple or chili as garnish*

Instructions for a „Devil's Tears":

1. **Alle Zutaten,** abgesehen vom Bitter, in den Shaker geben und mit viel Eis shaken.
2. In einem „Nick & Nora"-Glas abseihen.
3. **Chipotle Bitter** hinzugeben.
4. Mit einem **Stück Apfel oder Chili** garnieren..

1. *Add all ingredients, except the bitters, to the shaker and shake with plenty of ice.*
2. *Strain into a "Nick & Nora" glass.*
3. *Add **chipotle bitters.***
4. *Garnish with a **piece of apple or chili.***

MICHAELA DIETRICH RECOMMENDS:

YUZU BLIZZARD

Michaela Dietrich

... gehört seit der Eröffnung des House of Gin zum Team der legendären Bar. Fasziniert von der Wandelbarkeit von Spirituosen in Cocktails eignete sie sich das Bartender-Handwerk an. Die Leidenschaft für Gin begleitet sie seit Beginn ihrer Barkarriere. Zu ihren Lieblingsdrinks zählt unter anderem der Gimlet aber natürlich auch der eigens kreierte Yuzu Blizzard.

.. has been part of the legendary bar's team since the House of Gin opened. Fascinated by the mutability of spirits in cocktails, she taught herself the bartending craft. A passion for gin has accompanied her since the beginning of her bar career. Among her favorite drinks is the Gimlet and of course the Yuzu Blizzard.

Temperament:
Harmonious, fruity, with a subtle tartness.

Recommended glass:
Cocktail saucer or coupette

Ingredients:

5 cl	**mit Sechuan Buttons Infused London Dry Gin** *London Dry Gin infused with Sechuan buttons*
2 cl	**Yuzu-Likör** *yuzu liqueur*
1,5 cl	**Limettenwasser** *lime water*
1,5 cl	**Grapefruit-Lemongrass-Sirup** *grapefruit-lemongrass syrup*
A touch	**Lemongrass-Spray** *lemongrass spray*
	getrocknete Zitronenscheibe *dried lemon slice*

Instructions for a „Yuzu Blizzard":

1. **Alle Zutaten** mit einem Jigger abmessen und in einen Shaker füllen.
2. Eiswürfel dazugeben und kräftig shaken, bis der Shaker von außen kalt ist.
3. Mit Double Strain in eine Cocktailschale/ Coupette abseihen.
4. Mit einer **getrockneten Zitronenscheibe** garnieren.

1. *Measure **all ingredients** with a jigger and pour into shaker.*
2. *Add ice cubes and shake vigorously till outside of shaker is cold.*
3. *Double strain into a cocktail saucer / coupette.*
4. *Garnish with a **dried lemon slice.***

MICHAELA DIETRICH RECOMMENDS: YUZU BLIZZARD

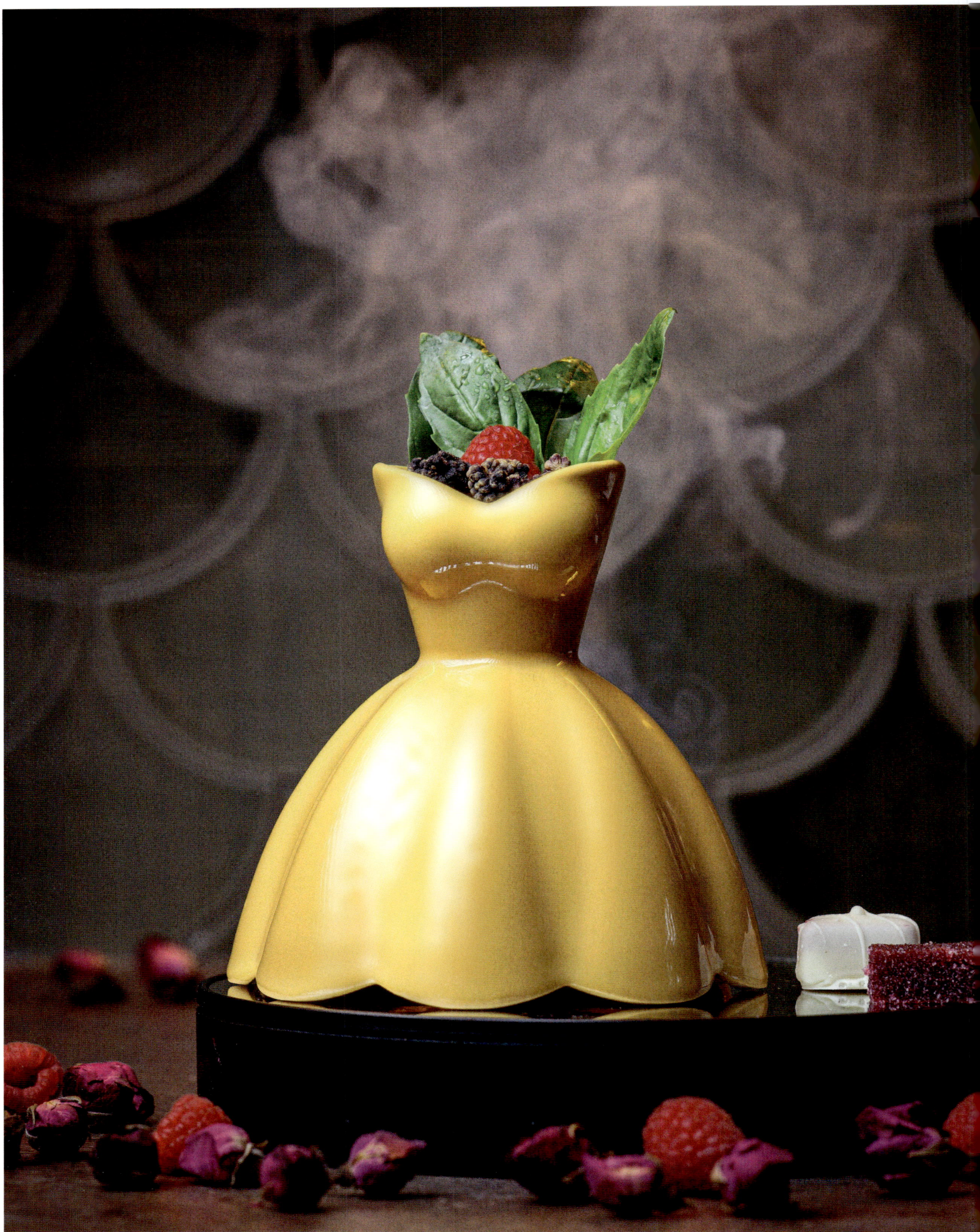

ARIEL LEIZGOLD RECOMMENDS:

BALLROOM BEAUTY

Ariel Leizgold

… ist ein gefeierter Barkeeper, Geschichtenerzähler und Visionär. In seiner Heimat Israel gehört er zu den 50 einflussreichsten Persönlichkeiten und ist zeitgleich der bis dato meist prämierte Bartender aller Zeiten. Er wurde neun Mal in Folge zum besten Barkeeper Israels ernannt. Als Meister der Aromen und Illusionen räumt er einen internationalen Award nach dem nächsten ab. Er liebt ausgefallene Bar-Konzepte; als Geschäftsführer der Bellboy Group hat er sich zuletzt in der Bellboy Bar Berlin verwirklicht.

… is a celebrated bartender, storyteller and visionary. In his native Israel, he is one of the 50 most influential personalities and at the same time the most highly awarded bartender of all time to date. He has been named Israel's best bartender nine times in a row. As a master of flavors and illusions, he collects one international award after the next. He loves unusual bar concepts and, as managing director of the Bellboy Group, he most recently realized his dream at Bellboy Bar Berlin.

Best enjoyed with a small candy.

Temperament:
Dominating acidity, noble sweetness, discreetly bitter, spirited.

Recommended glass:
Coupette

Ingredients:

5cl	**mit rosa Pfeffer und Maulbeere infusionierter Gin** *gin infused with pink pepper and mulberry*
1,5cl	**frischer Zitronensaft** *fresh lemon juice*
1cl	**Ingwer-Sirup** *ginger syrup*
1cl	**Himbeer-Sirup** *raspberry syrup*
4cl	**Sodawasser** *soda water*
8	**Blätter frisches Basilikum** *fresh basil leaves*
	einige Spritzer Brombeeressig *a few dashes of blackberry vinegar*
some	**getrocknete Maulbeeren** *dried mulberries*
some	**(getrockneter) Ingwer-Puderzucker-Mix** *mix of (dried) ginger and icing sugar*

Instructions for a „Ballroom Beauty":

1. **Alle Zutaten**, außer Sodawasser, zusammen shaken, in ein Glas füllen und mit Crushed Eis toppen. Mit **Sodawasser** auffüllen.
2. Das Glas mit **Basilikum, getrockneten Maulbeeren** und einer **essbaren Blume** garnieren und mit einem **(getrockneter) Ingwer-Puderzucker-Mix** im Verhältnis 5:1 bepudern.

1. *Shake **all ingredients** together except soda water, pour into a glass, top with crushed ice, and fill with soda water.*
2. *Garnish the glass with **basil, dried mulberries** and an **edible flower**, and dust with a 5:1 **mix of (dried) ginger and icing sugar**.*

NIC SHANKER RECOMMENDS:

ROSEHIP RENAISSANCE

Nic Shanker

… war gerade einmal 17 Lenze jung, als er das erste Mal in einer Bar jobbte. Drei Jahre und einen Bar-Kurs später wandelte sich der Düsseldorfer vom Runner zum Cocktailmixer. Eine Aufgabe, die ihm so sehr gefiel, dass er 2005 sein BWL-Studium schmiss, um sich voll und ganz seiner Leidenschaft hinzugeben – und zwar mit seinem bundesweit tätigen Cocktail-Catering-Service Starkeepers. Dabei dürfte Nics Antlitz dem einen oder anderen vor allem aus dem Fernsehen bekannt sein. Er ist unter anderem der Cocktailexperte für „Volle Kanne" im ZDF und steht bei VOX für „First Dates" hinter der Bar.

… was just 17 years young when he first worked in a bar. Three years and one bar course later, this native of Dusseldorf transformed himself from runner to cocktail mixer, a job he liked so much that he quit his business studies in 2005 to devote himself entirely to his passion – with his nationwide cocktail catering service, Starkeepers. Nic's face may be familiar to some people, especially from television. Among other things, he is the cocktail expert for "Volle Kanne" on ZDF and is behind the bar for "First Dates" on VOX.

Temperament:
Sweet, sparkling, slightly acidic, fruity & feisty.

Recommended glass:
Highball glass

Ingredients:

6 cl	**mit Hagebuttentee infusionierter Gin** *gin infused with rosehip tea*
30	**rote Johannisbeeren** *redcurrants*
3 cl	**naturtrüber Apfelsaft** *naturally cloudy apple juice*
1,5 cl	**frischer Limettensaft** *fresh lime juice*
1 cl	**Licor 43**
1 cl	**Amarena-Kirsch-Sirup aus dem Glas** *Amarena cherry syrup from jar*
3 cl	**Tonic Water**

Instructions for a „Rosehip Renaissance":

1. Für die Gin-Infusion vier Beutel **Hagebuttentee** mit 0,7 Liter **Gin** für 20 Minuten ziehen lassen.
2. **Johannisbeeren** im Shaker mörsern. Einige als Dekoration beiseite legen.
3. **Alle weiteren Zutaten,** bis auf das Tonic Water, hinzugeben und mit viel Eis shaken.
4. Die Flüssigkeit in ein Longdrinkglas mit frischen Eiswürfeln doppelt abseihen.
5. Mit **Tonic Water** aufgießen und mit Johannisbeeren dekorieren.

1. For the gin infusion, infuse four bags of **rosehip tea** with 0.7 liters of **gin** for 20 minutes.
2. Grind the **redcurrants** in a shaker. Set aside some as garnish.
3. Add **all other ingredients** except the tonic water and shake with plenty of ice.
4. Double strain the liquid into a highball glass with fresh ice cubes.
5. Top with **tonic water** and garnish with redcurrants.

COCKTAILS

NIC SHANKER RECOMMENDS: ROSEHIP RENAISSANCE

497

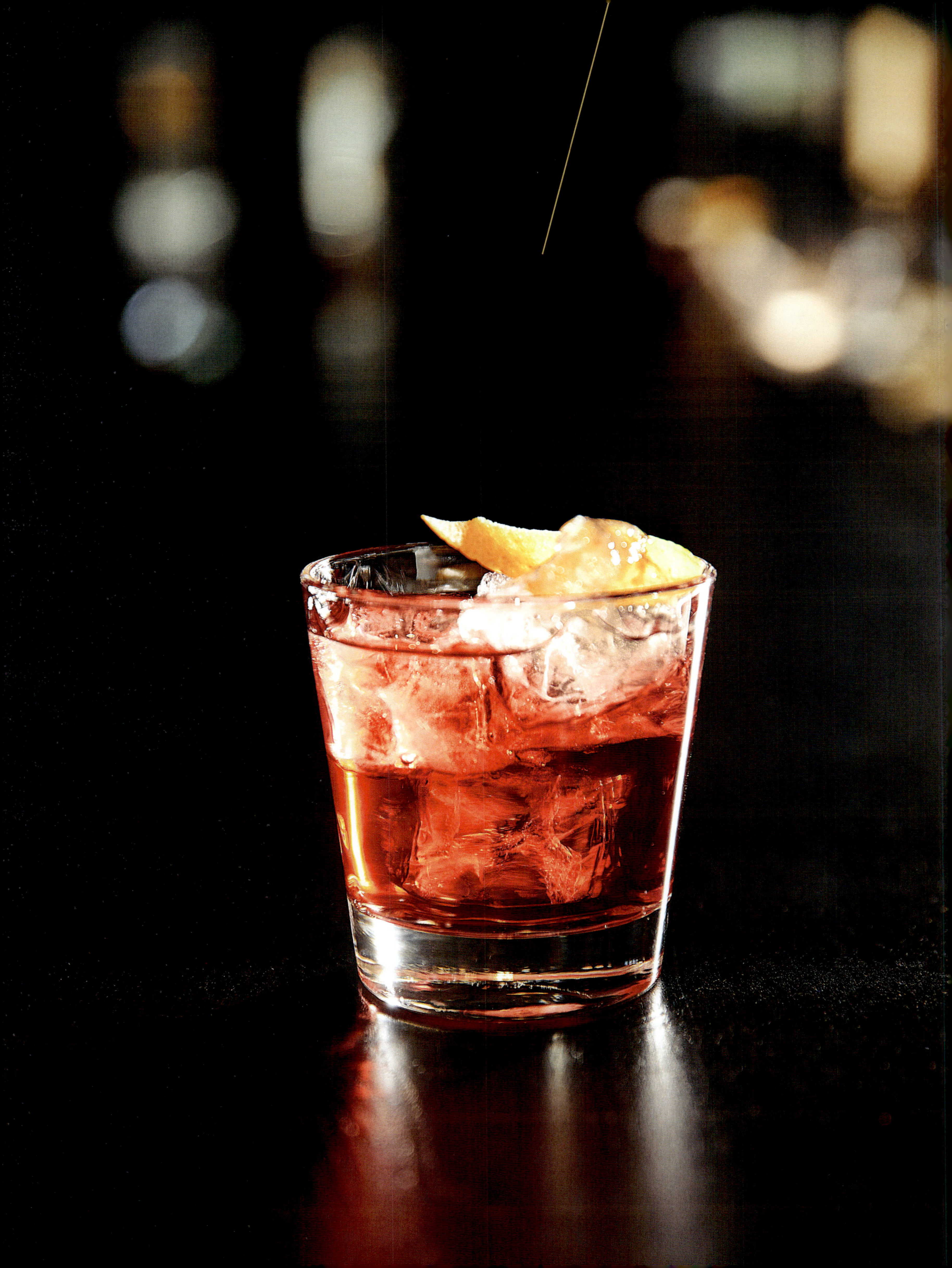

KONSTANTIN HENNRICH RECOMMENDS:

THE MILKY WAY

Temperament:
Dominant sweetness, slightly sour & subtly bitter.

Recommended glass:
Copa glass

Ingredients for 1 l:

45 cl	**aufgebrühter Hibiskustee**	*brewed hibiscus tea*
30 cl	**Gin**	
5 cl	**Bergamotte-Likör**	*bergamot liqueur*
9 cl	**Zitronenwasser oder -saft**	*lemon water or juice*
80 g	**Zucker**	*sugar*
23 cl	**Milch**	*milk*

Konstantin Hennrich

… ist kein Unbekannter in der Berliner Bar-Szene. Seine Gastro-Karriere begann in Münchens legendärem P1-Club. Er war Bartender in der Amano Bar, zu einer Zeit , in der sowohl diese als auch das Bar-Team als die Besten des Jahres ausgezeichnet wurden. Von hier führte ihn sein Weg in den Curtain Club und schließlich in das Fragrances im Ritz-Carlton Hotel Berlin. Inzwischen ist er selbst Barbesitzer. In der Stairs Bar bringt er ausgefallene und klassische Drinks auf die Karte. Gleichzeitig ist er Gründer und Geschäftsführer des Cocktail Lieferdienstes Cocktailando.

… is no stranger to the Berlin bar scene. His catering career began in Munich's legendary P1 club. He was a bartender at Amano Bar, at a time when both it and the bar team were named the best of the year. From there, his path led him to the Curtain Club and finally to Fragrances at the Ritz-Carlton Hotel Berlin. He has since become a bar owner himself. At Stairs Bar, he puts unusual and classic drinks on the menu. At the same time, he is founder and CEO of the cocktail delivery service, Cocktailando.

Instructions for a „The Milky Way":

1. Den **Tee** zubereiten und abkühlen lassen.
2. **Alle Zutaten**, bis auf die Milch, zu einem Punsch zusammenrühren.
3. Das Gemisch auf die **Milch** geben und gut umrühren.
4. Milk Punch für ca. zwei Stunden ruhen lassen und anschließend durch einen Kaffeefilter abseihen.

1. *Prepare the **tea** and let it cool down.*
2. *Stir **all the ingredients**, except the milk, to make a punch.*
3. *Pour the mixture on the **milk** and stir well.*
4. *Let the milk punch rest for about two hours and then strain through a coffee filter.*

Note: This drink needs some prep time, be patient and watch what happens.

JULIAN KUNZMANN RECOMMENDS:

BERLIN BREAKFAST CLUB

Julian Kunzmann

… kennt das Berliner Nachtleben wie seine Westentasche. Nach mehreren Jahren in der Szene und einem intensiven Erfahrungsaustausch in der Eventbranche war er an der Eröffnung des „Coda Dessert Dining" beteiligt. Inzwischen hat es ihn in die Bar „Franzotti" verschlagen, in der er seit 2021 sein Know-how als Bar Manager einbringt.

… knows Berlin's nightlife like the back of his hand. After several years on the scene and intensive experience in the event industry, he was involved in the opening of "Coda Dessert Dining". Since then, he's moved to the "Franzotti" bar, where he's been contributing his know-how as bar manager since 2021.

Temperament:
Pleasantly sweet. Interesting. Full-bodied.

Recommended glass:
Tea cup

Ingredients:

4,5 cl	**New Western Dry Gin**
4 cl	**Manzanilla Sherry**
10 cl	**Verjus**
0,5 cl	**Waldmeister-Essenz** *waldmeister essence*
1 bsp	**Aprikosenkonfitüre** *apricot jam*

Instructions for a „Berlin Breakfast Club":

1. **Alle Zutaten** gemeinsam in einen Shaker geben und etwa zehn Sekunden kalt shaken.
2. Doppelt in eine Teetasse abseihen.

1. *Put **all ingredients** together in a shaker and shake cold for about ten seconds.*
2. *Double strain into a tea cup.*

JULIAN KUNZMANN RECOMMENDS: BERLIN BREAKFAST CLUB

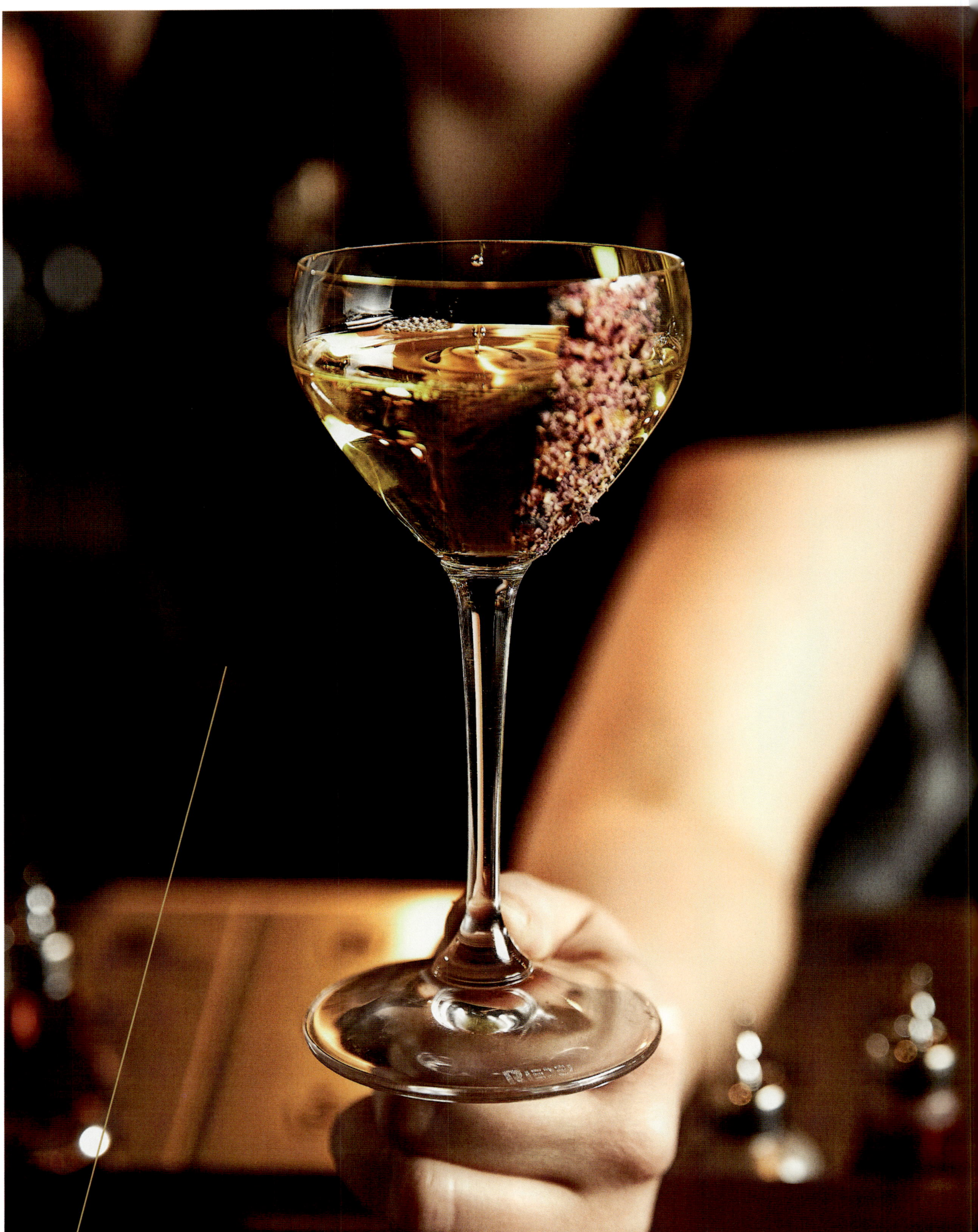

ERIC BERGMANN RECOMMENDS:

THE FRAGRANCE

Eric Bergmann

... ist ausgezeichnet. Als Bartender. Mehrfach. Der einstige Yo-Yo-Meister, der während seines Informatikstudiums in einer Kneipe arbeitete und währenddessen seine Kompetenzen im Flair-Bartending perfektionierte sowie Gefallen an der Mixologen-Szene fand, ist inzwischen nicht nur Inhaber eines Getränke-Catering-Services, Mitglied der Deutschen Barkeeper-Union und IHK-zertifizierter Barmeister, sondern auch Mitbesitzer der Jigger & Spoon Bar in Stuttgart. Letztere entführt die Gäste in die ehemaligen Tresorräume einer Bank.

... has achieved distinction. As a bartender. Several times. The former yo-yo master, who worked in a pub during his computer science studies while perfecting his skills in flair bartending and taking a liking to the mixology scene, is now not only the owner of a beverage catering service, a member of the German Bartenders' Union and an IHK-certified bar master, but also the co-owner of the Jigger & Spoon Bar in Stuttgart. The latter takes guests into the former vaults of a bank.

Temperament:
Sweet. Subtle acidity. Delicate bitterness.

Recommended glass:
„Nick & Nora" glass

Ingredients:
- 2 cl   **Rye Dry Gin**
- 3 cl   **Martini Floreale**
- 1 cl   **Italicus**
- 1 cl   **Peach Tree**
- 1 dash   **Rosenwasser**
  of rose water

Instructions for a „The Fragrance":

1. **Alle Zutaten** in einem Rührglas auf doppelt gefrostetem Eis kalt rühren.
2. „Nick & Nora"-Glas mit Blüten präparieren.
3. Den Drink in das vorbereitete Glas abseihen.
4. Auf einer Petrischale mit Sandelholz, das mit dem Eau de Parfum von Karo Kauer eingesprüht wurde, servieren.

1. *Stir **all ingredients** cold in a mixing glass with double-frosted ice.*
2. *Prepare "Nick & Nora" glass with blossom.*
3. *Strain the drink into the prepared glass.*
4. *Serve on a petri dish with sandalwood sprayed with Karo Kauer's Eau de Parfum.*

THANG VIET TRINH RECOMMENDS:

FAYE'S VALENTINE

Thang Viet Trinh

… ist einst als Quereinsteiger an die Bar gekommen. Er war jung, neugierig und brauchte das Geld. Aus dem anfänglichen Nebenjob wurde eine Berufung. Mit Leidenschaft arbeitet Thang inzwischen in Vollzeit im Nachtleben, zunächst als Bartender in der Twist Bar und inzwischen als Bar Manager in der neuen SHIKI Cocktail-Bar in Dresden, die sich auf japanische Kulinarik spezialisiert hat. Dort serviert er asiatisch angehauchte Cocktails mit eigener Handschrift. Als „Travelin Bartender" ist er darüber hinaus viel in der deutschen Bar-Szene unterwegs, um sich mit den Kollegen aus ganz Deutschland auszutauschen.

… originally came to bartending by way of a career change. He was young, curious and needed the money. What was initially a sideline job turned into a vocation. With passion, Thang now works full-time in the world of nightlife, initially as a bartender at Twist Bar and now as bar manager at the new SHIKI cocktail bar in Dresden, which specializes in Japanese cuisine. There he serves Asian-influenced cocktails with his own signature. As a "Traveling Bartender" he also travels a lot on the German bar scene to exchange ideas with colleagues from all over Germany.

Temperament:
Pleasantly sweet, with a tangy acidity, gently bitter chocolate note.

Recommended glass:
(Porcelain) Tumbler

Ingredients:

4,5 cl	**London Dry Gin**
1,5 cl	**Pistazien-Sirup** *pistachio syrup*
1,5 cl	**„Mozart Dark Chocolate"-Likör** *"Mozart Dark Chocolate" liqueur*
1,5 cl	**Limettensaft** *lime juice*
3 cl	**schwarzes Johannisbeeren-Püree** *blackcurrant puree*
	einige Stücke Schokolade *a few pieces of chocolate*

Instructions for a „Faye's Valentine":

1. **Alle Zutaten** mit Eiswürfeln shaken.
2. Den Drink auf Eiswürfel abseihen.
3. **Schokolade** auf einen Spieß aufreihen (alternativ: Glasrand in geschmolzene Schokolade eintauchen).
4. Das Getränk mit dem Spieß oben auf dem Glas servieren.

1. *Shake **all ingredients** with ice cubes.*
2. *Strain the drink over ice cubes.*
3. *Arrange the on a skewer (or: dip the glass in melted chocolate).*
4. *Serve the drink with the skewer on top of the glass.*

Portrait © Natalia Kepesz

THANG VIET TRINH RECOMMENDS: FAYE'S VALENTINE

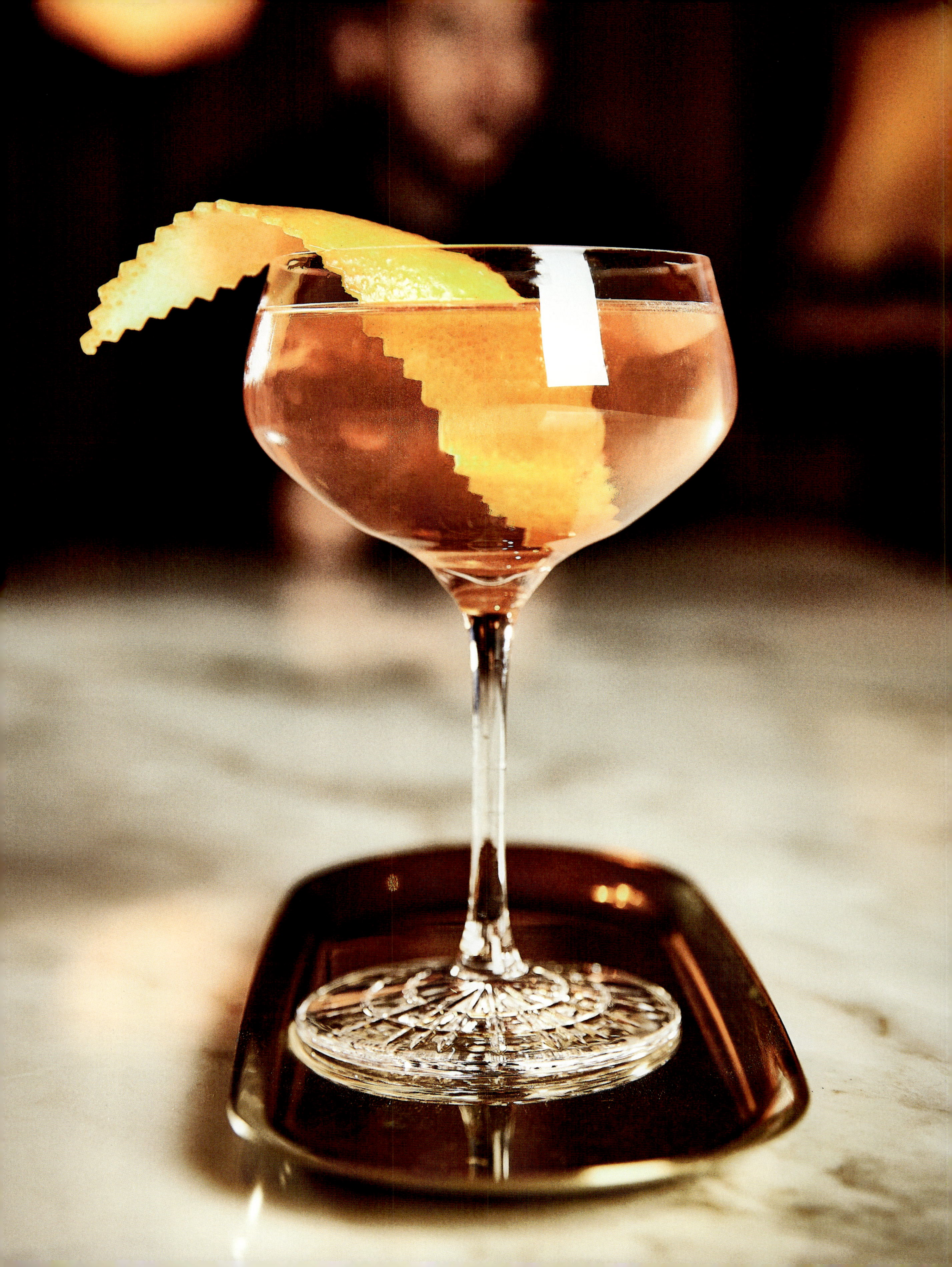

MICHAEL SCHEFFLER RECOMMENDS:

ROYAL FASHION

Temperament:
Bitter, subtly sweet & sparkling

Recommended glass:
Coupette

Ingredients:

5 cl	**fassgelagerter Gin**
	barrel-aged gin
3 dashes	**Angostura Bitters**
0,5 cl	**Chartreuse Verte**
0,75 cl	**1:1-Zucker-Sirup**
	1:1 sugar syrup
	Champagner Brut
	Orangenzeste
	orange zest

Instructions for a „Royal Fashion":

1. **Gin, Bitters, Chartreuse** und **Zucker-Sirup** in einem Mixing-Glas auf Eiswürfeln kalt rühren.
2. In ein vorgekühltes Coupette-Glas abseihen und mit Champagner auffüllen.
3. Mit einer **Orangenzeste** garnieren.

1. *Stir **gin, bitters, chartreuse** and **sugar syrup** in a mixing glass on ice cubes till cold.*
2. *Strain into a chilled coupette glass and top up with champagne.*
3. *Garnish with **orange zest**.*

Michael Scheffler

... ist einer der aktivsten Dresdner Barkeeper. Nach dreijährigem Exkurs in die Barwelt Österreichs und einer folgenden Anstellung als Bar Manager der Dachbar Dresden hatte er von 2019 bi 2022 im Gin House der sächsischen Landeshauptstadt. Inzwischen ist er als Head Bartender in der Widder Bar in Zürich tätig. Bekannt wurde er durch zahlreiche Cocktailwettbewerbe, an denen er seither überaus erfolgreich teilnimmt. So wurde er unter anderem Erster beim „Artisans of Taste" 2021 und der „No. 3 Gin Competition" 2020 sowie Zweiter bei der „World Class" 2021.

... is one of Dresden's most active bartenders. After a three-year excursion into the bar world of Austria and a subsequent stint as bar manager at Dachbar Dresden, he has worked at Gin House in the Saxon capital from 2019 to 2022. In the meantime he has moved on to a new adventure as head bartender at the Widder Bar in Zurich. He made his name in a series of cocktail competitions, followed by extremely success- ful participation ever since. Among other things, he came first at the "Artisans of Taste" 2021 and the "No. 3 Gin Competition" 2020 and second at the "World Class" 2021.

ISMAIL KARAKAYA RECOMMENDS:

TOUCH OF WINTER

Ismail Karakaya

… besser bekannt als „Isi", ist Berliner durch und durch. Nicht nur weil er in der deutschen Hauptstadt geboren ist, sondern weil er in jedem Stadtteil Berlins eine Ecke zum Wohlfühlen findet. In Charlottenburg ist das die Vesper Bar im Hotel Louisa's Place, in der er seit 2018 als Bar Manager tätig ist. Direkt nach seiner Ausbildung in der Hotellerie war Ismail klar, dass er hinter den Bartresen gehört. Nach Stationen in Kreuzberg und Mitte landete er schließlich auf dem Kurfürstendamm. In der Vesper Bar kann er seine Erfahrungen mit seiner Leidenschaft für das Bartender-Handwerk in Perfektion kombinieren.

… better known as "Isi", is a Berliner through and through. Not just because he was born in the German capital, but because he finds a niche where he feels good in every district of Berlin. In Charlottenburg it's the Vesper Bar at Hotel Louisa's Place, where he has been bar manager since 2018. Immediately after his training in the hotel industry, it was clear to Ismail that he belonged behind the bar counter. After working in Kreuzberg and Mitte, he finally landed at Kurfürstendamm. At Vesper Bar, he can combine his experience with his passion for the bartending craft to perfection.

Temperament:
Dominant sweetness and tartness, slightly bitter.

Recommended glass:
„Nick & Nora" glass or Coupette

Ingredients:

4 cl	**Gin**
1 cl	**Feigen-Sirup** *syrup of figs*
1 cl	**Amaretto**
1,5 cl	**Zitronensaft** *lemon juice*
1 cl	**krause Minze** *curly mint*
2 dashes	**Pflaumen-Bitters** *of plum bitters*
	Orangenzeste *orange zest*

Instructions for a „Touch of Winter":

1. **Alle Zutaten** in einen Shaker geben und kräftig shaken.
2. Doppelt in ein „Nick & Nora"-Glas abseihen.

1. *Pour **all ingredients** into a shaker and shake vigorously.*
2. *Double strain into a "Nick & Nora" glass.*

ISMAIL KARAKAYA RECOMMENDS: TOUCH OF WINTER

COCKTAILS

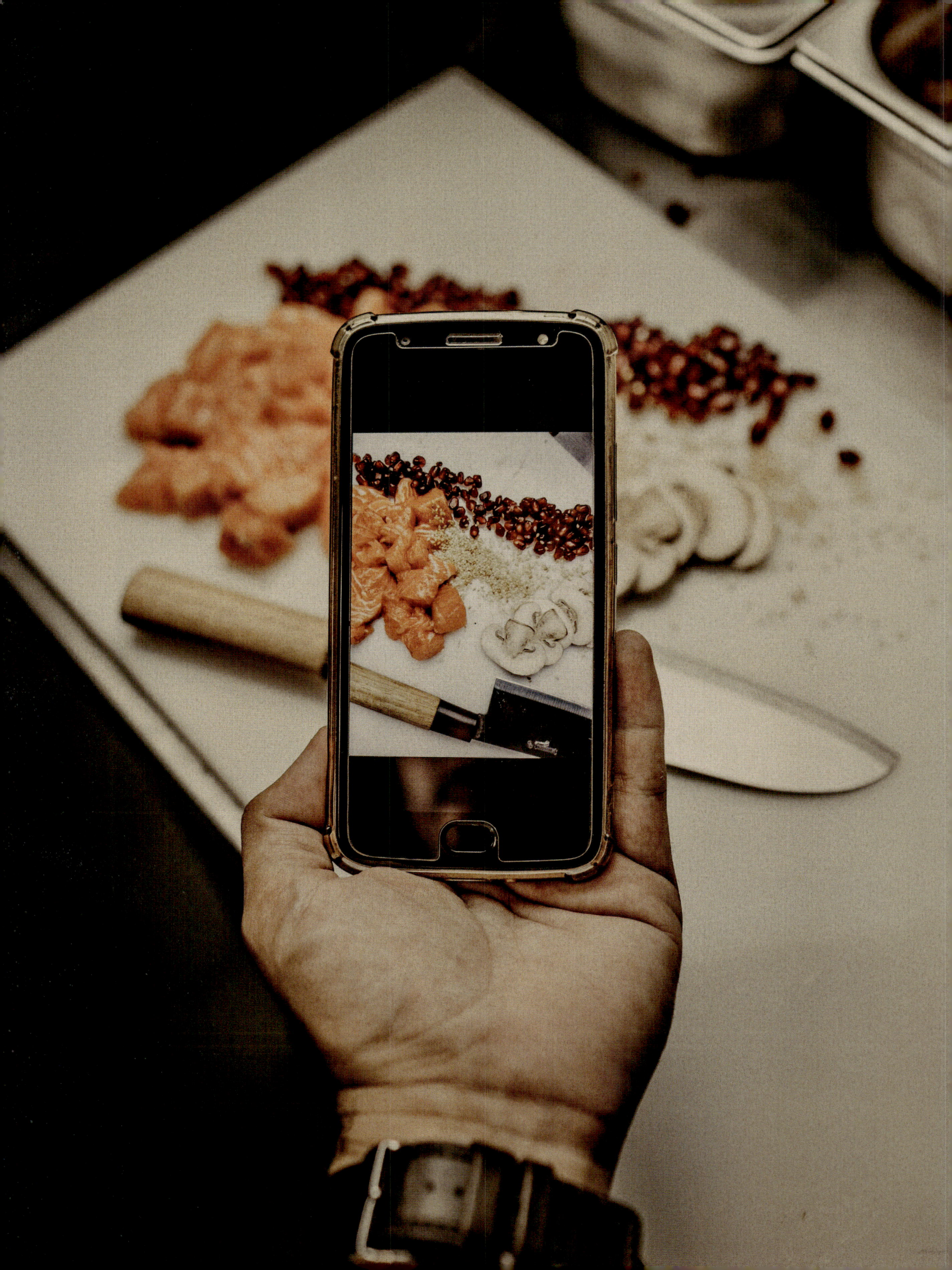

8

GIN & FOOD

EXPERT CONTRIBUTION BY KRISTOF MULACK:

FROM INSURANCE SALESMAN TO CATERING HERO

How Kristof Mulack is shaking up the culinary world whilst not giving up on gin

Wer rund um die Uhr ans Essen denkt, dem wird normalerweise nachgesagt, ein Problem zu haben. Es sei denn, derjenige gehört zu den renommiertesten Köchen und Restaurant-Konzeptentwicklern Berlins – so wie Kristof Mulack. 2015 gewann er im Team von Tim Mälzer die Koch-Show „The Taste". Er verhalf Restaurants wie dem „TISK" und dem „Lausebengel" zu Ruhm und Ehre und ist nebenbei mit seinem Ein-Mann-Catering, als Privatkoch, Rezeptentwickler und Food-Stylist überaus erfolgreich. Doch wer ist eigentlich dieser Kristof Mulack, der einst als Beat-Produzent durchstarten wollte, dann Versicherungskaufmann und schließlich einer der gefragtesten Gastro-Consulter seiner Zeit wurde? Im Gespräch mit dem VT-Verlag verrät er, wie es ihm gelingt, mehrere Bälle gleichzeitig zu jonglieren, Familie und Beruf unter einen Hut zu bekommen, und warum Gin nicht nur unter Bartendern, sondern auch unter Köchen so gefragt ist.

Anyone who thinks about food around the clock is usually said to have a problem. Unless, that is, that person is one of Berlin's most renowned chefs and restaurant concept developers – like Kristof Mulack. In 2015, he won the cooking show "The Taste" as part of Tim Mälzer's team. He helped restaurants like "TISK" and "Lausebengel" to fame and glory and is also extremely successful with his one-man catering operation, as a private chef, recipe developer and food stylist. But who is this Kristof Mulack, who once wanted to make it as a beat producer, then became an insurance salesman and ultimately one of the most sought-after catering consultants of his time? In an interview with VT-Verlag, he reveals how he manages to juggle several balls at once, reconcile family and career, and why gin is so in demand not only among bartenders but also among chefs.

Lieber Kristof, bei dir dreht sich alles darum, dass es schmeckt und dass Konzepte, die du für die Gastro entwirfst, funktionieren. Beinahe täglich lässt du dich auf neue kleinere und größere Abenteuer ein. Was treibt dich an?

Kristof Mulack: Ich mag keine Langweile. Am Ende des Tages bin ich immer irgendwie Koch. Aber ein etwas besser bezahlter Koch, der sich seine Arbeitszeiten und Arbeitgeber aussuchen kann. Irgendwann hat mich einfach genervt, jeden Tag die gleichen Tagesabläufe zu durchleben. Ich bin immer zu flügge gewesen und fand zu viele andere Sachen auch interessant, als dass ich mich festlegen wollte. Ich mag die asiatische Küche, liebe es, italienisch zu kochen, genieße die deutsche Hausmannskost ebenso wie die Sterneküche. Wenn du ein Konzept für ein Restaurant entwickelst, in dem du selbst in der Küche stehst und Inhaber bist, dann kannst du das nicht mehr so schnell ändern. Dann musst du 2000-prozentig dahinterstehen und das mindestens die nächsten drei Jahre. Ich bin zwar auch für eine gewisse Zeit immer mal wieder für jemanden tätig und konzentriere mich dann auf eine Richtung, aber das ist dann nur temporär.

Wenn du ein Restaurant auf seinem Weg zum Erfolg begleitest, konzentrierst du dich dann voll und ganz darauf oder schaffst du es, mehrere Projekte gleichzeitig zu handhaben?

Ich habe auch schon mal drei Projekte gleichzeitig koordiniert, nicht nur in Berlin. Das war sehr anstrengend, auch weil ich parallel noch Caterings umgesetzt habe. Das erste Projekt, das ich realisiert habe, war das „Bonvivant" in Berlin-Schöneberg. Ich habe zeitgleich noch ein zweites Projekt in Berlin-Kreuzberg angenommen und bin dann tagsüber hin- und hergependelt. Die Share-Now-Rechnung lag bei etwa 1.000 Euro im Monat. So viel bin ich durch Berlin getingelt. Zuletzt habe ich eineinhalb Jahre das „Bless" unterstützt und zusätzlich Projekte in Frankfurt am Main und München abgewickelt. Für mich hat es einen positiven Effekt, wenn ich parallel zu einem Projekt noch ein anderes mit einer anderen Küche auf der Agenda habe. Dann bleibt mein Job spannend.

Zu welchem Zeitpunkt kommen die Restaurantbesitzer auf dich zu? Wenn es nicht mehr läuft und sie ein Re-Opening planen?

Tatsächlich waren die Restaurants bisher alle noch nicht eröffnet. Aber ich habe auch mal für einen Schnitzelladen gearbeitet, in dem Dutzende aus Bosnien stammende Köche mehrere Hundert Schnitzel am Tag in die Pfanne hauen. Das konnten und können die auch sehr gut. Nur war hier recht schnell klar, wo die Kreativität anfängt und wo sie endet. Ihnen habe ich gezeigt, mit einfachen Mitteln positive geschmackliche und optische Veränderungen zu erzielen. Hinter die Kulissen eines Schnitzel-Riesens zu schauen ist aber nicht mein Tagesgeschäft. Normalerweise begleite ich eine Gastronomie von Anfang an als derjenige, der das Konzept entwickelt und somit das Gesicht der Gastronomie prägt.

Geht es bei den Konzepten nur um die Küche oder auch um die Getränkekarte oder das Design der Location?

Das ist sehr unterschiedlich. Ich habe das Glück, dass ich extrem vielfältig bin und mir aufgrund meiner Leidenschaft gegenüber allem, was die Gastronomie betrifft, sehr viel Wissen angeeignet und mit sehr vielen guten Leuten zusammengearbeitet habe. Ich habe auf Events der Fashion- und Musikbranche das Catering auf die Beine gestellt, mit Parfümeuren Kreativdinner veranstaltet oder mit Bartendern Cocktails entworfen. Ich habe

> **I don't like to be bored [...] and found too many other things interesting.**

Dear Kristof, for you it's all about making sure that things taste good and that concepts you design for catering really work. Almost every day you embark on new adventures, small and large. What drives you?

KRISTOF MULACK: *I don't like boredom. At the end of the day, I remain a chef in some way. But a slightly better-paid chef who can choose his working hours and employer. At some point, I just got annoyed with going through the same daily routines.*

I've always been too flighty, and found too many other things interesting as well, to want to commit. I like Asian cuisine, love cooking Italian, enjoy German home cooking as much as star cuisine. When you develop a concept for a restaurant in which you yourself are in the kitchen and are the owner, then you can't change that so quickly. Then you have to stand behind it 2,000 percent, and do so for at least the following three years. I do work for someone from time to time for a while and then concentrate on one direction, but that's just temporary.

513

einfach unfassbar viel gesehen und gemacht. Deshalb kann es auch sein, dass ich Drinks mitentwickle – insbesondere dann, wenn ein Betreiber möchte, dass diese zur Menükarte passen, dass sich das Essen und die Getränke auf Augenhöhe begegnen. In einem Lokal in Frankfurt haben wir zu den Signature Drinks kleine Gerichte als Garnitur kreiert. Manchmal übernehme ich auch das Koch-Coaching. Ich zeige den Köchen, wie bestimmte Gerichte gekocht werden müssen und wie diese auf dem Teller angerichtet werden.

Funktionieren denn alle Läden, an denen du mitgewirkt hast?

Tatsächlich ja. Natürlich ist nicht immer alles gleich von Anfang an durchgestartet, auch bedingt durch die Corona-Pandemie. Das „Bonvivant" hatte es zum Beispiel schwer. Der erste Koch war sehr teuer und dann brauchten sie einen neuen. Inzwischen haben sie sich gefangen, das Essen ist genial und ich bin mir sicher, das „Bonvivant" wird früher oder später ein vegetarisches Sternerestaurant.

Was ist die Quelle deiner Kreativität?

90 Prozent meines Inputs schlummern in mir selbst. Das fängt an bei Magazinen, die ich regelmäßig durchblättere, geht über

When you accompany a restaurant on its way to success, do you concentrate fully on it or do you manage to handle several projects at the same time?

There have been times when I coordinated three projects at once, not just in Berlin. That was very exhausting, also because I was still implementing catering services at the same time. The first project I realized was the "Bonvivant" in Berlin-Schöneberg. At the same time, I took on a second project in Berlin-Kreuzberg and then commuted back and forth during the day. The share-now bill was about 1,000 euros a month. That's how much I've been touring Berlin. Most recently, I supported "Bless" for a year and a half and also handled projects in Frankfurt am Main and Munich. For me, it has a positive effect when I have another project with a different cuisine on the agenda at the same time. That keeps my job exciting.

At what point do restaurant owners approach you? When things are no longer going well and they're planning a re-opening?

Actually, none of the restaurants had opened yet. But I once worked for a schnitzel store where dozens of chefs from

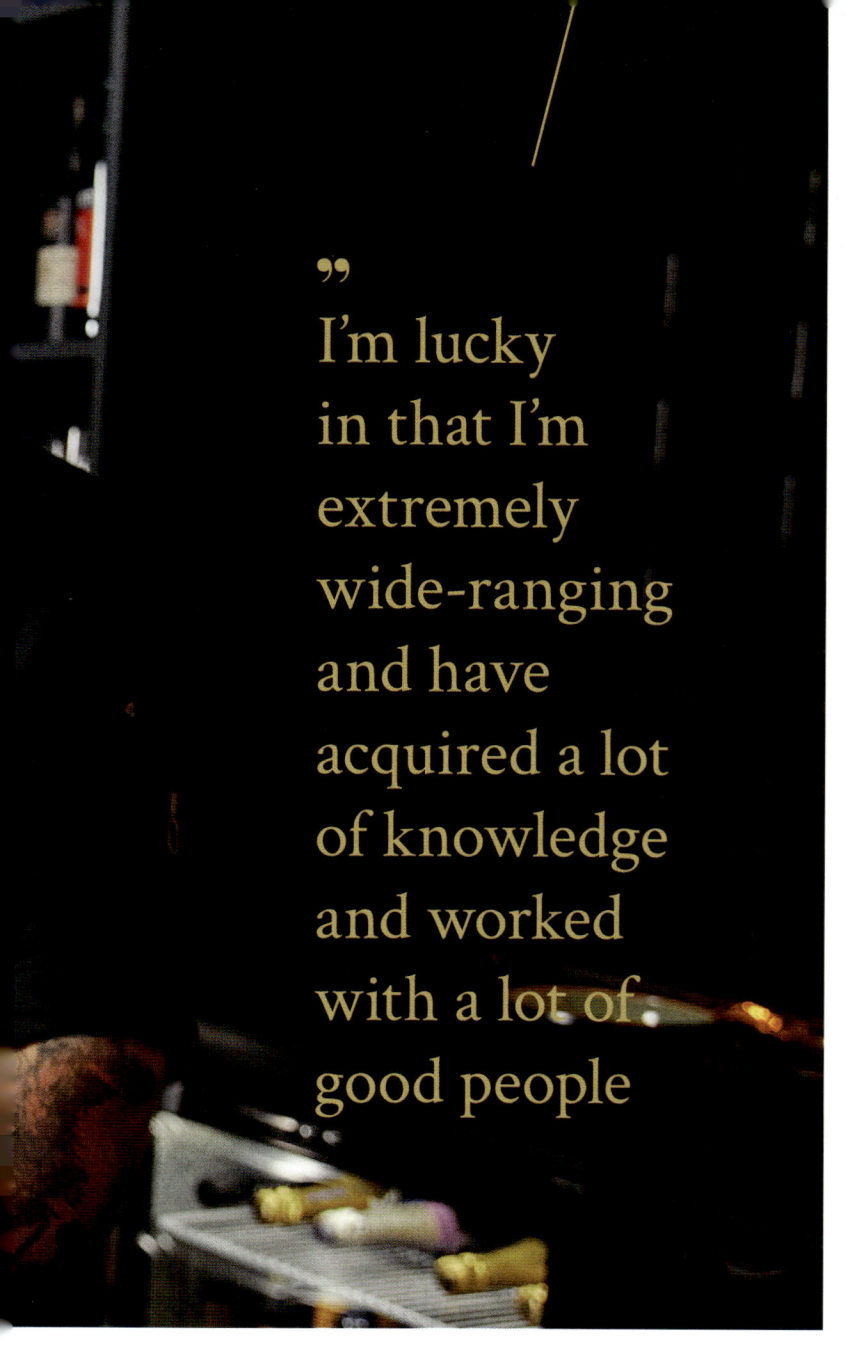

> "I'm lucky in that I'm extremely wide-ranging and have acquired a lot of knowledge and worked with a lot of good people"

Bosnia fry up several hundred schnitzels a day. They could and can do that very well. But it quickly became clear where creativity begins and ends. I showed them how to achieve positive changes in taste and appearance with simple means. However, looking behind the scenes of a schnitzel giant is not my day-to-day business. Normally, I accompany a restaurant from the very beginning as the person who develops the concept and thus shapes the face of catering there.

Are the concepts only about the cuisine or also about the drinks menu or the design of the location?

That varies a lot. I'm lucky in that I'm extremely wide-ranging and have acquired a lot of knowledge and worked with a lot of good people because of my passion for everything related to catering. I've catered at events in the fashion and music industries, hosted creative dinners with perfumers, and designed cocktails with bartenders. I've simply seen and done an incredible amount. That's why it can also be that I help develop drinks – especially when an operator wants them to match the menu, so that the food and drinks match up. In one restaurant in Frankfurt, we created small dishes as garnishes for the signature drinks. Sometimes I also do the chef coaching. I show the chefs how certain dishes have to be cooked and how to arrange them on the plate.

Do all the businesses on which you've collaborated work?

As a matter of fact, yes. Of course, not everything took off right from the start, partly due to the Corona pandemic. "Bonvivant", for example, had a hard time. The first chef was very expensive and then they needed a new one. In the meantime they have caught on, the food is brilliant and I'm sure the "Bonvivant" will become a vegetarian star restaurant sooner or later.

What is the source of your creativity?

Ninety percent of my input is dormant within me. It starts with the magazines I regularly flip through, continues through the series I watch on Netflix and the like, and ends with my interest in art and culture. I'm someone who walks through the world with my eyes open, always focusing on food in my mind. When I travel, I visit the markets there and of course the restaurants. I like to eat out a lot. I cook a lot, try out a lot and try to keep up with the times as well as observe the trends. Where are people cooking right now and how? Which restaurants are currently the best for what reasons? Who is new on the scene? I do a lot of research on my sector.

Your life sounds like it's lived in the fast lane. You have a daughter and decided in 2019 that you wanted to spend more time with your family. How well do you manage that among all your responsibilities?

I co-opened "TISK" at the time as a partner. That was very successful, but also consumed a lot of my time. I lived above the restaurant, I was there 16 hours a day, six or even seven days a week. That drained me. So much so that only a radical

Aber im Herzen bleibst du Koch?

Ja und nein. Wenn ich als Konzeptentwickler arbeite, bin ich kein Koch. Für mein Catering und für Events bin ich gern Koch. Das ist ein wunderbarer Beruf, der in mir eine Hassliebe hervorruft. Als Koch hast du immer Überstunden, du bist immer im Stress, aber es macht Spaß, mit Lebensmitteln zu arbeiten, das Resultat deiner Arbeit auf dem Teller zu sehen und das Feedback der Gäste zu hören. Köche haben den geilsten Job der Welt, aber es ist hart. Das sage ich als branchenfremder Autodidakt, der eigentlich aus der Versicherungsbranche kommt. Ich verstehe die Kolleginnen und Kollegen nicht, die ihre Ausbildung machen, in dem Restaurant dann die nächsten 20 Jahre festhängen und jeden Tag das Gleiche machen, am besten in irgendeinem Keller mit weiß gekachelten Wänden. Das ist brutal. Ich habe großen Respekt davor, denn das sind diejenigen, welche die Standardgastronomie am Leben halten. Aber das hat mit meiner Gastro-Welt nichts zu tun.

Nach welchen Grundsätzen arbeitest du?

Im Sommer habe ich mit einem Kumpel einen Foodtruck am Alten Strom in Warnemünde bei Rostock aufgestellt. Da war es uns wichtig, die Zutaten sehr nachhaltig zu wählen. Wir haben Rostocker Edelmatjes verkauft, Räucherlachs aus den Manufakturen lokaler Produzenten, Nordseekrabben aus Holland. Ich finde es sehr wichtig, sich damit zu befassen, ein möglichst nachhaltiges Produkt auf den Teller zu bringen, zum Beispiel nur Fleisch von Tieren zu verwenden, die artgerecht gehalten wurden. Ich muss aber auch gestehen, dass es nicht allen in jeder Küche möglich ist, nach diesem Grundsatz zu arbeiten, weil die entsprechenden Zutaten entweder nicht regional zu beschaffen sind oder weil es für ein Restaurant

cut helped. I did nothing for two months and then took the path as a consultant.

But you're still a chef at heart?

Yes and no. When I work as a concept developer, I'm not a chef. For my catering and events, I like being a chef. It's a wonderful profession that brings out a love-hate relationship in me. As a chef, you're always working overtime, you're always stressed, but it's fun to work with food, to see the result of your work on the plate and to hear the feedback from the guests. Chefs have the most awesome job in the world, but it's hard. I say that as an autodidact from outside the sector who actually comes from the insurance industry. I don't understand colleagues who do their training, then get stuck in that restaurant for the next 20 years doing the same thing every day, maybe even in some basement with white-tiled walls. That's brutal. I have a lot of respect for that sure, because they're the ones who keep regular catering alive. But that has nothing to do with my catering world.

What principles do you work by?

In the summer, I set up a food truck with a buddy at the Alter Strom in Warnemünde near Rostock. There, it was important to us to choose ingredients that were very sustainable. We sold local specialty pickled herring, smoked salmon from local producers, North Sea crabs from Holland. I think it's very important to deal with putting a product on the plate that is as sustainable as possible, for example, only using meat from animals that have been reared in a species-appropriate manner. But I also have to admit that it is not possible for everyone in every kitchen to work according to this principle, either because the relevant ingredients cannot be procured

finanziell nicht darstellbar ist, zum Beispiel nur bio einzukaufen. Wirtschaftlichkeit ist in der Gastronomie sehr wichtig, aktuell mehr denn je.

Du hast dir die Gastronomie ausgesucht wegen ihrer Vielfalt und der zahlreichen Möglichkeiten zu experimentieren. Gehört das Kochen mit Gin dazu?
Gin ist in der Küche schon vollständig angekommen. Die ersten Köche haben schon vor Jahren angefangen, Gin zu benutzen. Zu meinen persönlichen Favoriten gehört zum Beispiel in Vakuum gezogener gingebeizter Lachs. Gin funktioniert ausgezeichnet in einer Vinaigrette oder in Marinaden durch die schön würzige Note des Wacholders. Gin lässt sich aber auch gut einkochen, unter anderem zu einer Jus. Für eine Fischsoße wird in der französischen Küche beispielsweise ganz klassisch Pastis genutzt, in der norddeutschen hingegen Aquavit oder Gin. Ich nutze grundsätzlich gern Wacholder, um Fischfonds zu kochen. Mit Gin geht Einiges. Gin ist aber per se nichts, was für die leichten Geschmäcker gedacht ist. Häufig werden durch die zugegebenen Botanicals kräftige, kräuterige Noten erzeugt.

Gibt es einen Gin, der besonders gut zum Kochen geeignet ist?
Generell kann jeder Gin genutzt werden, der auch als Getränk genießbar ist – unabhängig vom Preis. Aber als Koch gibt es gewisse Regeln. Wenn ich einen Gin in einem Gericht verkoche, dann greife ich eher zu einem, der nicht ganz oben im Regal steht. Das gilt aber auch für Wein. Der Geschmack geht durch das Verkochen in Teilen verloren, ebenso wie der Alkohol. Ein Gin zum Abschmecken für eine Soße sollte höherwertig sein.

regionally or because it isn't financially feasible for a restaurant to buy only organic, for example. Profitability is very important in catering, now more than ever.

You chose catering because of its diversity and the many opportunities to experiment. Is cooking with gin one of them?
Gin has already well-and-truly arrived in the kitchen. The first chefs started using gin years ago. For example, one of my personal favorites is vacuum-pulled gin-pickled salmon. Gin works great in a vinaigrette or in marinades due to the nice spicy note of juniper. But gin can also be boiled down well, among other things to a jus. In French cuisine, for example, pastis is traditionally used for a fish sauce while, in northern German cuisine, aquavit or gin is used. I generally like to use juniper to cook fish stocks. A lot can be done with gin. However, gin per se is not something that is intended for light tastes. Often, the added botanicals create strong, herbal notes.

Is there a gin that is particularly well suited for cooking?
In general, any gin can be used that's also enjoyable as a drink – regardless of price. But as a chef, there are certain rules. If I'm going to use a gin in a dish, I tend to go for one that's not top-shelf. But that's also true for wine. The flavor is lost in part by reducing it, as is the alcohol. A gin to add taste to a sauce should be higher quality. At best, choose a gin here that is mild and blends well.

Do you think the hype around gin is justified?
The hype around gin is crazy. That's already clear from the fact that there are so many gin bars. I've really tried a lot of

Bestenfalls wählt man hierbei einen Gin, der sich mild und gut einfügt.

Findest du den Hype um Gin gerechtfertigt?
Der Hype um Gin ist verrückt. Das wird schon daran deutlich, dass es so viele Gin-Bars gibt. Ich habe wirklich viele Gins probiert mit der Erkenntnis, dass sie sich im Geschmack sehr ähneln. Um Gin ist ein regelrechter Kult entstanden. Ich habe schon vor dem Trend Gin Tonics getrunken. Da gab es das Phänomen noch nicht, dass Tausend verschiede Sorten zur Auswahl standen. Von den Mainstream-Gins ist der Monkey 47 mein gebliebener Favorit. Er überzeugt durch seine gute Balance der verwendeten Botanicals

gins and come to realize they're very similar in taste. A real cult has grown up around gin. I was drinking gin tonic even before the trend. This phenomenon of having a thousand different varieties to choose from didn't exist then. Of the mainstream gins, "Monkey 47" has remained my favorite. It wins me over with its good balance of the botanicals used and the alcohol, which makes it easy to drink neat. It also has a decisive advantage: it is available almost everywhere. Albeit, the sloe edition tastes almost better than the classic.

Do you have any other gin recommendations?
I like local, German, regional varieties. "Mampe Gin" from Berlin is good. But "Gin Sul" from Hamburg also works well.

Is it mandatory for trendy restaurants to have gin on the menu?
I think so. At least the creative version of a gin tonic should be on offer.

Which is more important: the gin or the tonic?
Definitely the gin. Ultimately, a cocktail is always about the alcohol. The spirit that ends up in a highball, which consists of two ingredients, should be of high quality. The tonic is the tip of the iceberg. I'm basically very open-minded when it comes to making a gin tonic, and sometimes drink it with cucumber. But I generally like to be more experimental, drinking my gin tonic with a sprig of rosemary, for example. As long as it tastes good: whatever! After the third mixed drink, it doesn't matter anyway if the cucumber floats on top.

Now that that's settled, let's allow ourselves a peek into the crystal ball. What does the future hold for Kristof Mulack? An interesting television career, perhaps?
Among the things I've done on and off in recent years are television appearances as a chef. That's always been a lot of fun for me. I'm at an age now where I'm thinking of maybe trying something completely different. This consulting job is cool, partly because I realize exciting projects in the process, but I think I function well as a guy in the media who can cook and talk well at the same time. In a new format, I'll be appearing as a host who tracks down the culinary hotspots of Berlin and Germany, looking for leads with the nerds from the catering world. There's already a title: "Kristof Mulack's Food Nerds". The plan is in place, but it won't start until someone supports the project with money. It all costs a lot of money, not least because of our high-quality demands. I have a top team at my side that has already accompanied star chef Harald Wohlfahrt's Master Class. Soon we'll have a few pitches with our idea to major streaming services. But there are also a few smaller things planned, including a mini cooking show with TV Berlin in cooperation with "Frischeparadies". There's also "Grill den Henssler" on my agenda. I was a coach on the show last year, and I've also been asked to coach the new season. So I'll be screening somewhere on and off. The older, seasoned TV chefs aren't getting any younger. Someone will have to step up at some point.

und den Alkohol, wodurch er sich entspannt pur trinken lässt. Außerdem hat er einen entscheidenden Vorteil: Er ist fast überall erhältlich. Die Schlehen-Edition schmeckt mir aber fast noch besser als der Klassiker.

Hast du noch eine weitere Gin-Empfehlung?
Ich mag lokale, deutsche, regionale Sorten. Mir gefällt der Mampe Gin aus Berlin. Aber auch der Gin Sul aus Hamburg funktioniert gut.

Ist es in Trend-Restaurants verpflichtend, Gin auf der Karte zu haben?
Ich denke schon. Mindestens die kreative Version eines Gin Tonics sollte angeboten werden.

Was ist wichtiger: Der Gin oder das Tonic?
Definitiv der Gin. Bei einem Cocktail geht es letztlich immer um den Alkohol. Die Spirituose, die in einem Highball landet, der aus zwei Zutaten besteht, sollte von hoher Qualität sein. Das Tonic ist die Spitze des Eisbergs. Ich bin grundsätzlich sehr offen, was die Zubereitung eines Gin Tonics betrifft, und trinke ihn auch mal mit Gurke. Ich mag es aber grundsätzlich, experimenteller ranzugehen, meinen Gin Tonic zum Beispiel mit angeschlagenem Rosmarin-Zweig zu trinken. As long as it tastes good: Fuck off! Ab dem dritten Mixgetränk ist es sowieso egal, ob die Gurke oben schwimmt.

Jetzt, wo das geklärt ist, lass uns einen Blick in die Kristallkugel wagen. Was hält die Zukunft für Kristof Mulack bereit? Eine interessante Fernsehkarriere vielleicht?
Zu den Dingen, die ich in den vergangenen Jahren immer mal wieder gemacht habe, zählen Fernsehauftritte als Koch. Das hat mir immer sehr viel Spaß gemacht. Ich bin jetzt in einem Alter, in dem ich daran denke, vielleicht noch einmal etwas ganz anderes auszuprobieren. Dieser Beratungsjob ist cool, auch weil ich dabei spannende Projekte realisiere, aber ich glaube, dass ich als Typ medial gut funktioniere, der gleichzeitig kochen und gut quatschen kann. In einem neuen Format trete ich als Host auf, der die kulinarischen Hotspots Berlins und Deutschlands ausfindig macht und mit den Nerds aus der Gastro auf Spurensuche geht. Einen Titel gibt es auch schon: „Kristof Mulacks Food Nerds". Der Plan steht, es geht aber erst dann los, wenn jemand das Projekt mit Geld unterstützt. Das kostet alles sehr viel Kohle, nicht zuletzt wegen unserer hochwertigen Ansprüche. Ich habe ein Top-Team an meiner Seite, das schon die Master Class von Sternekoch Harald Wohlfahrt begleitet hat. Demnächst haben wir mit unserer Idee ein paar Pitches bei großen Streaming-Diensten. Es sind aber auch ein paar kleinere Sachen geplant, unter anderem eine Mini-Kochshow mit TV Berlin in Kooperation mit „Frischeparadies". Daneben steht „Grill den Henssler" auf meiner Agenda. Die Show habe ich im vergangenen Jahr schon als Coach begleitet und für die neue Staffel wurde ich auch angefragt. Ich werde also immer mal wieder irgendwo aufflimmern. Die älteren, gestandenen Fernsehköche werden nicht jünger. Da muss irgendwann jemand nachrücken.

"
So much for the theory! Turn the page and you will discover one of Kristof's secret recipes – enjoy!

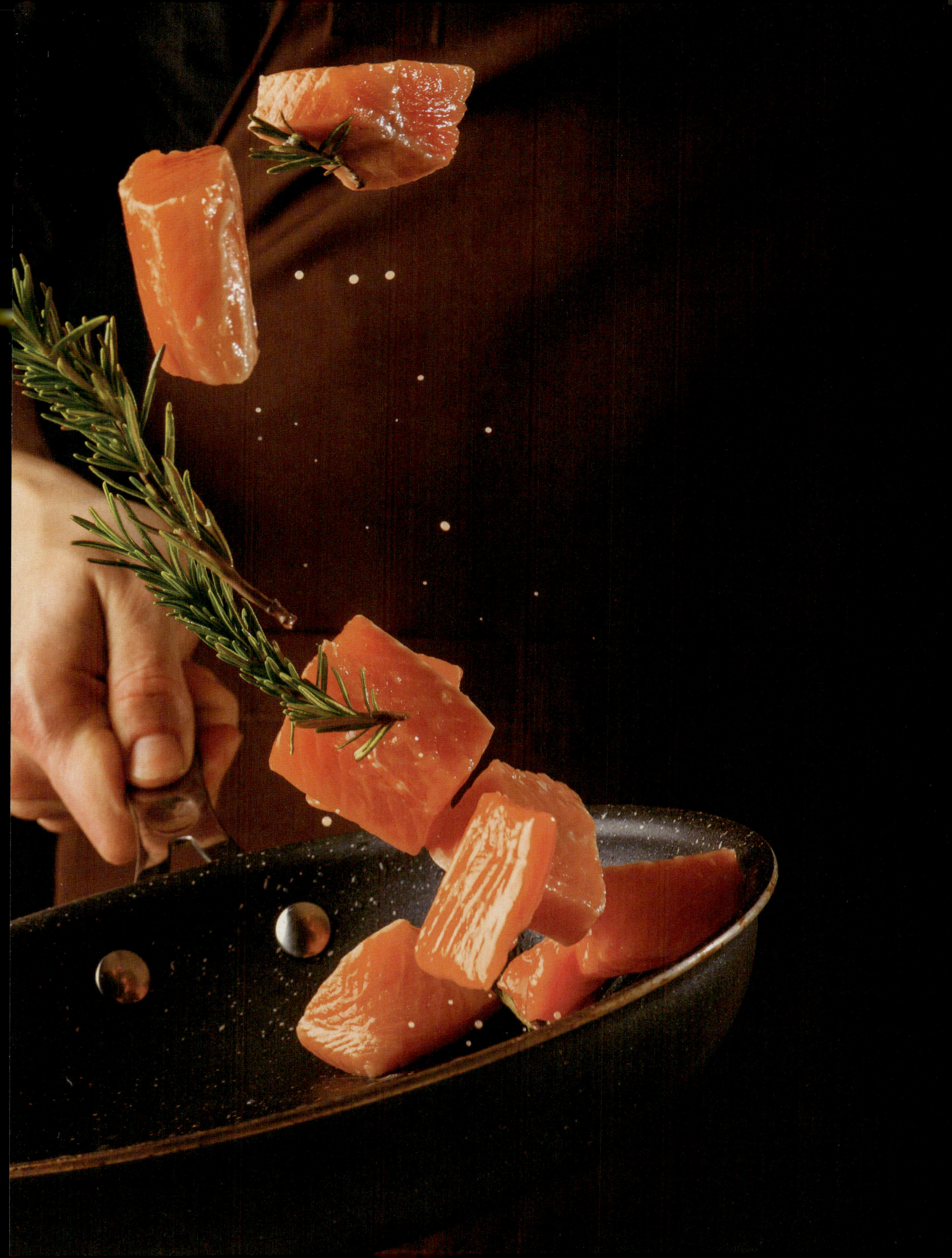

SALMON WITH GIN-SCHWIPS ON CUCUMBER-APPLE SALAD

Salmon is an all-round talent in the kitchen. Whether grilled, fried, steamed or raw - the fish, which comes mainly from Norwegian waters, tastes great and is practically always a success. Moreover, it's celebrated as an important source of nutrients because of the healthy omega-3 fatty acids it contains. Fish that is so good for the heart and the palate gets a place of honor on our appetizer plate - made by Kristof Mulack.

Ingredients for 4 people:

150 g	**Sashimi-Lachs**	*Sashimi salmon*
4	**Wacholderbeeren**	*juniper berries*
1 tbsp	**Senfkörner**	*mustard seeds*
1 cl	**Gin**	
1 tbsp	**Rapsöl**	*canola oil*
1 tbsp	**Meersalz**	*sea salt*
1 tbsp	**Zucker**	*sugar*
2	**Minigurken**	*Mexican sour gherkins*
1	**Granny Smith Apfel**	*Granny Smith apple*
2 bunches	**Schnittlauch**	*chives*
2	**Gewürzgurken**	*pickled gherkins*
250 g	**Griechischer Joghurt (10 %) oder Crème fraîche**	*Greek yoghurt (10 % fat) or crème fraîche*
2	**Limetten**	*limes*
6	**Körner schwarzer Pfeffer**	*black peppercorns*
1	**rote Zwiebel**	*red onion*
2 pkg	**frische, grüne (Senf-) Kresse**	*mustard cress*

Instructions for „Salmon with gin-schwips on cucumber-apple salad":

Zunächst zaubert ihr die Marinade für den **Lachs.** Hierzu die **Wacholderbeeren** und die **Senfkörner** gemeinsam in einem Topf anrösten und mit **Gin** ablöschen. Einreduzieren und etwas **Rapsöl** sowie **Salz und Zucker** hinzugeben. Die Marinade lauwarm zusammen mit dem Lachs in einen Vakuumbeutel geben und alles für mehrere Stunden, gerne auch über Nacht, einvakuumieren. **Minigurken** und den **Apfel** in Streifen schneiden und mit **Salz, Zucker, Rapsöl und Schnittlauch** vermengen. Die **Gewürzgurken** in Scheiben schneiden und anrichten. Den **Griechischen Joghurt** oder die **Crème fraîche** mit dem **Limettensaft,** etwas **Salz und Zucker** glattrühren. Den Lachs aus der Marinade holen, in Streifen schneiden und auf dem Teller neben dem Apfel-Gurkensalat sowie der Crème anrichten. Mit **Senfkresse** garnieren. Abschließend mit einem Esslöffel Marinade übergießen.

*First, prepare the marinade for the **salmon**. To do this, roast the **juniper berries** and **mustard seeds** together in a pot and quench with **gin**. Reduce and add some **canola oil, salt and sugar**. Put the marinade together with the salmon into a vacuum bag while it is still lukewarm and vacuum seal everything for several hours; overnight is fine. Cut the **Mexican sour gherkins** and **apple** into strips and mix with **salt, sugar, canola oil and chives**. Slice the **pickled gherkins** and arrange them. Mix the **Greek yogurt** or **crème fraîche** with the **lime juice**, some **salt and sugar** until smooth. Remove the salmon from the marinade, cut into strips and arrange on the plate next to the apple and cucumber salad and the crème. Garnish with mustard cress. Lastly, pour a tbsp. of marinade on top.*

SALMON WITH GIN-SCHWIPS ON CUCUMBER-APPLE SALAD

APPETIZER

523

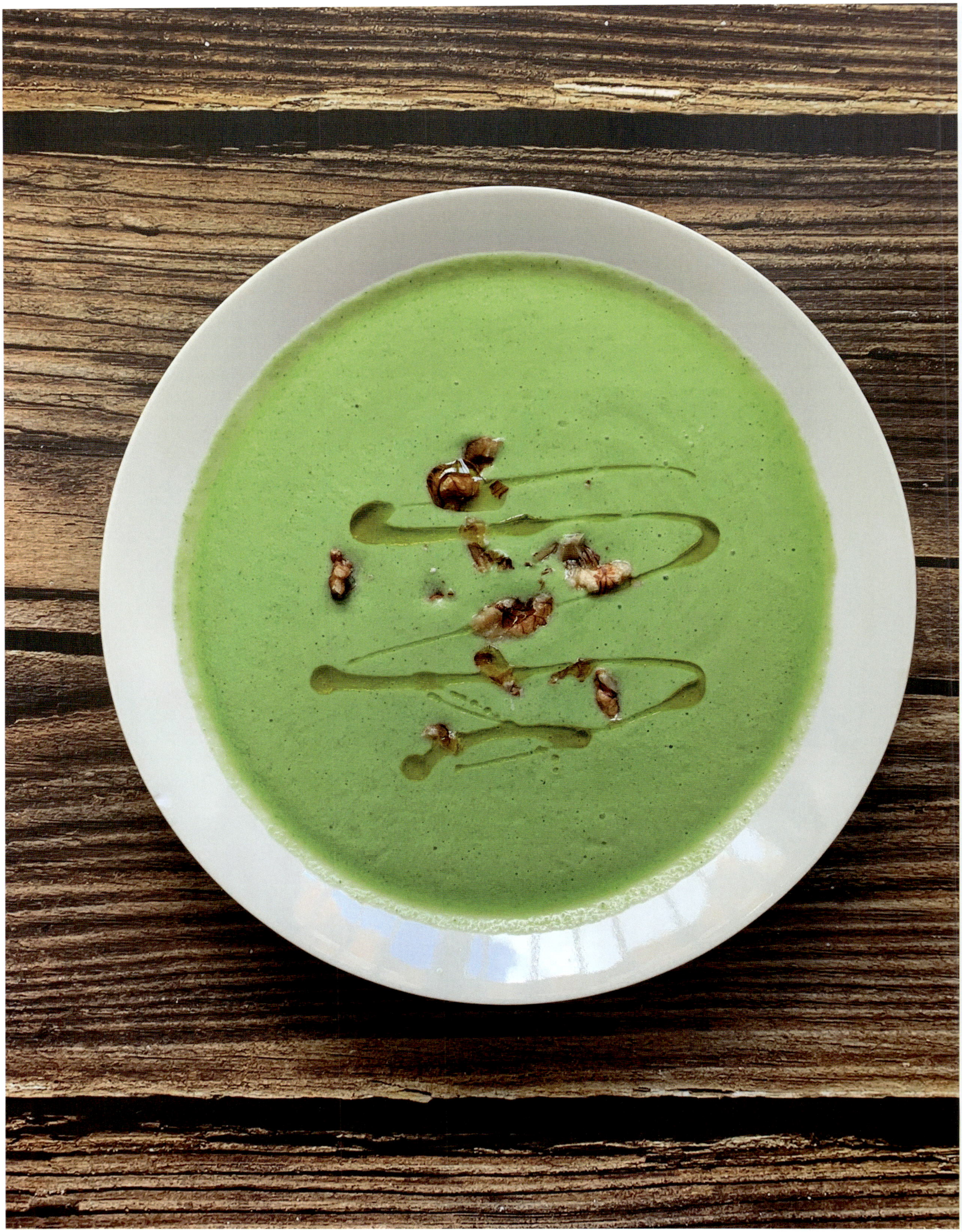

COLD VEGAN BASIL & COCONUT SOUP WITH GIN AND CARAMELIZED WALNUT CRUNCH

Normally, before a cozy meal with friends, family or acquaintances, you might serve an aperitif in the form of an alcoholic drink as a small appetizer. But a little variety never hurt anyone. How about a "gintastic" soup?

Ingredients for 4 people:

1 large	**Salatgurke**	*cucumber*
2	**Knoblauchzehen**	*garlic cloves*
5 handfuls	**Basilikumblätter**	*basil leaves*
2 tbsp	**Kokosmilch**	*coconut milk*
1 tbsp	**Apfelessig**	*cider vinegar*
3 tbsp	**Olivenöl**	*olive oil*
	Chili	
	getrockneter Oregano	*dried oregano*
6 tbsp	**Gin**	
	Salz und Pfeffer	*salt and pepper*

And for the caramelized walnuts:

100 g	**Walnusshälften**	*walnut halves*
70 g	**Zucker**	*sugar*
7 cl	**Wasser**	*water*

Instructions for „Cold vegan basil & coconut soup with gin and caramelized walnut crunch":

Die **Gurke** und den **Knoblauch** schälen und in Stücke schneiden. Die **Basilikumblätter** waschen und trocken tupfen. Gurke, Basilikum, **Kokosmilch** und Knoblauch zusammen fein pürieren. **Apfelessig** und **Olivenöl** hinzufügen und nochmals pürieren. Mit **Gewürzen** und **Gin** abschmecken und für drei Stunden kalt stellen. Für die karamellisierten **Walnüsse Wasser mit Zucker** aufkochen, bis der Zucker anfängt leicht braun zu werden. Die Walnüsse dazugeben, die Hitze reduzieren und die Walnusshälften unter ständigem Rühren im Karamell wälzen, bis sich ein schöner Überzug bildet. Die Walnüsse auf einem Backpapier einzeln verteilt auskühlen lassen. Anschließend zerkleinern.

Die Suppe in Gläsern anrichten und mit dem Walnuss-Crunch servieren.

*Peel the **cucumber** and **garlic** and cut them into pieces. Wash the **basil leaves** and pat dry. Finely puree the cucumber, basil, **coconut milk** and garlic together. Add **cider vinegar** and **olive oil** and puree again. Season to taste with **spices** and **gin** and refrigerate for three hours. For the caramelized **walnuts**, boil **water with sugar** until the sugar starts to brown slightly. Add the walnuts, reduce the heat and turn the walnut halves in the caramel, stirring constantly, until a nice coating forms. Allow the walnuts to cool, spread out individually on a sheet of baking paper. Then crush them.*

Arrange the soup in glasses and serve with the walnut crunch.

SPAGHETTI WITH GIN & TOMATO SAUCE AND MEATBALLS

At last! Here it is, the scientific explanation for why we're so fond of pasta, and it lies on our tongues. US researchers have discovered the "starchy" sense of taste right there. It's triggered by starchy food, so primarily when we eat carbohydrates. Sounds logical, doesn't it? Then get the pasta pot and conjure up a dish to fall in love with – à la Lady and the Tramp.

Ingredients for 4 people:

400 g	**rote & gelbe Kirschtomaten**	*red & yellow cherry tomatoes*
1	**Gemüsezwiebel**	*white onion*
	Olivenöl	*olive oil*
2 tsp	**Agavendicksaft**	*agave syrup*
3 tsp	**Tomatenmark**	*tomato puree*
500 g	**Spaghetti**	
100 g	**Pecorino**	
250 ml	**Gemüsebrühe**	*vegetable stock*
	frischer Thymian & Oregano	*fresh thyme & oregano*
4 cl	**Gin**	

And for 16 meatballs:

500 g	**Rinderhackfleisch**	*ground beef*
100 g	**Semmelbrösel**	*breadcrumbs*
2	**Eier**	*eggs*
80 g	**Schafskäse**	*sheep cheese*
1	**Knoblauchzehe**	*garlic clove*

Instructions for „Spaghetti with gin & tomato sauce and meatballs":

Die **Tomaten** waschen. Die **Zwiebel** schälen und fein würfeln. **Öl** erhitzen. Zwiebelwürfel und Kirschtomaten darin anbraten, mit **Agavendicksaft** leicht karamellisieren und mit **Tomatenmark** vermengen. **Spaghetti** kochen. Für die Fleischbällchen das **Rinderhackfleisch** mit den **Eiern** und den **Semmelbröseln** zu einer geschmeidigen Masse verkneten. Den **Knoblauch** fein hacken und untermischen, mit **Salz und Pfeffer** würzen Aus der Hackfleischmasse mit angefeuchteten Händen Bällchen formen. **Schafskäse** klein würfeln und jeweils ein Stück in die Mitte der Fleischbällchen drücken. Die **frischen Kräuter** waschen und fein hacken. Mit Salz und Pfeffer zu den Tomaten geben. Mit **Gemüsebrühe** und **Gin** ablöschen und alles darin für wenige Minuten köcheln lassen. Öl in einer Pfanne erhitzen und die Fleischbällchen bei mittlerer Hitze portionsweise 8–10 Minuten rundherum goldbraun anbraten. Die gegarten Nudeln sowie die Fleischbällchen in die Tomatensoße geben, alles anrichten und mit gehobeltem **Pecorino** servieren.

*Wash the **tomatoes**. Peel and finely dice the **onion**. Heat the **oil**. Fry the onion cubes and the cherry tomatoes in it. Lightly caramelize with **agave syrup** and mix with tomato paste. Cook the **spaghetti**. For the meatballs, knead the **ground beef** with the **eggs** and **breadcrumbs** until smooth. Finely chop the **garlic** and mix it in, season with **salt and pepper**. Form balls from the ground meat mixture with moistened hands. Cut the **sheep cheese** into small cubes and press a piece into the center of each meatball. Wash and finely chop the **fresh herbs**. Add to tomatoes with salt and pepper. Add the **vegetable broth** and **gin** and simmer for a few minutes. Heat the oil in a frying pan and fry the meatballs in batches over medium heat for 8-10 minutes until golden brown. Add the cooked pasta and meatballs to the tomato sauce, arrange everything and serve with grated **pecorino**.*

"
A dish to fall in love
with – à la Lady and
the Tramp.

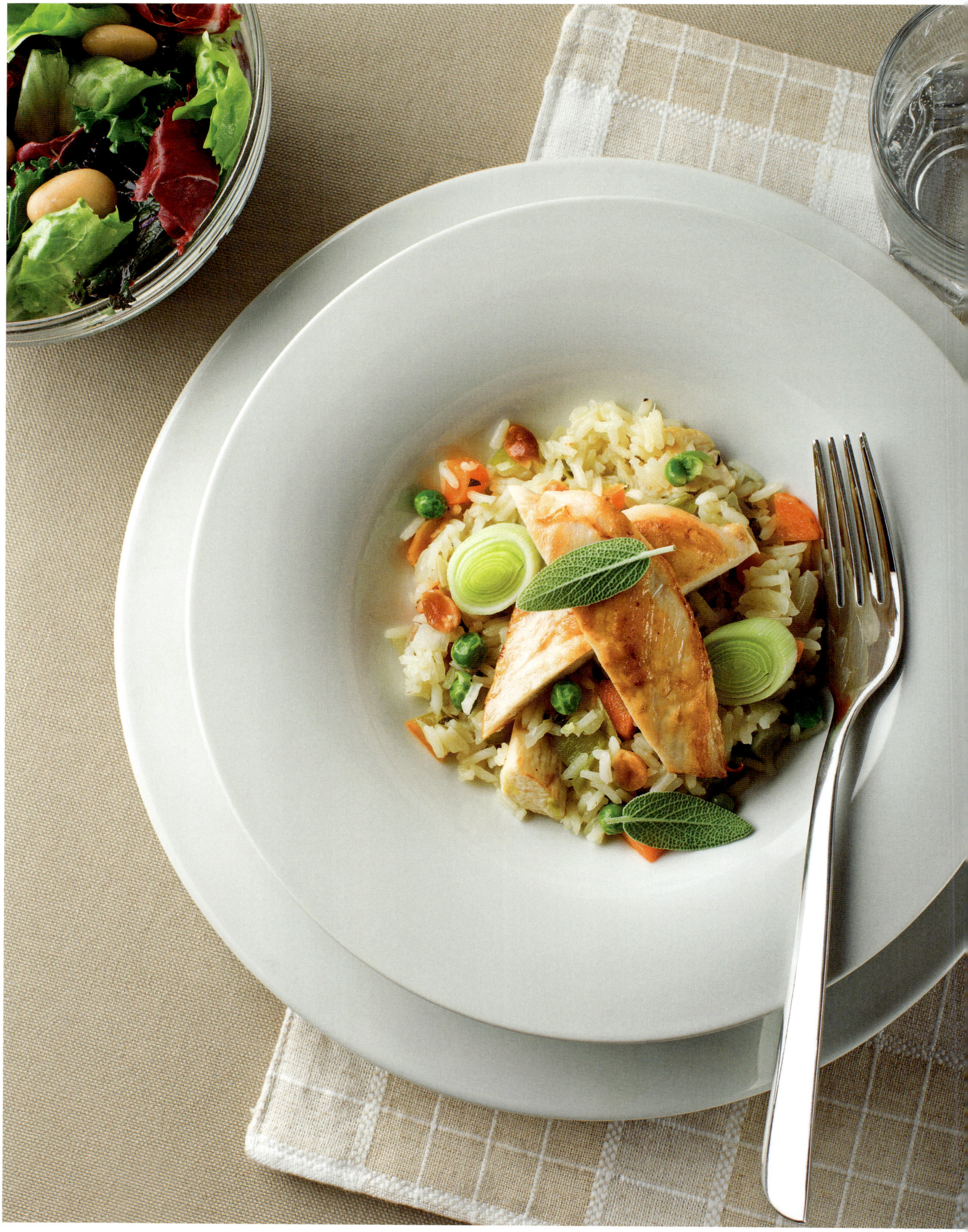

GIN-CHICKEN WITH SAGE RISOTTO WITH LEEKS AND PEAS

Mediterranean cuisine is celebrated internationally, always conveying a subtle allusion to vacation. Especially on cold rainy days, we long for T-shirt weather, sunshine, the sound of the sea and the diverse flavors of the Mediterranean. But we can do something about our yearning for faraway places – cooking, for example. Buon appetito!.

Ingredients for 4 people:

4	**Hähnchenbrüste**	*chicken breasts*
100 ml	**Gin**	
2 tbsp	**Olivenöl**	*olive oil*
	Mediterrane Kräuter	*Mediterranean herbs*
2	**Schalotten**	*shallots*
1	**Knoblauchzehe**	*garlic clove*
1	**Lauch**	*leek*
1 bunch	**Salbei**	*sage*
50 g	**Butter**	*butter*
250 g	**Risotto-Reis**	*risotto rice*
150 ml	**Weißwein**	*white wine*
1 handful	**Erbsen**	*peas*
750 ml	**Gemüsebrühe**	*vegetable stock*
2 handfuls	**Cocktail-Tomaten**	*cocktail tomatoes*
1 pack	**Pinienkerne**	*pine nuts*
100 g	**Grana Padano**	
	Salz & Pfeffer	*salt & pepper*

Instructions for „Gin-chicken with sage risotto with leeks and peas":

Die **Hähnchenbrust** in einer **Gin-Kräuter-Marinade** – bestehend aus Gin, einem Schuss **Olivenöl, Thymian, Olivenkraut und Rosmarin** – einlegen und einen Tag im Kühlschrank ruhen lassen. Für das Risotto zunächst die **Schalotten** und den **Knoblauch** schälen und fein würfeln bzw. hacken. Den **Lauch** in feine Ringe schneiden. Die **Salbeiblätter** von den Zweigen lösen und in Streifen schneiden. Vier Zweige beiseitelegen. **Butter** in einem Topf erhitzen. Die Salbeizweige darin anbraten und anschließend wieder herausnehmen. Die Schalottenwürfel und die Knoblauchstücke ebenfalls darin anbraten. Nun auch den **Risotto-Reis** zugeben und mit dem **Weißwein** ablöschen. Anschließend die **Erbsen** hinzugeben. Den Reis so lange köcheln lassen, bis die Flüssigkeit verdampft ist. Mit **Gemüsebrühe** aufgießen, bis der Reis knapp bedeckt ist. Etwa weitere 25 Minuten köcheln lassen und dabei nach und nach Gemüsebrühe hinzugießen und immer wieder umrühren. Das Fleisch von beiden Seiten in Olivenöl goldbraun anbraten. Die **Tomaten** und die restlichen Salbeistreifen in einer Pfanne mit etwas Olivenöl kurz anbraten. **Pinienkerne** rösten. Die Hälfte vom **Grana Padano** unter das Risotto mischen, **salzen und pfeffern.** Mit den angebratenen Tomaten, den Pinienkernen, dem restlichen Grana Padano und dem angerösteten Salbei servieren.

*Marinate the **chicken breasts** in a gin and herb marinade consisting of **gin,** a dash of **olive oil, thyme, olive herb and rosemary** and let it rest in the refrigerator for a day. For the risotto, first peel and finely dice or chop the **shallots** and **garlic.** Cut the **leeks** into thin rings. Remove the **sage leaves** from the sprigs and cut into strips. Set aside four sprigs. Heat the **butter** in a saucepan. Sauté the sage sprigs in it and then remove them. Sauté the shallot cubes and the garlic pieces in it as well. Now add the **risotto rice** and the **white wine.** Next, add the **peas.** Let the rice simmer until the liquid has evaporated. Pour in **vegetable stock** until the rice is just covered. Simmer for about another 25 minutes, gradually adding broth and stirring frequently. Brown the meat on both sides in olive oil until golden brown. Briefly sauté the **tomatoes** and remaining sage strips in a pan with a little olive oil. Roast the **pine nuts.** Mix half of the **Grana Padano** into the risotto, add **salt and pepper.** Serve with the sautéed tomatoes, the pine nuts, the remaining Grana Padano and the toasted sage.*

TIPSY PRALINES IN CHOCOLATE COATING

"Life is like a box of chocolates. You never know what you're going to get." Even the movie character Forrest Gump enjoyed the little sweet treats in his namesake blockbuster. Of course, the unexpected has its appeal, but sometimes the taste is good even in the absence of chance. Like these wonderful truffle pralines that scream gin and chocolate.

Ingredients for 25 delicious gin & tonic truffles:

- 200 g **Zartbitterschokolade**
  dark chocolate
- 50 g **Butter**
  butter
- 2 tbsp **Gin**
- 1 tbsp **Tonic Water**
- ½ **Bio-Limette – hier braucht ihr den Saft und den Abrieb**
  organic lime – you need the juice and the zest
- 200 g **weiße Schokolade**
  white chocolate

For the little extra:

- a pinch **essbarer Goldstaub**
  edible gold dust

Instructions for „Tipsy pralines in chocolate coating":

Die **Zartbitterschokolade** zusammen mit der **Butter** über einem heißen Wasserbad erhitzen. Leicht abkühlen lassen. **Gin, Tonic** sowie **Limettensaft** unterrühren. Alles für mindestens drei Stunden in den Kühlschrank geben. Aus dem Kühlschrank kommt eine homogene Masse, von der nun mit einem Messer kleine Stücke abgetrennt werden. Die Stückchen zu Kugeln formen, die anschließend für 30 Minuten in das Gefrierfach kommen. Die **weiße Schokolade** schmelzen. Die Zartbitterkugeln in die weiße Schokolade eintauchen, mit **Limettenabrieb** garnieren und noch einmal für 30 Minuten in den Kühlschrank stellen.

Für das kleine bisschen Extra: Bestäube die Pralinen mit feinem, **essbarem Goldstaub** – et voilà.

*Heat the **dark chocolate** together with the **butter** over a hot water bath. Allow to cool slightly. Stir in the **gin, tonic** and **lime juice.** Put everything in the refrigerator for at least three hours. Out of the refrigerator comes a homogeneous mass, from which now small pieces are separated with a knife. Form the pieces into balls, which are then placed in the freezer for 30 minutes. Melt the **white chocolate.** Dip the dark chocolate balls into the white chocolate, garnish with **lime zest** and place in the refrigerator for another 30 minutes.*

*For that little bit extra: Dust the chocolates with fine, **edible gold dust** - et voilà.*

" Don't fight with me over chocolate, I am not someone to be truffled with.

GIN & TONIC CAKE WITH LEMON CREAM

This classic long drink isn't served in a glass, but lands instead straight on a cake stand. Here, gin and tonic make friends with flour, sugar, butter, and all the other tempting ingredients that go into a delicious cake. It's gin & cake o'clock!

Ingredients to achieve your multi-tiered masterpiece (makes 12 pieces)

For the cake layers (20 cm diameter):

6	**Eier**	*eggs*
250 g	**Zucker**	*sugar*
1 pack	**Vanillezucker**	*vanilla sugar*
1 pinch	**Salz**	*salt*
70 ml	**London Dry Gin**	
150 ml	**Tonic Water**	
100 ml	**Mineralwasser**	*mineral water*
300 ml	**Backöl**	*cooking oil*
1 pack	**Backpulver**	*baking powder*
50 g	**Mehl**	*flour*

For the lemon cream:

1 pack	**Sahne**	*cream*
250 g	**Frischkäse (Doppelrahmstufe)**	*(double) cream cheese*
1	**Bio-Zitrone**	*organic lemon*
50 g	**Puderzucker**	*icing sugar*

For the butter cream:

500 g	**weiche Butter**	*soft butter*
6 tbsp	**Puderzucker**	*icing sugar*
4 tbsp	**Griechischer Joghurt**	*Greek yoghurt*
1 pinch	**Salz**	*salt*
1	**Vanilleschote**	*vanilla pod*

Instructions for „Gin & tonic cake with lemon cream":

Die Böden: Den Backofen auf 180 Grad (Ober- und Unterhitze) vorheizen. Eine Springform fetten oder mit Backpapier auskleiden. Die **Eier** gemeinsam mit dem **Zucker, Vanillezucker** und einer Prise **Salz** schaumig aufschlagen. Den **Gin**, das **Tonic Water**, das **Mineralwasser** und das **Backöl** dazugeben. Zuletzt das **Backpulver** mit dem **Mehl** mischen und unter die Masse heben. Den Teig in zwei Chargen in der Springform für jeweils rund 40 Minuten backen. Alternativ könnt ihr zwei Springformen befüllen. Die Stäbchenprobe zeigt euch, ob die Böden fertig sind. Ist das der Fall, müsst ihr sie anschließend vollständig abkühlen lassen. Während die Böden backen, könnt ihr die Füllungen zubereiten.

Die Zitronencreme: Zunächst die **Sahne** steif schlagen. Den **Frischkäse** unterheben und den **Saft der Zitrone** hinzufügen. Zum Schluss den **Puderzucker** einrieseln lassen. Alles vermengen.

Die Buttercreme: Die **Butter, den Puderzucker, das Mark der Vanilleschote und die Prise Salz** etwa fünf Minuten cremig aufschlagen. Den **Joghurt** dabei esslöffelweise unterrühren.

Die Torte bauen: Die abgekühlten Böden horizontal halbieren, sodass ihr vier gleich dicke Böden habt. Den ersten Boden mit **Gin** bepinseln und gleichmäßig mit **Buttercreme** bestreichen. Vorsichtig einen weiteren Boden auflegen und ganz leicht festdrücken. Diesen Boden wieder mit **Gin** bepinseln und mit **Zitronencreme** bestreichen. Dann den nächsten Boden auflegen. Wieder die **Buttercreme** verwenden. Schließlich den vierten Boden auflegen, sodass die untere Seite oben ist. Die Torte mit einer dünnen Schicht **Zitronencreme** einstreichen und für mindestens eine Stunde kalt stellen. Anschließend üppig weitere Creme auftragen und mit einem Teigspachtel glatt streichen. Bei einem Naked Cake wie diesem dürfen die Böden etwas durchscheinen. Die Torte noch einmal in die Kühlung geben und anschließend nach Belieben dekorieren, zum Beispiel mit **Zitronenscheiben, Rosmarin und Strohhalmen** – wie bei einem Cocktail.

*The Layers: Preheat the oven to 180 °C (top and bottom heat). Take a springform pan and grease or line with baking paper. Beat the **eggs** together with **the sugar, vanilla sugar and pinch of salt** until foamy. Add the **gin, tonic water, mineral water** and baking oil. Finally, mix the **baking powder** with the **flour** and fold into the mixture. Bake the mixture in two batches in the springform pan for about 40 minutes each. Alternatively, you can fill two springform pans. A skewer test will show you if the layers are ready. If they are, let them cool completely. While the layers are baking, you can prepare the fillings.*

*Lemon cream: First, whip the **cream** until stiff. Fold in the **cream cheese** and add the **juice of the lemon**. Finally, sprinkle in the **powdered sugar**. Mix everything together.*

*Butter cream: Beat the **butter, icing sugar, vanilla bean seeds and pinch of salt** for about five minutes until creamy. Stir in the **yogurt** by the tablespoonful as you go.*

*Build the cake: Cut the cooled cake layers in half horizontally so that you have four layers of equal thickness. Brush the first cake layer with **gin** and spread evenly with **butter cream**. Carefully place another layer on top and press down very lightly. Brush this layer again with **gin** and spread with **lemon cream**. Then place the next layer on top. Again use the **butter cream**. Finally, place the fourth cake layer on top, so that the bottom side is on top. Spread a thin layer of **lemon cream** on the cake and chill for at least one hour. Then spread on more cream generously and smooth with a pastry spatula. For a naked cake like this, the layers can show through a bit. Refrigerate the cake once more and then decorate as desired, for example with **lemon slices, rosemary and straws** – just like a cocktail.*

> "
> I tried to say no to gin – but
> it's 42.5 % stronger than me.